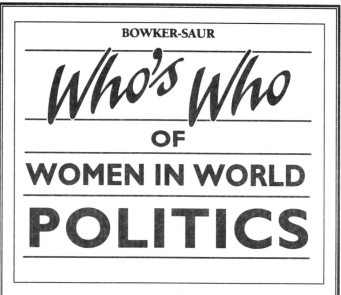

BOWKER-SAUR

Who's Who

OF
WOMEN IN WORLD

POLITICS

OTHER BOWKER-SAUR

Who's Who

PUBLICATIONS

Who's Who in European Politics
Who's Who in Asian and Australasian Politics
Who's Who in the People's Republic of China
Who's Who in South African Politics
Who's Who in the Arab World
Who's Who in American Politics
Who's Who in the Soviet Union
Who's Who in International Organisations

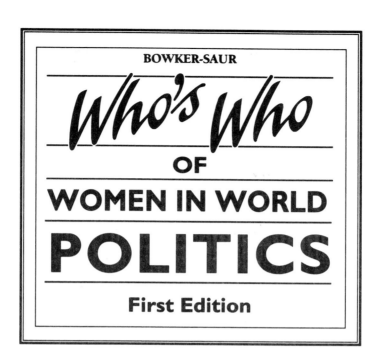

BOWKER-SAUR

London • Melbourne • Munich • New York

© BOWKER-SAUR LTD, 1991
60 Grosvenor Street, London W1X 9DA, United Kingdom
Tel: 071 493 5841 Fax: 071 580 4089

Bowker-Saur is part of the Professional Publishing Division of Reed International Books.

Bowker-Saur has used its best efforts in collecting and preparing material for Who's Who of Women in World Politics but does not warrant that the information is complete or accurate, and does not assume, and hereby disclaims, any liability to any person for any loss or damage caused by errors or omissions in Who's Who of Women in World Politics whether such errors or omission result from negligence, accident or any other cause.

British Library Cataloguing in Publication Data

Who's who of women in world politics.
  323.34

ISBN 0-86291-627-5

Library of Congress Cataloging-in-Publication Data
  Available on request

Cover design by Robin Caira, Typographics, Whitstable
Computer controlled typesetting by Microgen Ltd, Welwyn Garden City
Printed and bound by Antony Rowe, Chippenham

Printed on acid-free paper.

CONTENTS

FOREWORD

In 1971, when Rutgers University established the first research center to study women's political participation in the US., one of our earliest tasks was to begin collecting information about the numbers and status of women in public office. Without basic data, we could not design research projects to ask important questions about the nature of women's political roles: we could not convene conferences or seminars to identify and discuss key issues affecting women's political position: we could not develop educational programs and materials to stimulate enhanced participation in politics and government.

The counting process was enlightening. At the Center for the American Woman and Politics (CAWP), we learned that women's sparse representation at the most powerful and visible levels of public life was duplicated throughout the political system. Our count revealed that women did not count - at least not in politics. As late in the twentieth century as the 1970s, women were not present in significant numbers as decision-makers and public leaders anywhere in the United States. Thus, counting helped us to identify the women who held office as well as to recognise the scope of the problem of women's absence from politics.

Twenty years later, the importance of counting, naming, and sharing basic information about women in politics remains. While some individual nations have collected and issued data about their female public leaders, the data are uneven and much work remains before we have a good understanding about the extent and nature of women's participation in various political systems. What we do know is that nowhere in the world have women achieved a status nearing parity with men in exercising power or holding public leadership positions. We also know that in some nations an often small but nonetheless visible group of political women have gained important positions of leadership. Now with the publication of *Who's Who of Women in World Politics* the rest of the world will have an opportunity to become acquainted with these pioneers.

Who's Who of Women in World Politics is an important publication. It tells us something about prominent political women across the globe, which types of positions they seem to acquire, which interests and activities are often associated with them and which areas of the public arena they emerge in most frequently. This volume is a resource directory for people interested in locating the small minority of women who have attained prominence as public leaders. It will be of particular value to those political women who are interested in developing contacts, sharing information and building networks with women in similar positions. For those of us who are especially concerned with encouraging and expanding women's public leadership roles, *Who's Who of Women in World Politics* is both a sobering reminder of how much work remains to be done and an inspirational tool for pushing forward to add many more exciting pages to the next edition.

Ruth B. Mandel, Director
Center for the American Woman & Politics
Eagleton Institute of Politics
Rutgers University
New Brunswick, New Jersey
U S A

PREFACE

Women constitute more than half of most electorates throughout the world, yet are represented by little more than 10% of female politicians at national level in the developed regions and even fewer in other regions. Our research has shown that, while the number of women politically active in government or legislature is gradually increasing, there is still a long way to go before parity with men is achieved.

A survey of the biographical entries contained in this work will show that the main areas of women's political expertise are: education, social welfare, peace and the environment, which have far more impact on our global future than is apparent from statistics alone. Even more revealing have been the many letters of encouragement, regret and hope that we have received from the women themselves, during the compilation of this book. Of particular note are the words of a Soviet poet and senior politician:

"What personally concerns me .... is the fact that I do not practise politics, but politics is practised on me. I consider that all the cruelty of politics passes through the destiny of a woman and her children. Thus I am a politician against my will. Yet this does not mean that I consider any less that the future age will be the age of women presidents and leaders of all ranks."

It is usually impossible to find biographical details for any but the best known politicians in many countries. It is even harder to find details relating to the lives of politically active women. The aim of *Who's Who of Women in World Politics* has been to provide biographical and statistical information of women active on the global arena with contact addresses, including all leading figures, in one language and one volume, to be regularly updated.

In Part I, over 1500 biographies (each with a contact address) are given in alphabetical order, all of which have been sent for approval to the entrants themselves. Coverage includes virtually all top political leaders as well as a whole host of active politicians not yet dominating the headlines but still with important roles to play. The biographies aim to cover the main aspects of an entrant's personal and political life, with special emphasis on political career and interests. Inevitably, the fullness of the individual biographies varies. There are also constraints involved in translating posts and career equivalences from over 115 countries and 25 different languages and national systems. However, as far as possible the information has been updated to the end of July 1991.

Entry criteria:
To be included in the book an individual must belong to at least one of the following categories: head of state, member of government, member of national legislature, party or trade union federation leadership, or regional leader. A list of the countries covered in this volume is given on the Contents page, supplemented by the map at the beginning of the book.

Part II contains unique statistics relating to the numbers of women holding positions as Head of State, Prime Minister or equivalent, member of the Cabinet or of the national legislature, with relevant historical data including year of women's enfranchisement.

Part III contains a comprehensive Biographical Index arranged alphabetically by country and including primary political position in each listing.

A work of this magnitude is not possible without the assistance of many people. Special thanks must be given to the small army of researchers and translators who helped compile this First Edition and to the many embassies, government departments and party HQs who have been so patient in the dealing with our many inquiries. In particular we wish to acknowledge Lucy Baruch and Ruth Mandel of the Center for the American Woman and Politics for their help in compiling the list of American entrants and for the Foreword respectively. Our final thanks should go to the entrants themselves, without whose co-operation this publication would not have been possible.

Yolanda Dolling
Managing Editor

EDITOR'S NOTE

A proof of each biography is sent to the entrant for updating and amendment. Where necessary, responses are translated into English. While every care is taken, neither the publishers nor the printers can admit liability for any loss incurred through misprint or other circumstances.

If we do not yet include a potential entrant, who must be a current serving national or regional politician, party activist or trade union leader the editor is only too keen to receive the relevant details. (Please send Curriculum Vitae to *Who's Who of Women in World Politics,* Bowker-Saur Ltd., 60 Grosvenor Street, London W1X 9DA, UK).

It cannot be stated too emphatically that inclusion in *Who's Who of Women in World Politics is* not a matter for payment or of obligation to purchase the book.

NOTE DE L'ÉDITEUR

Une épreuve de sa biographie est envoyée au politicien entré pour chaque édition à des fins de mise à jour et de correction. Les réponses sont traduites en anglais, lorsque cela est nécessaire. Bien que le plus grand soin ait été pris, les éditeurs et imprimeurs ne peuvent pas admettre de responsabilité pour toute perte encourue en raison de faute d'impression ou de toute autre circonstance.

Au cas ou un politicien pouvait être entré dans ce Botin, et qui doit pour cela être en service actuellement au niveau national, régional, ou bien être ou dirigeant politique ou syndical n'y figure pas encore, l'éditrice sera très heureuse de recevoir les détails appropriés. (Veuillez envoyer votre Curriculum Vitae à *Who's Who of Women in World Politics*, Bowker-Saur Ltd., 60 Grosvenor Street, London W1X 9DA, Royaume-Uni.)

Nous n'insisterons jamais assez sur le fait que l'inclusion dans *Who's Who of Women in World Politics* n'implique aucun paiement ni l'achat de l'ouvrage.

ANMERKUNG DES HERAUSGEBERS

Dem betreffenden Aufgeführten wird jeweils ein Abzug der entsprechenden Biografie zugesandt, sodaß diese auf den neuesten Stand gebracht und gegebenfalls berichtigt werden kann. Wo nötig, werden die Antworten in die englische Sprache übersetzt. Obgleich große Sorgfalt waltet, können weder der Verlag noch die Druckerei für etwaige Verluste durch Druckfehler oder andere Umstände haften.

Ist ein potentieller Kandidat noch nicht vertreten, der ein im Augenblick im Amt befindlicher nationaler beziehungsweise regionaler Politiker, Parteitätiger oder Gewerkschaftsführer sein sollte, würde sich der Herausgeber freuen, die entsprechenden Einzelheiten entgegenzunehmen. (Bitte senden Sie einen Lebenslauf an *Who's Who of Women in World Politics*, Bowker-Saur Ltd., 60 Grosvenor Street, London W1X 9DA, GB).

Es kann nicht audrücklich genug betont werden, daß die Aufnahme in *Who's Who of Women in World Politics* keinerlei Zahlung erforderlich macht oder zum Kauf des Buches verpflichtet.

NOTA DEL EDITOR

Se envía una prueba de la biografía a participante para su actualización y corrección. Cuando es necesario, las respuestas se traducen al inglés. Aunque se ha puesto el mayor cuidado, ni la editorial ni los impresores admiten responsabilidad en caso de posibles pérdidas debido a errores tipográficos u otras circunstancias.

Si aun no hemos incluído a algún participante potencial, el cual deberá ser un político nacional actualmente en servicio, activista de partido o líder de sindicato, el editor estaría muy interesado en recibir los datos relevantes. (Por favor sírvase enviar el Curriculum Vitae a *Who's Who of Women in World Politics*, Bowker-Saur Ltd., 60 Grosvenor Street, London W1X 9DA, Inglaterra.)

Debemos insistir en que la inclusión en *Who's Who of Women in World Politics* no conlleva pago alguna u obligación de comprar el libro.

編集者の注記

各掲載事項の校正刷りが、更新及び修正のためにそれぞれの掲載人物に送付され、返答は必要に応じて英語に翻訳されます。あらゆる努力を払って誤りのないようにしていますが、印刷の誤り、或はその他の事情によって発生した損失に対して、出版者或は印刷者は責任を負い兼ねます。

現在、全国或は地方政治家、党活動家、労働組合指導者で、このディレクトリーに含まれていない人物がいれば、当編集部に詳細お知らせくだされば、幸甚です。（履歴書を、*Who's Who of Women in World Politics*, Bowker-Saur Ltd., 60 Grosvenor Street, London W1X 9DA, U.K.）までお願いします。

「アジア及びオーストラレーシア政治のフーズフー」への掲載は金銭の支払、或は本を購入する義務とは無関係であることを特に強調しておきたいと思います。

KEY TO BIOGRAPHIES

CLEF DES BIOGRAPHIES, ERLËAUTERUNG ZU DEN BIOGRAFIEN, CLAVE PARA LAS BIOGRAFICAS,　記載事項区分

[1]TARJAN, Dr. Anna; **[2]**Hungarian, Member of Parliament; **[3]** *born:* 27 August 1932, Lenti, Hungary; **[4]** *parents:* József Tajnafoi and Anna Tajnafoi (née Keseru); **[5]** *married:* Dr. László Tarján; **[7]** *year married:* 1957; **[8]** *public role of spouse:* Doctor; **[9]** *children:* Katalin, Zsuzsanna; **[10]** *religion:* Roman Catholic; **[11]***languages:* Hungarian, German, Latin, English; **[12]***education:* Univ of Forestry, Sopron, M.Sc., forestry, 1955, environmental engineering, 1977, Dr.Sc., 1982; **[13]** *Party membership:* Independent Small-Holders' Party (ISHP); **[14]** *Primary position:* Political Secretary of State at the Ministry for the Environment and Regional Policy; **[15]** *political career:* political Sec.-of-State, 1990-; Mem., National Board Political Commission, ISHP, 1990-; Mem., of Parliament, 1990-; **[16]** *political interests:* economic politics; **[17]** *memberships:* National Assn. of Forestry; **[18]** *professional career:* forest engineer, Somogy County, 1955-60; Senior Officer, Forestry Office, 1960-77; Inspector, National Authority for the Environment and Nature Conservation, Somogy County, 1977-79; Sec., Environment and Nature Conservation, Somogy County Cncl., 1979-89; Dir., Forest Economy, Forest Office, Somogy County, 1989-90; **[19]** *honours & awards:* Széchenyi Medal, National Environmental Authority, 1977; Medal for the Development of the Human Environment, NEA, 1987; Pro Urbe Medal, Hungarian Assn. of Architects, 1989; **[20]** *publications:* Dél-Balaton és környéke, 1984; Somogy megye védett természeti értékei, 1989; around 30 technical articles, since 1970; **[21]** *clubs:* Environmental Protection Club; **[22]** *recreations:* active in tourism clubs; **[23]** *private address:* H-1054., Budapest, Bank u. 3., Hungary; **[24]** *office address:* Dr. Anna Tarján, Országgyülés, Kossuth L. tér 1-3, Budapest V, Hungary: **[24]** *tel:* 22 5058; 22 5059.

---

1. Surname followed by first name(s) / initial(s)
2. Nationality of domicile followed by primary political position
3. Date of birth followed by place of birth
4. Father's full name followed by mother's full name
5. Full name of spouse
6. Maiden name of spouse, where applicable
7. Year of marriage
8. Prominent public role of spouse
9. Children, listed by name(s), gender(s) or number
10. Religious denomination, where applicable
11. Languages written or spoken, including first language or local dialect(s), where applicable.
12. School(s), college(s) or university(s) attended, with subjects, qualifications and dates of attendance.
13. Current political party membership.
14. Primary political position

15. Political career details in chronological order including current position.
16. Political, academic or professional interests.
17. Membership of business, professional or academic bodies/organisations.
18. Details of non-political career.
19. Honours and awards for academic, civil, military or other achievement.
20. Books, articles or other published works
21. Membership of social or leisure clubs
22. Recreations, hobbies or leisure interests
23. Private address, where provided.
24. Postal title and name with office address, followed by telephone, telex and fax numbers.

Note: In many cases it has not been possible to compile a complete entry, in which case all available data is included and sections for which no data are available have not been printed.

1. Nom suivi de prénom(s) / initiale(s)
2. Nationalité, suivie de fonction politique la plus importante
3. Date et lieu de naissance
4. Nom du père en entier et nom de la mère en entier
5. Nom d'époux/épouse en entier
6. Nom de jeune fille d'épouse (si cela s'applique)
7. Année de marriage
8. Fonction publique importante d'époux/épouse
9. Enfants, prénoms, sexe ou nombre
10. Dénomination religieuse (si cela s'applique)
11. Langues écrites ou parlées, y compris langue maternelle ou dialecte régionale, si cela s'applique
12. Écoles(s), collège(s) ou université(s)
13. Adhésion actuelle au parti politique
14. Fonction politique la plus importante
15. Détails de carrière politique, par ordre chronologique, fonction actuelle y compris
16. Domaines d'intérêt politiques, académiques et professionels
17. Adhésion aux organisations professionelles/académiques/commerciales
18. Détails de carrière (à l'exclusion de la carrière politique)
19. Honneurs et prix académiques, civils, militaires etc.
20. Livres, articles ou autres oeuvres publiés
21. Adhésion aux sociétés sportives ou culturelles/de loisir
22. Récréations, passetemps, loisirs
23. Adresse privé, (avec permission)
24. Titre postal, suivi de nom, adresse pour courrier, numéro de téléphone, télex et fac-similé

Note:
Dans plusieurs cas on n'a pas pu composé une biographie complète, par manque d'information matérielle; dans ces cas on n'a imprimé que les titres de catégories pour lesquelles on a d'information.

---

1. Nachname gefolgt von dem/den Vornamen / Initialen
2. Staatsangehörigkeit des Wohnortes gefolgt von wichtigster politischer Stellung
3. Geburtsdatum gefolgt vom Geburtsort
4. Vollständiger Name des Vaters gefolgt vom vollständigen Namen der Mutter
5. Vollständiger Name des Ehepartners
6. Mädchenname der Ehefrau, falls zutreffend
7. Datum der Eheschließung
8. Prominente öffentliche Funktion des Ehepartners
9. Kinder, aufgeführt nach Namen, Geschlecht oder Anzahl
10. Religion, falls zutreffend
11. Fremdsprachenkenntnisse in Schrift oder Wort, einschließlich Muttersprache bzw. örtlicher Dialekt, falls zutreffend
12. Besuchte Schulen, Colleges bzw. Universitäten, mit Angabe der Fächer, Abschlüsse und Studienzeit
13. Augenblickliche politische Parteizugehörigkeit
14. Wichtigste politische Stellung
15. Politischer Werdegang in chronologischer Reihenfolge einschließlich der gegenwärtigen Stellung
16. Politische, akademische bzw. professionelle Interessengebiete
17. Mitgliedschaft bei geschäftlichen, professionellen bzw. akademischen Körperschaften/Organisationen
18. Einzelheiten der nicht-politischen Laufbahn
19. Preise und Auszeichnungen für akademische, zivile, militärische oder andere Leistungen
20. Bücher, Artikel bzw. anderweitige Veröffentlichungen
21. Zugehörigkeit zu Gesellschafts- bzw. Freizeitklubs
22. Freizeitbeschäftigungen, Hobbies und persönliche Interessen
23. Privatadresse, falls angegeben
24. Postanschrift mit Namen und Büroadresse, gefolgt von Telefon-, Telex- und Telefaxnummern

In vielen Fällen war es nicht möglich, einen vollständigen Eintrag zusammenzustellen, in welchem Fall alle vorliegenden Daten aufgenommen wurden und die Abschnitte, für die keine Informationen zur Verfügung standen, nicht gedruckt wurden.

---

1. Apellido seguido por nombre(s) / iniciales.
2. Nacionalidad del domicilio seguida por posición política principal.
3. Fecha de nacimiento seguida por lugar de nacimiento.
4. Nombre completo del padre seguido por nombre completo de la madre.
5. Nombre completo del cónyuge.
6. Nombre de soltero/a del cónyuge, donde proceda.
7. Año del matrimonio.
8. Papel público prominente del cónyuge.
9. Hijos, en lista por nombre(s), género(s) o número.
10. Denominación religiosa, donde proceda.
11. Lenguas escritas o habladas, incluídas la lengua primera o dialecto(s) locales, donde proceda.
12. Escuela(s), colegios(s) o universidad(es) asistidas, con materias, cualificaciones y fechas de asistencia.
13. Militancia actual en partidos políticos.
14. Cargo político primario.
15. Detalles de la carrera política, en orden cronológico incluyendo el cargo actual.
16. Intereses políticos, académicos o profesionales.
17. Calidad de miembro de cuerpos/organizaciones comerciales, profesionales o académicas.
18. Detalles de la carrera no política.
19. Honores y premios por logros académicos, civiles, militares u otros.
20. Libros, artículos u otros trabajos publicados.
21. Pertenencia a clubs sociales o recreativos.
22. Recreo, aficiones o intereses de tiempo libre.
23. Dirección privada, donde se facilite.
24. Título y nombre postal con dirección de oficina, seguido por números de teléfono, telex y fax.

En muchos casos no ha sido posible compilar una entrada completa, en cuyo caso se han incluido todos los datos disponibles y las secciones para las cuales no existen datos no han sido impresas.

1　姓に続いて名／イニシャル
2　国籍（定住地）に続いて主要政治的地位
3　生年月日に続いて生誕地
4　父親の姓名に続いて母親の姓名
5　配偶者の姓名
6　配偶者の結婚前の名前（該当する場合のみ）
7　結婚年月日
8　配偶者の顕著な公的役割
9　子供の名前、性別、或は数
10　宗教（該当する場合のみ）
11　第一母国語或は方言（該当する場合のみ）を含めて、（書き言葉或は話し言葉）
12　卒業の学校、大学を含めた高等教育、専攻分野、取得資格、在学年月日
13　現在の政党所属
14　主な政治的地位
15　現在の地位をも含めた、政治的履歴
16　政治、学問、或は職業上の興味
17　ビジネス、職業、或は学問上の団体／組織への所属
18　非政治的履歴
19　学業、公務、軍事的栄誉、その他の実績
20　本、記事、その他の出版物
21　社交或はレジャー・クラブへの所属
22　レクリエーション、趣味、レジャーへの興味
23　自宅の住所（提供された場合のみ）
24　郵送時の称号、名前、職場住所、電話、テレックス、ファックス番号

＊多くの場合、全ての区分にわたって編纂することは困難でしたが、そのような場合には、入手可能な情報は全て含め、情報の存在しない部分は印刷されていますん。

ABBREVIATIONS

A

ADC	Aide-de-Camp
admin.	administration, administrative, administrator
AEC	Atomic Energy Commission
AFHQ	Allied Forces Headquarters
AIB	Associate of the Institute of Bankers
AICA	Associate Member, Commonwealth Institute of Accountants
AICE	Associate of Institute of Civil Engineers
AID	Agency for International Development
AIL	Associate of the Institute of Linguistics
AIME	Associate of the Institute of Mining Engineers
AIMM	Associate of the Institute of Mining and Metallurgy
A. Inst. CE	Associate of the Institute of Civil Engineers
Amb. Ex. & Plen.	Ambassador Extraordinary and Plenipotentiary
APEX	Association of Professional, Executive, Clerical and Computer Staff
approx.	approximately
apptd.	appointed
Apr.	April
ARCVS	Associate of the Royal College of Veterinary Surgeons
ARIC	Associate of the Royal Institute of Chemistry
Assn.	Association
Assoc.	Associate
Asst.	Assistant
Aug.	August

B

BA	Bachelor of Arts
barr.	barrister (lawyer)
B.Agr.	Bachelor of Agriculture
B.Arch.	Bachelor of Architecture
BA.Sc.	Bachelor of Applied Science
BAO	Bachelor of Art of Obstetrics
BBA	Bachelor of Business Administration
BBC	British Broadcasting Corporation
BCE	Bachelor of Civil Engineering
B.Ch.	Bachelor of Surgery
B. Chir.	Bachelor of Surgery
B. Comm.	Bachelor of Commerce
BD	Bachelor of Divinity
Bd.	Board
BD.Sc.	Bachelor of Dental Science
BE&A	Bachelor of Engineering and Architecture
B.Ed.	Bachelor of Education
BEE	Bachelor of Electrical Engineering
BEF	British Expeditionary Force
BEM	British Empire Medal
BIM	British Institute of Management
BIS	Bank for International Settlements
B.Litt.	Bachelor of Letters
BMA	British Medical Association
B.Phil.	Bachelor of Philosophy
Bros.	Brothers
BS	Bachelor of Surgery
BSA	Bachelor of Science in Agriculture
B.Sc.	Bachelor of Science
B.Soc.Sc.	Bachelor of Social Sciences
Bt.	Baronet

B.V.Sc.	Bachelor of Veterinary Science

C

CA	Chartered Accountant
Capt.	Captain
CB	Companion of the Order of the Bath
CBE	Commander of the Order of the British Empire
CBI	Confederation of British Industry
CE	Civil Engineer
CGIA	City and Guilds of London Insignia Award
CH	Companies of Honour
Ch.B.	Bachelor of Chemistry
Ch.D.	Doctor of Chemistry
Chllr.	Chancellor
Ch.M.	Master of Surgery
Chmn.	Chairman
Chwn.	Chairwoman
CIE	Companion of the Order of the Indian Empire
CIGS	Chief of the Imperial General Staff
C-in-C	Commander-in-Chief
CIO	Congress of Industrial Organisation
Cllr.	Councillor
CM	Master in Surgery
Cmdr.	Commander
Cmdre.	Commodore
CMG	Companion of the Order of St. Michael and St. George
Cmmw.	(The) Commonwealth
Cmn.	Commission
Cmnr.	Commissioner
Cncl.	Council
CND	Campaign for Nuclear Disarmament
CO	Commanding Officer
Co.	Company
Coll.	College
Co-op.	Co-operative
Corp.	Corporation
CSI	Companion of the Order of the Star of India
C.St.J.	Commander of the Order of St. John of Jerusalem

Cttee(s).	Committee(s)
CVO	Commander of the Royal Victorian Order

D

d.	daughters, (filles, Töchter, hijas)
DBA	Doctor of Business Administration
DBE	Dame Commander of the Order of the British Empire
D.Comm.	Doctor of Commerce
D.Com.L.	Doctor of Commercial Law
DCS	Doctor of Commercial Sciences
DDR	Deutsches Demokratische Republik
DDS	Doctor of Dental Surgery
DD	Doctor of Divinity
decd.	deceased
Dec.	December
D.Econ.	Doctor of Economics
Deleg.	Delegation
Dep.	Deputy
dept.	department
dev.	development
DFC	Distinguished Flying Cross
DFM	Distinguished Flying Medal
DHL	Doctor of Humane Letters
Dir.	Director
Dir.-Gen.	Director-General
DL	Deputy Lieutenant
D.Litt.	Doctor of Literature
D.Psych.	Doctor of Psychology
Dr.	Doctor(ate)
Drs.	Doctor Doctor; Doctorates
DSC	Distinguished Service Cross
D.Sc.(Agric.)	Doctor of (Agricultural) Science
DSM	Distinguished Service Medal
DSO	Distinguished Service Order
DV.Sc.	Doctor of Veterinary Science
D.Zool.	Doctor of Zoology

E

EBU	European Broadcasting Union
EC	European Community
ECA	Economic Co-operation Administration
ECE	European Central Inland Transport Association
econ.	economics
ECOSOC	Economic and Social Council for the United Nations
EEC	European Economic Community
EFTA	European Free Trade Association
En.Ex.& Min.Plen.	Envoy Extraordinary and Minister Plenipotentiary
EP	European Parliament
ERD	Emergency Reserve Decoration (Army)
est.	established
e.t.	en titre
etc.	et cetera (and so on)
EURATOM	European Atomic Energy Community
Exec.	Executive

F

FAO	Food and Agriculture Organisation
FBA	Fellow of the British Academy
FCA	Fellow of the Institute of Chartered Accountants
FCIB	Fellow of the Corporation of Insurance Brokers
FCO	Foreign and Commonwealth Office
FCWA	Fellow of the Institute for Cost and Works Accountants
Feb.	February
Fed.	Federation, Federal
F.Eng.	Fellowship in Engineering
FICE	Fellow, Institute of Civil Engineers
fmr.	former
fmrly.	formerly
FRAe.S	Fellow, Royal Aeronautical Society
FRHS	Fellow, Royal Historical Society
FRICS	Fellow, Royal Institute of Chartered Surveyors
FRS	Fellow, Royal Society
FRSL	Fellow, Royal Society of Literature
FSE	Fellow, Society of Engineers
FSM	Federal States of Micronesia

G

GATT	General Agreement on Tariffs and Trade
GB	Great Britain
GBE	Knight (or Dame) Grand Cross of the Order of the British Empire
GCB	Knight Grand Cross of the Order of the Bath
GCIE	Knight Grand Commander of the Order of the Indian Empire
GCMG	Knight Grand Cross of the Order of St Michael and St George
GCSI	Knight Grand Commander of the Order of the Star of India
GCVO	Knight Grand Cross of the Royal Victorian Order
GDR	German Democratic Republic
GOI	Government of India
GM	George Medal
GMB	General and Municipal Boilermakers Union
GNP	Gross National Product
Govt.	Government
Gp.	Group
GPO	General Post Office

H

h.c.	honoris causa
HE	Her Eminence, Her Excellency
HM	Her Majesty('s)
Hon.	Honourable, Honorary
Hon.Consul.	Honourable Consul
Hosp.	Hospital

HQ	Headquarters	KCIE	Knight Commander of the Order of the Indian Empire
HRH	Her Royal Highness		
HSH	Her Serene Highness		
		KCMG	Knight Commander of the Order of St Michael and St. George

I

		KCSG	Knight Commander of the Order of St Gregory
IAEA	International Atomic Energy Agency		
IATA	International Air Transport Association	KCSI	Knight Commander of the Order of the Star of India
IBA	Institute of British Architects	KCVO	Knight Commander of the Royal Victorian Order
IBC	International Broadcasting Corporation	KG	Knight of the Order of the Garter
IBRD	International Bank for Reconstruction and Development	KLJ	Knight, St. Lazarus of Jeruselem
		KSG	Knight of St Gregory the Great
ICAO	International Civil Aviation Organisation	K.St.J.	Knight of the Order of St John of Jerusalem
ICE	Institute of Civil Engineers	KT	Knight of the Order ot the Thistle
ICRC	International Committee of the Red Cross	Kt.	Knight
ILO	International Labour Office		
	International Labour Organisation		

L

IMCO	Inter-governmental Maritime Consultative Organisation	LDP	Liberal Democratic Party
		LHB	Bachelor of Humane Letters
IMF	International Monetary Fund	LHD	Doctor of Humane Letters
Inc.	Incorporated	Lt.	Lieutenant
Inst.	Institute	LLB	Bachelor of Laws
Instn.	Institution	LLD	Doctor of Laws
Int.	International	LLL	Licentiate of Laws
IPU	Inter-Parliamentary Union	LLM	Master of Laws
		LSE	London School of Economics
		Ltd.	Limited

J

M

Jan.	January	MA	Master of Arts
JP	Justice of the Peace	Man. Dir.	Managing Director
Jr.	Junior	Mar.	March
Jul.	July	MB	Bachelor of Medicine
Jun.	June	MBA	Master of Business Administration
		MBE	Member of the Order of the British Empire

K

KBE	Knight Commander of the Order of the British Empire	MC	Military Cross
		MCC.	Marylebone Cricket Club
KCB	Knight Commander of the Order of the Bath	M.Ch.	Master of Surgery
		MCL	Master of Civil Law

MCS	Master of Commercial Science	**P**	
MD	Doctor of Medicine	**Parly.**	Parliamentary
ME	Master of Engineering	**PEN**	Poets, Playwrights, Essayists, Editors and Novelists (Club)
M.Ec.	Master of Economics		
Mem.	Member		
Mgr.	Manager	**PGCE**	Post Graduate Certificate of Education
Min. Plen.	Minister Plenipotentiary		
Min.	Ministry	**Ph.D.**	Doctor of Philosophy
MM	Military Medal	**PLO**	Palestine Liberation Organisation
MP	Member of Parliament		
M.Phil.	Master of Philosophy	**Pref.**	Prefecture
MACGP	Master of Royal College of General Practitioners	**Pres.**	President
		PRO	Public Relations Officer
MRCS	Member of the Royal College of Surgeons	**Prof.**	Professor
MRI	Member of the Royal Institution	**Q**	
		QC	Queen's Counsel
MS	Master of Sciences, Master of Surgery		
M.Sc.	Master of Science	**R**	
Mt.	Mount	**RA**	Royal Academy, Royal Artillery
		RAC	Royal Automobile Club
N		**RAF**	Royal Air Force
		RC	Roman Catholic
Nat.	National	**RD**	Royal Naval and Marine Forces Reserve Decoration
NATO	North Atlantic Treaty Organization		
NEC	National Executive Committee	**Regt.**	regiment
		rep.	representative
née	refers to maiden name	**resd.**	resigned
NI	Non-attached	**retd.**	retired
Nov.	November	**Rev.**	Reverend
		RFC	Rugby Football Club
O		**RIBA**	Royal Institute of British Architects
		RIIA	Royal Institute of International Affairs
Oct.	October		
OECD	Organisation for Economic Co-operation and Development	**RMC**	Royal Military College
		RN	Royal Navy
		ROC	Republic of China
OM	Member of the Order of Merit	**Rt.Hon.**	(The) Right Honourable
		Rt.Rev.	(The) Right Reverend
OPEC	Organisation of Petroleum Exporting Countries	**S**	
opp.	opposition		
O.St.J	Officer of the Most Venerable Order of the Hospital of St. John of Jerusalem	**s.**	sons, (fils, Söhne, hijos)
		Sch.	School
		Scot.	Scotland
		Sec.	Secretary
Oy.	Osakeyhtio (Limited Company)	**Sec.-Gen.**	Secretary-General
		Sep.	September

Soc.	Society	UNRRA	United Nations Relief and Rehabilitation Administration
Sr.	Senior		
St.	Saint, Street		
Supt.	Superintendent	UPA	Universal Postal Union
		USA	United States of America

T

V

TD	Territorial Decoration		
Treas.	Treasurer	VC	Victoria Cross
TUC	Trades Union Congress	Vice-Chmn.	Vice-Chairman
TV	Television	Vice-Pres.	Vice-President

U

W

UK	United Kingdom	WEU	Western European Union
UNDP	United Nations Development Programme	WFTU	World Federation of Trade Unions
UNESCO	United Nations Educational, Scientific and Cultural Organisation	WHO	World Health Organisation

Y

UNIDO	United Nations Industrial Development Organisation	YMCA	Young Men's Christian Association
Univ.	University	YWCA	Young Women's Christian Association
UN(O)	United Nations (Organisation)		

PART I
BIOGRAPHIES

A

ABAIJAH, Josephine; Papua New Guinean, Leader of Papua Besena; *party:* Papua Besena (PB); *office address:* Ms Josephine Abaijah, Papua Besena, POB 661, Port Moresby, Papua New Guinea.

ABBOTT, Diane Julie; British, Member of Parliament; *born:* 27 September 1953; *education:* Newnham College, Cambridge; *party:* Labour Party, 1971; *political career:* Mem., Westminster City Council, 1982-86; MP for Hackney North and Stoke Newington, 1987-; *office address:* Ms Diane Abbott, House of Commons, London, SW1A OAA, England.

ABDULLAH, Anna; Tanzanian, Minister of Agriculture, Livestock Development and Co-operatives; *office address:* Ms Anna Abdullah, Ministry of Agriculture and Livestock Development, PO Box 9192, Dar-es-Salaam, Tanzania.

ABZUG, Bella S.; American, Member of the Democrat National Committee; *born:* 24 July 1920, New York City, USA; *parents:* Emanuel Savitzky and Esther Savitzky; *married:* Martin Abzug, 1944; *children:* Eve Gail, Isobel; *education:* Hunter College, AB; Columbia Law School; Jewish Theological Seminary; *party:* Democratic Party; *political career:* Mem., House of Reps. for New York, 1971-77; delegate Democrat National Convention, 1972, 1976, 1980 and 1984; Co-Chwn., President's National Advisory Cttee. for Women, 1978; Mem., Democrat National Cttee; *professional career:* former, daily news commentator on CNN; currently, practising attorney and lecturer; *publications:* Bella! Ms Abzug Goes to Washington, 1972; Gender Gap; Bella Abzug's Guide to Political Power for American Women; *office address:* Mrs Bella Abzug, Two Fifth Avenue, New York City, New York 10011, USA.

ACOSTA, Hon. Socorro O.; Filipino, Congresswoman; *born:* 17 November 1934, Bohol, The Philippines; *married:* Dr. Juan C. Acosta; *children:* Juan Benedict, Juan Romeo Nereus, Maria Lourdes; *education:* UP Los Banos, BS, Home Technology, MS, Poultry Nutrition; Univ. of Hawaii, MS, Animal Nutrition; Iowa State Univ., USA, Doctorate, Products Technology; *political career:* former Councillor, then Mayor for seven years, Manolo Fortich, Bukidnon; Congresswoman; *honours and awards:* Altrussan International Award, 1960; Most Outstanding Kagawad, 1979; 'Most Outstanding Mayor', Region X and Bukidnon Province, 1983 and 1985; *office address:* The Hon. Ms Socorro Acosta, The Congress of the Philippines - House of Representatives, Batasang Pambansa Bldg., Quezon City, Manila, The Philippines.

ADAM-SCHWÄTZER, Dr. Irmgard; German, Minister of State for Regional Planning, Building and Urban Development; *born:* 1942; *education:* Univs. of Passau, Münster and Bonn, pharmacy, 1961-67; Univ. of Bonn, Dr. rer. nat., 1971; *party:* Freie Demokratische Partei (FDP, Free Democratic Party), 1975; *political career:* Mem., Northrhine-Westphlia Land Exec., 1975-; Mem., Bundestag, 1980-; Sec.-Gen., FDP, 1982-84; Fed. Treasurer and Chwn., working group for social policy, FDP Parly. Party, 1984-87; Minister of State, Foreign Office, 1987-91; Minister of State for Regional Planning, Building and Urban Development, 1991-; *professional career:* pharmacist; *private address:* 5160 Düren, Germany; *office address:* Dr. Irmgard Adam-Schwätzer, Ministry of Regional Planning, Construction and Urban Development, 5300 Bonn 2, Deichmannsaue, Germany.

ADLER, Brigitte; German, Member of the Bundestag; *born:* 22 April 1944, Drangstedt, Wesermünde; *religion:* Protestant; *education:* Wertheim High School, intermediary examination; banking training; Heidelberg teacher training college, aptitude test for primary teaching; Weingarten/Tettnang Primary Teachers' Inst., teacher training examination, Parts I and II; *party:* Sozialdemokratische Partei Deutschlands (SPD, Social Democratic Party of Germany), 1970; *political career:* municipal councillor, Mauer, 1975-84; mem. of Landtag, Baden-Württemberg, 1980-87; mem. of Land cttee. Baden-Württemberg since 1981; mem. of Bundestag (Baden-Württemberg list); *professional career:* banking, 5 years; Elementary school teacher in Radolfzell, Neckargemünd and Heidelberg, Rohrbach; Rehabilitation Foundation Heidelberg, 6 years; mem. of GEW, AWO, Friends of Nature, BUND, German Society for the Protection of Birds, Society for the Protection of Children, Women help Women Assn. e.V., Polio Aid Kenya, EU, Pro Familia e.V., Amnesty International, Marie-Schlei Support Assn. e.V.; Land chwn., Working Group of Socialist Women, Baden-

Württemberg since 1983; *office address:* Frau Brigitte Adler, Bundeshaus, 5300 Bonn 1, West Germany.

AELVOET, Magda; Belgian, Senator; *born:* 4 April 1944, Steenokkerzeel; *parents:* Willem Aelvoet and Julia Endriatis; *married:* Henrard Raymond, 1969; *public role of spouse:* Member of staff of the VVI; *children:* three; *religion:* Christian; *languages:* Dutch, French, German, English, Spanish; *education:* German philology and political and social sciences; *party:* Anders Gaan Leven (Agalev, Dutch speaking Ecologist Party); *political career:* Provincial Senator Antwerp, 1985-; former member of the steering group and the Exec. committee; member, senate Cttee. on aid to developing countries; member, senate Cttee. on foreign relations; member, senate Cttee. on institutional reform; member without voting rights, senate Cttee. on infrastructure; *interests:* foreign affairs, development co-operation, women's emancipation; *professional career:* Vice chairman University Parish; staff co-worker of Misereor, Coopibo, Wereldverbond van de Arbeid en Broederlijk Delen.; member, adult education institute Dialoog; *publications:* a number of articles about womens emancipation, abortion, Vrije Tribunes, South Africa, Zaire, etc; *recreations:* ping-pong; *private address:* Koningin Astridlaan 39, 3200 Leuven, Belgium; *office address:* Ms Magda Aelvoet, Senate, Palais de la Nation, Place de a Nation 1, 1000 Brussels, Belgium.

AF UGGLAS, Margaretha; Swedish, Member of the Riksdag; *born:* 5 January 1939, Stockholm, Sweden; *parents:* Hugo Stenbeck and Märtha Stenbeck (née Odelfeldt); *married:* Bertil af Ugglas, 1966; *religion:* Protestant; *languages:* English, German, French; *education:* Harvard-Radcliffe Program, Business Administration, 1961; Stockholm School of Economics, MBA, 1964; *party:* Moderata Samlingsparteit (Moderate Party); *political career:* Member, Cttee. on Foreign Affairs; Board member, Swedish Aid Agency; Delegate to the Council of Europe; Spokesman for Foreign Affairs; Chwn., European Union of Women, (Swedish section); mem. of the Riksdag, 1974-; *professional career:* editorial writer, Svenska Dagbladet, 1968-74; Board member, STORA, Skandinavinvest; editor, Svensk Tidskrift; *office address:* Ms Margaretha af Ugglas, Riksdag, Fack, S-100 12 Stockholm, Sweden.

AGANA, Hon. Venecia B; Filipino, Congresswoman; *parents:* Former Ambassador Jacinto Castelar Borja (decd.) and Natividad Lopez Borja; *married:* Marcelino A. Agana Jr; *children:* Patricia, Marcelino, Natividad, Jacinto, Asuncion, Roberto; *religion:* Catholic; *languages:* Filipino, Spanish, English; *education:* Univ. of Sto. Tomas, B.Sc., Philosophy; *party:* Laban ng Demokratikong Pilipino (LDP); *political career:* Congresswoman; Mem., Women's Rights Movement of the Philippines; Mem., the Green Coalition; Mem.,

Philippine Legislators Cttee. on Population and Development Foundation Inc; *professional career:* Pres., Venecia Commercial Corp.; Vice Pres. and Treasurer, First Integrated Insurance and Bonding Co.; Dir., Iligan Light and Power Corp.; Chairperson, UNIDO and LABAN, Bohol; Dir. and Treasurer, Mosares Foundation, St. Paul's College; *clubs:* Manila Polo Club; Baguio Country Club; Cursillo Movement, Laguna; Rotar Ann; Tarlac; Casino Espanol, Manila; *recreations:* dancing, reading; *private address:* 16, 13th St., New Manila, Quezon City, the Philippines; *office address:* The Hon. Ms Venecia Agana, The Congress of the Philippines - House of Representatives, Batasang Pambansa Bldg., Quezon City, Manila, The Philippines.

AGLIETTA, Maria Adelaide; Italian, Member of the European Parliament; *born:* 4 June 1940, Turin, Italy; *languages:* Italian, French; *education:* General Certificate of Education; *party:* Partito Radicale (PR, Radical Party); *political career:* Nat. Secretary, PR, 1976; and 1977; Nat. Treasurer, PR, 1979; mem. Chamber of Deputies 1979; elected Deputy, for Turin-Novara-Vercelli, 1979; Pres. of Parliamentary Group of Radical Deputies; mem., Cttee., Interior; re-elected Deputy, Verona-Padova-Vicenza-Rovigo, 1983; mem. Supervisory Parliamentary Committee; mem., Cttee. on Justice; Resigned, August 1986; mem. Federal secretariat of PR, 1983-87; re-elected Deputy, Turin-Novara-Vercelli, 1987; mem., Cttee. on Environment, Land, and Public Works; elected to the European Parliament, on the Green Rainbow list, 1989; Mem., Institutional Affairs Cttee.; Mem., R.E.X. Sub-Cttee. on Human Rights; Co-Pres., Green Group; *interests:* women's and prisoner's rights, penal law; *office address:* Ms Maria Aglietta, European Parliament, Rue Belliend, 97/113 B-1040, Bruxelles, Belgium.

AGNELLI, Susanna; Italian, Senator; *born:* 24 April 1922, Turin, Italy; *children:* six; *party:* Partito Repubblicano Italiano, (PRI, Italian Republican Party), 1976; *political career:* Town Councillor, Monte Argentario, and Mayor, 1974-84; Deputy, Parliament, 1976, re-elected 1979; mem. of European Parliament 1979-81; elected Senator 1983-; Under-Sec. of State for Foreign Affairs, responsible for South and North American Affairs from 1983; mem. independent Commission on International Humanitarian Issues, Geneva 1984-87; mem. World Commission on Environment and Development, Geneva, 1984-87; mem. Founding Cttee., International Baccalaureate Office, Geneva; mem. International Council University for Peace, Costa Rica; mem. Board of International Institute on Ageing (Malta); mem. Rockefeller University Council, New York; *honours and awards:* Honorary Degree, Doctor of Laws Mount Holyoke College, Massachusetts, 1984; *publications:* articles in magazines and newspapers; Author of best-seller. 'We always wore sailor suits', 1975; 'Remember

Gualeguaychui', 1982; 'Addio, addio, mio ultimo amore', 1985; *office address:* Ms Susanna Agnelli, Senato della Repubblica, Palazzo Madama, 00100 Rome, Italy.

AGUIAR, Maria Manuela Aguiar Dias Moreira; Portuguese, Deputy; *born:* 9 June 1942, Oporto; *parents:* Joao Fernandes Dias Moreira and Maria Antonia Barbosa Aguiar (née Barbosa Aguiar); *married:* Manuel Vitorino de Queiroz, 1965: divorced; *religion:* Roman Catholic; *languages:* fluent English and French; Spanish, Italian; *education:* Liceu Rainha Santa Isabel, Oporto (Secondary School), 1958-60; Licenciate of Law with Distinction, Coimbra Univ., 1960-65; Higher Diploma of Law Studies and Research, Faculty of Law, Catholic Institute of Paris, France; *party:* Partido Social Democrata (PSD, Social Democratic Party), 1980; *political career:* Secretary of State for Labour, 1978-79; Secretary of State for Emigration and Portuguese Communities, 1980-81; Deputy, Assembly of the Republic, 1980-; Secretary of State for Emigration, 1983-85; Secretary of State for Portuguese Communities, 1985-87; elected Vice-Pres. Assembly of the Republic, 1987-90; Pres., Parly. Cttee. on Women, 1987-88; mem., Parly. Cttee. on Foreign Affairs; mem., PSD National Council; *interests:* Foreign Affairs; International Relations; Emigration; Human Rights; Women's Rights; Labour Law; Civil Law; *professional career:* researcher, Ministry of Labour Study Centre, 1967-74; Lecturer; Faculty of Human Sciences, Catholic Univ., Lisbon, 1972-73; Lecturer, Faculty of Law, Coimbra Univ., 1974-76; Legal Adviser, Ombudsman's Office, 1976-78; *honours and awards:* Grand Cross of the Order of Merit, Italy, 1980; Grand Cross of the Order of Merit, West Germany, 1980; Grand Cross, Order of the Phoenix, Greece, 1981; Grand Cross of the Order of Merit of Luxembourg; Grand Cross of the Order of the White River, Brasil; Grand Cross of the Order of Francisco Miranda, Venezuela; Grand Officer, Order of Merit, France; Grand Cross of the Southern Cross of Brasil, 1981; Grand Cross of Leopold II of Belgium, 1985; Grand Cross of the British Empire, 1985; *publications:* Politica de Emigraçao e Comunidades Portuguesas, 1986; Emigration Policy and Portuguese Communities, 1987; and numerous articles on labour law, emigration etc. in specialized journals; *clubs:* Elos Club of Porto; Euro-Atlantic Institute; Afro-Luso Foundation; mem. of the Luso Academy of Sciences, Arts and Humanities of Sao Paulo; Polytechnical School of Lisbon; Fontes Pereira de Melo Institute; Association for Citizen's Promotion and Defence; Parliamentarians for East Timor; *recreations:* sports, cinema, music, reading; *private address:* Ruga 7, 307-Espinho, Portugal; *office address:* Ms Maria Aguiar, Assembléia da República, Palacia de S Bento, 1296 Lisboa Codex, Portugal.

AHEARN, Theresa Mary; Irish, Member of the Dáil Éireann; *born:* 11 May 1951, Tipperary, Ireland; *parents:* John Scott and Katherine Scott (née Lonergan); *married:* Liam Ahearn, 1976; *public role of spouse:* President of Calik Lions Club; *children:* Patrick, Garret, Liam, Scott; *religion:* Roman Catholic; *languages:* English, Irish, French; *education:* Golden Nat. School, 1956-64; Presentation Convent, Cashel, 1964-69; Univ. College, Dublin, 1969-71; St. Patrick's College, Maynooth, 1971-72; *party:* Fine Gael, 1979; *political career:* Mem., South Tipperary Council, 1983-; Mem., South Tipperary Cttee. of Agriculture, 1983-85; Mem., local health cttee., 1983-88; Mem., Cospoir, 1985-; Mem., Dáil, June 1989-; Mem., South Tipperary VEC; spokesperson on Third Level Education; *interests:* agriculture, education, environment; *professional career:* maths teacher, Central Technical Institute, Clonmel, 1972-89; *honours and awards:* All-Ireland semi-finalist in public speaking and debating; *clubs:* Teachers Union of Ireland, IFA, Macra-na-Feirme; *recreations:* reading, swimming, walking; *private address:* Ballindoney Grange, Clonmel, Co. Tipperary, Ireland; *office address:* Ms Theresa Ahearn, Dáil Éireann, Lenister House, Kildare Street, Dublin 2, Ireland.

AHLOKOBA, Aissa; Togo, Minister of Social and Women's Affairs; *office address:* Ms Aissa Ahlokoba, Ministry of Social and Women's Affairs, rue Branly, Lomé, Togo; *phone:* 21 29 83.

AHOYO, Véronique; Benin, Minister of Labour and Social Welfare; *office address:* Ms Véronique Ahoyo, Ministry of Labour and Social Welfare, BP 907, Cotonou, Benin.

AIREY OF ABINGDON, Baroness (cr. 1979, Life Peer) Diana Josceline Barbara Neave Airey; British, Member of the House of Lords; *born:* 7 July 1919; *parents:* the late Thomas Arthur Walter Gifford; *married:* the late Airey Middleton Sheffield Neave, 1942; *children:* two s., one d; *education:* privately and abroad; *party:* Conservative Party; *political career:* House of Lords, 1979-; mem., North Atlantic Assembly, 1983-84; fmr. Pres., Anglo-Polish Cons. Soc; *interests:* Arts and heritage, defence, industry; *professional career:* RAF Hospital, Foreign Office and Polish Min. of Information, 1939-45; trustee, Nat. Heritage Memorial Fund, 1980-88; *clubs:* Dorneywood Trust (trustee); Stansted Park Foundation (trustee); City of London (Freeman); Imperial War Museum (trustee); *recreations:* reading, theatre, opera; *office address:* Baroness Airey of Abingdon, House of Lords, London SW1A 0PW.

AISSATOU, Yaou; Cameroon, Minister of Social Affairs and Women's Affairs; *education:* Univ. of Brussels; MA Economic, USA; *political career:* Minister of Social Affairs and Women's Affairs; *professional career:* Bank of Société Nationale d'Investissement

(BSI, National Investment Corporation); *office address:* Mme. Yaou Aissatou, Ministry of Social Affairs and Women's Affairs, Yaoundé, Cameroon.

AKRITA, Silva; Greek, Member of Parliament; *children:* Elena; *party:* Panelliniou Socialistikou Kinema (PASOK, Panhellenic Socialist Movement); *political career:* MP, 1974-77; MP, 1981-85, MP, B' Athens, 1989; Alternate Minister of Health, Welfare and Social Security, 1987; *professional career:* sociologist; *office address:* Vouli, Parliament Building, Syntagma, Greece.

AKUE, Sokewoe; Togo, Member of the National Assembly; *office address:* Ms Sokewoe Akue, Assemblée Nationale, B.P. 3227, Lomé, Togo; *phone:* 21 20 61; 21 20 63; 21 00 62.

AKUOKO SARPONG, Nana; Ghana, Minister of Health; *office address:* Ms Nana Akuoko Sarpong, Ministry of Health, PO Box M 44, Accra, Ghana.

AKYOL, Türkan; Turkish, Member of the National Assembly; *office address:* Ms Türkan Akyol, National Assembly, TBNN, Ankara, Turkey.

al-ATTAR, Najah; Syrian, Minister of Culture; *office address:* Ms Najah al-Attar, Ministry of Culture and National Guidance, Rawda Street, Damascus, Syria.

ALBANESE MORELLA, Constance; American, Member of the House of Representatives; *born:* 12 February 1901, Bethesda, Mass., USA; *parents:* Salvatore Albanese and Christine Albanese (née Fallette); *married:* Anthony Morella, 1954; *children:* Paul, Mark, Laura; *religion:* Roman Catholic; *education:* Boston Univ., AB, 1954; American Univ., MA, 1967; *party:* Republican Party; *political career:* Mem., Montgomery County Commission for Women, 1972-75, Pres., 1974-75; Mem., C&O Canal Park Advisory Commission, 1976-82, Vice-Chwn., 1977-82; Mem. and Education Chwn., Maryland International Women's Year Co-ordinating Cttee., 1976-77; Maryland State Delegate, District 16, 1979-86; Mem., House of Reps., Maryland District 8, 1987-; currently: Mem., Post Office and Civil Service, Science, Space and Technology Cttees; *memberships:* League of Women Voters; American Assn of Univ. Women; Maryland Consumer Cncl.; Hon. Mem., Montgomery County Hospice Society; *professional career:* prof., Montgomery College, Rockville, Maryland, 1970-; trustee, Capitol Inst. of Technology, Kensington, Maryland and Trinity College, Washington DC; Board Mem., Shady Grove Hosp. Foundation; *honours and awards:* American Univ. Distinguished Alumna Award, 1980 and 1982; Distinguished Legislator Award, Maryland Victims Advocacy Network; Collegium of Distinguished Alumni, Boston Univ; *publications:* The History of the American Woman and Alcoholism, Alcoholism Digest, 1974; *clubs:* Hon. Mem., Zonta International; *private address:* 6601 Millwood Road, Bethesda, Maryland 20817, USA; *office address:* Mrs Constance Albanese Morella, 1024 Longworth Bldg., Washington DC, 20515, USA.

ALBERICI, Aureliana; Italian, Senator; *born:* 16 September 1941, Bologna, Italy; *education:* Bologna University, Degree in Pedagogics; and Lecturing qualification in Pedagogics; *party:* Partito Democratico della Sinistra (PDS, Party of the Democratic Left); *political career:* Assessor for Public Instruction on Bologna Council, 1975-1983; Nat. Head, School and University Section, PCI Leadership, from 1983; mem. Central Cttee., PCI; elected Senator, Bologna (III)-Imola, 1987; mem. Cttee. on Public Instruction and Cultural Heritage; *professional career:* Lecturer, Pedagogics, Bologna University, until 1986; Lecturer in Adult Education, 'La Sapienza' University, Rome, from 1986; *office address:* Ms Aureliana Alberici, Senato della Repubblica, Palazzo Madama, 00100 Rome, Italy.

ALEMANY I ROCA, Joaquima; Spanish, Member of the Executive National Committee of the Democratic Convergence of Catalonia; *born:* 19 May 1942, Barcelona, Spain; *parents:* Joan Alemany and Julia Roca; *married:* Josep Ma. Sust, 1968; *public role of spouse:* businessman; *children:* Josep Ma., J. Antoni, Mireia; *religion:* Catholic; *languages:* Catalan, Spanish, French, English; *education:* Univ. of Barcelona, Admin. Law, 1960-65; *party:* Democratic Convergence of Catalonia (CDC), 1977; *political career:* District Cncl. Woman, 1983-87; Mem., Commission for the Advancement of Women, 1987-89; Senator for Barcelona, 1989; Vice-Pres., Women's Inst. of Catalonia, 1990; Mem., European Assn. for the Development and Training of Women, 1990; *interests:* the advancement of women; *professional career:* civil servant, county Govt., 1971; *honours and awards:* Leading Lady, Liderman Cirt International, 1988; Golden Madrone, House of Madrid in Barcelona, 1990; *publications:* Feine de Dones, 1989; L'Evolució de la Familia a Catalunya, 1989; El Paper de la Dona a Les Forces Armades, 1991; *clubs:* Club Nautico de Arenys de Mar Club Deportivo St. Pol; *recreations:* reading, painting, music; *private address:* Roger de Llúria 117 6è 1a., 08037 Barcelona, Spain; *office address:* Ms Joaquima Alemany i Roca, Senado, Plaza de la Marina Española 8, Madrid 13, Spain; *phone:* (01) 446 1013.

ALHO, Arja; Finnish, Member of the Eduskunta; *born:* 21 March 1954, Hartola, Finland; *parents:* Aarre Kaj-Erik Alho and Annikki Alho (née Iso-Somppi); *married:* Petteri Väänänen; *religion:* Lutheran; *languages:* Swedish, English, German; *education:* nursing school, Lahti, qualified nurse, 1977; Univ. of Helsinki, Master of Social Sciences, 1989; *party:* Suomen Sosialidemokraattinen Puolue (SDP, Finnish Social Democratic Party), 1970; *political career:* mem. City Council, Helsinki, 1980-, then Chmn. 1989-; elector of the Pres., 1980 and 1988; MP, 1983-; *office address:* Ms Arja Alho, Eduskunta, 00102 Helsinki, Finland.

ALI al-URAYBI, Salmin; Lybian, Assistant Secretary-General of the General People's Congress; *party:* Arab Socialist Union (ASU); *office address:* Ms Salmin Ali al-Uraybi, General People's Congress, C/0 Secretariat of the People's, National Congress, Tripoli., Lybia; *phone:* (21) 30777.

ALIOTO, Angela; American, California State Democratic Chairperson; *born:* San Francisco, California, USA; *married:* Adolfo Veronese, 1968; *children:* Angela Mia, Adolfo, Joseph, Gian-Paolo; *education:* Lone Mountain College, degree (Hons.), 1971; Univ. of San Francisco Law School, LLD, 1983; *political career:* Co-Chwn., Platform Cttee., California State Democratic Party, 1987-; currently Vice-Chwn., California State Democratic Party; Chwn., Special Elections; elected to the San Francisco Board of Supervisors; Chwn., City Services Cttee. and Transportation Authority; Mem., Outer-Continental Shelf Board of Control; *memberships:* Mem., California Bar Assn.; Mem., Political Action Cttee., Raoul Wallenberg Jewish Democratic Club; Board of Dirs., South of Market Business Assn.; Vice-Pres. and Dir., Barr Inst. for Under-priveleged Children; Mothers Against Drunk Driving; National Women's Political Caucus; Women's Campaign Fund; Italian American Bar; *professional career:* owner/manager, travel agency, early 1970's; lawyer, Alioto & Alioto; *clubs:* Harvey Milk Lesbian and Gay Democratic Club; Alice B. Toklas Club; City Democratic Club; City Club; Pro Bono Club; *office address:* Ms Angela Alioto, 400 Van Ness, City Hall Rm 250, San Francisco, California 94102, USA.

ALLIOT-MARIE, Michèle Yvette Marie-Thérèse; French, Member of the European Parliament; *born:* 10 September 1946, Villeneuve-le-Roi, Seine-et-Oise, France; *parents:* Bernard Marie and Renée Marie (née Lekyo); *languages:* English, Spanish; *education:* Folie Saint-James High School, Neuilly-sur-Seine; Laureate, Faculty of Law and Economics, Paris; Certificate of Legal Studies, 1968; second degrees in private law, political science, 1969; second degree in history of law, 1970; bar examination, 1970; certificate of law and economics of African nations, 1970; Masters degree in ethnology, 1970; Doctor of law, 1973; Doctor of political science, 1982; candidate for public law faculty, 1983; *party:* Rassemblement pour la République (RPR, Rally for the Republic); *political career:* technical advisor to Edgar Faure, Minister for Social Issues, 1972-73; representative to office of Bernard Stasi,

Minister of Overseas Territories and Departments, 1973-74; representative to Sec. of State for Tourism, 1974; technical advisor to Jean-Pierre Soisson, Sec. of State for Universities, 1974-76; Principal Private Sec. to Alice Saunier-Seïté, Sec. of State, then Minister for Universities, 1976- 78; member of board, then Chmn. and Managing Director of Uta-Indemnité, 1979-85; RPR representative for administrative and civil service matters, 1981-84; Deputy Secretary-General of Consultative Legal Cttee., 1984-; member of central committee, 1984-, and executive commission, 1985-; RPR National Sec. for teaching and research, 1985-; Deputy for Pyrénés-Atlantiques, 1986, resigned in favour of Alain Lamassoure, re-elected, 1988; Sec. of State to Minister for Education, responsible for teaching, 1986-88; National Sec. of RPR (plan), 1988-; Town Councillor for Ciboure, 1983-; Deputy for Pyrénées-Atlantiques, 1988-; Town Cllr., Biarritz, 1989-; Vice Gen. Sec. for foreign affairs of the RPR, 1990; *memberships:* Mem., then Pres., Information Centre for Family and Women, 1976; Mem., organising Cttee., Biarritz, Iberian and Latin-American Film Festival, 1978; Pres., Cttee. for Defence of Rights and Liberties, 1980; Gen.-Sec., Cncl. of French Assn. of Women Univ. Grads., 1984; *professional career:* assistant in Faculty of Law and Economics, then at University of Paris I, 1970-84; senior lecturer, University of Paris I-Panthéon-Sorbonne, 1984-; member Committee of Working Women, 1974-81; member, then President, Information Centre for Family and Women, 1976-; member, organising cttee., Biarritz, Iberian and Latin-American Film Festival, 1978-; President, Cttee. for Defence of Rights and Liberties, 1980-; Gen. Sec., council of French association of women university graduates, 1984; *honours and awards:* Commander of the Order of the Equatorial Star (Gabon); Commander of the Anjouan Star, Comores and of National Educational Merit (Ivory Coast); Order of the Republic (Egypt); Palmes Académiques, 1st class (Peru), for services to education; *publications:* L'abandon des normes générales de référence dans la jurisprudence du conseil d'Etat; L'administration des DOM - une administration de développement IIAP, 1984; Familles et Droit, 1975; l'Actionnariat des salariés, 1975; la Décision politique: attention une République peut en cacher une autre, 1983; *office address:* Mme. Michèle Alliot-Marie, European Parliament, Centre Européen, Plateau de Kirchberg, BP 2929, Luxembourg.

ALMARIO, Hon. Thelma Z.; Filipino, Congresswoman; *born:* 21 April 1933, Barili, Cebu, The Philippines; *married:* Vicente P. Almario Jr; *children:* Vittorio, Cynthia, Leah, Don, Joy, Mayo, Alma; *education:* Univ. of the East, B.Sc., Business Administation (Accountancy); Certified Public Accountant Exam., 1955; Univ. of Birmingham, England, urban and rural government administration and management; *political career:* former Mayor of

Mati; Congresswoman; *honours and awards:* Outstanding Mayor of the Philippines award, 1970; *office address:* The Hon. Ms Thelma Almario, The Congress of the Philippines - House of Representatives, Batasang Pambansa Bldg., Quezon City, Manila, The Philippines.

ALONI, Shumalit; Israeli, Chairperson of the Civil Rights and Peace Movement; *born:* 1929, Tel-Aviv, Israel; *married:* Reuven Aloni; *public role of spouse:* Director of Israel Lands Authority; *children:* Dror, Nimrod, Udi; *religion:* Jewish; *languages:* Hebrew, English; *education:* David Yellin Teacher's College, Diploma; Hebrew Univ. of U'lem, LLD; *party:* Israeli Labor Party; Ratz (Civil Rights and Peace Movement), since 1973; *political career:* Chwn. and founder, Ratz, 1973-; Mem., Knesset, 1965-; Mem., constitution and Legal Cttee., 1973-; Minister without Portfolio-Labor led Govt., 1974; Mem., Education and Culture Cttee., 1984-; Mem., Finance Cttee., 1988-; *memberships:* Chwn., Israel Cncl. for Consumer Rights, 1966; Board Mem., Centre for Peace in the Middle East and Israel Women's Network; *publications:* The Citizen and His/Her Country; Rights of the Child in Israel; Women as Human Beings; The Arrangement-A State of Law Against a State of Religion; *recreations:* reading, history, tennis; *office address:* Mrs Shumalit Aloni, Ratz, 21 Tchernihovsky Street, Tel-Aviv 63291, Israel; *phone:* 03-5101847; *fax:* 03-661943.

ALQUIER, Jacqueline Lucienne; French, Deputy; *born:* 29 July 1947, Vabre, Tarn, France; *parents:* Emile Bardou and Julia Bardou (née Loup); *married:* André Alquier, 1968; *party:* Parti Socialiste (PS, Socialist Party); *political career:* Deputy mayor, 1977-, and Departmental Councillor, 1979-, for Labruguière; Vice-Chmn. of Departmental Council for Tarn, 1982-85; Deputy for Tarn, 2nd constituency: Castres, replacing Jean-Pierre Gabarrou, deceased, 1985-86; Regional Councillor for Midi-Pyrénées, 1986-; Deputy for Tarn, 1988-; *professional career:* secretary, 1968; *private address:* Les Auriols, 81290 Labruguière, France; *office address:* Mme. Jacqueline Alquier, L'Assemblée Nationale, 126 rue de L'Université, 75355 Paris, France.

ALVA, Margaret; Indian, Member of the Rajya Sabha; *born:* 14 April 1942, Mangalore; *parents:* P.A. Nazareth and Elizabeth Nazareth; *married:* Niranjan Alva; *children:* three s., one d; *education:* BA; BL; *political career:* Gen. Sec., All India Catholic Univ. Federation, 1961; Joint Sec., Govt. Law College Students' Union, 1964; State Convenor, Congress Women's Front, 1972-73; Mem., Rajya Sabhya, 1974-; Mem., Indian Delegation to United Nations Conference, Mexico, 1975; Convenor, Congress Party Standing Cttee. on Information and Broadcasting, 1975-76; Mem., All-India Congress Cttee.; Mem., CPP Executive, 1975-76;

Pres., Delhi YWCA, 1975-78; Mem., United Nations General Assembly, 1976; Mem., Central Youth Advisory Board, 1976; Mem., General Council of ICCR; Joint Sec., All-India Congress Cttee., 1976-77; Mem., International Federation of Women Lawyers; Mem., National Children's Board, 1977-78; Mem., National Adult Education Board, 1978-79; Gen. Sec., Karnataka Pradesh Congress Cttee., 1978-80; Convenor, Mahila Congress, 1983-88; Minister of State for Parly. Affairs, 1985; Minister of State for Youth Affairs, Sports and Child Development, Govt. of India, 1985-89; Pres., World Women Parliamentarians for Peace, 1986-87; *professional career:* former lawyer, Supreme Court; *private address:* 3 Ware Road, Frazer Town, Bangalore - 560005, India; *office address:* Shrimati Margaret Alva, 23 Safdarjung Road, New Delhi, India.

AMANOVA, Maral Bazarovna; Soviet, Member of the Council of the Union; *party:* Communist Party of the Soviet Union; *political career:* elected from the Soviet Women's Cttee. to the Cncl. of the Union; Mem., Cncl. of the Union Commmissions on Labour, Prices and Social Policy; *interests:* enhancing women's social conditions, ecology; *professional career:* Dept. Head, A.M. Gorki Turkmen State Univ., Ashkhabad; *office address:* Ms Maral Bazarovna Amanova, Turkmen A.M. Gorki State University, 744014 Turkmen SSR, Ashkhabad, Pr. Lenina 31, USSR.

AMATHILA (APPOLUS-AMATHILA), Dr. Libertine; Namibian, Minister of Local Government and Housing; *born:* 10 December 1940, Fransfontein, Namibia; *children:* two; *education:* Augustineum Training College, Okahandja, 1955-57; Wellington High School, Cape, South Africa, 1957-59; Warsaw Medical Academy, Poland, MB, Ch.B., 1969; Muhimbili Teaching Hospital, Dar-es-Salaam, Tanzania, 1969-70; London School of Hygiene and Tropical Medicine, UK, Postgraduate Diploma in Nutrition, 1972, Postgraduate Diploma in Public Health, 1977-78; St. Goran Barn Clinic, Stockholm, Sweden, MB, Ch.B.; Bamako Medical Faculty, Mali, Diploma in Epidemiology, 1983; *party:* South West Africa People's Organisation of Namibia (SWAPO); *political career:* Dir., SWAPO Women's Council, until 1976; Deputy Sec. for Health and Welfare, SWAPO Central Cttee., until present; Dir. for Health, SWAPO Election Directorate, June 1987; appointed Minister Delegate of Local Govt. and Housing, 1987; Minister of Local Govt. and Housing, March 1991-; Mem., SWAPO Politbureau, March 1991-; Member of Parliament; *memberships:* Mem., Medical Women's International Association (MWIA), 1980-; *professional career:* Namibian Rep., World Health Organisation (WHO), 1974-89; Volunteer work in Namibian Refugee Camps, Zambia, 1975-79; Dir., Children's Centre, Kwanze Norte, Angola, 1979; worked in Angola, until 1988; *honours and awards:* Awarded SWAPO's highest medal, The Ongulambashe Medal for Bravery and Long Service, 1987; *private address:* 197 Klein Windhoek Road, Private Bag 13289, Windhoek, Namibia; *office address:* Dr. Libertine Amathila (Appolus-Amathila), Ministry of Local Government and Housing, Windhoek, Namibia.

AMIN, Angela Regina Heinzen Helou; Brazilian, Federal Deputy; *born:* 20 December 1953, Indaial, SC, Brazil; *parents:* Pedro Joao Heinzen and Petronila Marta Schmitt Heinzen; *married:* Esperidiao Amin Helou Filho; *children:* Joao António, Maria, Joana; *education:* UFSC, Florianópolis, Maths., 1973-76, partially completed post-grad. course in Applied Maths., 1977; *party:* Partido Democrático Social (PDS, Social Democrat Party); *political career:* Town Cllr., Florianópolis, 1989-91; Pres. of the Education Cttee., Vice-Pres. of the Environment Cttee., 1989-90; Federal Deputy for Santa Catarina, 1991-95; *office address:* Ms Angela Amin, Chamber of Deputies, Praça dos 3 Poderes, Ed. Principal, 70160 Brasilia, DF, Brazil; *phone:* (61) 225 2885.

AMIR, Nawal; Egyptian, Member of the General Federation of Arab Women; *office address:* Mrs Nawal Amir, People's Assembly, Magles Al-Shaab Street, Cairo, Egypt; *phone:* (02) 3545000.

ANDERSEN, Else Winther; Danish, Minister for Social Affairs; *born:* 5 April 1941; *education:* Alborg Univ. Centre, Social Work; *party:* Liberal; *political career:* candidate for Parliament, Liberal Party, Randers, 1985-88; candidate for Grená; Minister for Social Affairs, 1990-; *professional career:* teacher, Videbæk municipal education system, 1956-61; Principal of College, teacher, Agricultural Information and Conference Services, 1974; Mem., Danish Agricultural Youth Management, 1968-76; Chairperson, Youth Board and Mem. School Commission, Nibe, 1972-80; social worker, municipality of Randers, 1983-90; *office address:* Ms Else Winther Anderson, Ministry of Social Affairs, Slotsholmsgade 6, 1216 Copenhagen K, Denmark; *phone:* (01) 12 25 17; *fax:* (01) 932518.

ANDERSEN, Hanne; Danish, Member of the Folketing; *born:* 2 April 1939, Copenhagen, Denmark; *parents:* David Duemose and Karen Duemose; *married:* Ole Andersen, 1960; *children:* Lars, Jens; *religion:* Protestant; *languages:* Danish, English; *education:* Randersgade Realskole (Grammar School), 1956; course in Social Politics, 1964; *party:* Socialdemokratiet, (Socialist Democratic Party), 1957; *political career:* employed by Copenhagen Regional Council, 1982-84; member of the Folketinget, 1984-; *interests:* social and health politics, culture politics, municipal politics; *professional career:* assistant in public authority administration, 1960-84; *office address:* Ms Hanne Andersen, Christiansborg, 1240 Copenhagen K, Denmark.

ANDERSON GROWE, Joan; American, Secretary-of-State for Minnesota; *born:* 28 September 1935, Minneapolis, Minnesota, USA; *parents:* Arthur F. Anderson and Lucille Anderson (née Brown); *children:* Michael, Colleen, David, Patrick; *religion:* Catholic; *education:* St. Cloud State College, BS, 1956; Univ. of Minnesota, Special Education Certificate; Harvard Univ., 1979; *political career:* Minnesota State Rep., 1973-74; Sec.-of-State, Minnesota, 1975-; currently: Mem., State Board of Investment, State Exec. Cncl. and Governor's Commission on Poverty; *memberships:* League of Women Voters; National Women's Political Caucus; National Organisation of Women; National Assn. of Secs.-of-State; Business and Professional Women's Club; American Assn. of Univ. Women; NAACP; *professional career:* elementary teacher, Bloomington Public School, Minnesota, 1956-58; elementary teacher for exceptional children, Christ Childrens School, St. Paul, 1964-65; Special Education Teacher, St. Anthony Public School, 1965-66; *honours and awards:* Minnesota Schools Bell Award, MEA, 1977; YWCA Outstanding Achievement Award for Govt. and politics, 1978; National Leadership Award, NASS, 1983; Charlotte Striebel Long Distance Runner Award, Minnesota NOW, 1985; *private address:* 15 S. First Street, Minneapolis, Minnesota 55155, USA; *office address:* Ms Joan Anderson Growe, 180 State Office Bldg., St. Paul, Minnesota 55155, USA.

ANDERSON LONG, Dee (Devona); American, Minnesota State Representative; *born:* 5 April 1939, Minneapolis, Minnesota, USA; *parents:* Elder Carl Anderson and Emma Anderson (née Strom); *married:* Nicholas Kinsey Long, 1966; *children:* Catherine Emma, Nicholas Kinsey; *religion:* Congregational; *education:* Northwestern Univ., Evanston, Illinois, 1957-59; Univ. of Minnesota, BA, 1961; *party:* Democratic Party - Farmer-Labor (DFL); *political career:* Minnesota State Rep., District 59A, 1979-; *interests:* environment; *memberships:* Minnesota Women's Political Caucus; DFL Feminist Caucus; Citizens League; East Isles Residents Assn; *professional career:* teaching Asst., Univ. of Minnesota, 1961-63, Instuctor, 1963-68; teacher, Galashiels Academy, Scotland, 1968-69; community faculty, Metropolitan State Univ., 1973-; *honours and awards:* National Merit Scholar, National Merit Corp., 1957; Environmentalist of the Year, Sierra Club, 1983; Conservationist of the Year, Audubon Society, 1984; *clubs:* Sierra Club; *private address:* 459 State Office Bldg., St. Paul, Minnesota 55155, USA; *office address:* Mrs Dee Anderson Long, 2409 Humboldt Avenue S., Minneapolis, Minnesota 55405, USA.

ANDERSSON, Alfhild Marianne; Swedish, Member of the Riksdag; *born:* 26 May 1942, Alingsis, Sweden; *parents:* Erik Verner Andersson and Hanna Ottilia Maria Andersson; *married:* Svan Ivan Andersson, 1963; *children:* Pra Katarina, Pår Magnus; *religion:* Protestant; *languages:* English; *education:* Gothenburg School of Commerce, Degree in Economics, 1978-81; *party:* Centerpartiet (Centre Party), 1975; *political career:* Member of Riksdag for Norra Älvsborg's Constituency, 1985-; member, Education Cttee.; Deputy Member, Labour Market Committee; Board member of the Rescue Dept.; Board member of the Centre Party Women's Assoc; *interests:* environmental affairs, equality-feminism, finance; *clubs:* Centre Party Women's Assoc.; Swedish Society for Protection of the Environment; Amnesty International; *office address:* Ms Alfhild Andersson, Riksdag, Fack, S-100 12 Stockholm, Sweden.

ANDRÉ, Michèle Marie Claude; French, former Secretary of State for Women's Rights; *born:* 6 February 1947, Saint-Jacques d'Ambur, Puy de Dôme; *married:* Max André, 1968; *party:* Parti Socialiste (PS, Socialist Party); *political career:* Dir., Institute for Deaf Youth, Clemont-Ferrand, 1975-88; regional delegate on women's rights, 1981-83; Deputy Mayor, Clemont-Ferrand, responsible for Public Well-Being, Youth and Sports, 1983-; mem. Exec. Cttee., PS, 1983-; Sec. of State for Women's Rights, 1988; *office address:* Mme. Michèle André, Secrétariat d'Etat chargé des Droits des Femmes, 14 Boulevard de la Madeleine, 75008 Paris, France.

ANDRUNACHE, Emilia; Romanian, Member of the Grand National Assembly; *party:* Romanian Communist Party (RCP); *political career:* First Sec., Foscani RCP Municipal Cttee., Chairperson, Municipal People's Cncl., 1979-84; full Mem., RCP Central Cttee., 1984; Sec., Galati RCP District Cttee. in charge of Propaganda affairs, Dec. 1984-; Mem., Nat. Cncl. of Science and Instruction, 1985-; Deputy, Grand Nat. Assembly for Galati, 1985-; *office address:* Ms Emilia Andrunache, Marea Adunare Nationala, Aleea Marii Adunari Nationale, Bucharest, Romania; *phone:* 16 21 50.

ANGELONI, Luana (Rodano Luana); Italian, Deputy; *born:* 13 March 1952, Monterado, Ancona; *party:* Partito Democratico della Sinistra (PDS, Party of the Democratic Left); *political career:* mem. of Women's Movement; Mayor of Monterado, 1975-83; Regional Councillor for the Marche 1983-87; Deputy, Parliament, Ancona-Pesaro-Macerata-Ascoli, Piceno, 1987; mem. Cttee. on Environment Territory and Public Works; *professional career:* Teacher; *office address:* Ms Luana Angeloni, Camera dei Deputati, Montecitorio, 00186 Rome, Italy.

ANSELMI, Dott. Tina; Italian, Deputy; *born:* 25 March 1927, Castelfranco Veneto, Treviso; *education:* Catholic University, Milan, Degree in letters; *party:* Partito della Democrazia Cristiana (DC, Christian Democrat Party), 1944; *political career:* Leader, textile worker's Union, 1945-48; Leader, teacher's Union 1948-55; Leader, DC Young Women, 1958-64; Participant, 1st World Congress of DC Youth, Caracas, Venezuela; National Councillor, DC from 1959; on National advisory Cttee. DC, for Agriculture; National Vice-Delegate for Women's Section of the DC, from 1964; mem. Leadership Cttee. of Women's Union (international Christian and Democratic Women) Munich, 1967; Vice-Pres. of European Women's Union, Stockholm, 1967; Re-confirmed Vice-Pres. European Women's Union at Paris Congress, 1971; Deputy, Parliament, Venice-Treviso, 1968; mem. Cttee., Work and Social Security; Under-Sec. State for Work and Social Security in 5th Rumor government and 4th and 5th Moro governments; re-elected Deputy, 1976; Minister for Work and Social Security in 3D Andreotti government; re-elected Deputy, 1979; Pres. of Cttee. of Parliamentary Inquiry into P.2 Masonic Lodge; re-elected Deputy, 1983; mem. Cttee. on Health and Hygene; Re-confirmed Pres. of Cttee. of Parliamentary Inquiry into P.2 Masonic Lodge; re-elected Deputy, 1987; mem. of Cttee. on Social Affairs; *professional career:* Primary School Teacher; *office address:* Dott. Tina Anselmi, Camera dei Deputati, Montecitorio, 00186 Rome, Italy.

ANTILLE, Rosemarie; Swiss, Member of the Nationalrat; *born:* 20 April 1949, Chalais, Switzerland; *parents:* Clovis and Josephine; *religion:* Catholic; *languages:* French; *education:* further education at Sion; graduate in teacher training; *party:* Parti Radical-Démocratique Suisse (Freisinnig-Demokratische Partei der Schweiz, Liberal Democratic Party of Switzerland); *political career:* reserve Deputy for Canton of le Valais, 1981-89, Deputy, 1989-; *interests:* equal rights, Europe, narcotics; *professional career:* teacher; *recreations:* travel, history, sports (particularly football, skiing and cycling); *private address:* Monthéolo 14 b, 1870 Monthey, Switzerland; *office address:* Mme. Rosemarie Antille, Nationalrat/Conseil National, Secretariat-General, Parlamentsgebäude, 3003 Berne, Switzerland; *phone:* Berne 619711.

ANTTILA, Sirkka-Liisa; Finnish, Member of the Eduskunta; *born:* 20 December 1943, Marttila, Finland; *parents:* Paavo Artturi Ojala and Ellen Sofia Ojala (née Jalonen); *married:* Risto Into Einari Anttila, 1967; *children:* Hanna-Maija, Heli Sisko; *religion:* Evangelical-Lutheran; *languages:* Finnish, English, Swedish; *education:* secondary school, graduated 1963; degree, training programme for civil service, 1967; Univ. of Tampere, course in Health Care Administration, 1979; *party:* Suomen Keskusta (Finnish Centre Party); *political career:* mem. Forssa

City Council, 1977-; mem. Forssa City Board, 1977-78, 1981-83 and 1989-90; Vice-Chwn., Forssa City Cncl., 1991-; Representative, Häme Province Association, 1978-; mem. Forssa Council of Evangelical-Lutheran parishes, 1979-; mem. Parly. Consumer Cncl., 1979-83; Chmn., Board of South Häme district of the KP, 1981-83; mem. governing board, KP, 1982-84; presidential elector, 1982 and 1988; MP, 1983-; *professional career:* elementary school teacher, Martilla, 1963-64; office assistant, Southwest Häme mental hospital, 1969-72; financial manager, vocational training centre, Kankaanpää, 1972-73; office sec., Urjala municipality, 1973- 74; assistant financial manager, Southwest Häme Health Centre, 1974-82; *office address:* Ms Sirkka-Liisa Anttila, Eduskunta, 00102 Helsinki, Finland.

APFELBECK, Ute; Austrian, Member of the Nationalrat; *born:* 25 January 1943, Königsberg; *education:* secondary school, matriculation, 1961; *party:* Freiheitliche Partei Österreichs (FPÖ, Freedom Party of Austria); *political career:* district Chairperson, FPÖ, Graz district; district councillor, Stattegg, 1980-; Mem. of Nationalrat for Kärnten, Upper Austria, Salzburg, Steiermark, Tirol and Vorarlberg, 1988-; *professional career:* trained as medical assistant; *office address:* Frau Ute Apfelbeck, Nationalrat, Dr. Karl Renner Ring 3, 1017 Vienna, Austria.

AQUINO, Hon. Corazon C.; Filipino, President of the Republic of the Philippines; *born:* 25 January 1933, Manila, The Philippines; *parents:* José Cojuangco Sr; *married:* the late Benigno S. Aquino, Jr., (assasinated 1983); *children:* one s., four d; *languages:* English; *education:* College of Mount Saint Vincent, BA, major in French, minor in Mathematics; New York, 1953; *party:* United Nationalist Democratic Organisation (UNIDO), 1983; *political career:* entered politics after her husband's assassination, 1983; stood against Marcos in the impromptu Presidential election and won, 1986-; *honours and awards:* Time Magazine and Japan Broadcasting Corp. (NHK) named her 1986 Woman of the Year; many other awards and distinctions earned as President; *office address:* The Hon. Ms Corazon Aquino, Office of the President, Premiere Guest House, Malacañang Palace Compound, JP Laurel St., San Miguel, Manila, The Philippines; *phone:* (02) 5212301.

AQUINO-ORETA, Teresa; Filipino, Congresswoman; *born:* 28 June 1944, Concepcion, Tarlac; *parents:* Benigno Aquino Sr. and Aurora S. Aquino; *married:* Antolin M. Oreta Jr; *children:* Rissa, Len, Karmela; *education:* Assumption Convent, AB, Major in Literature and History; Cludad Ducal, Avila, Spain, Bachelors, International Studies; *political career:* Congresswoman; *honours and awards:* Marie Eugenie Award for Leadership; *office address:* Ms Teresa Aquino-Oreta, The Congress of the Philippines - House

of Representatives, Batasang Pambansa Bldg., Quezon City, Manila, The Philippines.

ARAD, Nava; Israeli, Member of the Knesset; *born:* 4 December 1938, Kibutz Hulda, Israel; *married:* Arieh, 1960; *children:* Ely; *religion:* Jewish; *languages:* Hebrew, English; *education:* Teacher's Seminary, B.Ed.; Hebrew Univ., Jerusalem, BA, social work, MA, social admin.; London School of Economics, UK, social work; *party:* Israeli Labor Party; *political career:* Chwn., National Social Workers Union, 1964-70; Head of NAAMT (Israel's largest women's movement), 1977-81; Chwn., Pioneers Women, Labor Zionist Movement; Mem., Presidium, World Zionist Organisation for Women; Mem., Knesset, 1981-; Chwn., Knesset lobby for Senior Citizens; Vice-Pres., Socialist International Women, Middle East Region; *interests:* finance, immigration, health and education, women's affairs, old age citizens; *memberships:* Chwn., Mishan (Israel's largest network of homes for the aged); *professional career:* juvenile probation officer, 1963-84; welfare sergeant of airbourne Nahal unit, 1958-60; *office address:* Ms Nava Arad, Knesset, Hakirya, Jerusalem 91000, Israel; *phone:* (02) 661211.

ARBELI-ALMOZLINO,   Soshana;   Israeli, Chairperson of the Knesset Select Committee on the Economy; *born:* 1929, Iraq; *party:* Ma'arach (Israeli Labour Party); *political career:* Mem., Knesset; Dep. Speaker, Knesset, 1977-81; former Minister of Health; Chwn., Knesset Select Cttee. on the Economy; *professional career:* teacher; *office address:* Ms Soshana Arbeli-Almozlino, Knesset, Hakirya, Jerusalem 91000, Israel; *phone:* (02) 661211.

ARMSTRONG, Hilary Jane; British, Member of Parliament; *born:* 30 November 1945; *party:* Labour Party; *political career:* MP for Durham North West, 1987-; *professional career:* social worker and lecturer; *private address:* Deneholme, Plantation Terrace, Howden-le-Wear, near Crook, County Durham DL15 8AD; *office address:* Ms Hilary Armstrong, House of Commons, London, SW1A OAA, England.

ARNABOLDI, Patrizia; Italian, Deputy; *born:* 27 November 1946, Milan, Italy; *education:* Classical School; University of Milan, Studied Philosophy; *party:* Democrazia Proletaria (DP, Proletarian Democracy Party); *political career:* Student Movement 1968; In Democrazia Proletaria from its foundation; Nationally responsible for information section of D.P.; Deputy, Parliament, Milan-Pavia, 1987; Vice-Pres. of Parliamentary Group; mem. Cttee. on Culture, Science and Training; *interests:* School and Student Affairs; *office address:* Ms Patrizia Arnaboldi, Camera dei Deputati, Montecitorio, 00186 Rome, Italy.

11

ARNDT, Mary Jo; American, Committeewoman for the Republican National Committee of Illinois; *born:* 18 September 1933, Chicago, Illinois, USA; *parents:* Holger Hans Larsen and Georgia E. Larsen (née Weede); *married:* Paul W. Arndt, 1956; *children:* Kristi, Kerri, Georgianne; *religion:* Christian; *education:* Northern Illinois Univ., BS, 1955; *party:* Republican Party; *political career:* Illinois Publicity Chwn., National Republican Womens Conference, Washington DC, 1969; precinct committeewoman, DuPage County; Mem., Illinois Federation of Republican Women, 1970-74, First Vice-Pres., 1975-76, Pres., 1977-81; Mem., Exec. Cttee., Republican Women in Power, 1971-76; Mem., Advisory Cttee., State Superintendent for Public Instruction, 1974-78; Mem., 14th Congressional District Senators Advisory Cttee., 1975-82; Mem., IWY, Illinois Co-ordinating Cttee., 1977-; delegate-at-large, Republican National Convention 1980 and Mem., Permanent Organisation Cttee.; Committeewoman, Illinois State Republican Central Cttee., Sixth Congressional District, 1982-88; Mem., National Advisory Cncl., Women's Educational Programs, 1982-88; Treasurer, National Federation of Republican Women, 1984-85; Chwn., Women's Education Equity Act Cttee., 1984-87; delegate, Republican National Convention, 1980, 1984 and 1988; Co-Chwn., Illinois, Republican Platform Cttee., 1984 and 1988; Co-Chwn., Arrangements Cttee., Illinois Republican Convention, 1986; Mem., Pres. Commission on White House Fellowship, 1987-; 3rd Vice-Pres., National Federation of Republican Women; Mem., Illinois National Republican Cttee; *memberships:* Trustee, Mid-West College of Engineering; Board of Overseers, Illinois Inst. of Technology, 1986-; National, Illinois and Chicago Veterans Medical Auxillaries; Lincoln Park Zoo Society; Lombard Bi-Centennial Commission; Suburban Press Club, Chicago; League of Women Voters; Chicago Women in Govt. Relations; *professional career:* Elementary Teacher, Villa Park and Urbana Schools, Illinois, 1955-59; partner and financial Vice-Pres., Arndt Business Enterprises, 1959-; stringer, Press Publications, 1974; freelance writer; *honours and awards:* Citizen of the Week, Press Publications, 1970; Republican Woman of the Year, DuPage County Federation of Republican Women, 1973; Outstanding Leader in Govt. and Politics, YWCA, 1988; *publications:* Columnist, Politics and Pollywogs; *office address:* Mrs Mary Jo Arndt, 35 S. Stewart, Lombard, Illinois 60148, USA.

AROZ I IBAÑEZ, Mercedes; Spanish, Deputy; *born:* 21 September 1944, Zaragoza, Spain; *party:* Partido Socialista Obrero Español (PSOE, Spanish Socialist Workers' Party); *political career:* Deputy, PSOE, Barcelona, re-elected 1989-; *office address:* Ms Mercedes Aroz i Ibañez, Congreso de los Diputados, Fernán Flor 1, Madrid 14, Spain.

ARSENI, Maria; Greek, Member of Parliament; *party:* Panelliniou Socialistikou Kinema (PASOK, Panhellenic Socialist Movement), 1989; *political career:* MP, PASOK, Pieria, 1989; member of the Central Cttee. of PASOK, 1974; Prefect of Pieria, 1982-84; General Secretary of Youth, 1986-87; *professional career:* philologist; *office address:* Vouli, Parliament Building, Syntagma, Greece.

ARTIOLI, Prof Rossella; Italian, Deputy; *born:* 26 January 1944, Rome, Italy; *education:* Degree in Foreign Languages and Literature; *party:* Partito Socialista Italiano (PSI, Italian Socialist Party); *political career:* mem. Central Cttee. PSI from 1972; civil secretary of PSI, Milan from 1980; Deputy, Parliament,-Milan-Pavia, 1983; mem. Cttee., Hygene and Public Health; re-elected Deputy, 1987; mem. Committees on Public and Private Works; and Social Affairs; *professional career:* English teacher; *office address:* Prof. Rossella Artioli, Camera dei Deputati, Montecitorio, 00186 Rome, Italy.

ARUTYUNYAN, Lyudmila Akopovna; Soviet, Member of the Council of Nationalities; *born:* Armenia, USSR; *party:* Communist Party of the Soviet Union; *political career:* Mem., Cncl. of Nationalities, elected from the Soviet Women's Cttee.; Mem., Congress of People's Deputies Commissions on Molotov-Ribbentrop Pact, Nationalities, Nationality Policy and Inter-ethnic Relations; *interests:* new mechanisms for mediating inter-ethnic disputes; *professional career:* teacher, philosophy; *office address:* Ms Lyudmila Akopovna Arutyunyan, Yerevan State University, 375049 Armenian SSR, Yerevan, Ul. Mravyana 1, USSR.

ARYEE, Joyce; Ghana, Secretary in the PNDC for the National Commission for Democracy; *office address:* Ms Joyce Aryee, National Commission for Democracy, The Castle, Osu, PO Box 1627, Ghana.

ASLAOUI, Leila; Algerian, Minister of Youth and Sport; *born:* Algiers; *education:* LLB; diploma Institute of Political Studies; *political career:* Cllr. of Supreme Court; Pres. of Court of Appeal; Head of Studies and Censuses, Cabinet of Ministry of Justice; *professional career:* judge; *office address:* Ms Leila Aslaoui, Ministry of Youth and Sports, 3 rue Mohammed Belouizdad, Algiers.

ASTALA, Heli Hellevi; Finnish, Member of the Eduskunta; *born:* 3 November 1937, Salo, Finland; *parents:* Viljo August Valdemar Lehtisalo and Alli Elina Lehtisalo (née Koskinen); *married:* Alpo Tuomo Antero Astala, 1961; *education:* BA, 1961; *party:* Suomen Kommunistinen Puolue (SKP, Communist Party of Finland); *political career:* Mem., Turku City Council, 1969; mem., Turku City Board, 1969-70 and 1973-74; 2nd Vice-Chmn, Turku City Council, 1975-76 and 1st

Vice-Chmn, 1977; mem., Presidential Electorate, 1978 and 1982; mem. of Eduskunta, 1979-; Chmn, Cultural Commission, 1983; *professional career:* Clerk, Turku Workers' Savings Bank, 1956-61; training officer, 1966-69; teacher, Kesälahti Municipal Middle School, 1961-62; Information Officer, Tarmola Co-Operative Soc., 1969-77; Sec.-Gen., Democratic Federation of Finnish Women, 1977-80; *recreations:* cultural pursuits; *office address:* Ms Heli Astala, Eduskunta, 00102 Helsinki, Finland.

AUBRY, Geneviève; Swiss, Member of the Nationalrat; *born:* 4 March 1928; *parents:* Dr. Virgile Moine; *married:* Paul Aubry, 1949; *education:* teacher; *party:* Parti Radical-démocratique suisse (Radical-Democratic Party); *political career:* Mem., Economy Cttee., Interparliamentary Union; mem. of Nationalrat; mem. of Military Cttee. of Federal Cncl; *professional career:* political journalist; President, World Anticommunist League, 1988-90; Board Banc Albis, Uniiabs; *publications:* Jura: Le Temps des Imposteurs, (French and German); Mon Aïeule derrière ses fourneaux, Ageco-Presse; Sous la Coupole, pas sous la coupe, (French and German); Toques et Politique; *clubs:* Albert Einstein Foundation; Swisstransplant; National Swiss Foundation; *recreations:* collector of semi-precious stones and antique furniture; *private address:* 4 Niesenweg 3012, Berne, Switzerland; *office address:* Frau Geneviève Aubry, Nationalrat/Conseil National, Secretariat-General, Parlamentsgebäude, 3003 Berne, Switzerland.

AUBRY, Martine; French, Minister of Labour, Employment and Professional Training; *born:* 8 August 1950, Paris 17e, France; *parents:* Jacques Delors, President of the Commission of the European Communities and Marie Delors (née Lephaille); *married:* Xavier Aubry, 1973; *public role of spouse:* Expert accountant/commissioner; *children:* Clémentine; *education:* Institue Saint-Pierre-Fourier; Lycée Paul-Valéry; Faculty of Law, Paris; graduate in economic science, diploma from Employment Institute of Social Science; diploma from Institute of Political studies, Paris; *political career:* deputy dir., cabinet of Jean Auroux, Minister of Labour, 1981; researcher, to Minister of Social Affairs and National Solidarity, 1983-84; Dir. of industrial relations, Ministry of Labour, Employment and Professional Training, 1984-87; Dir. Gen., Pechiney group, 1989-; Minister of Labour, Employment and Professional Training; *professional career:* civil administrator, Ministry of Labour, head of section on general employment policy, researcher for director of industrial relations, 1975-79; lecturer, École Nationale d'administration (National School of Administration), 1978-; civil administrator, council of state, 1980-81; *publications:* articles on industrial relations and working conditions; *clubs:* Club Echanges and Projects; *recreations:* tennis, ski-ing; *private address:* 2 bis square du Croisic, 75015 Paris,

France; *office address:* Mme. Martine Aubry, La Défense 5, 10 place des Vosges, cedex 68 92048 Paris, La Défense et Pechiney, France.

AULAS, Marie-Christine; French, Member of the European Parliament; *born:* 10 March 1945; *party:* Verts (Green Party); *political career:* MEP, 1989-; *professional career:* journalist; *private address:* 16 rue Vandrezanne, 74013 Paris, France; *office address:* Mme. Marie-Christine Aulas, European Parliament, Centre Européen, Plateau de Kirchberg, BP 2929, Luxembourg; *phone:* Luxembourg 43001.

AUNG SAN SUU KYI; Burmese, Secretary-General of the National League for Democracy; *born:* 1945; *parents:* Aung San (assassinated 1947); *married:* Michael Aris, 1972; *public role of spouse:* Prof., Oxford Univ., UK; *children:* Alexander (s.), Kim (s.); *education:* St. Hugh's College, Oxford Univ., UK, politics, philosophy, economics; *party:* National League for Democracy (NLD); *political career:* returned to Burma in time for pro-democracy demonstrations and decided to enter politics, 1988; achieved almost instant popularity with the people as the symbol of Burma's drive for democracy; after constantly criticising the Ne Win regime she was disqualified as a candidate, for having married a foreigner and placed under house arrest, 1989; National League for Democracy won a landslide victory in general election of May 1990, but ruling army council refused to honour this result; *interests:* individual responsibility, for oneself and towards society; individual rights; the rule of law; *professional career:* United Nations, New York USA; relief worker, Algeria and Bhutan; *honours and awards:* nominated for Nobel Peace Prize, 1991; awarded European Parliament's Andrei Sakharov Human Rights Prize, July 1991; *office address:* Ms Aung San Suu Kyi, National League for Democracy, 54-56 University Avenue, Rangoon, Myanma.

AUSTIN, Hon. Margaret Elizabeth; New Zealander, Member of Parliament; *born:* 1 April 1933; *parents:* Thomas Leonard and Margaret Leonard; *married:* John Maurice Austin, 1955; *public role of spouse:* reader in Chemistry, Canterbury Univ; *children:* three; *religion:* Roman Catholic; *languages:* English; *education:* Canterbury Univ., also in London; *party:* Labour Party; *political career:* Chairperson, Avonhead branch of the Labour party in Yaldhurst, until 1984; mem. of the Communication and Road Safety Select Cttee., Chairperson, Caucus subcommittee on Communications; also served on the education, employment, transport and works, regional development caucus committees; Leader of the NZ parliamentary Delegation to the Council of Europe and the European Parliament, 1985; mem. of an Australian and NZ parliamentary party that visited the USA 1987; Minister of Internal Affairs, Minister of Arts and

Culture, Minister of Civil Defence and Minister of Research Science and Technology, with additional responsibility for the New Zealand Symphony Orchestra, 1990; *interests:* education, science and technology, arts, communications; *professional career:* taught in various Christchurch Schools; Head of Science, Christchurch Girls' High School, 1971; Senior Mistress, Riccarton High School, 1977; curriculum development and education administration; *honours and awards:* Fellowship in biology, Univ. of Canterbury, Christchurch, 1970; Commonwealth Trust Fellowship (to research on the structure of secondary school curriculum at the Institute of Education in London), 1980; *recreations:* Classical musical, theatre, tramping, New Zealand flora and birdlife; *private address:* 11a St. Clio Street, Christchurch 8004, New Zealand; *office address:* The Hon. Ms Margaret Austin, C/O Parliament House, Wellington, New Zealand.

AVICE, Edwige; French, Minister for Co-operation and Development; *born:* 13 April 1945, Nevers, Nièvre, France; *parents:* Edmond Bertrant and Hélène Bertrant (née Guyot); *married:* Etienne Avice, 1970; *education:* Pothier High School, Orléans; University of Paris, Sorbonne, first degree in literature; Faculty of Law, Paris, first degree in public law; Institute of Political Studies, Paris, diploma; Institute of International Trade, diploma; *party:* Parti Socialiste (PS, Socialist Party); *political career:* member of National Cttee. for Improvement of Accommodation, 1970; employed in international sector of Crédit Lyonnais, 1970-73; employed in office of Managing Director of Paris Hospitals, 1972-73; member of Executive Office, 1977; member of National Secretariat of Socialist Party, 1987-; National Delegate of Socialist Party, responsible for National Service; Deputy for Paris, 14th arrondissement, 1978, re-elected 1981, gave up seat to Roger Rouquette; Minister of State to Minister for Leisure, responsible for Youth and Sport, 1981-83; Minister of State for Leisure, Youth and Sport, 1983-84; Councillor for Paris, 1983-; Sec. of State to Minister of Defence, 1984-86; Deputy for Paris, 1986-88; Deputy for Isère, 5th constituency, 1988, gave up seat to Jean-François Delahais; Minister of State, Ministry of Foreign Affairs, 1988; Minister for Co-operation and Development; *recreations:* travel, music, swimming, hiking, fencing; *office address:* Mme. Edwige Avice, Ministry of Co-operation and Development, 20 rue Monsieur, 75700 Paris, France.

AXDAHL, Evelyn Irene; American, Chairwoman of the Fourth District Independant-Republican Committee of Minnesota; *born:* 28 March 1929, Emmetsburg, Iowa, USA; *parents:* Ted Barkve and Gunellia Gjerde Barkve (née Smith); *married:* Lester Glen Axdahl, 1950; *children:* Gwen, Lee Olin, Jane L., Ann M; *religion:* Lutheran; *education:* Emmetsburg Jr. College, 1948-49; Univ. of Minnesota, 1949; *party:* Independent; *political career:* Chwn., 4th District Independent-Republican

Cttee., Minnesota, 1979-; Mem., Arrangements Cttee., 1975 and 1976; delegate, Republican National Convention, 1980; *memberships:* Maplewood Fine Arts; PTA; Lakeview Lutheran Education Board; American Lutheran Church Women; Maplewood Boosters; *office address:* Mrs Evelyn Axdahl, 2209 Payne Avenue, St. Paul, Minnesota 55117, USA.

AYKUT, Imren; Turkish, Minister of Labour and Social Security; *born:* 1941, Adana; *languages:* English; *education:* Istanbul Univ., Faculty of Economics; Oxford Univ., specialized in employee/employer relations and trade unions; USA, UK and Oslo University, research; Istanbul University, Faculty of Economics, Ph.D degree; *party:* National Democracy Party; Anavatan Partisi (ANAP, Motherland Party); *political career:* Sec.-Gen., Paper Industry Employers' Union; elected to the Consultative Assembly, 1981; National Democratic Deputy for Istanbul, 1983; joined ANAP after dissolution of National Democracy Party; re-elected Deputy for Istanbul, 1987-; Minister for Labour and Social Security, 1987-; first woman Minister ever elected in the history of the Turkish Republic; *professional career:* Man., Collective Agreements and Research Office of Maden-İş and Teksif (Trade Unions); industrial relations expert, Turkish glass and crystal industry; Sec.-Gen., Paper Industry Employers' Union; *office address:* Ms Imren Aykut, Ministry of Labour and Social Security, Calisma ve Sosyal Guvenlik Bakanligi, Mithat Pasa Cad., Ankara, Turkey.

AZIZBEKOVA, Pyusta Azizaga kyzy; Soviet, Member of the Council of Nationalities; *born:* 29 December 1929, Azerbaijan, USSR; *party:* Communist Party of the Soviet Union; *political career:* Mem., Cncl. of Nationalities; Mem., Cncl. of Nationalities Commission on Development of Culture, Language, National and Inter-ethnic Traditions and Preservation of Historical Heritage; *memberships:* corresponding Mem., Azerbaijan SSR Academy of Sciences; *professional career:* professor of history; Dir., Museum of History of Azerbaijan, Baku; *office address:* Ms Pyusta Azizaga kyzy Azizbekova, Museum of History of Azerbaijan, Azerbaijan Academy of Sciences, Baku, Ul. Malygina, Azerbaijan, USSR.

AZIZE, Beth (Elizabeth); Brazilian, Federal Deputy; *born:* 11 January 1940, Manacapuru, Amazonia, Brazil; *parents:* Rafael Azize Abrahim and Olga Fraiji Abrahim; *education:* School of Law, Amazon Univ., 1960-64; Lisbon Univ.,Portugal, further studies, 1971; *party:* Partido Democrático Trabalhista (PDT, Centre Left Party); *political career:* Town Cllr., Manaus, 1977-78; State Deputy for Amazonia, 1979-83, re-elected 1983-87; founder and Pres., PDT Amazonia, 1985; Chwn., Sub-Cttee. for the Rights of Workers and Public Servants, 1987; Federal Deputy for Amazonia, 1987-

91, re-elected, 1991-95; visited Libya, 1989; Chwn., Cttee. for Justice and the Constitution, 1990-91; Pres., PDT, Amazonia; *memberships:* Pres., Political Reporters' Club, 1975; Vice-Pres., Law Soc. of Brazil, Amazon section; *professional career:* judge, 1966-70; attorney, Manaus, 1971-76; journalist; *office address:* Ms Beth Azize, Chamber of Deputies, Praça dos 3 Poderes, Ed. Principal, 70160 Brasilia, DF, Brazil; *phone:* (61) 225 2885.

B

BA, Sy Maimouna; Mali, Minister of Rural Development and the Environment; *party:* Transition Committee for the Salvation of the People (CTSP); *office address:* Mme. Sy Maimouna Ba, c/o Office of the President, B.P. 1463, Bamako, Mali.

BAARVELD-SCHLAMAN, E.M.P; Dutch, Member of the First Chamber; *born:* Arnhem, Netherlands; *education:* secondary school; *party:* Partij van de Arbeid (PvdA, Labour Party); *political career:* Mem. of town council, Lelystad, 5 years; active Mem. of town council, Lelystad, 3 years; international secretary, Red Women in PvdA, 4 years; Mem. of First Chamber, 1981-; *private address:* Heidelaan 30, 3851 EZ Ermelo, the Netherlands; *office address:* Mevr. E.M.P Baarveld-Schlaman, Eerste Kamer der Staaten-Generaal, Binnenhof 22, Postbus 20017, The Hague, Netherlands.

BACHELOT-NARQUIN, Roselyne; French, Deputy; *born:* 24 December 1946, Nevers, Nièvre, France; *parents:* Jean Narquin and Yvette Narquin (née Le Du); *married:* Jacques Bachelot, 1968; *children:* Pierre; *religion:* Roman Catholic; *languages:* English, Arabic; *education:* Sainte Agnès School, Angers, university entrance examination, 1956-64; Faculty of Medicine, Angers, first year medical studies, 1965-66; Faculty of Pharmacy, Angers, doctor of pharmacy, 1976-81; *party:* Rassemblement pour la République (RPR, Rally for the Republic), 1976; *political career:* Departmental Councillor for Maine et Loire, 1982-88; Vice-Chmn. of Regional Council for Pays de la Loire, 1986-; Deputy for Maine et Loire, 1988-; *interests:* social issues, family, education, health, Third World, Arab and African culture; *professional career:* pharmacist, Angers, 1984-; *publications:* Sphère de coordination de l'atome métallique dans les gluconates par spectrophotometrie IR, 1982; *clubs:* Club L international; *recreations:* literature, music; *private address:* 14 rue Brémont, 49100 Angers, France; *office address:* Mme. Roselyne Bachelot-Narquin, L'Assemblée Nationale, 126 rue de L'Université, 75355 Paris, France.

BACHER, Ingeborg; Austrian, Member of the Bundesrat; *born:* 3 July 1937, Rothenthurn; *education:* teacher training college, Klagenfurt; *party:* Sozialistische Partei Osterreichs (SPÖ, Socialist Party of Austria); *political career:* women's consultant, district vice chairperson for women, Villach; mem. of central Cttee., Province of Kärnten; mem. of Kärnten Provincial Assembly, 1984-; sent to Bundesrat from Kärnten Provincial Assembly, mem. of Bundesrat, 1989-; *professional career:* primary school teacher, 1957-; visiting teacher for students of the Academy of Pedagogy; headmistress, Ferndorf Primary School, 1987; staff representative for teachers; *office address:* Frau Ingeborg Bacher, Bundesrat, Dr. Karl Renner Ring 3, 1017 Vienna, Austria.

BACON, Baroness (cr. 1970, Life Peer) Alice Martha Bacon; British, Member of the House of Lords; *parents:* the late Benjamin Bacon; *education:* Normanton Girls' School; Stockwell College; London Univ. (external); *party:* Labour Party; *political career:* mem., Lab. Nat. Exec. Cttee., 1941-70; Member of Parliament, 1945-70; Chmn., Standing Joint Cttee. of Working Women's Organisations, 1946-47; mem., Consultative Assembly of Council of Europe, 1950-53; Chmn., Labour Party, 1950; Chmn., Lab. Conference, 1951; Minister of State, Home Office, 1964-67; PC, 1966-; Minister of State, Education and Science, 1967-70; House of Lords, 1970-; mem., North Atlantic Assembly, 1974-80; *professional career:* teacher; *honours and awards:* CBE, 1953; Hon. LLD, Univ. of Leeds, 1972; Dep. Lieut., West Yorkshire; *private address:* 53 Snydale Road, Normanton, West Yorkshire, WF6 1NY, UK; *office address:* Baroness Bacon, House of Lords, London SW1A 0PW.

BADAMHAAMB, Her Excellency Ch.; Mongolian, Minister of Labour; *office address:* HE Ch. Badamhaamb, State Labour and Social Security Committee, Ulan Bator, Mongolia.

BADOMBE, Betty; Ugandan, Minister of State in the Prime Minister's Office; *office address:* Office of the Prime Minister, POB 341, Kampala, Uganda.

BAINUN BINTI MOHD ALI, Her Majesty Raja Permaisuri Agong Tunku; Malaysian, Raja Permaisuri Agong; *born:* Penang; *education:* St. George School, Penang; Kirby Teachers College, England, 1952-54; *political career:* became the Raja Permaisuri Perak Darul Ridzuan, 1984; currently, Raja Permaisuri Agong of Malaysia, 1989; *professional career:* teacher: St. George School, Penang; Batu Road Primary School, Kuala Lumpur; King George V Primary School,

Seremban; Sultan Mahmud School, Raub, Pahang; King Edward VII School, Taiping; Raja Perempuan School, Ipoh and Methodist Girls School, Kuantan, Pahang; *honours and awards:* The Most Honourable Family Order of Pahang; *private address:* Istana Negara, Jalan Istana, 50500 Kuala Lumpur; *office address:* HM Raja Permaisuri Agong Tunku Bainun Binti Mohd Ali, Dewan Rakyat, Parliament Building, 50680 Kuala Lumpur, Malaysia; *phone:* (03) 2321955.

BAIRD ANSTINE, Anna; American, Member of the Republican State Committee of Pennsylvania; *born:* 27 March 1924, Lock Haven, Pennsylvania, USA; *parents:* Clarence Eugene Baird and Roseanna Baird (née Kalmbach); *married:* John Brindle Anstine Sr., 1944; *children:* Elizabeth, John Jr., Rachel; *religion:* Lutheran; *education:* Pennsylvania State Univ., 1944-45; *party:* Republican Party; *political career:* Mem., Mifflin County Leadership Cttee., Pennsylvania; Mem., Republican State Cttee., Pennsylvania; *professional career:* Sec. and treasurer, Annlick Farm Supply Inc., 1974-; *clubs:* Women's Civic Club; *office address:* Mrs Anna Baird Anstine, 603 Ninth Street, Port Royal, Pennsylvania 17082, USA.

BAIRD WHITTLESEY, Eunice; American, Member of the Republican National Committee for New York State; *born:* Yorkville, New York, USA; *parents:* Stuart John Baird Sr. and Susanna Kennerknecht Baird; *married:* Joseph Insull Whittlesey, 1947; *children:* Anne; *religion:* Presbyterian; *education:* State Univ. New York, Albany, BA; *party:* Republican Party; *political career:* Mem., Republican National Cttee., New York, 1977-; appointed by Pres. Bush to the Presidential delegation to the Bulgarian elections, June 1990; *memberships:* Mem., Alumni of State Univ., Albany, New York; American Assn. of Univ. Women; New York State Legislative Forum; *honours and awards:* Excellence in Service Award, New York State Univ., 1979; *office address:* Mrs Eunice Baird Whittlesey, 118 Acorn Drive, Scotia, NY 12302, USA.

BAJOIE, Diana E.; American, Louisiana State Representative; *born:* 8 February 1948; *party:* Democratic Party; *political career:* Louisiana State Rep., District 91, 1976-; alternate delegate, Democrat National Party Conference, 1978; *private address:* 4129 S. Liberty Street, New Orleans, Louisiana 70115, USA; *office address:* Ms Diana Bajoie, P.O. Box 15168, New Orleans, Louisiana 70126, USA.

BAJPAI, Dr. Rajendra Kumari; Indian, Member of the Lok Sabha; *born:* 8 February 1925, Laloochak, Bhagalpur District, Bihar; *parents:* Shree Krishna Mishra; *married:* D.N. Bajpai; *children:* one s., one d; *education:* BA; MA; D.Phil.; PhD; *party:* Congress Party; *political career:* participated in Quit India Movement; Mem., UP Legislative Assembly, 1962-77;

State Education Minister of UP, 1970; State Health Minister of UP, 1971; Pres., UPCC, 1971-72; Chmn., Sampradayikta Virodhi Samiti; Minister of Food and Civil Supplies for LSG, 1973-75; Minister of Power and Labour for LSG, 1976-77; former Mem., Indian delegation to ILO Conference in Geneva; Mem. of Lok Sabha, 1980-; General Sec., AICC, 1980-85; Minister of State for Welfare, GOI, 1985-89; *office address:* Dr. Rajendra Bajpai, Lok Sabha, Parliament House, New Dehli 110 011, India; *phone:* (11) 381825; 377102.

BAKER, Roz (Rosalyn); American, Hawaii State Representative; *born:* 20 September 1946, El Campe, Texas, USA; *education:* Southwest Texas State Univ., BA, 1968; Univ. of Southwest Louisiana, MA, 1969; *party:* Democratic Party; *political career:* delegate-at-large, Democrat National Convention, 1984; Mem., Exec. Commission, Maui County Democratic Cttee., 1986-88; Hawaii State Rep; *memberships:* Mem., American Cancer Society; Work Day Volunteers; *professional career:* instructor, Univ. of Southwest Louisiana, 1968-69; lobbyist and Asst. Dir., Govt. Relations National Education Assn., Washington DC, 1969-80; owner of a sporting goods store, Maui, 1980-87; currently, Vice-Chwn., Maui Service Area Board on Mental Health and Substance Abuse; *office address:* Ms Roz Baker, State Capitol, 415 South Beretania Street, Honolulu 96813, Hawaii.

BAKOYIANNIS, Dora; Greek, Under Secretary to the Prime Minister's Office; *parents:* Prime Minister of Greece; *office address:* Ms Dora Bakoyiannis, Prime Minister's Office, Maximou Megaro, Athens, Greece.

BAKSH, Salisha; Trinidad and Tobago, Senator; *political career:* represents the United Nations Congress in Senate; has never contested elections; *professional career:* freelance journalist; *office address:* Ms Salisha Baksh, Senate, Red House, St. Vincent Street, Port-of-Spain, Trinidad and Tobago; *phone:* (62) 32971/76.

BAKUNAWA, Hon. Luz Cleta R.; Filipino, Congresswoman; *born:* Tacloban City; *parents:* Francisco Reyes Sr. and Irene Ondez; *married:* Manuel Bakunawa Jr; *children:* Manuel III, Isidoro, Mandel Andres, Mona Liza, Rosolo, Jose Manolo, Anthony Jude Francis; *political career:* former Exec. Assistant, Office of the Pres., Malacañang; Congresswoman; *memberships:* An Leyteño Inc.; An Taclobanon; Circulo Masbateño; *clubs:* Garden Club of the Philippines; *office address:* The Hon. Ms Luz Bakunawa, The Congress of the Philippines - House of Representatives, Batasang Pambansa Bldg., Quezon City, Manila, The Philippines.

BALBO, Prof. Dott Ceccarelli Laura; Italian, Deputy; *born:* 30 November 1933, Padua, Italy; *children:* three; *party:* Independent Left; *political career:* Deputy,

Parliament Milan-Pavia, as Independent on PCI Lists, 1983; mem. Committee; Work; re-elected Deputy, 1987; mem. Committee; Public and Private Work; *professional career:* Professor of Sociology, has taught at University of Milan and Ferrara, and in the USA; Research on society, the family and work, women for GRIFF (Interdisciplinary Research Group on the Family and Women's Position), University of Milan; *publications:* Collaborator on magazines on sociology, and politics: Stato & Mercanto, Inchiesta, Democrazia & Diritto, Politica ed Economia, Rinascita and L'Unità and Manifesto; Books: Stato di Famiglia (1976); Interferenze: Lo Stato, la vita familiare, la vita privata (1979); Time to Care: politiche del tempo & diritti quotidiani (1987); *office address:* Prof. Dott. Ceccarelli Laura Balbo, Camera dei Deputati, Montecitorio, 00186 Rome, Italy.

BALI, Vyjayanthimala; Indian, Member of the Lok Sabha; *born:* 13 August 1933, Madras, India; *parents:* M D Raman; *married:* Dr. Chaman Bali, 1968; *children:* one s; *education:* graduate; *party:* Congress (I); *political career:* Mem., Lok Sabha for Tamil Nadu, Madras South, 1984-; *interests:* working for the improvement of conditions for the underprivileged and disadvantaged sections of society, particularly for women; *professional career:* founded the NATYALAYA, Academy of Bharat Natyam and Music; actress; first Indian dancer invited to give performance at United Nations in celebration of Human Rights Day; performed at Sydney Opera House, PATA Conference on behalf of Government of India; dance recitals at Royal Opera Ballet Festival, Stockholm, Sweden, Autumn Festival, Paris, France and other festivals in the USSR before several heads of state; *honours and awards:* Padra Shri, for her services in the field of Bharat Natyam, 1968; Sangeet Natak Award, 1983; State Artiste Award in Bharat Natyam, Government of Tamil Nadu; three Film Fare Awards for best actress; conferred titles of Nritya Siromani, Natyakala Sikhamani, Nritya Nirupama Visarade by leading cultural organisations in recognition of her talent; *publications:* LP records on Bharata Natyam; book on Rare Temples of Ritual Dances, Nava Sandhi and Kawthuvams, Mela Prapti, Todaya Mangaiayam; *clubs:* golf clubs of Bombay, Delhi, Madras; *recreations:* reading, writing, golf, research in classical Bharat Natyam; *private address:* 80, Dr. C. P. Ramaswami Iyer Road, Alwarpet, Madras-18, India; *office address:* Shrimati Vyjayanthimala Bali, Lok Sabha, Parliament House, New Dehli 110 011, India; *phone:* (11) 381825; 377102.

BALLETBO I PUIG, Anna Maria; Spanish, Deputy; *born:* 15 December 1943, Santpedor, Barcelona, Spain; *parents:* Juan and Antonia; *children:* Eugeni, Marti, Aina, Bernat; *religion:* Catholic; *languages:* Catalan, Spanish, English, French, German; *education:* degrees in journalism and modern and contemporary history; *party:* Partido Socialista Obrero Español (PSOE,

Spanish Socialist Workers' Party), 1974; *political career:* Deputy, PSOE, Barcelona, 1979, re-elected 1982, 1986, 1989-; Mem. Cttee. on Control of RTVE, Foreign Affairs and Industry; *interests:* mass communication, women's rights, disarmament; *memberships:* Sec.-Gen., Olaf Palme Int. Foundation; *professional career:* Professor of Information Science, School of Sciences, Autonomous Univ. of Barcelona; as a journalist has worked for RTVE, Radio Nacional and Tele-Exprés newspaper; writer for El Periodico and La Vangurrdia newspapers; *publications:* Mujer Bajo la Dictadura; Mujer y Nuevas Telnologias; La Mujer en la Politica; La Dona a Catalunya Avui; El Estatuto Juridico de la Radio y la Television; Prensa Femenina; Cap Una Xarxa Unica de Telecomunicacions; The Increasing Role of the Relations Between Spain-USA; *clubs:* Barcelona Football Club; Federacion Española Esqui; *recreations:* skiing, cycling, tennis; *private address:* C/ Nicaragua, 75/08029, Barcelona, Spain; *office address:* Ms Anna Balletbó i Puig, Congreso de los Diputados, Fernán Flor 1, Madrid 14, Spain.

BANDARANAIKE, Sirimavo R.D.; Sri Lankan, President of the Sri Lanka Freedom Party; *born:* 17 April 1916, Ratnapura, Sabaragamuwa Province; *parents:* Barnes Ratwatte and Rosemund Mahawalatenne Ratwatte; *married:* S.W.R.D. Bandaranike, 1940; *public role of spouse:* former Prime Minister of Ceylon, 1956-59; *children:* one s., two d; *education:* St. Bridget's Convent, Colombo; *party:* Sri Lanka Freedom Party; *political career:* Pres., Sri Lanka Freedom Party, 1960-; Prime Minister, Minister of Defence and External Affairs, 1960-65; Mem., Senate until 1965; Leader of the Opposition, 1965-70; Prime Minister, Minister of Defence and Foreign Affairs, Planning, Economic Affairs and Plan Implementation, 1970-77; *memberships:* Pres., Sri Lanka Nidahas Sewaka Sangamaya; *recreations:* gardening, reading, cooking; *private address:* 65 Rosmead Place, Colombo 7, Sri Lanka; *office address:* Mrs Sirimavo Bandaranaike, Sri Lanka Freedom Party, 301 Darley Road, Colombo 10, Sri Lanka; *phone:* (1) 686025.

BANDEIRA, Alda; , Minister of Foreign Affairs; *party:* Movimento de Libertaçao de Sao Tomé e Príncipe (MLSTP, Movement for the Liberation of Sao Tomé and Príncipe); *office address:* Ms Alda Bandeira, Ministry of Foreign Affairs, Sao Tomé, Sao Tomé and Príncipe; *phone:* 21446.

BANKEWAKA, Anna Danuta; Polish, Member of the Sejm; *office address:* Ms Anna Danuta Bankewaka, Sejm PRI, ul. Wiejska 4/6/8, 00-489 Warsaw, Poland; *phone:* (22) 28 70 01; 28 40 31.

BANOTTI, Mary; Irish, Member of the European Parliament; *born:* 29 May 1939; *party:* Fine Gael (FG, United Ireland Party); *political career:* MEP, 1984-;

19

office address: Mary Banotti, European Parliament, Centre Européen, Plateau de Kirchberg, BP 2929, Luxembourg; *phone:* Luxembourg 43001.

BAPPOO, Sheilabai; Mauritius, Minister of Employment, Industrial Relations, Women's Rights and Family Welfare; *children:* two; *education:* Henry Buswell CEA school; Queen Elizabeth College; MIE diploma in Home Economics; *party:* Mouvement socialiste mauricien (MSM, Mauritian Socialist Movement); *political career:* entered politics, 1970; Pres., MMM, 1973; candidate for MMM in general election, Belle Rose/Quatre Bornes, 1976; municipal Cnclr., MMM, Beau Bassin/Rose Hill, 1977; Dep. Mayoress, Beau Bassin/Rose Hill, 1977-78; left MMM to join MSM, 1983; elected for Savanne/ Riviere Noire, 1983, 1987; Minister of Employment, Industrial Relations, Women's Rights and Family Welfare; *professional career:* teacher, 1966-83; *office address:* Mme. Sheilabai Bappoo, Ministry of Employment, Industrial Relations, Women's Rights and Family Welfare, Government House, Port Louis, Mauritius; *phone:* 011195.

BARBIERI, Tagliavini Silvia; Italian, Deputy; *born:* 13 November 1938, Ferrara, Italy; *education:* Doctor of Jurisprudence; *party:* Partito Democratico della Sinistra (PDS, Party of the Democratic Left); *political career:* Mayor of Argenta, Ferrara; Deputy, Parliament, Bologna- Ferrara-Ravenna-Forli, 1987; mem. of Federal Cttee. of PCI, Ferrara; Vice-Pres. of Cttee. on Constitutional Affairs, Presidency of the Council and Internal Affairs; *professional career:* School Teacher, Jurisprudence and economics; *office address:* Ms Tagliavini Barbieri, Camera dei Deputati, Montecitorio, 00186 Rome, Italy.

BARNES, Rosie (Rosemary) Susan; British, Member of Parliament; *born:* 16 May 1946; *party:* Social Democratic Party (SDP); *political career:* MP for Greenwich, Feb. 1987-; *office address:* Mrs Rosie Barnes, House of Commons, London, SW1A OAA, England.

BARROW, Dame Nita; Barbados, Governor-General of Barbados; *education:* Columbia Univ., New York; Univ. of Toronto; Univ. of Edinburgh; *political career:* Permanent Mission of Barbados to UN, 1986-90; Gov.-Gen., Barbados, June 1990-; *memberships:* Commonwealth Group of Eminent Persons, (EPG), 1986; *professional career:* various staff, teaching and admin. posts in nursing and public health, Barbados and Jamaica, 1940-56; Principal Nursing Officer, Jamaica, 1956-62; Nursing Adviser, Pan American Health Organization, 1967-71; Associate Dir., Christian Medical Commission of WCC, Geneva, 1971-75, Dir., 1975-80; Health Consultant, WHO, 1981-86; Pres., World YWCA, 1975-83; Pres., Int.

Cncl. for Adult Education, 1982; Pres., WCC, 1983; *office address:* Dame Nita Barrow, Office of the Governor-General, Government House, Saint Michael, Barbados.

BAR-SCHWAB, Muri; Swiss, Member of the Nationalrat; *born:* 1 December 1947, Biel; *children:* one; *education:* Business school; *party:* Grüne Partei der Schweiz (Green Party); *political career:* Mayoress of Richterswil and Siselen BE; Mem., Great borough Cncl. of Muri, 1981-86, Pres., 1985; Mem., Great Cncl. of Muri, 1982-87; Mem. of the Nationalrat for Muri, Canton of Bern, 1987-; *professional career:* housewife; secretary; *office address:* Frau Muri Bär-Schwab, Nationalrat/Conseil National, Secretariat-General, Parlamentsgebäude, 3003 Berne, Switzerland; *phone:* Berne 619711.

BASABARAJESWARI, S.M.T.; Indian, Member of the Lok Sabha; *born:* 1928, Harunapuram Village, Anatapur District, Andhra Pradesh, India; *parents:* D. Veera Reddy; *married:* Sharana Basava Raj, 1948; *children:* four s., four d; *party:* Congress (I); *political career:* Deputy Minister for Social Welfare and Minor Irrigation, Government of Karnataka, 1967; founding Vice-Pres., Institute of Parly. Affairs; Mem., Karnataka Legislative Assembly, 1957-62, 1962-67, 1967-72; Mem., Karnataka Legislative Cncl., 1976-80, 1982-84, Chair, 1976-80; Mem., India Parly. Delegation Commonwealth Parly. Assn. Conference, Lusaka; led farmers Delegation to Japan, Hong Kong, Singapore; Mem., panel of Chairmen; Mem., Lok Sabha for Karnataka, Bellary, 1984-; *interests:* social service, serving the poor uneducated women of village areas, issues affecting farmers, agriculture, dairy development, horticulture; *professional career:* founding Pres., Tagore Memorial Education Soc., Raichur; Exec. Pres., Karnataka Krishik Samaj, Bangalore; sponsored mini steel plant, Bellary, and was its first Managing Dir.; Mem., Senate of Karnataka Univ.; Mem., Board of Regent, Agricultural Univ.; educationalist and social worker; *recreations:* agriculture; *private address:* Ghanda Nagar, 3rd Cross, Bellary, Karnataka, India; *office address:* Shrimati S.M.T. Basbarajeswari, Lok Sabha, Parliament House, New Dehli 110 011, India; *phone:* (11) 381825; 377102.

BASSI MONTANARI, Franca; Italian, Deputy; *born:* 20 January 1956, Piacenza; *party:* Federazione Nazionale per Le Liste Verdi (Green Party); *political career:* Activist in student movement and early feminist colletives, Piacenza; 1970's; activist, Democrazia Proletaria; activist Peace and anti-Nuclear Movements, 1980's; Promoter of Green Lists, Piacenza; elected Councillor in charge of the area of the historic centre, Piacenza, 1985; Deputy, Parma- Piacenza-Modena-Reggio Emilia, 1987; mem. Cttee. on Health; *interests:* Children, adolescents with problems/handicaps, environment; *office address:* Ms Franca Bassi Montanari, Camera dei Deputati, Montecitorio, 00186 Rome, Italy.

BAUER, Rosemarie; Austrian, Member of the Nationalrat; *born:* 15 July 1944, Roggendorf bei Melk, Austria; *education:* Vocational high school with leaving examination certificate; *party:* Österreichische Volkspartei (ÖVP, Austrian People's Party); *political career:* ÖVP regional representative for Lower Austria, 1980-; leader of Lower Austrian region women's movement, 1983-; General Sec. of ÖVP women's movement, 1984-; member of Bundesrat 1983-85; member of Nationalrat 1985-; *professional career:* technical college headmistress; towncouncillor, 1972-75; Hollabrunn district councillor, 1972-85; headmistress of Mittergrabern agricultural college, 1981-; *office address:* Frau Rosemarie Bauer, Nationalrat, Dr. Karl Renner Ring 3, 1017 Vienna, Austria.

BAUMAN EISENSTADT, Pauline; American, New Mexico State Representative; *born:* 31 December 1938, New York City, USA; *parents:* Morris Bauman and Ann Bauman (née Lautenberg); *married:* Melvin Eisenstadt, 1960; *children:* Todd, Keith; *education:* Univ. of Florida, BA, 1960; Univ. of Arizona, MA, 1964; *party:* Democratic Party; *political career:* Board Mem., Solar Utilisation Network of New Mexico, 1977-79; alternate delegate, Democrat National Party Conference, 1978; Board Mem., New Mexicans for Tribal Development, 1978-79 and Govt. Geo-thermal Advisory Cttee. 1979-; Mem., New Mexico State Democrat Central Cttee.; New Mexico State Representative, District 44; Chwn., Business Cttee.; Mem., Education and Judiciary State Cttees; *memberships:* Federal Energy Admin.; League of Women Voters; Pan American Round Table II; *professional career:* Vice-Pres., National Centre for Appropriate Technology; Pres., Eisenstadt Enterprises; *publications:* Corrales, Portrait of a Village; *clubs:* New Mexico Poetry Society; Sandoval County Democrat Women's Club; *office address:* Mrs Pauline Bauman Eisensdadt, P.O. Box 658, Corrales, New Mexico 87048, USA.

BAUMLIN, Ursula; Swiss, Member of the Nationalrat; *born:* 12 May 1938, Bern, Switzerland; *education:* Graduate, Philosophy, History, Theology, Univ. Bern; *party:* Sozialdemokratische Partei der Schweiz (SDP, Social Democratic Party of Switzerland); *political career:* Mayoress of Bonau TG, and Zürich; city Cllr., 1985-87; Mem. of the Nationalrat for Bern, 1987-; *professional career:* housewife; *office address:* Frau Ursula Bäumlin, Nationalrat/Conseil National, Secretariat-General, Parlamentsgebäude, 3003 Berne, Switzerland; *phone:* Berne 619711.

BAUMRUKOVA, Dr. Nasta; Czechoslovakian, former Minister of Labour and Social Affairs; *education:* Politic Univ. of Central Cttee., CP CSSR, Prague, 1964; *party:* Komunistická Strana Ceskoslovenska (KSC, Communist party of Czechoslovakia); *political career:* Section Chief, Central Cttee., CP CSSR, Prague 1964-72; Sec. Cttee. for Social Politic of Parliament of CSSR, 1972-84; Vice-Minister of Labour and Social Affairs, CSR, 1984-86; Minister of Labour and Social Affairs, CSR 1986-88; *professional career:* apprenticeship as shop assistant; *honours and awards:* Honour for Merits and Progress, 1975; Order of Labour, 1985; *office address:* Dr. Nasta Baumrukova, Ministry of Labour and Social Affairs, W. Piecka 98, 120, 37, Prague 10, Czechoslovakia.

BAZAROVA, Roza Atamuradovna; Soviet, Member of the Council of Nationalities; *born:* July 1933; *education:* Doctor of History; *party:* Communist Party of the Soviet Union; *political career:* Chwn., Presidium, Turkmen SSR Supreme Soviet, Ashkhabad; former Prime Minister and Minister of Foreign Affairs of Turkmenia; currently: Mem., Cncl. of Nationalities; Mem., Congress of People's Deps. Drafting Commission; Dep.-Chwn., Supreme Soviet Presidium; advocates granting real power to local Soviets to achieve socio-economic development of their regions; *publications:* co-author, two-volume history of Soviet Turkmenistan; *office address:* Ms Roza Atamuradovna Bazarova, Council of Nationalities, Kremlin, Moscow, USSR.

BEATRIX, Queen of the Netherlands, Beatrix Wilhelmina Armgard; Dutch, Queen of the Netherlands; *born:* 31 January 1938, Baarn; *parents:* Bernhard, Prince of the Netherlands and Queen Juliana; *married:* Claus George Willem Otto Frederik Geert von Amsberg, 1966; *children:* Prince Willem-Alexander Claus George Ferdinand, Prince of Orange; Prince Johan Friso Bernhard Christiaan David; Prince Constantijn Christof Frederik Aschwin; *education:* Baarn Grammar School; Leiden State Univ; *political career:* succeeded to the throne on the abdication of her mother, 30 April 1980; *office address:* HM Queen Beatrix of the Netherlands, Office of the Private Secretary, Pateis Noordeinde, 68 PO Box 30412, 2500 GK The Hague, The Netherlands.

BEAUDEAU, Marie-Claude; French, Senator; *born:* 30 October 1937, Saint-Vincent-de-Connezac, Dordogne, France; *parents:* Pierre Rivière and Françoise Rivière (née Chauny); *married:* Emilien Beaudeau, 1956; *party:* Parti Communiste (PC, Communist Party); *political career:* Town Councillor for Sarcelles, 1972; Deputy Mayor of Sarcelles, 1977-83; Departmental Councillor for Val d'Oise, Sarcelles canton, 1977; Senator for Val d'Oise, 1979, replacing Fernand Châtelain, deceased; Senator for Val D'Oise, 1986-; *professional career:*

director's secretary; *private address:* 19-21 bd Henri-Poincaré, 95200 Sarcelles, France; *office address:* Mme. Marie-Claude Beaudeau, Sénat de la République Française, Palais du Luxembourg, 75291 Paris Cedex 06, France.

BECCHI, Prof. Dott Ada; Italian, Deputy; *born:* 30 May 1937, Turin, Italy; *parents:* Covelo Bechhi and Costamagna Bechhi (née Grazia); *languages:* Italian, English, French; *education:* Univ. degree; *political career:* Equal Opportunities Commissioner, Regional Employment Commission Campania; Employee FIOM-CGIL 1969-77; Deputy, Parliament, Naples-Caserta, 1987-; mem. Cttee. Budget, Treasury and Planning; *interests:* Problems of work, employment urban economy, The South, Developing nations; *professional career:* Professor of Urban and Regional Economy University of Architecture, Venice; *publications:* books and articles; *private address:* Via Daeudolo 74, 00153 Rome, Italy; *office address:* Prof. Dott. Ada Becchi, Camera dei Deputati, Montecitorio, 00186 Rome, Italy.

BECKER-INGLAU, Ingrid; German, Member of the Bundestag; *born:* 20 November 1946, Essen, West Germany; *married:* Dietmar, 1971; *languages:* English, French, Latin; *education:* High school leaving examination, 1967; Teaching examinations Part I, 1971; Part II, 1972; *party:* Sozialdemokratische Partei Deutschlands (SPD, Social Democratic Party of Germany); *political career:* mem. of council, Essen, 1979-87; mem. of Bundestag; *professional career:* Teacher at primary level; former headmistress; *recreations:* literature, Drama, Painting; *office address:* Frau Ingrid Becker-Inglau, Bundeshaus, 5300 Bonn 1, West Germany.

BECKERS-DE-BRUIJN, Drs. Ria; Dutch, Member of the Second Chamber; *born:* 2 November 1938, Driebergen-Rÿsenburg; *married:* K.J. Beckers, 1965; *children:* three ch; *languages:* Dutch, English; *education:* State University Utrecht, Drs. of Classic Literature, 1956-62; *party:* Politieke Partij Radikalen (PPR, Political Party of Radical Democrats), 1962; Groen Links (Green Left), 1989; *political career:* Mem. of Second Chamber, 1977-; Pres. of Green Left Group, 1989-; *office address:* Mevr. Drs. Ria Beckers-de-Bruijn, Tweede Kamer der Staaten-Generaal, Binnenhof 1A, Postbus 20018, The Hague, Netherlands.

BECKETT, Margaret; British, Member of Parliament; *born:* 15 January 1943; *parents:* Cyril Jackson; *married:* Lionel Arthur Beckett, 1979; *children:* two stepsons; *education:* Notre Dame High School, Norwich; *party:* Labour Party; *political career:* Research Asst., Labour Party, 1970-74; Member of Parliament for Lincoln, 1974-79; Political Adviser, Min. of Overseas Development, 1974; PPS to the Rt. Hon. Judith Hart

MP, 1974-75; Asst. Government Whip, 1975-76; Parliamentary Under-Sec. of State, Dept. of Education and Science, 1976-79; Member of Parliament for Derby South, 1983-; Shadow Minister for Social Security, 1984-89; Shadow Chief Sec. to the Treasury, 1989-; mem. of the National Exec. Cttee., 1980-81, 1985-86, 1988-89; *interests:* Industry; *professional career:* Student apprentice in Metallurgy, AEI Manchester, 1961-66; Experimental Officer, dept. of Metallurgy, University of Manchester, 1966-70; Principal Researcher, Granada Television, 1979-83; *clubs:* Transport and General Workers Union; National Union of Journalists; Association of Cinematography and Allied Technicians; Fabian Society; CND; Anti-Apartheid Movement; Tribune Group; Socialist Education Association; Labour Womens Action Committee; Derby Co-op Party; Socialist Environment and Resources Association; Amnesty International; Common Market Safeguards Campaign; *office address:* Ms Margaret Beckett, House of Commons, London SW1A OAA.

BECK-OBERDORF, Marieluise; German, Member of the Bundestag; *born:* 25 June 1952, Bramsche/Osnabrück, West Germany; *education:* grammar school, Abitur (advanced matriculation examination), Osnabrück, 1970; Universities of Bielefeld and Heidelberg; German, history, social studies; *party:* Die Grünen (Green Party), Mar. 1980; *political career:* regional chairperson, Die Grünen, Baden-Württemberg, Nov. 1980-Jun. 82; Speaker of Green parly. group, 1983-84; mem. of Bundestag, party list of Bremen; *professional career:* teacher, Konrad Adenauer Secondary School, Pforzheim; member of Gewerkschaft Erziehung und Wissenschaft (GEW, Trade Union for Education and Science); *private address:* 2800 Bremen 1, West Germany; *office address:* Frau Marieluise Beck-Oberdorf, Bundeshaus, 5300 Bonn 1, West Germany.

BEEBE TARANTELLI, Carole Jane; Italian, Deputy; *born:* 12 July 1942, Elizabeth, New Jersey, USA; *children:* one s; *education:* B.A. Wellesley College; M.A. University of Michigan; Ph.D. Bauders University; *party:* Independent Left Parly. Group; *political career:* Women's movement activist; Deputy, Rome Viterbo-Latina-Frosinone, 1987; mem. Cttee. on Justice; *professional career:* Professor, Faculty of Letters, English Department, University of Rome; Psychoanalist at Italian Centre of Analytic Psychology; *office address:* Ms Carole Beebe Tarantelli, Camera dei Deputati, Montecitorio, 00186 Rome, Italy.

BEER, Angelika; German, Member of the Federal Executive Committee of the Green Party; *born:* 24 May 1957, Kiel, West Germany; *education:* Mittlere Reife (intermediate high school certificate); *party:* Die Grünen (Green Party); *political career:* Mem. of

Bundestag, party list of Schleswig-Holstein, 1987-90; Mem., Federal Exec. Cttee., Green Party, 1991-; *interests:* foreign and defence policy, human rights; *professional career:* trained doctor's asst., lawyer's asst. and notary's clerk; lawyer's asst; *private address:* 2350 Neumünster, Germany; *office address:* Ms Angelika Beer, Die Grünen, Bundesgeschäftsstelle, Postfach 14 22, D-5300 Bonn 1, West Germany.

BEIM, Helen; Danish, Member of the Folketing; *born:* 24 April 1943, Copenhagen, Denmark; *parents:* Bror Ossian Hansson and Olga Hansson (née Petersen); *married:* Werner August Wilhelm Beim, 1963; *children:* Anne, Tine, Peter; *religion:* Protestant, Lutheran-Evangelical; *languages:* English, German; *party:* Socialdemokratiet (Social Democratic Party), 1964; *political career:* Member of Folketing; *private address:* Sognevoj 3, Gundsomagle 4000, Roshilde, Denmark; *office address:* Ms Helen Beim, Christiansborg, 1240 Copenhagen K, Denmark.

BEKE, Kata; Hungarian, Member of the Országgyülés; *party:* Hungarian Democratic Forum (MDF); *office address:* Ms Kata Beke, Országgyülés, Kossuth L. tér 1-3, Budapest V, Hungary; *phone:* 22 5058; 22 5059.

BEKI, Gabriella; Hungarian, Member of the Országgyülés; *party:* Alliance of Free Democrats (SZDSZ); *office address:* Ms Gabriella Béki, Országgyülés, Kossuth L. tér 1-3, Budapest V, Hungary; *phone:* 22 5058; 22 5059.

BELCHER, Jennifer M.; American, Washington State Rereresentative; *born:* 4 January 1944, Beckley, West Virginia, USA; *parents:* Grover Marion and Virginia Marion; *languages:* French, German; *education:* Bethany College, West Virginia; Harvard Univ., grad. programme for Senior Execs. in State and Local Govt., 1986; *party:* Democratic Party; *political career:* Washington State Rep., 1983-; *interests:* natural resource issues, human rights issues; *memberships:* Washington Women's Political Caucus; Business and Professional Women; The Nature Conservancy; *professional career:* Pres., Management Dynamics; *office address:* Ms Jennifer Belcher, JLOB 406, Olympia, Washington 98504, USA.

BELDE, Cameluta; Romanian, Secretary of the Grand National Assembly Commission for Education, Science and Culture; *party:* Romanian Communist Party (RCP); *political career:* candidate mem., RCP Central Cttee., 1984-; Deputy, Grand Nat. Assembly, Iolomita district, 1985; Sec., Grand Nat. Assembly Commission for Education, Science and Culture, 1985-; full Mem., RCP Central Cttee., 1988-; *professional career:* Rector, Iasi Polytechnic Institute, 1987; *office address:* Ms Cameluta Belde, Marea Adunare Nationala, Aleea Marii Adunari Nationale, Bucharest, Romania; *phone:* 16 21 50.

BELL, Jeannette Lois; American, Wisconsin State Representative; *born:* 2 September 1941, Milwaukee, Wisconsin, USA; *parents:* Harold Arthur Jeske and Luella Ruth Jeske (née Block); *married:* Chester Robert Bell (née 1962); *children:* Chester III, Colleen, Edith; *religion:* Presbyterian; *education:* Univ. of Wisconsin, Milwaukee, BA, 1988; *party:* Democratic Party; *political career:* Wisconsin State Rep., District 23, 1983-; *memberships:* League of Women Voters; *professional career:* former nursing home aide; *office address:* Ms Jeannette Bell, 1415 S. 60th Street, West Allison, Wisconsin 53214, USA.

BELO, Maria; Portuguese, Member of the European Parliament; *born:* 27 April 1938; *party:* Partido Socialista (PS, Socialist Party); *political career:* MEP, 1988; *interests:* co-operation and development, foreign relations; *private address:* Largo Jean Monnet 1-6, 1200 Lisbon, Portugal; *office address:* Ms Maria Belo, European Parliament, Centre Européen, Plateau de Kirchberg, BP 2929, Luxembourg; *phone:* Luxembourg 43001.

BENAKI-PSAROUDA, Anna; Greek, Alternate Minister of Culture; *born:* 12 December 1934; *parents:* Evangelos and AiKaterini; *married:* Línos Benakis, 1957; *public role of spouse:* Vice President of the Jonian University Corfou; *religion:* Greek Orthodox; *languages:* English, German, French; *party:* Nea Demokratia (ND, New Democracy Party); *political career:* MP of State, 1981; MP, A' Athens, 1985; MP A' Athens, 1989; Alternate Minister of Education, 1989; Alternate Minister of Culture, 1990-; *interests:* justice, education, culture; *memberships:* Athens Bar Assn; *professional career:* University professor (Penal Law); Attorny at Law; *publications:* four books and several articles on politics and criminal matters; *recreations:* swimming - water sports; *private address:* Sina 58, 106 72 Athens, Greece; *office address:* Ms Anna Benaki-Psarouda, Ministry of Culture, Odos Aristidou 14, 101 86 Athens, Greece.

BENNEDSEN, Dorte; Danish, Member of the Folketing; *born:* 2 July 1938, Frederiksberg; *parents:* Hal Koch and Bodil Koch (née Thastum); *married:* Jorgen Bennedsen, 1961; *children:* Mette, Mads, Morten; *religion:* Lutheran Evangelist; *languages:* Danish, English, Swedish, Norwegian; *education:* Metropolitan School, 1953-56; Univ. of Copenhagen, Bachelor of Divinity, 1956-64; *party:* Socialdemokratiet (Socialist Democratic Party), 1964; *political career:* member of the Town Council in Frederiksberg, 1970; Minister of Ecclesiastical Affairs, 1971-73; member of the Folketinget, 1975-; Minister of Education, 1979-82; *professional career:* Priester, Holmens Church 1964-68;

General Secretary, Danish Youth Community, 1968-71; *clubs:* Chairman of the Consumers Advisory Council, 1974-1979, Chairman of Nordic Association, 1984-; *office address:* Ms Dorte Bennedsen, Christiansborg, 1240 Copenhagen K, Denmark.

BENTLEY, Helen Delich; American, Member of the House of Representatives; *born:* 28 November 1923, Ruth, Nevada, USA; *parents:* Michael Delich and Mary Kovich; *married:* William Roy Bentley, 1959; *religion:* Greek Orthodox; *education:* Univ. of Nevada, 1941-42; George Washington Univ., 1943; Univ. of Montana, JB, 1944; *party:* Republican Party; *political career:* Campaign manager, the late Senator James Scrugham, White Pine County, Nevada, 1942; Chwn., Federal Maritime Commission, 1969-76; Chwn., American Bicentennial Fleet Inc., 1973-76; Republican Nominee for Congress, 2nd District, Maryland, 1980 and 1982; Member of the House of Reps. for Maryland; *memberships:* Newspaper Women's CLub; American Women in Radio and TV; Maryland Historical Society; National Federation of Press Women; *professional career:* reporter, Ely Record, Nevada, 1940-42; bureau Mgr., United Press, Fort Wayne, Indiana, 1944-45; reporter, Baltimore Sun, Maryland, 1945-53; maritime editor, 1953-69; TV producer, world trade and maritime shows, 1950-65; public relations adviser, American Assn. of Port Authorities, 1958-62 and 1964-67; *honours and awards:* Only Woman to Trek the North-West Passage aboard USS Manhattan, 1969; GOP Woman of the Year, 1972; American Legion Distinguished Service Medal, 1973; Robert M. Thompson Award, Navy League of US, 1973; Jerry Land Medal, 1974; *office address:* Helen Delich Bentley, 408 Chapelwood Lane, Lutherville, Maryland 21093, USA.

BERGÉ-LAVIGNE, Maryse; French, Senator; *born:* 29 January 1941, Pamiers, Ariège; *parents:* Jean Bergé and Alice Bergé (née Durrieu); *married:* Paul Lavigne; *children:* Pierre, Jean-Louis; *education:* Lycée Raymond Naves, Toulouse; certificate in the teaching of children with learning difficulties; *party:* Parti Socialiste (PS, Socialist Party); *political career:* regional Cllr., Midi-Pyrénées, 1986-; elected Senator, Haute-Garonne, 1989-; Mem., League for the Rights of Man; Mem., Regional Agency for the Environment, Midi-Pyrénées; *professional career:* teacher; *recreations:* reading, walking; *private address:* 6 rue Henri Molins, 31100 Toulouse, France; *office address:* Mme. Maryse Bergé-Lavigne, Sénat, Palais du Luxembourg, 75291 Paris Cedex 06, France; *phone:* Paris 42 34 20 00; *fax:* Paris 43 29 86 47.

BERGHOFER-WEICHNER, Dr. Mathilde; German, Deputy Member of the Bundesrat; *married:* the late Robert, 1969; *party:* Christlich Soziale Union (CSU, Christian Social Union); *political career:* Secretary of State for Teaching and Culture until 1986; mem. Municipal Council, Gauting; mem. of County Council, Starnberg; Minister of State for Justice, 1986-; mem. of Landtag; mem. of Bundesrat, 1974-; *office address:* Dr. Mathilde Berghofer-Weichner, Bundesrat, 5300 Bonn 1, West Germany.

BERGLIN, Linda; American, Minnesota State Senator; *born:* 29/10/44 Oakland, California, USA; *parents:* Freeman Waterman and Norma Waterman (née Lund); *education:* Minneapolis College of Art and Design, BFA, 1967; *party:* DFL; *political career:* Minnesota State Rep., 1973-80; Minnesota State Senator, District 60, 1981-; Chwn., Health and Human Services Senate Cttee.; Mem., Judiciary, Rules and Admin., Taxes and Tax Law Senate Cttees; *office address:* Ms Linda Berglin, 2309 Clinton Avenue S., Minneapolis, Minnesota 55404, USA.

BERNASCONI, Dott. Anna Maria; Italian, Deputy; *born:* 4 January 1945; *parents:* Onorato Bernasconi and Albertina (née Rossi); *languages:* English; *education:* University Degree in Medicine and Surgery; *party:* Partito Democratico della Sinistra (PDS, Party of the Democratic Left); *political career:* mem. of the commission for Social Affairs in the House of Deputies; Deputy of the Communist Parliamentary Group 1976; Councilor, (Milan) mem. Assembly of USL, 1964; *interests:* domestic and social politics; *professional career:* Medical Assistant, S. Gerardo Hospital, Rome, 1987-; *publications:* Various scientific publications on gastroenterology and internal medicine; *clubs:* mem. CGIL trade union; mem. Assembly of USL; *office address:* Dott. Anna Maria Bernasconi, Camera dei Deputati, Montecitorio, 00186 Rome, Italy.

BERNOCCO GARZANTI, Dott. Luigina (Gina Lagorio); Italian, Deputy; *born:* 6 January 1922, Bra, Cuneo, Italy; *party:* Independent Left Parly. Group; *political career:* Deputy, Parliament, Genoa-Imperia-La Spezia-Savona, 1987-; mem. Cttee. on Culture, Science and Teaching; *professional career:* Writer, novels, studies, plays; *office address:* Dott. Luigina Bernocco Garzanti, Camera dei Deputati, Montecitorio, 00186 Rome, Italy.

BERTONE, Pinuccia (Giuseppina); Italian, Deputy; *born:* 21 October 1938, Rivoli, Turin, Italy; *party:* Independent Left Parly. Group; *political career:* Provincial Councillor ACLI Turin, 1963; mem. Provincial Presidency ACLI from 1963-87; National Councillor, ACLI, 1966-75; Dir., Benevolent Fund, ACLI; Deputy, Parliament, Turin-Novara-Vercelli, 1987; mem. Cttee., Social Affairs; *office address:* Ms Pinuccia Bertone, Camera dei Deputati, Montecitorio, 00186 Rome, Italy.

BESSEROVA, Ladislava; Czechoslovakian, Deputy to National Assembly; *born:* 27 June 1912, Benesov, near Prague, Czecholslovakia; *education:* intermediate school; Lenin School, Moscow, 1932-37; *party:* Komunistická Strana Ceskoslovenska (KSC, Communist party of Czechoslovakia); *political career:* Sec., CP Czechoslovakia Regional Cttees., Prague, Olomouc, Hradec Králové, 1934-37; Mem., CP Central Cttee., 1937-38; prisoner, Nazi concentration camp, 1940-45; Mem., CP CSSR Central Cttee., 1945-53; Mem., Bohemian Prov. Nat. Cttee., 1945-58; Mem., Secretariat of CSSR-USSR Friendship Soc., 1945-48; Mem., CP CSSR Central Cttee., 1946-68; Head, Social Services Branch, Bohemian Provincial Nat. Cttee., 1946-48; Mem., Presidium and Secretariat, Central Action Cttee., Nat. Front, 1948-53; Deputy, National Assembly, 1948-; Chairperson, Prague Regional Cttee., CSSR-USSR Friendship Soc., 1950-60; Mem., CSSR-USSR Friendship Soc. Central Cttee.., 1950-; Mem., Presidium and Chief Section of Nat. Front Central Cttee., 1953-68; Mem., Presidium of Nat. Assembly, 1954-68; Mem., CSSR Cttee. of Peace Defenders, 1958-68; Mem., Cttee. for Socialist Culture, 1960-62; Chairperson, Parly. Group for Africa, Nat. Assembly, 1962-68; Chairperson, CSSR Cttee. for Solidarity with Nations of Africa and Asia, 1964-; Mem., Secretariat CP CSSR Central Cttee., 1964-66; Mem., World Peace Cncl., 1956-69; Mem., Central Cttee. of CSSR Union of Women, 1966-68; Mem., Chamber of People, Federal Assembly of CSSR; Mem., Cttee. for Agriculture and Food, 1969-; *professional career:* employee of various private firms; *honours and awards:* Czechoslovak War Cross, 1939, 1945; Order of 25th February First Class, 1949; Order of the Republic, 1955, 1962; Commemoration Medal, 20th Anniversary of Liberation of CSSR, 1965; Czechoslovak Peace Prize, 1967; *office address:* Ms Ladislava Besserova, Cttee. for Agriculture and Food, Ministry of Agriculture and Food, Tesnov 17, 117 05 Prague 1, Czechoslovakia.

BEVILACQUA, Cristina; Italian, Deputy; *born:* 9 March 1962, Broni, Pavia, Italy; *children:* one s; *party:* Communist Party Parly. Group; *political career:* Provincial Secretary, FGCI; Deputy, Parliament-Milan-Pavia, 1987; mem. Cttee. on Environment, Land, and Public Works; *office address:* Ms Cristina Bevilacqua, Camera dei Deputati, Montecitorio, 00186 Rome, Italy.

BEZERRA, Zila (Maria Zila Frota Bezerra de Oliveira); Brazilian, Federal Deputy; *born:* 7 May 1945, Rio de Janeiro; *parents:* Giucippe Genuense Frota and Maria Julia Lopes Frota; *children:* Natasha; *education:* UNB, Brasilia, Letters, 1971-81; *party:* Partido do Movimento Democrático Brasileira (PMDB, Party of the Brazlian Democratic Movement); *political career:* Co-ordinator for the agricultural development of the Juruá valley, 1985-89; Sec. for Government Affairs, 1987-90; Federal Deputy for Acre, 1991-95; *professional career:*

professor; *office address:* Ms Zila Bezerra, Chamber of Deputies, Praça dos 3 Poderes, Ed. Principal, 70160 Brasilia, DF, Brazil; *phone:* (61) 225 2885.

BHUTTO, Benazir; Pakistani, Member of the National Assembly and Chairwoman of the Pakistan People's Party; *born:* 21 June 1953; *parents:* the late Zulfikar Ali Bhutto (decd.1979) and Begum Nusrat Bhutto; *married:* Asif Ali Zardari, 1987; *children:* one s., one d; *education:* Harvard Univ., USA; Lady Margaret Hall, Oxford, UK; *party:* Pakistan People's Party (PPP); *political career:* under House arrest, 1977-84; joint leader (with her mother) in exile of the PPP and involved in the Movement for the Restoration of Democracy in Pakistan, 1984-; returned to Pakistan, 1986; Prime Minister, 1988-90; *honours and awards:* Dr.h.c., Harvard Univ., USA and Lady Margaret Hall, Oxford, UK, 1989; *publications:* Daughter of the East, 1988; *office address:* Mrs Benazir Bhutto, Pakistan People's Party, 70 Clifton, Karachi 75600, Pakistan.

BHUTTO, Begum Nusrat; Pakistani, Member of the National Assembly and Chairwoman of the Pakistan People's Party; *born:* 1934; *married:* the late Zulfikar Ali Bhutto (decd. 1979); *children:* two s., two d; *party:* Pakistan People's Party (PPP); *political career:* former First Lady of Pakistan; co-chair, PPP (with daughter Benazir Bhutto); involved in Movement for the Restoration of Democracy in Pakistan, 1984-; *office address:* Begum Nusrat Bhutto, Pakistan People's Party, 70 Clifton, Karachi 75600, Pakistan.

BIBA, Gjela Marku; Albanian, Deputy Chairperson of the People's Assembly; *party:* Albanian Workers' Party (AWP); *political career:* Mem., AWP Central Cttee., 1978; Dep. Chairperson, Albanian Democratic Front, 1979-; Dep., People's Assembly, Mirdite constituency district, 1982-; Dep. Chairperson, People's Assembly, 1982-; First Sec., Mirdite Rreth district AWP, 1983-; *office address:* Ms Gjela Biba, Kuvënd Popullore, Tirana, Albania.

BIDARD-REYDET, Danielle Louise; French, Senator; *born:* 8 December 1939, Paris, France; *parents:* Reydet and Georgette Reydet (née l'Hospitalier); *children:* Christine; *education:* agrégation in geography (highest competitive examination for teachers); *party:* Parti Communiste (PC, Communist Party); *political career:* Senator for Seine-Saint-Denis, 1978-; *professional career:* secondary school teacher; *office address:* Mme. Danielle Bidard-Reydet, Sénat de la République Française, Palais du Luxembourg, 75291 Paris Cedex 06, France.

BIDWELL, Arline M.; American, Chair of Connecticut State Democratic Committee; *born:* 6 August 1940, Tariffville, Connecticut, USA; *parents:* James Anthony Bidwell and Margaret Bidwell (née Quinn); *religion:*

Catholic; *education:* Hartford Fire Instruction School, 1958; *party:* Democratic Party; *political career:* Chair, Simsbury Democratic Town Cttee., Connecticut, 1961-66, Vice-Chair, 1976; Committeewoman, Eighth Senatorial District Democratic Cttee., Chair, 1976-78; Chair, Connecticut State Democratic Central Cttee; *professional career:* Assc. Admin., Hartford Board of Education, Connecticut, 1969-; *honours and awards:* Home Town Hero Award, Simsbury, Connecticut, 1986; *office address:* Ms Arline Bidwell, 24 Elm Street, Tariffville, Connecticut 06081, USA.

BIE, Helen; American, Member of the Republican National Cttee., Wisconsin; *party:* Republican Party; *political career:* Delegate, Republican Nat. Convention, 1980-; currently, Mem., Republican Nat. Cttee., Wisconsin; *office address:* Ms Helen Bie, 135 E Whitney Green Bay, Wisconsin 5430, USA.

BIENKOWSKA, Alicja; Polish, Member of the Sejm; *office address:* Ms Alicja Bienkowska, Sejm PRl, ul. Wiejska 4/6/8, 00-489 Warsaw, Poland; *phone:* (22) 28 70 01; 28 40 31.

BILDA, Barbara; Polish, Member of the Sejm; *office address:* Ms Barbara Bilda, Sejm PRl, ul. Wiejska 4/6/8, 00-489 Warsaw, Poland; *phone:* (22) 28 70 01; 28 40 31.

BINDI, Rosaria; Italian, Member of the European Parliament; *born:* 12 February 1951; *party:* Partito della Democrazia Cristiana (DC, Christian Democrat Party); *political career:* MEP, 1989-; *office address:* Ms Rosaria Bindi, European Parliament, Centre Européen, Plateau de Kirchberg, BP 2929, Luxembourg; *phone:* Luxembourg 43001.

BIRK, Baroness (cr. 1967, Life Peer) Alma Birk; British, Member of the House of Lords; *parents:* the late Barnett Wilson; *married:* Ellis Birk; *children:* one s., one d; *education:* South Hampstead High School; London School of Economics, B.Sc., economics; *party:* Labour Party; *political career:* Parly. candidate, 1950, 1951, 1955; Leader, Lab. Group, Finchley Borough Council, 1950-53; mem., Hendon Group Hospital Management Cttee., 1951-59; Sec., Fabian Soc. Research Cttee. on Marriage and Divorce, 1951-52; House of Lords, 1967-; mem., Youth Service Development Cncl., 1967-71; Vice-Pres., Cncl. for Children's Welfare, 1968-75; Chmn., Health Education Cncl., 1969-72; Vice-Pres., Divorce Law Reform Union, 1969-; Baroness-in-Waiting (Government Whip), 1974; Parly. Under-Sec. of State, 1974-79; Minister of State, 1979; Chief Opposition Front Bench Spokesman on Environment, 1979-86; Vice-Pres., Assn. of Metropolitan Authorities, 1982; Vice-Pres., Assn. of District Councils; Chief Opposition Spokesman on Arts, Libraries, Heritage, Broadcasting and Cable, 1986-; *professional career:* JP, 1952; Assoc. Editor, Nova, 1965-70; Panel mem.,

Pregnancy Advisory Service, 1968-; Governor, London School of Economics, 1971-; Dir., New Shakespeare Co., 1979-; Governor, British Film Inst., 1981-87; trustee, Health Promotion Research, 1983-; trustee, Stress Syndrome Foundation, 1983-; Pres., Confederation of Art and Design Assns., 1984-88; *publications:* co-author, Family Service And Family Courts; co-author, Families With Problems; *clubs:* Howard league for Penal Reform Council; Albany Trust (cttee.); H.G. Wells Socy. (Vice-Pres.); Redbridge Jewish Youth Centre (Vice-Pres.); Royal Socy. of Arts (Fellow); Georgian Group (cncl.); Assn. of Art Inst. (Pres.); Craft Arts Design Assn. (Pres.); *private address:* 3 Wells Rise, Regent's Park, London NW8 7LH, UK; *office address:* Baroness Birk, House of Lords, London SW1A 0PW.

BISHOP, Bronwyn Kathleen; Australian, Senator; *born:* 19 October 1942, Sydney, Australia; *education:* qualified as a solicitor; *party:* Liberal Party; *political career:* Pres., Liberal Party Balmoral Branch, 1973-79; Vice-Pres., Warringah Federal Electoral Conference, 1978-80; Pres., Mosman State Electorate Conference, 1978-81; Vice-Pres., Liberal Party Women's Group, NSW, 1978-81; Mem., Liberal Party State Executive, 1980-; Chairperson, Liberal Party Annual State Convention, NSW, 1981-85; Metropolitan Vice-Pres., Liberal Party, NSW, 1982-85; Pres., Liberal Party, NSW, 1985-87; elected to the Senate for NSW, 1987-; Committee Service: Mem. of the Senate Standing Cttee. for Regulations and Ordinances, 1987-; Mem. of the Senate Estimates Cttee. A, 1987-; Mem. of the Joint Statutory Cttee. for Public Accounts, 1987-; *professional career:* solicitor; company dir; *office address:* Ms Bronwyn Bishop, Senate, Parliament House, Room M13, Canberra, ACT 2600, Australia; *phone:* (062) 727111.

BJARTVEIT, Erna Eleonore; Norwegian, former Minister for Church and Cultural Affairs; *born:* 11 July 1924, Alta, Norway; *parents:* Havdan Waage and Frida Waage (née Holmboe); *married:* Kjell Bjartveit, 1951; *children:* Marit, Gro, Kristin, Steinar; *education:* Cand. med., 1951; studies, USA, Canada, 1961-1962; Recognised Specialist, Rehabilitation Medicine, 1965; Recognised Specialist, Geriatric, 1976; *party:* Kristelig Folkeparti (KrF, Christian Democratic Party); *political career:* mem., various Cttees. in the Health and Social Sector, Oslo; Vice-Chmn., Social Services Board of Control, 1976-79; mem. Social Services Cttee., 1976-83; Chmn., Religious Council, Furuset, 1979-81; mem., City Board of Control, Oslo, 1980; Deputy Member of Storting, 1981-82, 1982-83; Deputy mem., State Outdoor Life Council, 1983; Deputy mem., The Land Council, 1983; mem., Christian Democratic Party County Board of Control, Oslo, 1981-82; Vice-Pres., Storting, Odelstinget, Lower House of Norwegian Legislature, 1985-86; mem., Justice Cttee., 1985-86; 1st Deputy Representative, Oslo, 1986-89; Minister,

Church and Cultural Affairs, 1989-Oct.1990; *professional career:* doctor, Gaustad Hospital, Gaustad, 1951-52; doctor, Bindal District, 1952-53; doctor, Sanatorium, Landeskogen, 1953-57; doctor, Kongsberg Hospital, Kongsberg, 1953-57; assistant doctor, State Rehabilitation Institute, Oslo, 1958-59; reserve doctor, Oslo, 1959-62; doctor, Social Medicine Department, Health Council, Oslo, 1962-67; doctor mem., Social Insurance Tribunal, 1967-; part-time geriatrics' hospital doctor, 1968-79; *office address:* Ms Eleonore Bjartveit, Ministry of Church and Education, Akersgt. 42, POB 8119 Dep., 0032 Oslo 1, Norway.

BJELKE-PETERSEN, Lady Florence Isabel; Australian, Senator; *born:* 11 August 1920, Brisbane, Australia; *party:* National Party of Australia; *political career:* Public Relations Officer, Barambah Electorate Council, 1971-81; chosen to represent Queensland, 1981-; Committee Service: Mem. of the Senate Standing Cttee. for the House, 1985-; Mem. of the Senate Legislative and General Purpose Standing Cttee. for National Resources, 1981-83; for Social Welfare, 1983-87; Mem. of the Senate Select Cttee. for Private Hospitals and Nursing Homes, 1981-85; Mem. of the Senate Estimates Cttee. C, 1981-82; B, 1983-85; Mem. of the Joint Standing Cttee. for Foreign Affairs and Defence, 1981-83; temporary Chairperson of Cttees., 1985-; Conferences, Delegations and Visits: Mem., Parly. Delegation to the European Parly. Institutions, Strasbourg and Berlin, 1985; Dep. Leader, National Party of Australia, in the Senate, 1985-; *professional career:* Private Sec. to the Queensland Commissioner for Main Roads; *office address:* Lady Florence Bjelke-Petersen, Senate, Parliament House, Room M13, Canberra, ACT 2600, Australia; *phone:* (062) 727111.

BJERREGAARD, Ritt Jytte; Danish, Member of the Folketing; *born:* 19 May 1941, Copenhagen, Denmark; *parents:* Gudmund Bjerregaard and Rita Bjerregaard (née Hærslev); *married:* Soeren Moech, 1966; *public role of spouse:* Lecturer; *religion:* Christian; *languages:* Danish, German, English, French; *education:* Enghave Plads Skole, primary school, 1948-53; Christianshavns Gymnasium, High school, 1953-58; Emdrupborg Seminar, college of Education, 1964; *party:* Socialdemokratiet (Social Democratic Party); *political career:* Minister for Education, 1973; Minister for Social Affairs, 1975-79; Mem., Board of Dirs., Nat. Bank of Denmark, 1981; Chairperson, Social Democratic Party Parly. Group, 1981-; Vice-Chairperson, Social Democratic Parly. Group, 1987 and Chairperson; Auditor, Public Accounts Cttee., 1982, Chairperson, 1990; *professional career:* teacher in secondary schools, 1964-82; *recreations:* gardening, travel; *office address:* Ms Ritt Bjerregaard, Folketing, Christiansborg, 1240 Copenhagen K, Denmark.

BLACKSTONE, Baroness (cr. 1987, Life Peer) Tessa Ann Vosper Blackstone; British, Member of the House of Lords; *born:* 27 September 1942, London, UK; *parents:* Geoffrey Vaughan Blackstone and Joanna Blackstone (née Vosper); *married:* Tom Evans, 1963, marriage dissolved; *children:* Benedict, Liesel; *languages:* French, German; *education:* London School of Economics, B.Sc., 1964, Ph.D., 1969; *party:* Labour Party, 1962; *political career:* mem., Science and Education Sub-Cttee., Lab. National Exec. Cttee., 1974-75, 1978-83; House of Lords, 1987-; Opposition Front Bench Spokesperson on Education and Science; *interests:* social and educational policy, foreign policy, the arts and the media; *memberships:* Dir., Thames Television; Royal Inst. of Public Admin.; Fabian Soc.; Royal Opera House (Dir.); Chairperson, Inst. for Public Policy Research; *professional career:* Assoc. lecturer, Enfield College, 1965-66; Asst. lecturer and lecturer in social admin., London School of Economics, 1966-75; adviser, Central Policy Review Staff, Cabinet Office, 1975-78; Prof. of educational admin., Inst. of Education, 1978-83; Dep. Education Officer, then clerk and Dir. of Education, Inner London Education Authority, 1983-86; Fellow, Policy Studies Inst., 1986-87; Master, Birkbeck College, 1987-; *honours and awards:* Hon. Dr. Litt; *publications:* joint author, Students In Conflict, 1970; A Fair Start, 1971; Education And Day Care For Young Children In Need, 1973; Academic Labour Market, 1974, joint author; Disadvantage And Education, 1982, joint author; Educational Policy And Educational Inequality, 1982, joint author; Response To Adversity, 1983, joint author; Testing Children, 1983, joint author; Inside The Think Tank, 1988, joint author; Prisons and Penal Reform, 1990; *recreations:* ballet, opera, tennis; *private address:* c/o Birkbeck College, Malet Str., London WC1E 7HX, UK; *office address:* Baroness Blackstone, House of Lords, London SW1A 0PW.

BLAND BAXTER, Elaine; American, Secretary-of-State of Iowa; *born:* 16 January 1933, Chicago, Illinois, USA; *parents:* Clarence Arthur Bland and Margaret Bland (née Clark); *married:* Harry Youngs Baxter, 1954; *children:* Katherine, Harry, John; *education:* Univ. of Illinois, BA, 1954; Iowa Wesleyan College, Teaching Certificate, 1970; Univ. of Iowa, MS, 1978; *party:* Democratic Party; *political career:* City Cncl. Mem., Burlington, Iowa, 1973-75; Dir., League of Iowa Municipality, 1973-75; delegate, Democrat National Convention, 1974 and 1988; Senior Liaison Officer, Legislative and Congressional Relations, HUD, Washington DC, 1979-81; Iowa State Rep., District 60, 1982-86; Mem., Foreign Trade Task Force, National Conference of State Legislators, 1985; Sec.-of-State, Iowa, 1987-; National Chwn., Dukakis-Bentsen Presidential Campaign, 1988; Mem., Advisory Board, Coalition for Women's Appointments; *memberships:* Dir., Women's Equity Action League; American Society for Public Admin.; Women Execs. in State

Govt.; Urban Land Inst.; Victoria Society, Iowa; Foundation of Iowa Children and Family Services; *professional career:* history teacher, Burlington Community High School, Iowa; Consultant, economic development; *honours and awards:* Women Exec. in State Govt. Fellowship, Senior Execs. in State and Local Govt. Program, J. F. Kennedy School of Govt., Harvard Univ., 1988; Hon. Residential Chair, Iowa Chapter, American Heart Assn., 1989; *publications:* North Side Neighbourhood Preservation Study: Historic Structures Inventory, Inst. of Urban and Regional Research, Univ. of Iowa, 1977; Cities and Voter Registration, Iowa Municipalities, 1988; Running for Statewide Office is not for Beginners, Iowa Democrat Quarterly, 1988; *private address:* 1016 N. 4th Street, Burlington, Iowa 52601, USA; *office address:* Mrs Elaine Bland Baxter, State House, Des Moines, Iowa 50319, USA.

BLATCH, Baroness (cr. 1987, Life Peer) Emily May Blatch; British, Minister of State for the Environment; *born:* 24 July 1937; *parents:* the late Stephen Triggs and the late Sarah Triggs; *married:* John Richard Blatch, AFC, 1963; *children:* two s. (one decd.), one s., one d. (twins); *religion:* Church of England; *education:* Prenton Girls School, Birkenhead; *party:* Conservative Party; *political career:* Leader, Cambridgeshire County Council, 1981-85; mem., Peterborough Development Corp., 1984-85; mem., European Economic and Social Cttee., 1986-87; House of Lords, 1987-; Baroness in Waiting to H.M. the Queen, 1990-91; Parly. Under-Sec. for the Environment, 1991; Minister of State for the Environment, 1991-; *interests:* local government management, education, Anglo-American relations; *professional career:* secretarial training and office work, 1953-55; Air Traffic Control, WRAF, 1955-59, civilian, 1959-63; Pres., National Benevolent Institute; *honours and awards:* CBE, 1983; *clubs:* RAF Club; Royal Socy. of Arts (fellow); *recreations:* family, music, theatre; *office address:* Baroness Blatch, Department of the Environment, 2 Marsham Street, London SW1P 3EB, United Kingdom.

BLOMME, Jeannine; Belgian, Senator; *born:* 25 January 1936, Brussels, Belgium; *parents:* deceased; *married:* Jules Hermans, 1959; *public role of spouse:* Provincial Councillor for Brabant; *children:* one; *religion:* secular; *languages:* French; *education:* Funks School, Commercial Studies, 1948-54; *party:* Parti Socialiste (PS, Socialist Party); *political career:* PS activist, 1955-; Cabinets of Ministers Larock and Janne, Nat. Education, 1962-65; trade union activist, 1966-; Deputy Mayor for Social Affairs and Youth, Bercham-Sainte-Agathe, 1977-; co-opted Senator, 1988-; mem.of PS Exec., Brussels Federation; mem. of Senate Commissions; *interests:* social affairs, youth affairs, finance, economics, co-operation development; *professional career:* accountant, Codu, 1954-60; Nat. Secretary, Faucons Rouges Movement,1960-62; Fund

for Educational Buildings, 1965-88; *honours and awards:* Knight of the Order of the Crown; *recreations:* music; *private address:* 64, Rue des Soldats, 1080 Bruxelles (Berchem-Sainte-Agathe), Belgium; *office address:* Mme. Jeannine Blomme, Senate, Palais de la Nation, Place de a Nation 1, 1000 Brussels, Belgium.

BLUNCK, Lilo (Lieselott); German, Member of the Bundestag; *born:* 19 November 1942, Bad Segeberg; *children:* one d; *education:* grammar school, Mittlere Reife (intermediate high school certificate), 1959; qualifying examination for commercial clerk, 1961; College of Education, Schleswig, state examination in education, 1972-74; *party:* Sozialdemokratische Partei Deutschlands (SPD, Social Democratic Party of Germany), 1971; *political career:* dep. district chmn., SPD, 1974-76; chmn., Local Group of the SPD, 1979-80; mem. of Bundestag, party list of Schleswig-Holstein; *professional career:* trained commercial clerk; educationist; worked for Arbeiterwohlfahrt (AWO, Labour Welfare Organisation), 1973-77; member of AWO, since 1977; worked for Arbeitsgemeinschaft Deutsches Schleswig (Working Group German Schleswig), 1977-81; dep. chmn., Marie Schlei Society; member of Gewerkschaft Handel, Banken und Versicherungen (HBV, Trade Union for Commerce, Banks and Insurance); *honours and awards:* honorary judge, administrative court, Schleswig, 1978-81; *private address:* 2082 Uetersen, West Germany; *office address:* Frau Lilo Blunck, Bundeshaus, 5300 Bonn 1, West Germany.

BOBU, Maria; Romanian, Minister of Justice; *married:* Emile Bobu; *party:* Romanian Communist Party (RCP); *political career:* Mem., Bureau of Women's Nat. Cncl., 1974; Prosecutor, Gen. Prosecutor, 1975; Mem., Higher Sanitary Cncl., Vice Chairperson, Women's Nat. Cncl., 1977; Prosecution-Inspector, Gen. Prosecutor's Office and Mem., Exec. Bureau, Romanian Assn. of Jurist, 1976; Mem., Nat. Cncl. of Socialist Democracy and Unity Front, 1980-; Vice Chairperson, Fatherland's Falcons Organisations, 1980-; Deputy Minister of Justice, 1982; Minister of Justice, 1987- full Mem., RCP Central Cttee., 1984; Deputy to Grand Nat. Assembly for Constanta constituency, 1985; *office address:* Ms Maria Bobu, Ministry of Justice, Blvd. Gheorghe Gheorghiu - Dej. 33, Bucharest, Romania.

BOERS-WIJNBERG, Drs. Mieke H.A.; Dutch, Member of the Second Chamber; *born:* 20 February 1946, Velsen, Netherlands; *education:* Univ. of Amsterdam, masters in economics; *party:* Christen Democratisch Appel (CDA, Christian Democratic Appeal); *political career:* secretary CDA group, Amerongen; Mem. Provincial Board, CDA Utrecht; vice-Pres. CDA foundation Frame and form work; Mem. of Second Chamber, 1986-; *professional career:*

teacher of economics, Koningen Wilhelmina College, Culemborg; *clubs:* pres CHU choosing association, Amerongen, secretary CHU general board; *private address:* Prof. Gimbrèrelaan 172, 5037 EN Tilburg, the Netherlands; *office address:* Drs. Nieke Boers-Wijnberg, Tweede Kamer der Staaten-Generaal, Binnenhof 1A, Postbus 20018, The Hague, Netherlands.

BOGUCKA-SKOWRONSKA, Anna Teresa; Polish, Senator; *office address:* Ms Anna Teresa Bogucka-Skowronska, Senat, ul. Ogrodowa 6, 00-896 Warsaw, Poland; *phone:* (22) 20 03 71.

BOHLIN, Britt Eva Irene; Swedish, Member of the Riksdag; *born:* 10 February 1956, Dalskog, Sweden; *parents:* Åke Karlsson and Gunvor Karlsson (née Johansson); *married:* Kent Bohlin, 1983; *children:* Johan; *religion:* Protestant; *languages:* English; *education:* Continuation School, Vänersborg, Mental Nurse, 1974-75; *party:* Sveriges Socialdemokratiska Arbetarepartiet (SAP, Swedish Social Democratic Labour Party), 1975; *political career:* Member of Riksdag, 1988-; Member of the Defence Committee; *professional career:* Member of the Superior board of the Union of Swedish Local Government Workers; *clubs:* Chairwoman of the Union of Swedish Local Government Workers, Chapter 21; *office address:* Ms Britt Bohlin, Riksdag, Fack, S-100 12 Stockholm, Sweden.

BOHLIN, Görel Ruth Charlotte; Swedish, Member of the Riksdag; *born:* 6 November 1930, Östersund, Sweden; *parents:* Uno Fredman and Astrid Fredman (née Obberlind); *married:* Carl Lennart Bohlin, 1960; *children:* Marià, Charlotte, Görel Johanna; *religion:* Protestant; *languages:* English, German; *education:* Uppsala Univ., B.Sc., 1973; *party:* Moderata Samlingspartiet (Moderate Party) 1948; *political career:* Board mem. National Railways Women Civil Servants Union, 1951-54; Chmn. National Water Works Womens Civil Service Union, 1954-59; Board mem., Sigtuna, 1966-82 and Chmn., 1970-72, Vice-Chmn. 1976-82; municipal cnclr., Sigtuna, 1971-85, and 1988-, Pres., 1989-; mem. Social Central Council, 1973-82, Chmn., 1973-79; MP, 1979-; dep. mem., Parly. Social Insurance Cttee., and the Labour Market Cttee., 1979-82; mem., Parly. Cttee. for Transport and Communications, 1982-; Vice Chmn., Stockholm County Moderate Party; Board Mem., Moderate Party Parly. Group; *interests:* defence, equality, national insurance; *professional career:* Clerk, National Railway, 1948-54; director's sec., National Water Works, 1954-59; ASAB, 1956-61; teacher of business studies for Bar-Lock Institute, 1965-75; instructor and head WAAC, voluntary defence, 1947-63; Vice-Chmn., Dance Academy, 1978-; Vice-Chmn., Stockholm County National Insurance Office, 1979-; Board mem., Märsta Electricity Board Ltd., 1972-73; Church Warden, Saint

Olof Parish, Sigtuna, 1971-74; Board mem., Tingsätra Old Peoples Home, 1974-79; Board mem., Sigtuna Power Station Ltd., 1977-79; Alderman, Stockholm County Court, 1979; Board mem., Swedish Road Safety Office, 1985-89; Board mem., Swedish Road and Traffic Research Institute, 1988-89; Board mem., Civil Aviation Administration, 1989-; Vice Chmn., Stockholm County Moderate Party; *publications:* Region for the Future, 1978; *clubs:* Swedish WAAC, Art Councils, Red Cross; *recreations:* art, music; *private address:* Jarlers väg 21, 19300 Sigtuna, Sweden; *office address:* Ms Görel Bohlin, Riksdag, Fack, S-100 12 Stockholm, Sweden.

BÖHRK, Gisela; German, Deputy Member of the Bundesrat; *born:* 8 June 1945, Leipzig; *education:* Ann Arbor High School; Mathematical-technical assist. training, 1965-66; *party:* Sozialdemokratische Partei Deutschlands (SPD, Social Democratic Party of Germany), 1973; *political career:* Dep. Chmn, Young Socialists, Land Group since 1974; 2nd Dep. Chmn., SPD-Landtag Group since 1983; Minister for Women, Schleswig-Holstein since 1988; mem. of Bundesrat, 1988; *professional career:* Temporary Programmer, Teacher Training College, Kiel, 1966-69; Teacher since 1969; *office address:* Frau Gisela Böhrk, Bundesrat, 5300 Bonn 1, West Germany.

BOLANDER, Gunhild Anna Maria; Swedish, Member of the Riksdag; *born:* 26 September 1932, Atlingbo, Sweden; *parents:* Karl Bernhard Johnsson and Alvina Tyra Anna Maria (née Pettersson); *married:* Karl Allan Niklas Bolander, 1952; *children:* Magnus, Elizabeth; *religion:* Protestant; *education:* Hemse Elementary School, 1949-50; Lövsta Agricultural School, 1950-51; *party:* Centerpartiet (Centre Party), 1952; *political career:* Gotland Provincial Cllr., 1981-; mem. of Riksdag, 1981; mem., Defence Cttee. and dep. mem., Labour Market Cttee.; mem., Construction Board, 1986-; War Material Inspectorates Advisory Councillor, 1986-; mem., MOD's Institute of Rationalisation Board, 1989-; *interests:* defence, regional policies, the disabled; *clubs:* Defence Policy Forum; Centre Party Women's Assoc.; Professional Women's Club; the Lotta Corps; *office address:* Ms Gunhild Bolander, Riksdag, Fack, S-100 12 Stockholm, Sweden.

BOLDING, F.; Dutch, Member of the First Chamber; *born:* 18 September 1958, Beilen, Netherlands; *education:* academy of Art, Groningen; history, Utrecht; *party:* Groen Links (Green Left); *political career:* Mem. of CPN-party board, 1982-; Mem. daily ruling Board CPN, 1984-; Mem. First Chamber, 1986-; Pres. of Groen Links group in First Chamber; *professional career:* social worker, Lelystad, until 1985; *private address:* Plantage 140, 8212 VJ Lelystad, the Netherlands; *office address:* Mevr. F. Bolding, Eerste

Kamer der Staaten-Generaal, Binnenhof 22, Postbus 20017, The Hague, Netherlands.

BONFATTI PAINI, Marisa; Italian, Deputy; *born:* 3 November 1947, Mantua, italy; *education:* Licentiate of Science, Mantua; Florence University, Faculty of Architecture, specialist town-planning, degree, 1971; restoration courses at Milan, Lucca and Bergamo; *party:* Communist Parly. Group; *political career:* Deputy, Parliament, Mantova-Cremona, 1987; mem. Committee on Environment, Territory and Public Works; *professional career:* Head of Technical Office, Suzzara Council, Milan, 1975-79; Head of Economic and Popular Housing, Mantua Council, 1979-1986; private practice, 1986-; *office address:* Ms Marisa Bonfatti Paini, Camera dei Deputati, Montecitorio, 00186 Rome, Italy.

BONIVER, Margherita; Italian, Deputy; *born:* 11 March 1938, Rome, Italy; *children:* one d; *education:* University of Georgetown, Washington, Faculty of Political Science; *party:* Partito Socialista Italiana (PSI, Italian Socialist Party), 1961; *political career:* Activist, Women's movement; Activist, Amnesty International; , from 1975; Pres., Italian Section, Amnesty International; mem. International Exec. Cttee. of Amnesty International, 1978-80; elected Senator, Milan, 1980; Vice-Pres. of the Commission on Foreign Affairs; mem. Council of Europe; mem. Western European Union; mem. Parliamentary Assembly of Nato; Head of Foreign Section, National Leadership of PSI, 1981; mem. of Trilateral Cttee., from 1982; elected to Nat. Exec. of PSI, 1984, Head of International Socialist Section; mem. Commission for Human Rights of the Presidency of the Council and Vice Pres. of the Atlantic Committee; Deputy, Parliament, Cuneo-Alessandria-Asti, 1987; Vice-Pres. of Cttee. on Foreign and Community Affairs; *professional career:* Co-founder, with Gisèle Halimi, the Italian section of Choisir group to campaign for the liberalisation of abortion and contraception; *office address:* Ms Margherita Boniver, Camera dei Deputati, Montecitorio, 00186 Rome, Italy.

BOOTHROYD, Betty; British, Deputy Speaker; *born:* 8 October 1929; *parents:* Archibald Boothroyd and Mary Boothroyd; *education:* Dewsbury College of Commerce and Art; *party:* Labour Party; *political career:* Personal and political asst to Labour Ministers and mem. of foreign conference delegations, legislative asst. to United States Congressman, 1960-62; Cllr., Hammersmith Borough Council 1965-68; Chmn., Hammersmith Race Relations Employment Cttee., 1967-72; Member of Parliament for West Bromwich West since 1973; Member of European Parliament, 1975-77; Asst. Government Whip, 1974-76; Mem., Speaker's Panel of Chairmen 1979-87; former mem., Select Cttee. on Foreign and Commonwealth Affairs;

mem., House of Commons Commission, 1983-87; mem., Labour Party National Exec. Cttee., 1981-87; Second Dep. Chmn., Ways and Means; Deputy Speaker, 1987; *office address:* Ms Betty Boothroyd, House of Commons, London SW1A OAA.

BORAWAKA, Marianna; Polish, Member of the Sejm; *office address:* Ms Marianna Borawaka, Sejm PRI, ul. Wiejska 4/6/8, 00-489 Warsaw, Poland; *phone:* (22) 28 70 01; 28 40 31.

BOS-BEERNINK, B.F.; Dutch, Member of the First Chamber; *born:* 11 August 1931, Huttwil, Switzerland; *education:* Classical College, Lausanne; diploma translator and interpreter; *party:* Christen Democratische Appel (CDA, Christian Democratic Appeal); *political career:* Mem. First Chamber 1987-; *clubs:* Dutch Women's Council; Nat. committee European Cultural Foundation; Protestant-Christian school; pres. Dutch Red Cross in Katwÿk; *private address:* Nieuwe Duinweg 10, 2224 EC Katwÿ, the Netherlands; *office address:* Mevr. B.F. Bos-Beernink, Eerste Kamer der Staaten-Generaal, Binnenhof 22, Postbus 20017, The Hague, Netherlands.

BOSCAGLIA, Clara; San Marino, Secretary of State for Finance and Budget; *party:* Partito Democratico Cristiano Sammarinese (PDCS, San Marino Christian Democratic Party); *office address:* Ms Clara Boscaglia, Ministry of Finances, Budget, Programming, and Information, Palazzo Begni, Contrada Omerelli, 47031 San Marino.

BOSELLI, Anna; Italian, Deputy; *born:* 21 September 1943, Reggio Emilia, Italy; *education:* Doctor in Biological Science; *party:* Partito Democratico della Sinistra (PDS, Party of the Democratic Left); *political career:* Councillor, Federal Cttee. of Provincial Secretariat, PCI; Deputy, Parliament, Verona-Padua-Vicenza-Regio Emilia 1983; mem. Cttee. on Public Works; re-elected Deputy, 1987; mem. Cttee. Environment, Land and Public Works; *professional career:* Teacher; *office address:* Ms Anna Boselli, Camera dei Deputati, Montecitorio, 00186 Rome, Italy.

BOSSANYI, Katalin; Hungarian, Member of the Országgyúlés; *party:* Hungarian Socialist Party (MSZP); *office address:* Ms Katalin Bossányi, Országgyúlés, Kossuth L. tér 1-3, Budapest V, Hungary; *phone:* 22 5058; 22 5059.

BOTOS, Katalin; Hungarian, Minister without portfolio; *party:* Hungarian Democratic Forum (MDF); *political career:* deals with the tasks of the Govt. concerning the financial institutional system; *office* *address:* Ms Katalin Botos, Országgyűlés, Kossuth L. tér 1-3, Budapest V, Hungary; *phone:* 22 5058; 22 5059.

BOTTOMLEY, Virginia Hilda Brunette Maxwell, JP; British, Minister for Health; *born:* 12 March 1948; *parents:* John Garnett, CBE; *married:* Peter James Bottomley; *children:* one s., two d; *education:* Essex University (BA); London School of Economics (M.Sc.); *party:* Conservative Party; *political career:* Member of Parliament for Surrey South West, 1984-; Sec., Backbench Employment Cttee., 1985-86; Sec., All Party Social Science and Policy Cttee, 1984-86; PPS to Mr. Chris Patten, Minister of State, Dept. of Education and Science, 1985-86 and then Minister of State, Foreign and Commonwealth Office and Minister for Overseas Development; PPS to Sir Geoffrey Howe QC, Sec. of State for Foreign and Commonwealth Affairs, 1987-88; Parliamentary Under-Sec., Dept. of the Environment, 1988-89; Minister of State for Health, Nov. 1989-; Govt. Co-Chwn., Women's National Commission, Jan. 1991-; *interests:* child care law; education; overseas aid; health service; penal affairs; *professional career:* researcher, Child Poverty Action Group, 1971-73; tutor, further education, 1971-73; psychiatric social worker in Child Guidance Unit, 1973-84; Inner London Magistrate (Juvenile) 1975-84; Chmn., Lambeth Juvenile Court, 1980-84; Dir., Mid Southern Water Company, 1987-88; mem. of Court of Governors, London School of Economics, 1985-; Freeman, City of London, 1989-; *clubs:* Industry and Parliament Trust (Fellow); *office address:* Mrs Virginia Bottomley, Department of Health, Richmond House, 79 Whitehall, London SW1.

BOUCHARDEAU, Huguette; French, Deputy; *born:* 1 June 1935, Saint-Étienne; *party:* Parti Socialiste (PS, Socialist Party); *political career:* fmr. Minister; Deputy, 1986, 1988-; *professional career:* teacher; *office address:* Mme. Huguette Bouchardeau, L'Assemblée Nationale, 126 rue de L'Université, 75355 Paris, France.

BOURDARA, Kelly; Greek, Under Secretary of State for Education and Religion; *party:* Nea Demokratia (ND, New Democracy Party), 1989; *political career:* MP, ND, B' Athens, 1989; member of the Section of Women's Issues of ND; Under Sec. of State for Education and Religion, 1990-; *professional career:* Assistant Professor of the Law School of Athens; *office address:* Ministry of Education and Religion, Odos Metropoleos 15, Athens, Greece.

BOURGAULT, Lise; Canadian, Member of the House of Commons and Parliamentary Secretary to the Minister of National Health and Welfare; *office address:* Mrs Lise Bourgault, House of Commons, Parliament Buildings, Wellington Street, Ottawa, Ontario K1A OA6, Canada; *phone:* (613) 957 3744; *fax:* 952 0874.

BOURNE, Vicki Worrall; Australian, Senator; *born:* 22 October 1954, Sydney, New South Wales, Australia; *education:* B.Sc., M.Sc., (NSW); *party:* Australian Democrats; *political career:* Mem., Campaigns Team, Australian Democrats, NSW, 1980-, Assistant Campaign Manager, 1984; Mem., NSW Constitutional Review Cttee. of Australian Democrats, 1988-90; Spokesperson for Australian Democrats on Foreign Affairs, Customs, Antartica, Housing and Arts, 1990-; Senator for NSW, 1990-; Mem., Senate Standing Cttee. on Privileges, Scrutiny of Bills, 1990-; Mem., Senate Legislative Cttee. and General Purpose Standing Cttee., Mem., Cttees. on the Environment, Recreation and the Arts, Foreign Affairs, Defence and Trade, 1990-; Mem., Senate Cttee. on Migration Regulations, 1991-; *interests:* foreign affairs, human rights, environment, arts; *professional career:* Research Officer and Private Sec. to Senator C. Mason, 1978-87; Research Officer to Senator P. McLean, 1987-90; *office address:* Ms Vicki Bourne, Senate, Parliament House, Room M13, Canberra, ACT 2600, Australia; *phone:* (062) 727111.

BOUTIN, Christine; French, Deputy; *born:* 6 February 1944, Levroux; *parents:* Martin and Bernadette (née Durand); *married:* Louis Boutin, 1967; *children:* Loïc, Armelle, Pierre Yves; *religion:* Catholic; *languages:* English; *education:* Faculty of Law, Paris, until 1964, degree in public law; *party:* Union Centriste (UC, Centrist Union); *political career:* Gen. Cllr. Rambouillet, Yvelines; Vice-Pres., Gen. Cncl. of Yvelines; Deputy Mayor, Rambouillet; Deputy, Yvelines, 1986-; *interests:* family, audiovisual, media, bio-ethics; *professional career:* journalist; *publications:* Une Éthique sans citoyen; *private address:* 40 bis Ave. Foch, 78120 Rambouillet, France; *office address:* Mme. Christine Boutin, L'Assemblée Nationale, 126 rue de L'Université, 75355 Paris, France.

BOWSER, Anita Olga; American, Indiana State Representative; *born:* 18 August 1920, Canton, Ohio, USA; *parents:* Nicholas B. Albu and Karoline Albu (née Stobbe); *married:* Russell A. Bowser, 1948; *religion:* Lutheran; *education:* Kent State Univ., AB, 1945; William McKinley School of Law, LLB, 1949; Purdue Univ., MS, 1967; Notre Dame, MA, Ph.D., 1976; *party:* Democratic Party; *political career:* State Delegate, Democratic National Convention, 1956-80; Mem., Indiana House of Reps., 1980-; delegate, Democrat National Convention, 1984; Mem., Democrat National Platform Cttee; *memberships:* Business and Professional Women's Assn.; American Assn. of Univ. Women; League of Women Voters; Women's Democratic Caucus; *professional career:* professor, Political Science, Purdue Univ., 1950-; *honours and awards:* Standard Oil Award for Outstanding College Teaching, 1969; Indiana State Bar Assn. Award, 1976; Outstanding Woman, Business and Professional Women's Assn; *publications:* Delimiting Religion in the Constitution, Valparaiso Law Journal, 1977; *office* *address:* Mrs Anita Bowser, 1912 E. Coolspring, Michigan City, Indiana 46360, USA.

BOXER, Barbara; American, Member of the House of Representatives; *born:* 11 November 1940, Brooklyn, New York; *parents:* Ira D. Levy and Sophie Levy; *married:* Stewart W. boxer, 1962; *children:* Douglas, Nicole; *religion:* Jewish; *education:* Brooklyn College, BA, 1962; *party:* Democratic Party; *political career:* Mem., Board of Supervisors, Marin, California, 1976-82; Pres., 1980-81; Dir., Bay Area Quality District, 1977-82, Pres., 1979-81; Dir., Golden Gate, Highway and Transport District, 1978-82; Mem., House of Reps. for District 6, California, 1983-; Mem., Budget, Govt. Operations Cttees.; Mem., House of Reps. Select Cttee. on Children Youth and Families; Vice-Chair, Federal Govt. Service Task Force; Mem., Exec. Cttee., Congressional Caucus on Women's Issues; Mem., Democratic Leadership Task Force on Nicaragua; *memberships:* Marin County Education Corp.; Marin National Womens' Caucus; *professional career:* stock broker and economic researcher, 1962-65; journalist and Assc. editor Pac Sun Newspaper, 1972-74; *honours and awards:* Common Cause open Govt. Award, 1980; Congressional Patriot Award, Coalition to Stop Govt. Waste, 1985; Most Likeable Local Politician, Pac Sun Newspaper, 1986; *private address:* 450 Golden gate Avenue, Box 36024, San Francisco, California 94102, USA; *office address:* Mrs Barbara Boxer, 307 Cannon Bldg., Washington DC, 20515, USA.

BOZO, Naunka; Albanian, Deputy to the People's Assembly; *party:* Albanian Workers' Party (AWP); *political career:* Mem., AWP Central Cttee., 1976-; Dep., People's Assembly, Fier constituency, 1978-; First Sec., Librazhd Rreth (district) AWP Cttee., 1984-; *office address:* Ms Naunka Bozo, Kuvênd Popullore, Tirana, Albania.

BRAGA, Lúcia (Antonia Lúcia Navarro); Brazilian, Federal Deputy; *born:* 13 December 1934, Joao Pessoa, Paraíba; *parents:* Joao Navarro Filho and Maria Augusta de Toledo Navarro; *married:* Wilson Leite Braga; *children:* Marcelo, Patrícia; *education:* Faculty of Social Services, Joao Pessoa, 1955-59; AEUDF, Brazilia, law, 1969-73; *party:* Partido Democrático Trabalhista (PDT, Centre Left Party); *political career:* Federal Deputy, 1987-91 and 1991-95; *professional career:* welfare assistant; *office address:* Ms Lúcia Braga, Chamber of Deputies, Praça dos 3 Poderes, Ed. Principal, 70160 Brasilia, DF, Brazil; *phone:* (61) 225 2885.

BRAUN-MOSER, Ursula; German, Member of the European Parliament; *born:* 25 May 1937; *party:* Christlich Demokratische Union Deutschlands (CDU, Christian Democratic Union); *political career:* MEP, 1989-; *private address:* Erzweg 55, 6368 Bad Vilbel, Germany; *office address:* Ursula Braun-Moser, European Parliament, Centre Européen, Plateau de Kirchberg, BP 2929, Luxembourg; *phone:* Luxembourg 43001.

BREDA, Roberta; Italian, Deputy; *born:* 22 September 1952, Udine, Italy; *party:* Partito Socialista Italiano (PSI, Italian Socialist Party), 1970; *political career:* mem. Regional Secretariat of the Federation of Socialist Youth from 1972-73; Leader, CGIL, Udine, Health Department, 1973-77; Regional Leader, Socialist Women of Friuli-Venice Giulia, 1975-78; mem. Provincial Secretariat, Friuli, PSI, in charge of Health, Social Security and Protection of the Environment 1977-82; mem. Central Cttee. PSI, 1978; Councillor, Udine from 1980, re-elected 1985; Vice-President of USL, Udine from 1981; mem. Regional leadership PSI, Friuli-Venice Giulia; mem. Nat. Council of ANCI from 1982; Deputy, Parliament, Udine-Belluno-Gorizia-Perdenone, 1983; mem. Cttee. on Internal Affairs; re-elected Deputy, 1987; mem. Cttee. on Production, Commerce and Tourism; *professional career:* Administrator, Udine University; *office address:* Ms Roberta Breda, Camera dei Deputati, Montecitorio, 00186 Rome, Italy.

BREDIN, Frédérique; French, Minister of Youth and Sports; *born:* 2 November 1956, Paris, France; *parents:* Jean-Denis Bredin and Danièle Bredin (née Hervier); *education:* Institute of Political Studies, Paris, diploma; National School of Administration, 1978-80; *party:* Parti Socialiste (PS, Socialist Party); *political career:* Treasury Inspectorate, 1980-84; on detachment to Jack Lang, Minister of Culture, 1984-86; on detachment to the President of the Republic, 1986-88; Deputy for Seine-Maritime, 1988-; Minister of Youth and Sports; *private address:* 80 rue de Vaugirard, 75006 Paris, France; *office address:* Mme. Frédérique Bredin, Ministry of Youth and Sports, 110 rue de Grenelle, 75700 Paris, France.

BREPOELS, Frederika; Belgian, Member of the Chamber of Representatives; *born:* 7 May 1955, Mopertingen; *education:* Provincial higher institute for architecture, Hasselt, 1973-78; *party:* Volksunie (VU, People's Union); *political career:* alderman, Bilzen, 1983-; provincial councillor, Limburg, 1985-87; member of Chamber of Reps. for district of Tongeren-Maaseik, 1988-; alderman of town and country planning, the environment, housing and youth; Chamber of Reps. Cttee. on agriculture and small businesses; Chamber of Reps. Cttee. on infrastructure; Chamber of Reps. Cttee. on public health, the environment and families; Chamber of Reps. Cttee. on petitions; substitute representative, Chamber of Reps. Cttee. on social emancipation; member, Flemish council Cttee. on the environment, preservation of nature and rural planning; member, Flemish council

Cttee. on housing and urban renewal; member VU district council Tongeren-Maaseik; member VU district Cttee., Tongeren-Maaseik; member VU party council, member, VU party committee; *professional career:* self employed architect, 1978-; Regional Commission for advice on town and country planning; Provincial commission for landscape and monuments; *private address:* Kerkhoflaan 24, 3740 Bilzen (Eigenbilzen), Belgium; *office address:* Ms Frederika Brepoels, Kamer van Volksvertegenwoordigers, Palais de la Nation, Place de la Nation 2, 1000 Brussels, Belgium.

BRETHERTON, Dr. Di; Australian, Senator; *born:* 1943; *children:* Rebecca Cooney, Jason Cooney; *languages:* French, studying Vietnamese; *education:* Preshil Primary level 1; Melbourne Church of England Girls' Grammar School; Univ. of Tasmania, BA Psychology, Philosophy and Ancient Civilization, 1963; Univ. of Keele, Ph.D., research on Thesis on parental attitudes to obedience, 1969; Latrobe Univ., Dip. Ed., B.Ed., 1977; graduate Diploma in Movement and Dance, Institute of Early Childhood Development, 1982; *party:* Australian Democrats; *political career:* Mem., Peace Studies Task Force, 1985-86, helped establish Peace Education Resource Centre, Ministry of Education; toured Thailand, 1986; joined peace delegation to USSR, 1987; Mem., Victorian Inquiry into Anti-Social Toys, advising Ministry of Consumer Affairs, 1988; Senator for Melbourne Ports, 1990-; currently Spokesperson for Australian Democrats on Women's Issues; Mem., Victorian Cncl. Against Community Violence for Minister of Police; *memberships:* founding Mem., Australian Psychological Soc.; Mem., Community Psychologists' Board; Mem., Psychologists for the Prevention of War; Conflict Resolution Network; International Campaign for Disarmament; Pres., Nat. Action Against War Toys; Pres., Assn. of Women on Campus, Univ. of Melbourne; *professional career:* teacher and guidance officer, Univ. of Keele, 1964-69; research fellow, Univ. of Keele, 1966-69; professional psychologist, school counsellor, counsellor for nurses, 1970-75; lecturer, then senior lecturer, Psychology, Institute of Early Childhood Development and Melbourne College of Education (amalgamated with Univ. of Melbourne, 1989), 1975-88; former Chairperson, Psychology Dept., Institute of Early Child Development, Co-ordinator of Community Education; currently Senior Lecturer, Institute of Education, Univ. of Melbourne; spokesperson for various organisations; *publications:* author/co-author of 32 books, including most recent publications: Peace Education in your school, Melbourne, Peace Education Resource Centre, Ministry of Education, 1986; Changes in the USSR and their Implication for Disarmament and Peace, Melbourne, Campaign for Int. Co-operation in Disarmament, 1987; Dealing with Conflict, Melbourne, 1989; Peace Studies in Australia and New Zealand, Canberra, Australian Nat. Univ., 1989; Proceedings of the Australian School Library Assn. 11th Biennial Conference, Canberra CAE, 1989; Psychological Development: Perspectives Across the Life Span, North Holland, Elsevier Science Publishers, 1989; Social Applications and Issues in Psychology, North Holland, Elsevier Science Publishers, 1989; Peace education in your school, Melbourne, Peace Education Resource Centre, Ministry of Education, 1986; *office address:* Dr. Di Bretherton, House of Representatives, Parliament House, Room M80, Canberra ACT, 2600, Australia; *phone:* (062) 726383.

BREWER, Janice Kay; American, Arizona State Senator; *born:* 26 July 1944, Hollywood, California, USA; *married:* John L. Brewer; *religion:* Lutheran; *education:* DHL, 1970; *party:* Republican Party; *political career:* Arizona State Representative, District 19, 1983-86; Arizona State Senator, District 19, 1987-; Mem., Commerce, Labour, Insurance, Banking, Government and Appropriations Cttees.; Vice-Chair, Commerce and Labour, Aging, Rules, Health and Welfare and Environment Cttees.; Chair, Select Cttee. on Veterans Affairs; Co-Chair, Joint Legislative Cttee. to study the Homeless and Chronically Mentally Ill; Chair, Rules Cttee; *memberships:* National and Arizona Federation of Republican Women; National Conference of State Legislators; Republican Womens' Forum; Board Mem., Westside Mental Health Agency; National Order of Women Legislators; Mem., Advisory board, Phoenix General Hospital; *professional career:* Medical Asst. and Radiological Technician; Pres., Brewer Property and Investment; Exec. Dir., J.L. Brewer and Assc; *publications:* Woman of the Year, Chiropractor's Assn. of Arizona, 1982-83; Leadership Award, Cttee. American Freedom; *clubs:* PTA; *office address:* Ms Janice Brewer, 6835 West Union Hills Drive, Peoria, Arizona 85345, USA.

BREYER, Hiltrud; German, Member of the European Parliament; *born:* 22 August 1957; *party:* Grüne (Greens); *political career:* MEP, 1989-; *private address:* Ormesheimer Str 3, 6676 Mandelbachtal 5, Germany; *office address:* Ms Hiltrud Breyer, European Parliament, Centre Européen, Plateau de Kirchberg, BP 2929, Luxembourg; *phone:* Luxembourg 43001.

BRINEK, Dr. Gertrude; Austrian, Member of the Nationalrat; *born:* 4 February 1952, Hollabrun; *education:* College of Economic Women's Professions, matriculation, 1971; Federal Pedagogical Academy, Vienna; studied history of art, 1978; studied pedagogy and psychology, 1979; Institute of Educational Sciences, University of Vienna, PhD, 1987; *party:* Österreichische Volkspartei (ÖVP, Austrian People's Party); *political career:* district councillor, Vienna, Leopoldstadt, 1983-88; district Party Chairperson, ÖVP, Leopoldstadt, 1984-; Exec. Women's Chairperson, Austrian Workers' and Employees'

Federation, Vienna, 1985-; Mem. of Nationalrat, for Vienna, 1988-; *professional career:* primary school teacher, 1973-83; assistant to Institute of Educational Sciences, University of Vienna, 1983-; University assistant, 1987-; staff representative, departmental committee for compulsory school teachers, Vienna 2; *office address:* Dr. Gertrude Brinek, Nationalrat, Dr. Karl Renner Ring 3, 1017 Vienna, Austria.

BRISEPIERRE, Paulette Louise Fernande Mireille; French, Senator; *born:* 21 April 1917, Bordeaux, Gironde, France; *married:* Baron Lionel de la Fontaine; *children:* François-Xavier, Claude, Patrick, Jean-Eric, Anne, Marie-Dorée, Lionel; *education:* Lycée Molière and Victor Duruy, Paris, France; graduate, Univ. of Michigan, USA; *party:* Rassemblement pour la République (RPR, Rally for the Republic); *political career:* Mem., Superior Cncl. of French Nationals Abroad, 1968-, Vice-Pres., 1974-77; elected Senator representing French ex-patriots, 1989-; Mem., Economic and Social Cncl., 1976-78, 1980-82, 1986-88; Adviser on French External Trade, 1968-; *honours and awards:* Knight of the Legion of Honour; Officer of the order of National Merit; Knight of Agricultural Merit; *private address:* 18 rue de Bourgogne, 75007 Paris, France; *office address:* Mme. Paulette Brisepierre, Sénat, Palais du Luxembourg, 75291 Paris Cedex 06, France; *phone:* Paris 42 34 20 00; *fax:* Paris 43 29 86 47.

BROOKE OF YSTRADFELLTE, Baroness (cr. 1964, Life Peer) Barbara Brooke; British, Member of the House of Lords; *born:* 14 January 1908; *parents:* Rev. Canon A.A. Mathews; *married:* the late Rt. Hon. Henry Baron Brooke of Cumnor, CH, 1933; *children:* two s., two d; *education:* Queen Anne's School, Caversham; Glos. Training College of Domestic Science; *party:* Conservative Party; *political career:* mem., Hampstead Borough Council, 1948-65; Vice-Chmn., Conservative and Unionist Party, 1954-64; mem., N.W. Metropolitan Regional Hospital Board, 1954-66; House of Lords, 1964-; *professional career:* Chmn., Exec. Cttee., Queen's Inst. of District Nursing, 1961-71; Chmn. of Governors, Godolphin and Latymer Girls School, Hammersmith, 1961-78; mem., Management Cttee., King Edward's Hospital Fund for London, 1966-71; *honours and awards:* Hon. Fellow, Westfield College; DBE, 1960; *private address:* Romans' Halt, Mildenhall, Marlborough, Wiltshire, UK; *office address:* Baroness Brooke of Ystradfellte, House of Lords, London SW1A 0PW.

BROWES, Pauline A.; Canadian, Minister of State for the Environment; *party:* Progressive Conservative Party (PCP); *political career:* Member of the House of Commons and former Parliamentary Secretary to the Secretary of State of Canada and Minister of State for Multiculturalism and Citizenship; *office address:* Mrs Pauline Browes, House of Commons, Parliament Buildings, Wellington Street, Ottawa, Ontario K1A 0A6, Canada; *phone:* (613) 957 3744; *fax:* 952 0874.

BROWN, Leanna; American, New Jersey State Senator; *born:* 11 May 1935, Providence, Rhode Island, USA; *parents:* Harold Herbert Young and Esther Young (née Maurer); *married:* W. Stanley Brown, 1956; *children:* William, Stephen; *religion:* Protestant; *languages:* French; *education:* Smith College, BA, 1956; *party:* Republican Party; *political career:* Cllr., Chatham Borough, New Jersey, 1969-72; Mem., New Jersey State Assembly, District 26, 1980-83; New Jersey State Senator, District 26, 1984-; Mem., Revenue, Finance and Appropriations, Aging and Childrens Service State Senate Cttees.; delegate to Grand Old Party (GOP) National Conventions, 1984, 1988; *memberships:* trustee, Arts Cncl., Morris Area, 1973 and Morris Museum of Arts and Science, 1975-80 and 1982-; Mem., Board of Dirs., Chatham Trust, 1982-; New Jersey Assn. of Elected Women Officials; New Jersey Assn. of Counties; League of Women Voters; United Way of Morris County; *professional career:* Bank Dir.; host, Upbeat New Jersey; *honours and awards:* Woman of the Year, New Jersey Federation of Republican Women, 1978; Legislator of the Year, New Jersey Assn. of Counties, 1984; *office address:* Mrs Leanna Brown, 7 Dellwood Avenue, Chatham, New Jersey 07928, USA.

BROWN, Nancy Joyce; American, Kansas State Representative; *born:* 3 September 1942, Chicago, Illinois, USA; *parents:* Herman Hugo Becker and Katherine Becker (née Gralund); *married:* Myron Douglass Brown, 1968; *children:* Derek Douglass, Jason Alan; *religion:* Protestant; *education:* Barat College, Lake Forest, Illinois, BS, 1978; Univ. of Missouri, Kansas City, 1981; *party:* Republican Party; *political career:* Treasurer, Village of Riverwoods, Illinois, 1975-76, Trustee, 1976-80, Mem., Planning Commission, 1978; Kansas State Representative, 27th District, 1985-; Mem., National Hazardous Materials Transport Advisory Cttee.; Chwn., Community Development Block Grant Task Force; Mem., Kansas State Emergency Response Commission; Mem., State and Local Task Force; *memberships:* Board Mem., National Assn. of Towns and Townships, 1982-; League of Women Voters; American Society for Public Admin.; National Conference of State Legislation; Blue Valley Community Cncl; *professional career:* Consultant, TRW, Chicago, 1978-80; extension Asst., Univ. of Kansas, 1980-81; office Mgr., Gubernatorial Campaign, 1981-82; Exec. Dir., Kansas Assn. of Townships, 1983-; *honours and awards:* Outstanding Citizen Award, Village of Riverwoods, Illinois, 1980; Excellence in Education Award, Blue Valley School Ditrict, 1984; Outstanding Service Award, Kansas Assn. for the Deaf, 1988; Best Bets Environmental Award, Inst. of Public Policy; *clubs:* History Society of Blue Valley; *office address:* Mrs Nancy Brown, 15429 Overbrook Lane, Stanley, Kansas 66224, USA.

BRSOZOWSKA, Anna; Polish, Member of the Sejm; *office address:* Ms Anna Brsozowska, Sejm PRI, ul. Wiejska 4/6/8, 00-489 Warsaw, Poland; *phone:* (22) 28 70 01; 28 40 31.

BRUNDTLAND, Gro Harlem; Norwegian, Prime Minister; *born:* 20 April 1939, Oslo, Norway; *parents:* Dr. Gudmund Harlem; *married:* Arne Olav Brundtland; *children:* four; *education:* Oslo Univ., Degree in Medicine, 1963; Harvard Univ., Masters Degree in Public Health, 1965; *party:* Norwegian Labour Party; *political career:* Minister of the Environment, 1974-79; Prime Minister, Feb.-Oct. 1981, May 1986-Oct. 1989 and Nov. 1990-; led UN Commission on the Environment and Development, 1983-87-; Mem., Storting, 1977-; Mem., Standing Cttee. on Finance, Foreign Affairs and Constitutional Affairs; Chwn., Standing Cttee. on Foreign and Constitutional Affairs, 1980-81, 1981-86 and 1989-90; Parliamentary Leader of the Labour Party, 1981-86 and 1989; Dep. Leader of the Norwegian Labour Party, 1975, Leader, since 1981; Vice-Pres., Socialist International; *interests:* equal rights for women, the Environment; *professional career:* Medical Officer, Norwegian Directorate of Health, 1966-68; Asst. Senior Medical Officer, Oslo Board of Health, 1969-74; *honours and awards:* Third World Prize, 1988; Indira Gandhi Prize for Peace, Disarmament and Development, 1988; *publications:* numerous articles on political, environmental and development issues; *office address:* Ms Gro Harlem Brundtland, Office of the Prime Minister, Akersgaten 42, P.O. Box 8001 Dep, 0030 Oslo 1, Norway; *phone:* (02) 34 90 90; *fax:* 349500.

BRUNN, Anke; German, Member of the Bundesrat; *born:* 19 September 1942, Behlendorf Kreis Lauenburg; *children:* one; *education:* Univs. Hamburg, Paris and Cologne, Economic and Social Science, Economics, 1966; *party:* Sozialdemokratische Partei Deutschlands (SPD, Social Democratic Party of Germany), 1967; *political career:* mem. of Landtag North Rhine-Westphalia, 1970-81 and since 1985; Senator for Family, Youth and Sport, Berlin, 1981; Minister of Science and Research, North Rhine-Westphalia since 1985; mem. of Bundesrat; *professional career:* economist; research asst., Computer Centre, Univ. Cologne; *office address:* Frau Anke Brunn, Bundesrat, 5300 Bonn 1, West Germany.

BUCHAN, Jane O'Neil; British, Member of the European Parliament; *parents:* Joseph Kent and Christina Kent; *married:* Norman Findlay Buchan, 1945; *children:* one s; *education:* secondary school; commercial college; *party:* Labour Party; *political career:* MEP for Glasgow, 1979-; Regional Councillor, Strathclyde Regional Council, 1974-; *professional career:* housewife; occasional scriptwriting; journalism; chairman, Scottish Gas Consumers' Council; *recreations:* books, music, theatre, television; *private address:* 72 Peel Street, Glasgow G11 5LR, Scotland, UK; *office address:* Ms Jane Buchan, European Parliament, Centre Européen, Plateau de Kirchberg, BP 2929, Luxembourg.

BUDAK, Mary Kay; American, Indiana State Representative; *born:* Philadelphia, Pennsylvania, USA; *parents:* Francis McMahon; *married:* Michael S. Budak Jr., 1953; *children:* Kathy, Michael S. III, Patricia A; *religion:* Roman Catholic; *education:* Temple Univ., 1950-51; Purdue Univ., North Central Campus, 1968-80; *party:* Republican Party; *political career:* Sec. to Campaign Co-ordinator, Michigan City Mayor Campaign, Indiana, 1966-79; City Cncl. candidate, Michigan City, 1979; Indiana State Rep., District 9, 1980-; Mem., Ways and Means and Budget Cttee.; ranking majority Mem., Judiciary Cttee.; ranking Republican mem., Family and Children Cttee.; Mem., Human Affairs, Interstate Co-operatives, Roads and Transport Cttees.; Indiana house Rep; *memberships:* Miss Indiana Scholar Pagaent; League of Women Voters; Business and Professional Women's Club; VFW Auxillary; *professional career:* owner/Mgr., Budak Memorials Inc., 1960-81; Exec., Michiana Sheltered Workshop, 1981-86; *honours and awards:* Outstanding Woman in Politics, 1982; Outstanding Legislator for Fraternal Order of Police, 1983; *clubs:* LaPorte Republican Women's Club; LaPorte County Grange; LaPorte Homemakers Extension Club; *office address:* Mrs Mary Budak, 5051 Pawnee Trail, La Porte, Indiana 46350-8262, USA.

BUGGE FOUGNER, Else; Norwegian, former Minister for Justice and Police; *born:* 9 November 1944, Moss; *children:* three; *education:* law degree, 1971; *party:* Hoyre (Conservative Party); *political career:* active in local politics in Bærum, outside Oslo; former mem., and Chwn., Permanent Commission on Criminal Law; Chmn., Conservative Party health policy Cttee., 1985-87; mem., Conservative Party programme cttee., 1989-93; Minister for Justice and Police, Nov. 1989-Oct. 1990; *professional career:* fifth woman in Norway to become Supreme Court Advocate, 1975; partner in law firm, Hjort, Eriksrud & Co., 1977-; mem. boards for: National Hospital; Small Business Fund; Statoil (State owned oil corp.); Bergen Bank; permanent defence Counsel, Oslo City Court, until Nov. 1989; *office address:* Ms Else Bugge Fougner, Ministry of Justice, Akersgt. 42, POB 8005 Dep., 0030 Oslo 1, Norway.

BÜHRER, Esther; Swiss, Member of the Nationalrat; *born:* 30 March 1926, Schaffhausen, Switzerland; *children:* two; *education:* teacher training studies, Schaffhausen, Switzerland, Bogotà, Colombia; *party:* Sozialdemokratische Partei der Schweiz (SDP, Social Democratic Party of Switzerland); *political career:*

Mayoress of Schaffhausen, Bibern and Hofen; Mem. of the Schaffhausen Great Cncl., 1973-, Pres., 1978; Mem. of the Ständerat for Schaffhausen, 1979-; *professional career:* housewife; *office address:* Frau Esther Bührer, Ständerat/Conseil d'Etat, Secretariat-General, Parlamentsgebäude, 3003 Berne, Switzerland; *phone:* Berne 619711.

BUKATA, Aniela; Polish, Member of the Sejm; *office address:* Ms Aniela Bukata, Sejm PRI, ul. Wiejska 4/6/8, 00-489 Warsaw, Poland; *phone:* (22) 28 70 01; 28 40 31.

BUKEWAKA, Anna Teresa; Polish, Member of the Sejm; *office address:* Ms Anna Teresa Bukewaka, Sejm PRI, ul. Wiejska 4/6/8, 00-489 Warsaw, Poland; *phone:* (22) 28 70 01; 28 40 31.

BUKY, Dorottya; Hungarian, Member of the Országgyűlés; *party:* Alliance of Free Democrats (SZDSZ); *office address:* Ms Dorottya Búky, Országgyűlés, Kossuth L. tér 1-3, Budapest V, Hungary; *phone:* 22 5058; 22 5059.

BULMAHN, Edelgard; German, Member of the Bundestag; *born:* 4 March 1951, Minden/Westfalen; *education:* Petershagen secondary school, Abitur (advanced matriculation examination), 1972; University of Hannover, political science, English studies; first state examination, 1978; second state examination, 1980; long periods abroad in Israel and the United Kingdom; *party:* Sozialdemokratische Partei Deutschlands (SPD, Social Democratic Party of Germany), 1969; *political career:* various activities, Working Group of the Young Socialist (Jung-Sozialisten), 1969-72; member of district council, Hannover-Linden, 1981-86; dep. chmn., inquiry commission Technikfolgen-Abschätzung und-Bewertung (Assessment of the Effects of Technology); mem. of Bundestag city of Hannover II, 1987; *professional career:* retd. secondary school teacher (civil servant); teacher, Luther School, Hannover; member of Gewerkschaft Erziehung und Wissenschaft (GEW, Trade Union for Education and Science); member of Arbeiterwohlfahrt (AWO, Labour Welfare Organisation); *clubs:* Naturfreunde (Friends of Nature); Association for the Promotion of the Rambaff Theatre (Chmn.); *private address:* 3000 Hannover 91, West Germany; *office address:* Frau Edelgard Bulmahn, Bundeshaus, 5300 Bonn 1, West Germany.

BUMBOVA, Stanislava; Czechoslovakian, Member of the Narodni Rada (Czech National Council); *born:* 8 September 1948; *party:* Komunistická Strana Ceskoslovenska (KSC, Communist party of Czechoslovakia); *office address:* Ms Stanislava Bumbová, Ceská národní rada, Snemovní 4, 110 00 Praha 1, Czechoslovakia; *phone:* (02) 2105.

BUNTESKA, Vera; Yugoslavian, Member of the Central Committee of the League of Communists of Yugoslavia; *born:* 1943; *party:* League of Communists of Yugoslavia (LCY); *political career:* Mem., Central Cttee., LCY; *office address:* Ms Vera Bunteska, League of Communists of Yugoslavia, Novi Beograd, Bul. Lensina 6, Yugoslavia.

BURESOVA, Dr. Dagmar; Czechoslovakian, President of the Czech National Council; *born:* 19 October 1929, Prague, Czechoslovakia; *parents:* Dr. Josef Kubista and Marie Kubistová (née Köhlerová); *married:* Dr. Radim Bures, 1950; *children:* Zuzana, Lucie; *religion:* Czechoslovak Hussit Church; *languages:* Czech, German, English; *education:* Charles Univ. Faculty of Law, Prague, 1948-52; *party:* Obcanské hnutí (Civic Movement), 1990; *political career:* Minister of Justice, Czech National Govt., Dec. 1989-June 1990; Mem., Presidium, Civic Movement; Pres., Czech National Cncl., June 1990-; *memberships:* Assn. of Czech Lawyers; *publications:* articles on labour law in Bulletin Ceské Advokacie; *clubs:* Mayor of Czech Scouts; Masaryk Democratic movement; Sokol; *recreations:* reading, nature, skiing, scouting, sports; *private address:* Na Orechovce 59, Praha 6, Czechoslovakia; *office address:* Dr. Dagmar Buresová, Ceská národní rada, Snemovní 4, 110 00 Praha 1, Czechoslovakia; *phone:* (02) 2105.

BURGEON, Colette; Belgian, Member of the Chamber of Representatives; *born:* 11 February 1957, La Hestre; *parents:* Burgeon and Georgette (née Outlet); *children:* one d; *education:* District School of Haine-St-Pierre, Primary Education, Sep. 1963-Jun. 1969; Athena Provincial and Warocque joint Secondary School, Morlanwelz, School leaving certificate in humanities, Sep. 1969-Jun. 1975; Provincial Teacher Training College F. Hotyat Morlanwelz, Educational Psychology Section, qualified Primary School Teacher, Sep. 1976-Jun. 1978; *party:* Parti Socialiste (PS, Socialist Party), 1968-; *political career:* Deputy for Wallonia Region, Oct. 1985-; mem. of Nat. Exec. PS; Political Sec., Maine-Saint-Pierre Section; mem. of Exec. of Fereration for Soignies; mem. of Federal Cttee., Soignies; District Cllr., for La Louviere, Jan. 1989-; *interests:* social issues, the environment, education; *professional career:* temporary Primary School Teacher, teaching specifically moral education or working as superviser/tutor, in districts of La Louviere, Manage, Estinnes or in province of Hainaut, Sep. 1978-Oct. 1985; *clubs:* mem. of Administrative Cncl. of Federation of Socialist Mutualities of the Centre; mem. of Administrative Cncl. of Provident Socialist Women, Vice-Pres., 1989-; *private address:* Rue de la Fraternité 21, 7100 Haine-Saint-Paul, La Louvière, Belgium; *office address:* Ms Colette Burgeon, Kamer van Volksvertegenwoordigers, Palais de la Nation, Place de la Nation 2, 1008 Brussels, Belgium.

BURNHAM, Hon. Viola; Guyanan, Deputy Prime Minister and Vice President for Culture and Social Development; *party:* People's National Congress (PNC); *office address:* The Hon. Ms Viola Burnham, Office of the President, New Garden and South Streets, Georgetown, Guyana; *phone:* (02) 51330.

BURON, Martine; French, Member of the European Parliament; *born:* 12 January 1944, Neuilly-sur-Seine; *parents:* Robert Buron and Marie-Louise Buron (née Trouillard); *married:* Ahmad Adjari, 1967; *children:* Armand Martin; *languages:* English, Persian; *education:* School of Fine Art; graduate in architecture; higher diploma in English and in Oriental Languages; *party:* Parti Socialiste (PS, Socialist Party); *political career:* Member, executive of Socialist Party, 1974-87; National Sec. of the Women's Movement 1985-87; Member, European Parliament; *interests:* Women's movement; *professional career:* Town planner, Paris 1974-81; *private address:* 15 rue des Déportés-Résistants, 44110 Châteaubriant; *office address:* Mme. Martine Buron, European Parliament, Centre Européen, Plateau de Kirchberg, BP 2929, Luxembourg.

BURTON OF COVENTRY, Baroness (cr. 1962, Life Peer) Elaine Frances Burton; British, Member of the House of Lords; *born:* 2 March 1904; *parents:* the late Leslie Burton; *education:* Girls' Modern School; Training College, Leeds; *party:* fmr. Labour Party; Social Democratic Party (SDP); *political career:* Member of Parliament (Lab.) 1950-59; House of Lords, 1962-; Chmn., Domestic Coal Consumers' Cncl., 1962-65; mem. Independent Television Authority, 1964-69; mem., Sports Cncl., 1965-71; Chmn., Cncl. on Tribunals, 1967-73; SDP Spokesman on Civil Aviation and Consumer Affairs, 1983-; *professional career:* teacher, 1924-35; social worker, 1935-37; organiser, Nat. Fitness Cncl., 1937-39; Retail Trade Exec., 1940-45; Public Relations consultant, 1945-50; Dir., Consultancy Ltd., 1969-73; consultant, Courtaulds Ltd., 1960-73; Imperial Domestic Applicances Ltd., 1963-66; mem., Cncl. of Industrial Design, 1963-68; Chmn., Mail Order Publishers' Authority, 1970-84; mem., Airline User's Cttee., 1973-80, and Hon. Consultant, 1980-; Pres., Inst. of Travel Managers,

1977-86; *recreations:* politics, reading, travel, colour photography; *private address:* 47 Molyneux Street, London W1; *office address:* Baroness Burton of Coventry, House of Lords, London SW1A 0PW.

BUSH, Barbara Pierce; American, First Lady of the United States of America, 1989; *born:* 8 June 1925, Rye, New York, USA; *parents:* Marvin Pierce and Pauline Pierce (née Robinson); *married:* George Herbert Walker Bush, 1945; *public role of spouse:* President of the United States of America; *children:* four s., one d; *education:* Smith College; *party:* Republican Party; *memberships:* Board of Dirs., Reading is Fundamental, Business Cncl. for Effective Literacy; advisory Cncl., Memorial Sloane-Kettering Cancer Centre; Hon. Chwn., Advisory Cncl., Literacy Volunteers of America; Pres., Ladies of the Senate, 1981-88; *honours and awards:* numerous awards including: Outstanding Mother of the Year, 1984; Distinguished Leadership Award, United Negro College Fund, 1986; Distinguished American Woman Award, College of Mt. St. Joseph, 1987; *office address:* First Lady Mrs Barbara Bush, The White House, 1600 Pennsylvania Avenue, Washington DC 20501, USA.

BYRON, Beverly B.; American, Member of the House of Representatives; *born:* 27 July 1932, Baltimore, Maryland, USA; *parents:* Harry C. Butcher and Ruth Butcher (née Barton); *married:* the late Goodloe E. Byron (Decd. 1978); re-married B. Kiek Walsh, 1986, 1952; *children:* Goodloe E. Jr., Barton Kimball, Mary McComas; *religion:* Episcopal; *education:* Hood College, Maryland, 1963-64; *party:* Democratic Party; *political career:* Mem., House of Reps., District 6, 1979-; Mem., Armed Services Cttee.; Chwn., Disarmament and Arms Control Panel; *memberships:* Board of Asscs., Hood College; Mem., Board of Visitors, US Air Force Academy; Chwn., Maryland Physical Fitness Commission; Board of Trustees, Mt. Saint Mary's College; *honours and awards:* Hon. Degrees: LLD, Frostburg State College; LHD, Mt. Saint Mary's College; Healthy American Fitness Leader, Jaycees 1982; *private address:* 306 Grove Blvd., Freferick, Maryland 21701, USA; *office address:* Mrs Beverly Byron, 2430 Rayburn House Office Bldg., Washington DC, 20515, USA.

C

CACHEUX, Denise Jeanne Henriette; French, Deputy; *born:* 18 March 1932, Nancy, Meurthe-et-Moselle, France; *parents:* Georges Habigand and Marie-Thérèse Habigand (née Aubry); *married:* Pierre Cacheux, 1955; *children:* Pierre-Henri, Françoise, Paul; *education:* Jeanne d'Arc High School, Nancy; Rouen High School, university entrance examination; Departmental Schools of Nursing and Social Work, Rouen, state diplomas; *party:* Parti Socialiste (PS, Socialist Party); *political career:* Federal Sec. of Nord Socialist Party, 1971-81; member of management committee of Socialist Party, 1971-; Councillor for Urban Community of Lille, 1971-77; Deputy Mayor of Lille, 1977-; Regional Councillor for Pas-de-Calais, 1979-; Deputy for Nord, 16th constituency, Cambrai, replacing Jean Le Garrec on his entry to government, 1981-86; Quaestor of the National Assembly, 1985-86; Deputy for Nord, replacing Arthur Notebart, 1987-88; Deputy for Nord, elected 1988; *professional career:* social worker; *private address:* 1386 avenue de Paris, 59400 Cambrai, France; *office address:* Mme. Denise Cacheux, L'Assemblée Nationale, 126 rue de L'Université, 75355 Paris, France.

CALLARI GALLI, Matilde; Italian, Senator; *born:* 23 July 1934, Terracina, Latina, Italy; *education:* Degree in Ancient Letters (with emphasis on Archaeology); 3 terms at University of Pennsylvania, USA; Department of Anthropology, Philadelphia; Lecturing Qualification, Cultural Anthropology, 1968; *party:* Partito Democratico della Sinistra (PDS, Party of the Democratic Left); *political career:* elected Senator, Bologna II, 1987; mem. Cttee. on Public Instruction and Cultural Heritage; *professional career:* researcher for CNR, Rome; taught at University of Abruzzo, 1968-69; lecturer, Faculty of Teaching, Department of Education Science, University of Bologna, 1970; Researcher for CNR, MPI, IRPA (Regional Institute of the Psychology of Teaching of Apprenticeships) on: Quality of Life; Social Services; Women, Family, Communications/Information, Educational Models; Problems of emargination; Educational problems of developing countries; *honours and awards:* winner of a 'Bennett Fellowship' to University of Pennsylvania; *office address:* Ms Matilde Callari Galli, Senato della Repubblica, Palazzo Madama, 00100 Rome, Italy.

CALVANESE, Flora; Italian, Deputy; *born:* 16 July 1954, Sarno, Salerno, Italy; *education:* Degree in Jurisprudence; *party:* Partito Democratico della Sinistra (PDS, Party of the Democratic Left); *political career:* mem. Federal Leadership Cttee., Salerno; mem. Regional Cttee., PCI, Campania; Provincial Head, Cttee. on Women and Health; Deputy, Parliament, Benevento-Avellino -Salerno, 1983; mem. Cttee. on Constitutional Affairs; re-elected Deputy, 1987; Secretary of Cttee. on Constitutional Affairs, Presidency of the Council and Internal Affairs; *professional career:* Employee INPS; *office address:* Ms Flora Calvanese, Camera dei Deputati, Montecitorio, 00186 Rome, Italy.

CAMATA, Rita de Cassia Paste; Brazilian, Federal Deputy; *born:* 1 January 1961, Conceiçao do Castelo; *parents:* Antonio Paste and Anidis Venturim Paste; *married:* Gerson Camata; *children:* Enza Rafaela; *education:* UFES, Vitória, communications, 1981-85; *party:* Partido do Movimento Democrático Brasileira (PMDB, Party of the Brazlian Democratic Movement); *political career:* Federal Deputy for Espirito Santo, 1987-91 and 1991-95; Chwn., Sub-Cttee. for the Family and Minors, and Cttees. for Education, Culture and Sports, Science and Technology and Communications, 1987; substitute Mem., Sub-Cttee. of Rights and Individual Guarantees of the Cttee. for Sovereignty and Rights and Guarantees of Men and Women, 1987; substitute Mem., Cttees. for Science and Technology and for Information, 1989-90; Chwn., Special Cttee. for the Protection of Infants and Young People under the Children's and Adolescents' Act, 1989-90; Chwn., Cttee. for Social security and the family, 1990-91; substitute mem., Cttee. for Education, Culture and Sports, 1990-91; *professional career:* journalist; *office address:* Ms Rita Camita, Chamber of Deputies, Praça dos 3 Poderes, Ed. Principal, 70160 Brasilia, DF, Brazil; *phone:* (61) 225 2885.

CAMPBELL, Bonnie; American, Iowa Attorney-General; *born:* 9 April 1948, Norwich, New York, USA; *married:* Edward Campbell; *education:* Drake Univ., BA, 1982, JD, 1984; *party:* Democratic Party; *political career:* Chwn., Iowa State Democrat Party, 1987-; Attorney-General, Iowa; *professional career:* legal-clerk, Wimer, Hudson, Flynn and Neugent, Desmoines, Iowa, 1983-85, Assc., 1985-; *private address:* 300 Walnut

Street No. 187, Des Moines, Iowa 50309, USA; *office address:* Mrs Bonnie Campbell, 2116 Grand Avenue, Des Moines, Iowa 50312, USA.

CAMPBELL, Jane Louise; American, Ohio State Representative; *born:* 19 May 1953, Ann Arbor, Michigan, USA; *parents:* Paul Campbell and Joan Louise Campbell (née Brown); *married:* Hunter Morrison III, 1984; *education:* Univ. of Michigan, BA; Cleveland State Univ., Ohio, MS, 1980; *party:* Democratic Party; *political career:* Ohio State Rep., District 15, 1985-; Chwn., Children and Youth Cttee. and Mem., Ways and Means, Aging, Housing, Finance and Appropriations Cttees.; Pres., Women's Network and National Conference on State Legislation; *memberships:* Ohio Youth in Govt. Cttee; *office address:* Ms Jane Louise Campbell, 13815 Drexmore Road, Cleveland, Ohio 442120, USA.

CAMPBELL, Hon. Kim; Canadian, Minister of Justice and Attorney-General of Canada; *party:* Progressive Conservative Party (PCP); *office address:* The Hon. Ms Kim Campbell, Department of Justice, Justice Building, Wellington and Kent Streets, Ottawa, Ontario K1A OH8, Canada; *phone:* (613) 957 4222.

CAMPOS, Maria Aparecida; Brazilian, Federal Deputy; *born:* 4 September 1942, Sao Paulo; *parents:* Amandioda Conceiçao Barbosa Campos and Maria Tereza Barbosa Campos; *married:* Antonio Ricardo Venancio Straus; *children:* Maria Carolina, Ricardo; *party:* Partido Democrático Trabalhista (PDT, Centre Left Party); *political career:* Federal Deputy for Rio de Janeiro, 1991-95; *office address:* Ms Maria Campos, Chamber of Deputies, Praça dos 3 Poderes, Ed. Principal, 70160 Brasilia, DF, Brazil; *phone:* (61) 225 2885.

CANALES DE MENDIETA, Sonia; Honduran, Minister of Culture, Tourism and Information; *office address:* Ms Sonia Canales de Mendieta, Ministry of Culture, Information and Tourism, Costado Este del Palacio Legislativo, Tegucigalpa, Honduras; *phone:* 22 5867.

CANDIDO, Raquel; Brazilian, Federal Deputy; *born:* 17 June 1951, Guajará-Mirim, Rondonia; *parents:* Antonio Alipio e Silva and Eva Candido e Silva; *married:* Francisco Magnos Antunes Guimaraes; *children:* Evaliuce, Maria Oceano, Luciana, Walfredo Romano; *party:* Partido Democrático Trabalhista (PDT, Centre Left Party); *political career:* Town Cllr. for Porto Velho, 1983-87; Federal Deputy for Rondonia, 1987-91 and 1991-95; substitute Mem., Cttee. for Urban and Interior Development, 1989-90; Chwn., Cttee., for Mines and Energy, 1989-91; substitute Mem., Cttee. for Consumer Protection, the Environment and Minorities, 1990-91; *professional*

career: public servant and government functionary for the territory of Rondonia; *office address:* Ms Raquel Candido, Chamber of Deputies, Praça dos 3 Poderes, Ed. Principal, 70160 Brasilia, DF, Brazil; *phone:* (61) 225 2885.

CAPECCHI PALLINI, Maria Teresa; Italian, Deputy; *born:* 7 March 1948, Pistoia; *party:* Partito Democratico della Sinistra (PDS, Party of the Democratic Left); *political career:* Secretary, Region of Tuscany Cttee. of PCI; mem. Regional Leadership Cttee., PCI; Deputy, Parliament, Florence- Pistoia, 1983; mem. Cttee. on Budget; re-elected Deputy, 1987; Secretary of Cttee. on Defence; *office address:* Ms Maria Capecchi Pallini, Camera dei Deputati, Montecitorio, 00186 Rome, Italy.

CAPPIELLO, Agata Alma; Italian, Deputy; *born:* 16 January 1948, Milan, Italy; *education:* Degree in Jurisprudence; *party:* Partito Socialista Italiano (PSI, Italian Socialist Party); *political career:* Councillor, Milan; Pres. Cttee. on Civil Rights- Womens' issues; Deputy Head of PSI group, Palazzo Marino; mem. Legislative Office of the Presidency of the Council of Ministers; Nat. Co-ordinator of Equal Rights Cttee. in Presidency of the Council of Ministers; mem. Nat. Assembly PSI; Pres. of Regional Cttee. on Justice and Civil Rights, PSI; Deputy, Parliament, Milan-Pavia, 1987; mem. Cttee. on Constitutional Affairs, Presidency of the Council and Internal Affairs; mem. Cttee. for the Authorizations to Prosecute; *professional career:* Teacher of Economics and Law, Technical Institutes, Civil lawyer; *publications:* Co-authoress, Codice Donna; and Donne & diritto - due secoli di legislazione, 1796-1986, Co-director of magazine, Rivista di diritto scolastico; *office address:* Ms Agata Cappiello, Camera dei Deputati, Montecitorio, 00186 Rome, Italy.

CARDOSO de MELLO, Zelia; Brazilian, former Minister of Economics; *born:* 1954; *political career:* Minister of Economics, Mar.-May, 1991, resigned to return to teaching; *professional career:* prof., economic history; *office address:* Ms Zelia Cardoso de Mello, Chamber of Deputies, Praça dos 3 Poderes, Ed. Principal, 70160 Brasilia, DF, Brazil; *phone:* (61) 225 2885.

CARNEGY OF LOUR, Baroness (cr. 1982, Life Peer) Elizabeth Patricia Carnegy of Lour; British, Member of the House of Lords; *born:* 28 April 1925, London, UK; *parents:* Lt. Colonel Ughtred Elliott Carnegy of Lour and Violet Carnegy (née Henderson); *religion:* Scottish Episcopalian; *languages:* French; *education:* Downham School, Essex; *party:* Conservative Party, 1974; *political career:* Chmn., Further Education Cttee., Angus County Council, 1971-75; Chmn., Leisure and Recreation Cttee., Tayside Regional Council, 1974-76; Chmn.,

Working Party on Professional Training for Community Education in Scotland, 1975-77; Chmn., Education Cttee., Tayside Regional Council, 1977-81; mem., Scottish Economic Council, 1980-; Chmn., Scottish Cttee., Manpower Services Commission, 1981-83; Chmn., Scottish Council for Community Education, 1981-88; House of Lords, 1982-; mem., Select Cttee. on European Community, 1984-; mem., Council of the Open Univ., 1984-; trustee, Nat. Museums of Scotland, 1987-; *interests:* education, employment, training, local government, European Community affairs, countryside, youth work; *professional career:* farmer, Lour Farms, Angus, Scotland; *honours and awards:* Dep. Lieut., County of Angus, 1988; *clubs:* Royal Socy. of Arts (Fellow); Girl Guides Assn., Scotland (Pres.); Assn. of Cons. Peers; Scottish Peers Assn., Lansdowne Club; *private address:* Lour, Forfar, Angus, Scotland DD8 2LR, UK; *office address:* Baroness Carnegy of Lour, House of Lords, London SW1A 0PW.

CARNEY, Pat; Canadian, Senator; *born:* 26 May 1935, Shanghai, China; *children:* Patrick John Dickson, Jane Reid; *education:* Nelson High School, Nelson, BC; Univ. of British Colombia, BA Political Science and Economics, Univ. of British Colombia School of Community and Regional Planning, MA Regional Planning; *party:* Progressive Conservatives; *political career:* former Mem., Economic Cncl. of Canada; Mem. of the House of Commons for riding of Vancouver Centre, 1980; Opposition Critic for Energy, Mines and Resources, Finance and Sec. of State, 1980-84; Minister of Energy, Mines and Resources, 1984; Minister for Int. Trade, 1986-88, during which time Free Trade Agreement with US was negotiated and signed; Pres., Treasury Board, 1988; *memberships:* Assn. of Professional Economists of British Colombia; Mem., Canadian Institute of Planners; Hon. Mem., FRAIC (Fellow of the Royal Architects' Intitute of Canada); *professional career:* former economic journalist; established Gemini North Ltd., firm specializing in socio-economic impact studies in the North; *honours and awards:* Hon. LLD, Univ. of British Colombia, 1990; *publications:* foreword to Beneath the Veneer, 1988; *office address:* Ms Pat Carney, Senate, Parliament Buildings, Wellington Street, Ottawa, Ontario K1A OA4, Canada; *phone:* (613) 992 4416.

CAROLUS, Cheryl; South African, General Secretary of the Federation of South African Women; *married:* Graeme Bloch, 1989; *public role of spouse:* Lecturer, Univ. of Western Cape; former Exec. Mem., UDF Western Cape Region; *education:* Univ. of the Western Cape, BA; *party:* United Democratic Front (UDF); *political career:* active in the Black Consciousness South African Students' Organisation (SASO), detained for five months, 1976; Mem., Students' Representative Cncl., 1981; helped in formation of Western Cape region of UDF, 1983, Gen.-Sec.; UDF National

Executive, 1983-87; founder Mem., United Women's Organisation (later the United Women's Congress), Western Cape; Gen.-Sec., Federation of South African Women, (FEDSAW), Western Cape Region, UDF, 1983-; Mem., Interim Leadership Group, South African Party, 1990-; Mem., Interim Leadership Cttee., ANC, 1990-; invited as part of UDF delegation, International Centre for the Swedish Labour Movement, 1986, met official of Sweden's ruling Socialist Democratic Party, key labour figures and Ministers of Foreign Affairs and Development Aid; returned to South Africa and was detained under emergency regulations for three weeks, 1986; served with restriction order on her release; Spokesperson, Western Cape Defiance Campaign, 1989; Mem., Congress of South African Trade Unions; Mem., Nat. Education Crisis Cttee., 1989 Organisation of African Unity, Harare, this was first time South Africans from inside country had formally attended a meeting of this body, delegation supported ANC document setting out agreed preconditions for negotiations in South Africa; detained again, 1989 for two weeks; formed part of ANC team which met South African Govt. reps., Groote Schnurr, Cape Town, 1990; Mem., Interim Leadership Group, South African Communisty Party, 1990-; *professional career:* Churches Urban Planning Commission, 1982-83; *office address:* Ms Cheryl Carolus, Parliament, Cape Town, South Africa; *phone:* (012) 403-2911.

CARPENTER, Dorothy F.; American, Iowa State Representative; *born:* 13 March 1933, Ismay, Montana, USA; *parents:* Daniel A. Fulton and Mary Ann Fulton (née George); *married:* Thomas Ward Carpenter, 1955; *children:* Mary Ione, James Thonas; *religion:* Episcopal; *education:* Grinnell College, BA, 1955; *party:* Republican Party; *political career:* Iowa state Rep., District 82, Minority Floor Leader, 1982-88; Iowa House Rep; *memberships:* Iowa Women's Political Caucus; NOW; Common Cause; *office address:* Mrs Dorothy Carpenter, 1100 24th Street West, Des Moines, Iowa 50265, USA.

CASSANMAGNAGO-CERRETTI, Dott. Maria Luisa; Italian, Member of the European Parliament; *born:* 29 July 1940, Bergamo, Italy; *education:* Catholic Univ. of Milan, doctor of economics and commercial science; *party:* Democrazia Cristiana (DC, Christian Democratic Party); Group of the European People's Party, PPE; *political career:* mem. of DC Exec. for Nat. Women's Movement, 1963-; mem. of Italian Chamber of Deputies, 1972-79; MEP, 1976-; Vice Chairperson of PPE, 1980-; mem. of EC Cttees. on Political Affairs, Social Affairs, Employment Development Co-operation; mem. Institutional Cttee. and Inquiry Commission on Women's Rights; *private address:* Via Lulli 28, I-20131, Milan, Italy; *office address:* Dott. Maria Cassamagnago-Cerretti, European Parliament, Centre Européen, Plateau de Kirchberg, BP 2929, Luxembourg.

CASTELLINA, Dott. Luciana; Italian, Member of the European Parliament; *born:* 9 August 1929, Rome, Italy; *children:* two; *languages:* English, French, German; *education:* Law Degree; *party:* not affiliated since the dissolution of PCI, Feb. 1991; Partito Comunista Italiano (PCI, Italian Communist Party), 1964-69, expelled from PCI, 1969, founded the Manifesto Group, which became the PDUP (Proletarian Unity Party for Communism) and merged with PCI, 1985; Mem., EC Communist Group; *political career:* Mem., Directorate of Communist Youth; Mem., PDUP Exec.; President of Union of Democratic Women; Deputy, PCI, 1976, 1979, 1983; MEP, 1979, 1984-; Vice-Pres., International League for People's Rights; Mem., European Parl., 1979-; *interests:* international affairs, Third World, ecology; *memberships:* journalists union; *professional career:* editor, Nuova Generazione, weekly newspaper of Young Communist Federation, 1958-61; journalist; editor, Il Manifesto, daily newspaper; editor, Pace Eguerra, weekly newspaper; *publications:* Che cosa c'é in America?, 1973; Famiglia e Societa, 1974; Socialism on the Eve of Year 2000, 1988; The Future of Socialism, 1991; *office address:* Dott. Luciana Castellina, Lega dei Popli, Via Della Dogana Vecchia 5, Rome, Italy.

CATALA, Nicole; French, Deputy; *born:* 2 February 1936, Millau, Aveyron, France; *parents:* Charles Catala and Jeanne Catala (née Hugla); *children:* Marianne; *religion:* Catholic; *languages:* English; *education:* Faculties of Law and Letters, Montpelier; Faculty of Law, Paris; first degree in literature; agrégation in law (highest legal teaching qualification); *party:* Rassemblement pour la République (RPR, Rally for the Republic); *political career:* member, 1979, Chmn., 1981-84, of Work and Professional Relations Section of Economic and Social Council; Secretary of State to Minister of Education, responsible for professional training, 1986-88; Regional Councillor for Ile-de-France, 1986-; Deputy for Paris, 1988-; adjunct to the Mayor of Paris, 1989-; *interests:* the european community, juridicial questions, social questions, education, training; *memberships:* Vice-Pres., delegates of Club 89; *professional career:* senior lecturer, Faculty of Law, Dakar, Senegal, 1962-64; Professor, Faculty of Law, Dijon, 1964-69, Paris, 1969-70; Professor at Paris University of Law Economics and Social Sciences, 1970-; creator and Director of Interuniversity Centre for Personnel Training, 1971-86; *publications:* la Nature juridique du paiement, 1961; le Personnel et les intermédiaires de l'entreprise, 1971; le Travail temporaire, 1973; l'Enterprise, 1980; Droit social communautaire (with R. Bonnet), 1991; *clubs:* racing club; *recreations:* tennis, skiing, swimming; *private address:* 66 avenue de Breteuil, 75007 Paris, France; *office address:* Mme. Nicole Catala, L'Assemblée Nationale, 126 rue de L'Université, 75355 Paris, France.

CATARINO, Cecília Pita; Portuguese, Deputy; *born:* 21 April 1949, Lisbon, Portugal; *education:* Licenciate of Law; *party:* Partido Social Democrata (PSD, Social Democratic Party); *political career:* Deputy, Assembly of the Republic, 1979-; former Deputy Secretary, Assembly of the Republic; Mem., Directive Council, Portuguese Group, Interparliamentary Union; *professional career:* Senior Civil Servant, Regional Secretariat for Education and Culture, Madeira; *office address:* Ms Cecília Catarino, Assembléia da República, Palacia de S Bento, 1296 Lisboa Codex, Portugal.

CATASTA, Anna; Italian, Member of the European Parliament; *born:* 6 May 1952; *party:* Partito Democratico della Sinistra (PDS, Party of the Democratic Left); *political career:* trade unionist; MEP, 1989-; *office address:* Ms Anna Catasta, European Parliament, Centre Européen, Plateau de Kirchberg, BP 2929, Luxembourg; *phone:* Luxembourg 43001.

CATSELLI, Rina; Cypriot (Greek), Member of Parliament; *born:* 31 March 1938, Kyrenia; *parents:* Stavros and Eleni; *married:* Stelios Catsellis, 1959; *public role of spouse:* Mayor of Kyrenia, 1964-78 and Minister, 1978-85; *children:* two d; *religion:* Greek Orthodox; *languages:* Greek, English; *education:* Kyrenia Gymnasium, during which time she joined the 1955-59 National Liberation struggle, imprisoned 1958 by the British; *party:* Democratic Party; *political career:* fled to Limassol after Turkish invasion as a refugee, moved to Nicosia, 1978; Mem., Kyrenia District Cttee. of the Democratic Party, 1981; Mem. of Parliament, Democratic Party, 1981, 1985-; Dep. Chairperson, House Standing Cttee. on Education and Foreign Affairs; Mem., Standing Cttee. on Labour and Social Insurance; Mem. Cttee. on Refugees, Enslaved, Missing and Adversely Affected Persons; Mem., Cttee. on the Environment: Mem., Cttee. on Refugees, Enslaved, Missing Persons; *interests:* Cypriot problems, environment; *memberships:* writers union of Cyprus - Cyprus PEN; *professional career:* writer; *honours and awards:* State Literary Prizes for three novels; *publications:* works concerning Cypriot history, traditions and customs and suffering of Greek Cypriots displaced by Turkish invasion; *recreations:* swimming; *private address:* PO Box 5182, Nicosia, Cyprus; *office address:* Mrs Rina Catselli, House of Representatives, Nicosia, Cyprus; *phone:* Nicosia 403451.

CAVALCANTI, Sandra Martins; Brazilian, Federal Deputy; *born:* 30 August 1925, Belém; *parents:* Djalma Cavalcanti and Conceiçao Martins Cavalcanti *education:* PUC, Rio de Janeiro, law and post-grad studies in the Portuguese language, philosophy and linguistics; *party:* Partido Da Frente Liberal (PFL Liberal Alliance); *political career:* Town Cllr., Rio de Janeiro, 1954-58; State Deputy, Rio de Janeiro, 1960-62 and 1975-79; Sec. for Social Services, 1962-64; Pres.

BNH, 1964-65; Federal Deputy for Rio de Janeiro, 1987-91 and 1991-95; *professional career:* professor; *publications:* Rio - Viver ou Morrer, 1978; A Politica Nossa de Cada Dia, 1982; *office address:* Ms Sandra Cavalcanti, Chamber of Deputies, Praça dos 3 Poderes, Ed. Principal, 70160 Brasilia, DF, Brazil; *phone:* (61) 225 2885.

CAVIGLIASSO, Dott. Paola; Italian, Deputy; *born:* 2 October 1942, Murello, Cuneo, Italy; *education:* Degree in Literature; *party:* Partito della Democrazia Cristiana (DC, Christian Democrat Party); *political career:* Provincial leader, Women's Movement, Federation of Direct Cultivators, Turin for over 10 years; Councillor of the Piedmont Council for Agricultural Development; Deputy, Parliament, Turin-Novara-Vercelli, 1976; Secretary of Cttee. on Public Instruction and Fine Art; re-elected Deputy 1979; mem. Cttee. on Hygene and Public health; re-elected Deputy, 1983; Undersecretary of State for Health in 1st and 2nd Craxi government; Undersecretary of State for Cultural Heritage in 6th Fanfani government; re-elected Deputy, 1987; mem. Cttee. on Social Affairs; *professional career:* Teacher, State Technical Agricultural Institute, Turin; *office address:* Dott. Paola Cavigliasso, Camera dei Deputati, Montecitorio, 00186 Rome, Italy.

CAYZ, Barbara; Polish, Member of the Sejm; *office address:* Ms Barbara Cayz, Sejm PRI, ul. Wiejska 4/6/8, 00-489 Warsaw, Poland; *phone:* (22) 28 70 01; 28 40 31.

CECCATELLI, Anna Gabriella; Italian, Senator; *born:* 1 December 1927, Prato, Florence, Italy; *education:* Degrees in Chemistry and Political Science; *party:* Partito della Democrazia Cristiana (DC, Christian Democrat Party); *political career:* mem. Catholic Action, in both FUCI and Gioventù Studentesca (Student Youth); Delegate, Gioventù Studentesca, until 1961; Nat. Youth Delegate, DC Women's Movement; 1963-69; Nat. Vice-Delegate, Women's Movement, 1969-77; Nat. Delegate, DC Women's Movement, 1977, confirmed 1982; mem. Leadership and Nat. Council of DC; mem. Leadership, Women's Section Partito Popolare Europeo (European Popular Party), and of Unione Femminile Democratica Cristiana Europea (UEFDC, European Christian Democracy Women's Union); elected Senator, Alba-Bra-Savigliamo, 1983; mem. Cttee., Agriculture and mem. Supervisory Cttee. on Taxation; re-elected Senator, Rome VII, 1987; Under-Sec. for Environment in Goria govt; *professional career:* professional journalist; Dir., 'Donne e Società' (Women and Society magazine); *office address:* Ms Anna Ceccatelli, Senato della Repubblica, Palazzo Madama, 00100 Rome, Italy.

CECHOVA, Heda; Czechoslovakian, Member of the Narodni Rada (Czech National Council); *born:* 17 July 1928; *party:* Civic Forum; *office address:* Ms Heda Cechova, Ceská národní rada, Snemovní 4, 110 00 Praha 1, Czechoslovakia; *phone:* (02) 2105.

CECI BONIFAZI, Prof. Dott. Adriana; Italian, Member of the European Parliament; *born:* 9 December 1942, Barletta, Italy; *education:* Doctor of Medecine, specialist in Paediatrics and Haematology; *party:* Partito Democratico della Sinistra (PDS, Party of the Democratic Left); *political career:* Pres., Council on Health and Preventative Medicine, Bari; MP for Bari-Foggia, 1983, re-elected 1987; mem., Cttee. on Health; Vice-Pres. of the Cttee. on Social Affairs; MEP, 1989-; *professional career:* Doctor; University Professor; Clinical Assistant, for Paediatric onco-haemotology; *office address:* Prof. Dott. Adriana Ceci Bonifazi, Camera dei Deputati, Montecitorio, 00186 Rome, Italy.

CEDERSCHIÖLD, Charlotte (Ulla Margareta Charlotte); Swedish, Member of the Riksdag; *born:* 28 September 1944, Gävle, Sweden; *parents:* Nils Erik Axel Lundahl and Astrid Marianne Lundahl (née Lindberg); *married:* Carl Hugo Torsten Cederschiöld, 1972; *public role of spouse:* mayor of Stockholm; *children:* Anna, Sebastian; *religion:* Protestant, Church of Sweden; *languages:* English, German, French; *education:* Fil. Kand., Stockholm University, 1965-70; exams in Political Science, German Language, Economics and preparation course in Law; *party:* Moderata Samlingspartiet (Moderate Party), 1970; *political career:* Deputy member of Stockholm Admin. Province County Council, 1976-88, full mem., 1979-88, First Deputy Chairwoman, 1985-88 and mem. of Panel of lay assessors for Cultural Affairs and Cttee. of Administration, 1985-88; First Deputy member of the Civil Rights Cttee., 1988-; Third deputy member of the Labour Market Cttee., 1988-; MP, 1988-; *interests:* pensions and social security matters, family policies, tax, trade and industrial affairs, consitutional affairs; *professional career:* Secretary for Trade and Industrial Affairs, Entrepreneur's Association, 1987-; Information Manager for the Stockholm Site and Development Co., (marketing body for the City of Stockholm), 1973-87; *publications:* Family Policy, in Svenska Dagbladet, 1976, 1978, 1981, 1983; Widow's Pensions, in Svenska Dagbladet, 1983, 1988; Product Security, in SAF-Tidningen, 1989; and articles in many newspapers; *clubs:* European Union of Women, EUW; International Chwn., The Family Commission; Dep.-Chwn., The Moderate Women Assoc. in Sweden; *office address:* Ms Charlotte Cederschiöld, Riksdagen, S-100 12 Stockholm, Sweden.

CELISOVA, Dr. Kvétoslava; Czechoslovakian, Member of the Narodni Rada (Czech National Council); *born:* 11 April 1946; *education:* Paed. Dr; *party:* Komunistická Strana Ceskoslovenska (KSC, Communist party of Czechoslovakia); *office address:*

Ms Kvétoslova Celisova, Ceská národní rada, Snemovní 4, 110 00 Praha 1, Czechoslovakia; *phone:* (02) 2105.

CERNOVA, Darina; Czechoslovakian, Deputy Chairperson of the Central Committee of the Czechoslovak Union of Women; *born:* 2 July 1924, Bratislava; *education:* completed secondary school education; *political career:* dept. Head, Slovak Central Cttee., Czechoslovak Union of Youth (CSM), 1949-51; Mem., Presidium Central Cttee., CSM, 1949-54; Adviser, Commission for Heavy Industry, 1951-54; Mem., Staff Central Cttee., CP of Slovakia, 1954-60; studied Higher Party School, Institute of Social Sciences of Central Cttee. of CP CSSR, 1957-60; Sec., East Bratislava Regional Cttee., CP Slovakia, 1962-; Mem. Presidium, Slovak Cttee., Czechoslovak Union of Women (CSZ), 1963-67; *professional career:* editor, periodical Partizán (the Partisan), 1947-49; editor, newspaper, Hlas Ludu (Voice of the People), Bratislava, 1960-62; *honours and awards:* Slovak National Prize, 1949; *office address:* Ms Darina Cernová, Slovak Women's Union, Panaska 7, Prague 1, Czechoslovakia.

CHAFFIN, Charlie Cole; American, Arkansas State Senator; *born:* 13 September 1938, Little Rock, Pulaski County, Arkansas; *parents:* John W. Cole MD and Grace Francis Cole; *married:* Sam L. Chaffin, 1958; *children:* three; *religion:* Baptist; *education:* Univ., of Arkansas, BSE, MEd; *party:* Democratic Party; *political career:* Mem., Constitutional Convention, 1979-80; Arkansas State Senator, 1984-; Mem., Education, City, County and Local Affairs Cttees; *memberships:* Delta Kappa Gamma; *professional career:* eduacator; *honours and awards:* Outstanding Chemistry Teacher, Southwest Region, ACS; *clubs:* Zeta Tan Alpha; *office address:* Mrs Charlie Chaffin, 12180 I-30, Benton, Arkansas 72015, USA.

CHAKRAVARTY, Bijoya; Indian, Member of the Rajya Sabha; *born:* 7 October 1940, Baligaon, Jorhat, Assam; *parents:* Beda Kanta Thakur; *married:* Jiten Chakravarty, 1960; *children:* one d; *education:* Girl's High School, Jorhat; Banaras Hindu Univ., MA (English); *party:* Asom Gana Parishad (Assam); *political career:* involved in Students' Union activities from school days; Assistant Gen. Sec., JB College Students' Union, 1955-56; actively involved in Assam movement against foreign nationals since 1979; jailed on a number of occasions, 1980-82; externed to deep forest of Bhalukpung near Assam-Arunachal border, 1981; associated with Praja Socialist Party, 1965-77; Vice-Pres., All Assam Moina Parijat, 1969-71; Sec., District Mahila Saniti, Mangaldai, 1969-75; Pres., District Moina Parijat, Mangaldai, 1970-73; District Pres., Mangaldai, Harijan Santha, 1975-85; District Sec., Janata Party, Mangaldai Branch, 1977-78; Adviser, All Assam Mahila Parishad, 1985-86; Mem., Rajya Sabha,

1986-; Mem., Cttee. on Rules, Rajya Sabha, 1988-; *interests:* improvement in conditions of women, children and Harijans; *professional career:* lecturer in English, Mangaldai College, Assam; Joint Sec., All Assam Woman Writer's Assn., 1976-81; *publications:* poems, short stories, novels, features, write-ups and Light Essays; contributed work to Assam Tribune, 1964-68; three novels in Assanese entitled 'Nazal Phiringathi', 'Abhijan' and 'Karagar'; *recreations:* sports, social work, writing; *private address:* Santipur, Ward No. 3, P.O. Mangaldai Darrang, Assam - 784125, India; *office address:* Shrimati Bijoya Chakravarty, Rajya Sabha, Parliament House, New Dehli 110 011, India; *phone:* (11) 389977; 389997.

CHALKER, Rt. Hon. Lynda; British, Minister for Overseas Development at the Foreign and Commonwealth Office; *born:* 29 April 1942, Hitchin, UK; *parents:* Sidney Henry James Bates and Marjorie Kathleen Bates (née Randell); *married:* Clive Hugh Alexander Landa, 1981; *religion:* Church of England; *languages:* French, German; *education:* Roedean School; Heidelberg Univ., German for Science, 1961; London Univ., mathematics; Central London Polytechnic, statistics; *party:* Conservative Party, 1957; *political career:* mem., Cons. National Exec. Cttee., 1968-74; vice-Chmn., National Young Conservatives, 1970-71; Member of Parliament, 1974-; Opposition Spokesman on Social Services, 1976-79; Parly. Under-Sec. of State for Social Security, 1979-82; Parly. Under-Sec. of State for Transport, 1982-83; Minister of State for Transport, 1983-86; Minister of State for Foreign and Commonwealth Affairs, 1986-; PC and Dep. to Foreign and Commonwealth Sec., 1987-; Minister for Overseas Development, Office of Foreign and Commonwealth Affairs, 1989-; *interests:* European and African affairs, international exchange of information; *professional career:* statistical asst., Kodak Ltd., 1962-63; asst. statistician, Unilever, 1963-69; Dep. market research mgr., Shell Mex and BP, 1969-72; Chief Exec., Louis Haris Int. Inc., 1972-74; special adviser, Barclays Bank International plc, 1976-79; *publications:* Police in Retreat, 1969; Unhappy Families, 1976; We're Richer Than We Think, 1979; Africa Turning The Tide, 1989; *clubs:* Royal Statistical Socy. (Fellow); Market Research Socy. (Fellow); Royal Inst. for Int. Affairs; Tory Reform Group (patron); Bow Group; *office address:* The Rt. Hon. Ms Lynda Chalker, Foreign and Commonwealth Office, Downing Street, London SW1A 2AL.

CHAMORRO, H.E. Violeta Barrios de; Nicaraguan, President of Nicaragua and Minister of Defence; *born:* 18 October 1929, Rivas, Nicaragua; *married:* Pedro Joaquín Chamorro Cardenal (assassinated 1978), 1950; *public role of spouse:* Publisher of newspaper, La Prensa, which criticised the government of General Somoza; Pedro Chamorro was banished in 1957 for several years and assassinated on 10 Jan. 1978; *children:* Pedro, Claudia, Christiana, Carlos; *religion:* Roman Catholic;

education: Roman Catholic High School for Girls, San Antonio, Texas, USA; Blackstone College, Southside, Virginia, USA; *party:* Unión Nacional Opositora (UNO, National Opposition Union); *political career:* member of civilian junta after downfall of General Somoza, July 1979; resigned in 1980 due to disillusionment with new Sandinista government; after death of husband in 1978, she became publisher of La Prensa, using it to oppose the Sandinista government; became leader of opposition party, Unión Nacional Opositora (UNO), Sep. 1989; elected President, Feb. 1990, inaugurated April 1990, also became Minister of Defence, 1990; *professional career:* Publisher, La Prensa newspaper, 1978-; *office address:* H.E. Violeta Barrios de Chamorro, Office of the President, Casa de Gobierno, Apartado No. 2398, Managua, Nicaragua.

CHAN, Hon. Anson; Hong Kong, Member of Legislative Council; *born:* 1940; *education:* Hong Kong, BA (Hons.); *political career:* Member of Legislative Council, 1990; *professional career:* Admin. Officer, 1962, 1970, 1973, 1978, 1985-86, 1988; Asst. Sec., Govt. Secretariat, 1963, 1966; Asst., Financial Sec, 1970; Principal Asst. Financial Sec., 1972; Dep. Sec. for NT, 1975; Dep. Sec. for Social Services, 1976-79; Dir. of Social Welfare, 1980, 1982-84; Sec. for Economic Services, Govt. Secretariat, 1987; Sec., Govt. Secretariat, 1988-; *office address:* The Hon. Mrs Anson Chan, The Legislative Council, Government House, Hong Kong.

CHANDRASEKHAR, Maragatham; Indian, Member of the Lok Sabha; *born:* 11 November 1917, Madras, India; *parents:* the late Vidwan Kalathur Munuswamy Pillai; *married:* R. Chandrasekhar, 1950; *children:* one s., one d; *education:* Lady Willingdon Training College, Madras; King's College, London Univ., UK; National Training College of Domestic Science, London, UK; Westminster Training College, London, UK; London School of Journalism, UK; Middlesex Hospital, London, UK; HSS London diploma in freelance journalism, domestic science, dietetics course; specialised institutional management and degree course, London, UK; *party:* Congress (I); *political career:* associated with Nat. student movement and took active part in India League, London, 1946-50; Leader, official Indian cultural delegation to USSR, Czechoslovakia and Poland, 1954; Mem., first Lok Sabha, 1952-57; Union Deputy Minister of Health, 1952-57; Convener, South Indian Women Legislative Conference, Bangalore, 1957 and Bharat Sevak Samaj, Madras state, 1957-59; Union Deputy Minister in the Ministry of Home Affairs, 1962-64; Leader, offical Indian delegation to United Nations Seminar on Human Rights in Developing Countries, Kabul, elected Vice-Chair, 1964; Leader, Indian Delegation to XIII International Conference on Social Work, Washington, USA, 1966; Leader, Indian delegation to International Women's Conference, Mongolia; Mem., third Lok Sabha, 1962-67; Union Deputy Minister in the Department of Social Welfare, 1964-67; Mem., Rajya Sabha, 1972-76; Gen.,-Sec., All India Congress Cttee., 1972, Treasurer, 1978-80; Chair, Commission for Scheduled Castes and Scheduled Tribes, 1983; Union Minister of State for social and Women's Welfare, 1984-; Mem., Lok Sabha for Tamil Nadu, Sriperumbudur, 1984-; *interests:* social welfare; *professional career:* teacher; political and social worker; Mem., Central Cttee. of State Film Awards, 1961-62; Mem., First Court, Jawaharlal Nehru Univ.; Mem., Gandhi Sadan Cttee.; Mem., Standing Cttee., India Council of Child Welfare; Mem., Governing Cncl., Indo-German Social Service Soc.; Chair, Nat. Small Industries Corporation, 1959-62; Commissioner for Linguistic Minorities of India, 1967-70; Life Mem., British Univ. Soc. of South India and Indian Council of Child Welfare, and Mem. of its Exec. Cttee.; connected with various social welfare and educational institutions; *recreations:* reading, gardening; *private address:* No. 14 Crescent Road, Shenoynagar, Madras-600030, India; *office address:* Shrimati Margatham Chandrasekhar, Lok Sabha, Parliament House, New Dehli 110 011, India; *phone:* (11) 381825; 377102.

CHANDRAWATI; Indian, Lieutenant-Governor of Pondicherry; *born:* 3 September 1928, Dalavas Village, Charki Dadri Tehsil, Bhiwani District, Jat; *parents:* Choudhary Hazari Lal; *education:* Punjab and Delhi Univ., BA LLB; *party:* Janata Dal; *political career:* Mem. PEPSU Legislative Assembly, and Parly. Sec. PEPSU Gov., 1954-57; Parly. Sec., Gov. of Punjab, 1962-63; Mem., Punjab Legislative Assembly, 1962-67; Mem., Estimates Cttee., Punjab Legislative Assembly, 1963-64; Dep. Minister, Gov. of Punjab, 1964-66; Mem., Haryana Pradesh Congress Cttee., Haryana Pradesh Congress Exec. Cttee. and Haryana Pradesh Congress Election Cttee., 1968-72; Mem., Haryana Legislative Assembly, 1968-77; Chmn., Haryana Legislative Assembly Estimates Cttee. and Library Cttee., 1972-73; Minister of State, Gov. of Haryana, 1973-74; active leader of Congress in Haryana; joined Janata Party when Congress split; then the Lok Dal under Charan Singh and finally the Janata Dal; Mem., Haryana Legislative Assembly Cttees. on Public Undertakings and on Papers Laid on the Table; *interests:* promotion of education in rural areas, particularly for girls; rural economy; *professional career:* lawyer; *recreations:* reading Hindi and English literature, horticulture, travelling; *office address:* Shrimati Chandrawati, Lt. Governor of Pondicherry, Raj Bhawan, Pondicherry, India.

CHAPUT-ROLLAND, Solange; Canadian, Senator; *born:* 14 May 1919, Montreal, Quebec, Canada; *married:* the late André Rolland; *children:* Suzanne, Claude; *education:* Couvent d'Outremont; The Sorbonne; Catholic Institute of Paris; *party:* Progressive Conservative; *political career:* elected to Quebec Nat.

Assembly, 1979-81; Senator, 1988-; Mem., Cttee. on Legal and Constitutional Affairs; *professional career:* political writer and broadcaster; *recreations:* reading, music; *office address:* Mme. Solange Chaput-Rolland, Senate, Parliament Buildings, Wellington Street, Ottawa, Ontario K1A OA4, Canada; *phone:* (613) 992 4416.

CHARBONNEAU, Rhona Mae; American, Chairwoman of the Republican State Committee; *born:* 20 February 1928, Lowell, Mass., USA; *parents:* Daniel Francis Shay and Harriette Shay (née LaSalle); *married:* Claude Maurice Charbonneau, 1950; *children:* Claudia, Rhona, Richard, Mark, Alida; *religion:* Protestant; *education:* Univ. of Lowell, 1962, 1965, 1968 and 1981; Federal Grant Seminars, 1982; *party:* Republican Party; *political career:* New Hampshire State Rep., District 21, 1982-84; Asst. Chwn., Republican State Cttee; New Hampshire State Senator, District 14, 1984-90; Chwn., Republican State Cttee; *professional career:* Pres., Car Development Corp., 1977-; Pres., Continental Crimping Inc., 1964-; *honours and awards:* Woman of the Year, YWCA, 1985; *clubs:* Hudson Lioness Club; *office address:* Mrs Rhona Mae Charbonneau, Two Old Derry Road, Hudson, New Hampshire, 03051, USA.

CHARLES, (Mary) Eugenia; Dominican, Prime Minister; *born:* 15 May 1919, Pointe Michel; *parents:* John B. Charles and Josephine Charles (née Delauney); *party:* Dominica Freedom Party; *political career:* co-founder and first leader of the Dominica Freedom Party; Mem. of Parliament, 1975-; Leader of the Opposition, 1975-79; former Minister of Tourism and Development; former Dir., Dominica Co-operative Bank; Prime Minister, Minister of Foreign Affairs, Finance and Development, 1980-; *professional career:* legal practice, Barbados, Windward and Leeward Islands; *recreations:* reading, travel; *office address:* Ms Eugenia Charles, Office of the Prime Minister, PO Box 121, Roseau, Dominica.

CHARLES, Una; Trinidad and Tobago, Senator; *political career:* Government Senator; active local politics, 1980-; *office address:* Ms Una Charles, Senate, Red House, St. Vincent Street, Port-of-Spain, Trinidad and Tobago; *phone:* (62) 32971/76.

CHATTERJEE, Prof. Asima; Indian, Member of the Rajya Sabha; *born:* 23 September 1917, Calcutta; *parents:* Dr. I.N. Mukherjee; *married:* Prof. B. Chatterjee, 1945; *children:* one d; *education:* Bethune Collegiate School; Scottish Church College; Univ. of Calcutta, D.Sc., M.Sc., PRS; *political career:* Mem., Rajya Sabha, 1982-; Mem., Cttee. on Petitions, Rajya Sabha, 1984-85; Mem., Cttee. on Rules, Rajya Sabha, 1986-87; Mem., House Cttee., Rajya Sabha, 1988-; *professional career:* teacher, distinguished in the field of Chemistry; associated with Indian Council of Medical

Research and Indian Academy of Science; Prof. and Head of Department of Chemistry, Lady Brabourne College, Calcutta, 1940-54; Honorary Lecturer, Department of Pure Chemistry, Calcutta Univ., 1944-53; Reader in Chemistry, Univ. College of Science, Calcutta Univ., 1954-61; Khaira Prof. of Chemistry, Calcutta Univ., 1962-; Dean of Faculty of Science, Calcutta Univ., 1969-77; Head of Department of Pure Chemistry, Calcutta Univ., 1969-80; Project Co-ordinator, Special Assistance Programme 'Chemistry of Natural Products', Department of Pure Chemistry, 1972-; Chmn., Board of Dirs., Calcutta Chemical Company Limited, Calcutta; Chmn., Chemical Research Cttee. of CSIR, 1973-75; Convener, Chemistry Panel, UGC, 1980-82; Principal Co-ordinator, Regional Institute (Ayurveda) West Bengal, under Union Health Ministry; Sisir Kumar Mitra Lectureship of Indian National Science Academy, New Delhi, 1984; Santanu Memorial Lectureship, 1987; Programme Co-ordinator, Centre of Advanced Studies on the Chemistry of Natural Products, Univ. of Calcutta, 1985-90; mem.; SIGMA X1, USA; Indian Chemical Society; Indian Assn. for the Cultivation of Science (and mem. of the Council); Council of Indian Science Congress Assn.; Chemical Society, London; Council, Calcutta Univ.; Indian National Science Academy; Editorial Board, Indian Journal of Chemistry; National Commission, UNESCO, 1982-; Review Cttee., Central Universities in India, 1982-83; Board of Dirs., Organon (research centre), Calcutta, 1983-; Governing Body, National Chemical Laboratories (CSIR), Pune; Central Advisery Board of Education, 1983-84; Cttee. on DSA/CAS constituted by UGC, 1985; Chemistry Panel, UGC, constituted in 1985; Board of Dirs., Infar (Organon), 1985; Executive Council, Vishwa Bharati; Executive Council, Jadavpur Univ.; Executive Council, Burdwan Univ; *honours and awards:* Sir Shanti Swarup Bhatnagar Award, 1961; PADMA BHUSHAN, 1975; Sir C.V. Ramon Award for Physical Sciences by UGC, 1982, 1985; Doctor of Science (Honoris Causa), Banaras Hindu Univ. and Burdwan Univ; *publications:* 300 research publications; *recreations:* music, cooking, painting; *private address:* 108, Manicktala Main Road, Block 1, Flat No. 3, Calcutta-54, West Bengal, India; *office address:* Prof. Asima Chatterjee, Rajya Sabha, Parliament House, New Dehli 110 011, India; *phone:* (11) 389977; 389997.

CHEJONSKA, Irena; Polish, Member of the Sejm; *office address:* Ms Irena Chejonska, Sejm PRI, ul. Wiejska 4/6/8, 00-489 Warsaw, Poland; *phone:* (22) 28 70 01; 28 40 31.

CHEN MUHUA; Chinese, Vice Chairman of the Standing Committee of the National People's Congress; *born:* 1921, Qingtian County, Zhejiang Province; *education:* Studied building construction at Shanghai Jiaotong Univ; *party:* Chinese Communist Party; *political career:* Dep. Dir., Bureau of Integrated

Industrial Equipment, General Liaison Office of Economic Relations with Foreign Countries, 1962-64; Dep. Dir., Bureau of Integrated Industrial Equipment, State Commission for Economic Relations with Foreign Countries, 1964-70; Vice Minister of Economic Relations with Foreign Countries, 1970-77, Minister, 1977-82; Vice Premier, 1978-82; Alternate Mem., Politburo, 11th, 12th Central Cttees., 1977-87; Dir., Birth Planning Leading Group under the State Council, 1978-81; Minister, Commission for Family Planning, 1981-82; Minister for Foreign Economic Relations and Trade, 1982-85; State Councillor, 1982-88; Pres., People's Bank, 1985-88; Honorary Chmn., Board of Chairmen, Bank of China, 1985-; Mem., National People's Congress: 5th, Zhejiang; 7th, Liaoning, Vice-Chmn., Standing Cttee.; Mem., 10th, 11th, 12th, 13th Central Cttees., 1973-; *memberships:* Chairperson, Women's Federation; *professional career:* survived the Cultural Revolution unharmed; *office address:* Chen Muhua, National People's Congress, Standing Committee, Great Hall of the People, Beijing, People's Republic of China; *phone:* 667380.

CHEN SUZHI; Chinese, Alternate Member of the Chinese Communist Party 13th Central Committee; *born:* 1931, Liaoning Province; *education:* Primary School; Liaoning Univ; *party:* Chinese Communist Party, 1949; *political career:* Mem., Standing Cttee., Liaoning Province CCP, 1982-; Alternate mem., Chinese CCP 12th and 13th Central Cttees., 1982-; Vice-Governor, Liaoning Province, 1982-; Mem., 10th Executive Cttee., Federation of Trade Unions, 1983-; Dir., Trade Union Council, Liaoning Province, 1986-; *office address:* Chen Suzhi, The Communist Party of China, Beijing, The People's Republic of China.

CHEN YUJIE; Chinese, Alternate Member of the Chinese Communist Party 13th Central Committee; *born:* 1942; *party:* Chinese Communist Party; *political career:* mem., Standing Cttee., Hebei Province CCP, 1985-; Alternate mem., Chinese CCP 13th Central Ctte., 1987-; *office address:* Chen Yujie, The Communist Party of China, Beijing, The People's Republic of China.

CHEN YUYING; Chinese, Member of the Chinese Communist Party 13th Central Committee; *party:* Chinese Communist Party; *political career:* Sec., Changzhou City CCP, 1986-; Mem., CCP 13th Central Cttee., 1987-; *office address:* Chen Yuying, The Communist Party of China, Beijing, The People's Republic of China.

CHEN ZHILI; Chinese, Alternate Member of the Chinese Communist Party 13th Central Committee; *born:* 1943; *education:* Fudan Univ., 1964; *party:* Chinese Communist Party; *political career:* Alternate mem., Chinese CCP 13th Central Cttee., 1987-; Dir.,

Propaganda Dept., Shanghai CCP, 1988-; *interests:* Associate research fellow, Shanghai Scientific and Technological Commission, 1987-; *office address:* Chen Zhili, The Communist Party of China, Beijing, The People's Republic of China.

CHEUNG MAN-YEE; Hong Kong, Director of Broadcasting; *born:* 25 December 1946, Hong Kong; *parents:* Cheung Sin-Wong and Mo Ying-yin; *education:* Chung Chi College, Chinese Univ. of HK, 1964-68; BBC Training Course, UK, 1972; Administrative Staff College, UK, 1980; *political career:* Programme Officer to Controller, Radio Television HK (RTHK), 1972-83; Information Services Department, 1983 (Assistant Director, Public Relations, 1984 Deputy Director); RTHK, Director of Broadcasting, 1986-; *memberships:* Mem., HK Red Cross Advisory Council, 1984; Chairman, Henley Assn.; Council Mem., Family Planning Assn. of HK, 1985; Mem., Television Advisory Board, 1986; Executive Cttee. Mem., Society for the Relief of Disabled Children, 1986-; *professional career:* part-time script writer, Rediffusion (HK) Ltd., 1965; Assistant TV Producer and Part-time Compere, 1968-70; TV Producer, 1970-71; Account Executive, Young Nichol and Co. Ltd., 1971-72; *honours and awards:* 1980 Ten Outstanding Young Persons Award; *office address:* Ms Cheung Man-yee, RTHK, Broadcast Drive, Kowloon, Hong Kong.

CHIBA, Keiko; Japanese, Member of the House of Councillors; *born:* 11 May 1948; *education:* Chuo Univ; *party:* Japan Socialist Party (JSP); *political career:* former Vice Chairperson, JSP Kanagawa Prefectural HQ; elected for Kanagawa, 1990; Chmn., House of Cllrs. Cttee. on Audit and Dir., JSP Citizens Bureau, 1990-; *professional career:* lawyer; *office address:* Ms Keiko Chiba, House of Councillors, 1-7-1 Nagata-cho, Tokyo 100, Japan; *phone:* (03) 5813111.

CHIEPE, Hon. Dr. Gaositwe; Botswana, Minister of External Affairs; *office address:* The Hon. Dr. Gaositwe Chiepe, Ministry of External Affairs, Private Bag 001, Gaborone, Botswana; *phone:* 355 454; 355 441; 355 452; 356 065.

CHILD, Hon. Joan; Australian, Member of the House of Representatives; *born:* Melbourne, Australia; *party:* Australian Labor Party; *political career:* delegate, Labor Party State Council, Victoria, 1970-73; Sec., Heuty Federal Electorate Assembly, 1970-74; elected for Heuty, 1974-75; Pres., Heuty Federal Electorate Assembly, 1974-80; Committee Service: Mem. of the Joint Cttee. for Prices, 1974-75; Joint Chairperson for the New Parliament House, 1986-; Mem. of the House of Representatives Standing Cttee. for Library, 1986-; Chairperson for the House Cttee., 1986-; Chairperson of the Joint Statutory Cttee. for Broadcasting of Parly. Proceedings, 1986-; elected for Heuty, 1980-; delegate,

Labor Party Federal Conference, 1981; Vice-Pres., Heuty Federal Electorate Assembly, 1981-; Conferences, Delegations and Visits: Mem., Parly Delegation to Scandinavia, 1982; Mem., Parly. Delegation to the European Parliament Institutions, Strasbourg, the Hague and France, 1983; Dep. Chairperson of Cttees., 1983-84; Chairperson of Cttees. 1984-86; Dep. Speaker, 1984-86; Speaker of the House of Representatives, 1986-; *professional career:* electorate Sec.; executive officer of the Victorian State Colleges Staff Association, 1976-78; *office address:* The Hon. Ms. Joan Child, House of Representatives, Parliament House, Room M80, Canberra ACT, 2600, Australia; *phone:* (062) 726383.

CHIRIAC, Nelia; Soviet, Member of the Council of Nationalities; *born:* 1935, Moldavia, USSR; *party:* Communist Party of the Soviet Union; *political career:* Sec., Presidium, Moldavian SSR Supreme Soviet; Mem., Cncl. of Nationalities; Mem., Supreme Cttee. on Soviets of People's Deps., Development of Govt., and Self-Govt; *office address:* Ms Nelia Chiriac, Council of Nationalities, Kremlin, Moscow, USSR.

CHISHOLM-HARDWICK, Shirley; American, former Congresswoman; *born:* 30 November 1924, Brooklyn, New York, USA; *parents:* Charles St. Hill and Ruby St. Hill (née Seale); *married:* Conrad Chisholm (first, 1949); Arthur Hardwick (second), 1977; *public role of spouse:* former New York State Assemblyman; *religion:* Methodist; *languages:* English, Spanish; *education:* Brooklyn College, BA, Sociology, 1942-46; Columbia Univ., MA, childhood education,, 1947-51, Professional Diploma in Supervision and Admin. in Education, 1959-61; *party:* Democratic Party; *political career:* local district leader, Brooklyn, 1960-64; New York State Assemblywoman, Brooklyn, 1964-68; Mem., Democrat National Cttee., New York State, 1968-72; first black congresswoman, Brooklyn, 1968-82; first black woman to run for President, 1972; *memberships:* League of Women Voters; Democratic Workshop; National Assn. of College Women; Brooklyn Branch, NAACP; *professional career:* nursery school teacher, New York, 1946-52; private nursery Dir., 1952-53; Dir., Hamilton-Madison Child Care Centre; Education Consultant, 1959-64; *honours and awards:* 34 Hon. Law Degrees; Key Woman of the Year Award, 1963; Outstanding Service in Good Govt., 1965; Women of Achievement Award, 1965; Medal for Distinguished Service, Teachers College, 1969; Certificate of Merit, Penn State Univ., 1979; Louise Waterman Wise Award for Distinguished Service in the Field of Human Rights, 1969; American Women in Radio and Television Award for Contribution to Communication, 1971; Who's Who in American Women Award in the Field of Politics, 1969; Award of Honour, Brooklyn College, 1969; Award for Civic and Community Leadership, Cncl. of Churches of New York City, 1977; *publications:* Unbought and Unbossed, 1973; The Good Fight, 1973; Economic Injustice in America Today; The White Press: Racist and Sexist, 1973; A look at the Family, 1970; Children and Violence in American Society - The Societal Costs, 1980; numerous articles and speeches on education, health and welfare, women and politics; *office address:* Ms Shirley Chisholm-Hardwick, 48 Crestwood Lane, Williamsville, New York 14221, USA.

CHITEPO, Hon. Victoria; Zimbabwe, Minister of Information, Posts and Telecommunications; *office address:* The Hon. Ms Victoria Chitepo, Ministry of Information, Posts and Telecommunications, Liquenda House, 11th House, P.O. Box 8232, Causeway, Harare, Zimbabwe; *phone:* 703894/95.

CHOINACKI, Luci Teresinha; Brazilian, Federal Deputy; *born:* 17 March 1954, Descanso, Santa Catarina; *parents:* Tadeu Kosvoski and Rosa Kovaleski; *children:* Rudimar José, Tatiane Luci, Joao Paulo, Ezequiel; *party:* Partido dos Trabalhadores (PT, Independent Labour Party); *political career:* State Deputy, 1987-91; Federal Deputy for Santa Catarina, 1991-95; *honours and awards:* Best Parliamentary Performance, Journalists' Union of Santa Catarina, 1987 and the House of Journalists and Union of Radio and Television Employees of Florianópolis, 1989; *office address:* Ms Luci Choinacki, Chamber of Deputies, Praça dos 3 Poderes, Ed. Principal, 70160 Brasilia, DF, Brazil; *phone:* (61) 225 2885.

CHOWDHURY, Renuka; Indian, Member of the Rajya Sabha; *born:* 13 August 1954, Visakhapatnan, Andhra Pradesh; *parents:* Air Commodore, K.S. Rao; *married:* Sreedhar Chowdhury, 1974; *education:* Madras Univ.; Bangalore Univ.; MA (Industrial Psychology); Diploma in Marketing Management, Public Relations and Advertising; *party:* Teluga Desam (Andhra Pradesh); *political career:* Chmn., Student Federation, Andhra Pradesh; organised social welfare drives; regional organiser, Department of Women and Children's Welfare, Andhra Pradesh; District convener in Mahoob Nagar and Ranga Redaly, Andhra Pradesh; Mem., Municipal Corporation, Banjara Hills, Hyderabad; adviser to a number of private sector trade unions; Mem., Rajya Sabha, 1986; Mem., Cttee. on Privileges, Rajya Sabha, 1986-87, 1988-; *interests:* urban and slum reorganisation, women's roles and rights in society; *professional career:* social service in Tamil Nadu; directed cultural programmes; *honours and awards:* received certificate from Govt. of Tamil Nadu in recognition of service; *publications:* articles, short stories, dramas; *clubs:* Secunderabad Club; *recreations:* reading, organising, writing plays, benefit shows, painting, interior decoration, poetry; *private address:* Incon House, Univ. Past, Hyderabad - 500001, Andhra Pradesh, India; *office address:* Shrimati Renuka

Chowdhury, Rajya Sabha, Parliament House, New Dehli 110 011, India; *phone:* (11) 389977; 389997.

CHOW LIANG, Hon. Selina Shuk-Yee; Hong Kong, Member of the Legislative Council; *born:* 25 January 1945, Hong Kong; *married:* Joseph Ming-kuen Chow; *children:* two; *education:* St. Paul's Co-Educational College, Hong Kong; Univ. of Hong Kong, BA (Hons.), English; Rose Bruford College of Speech and Drama, United Kingdom, Post Graduate Diploma; LRAM, Drama, ADB; *political career:* Mem., Legislative Cncl; *honours and awards:* OBE, Justice of the Peace; *office address:* The Hon. Ms Selina Chow Liang, The Legislative Council, Government House, Hong Kong.

CHUNG, Hon. Fay; Zimbabwe, Minister of Education and Culture; *office address:* The Hon. Ms Fay Chung, Ministry of Education and Culture, Ambassador House, Union Avenue, P.O. Box 8022, Causeway, Harare, Zimbabwe; *phone:* 700791.

CIBILIS VIANA, Marcia Maria d'Avila; Brazilian, Federal Deputy; *born:* 26 August 1949, Porto Alegre; *parents:* Cibilis da Rocha Viana and Leda d'Avila Viana; *children:* Gabriela; *education:* UERJ, Rio de Janeiro, economics, 1969-73; UNB, Brasilia, MA, 1976-80; UNICAMP, Campinas, Ph.D., 1982; *party:* Partido Democrático Trabalhista (PDT, Centre Left Party); *political career:* Federal Deputy for Rio de Janeiro, 1991-95; Mem., Cttee. for Education, Culture, Sport and Tourism, 1989-91; *professional career:* Univ. prof. and economist; *office address:* Ms Marcia Cibilis Viana, Chamber of Deputies, Praça dos 3 Poderes, Ed. Principal, 70160 Brasilia, DF, Brazil; *phone:* (61) 225 2885.

CIMA, Dott Laura; Italian, Deputy; *born:* 4 August 1942, Turin, Italy; *children:* two; *education:* Turin Univ., Degree in Letters and Philosophy; *party:* Federazione Nazionale per Le Liste Verdi (Green Party); *political career:* Activist, Feminist movement and Gramsci Group, Extra-Parliamentary Left, 1970; Candidate for Democrazia Proletaria, 1976; Candidate, New United Left; Local election candidate on Green Lists, Turin 1985; mem. Provincial Leadership, School section, CGIL; mem. Regional Exec. CGIL-Professional Training; Deputy, Parliament, Turin-Novara-Vercelli, 1987; Vice-Pres. of Green group; mem. Cttee. on public and private work; *professional career:* Teacher, computing, Professional Training Centre; Mem. Documentation Centre on Women's Health, Simonetta Tosi; *office address:* Dott. Laura Cima, Camera dei Deputati, Montecitorio, 00186 Rome, Italy.

CISNEROS DE PEREZ, Dr. Imelda; Venezuelan, Minister of Development; *born:* 10 November 1946, Caracas, Venezuela; *parents:* Juan José Cisneros and Josefina Alzuru de Cisneros; *married:* Francisco Pérez Santana, 1974; *public role of spouse:* Superintendent of Strategic Planning, CORPOVEN, OIL FILIAL; *children:* Francisco, Adriana; *religion:* Catholic; *languages:* Spanish, English, French; *education:* School of Economics, Venezualan Central Univ., BA International Studies; Waterloo Univ. Ontario, Canada., MA Pol.Sc; *political career:* former Dir., Inter-American Affairs Dept., Central Office of Co-ordination and Planning of the Presidency (CORDIPLAN); Gen.-Dir., Ministry of State for Internatinal Economic Affairs; worked towards the co-ordination of industrial policies and an open economy in the Latin Amercian Continent as Gen.-Dir., Economic Affairs Cttee., Ministry of the Presidency and as Dir. of Consult and Co-ordination of the Latin American Economic System (SELA); Vice-Minister of Development, Feb. 1989, Minister, 1990; Mem. of several Presidential Commissions including Privitisation, Restructuring of State Enterprises and Social Programmes; *professional career:* former Dir., Venezuelan Investment Fund; currently, Dir., Venezuelan Central Bank and Pres., National Cncl. for Foreign Investment; *office address:* Dr. Imelda Cisneros de Perez, Ministry of Development, Edificio Sur, Piso 5, Centro Simón Bolivar, Caracas 1010, Venezuela; *phone:* (02) 562-5444; 562-0360.

CLAPP, Elinor; American, Member of the Republican National Cttee., Rhode Island; *born:* 10 September 1925; *married:* Judge Charles Clapp II; *education:* Swarthmore College, Pennsylvania, BA, 1946; *party:* Republican Party; *political career:* Delegate, Republican Nat. Convention, 1980, 1984, 1988; Pres., New England Republican Cncl., 1986-; Mem., Republican Nat. Cttee; *office address:* Ms Elinor Clapp, 162 Brown Street, Providence, Rhode Island 02906, USA.

CLARK, Rt. Hon. Helen Elizabeth; New Zealander, Member of Parliament; *born:* 26 February 1950, Hamilton, New Zealand; *education:* Epsom Girls' Grammar; Auckland Univ., MA (Hons.); *party:* Labour Party; *political career:* Mem., NZ Executive of the Labour Party, 1978-88; served on Party's Policy Council; Pres., Labour Youth Council; secretary, Labour Womens' Council, has represented Labour party at a number of international events; MP, Mt. Albert, 1981; chaired parly. Select Cttee. on Foreign Affairs and Defence; served on the Select Cttee. on Govt. Admin.; chaired the govt. caucus committee on foreign affairs and security, served on caucus committees on women, social welfare and justice; Minister of Housing and Conservation, 1987-89; Deputy Prime Minister, Minister of Health and Minister of Labour, 1989-90; *professional career:* lecturer in political studies, Auckland Univ., New Zealand, 1973-75 and 1977-81; *honours and awards:* Univ. grants Cttee., post graduate scholarship, 1976;

recreations: racquet sports, films, theatre and classical music; *office address:* The Rt. Hon. Ms. Helen Clark, Parliament House, Wellington, New Zealand.

CLARK, Nancy Randall; American, Maine State Senator; *party:* Democratic Party; *political career:* Maine State Senator, District 26; Majority Leader; Mem., Aging, Retirement and Veterans Cttees; *professional career:* business education teacher, Freeport High School, Maine; *office address:* Ms Nancy Randall Clark, R R 2 Box 37, Freeport, Maine 04032, USA.

CLARKE, Alyce Griffin; American, Mississippi State Representative; *born:* Yazoo City, Mississippi, USA; *married:* L.W. Clarke Jr; *children:* DeMarquis Johntrell; *religion:* Baptist; *education:* Alcorn State Univ., BS; Tuskegee Inst., MS; Jackson State Univ.; Mississippi College; *party:* Democratic Party; *political career:* Mississippi State Rep., District 69, 1985-; *professional career:* nutritionist; *clubs:* Jack and Jill of America; *office address:* Mrs Alyce Griffin Clarke, 1053 Arbor Vista Blvd., Jackson, Mississippi 39209, USA.

CLEMET, Kristin; Norwegian, Member of the Storting; *born:* 20 April 1957, Harstad; *education:* Norwegian School of Economics and Business Admin., graduated 1981; *party:* Hoyre (Conservative Party); *political career:* various posts, Conservative Party Youth Assn., Oslo and Hordaland County; Private Sec., Minister of Industry, 1981-83; group sec., Conservative Party parly. group, 1983-84; Information Sec., Conservative Party HQ, 1985; Private Sec./adviser, Prime Minister's Office, 1985-86; Dep. Member of Storting, 1985-89; Sec., Conservative Party programme Cttee., 1986-89; head, Oslo City Council Secretariat, 1987-88; head, Conservative Party HQ political affairs dept., 1988-89; Mem., Kleppe Cttee., to examine Norwegian monetary and credit policies, 1987-89; Chmn., Board of Conservative Party Telemarketing Ltd., 1988-; Member of Storting, 1989-; Minister of Labour and Government Administration, 1989-Nov. 1990; *professional career:* project co-ordinator, Finansbanken, 1986-87; *office address:* Ms Kristin Clemet, Storting, Karl johansg. 22, 0026 Oslo 1, Norway.

CLWYD, Ann; British, Member of Parliament; *born:* 1937; *parents:* Gwilym H. Lewis and Elizabeth Ann Lewis; *married:* Owen Roberts, 1964; *religion:* Presbyterian; *languages:* Welsh; *education:* Univ. College, Bangor; *party:* Labour Party; *political career:* Member of the European Parliament, 1979-84; mem., Labour Party National Exec., 1983-84; Member of Parliament for Cynon Valley, 1984-; Chmn., The Tribune Group, 1986-87; Shadow Minister for Education and Women's Rights, 1987-88; Shadow Secretary of State for Development and Co-operation;

professional career: journalist and broadcaster; mem., Arts Cncl., 1975-79; Vice-Chmn., Welsh Arts Cncl., 1975-79; mem., Royal Commission on the National Health Service, 1976-79; *office address:* Mrs Ann Clwyd, House of Commons, London SW1A OAA.

COCHRANE, Ethel M.; Canadian, Senator; *born:* 23 September 1937, Lourdes, Port Au Port, Newfoundland; *parents:* Edward Bungay and Mary Bungay; *married:* James Cochrane, 1956; *children:* Victoria, Rhonda, Rachelle, Denise, James Jr., Michael; *religion:* Roman Catholic; *education:* Our Lady of Lourdes High School; Prince of Wales College, St. John's, Newfoundland, BA Educ., 1974 and BA 1972; St. Francis Xavier Univ., Antigonish, NS M.Ed., 1984; *party:* Progressive Conservative; *political career:* Senator, 1986-; Mem., Internal Economy, Budgets and Admin. Cttee; *professional career:* teacher; *recreations:* skiing, reading, sewing; *office address:* Ms Ethel Cochrane, Senate, Parliament Buildings, Wellington Street, Ottawa, Ontario K1A OA4, Canada; *phone:* (613) 992 4416.

COFFIN, Violet; American, Chairwoman of the Vermont State Democratic Cttee; *born:* 2 December 1920; *married:* Edmund Coffin; *religion:* United Church of Christ; *education:* Smith College, BA; *party:* Democratic Party; *political career:* Chwn., Orange County Democratic Cttee., 1981-85; Chwn., Vermont State Democratic Cttee., 1988-; *office address:* Ms Violet Coffin, PO Box 61 Strafford Vermont 05072 USA.

COHEN, Geula; Israeli, Deputy Minister for Science and Technology and Deputy Leader of the Tehiya Party; *born:* 25 December 1927, Tel-Aviv, Israel; *parents:* Yosef Cohen and Miriam Cohen (née Levhar); *married:* Emmanuel Hanegbi, 1948; *public role of spouse:* Field Commander, Lehi; *children:* Tzachi; *religion:* Jewish; *languages:* Hebrew, Arabic, English; *education:* Hebrew Univ., philosophy and literature, MA, 1949-52; *party:* Herut, 1970-79; Tehiya-Zionist Revival Movement, 1979-; *political career:* Mem., Knesset, 1974-; Chwn., Immigration and Absorption Cttee., 1977-79; Mem., Tehiya Exec. Cncl., 1979-; Dep.-Minister for Science and Technology, 1990-; *memberships:* Chwn., Academy of National Studies; *publications:* Sipura shel Lochemet Mifgash Histeri, 1964; *office address:* Ms Geula Cohen, Ministry of Science and Technology, New Kirya, Clermont Gannot Street, Schech Jarah, Jerusalem 91180, Israel; *phone:* (02) 896518.

COHEN, Naomi Kurnitsky; American, Connecticut State Representative; *born:* 3 April 1941, Hartford, Connecticut, USA; *parents:* Hyman Kurnitsky and Sarah Kurnitsky (née Dubrow); *married:* Michael Norman Cohen; *children:* Joshua, Jonah, Matthew;

religion: Jewish; *education:* Forsyth School for Dental Hygienists, AS, 1961; *party:* Democratic Party; *political career:* Mem., Board of Education, Bloomfield, Connecticut, 1974-82; , Vice-Chair, 1975-82; Board Dir, Connecticut Board of Education Assn., Hartford, 1980-82; Mem., Task Force on Special Education, 1980-82; Connecticut State Rep., District 15, 1983-; Mem. Education Cttee., 1983; Chair, Special Education Sub-Cttee., 1983-; Mem., Human Services Cttee; *memberships:* Urban League; League of Women Voters; Board Dir., Cttee. for Developmentally Disabled, 1980-; *publications:* Co-editor, Reflections on Faith; Rabbi Philip Lozowski, 1983; *office address:* Mrs Naomi Cohen, 241 Duncaster Road, Bloomfield, Connecticut 06002, USA.

COLERIO, Maire Louise; Maltese, Secretary-General of the Malta Labour Party; *party:* Malta Labour Party (MLP); *office address:* Ms Marie Louise Colerio, Malta Labour Party, March 31st Street, Senglea, Malta; *phone:* 82 10 23; *fax:* 776804.

COLLINS, Barbara-Rose; American, Member of the House of Representatives; *born:* 13 April 1939; *children:* Cynthia Simpson, Christopher Collins, grandmother of Amber Rose, Bruce Simpson Jr. and Kwame Collins; *religion:* Shrine of the Black Madonna Church (Pan-African Orthodox Christian); *education:* Detroit public school; Wayne State Univ., Political Science and Anthropology; *party:* Democratic Party; *political career:* Mem., Michigan State House of Reps., 1975-81; Mem., Detroit City Cncl., 1982-91; sponsored and passes city ordinances on South African divesture, toxic waste, single room occupancy housing; Chairperson, Task Force on Teenage Violence and Juvenile Crime, Homelessness; Vice-Chairperson, Task Force on Litter, Clean-up Detroit; Mem., New Detroit's Minority Business Cttee.; State legislature, sponsored intiatives on sexual education and harassment, equal benefit for women's pensions, pituitary gland retrieval, food dating and Enterprise Zones; former Chairperson, House Standing Cttee., Urban Affairs; former Chairperson and founding Mem., Michigan Legislative Black Caucus; former Vice-Chairperson, Michigan Democratic Caucus; *professional career:* served on Detriot Region I Public School Board, 1971-73; *recreations:* playing the harp and piano, reading science fiction, opera, symphony music, portrait painting; *office address:* Ms Barbara-Rose Collins, Longworth House Office Building, Washington DC 20515, USA.

COLLINS, Cardiss; American, Member of the House of Representatives; *born:* 24 September 1924, St. Louis, Missouri, USA; *children:* Kevin; *religion:* Baptist; *education:* Northwest Univ., 1967; *party:* Democratic Party; *political career:* Committeewoman, Chicago 24th Ward Regular Democrat Organisation; Mem., House of Reps. for 7th District, Illinois, 1973-; Mem., Govt.

Operations, Energy and Commerce Cttees.; delegate, Democrat National Convention, 1976; Chwn., Congress Black Caucus; *memberships:* Lawndale Youth Commission; NAACP, Greater Lawndale Conservative Commission; *professional career:* stenographer, Illinois Dept. of Labour; Sec., Accountant and Revenue Auditor, Illinois Dept. of Revenue; *private address:* 1115 S. Plymouth Court, Chicago, Illinois 60605, USA; *office address:* Ms Cardiss Collins, 2264 Rayburn House Office Bldg., Washington DC, 20515, USA.

COLLINS, Martha Layne; American, Former Governor of Kentucky; *born:* 7 December 1936, Bagdad, Kentucky, USA; *parents:* Everet L. Hall and Mary Hall (née Taylor); *married:* Bill Louis Collins, 1959; *children:* Stephen Louis, Marla Ann; *religion:* Baptist; *education:* Univ. of Kentucky, BS, 1959; *party:* Democratic Party; *political career:* Sec., Kentucky State Democratic Central Cttee.; Democrat National Committeewoman, 1972-76; Mem., Democrat National Cttee., Fairness Cttee. and Vice Presidential Selection Process Commission; Lt.-Gov., Kentucky, 1979-83; Vice-Chwn., National Conference of Lt.-Govs., 1981-82, Chwn., 1982-83; Gov., Kentucky; Chwn. Democrat National Convention, San Francisco, 1984; former Chwn., Southern States Energy Board and Southern Regional Education Board; Chwn, Southern Growth Policies Board, 1986; currently Chwn., National Govs. Assn. Task Force on Drug and Substance Abuse; *memberships:* National Conference of Appellate Court Clerks; Business and Professional Women's Club; Kentucky Commission on Women; Eastern Star; Democrat Women's Club; National Governors' Assn; *professional career:* Public School Teacher 1959-63 and 1967-71; clerk, Kentucky Supreme Court; 1975-79; *office address:* Mrs Martha Collins, Box 1189 Lexington, Kentucky 40578-1890, USA.

COLLINS, Hon. Mary; Canadian, Associate Minister of National Defence and Minister responsible for the Status of Women; *party:* Progressive Conservative Party (PCP); *office address:* The Hon. Ms Mary Collins, Department of National Defence, 101 Colonel By Drive, Ottawa, Ontario K1A OK2, Canada; *phone:* (613) 992 8597.

COLOMBINI, Leda; Italian, Deputy; *born:* 10 January 1929, Fabbrico, Reggio Emilia, Italy; *party:* Partito Democratico della Sinistra (PDS, Party of the Democratic Left); *political career:* Councillor and Assessor, Regional of Lazio; mem. Leadership Cttee., PCI Lazio; mem. Federal Cttee., PCI; mem. Leadership Cttee. of the Secretariat of Rome PCI; Deputy, Parliament, Rome-Viterbo-Latina-Frosinone, 1983; mem. Cttee. on Internal Affairs; re-elected Deputy, 1987; Secretary of Cttee. on Social Affairs; mem. Election Cttee; *office address:* Ms Leda Colombini,

Camera dei Deputati, Montecitorio, 00186 Rome, Italy.

CONAWAY WILLIAMS, Ellen; American, Executive Director of the Republican Party of Kentucky; *born:* 23 November 1956, Tampa, Florida, USA; *parents:* Lt. Gen. John B. Conaway and the late Rosemary Conaway; *married:* Greg Williams, 1990; *children:* Samuel; *religion:* Methodist; *education:* Univ. of Kentucky, Lexington, USA, BA, Business Education; *party:* Republican Party; *political career:* Exec. Dir., Young Republican National Federation; Regional Field Dir., Voter Programs Division; Reagan/Bush Campaign, 1988; Regional Political Dir., Fund for America's Future; Regional Political Dir., National Republican Senate Commission; Exec. Dir., Republican Party of Kentucky; *professional career:* Dep. Campaign Manager, then Exec. Asst. for Senator Bob Kasten; *office address:* Mrs Ellen Conaway Williams, 438 Craigs Creek Road, Versailles, Kentucky 40383, USA.

CONDE, Rosa (Conde Gutiérrez del Alamo); Spanish, Government Spokesperson; *office address:* Ms Rosa Conde Gutiérrez del Alamo, Ministry-Government Spokesperson, Complejo de la Moncloa, Edificio Regionales, 28071, Madrid, Spain; *phone:* 4493528.

CONNELL, Kathleen; American, Secretary of State, Rhode Island; *born:* 24 May 1937, Newport, Rhode Island, USA; *parents:* Laurence Sullivan and Margaret Sullivan (née Byrnes); *married:* Gerald Connell, 1960; *children:* Laurence, Margaret, Kathleen; *religion:* Roman Catholic; *education:* Salve Regina College, Rhode Island, BS, 1958; Boston College, Univ. of Rhode Island and Rhode Island College, post-grad. studies; *party:* Democratic Party; *political career:* Delegate, Democratic Nat. Convention, 1984; mem., Democratic Nat. Cttee., 1985-; Mem., Women's Democratic Caucus, 1985-; Sec. of State, Rhode Island, 1987-; *professional career:* Registered Nurse, Rhode Island, 1970-86; *office address:* Ms Kathleen Connell, State House Room 217, Providence, Rhode Island 02903, USA.

CONRAD, Margit; German, Member of the Bundestag; *born:* 30 September 1952, Kusel; *education:* Abitur (advanced matriculation examination), 1972; University of the Saarland, medicine, sociology; state examination in medicine, 1981; *party:* Sozialdemokratische Partei Deutschlands (SPD, Social Democratic Party of Germany), 1978-; *political career:* Co-operation, Working Group of the Young Socialists (Jungsozialisten), 1972-; county Chmn., Jungsozialisten, for two years; member of county Exec. Cttee. of the Saar, Arbeitsgemeinschaft sozialdemokratischer Frauen (AsF, Working Group of Social Democratic Women), 1981-; dep. sub-disrict Chmn., SPD, city of Saarbrücken, 1985-; mem. of Bundestag, Saarbrücken I, 1987-; *private address:* 6600 Saarbrücken 1, West Germany; *office address:* Frau Margit Conrad, Bundeshaus, 5300 Bonn 1, West Germany.

CONTI, Laura; Italian, Deputy; *born:* 31 March 1921, Udine, Italy; *education:* Milan Univ; Degree in Medecine, 1948; *party:* Partito Democratico della Sinistra (PDS, Party of the Democratic Left); *political career:* Mem PSIUP, 1944-50; elected to leadership PSIUP, 1947; mem. Regional Cttee., PCI Lombardy, 1951; Provincial Councillor, Milan 1960-70; Regional Councillor, Lombardy, 1970-80; Deputy, Parliament, Florence-Pistoia, 1987; mem. Cttee. on Agriculture; *professional career:* Doctor, traumatologist for INAIL, then in School Medical Service of Milan Council as orthopaediatrician writer for L'Unità, Rinascità and other newspapers and magazines; *honours and awards:* Premio Pozzale (Pozzale Prize) for novel Cecelia e le Streghe, Turin; Premio Penne for Una lepre con la faccia di bambina; *publications:* Many publications, including: Assistenzae previdenza sociale, storia e problemi, Milan; La Resistenza in Italia, saggio bibliografico, Milan; Cecilia e le streghe, Turin (novel); La condizione sperimentale, Milan; Una lepre con la faccia di bambina, Rome; Several scientific works: Le frontiere della vita, Il dominio salla materia, Il corpo umano, Milan; Che cosè l'ecologia, Rome; Questo pianeta, Rome; *office address:* Ms Laura Conti, Camera dei Deputati, Montecitorio, 00186 Rome, Italy.

COOLS, Anne C.; Canadian, Senator; *born:* 1943, Barbados; *education:* Queen's College, Barbados; Thomas D'Arcy McGee High School, Montreal; McGill Univ., Montreal, degrees in Social Sciences, Sociology and Psychology major; *party:* Liberal; *political career:* Senator, 1984-; mem., Senate Cttees. on Legal and Constitutional Affairs, Nat. Finance, Official Languages Policy and Programs; *professional career:* social worker; *office address:* Ms Anne Cools, Senate, Parliament Buildings, Wellington Street, Ottawa, Ontario K1A OA4, Canada; *phone:* (613) 992 4416.

COORENS, Dr. Claudette; Belgian, Senator; *born:* 15 September 1940, Charleroi, Belgium; *education:* Free Univ., Brussels, Medicine, 1958-65; qualified in General Medicine, 1973-74; *party:* Parti Socialiste (PS, Socialist Party); *political career:* Local Cllr., Charleroi, 1971; Deputy Mayor, Charleroi, 1974; Senator, Province of Hainaut, 1981-; mem. of Senate Commissions; Vice-Pres., Intercommunal Social Work; *professional career:* doctor, 1965-; *private address:* 11, Rue Jean-Baptiste Ledoux, 6040 Jumet, Belgium; *office address:* Dr. Claudette Coorens, Senate, Palais de la Nation, Place de a Nation 1, 1000 Brussels, Belgium.

CORBISIER-HAGON, Anne-Marie; Belgian, Member of the Chamber of Representatives; *born:* 24 June 1947, Gosselies; *education:* UCL, Philosophy and Arts (Classics), until 1970; *party:* Parti Social Chrétien (PSC, Christian Social Party); *political career:* Local Cllr., Montigny-le-Tilleul, 1976-82; Temporary Deputy, 1978 and 1981; Deputy Mayor, Montigny-le-Tilleul, 1982-88; Provincial Cllr., 1985-87; Deputy, Charleroi, 1988-; mem. of Commissions, Chamber of Reps. and Cncl. of French Community; *professional career:* Teacher of Ancient Languages at Teacher Training College, Mons, 1970, Royal Secondary School, Marchienne-au-Port, 1971, Royal Secondary School, Gilly, until 1976 and Royal Secondary School, Charleroi I, until 1988; *private address:* Rue des Ronces 9, 6110 Montigny-le-Tilleul, Belgium; *office address:* Mme. Anne-Marie Corbisier-Hagon, Kamer van Volksvertegenwoordigers, Palais de la Nation, Place de la Nation 2, 1000 Brussels, Belgium.

CORDATI, Dott. Rosaia Luigia; Italian, Deputy; *born:* 15 February 1926, Barga, Lucca, Italy; *children:* two children; *education:* Degree in Mathematics and Physics; *party:* Partito Democratico della Sinistra (PDS, Party of the Democratic Left); *political career:* Councillor, La Spezia, 1965-; Assessor for Public Instruction, 1972-80; Regional Councillor, Lombardy, 1980-85; Deputy, Parliament, Genoa-Imperia-La Spezia-Savona, 1987; mem. Ctte. on Culture, Science and Teaching; *professional career:* Teacher, State Lycea; *office address:* Dott. Rosaia Cordati, Camera dei Deputati, Montecitorio, 00186 Rome, Italy.

CORNING, Joy; American, Lieutenant Governor of Iowa; *born:* 7 September 1932, Bridgewater, Iowa, USA; *parents:* Perry Sullivan and Ethel Marie Sullivan; *married:* Burton Eugene Corning, 1955; *children:* Carol, Claudia, Ann; *religion:* Christian; *education:* Univ., of North Iowa, BA, 1954; *party:* Republican Party; *political career:* Iowa State Senator, District 12, 1984-; Asst. Minority Leader; Lt.-Gov., Iowa; *memberships:* Iowa Assn. School Board; League of Women Voters; American Assn. of Univ. Women; Cedar Arts Forum; Black Hawk County Family and Childrens' Cncl.; Waterloo Community Playhouse Advisory Board; *professional career:* teacher, Greenfield Elementary School, 1951-53, Waterloo Community School, 1954-55; Mem., Iowa Housing Finance Authority, Des Moines, 1981-84; *honours and awards:* Citizen of the Year, Cedar Falls CofC, 1984; Alumni Achievement Award, Univ. of North Iowa, 1985; *office address:* Mrs Joy Corning, State Capitol, Des Moines, Iowa 50319, USA.

CORREIA, Natália de Oliveira; Portuguese, Deputy; *born:* 13 September 1923, Ponta Delgada, Azores; *party:* Partido Renovador Democrático (PRD, Democratic Renewal Party); *political career:* Deputy, Assembly of the Republic, 1987-; *professional career:* Writer; *honours and awards:* Grand Officer of the Order of St. James and the Sword; *publications:* author of numerous books of poetry, fiction, essays and plays; *office address:* Ms Natália Correia, Assembléia da República, Palacia de S Bento, 1296 Lisboa Codex, Portugal.

COSETENG, Hon. Anna Dominique 'Nikki' M.L.; Filipino, Congresswoman; *born:* 18 December 1952, Manila, The Philippines; *parents:* Emerson T. Coseteng and Alicia G. Marquez-Lim; *religion:* Catholic; *languages:* Pilipino, English, Chinese, several Philippine dialects; *education:* St. Maur's Convent, England; St. Paul's College, Quezon City; Maryknoll College, Quezon City; St. Theresa's College, Baguio City; Palo Alto Senior High, California; Notre Dame College, California; Brent School, Baguio City; St. Louis Univ., Baguio City; Univ. of the Philippines, College of Arts and Sciences, Diliman, Quezon City, the Philippines; *party:* Kababaihan Para sa Inang Bayan (KAIBA, Women for the Motherland, all women political party); *political career:* formerly: Chairperson, WOMB; National Council Mem., GABRIELA; Mem., August 21 Movement; presently: Mem., Campaign for a Sovereign Philippines; Congresswoman; *interests:* human rights, students, urban poor and peasant interests and welfare; *memberships:* Amnesty International; No Nukes; World Ecologists Foundation; Advocates for the Study and Ratification of the Constitution; Hon. Chairwoman, in support of LIFE (Local Initiatives for the Environment); Mem., Sisterhood is Global Institute, International Organization; *professional career:* formerly: Special Projects Manager, Ballet Philippines; Marketing Dir., Cultural Centre of the Philippines; Curator and Proprietress, Galerie Dominique; Owner and Manager, Marlwasu basketball team; Treasurer and Vice Pres., Basketball Assn. of the Philippines; radio commentator, Radyo ng Bayan; presently: television presenter, Womanwatch; Mem., Womanhealth; Mem., Ethics Cttee., Philippine Heart Centre for Asia; Special Projects Manager, Ballet Philippines; *honours and awards:* Ten Most Outstanding Represenative for two consecutive years, 1988, 1989; Outstanding Congresswoman for 1988, 1989; Federation of Provincial Press Club of the Philippines; Pilipino Reporter Magazine, Top Ten Lawmakers and Achievers, 1988; Unified Movement of Filipino News Correspondents; Top Twenty Legislators, 1990, Lawmakers Magazine; *clubs:* First Filipino woman Rotarian, Rotary Club of Diliman, Quezon City; first woman Mem., United Nations Walkers' Club; *private address:* 65 Ifugao St., La Vista Subdivision, Quezon City, The Philippines; *office address:* The Hon. Ms Anna Coseteng, Rm. 511 House of Representatives, Diliman, Quezon City, The Philippines.

COX, Baroness (cr. 1982, Life Peer) Caroline Anne Cox; British, Member of the House of Lords; *born:* 6 July

1937; *parents:* the late Robert John McNeill Love and the late Dorothy Bonland; *married:* Dr. Murray Newall Cox, 1959; *children:* two s., one d; *education:* Channing School; London Univ. (external student); London Hospital; B.Sc.; M.Sc.; RGN; FRCN; *party:* Conservative Party; *political career:* House of Lords, 1983-; Baroness-in-Waiting, 1985; a Dep. Speaker, House of Lords, 1985-; *interests:* education, health care, nursing; *professional career:* staff nurse, Edgware General Hospital, 1960; research asst., Newcastle Univ., 1967-69; lecturer, Sociology and Social Psychology, Polytechnic of Central London, 1967-69; lecturer, senior lecturer and principal lecturer, Polytechnic of North London, 1969-74; Head of Dept. of Sociology, 1975-77; Open University tutor, 1970-78; Governor, Southlands College, Roehampton Institute of Higher Education, 1975-82; Dir., Nursing Education Research Unit, Chelsea College, Univ. of London, 1977-84; external examiner, London University External Bsc. (Sociology), 1970-73; University of Manchester, Dept. of Nursing, 1978-82; mem., Education Cttee., Royal College of Midwives, 1978-81; mem. Research Cttee., UK Council for Nursing, Midwifery and Health Visiting, 1980-82; mem. Social Policy Cttee., Church of England Board of Social Responsibility, 1980-82; Dir., Centre for Policy Studies, 1983-85; Nurse representative, Brent Health Authority, 1983-84; external examiner, Nursing, New University of Ulster, 1984-85; Chair, Parental Allaince for Choice in Education, 1985-; visiting lecturer, Nursing, University of Surrey, 1986-87; Patron, Christian Solidarity Internat, 1989-; Governor, Dorset Institute of Higher Education, 1988-; non-executive Dir., Open College, 1989-; Chmn., Academic Cncl. for Peace and Freedom; Chmn., Jagiellonian Trust; Pres., Int. Management Centre, Buckingham; mem., Cncl. of Management, St. Christopher's Hospice; patron, Medical Aid for Poland Fund; Chmn., Health Studies Board, Council for National Academic Awards; *honours and awards:* Hon. Ph.D., Polish Univ. in London, 1988; Fellow, Royal College of Nursing, 1985; *publications:* co-editor, International Journal of Nursing Studies, 1980-; various publications on Nursing, Sociology, education and peace studies, 1975-89; *clubs:* Freedom Assn. (cncl.); Parental Alliance for Choice in Education (Chmn.); Inst. for European Defence and Strategic Studies (Advisory Cncl.); Royal College of Nursing (Fellow); Royal Commonwealth Socy.; Royal Overseas League; *office address:* Baroness Cox, House of Lords, London SW1A 0PW.

CRAIK, Christine; Australian, Senator; *born:* 1962, Brisbane, Australia; *children:* four; *education:* Heidelberg High School, HSC, 1979; Philip Institute of Technology, Bundoora, BA Social Work, 1988; *party:* Australian Democrats, 1988; *political career:* Senator; Convenor, Women's Policy Group; Mem., Communications Cttee., Australian Democrats; *professional career:* Bank Officer, Westpac, 1979-82;

full time Mother at home, 1982-87; Mill Park Play Group Cttee., Stables Kindergarten Cttee., 1986-87; Family Support Co-ordinator, Bundoora Nursing Mothers Assn.; Vice-Pres., PIT Child Care Co-operative Cttee.; Mem., Kids on Campus Cttee., PIT Anti-Fees Action Group, Students' Assn. Against Rape, Bundoora Koori Support Group, 1988-; researcher, Whittlesea Community House, 1989-; *office address:* Ms Christine Craix, Senate, Parliament House, Room M13, Canberra, ACT 2600, Australia; *phone:* (062) 727111.

CRAIMON DAIBER, Birgit; German, Member of the European Parliament; *born:* 22 August 1944, Ebingen, Württemberg, Germany; *parents:* Karl Daiber and Gertrud Daiber (née Müller); *children:* Nathalie, Lotta; *languages:* German, English, French, Italian, Dutch; *education:* Univ. Frankfurt/Main, teaching diploma; *party:* Die Grünen (The Greens); *political career:* MEP; Mem., Social Affairs Cttee., European Parliament; Mem., European Parliament Mashreg delegation; *interests:* social policy, women's policy, economics; *professional career:* researcher, educational sciences, Technical Univ. of Berlin, for eight years; Project Manager, Women's Projects, Berlin, for 10 years; Chairperson, Berlin Femininist Financial Network, Goldrausch Frauennetzwerk, Berlin, for three years; *publications:* Schwesternstreit, Reinbek, 1983; Was Wollen Frauen Lernen?, Frankfurt, 1983; Licht- und Schattenseiten, Forschungspraxis Mädchenarbeit, Munich, 1987; *office address:* Ms Birgit Craimon Daiber, European Parliament, Centre Européen, Plateau de Kirchberg, BP 2929, Luxembourg; *phone:* Luxembourg 43001.

CRASWELL, Ellen; American, Washington State Senator; *born:* 25 May 1953, Seattle, Washington, USA; *married:* Dr. Bruce Craswell; *children:* Richard Bruce, James Arthur, Patricia Louise, Jill Ellen; *religion:* Baptist; *education:* Univ. of Washington; Providence Hospital Medical Technology Internship; *party:* Republican Party; *political career:* Washington State Senator, District 23; *professional career:* Dir., Seattle Hearing and Speech Clinic; Dir., Great Northwest Federal Savings and Loan; *office address:* Ms Ellen Craswell, 8066 Chico Way, NW Bremerton, Washington 98312, USA.

CRAWFORD, Mary Catherine; Australian, Member of the House of Representatives; *born:* 12 April 1947, Toowoomba, Queensland, Australia; *education:* BA; Diploma in Education, Queensland; *party:* Australian Labor Party; *political career:* elected for Forde, 1987-; Committee Service: Mem. of the Joint Select Cttee. for Video Material, 1987-; various positions at Labor Party Branch level; *office address:* Ms Mary Crawford, House of Representatives, Parliament House, Room M80, Canberra ACT, 2600, Australia; *phone:* (062) 726383.

CRAWLEY, Christine Mary; British, Member of the European Parliament; *born:* 9 January 1950; *children:* three; *education:* Notre Dame Catholic Secondary Girls' School, Plymouth; Digby Stuart Training College, Roehampton; *party:* Labour Party; *political career:* MEP for Birmingham East, 1984-; Chair of European Parliament Women's Rights Committee, 1989-91; *professional career:* teacher, drama and history; *office address:* Ms Christine Crawley, European Parliament, Centre Européen, Plateau de Kirchberg, BP 2929, Luxembourg.

CREPAZ, Irene; Austrian, Member of the Bundesrat; *born:* 17 April 1945, Zell am Ziller, Austria; *party:* Sozialistische Partei Österreichs (SPÖ, Socialist Party of Austria); *political career:* Mem. of SPÖ district Praesidium, since 1985; mem. of SPÖ Provincial Party Exec., since 1985; district Women's leader, SPÖ, municipality of Innsbruck, since 1985; sent to Bundesrat from Tirol Provincial Assembly, mem. of Bundesrat, since 1986; *professional career:* apprenticeship in wholesale trade, 1960-63; clerk; housewife, since 1987; *office address:* Frau Irene Crepaz, Bundesrat, Dr. Karl Renner Ring 3, 1017 Vienna, Austria.

CRESSON, Edith; French, Prime Minister; *born:* 27 January 1934, Boulogne-sur-Seine, Seine, France; *parents:* Gabriel Campion and Jacqueline Campion (née Vignal); *married:* Jacques Cresson, 1959; *children:* Nathalie, Alexandra; *religion:* Catholic; *languages:* English, Spanish; *education:* Hautes Etudes Commerciales (advanced business school); doctorate in demography; *party:* Parti Socialiste (PS, Socialist Party); *political career:* assistant to Bernard Lafay, founder of Republican Centre; economist in various consultancies; member of Convention of Republican Institutions, 1965; responsible for the organisation of youth and students, National Secretariat of Socialist Party, 1975; Mayor of Thuré, 1977; Member of European Parliament, 1979-81; Minister of Agriculture, 1981-83; Minister of Foreign Trade and Tourism, 1983-84; Minister of Industrial Redeployment and Foreign Trade, 1984-86; Departmental Councillor for Chatellerault-Ouest, 1982-; Mayor of Chatellerault, 1983-; Deputy for Vienne, 1986, re-elected 1988, gave up seat to Guy Monjalon; Chmn. of Democratic Association for French Residents Abroad (ADFE), 1986; member of National Secretariat of Socialist Party, 1987; Minister of European Affairs, 1988-90; Prime Minister, 1991-; *professional career:* Research assistant at the Compagnie Français des Pétroles (CFP), 1958-60; Dir. of Studies, Private Economic Research Inst.; Managing Dir., Schneider Industries International Dept., 1990-91; *publications:* Avec le soleil, 1975; *clubs:* Chwn., Democratic Assn. for French Residents Abroad, 1986; *office address:* Mme. Edith Cresson, Prime Minister's Office, 57 rue de Varenne, 75007 Paris, France.

CROES, Lisette W.; Belgian, Senator; *born:* 28 February 1939, Hasselt, Belgium; *married:* Hugo Lieten, 1962; *children:* Ingrid, Sven; *languages:* French, Flemish; *party:* Socialistische Partij (SP, Socialist Party), 1957; *political career:* provincial Cllr., 1978-85; co-opted Senator, 1985-; *professional career:* gardener, 1957-78; *office address:* Mevr. Lisette Lieten-Croes, Senaat/Sénat, Palais de la Nation, Palaca de la Nation 1, 1000 Brussels, Belgium; *phone:* Brussels 5133800.

CROWLEY, Rosemary Anne; Australian, Senator; *born:* 30 July 1938, Melbourne, Australia; *children:* three s; *education:* Melbourne Univ., Bachelor of Medicine; Bachelor of Surgery; *party:* Australian Labor Party; *political career:* Senator for South Australia, 1983-; Chairperson, Senate Select Cttee. on Health Legislation and Health Insurance; Chairperson, Senate Standing Cttee. on the Environment, Recreation and the Arts; Mem., Senate Select Cttee. on Agriculture and Veterinary Chemicals; Mem., Senate Standing Cttees. on the Scrutiny of Bills and Community Affairs; Chairperson, Senate Estimates Cttee.; Sec., Caucus Cttees. on Community Services and Welfare and the Status of Women; Mem., Caucus Cttees. on Economics and Industrial Relations and Education, Employment and Training; co-convenor Caucus Working Group on Child Care; Chairperson, Joint House Sub.-Cttee. on Occupational Health and Safety; *memberships:* Board mem. and former Vice-Chair., Australian People for Health Education and Development Abroad (APHEDA); mem., ANZSEARCH/APHA Inc.; Doctors Reform Soc.; Australian Federation of Univ. Women; South Australia Medical Women's Soc.; Medical Practitioners Against War; Amnesty International (Parly. Group); Campaign Against Racial Exploitation; Course Advisory Cttee.; Primary Health Care; Flinders Univ. of South Australia; Parks Community Centre Youth Sports Fund; Vice Patron, Service to Youth Cncl.; Patron, Contax Netball Club Inc; *professional career:* Jnr. RMO, 1962; Snr. RMO, St. Vincent's Hospital, Melbourne, 1963; Pathology Registrar, Royal Children's Hospital, Melbourne, 1964; Jnr. Clerical Asst. Paediatrics Medicine Dept., Adelaide Childrens Hospital, 1970-71; Asst., Clinical Haemotology Institute, Medical and Veterinary Science South Australia, 1972-74; founding mem., South Australia, Mental Health Review Tribunal, 1979-83; *recreations:* jogging, theatre, gardening; *office address:* Ms Rosemary Crowley, Senate, Parliament House, Room M13, Canberra, ACT 2600, Australia; *phone:* (062) 727111.

CRUAÑES MOLINA, Asunción; Spanish, Deputy; *born:* 15 January 1925, Jávea, Alicante, Spain; *party:* Partido Socialista Obrero Español (PSOE, Spanish Socialist Workers' Party); *political career:* Deputy, PSOE, Alicante, 1977-89, re-elected 1989-; mem. Social Policy and Employment Cttee; *private address:* Complejo Vistahermosa, Bloque 2, V, 2° dcha., E-03016, Alicante, Spain; *office address:* Ms Asunción

Cruañes Molina, Congreso de los Diputados, Fernán Flor 1, Madrid 14, Spain.

CSEHAK, Dr. Judit; Hungarian, Member of the Országgyülés; *party:* Hungarian Socialist Party (MSZP); *office address:* Dr. Judit Csehák, Országgyülés, Kossuth L. tér 1-3, Budapest V, Hungary; *phone:* 22 5058; 22 5059.

CUENCA I VALERO, María Eugenia; Spanish, Deputy; *born:* 1948, Zaragoza, Spain; *married:* Ramón Pla Nadal; *children:* one; *education:* Univ. of Zaragoza, law degree; *party:* Convergencia Democratica de Cataluña (CDC, Democratic Party of Catalonia) 1976; Convergencia i Unió (CiU, Convergence and Union Party); *political career:* legal adviser, Councillor of Education and Culture, Catalan autonomous government, 1978; adviser, Mixed Commission on Central Government-Autonomous Government Transferences; secretary-general, Dept. of Education, Catalan autonomous government, 1982; Deputy, CDC, Barcelona, 1986-89, re-elected Deputy, CiU, Barcelona, 1989-; mem., Education and Culture Cttee; *professional career:* professor of administrative law, Autonomous Univ. of Barcelona, 1971-82; *office address:* Ms María Cuenca i Valero, Congreso de los Diputados, Fernán Flor 1, Madrid 14, Spain.

CULIKOVA, Vera; Czechoslovakian, Member of the Narodni Rada (Czech National Council); *born:* 4 May 1951; *party:* Civic Forum; *office address:* Ms Vera Culikova, Ceská národní rada, Snemovní 4, 110 00 Praha 1, Czechoslovakia; *phone:* (02) 2105.

CUNGU, Bukurije; Albanian, Deputy to the People's Assembly; *party:* Albanian Workers' Party (AWP); *political career:* candidate Mem., AWP Central Cttee., 1981-; Deputy, People's Assembly, Shkoder constituency district, 1982-; Sec., Shkoder Rreth district AWP Cttee., 1984; *office address:* Ms Bukurije Cungu, Kuvënd Popullore, Tirana, Albania.

CURRIE, Edwina; British, Member of Parliament; *born:* 13 October 1946, Liverpool, UK; *married:* Raymond Frank Currie, 1972; *children:* Deborah, Susannah; *education:* Liverpool Inst. for Girls; St. Anne's College, Oxford, 1965-69; London School of Economics, M.Sc., economic history, 1971-72; *party:* Conservative Party; *political career:* mem., Birmingham City Council, 1975-86; Chmn., Social Services Cttee., 1979-80; Chmn., Housing Cttee., 1982-83; mem., Birmingham Area Health Authority, 1975-82; Chmn., Central Birmingham Health Authority, 1981-83; Member of Parliament, 1983-; mem., Select Cttee. on Health and Social Services, 1983-86; mem., BBC General Advisory Council, 1984-85; PPS to Sir Keith Joseph, 1985-86; Parly. Under-Sec. of State at the Dept. of Health and Social Security, 1986-88; *interests:* health, economics, housing, transport and car industry; *professional career:* economic asst., Dept. of Trade and Industry, 1970-71; Head of Business Studies, Bromsgrove School, 1978-81; *publications:* Life Lines, 1989; *office address:* Mrs Edwina Currie, House of Commons, London SW1A 0AA.

CWEJDZINSKA, Gabriela; Polish, Senator; *office address:* Ms Gabriela Cwejdzinska, Senat, ul. Ogrodowa 6, 00-896 Warsaw, Poland; *phone:* (22) 20 03 71.

CYCMANICK, Carol George; American, Vice-Chair of the Florida State Democratic Party; *born:* 30 October 1944, Poughkeepsie, New York, USA; *parents:* Peter George and Margaret George (née NeJame); *children:* Christopher, Jonathan; *religion:* Catholic; *education:* Univ. of Florida, BA, 1968; Univ. of Central Florida, MA, 1983; *party:* Democratic Party; *political career:* Precinct Committeewoman, Orange County, Florida State Democratic Exec. Cttee., 1972-; State Committeewoman, 1980-, Vice-Chair, 1985; Mem., National Credentials Cttee., Democratic National Cttee., 1980-; Vice-Chair, 5th Congresional District Democratic Party, 1980-82, 11th Congressional District Democratic Cttee., 1983-84; Mem., Democratic National Cttee., 1984-; Vice-Chair, Florida State Democratic Party, 1984-; Mem., Exec. Cttee., Assn. of State Democratic Chmn., 1986-; *memberships:* Orange County Cncl. of International Reading Assn.; Women's Political Caucus; Centre for Independent Living; International Reading Assn.; Assn. for Supervision and Curriculum Development; Pres., Central Florida Assn. of Non Public Schools, 1990-91; *professional career:* teacher, Pinellas County School Board, 1966-68 and Education Development Centre, 1970-73, Park Maitland School, 1973-81; Asst. Dir., Park Maitland School, 1981-; *clubs:* Board Mem., Foundation for Communication in the Mid-East and Tiger Bay of Central Florida; *office address:* Ms Carol Cycmanick, 3430 Golfview Blvd., Orlando, Florida 32804, USA.

CZARNIK-SOJKA, Teresa; Polish, Member of the Sejm; *office address:* Ms Teresa Czarnik-Sojka, Sejm PRI, ul. Wiejska 4/6/8, 00-489 Warsaw, Poland; *phone:* (22) 28 70 01; 28 40 31.

CZENEZEK, Maria; Polish, Member of the Sejm; *office address:* Ms Maria Czenezek, Sejm PRI, ul. Wiejska 4/6/8, 00-489 Warsaw, Poland; *phone:* (22) 28 70 01; 28 40 31.

CZUPALA-HOLOGA, Stefania; Polish, Member of the Sejm; *office address:* Ms Stefania Czupala-Hologa, Sejm PRI, ul. Wiejska 4/6/8, 00-489 Warsaw, Poland; *phone:* (22) 28 70 01; 28 40 31.

D

DA COSTA SALEMA ROSETA, Maria Helena do Rego; Portuguese, Deputy; *born:* 23 December 1947, Lisbon, Portugal; *married:* Pedro Manuel Cruz Roseta; *education:* Architecture course, Escola de Belas Artes de Lisboa, Lisbon University; *party:* Partido Socialista (PS, Socialist Party); *political career:* Deputy, Constituent Assembly, 1975; elected Deputy, Assembly of the Republic, 1976, 1979, 1980 and 1987; Mayor of Cascais, 1983-85; *professional career:* former editor, Jornal Novo (national daily newspaper) and Povo Livre (PSD party newspaper); Executive, New University of Lisbon; *honours and awards:* Medal of Merit, Council of Europe; *office address:* Ms Maria da Costa Salema Roseta, Assembléia da República, Palacia de S Bento, 1296 Lisboa Codex, Portugal.

DAEPP-HEINIGER, Susanna; Swiss, Member of the Nationalrat; *born:* 20 August 1938, Eriswil, Switzerland; *children:* two; *party:* Schweizerische Volkspartei (Swiss People's Party); *political career:* Mayoress of Oppligen; Pres., Bern District Women's Assn.; Pres., Central Cttee. of Swiss National Women's Assn.; Mem. of the Nationalrat for Oppligen, Canton of Bern, 1988-, replacing Adolf Ogi on his election to the Bundesrat; *professional career:* home economics teacher; farmer; *office address:* Frau Susanna Daepp-Heiniger, Nationalrat/Conseil National, Secretariat-General, Parlamentsgebäude, 3003 Berne, Switzerland; *phone:* Berne 619711.

DAGRI DIABATE, Henriette Rose; Côte D'Ivoire, Minister of Culture; *born:* Bingerville; *children:* five; *languages:* English; *education:* primary school, Soubré, Dimbokra, Gagnoa; secondary school, Collège moderne des jeunes filles de Bingerville; École Normale des jeunes filles de Rufisque (Sénégal), school leaving examination, first part; Lycée classique de Cocody, school leaving examination, second part; Univ. of Dakar Fann, Cert. in study of general literature; Univ. of Aix-en-Provence; Univ. of Abidjan; Univ. of Paris-Sorbonne, BA history, MA history, doctorate of 3rd cycle, in history, State doctorate in history; *memberships:* founding Mem., Institute of African History, Art and Archeology, (IHAAA); founding Mem., Assn. of African Historians; Dep. Mem. of Bureau of Assn. of Part or Wholly French speaking Univs., (AUPELF); Mem., Assn. of writers in the French language; *professional career:* teacher, girls'

school, Thiés, 1959-60; Assistant, Univ. Nat. of Côte d'Ivoire, 1968-76; Dir. of Science, Houphouet-Boigny Foundation, 1976-84; Chief assistant in history, Univ. of Abidjan, head of conferences in history Dept., Prof. of history, 1984-90; *honours and awards:* Chevalier de Palmes académique (Knight of academic Palms); Knight of Merit of France; *publications:* numerous articles, television and radio broadcasts and seminars; books including: Origine du Sannvi, 1979; Le Sannvi, un royaume akan de la Côte d'Ivoire, 1701-1902, 1984; Aniaba, un Assinien à la cour de Louis XIV, Paris, ABC, Abidjan, NEA, 1975; La Marche des Femmes sur Grand-Bassam, Abidjan, NEA, 1975; Le Sannvin: Sources, oracles et histoire. Essai de Méthologie, Abijan, NEA, 1986; Mémorial de la Côte d'Ivoire, volume 1, époque précoloniale (direction et collaboration), AMI, 1987; Église et société africaine. Paroisse Saint-Pierre de Jacqueville, un siècle d'apostolat, Abidjan, NEA, 1988; Toujours plus haut..., Notre Abidjan, June 1991; working on three other books about the Côte d'Ivoire; *office address:* Mme Henriette Dagri Diabate, Ministry of Information, Culture, Youth and Sport, Adjamé-Avenue 13, Cité Administrative, Tour-L, B.P. V-138, Abidjan, Côte D'Ivoire; *phone:* 29 40 00.

DAHL, Birgitta; Swedish, Minister of the Environment; *born:* 20 September 1937, Råda, Sweden; *parents:* Sven Dahl and Anna-Brita Dahl (née Axelsson); *married:* E. Kokk; *children:* one s., two d; *languages:* English, French, German; *education:* Fil. Kand., Uppsala, 1960; *party:* Sveriges Sosialdemokratiska Arbetarepartiet (SAP, Swedish Social Democratic Labour Party); *political career:* First Under Sec. for Int. Development, 1964-68; then Principal Assistant Sec., 1968-82; assistant, Scandinavian Institute for African Studies, 1964-65; Board mem. Uppsala Student Association, 1963 and United Student Organisations of Sweden, 1964; Trustee, the Dag Hammarskjöld, 1965-67; Vice-Chmn., Workers' Education Federation, Uppsala County, 1968-74; MP, 1969-; dep. mem. Bank Cttee., Agricultural Cttee., 1969-70, Education Cttee., 1971-75 and Cttee. for Housing and National Resources, 1975-82; SAP board mem. Svartbäckens, Uppsala and Exec. Ctte. for Uppsala County, 1969-; mem., Nat. Board and Exec. cttee., SAP, 1975-; municipal Cnclr., Uppsala, 1974-79; mem. various cttees. on education, energy and housing; UN delegate, 1980-81; Cabinet Minister of the Ministry of Industry, for Energy, 1982-87 and for the

Environment, 1986-87; mem. War Delegation, 1986-; Minister of the Environment and of Energy, 1987-90; Minister of the Environment, 1990-; *interests:* environment, international affairs, living conditions of children; *publications:* Guinea-Bissau. Rapport om ett land och en befrielserörelse, 1971 (in co-operation with K. Andreassen); *office address:* Ms Birgitta Dahl, Ministry of the Environment and Energy, Fredsgt. 8, 103 33 Stockholm, Sweden.

DALES, Ien (CJ); Dutch, Minister for Home Affairs; *born:* 18 October 1931, Arnhem, Netherlands; *education:* Kerk en Wereld (Church and World) Academy, Driebergen, Diploma in Theology and Preaching; Amsterdam Univ., Education, 1975; *party:* Labour Party; *political career:* State Sec. for Social Affairs and Employment with special responsibility for Social Security, Sept. 1981-May 82; Labour Party Mem., lower House of States Gen.; Burgomaster of Nijmegen, 1987; Mem., Cttee. supervising Civil Service re-organisation; Minister of Home Affairs, Nov. 1989-; *memberships:* Policy and Retrenchment Advisory Cttee., Dutch Reformed Church; Supervisory Board, Electricity Companies Assn.; Dir., Netherlands Trade Fair and Social Questions Section, Dutch Cncl. of Churches; *professional career:* course teacher, Church and World Organisation, 1956; Dep.-Head, then Head, Church and World Education Dept.; Dir., Church and World Organisation, 1968-74; freelance researcher, 1975; Dir., Rotterdam Municipal Social Services, 1977-81; *office address:* Mevr. C. Ien Dalese, Ministry of Home Affairs, Schedeldoekshaven 200, POB 20011, 2500 EA The Hague, The Netherlands.

DALY, Margaret Elizabeth; British, Member of the European Parliament; *born:* 26 January 1938; *parents:* Robert Bell and Elizabeth Bell; *married:* Kenneth Anthony Edward Daly, 1964; *children:* one daughter; *religion:* Ecumenical; *languages:* French, German; *education:* Methodist College, Belfast; *party:* Conservative Party; *political career:* MEP for Somerset and Dorset West, 1984-; vice-Chmn., Development Cttee., European Parliament, 1987-89; Vice-Pres., Joint EEC/ACP (African, Caribbean, Pacific), Lomé Assembly; *interests:* Third World, social affairs, European Union in 1992; *professional career:* Departmental Head, Phoenix Assurance Co., 1956-60; Trade Union Official, Insurance Unions, 1960-71; Dir., Conservative Trade Unionist Organisations, 1980-84; *publications:* various political pamphlets; *recreations:* swimming, music, travel; *private address:* The Old School House, Aisholt, Spaxton, Bridgewater, Somerset; *office address:* Ms Margaret Daly, European Parliament, Centre Européen, Plateau de Kirchberg, BP 2929, Luxembourg; *phone:* Luxembourg 43001.

DALZIEL, Lianne; New Zealander, Member of Parliament; *born:* 7 June 1960; *education:* law degree;

party: Labour Party; *political career:* became involved with the Hotel and Hospital Workers Union while studying for Law degree; organiser then legal officer, Hotel and Hospital Workers Union, 1984; elected Union Sec., 1987; Canterbury Rep., National Cncl. of the NZCTU since its inception; Labour Party involvement began as Affiliate Rep. to the Christchurch Central electorate; Mem., various Labour policy Cttees.; Mem., Justice and Law and Electoral Law Reform Select Cttees.; Mem., Economic, Environment, Employment Caucus Cttees.; Mem., Domestic Issues Cttee. and Women's Caucus; Spokesperson on Customs, Audit and Assc. Justice; MP for Christchurch Central; *professional career:* solicitor and barrister, 1984; *recreations:* reading, music, tennis; *office address:* Ms Dalziel Lianne, House of Representatives, POB 18041, Wellington, New Zealand; *phone:* (04) 719199; *fax:* (04) 4990704.

DAMANAKI, Maria; Greek, Member of Parliament and President of the Left and Progress Coalition; *born:* 1952, Aghios Nikolaos, Crete; *parents:* Theodoros Damanakis and Heleftheria Damanaki; *married:* Dimitris Danikas, 1986; *public role of spouse:* journalist and cinema critic; *children:* two; *languages:* English, French; *education:* grad., Ethnikon Metsovion Polytechnion (Athens Polytechnic); *party:* Kommunistiko Komma Elladas (KKE, Communist Party of Greece); Sinaspismos Tis Aristeras Ke Tis Proodou (SAP, Coalition of Left and Progress), 1989; *political career:* student leader in polytechnic uprising, Nov. 1973; MP, 1977; MP, SAP, B' Athens, 1989; Vice-Pres., Parliament, 1985-90; Pres., Left and Progress Coalition, Mar. 1991-; *memberships:* Technical Chamber of Greece; *professional career:* chemical engineer; *publications:* Sychroni Epohi, essay for the Women's Liberation Movement, 1981; numerous articles in the Greek press; *recreations:* music, collector of classical LPs; *private address:* Gounari 4, Dionyssos 14565, Greece; *office address:* Ms Maria Damanaki, 7 Themistokleous Street, Athens, Greece 10677.

DAMBENZET, Jeanne; The Congo, Minister of Labour and Social Security; *office address:* Mme. Jeanne Dambenzet, Ministry of Labour and Social Security, Centre Administratif, Quartier Plateau, Brazzaville, People's Republic of the Congo.

DAMIAO VIEIRA, Elisa Maria Ramos; Portuguese, Deputy; *born:* 10 September 1946, Alcobaça, Portugal; *education:* Industrial Course; Secretarial Course; bi-lingual secretarial course; *party:* Partido Socialista (PS, Socialist Party); *political career:* Trade Unionist; National Secretary, Uniao Geral de Trabalhadores (General Workers Union); Pres., Union of Office, Commercial and Service Workers of Setúbal; Deputy, Assembly of the Republic, 1987-; *professional career:* secretary; *office address:* Ms Elisa Damiao Vieira,

Assembléia da República, Palacia de S Bento, 1296 Lisboa Codex, Portugal.

d'ANCONA, Hedy; Dutch, Minister of Welfare, Health and Culture; *born:* 1 October 1937, The Hague, Netherlands; *children:* two; *education:* grad., Amsterdam Univ., geography and sociology, 1963; *political career:* mem., Upper House, Labour, 1974-81 and 1982-83; State Sec. for Social Affairs and Employment with special responsibility for Women's Rights, Sep. 1981-May 1982; Mem., European Parly., 1984-89; Chwn., Women's Rights Cttee., until 1989 and Chwn., Social Affairs and Employment Cttee., since 1989; Minister of Welfare, Health and Cultural Affairs, Nov. 1989-; *memberships:* has sat on: Housing Cncl.; Provisional Cncl. for Research into the Built Environment; Praemium Erasmianum Foundation; Boekman Foundation; Labour Party Policy Principle's Cttee.; Action Group on Man, Woman and Society; Bolhuis Foundation; SAAM Cttee. (aid to Argentinian mothers); Against Her Will Foundation; Swarttouw Cttee.; Mem., Jury, Dutch Film Festival; Chwn., AKO Literature Prize Awards Cttee.; Board Mem., Dutch Centre for Foreigners; *professional career:* producer of women's TV programmes for VARA (Socialist Broadcasting Assn.), 1962-65; senior lecturer, social geography, Amsterdam Univ., 1965-75; Dir., CEBEON (a research centre advising on policy matters), Amsterdam, 1975-82; *publications:* numerous articles and several books on housing, town and country planning, women's rights and European Affairs; *office address:* Mevr. Hedy d'Ancona, Ministry of Welfare, Health and Cultural Affairs, Sir Winston Churchilliaan 370, POB 5406, 2280 EH Rijswik, The Netherlands.

DANKOWSKA, Adela; Polish, Member of the Sejm; *office address:* Ms Adela Dankowska, Sejm PRI, ul. Wiejska 4/6/8, 00-489 Warsaw, Poland; *phone:* (22) 28 70 01; 28 40 31.

DANOCHOWSKA, Maria; Polish, Member of the Sejm; *office address:* Ms Maria Danochowska, Sejm PRI, ul. Wiejska 4/6/8, 00-489 Warsaw, Poland; *phone:* (22) 28 70 01; 28 40 31.

DANUSER, Menga; Swiss, Member of the Nationalrat; *born:* 31 July 1951, Frauenfeld, Switzerland; *education:* Univ. of Zürich and Geneva; *party:* Sozialdemokratische Volkspartei der Schweiz (SDP, Social Democratic Party of Switzerland); *political career:* borough Cllr., Frauenfeld, 1975-83; Mem. of the Frauenfeld Great Cncl., 1976-; Mem. of the Nationalrat for Frauenfeld, Canton of Thurgau, 1987-; *professional career:* secondary school teacher; *office address:* Frau Menga Danuser, Nationalrat/Conseil National, Secretariat-General, Parlamentsgebäude, 3003 Berne, Switzerland; *phone:* Berne 619711.

DARCY DE KNAYTH, Baroness (18th in line, England, cr. 1332) Davina Marcia Ingrams (neé Herbert); British, Member of the House of Lords; *born:* 10 July 1938; *parents:* Mervyn, 17th Baron, Viscount Clive; *married:* the late Rupert George Ingrams, 1960; *children:* one s., two d; *education:* St. Mary's, Wantage; Italy; Sorbonne, Paris, FR; *party:* Independent; *political career:* House of Lords, 1943-; mem., General Advisory Cncl., Independent Broadcasting Authority; mem., Select Cttee. on Murder and Life Imprisonment, 1988-; *interests:* disability matters; *private address:* Camley Corner, Stubbings, Maidenhead, Berks, SL6 6QW, UK; *office address:* Baroness Darcy de Knayth, House of Lords, London SW1A 0PW.

DARLING, Elaine Elizabeth; Australian, Member of the House of Representatives; *born:* Brisbane, Australia; *parents:* John (Jack) Melloy and Elizabeth Maude Melloy; *married:* Robert Francis Darling, 1958; *children:* Mark, Russell, Vicky; *religion:* Uniting Church of Australia; *education:* BA; Diploma in Education, Queensland; *party:* Australian Labor Party; *political career:* Pres., Lilley Federal Divisional Electorate; Vice-Pres., Nudgee Electorate Executive Council; Pres. Labor Party Banyo, Northgate East Branch; elected to Lilley, 1980-; Committee Service: Mem. of the House of Representatives for Road Safety, 1980-84 and Chairperson, 1983-84; Chairperson for Transport Safety, 1985-; Dep. Chairperson of Cttees., 1983-; Chairperson, Caucus Education, Employment and Training Cttee., 1987-90; Dep.-Chairperson, Caucus, 1990; Mem., House of Reps. Standing Cttee. on Environment and on Sport, 1990-; Conferences, Delegations and Visits: Mem., 29th Commonwealth Parly. Association Conference, Nairobi, 1983; Mem., 73rd Inter Parly.-Union Conference, Togo 1985; Leader, Parly. Delegation, India and Sri Lanka, 1986; Mem., Australian War Memorial Council, 1983-87; Queensland State Co-ordinator, National Prices Network, 1986-90; delegate United Nations General Assembly, 1989; CPA Conference Harare and South Africa, 1990; *interests:* foreign affairs, aid and development, peace and disarmament, assistance for disabled, aboriginal rights, human rights, policies for the aged, health and community; *professional career:* graduate assistant to Dir., Brisbane Kindergarten Training College; teacher, English and secretarial skills; Pres., South Queensland Consumers Association, 1974-83; mem., Action for World Development, 1976-77; executive mem. and sec., Queensland Consumers Association, 1978-79; Vice-Pres., Banyo Community Association, 1978-80; Convener, Consumer Education Advisory Cttee., 1979-80; Australian Federation of Consumers Organisations, 1979-80; mem., World Vision, 1979-80; Trustee, Nudgee Kindergarten Association, 1980; Patron, Northside Benevolent Cttee., 1980; *recreations:* reading and writing; *office address:* Ms Elaine Darling, House of Representatives, Parliament House, Room

M80, Canberra ACT, 2600, Australia; *phone:* (062) 726383.

DA ROSA AMORIM, Dr. Maria Luísa Rodrigues Garcia (Maria Luísa Rodrigues Amorim Garcia); Portuguese, Deputy; *born:* 17 March 1946, Lisbon, Portugal; *education:* Licenciate of Medicine; Student of History, Lisbon Univ; *party:* Partido Comunista Portugues (PCP, Portuguese Communist Party); *political career:* former Mem., Lisbon Municipal Assembly; National Secretary and Mem., National Council and National Leadership of the Democratic Movement of Portuguese Women; Vice-Pres., International Democratic Federation of Women; Deputy, Assembly of the Republic, 1987-; *professional career:* Doctor; *office address:* Dr. Maria da Rosa Amorim, Assembléia da República, Palacia de S Bento, 1296 Lisboa Codex, Portugal.

DA SILVA, Benedita Souza; Brazilian, Federal Deputy; *born:* 26 April 1942, Rio de Janeiro, Brazil; *parents:* José Tobias de Souza and Maria da Conceiçao de Souza; *children:* Eunice Maria, Vanda, Admilton, Nilcea, Pedro Paulo; *education:* Faculty of Social Services, Rio de Janeiro, social services and sociology, 1980-84; *party:* Partido dos Trabalhadores (PT, Independent Labour Party); *political career:* leader of the Municipal Chamber of Rio de Janeiro, 1983-86 and Town Cllr., 1983-87; Chwn. of the Sub-cttee. for Negroes, Indiginous Population, the Disabled and Minorities, 1987; Substitute Chwn. of the Sub-cttee. for Nationality, Sovereignty and Int. Relations, 1987; Federal Deputy for Rio de Janeiro, 1987-91 and re-elected for 1991-95; Chwn., Cttees. for External Relations and for Social Welfare and Social Assistance, 1989-90; Chwn., Cttee. for Social Security and the Family, 1990-91; Substitute Chwn., Cttee. for Consumer Protection, the Environment and Minorities, 1990-91; Chwn., Cttee. for Justice, 1991-95; *professional career:* auxillary nurse; public servant; professor; social services worker; *honours and awards:* Friend of the City of Los Angeles, 1983; Woman of the Year, 1983; Community Award of the National Council of Brazilian Women,1984; Personality of the Year for 1984, Macaé journal, 1985; awarded title of Guest of Honour of the City of Managua, Nicaragua, 1985; *publications:* article on the community activities of women for the benefit of the needy, Rio de Janeiro, 1986; *office address:* Ms Benedita Da Silva, Chamber of Deputies, Praça dos 3 Poderes, Ed. Principal, 70160 Brasilia, DF, Brazil; *phone:* (61) 225 2885.

DA SILVA, Ercília Domingos Monteiro Pinto Ribeiro; Portuguese, Deputy; *born:* 4 February 1948, Pombal, Portugal; *education:* Secondary School diploma; *party:* Partido Social Democrata (PSD, Social Democratic Party); *political career:* former mem., Pombal Municipal Assembly; Mem. PSD Political Cttee.,

Pombal; Mem., PSD Leinia District Assembly; Deputy, Assembly of the Republic, 1987-; *professional career:* bank employee; *office address:* Ms Ercília da Silva, Assembléia da República, Palacia de S Bento, 1296 Lisboa Codex, Portugal.

DA SILVA, Eurides Brito; Brazilian, Federal Deputy; *born:* 28 February 1937, Capanema, Pará; *parents:* Alvino Alves de Brito and Maria Pinto de Brito; *married:* Adamor Nogueira da Silva; *children:* Harley, Ana Claudia; *education:* Federal Univ. of Para, B.Sc. geography and history, 1958-59; Federal Univ. of Parana, Dr. of Education, 1974; *party:* Partido dos Trabalhadores (PT, Independent Labour Party); *political career:* Federal Deputy; *office address:* Ms Eurides da Silva, Chamber of Deputies, Praça dos 3 Poderes, Ed. Principal, 70160 Brasilia, DF, Brazil; *phone:* (61) 225 2885.

DÄUBLER-GMELIN, Dr. Herta; German, Member of the Bundestag; *born:* 12 August 1943, Bratislava, Czechoslovakia; *married:* Prof. Dr. Wolfgang; *children:* two; *education:* Tübingen, Berlin, Law and Economics; 1968-72; Law examinations Part II, 1974; Dr. Jur; *party:* Sozialdemokratische Partei Deutschlands (SPD, Social Democratic Party of Germany), 1965; *political career:* Chwn., Work Community of Social Democratic Women, Baden-Württemberg, 1971; mem. of Bundestag, 1972-; Chwn., Law cttee. to 1982; dep. chmn. SPD Group, 1983-; *professional career:* lawyer; *publications:* various labour and economic law publications; *office address:* Dr. Herta Däubler-Gmelin, Bundeshaus, 5300 Bonn 1, West Germany.

DAUGREILH, Martine; French, Deputy; *born:* 11 September 1947, Talence, Gironde, France; *parents:* Roger Gasquet and Denise Gasquet (née Rous); *children:* Joachim, Alienor; *religion:* Roman Catholic; *languages:* English, Italian; *education:* University of Nice, Masters degree, history and geography; postgraduate diploma, history and geography; diploma in industrial geography; *party:* Rassemblement pour la République (RPR, Rally for the Republic); *political career:* Deputy, 1988-; Deputy Mayor responsible for town planning, Nice, 1989-; *interests:* town planning, geostrategy, defence; *professional career:* delegate with responsibility for regional development, Nice, 1973-88; *office address:* Mme. Martine Daugreilh, L'Assemblée Nationale, 126 rue de L'Université, 75355 Paris, France.

DAVID, Dr. Ibolya; Hungarian, Member of the Országgyülés; *party:* Hungarian Democratic Forum (MDF); *office address:* Dr. Ibolya Dávid, Országgyülés, Kossuth L. tér 1-3, Budapest V, Hungary; *phone:* 22 5058; 22 5059.

DAVID, Baroness (cr. 1978, Life Peer) Nora Ratcliff David; British, Member of the House of Lords; *born:* 23 September 1913; *parents:* George Blockley Blakesley and Annie Edith Blakesley; *married:* Richard William David, 1935; *children:* two s., two d; *education:* Ashby-De-La-Zouch Girls' Grammar School; St. Felix School, Southwold; Newnham College, Cambridge, MA; *party:* Labour Party; *political career:* mem., Cambridge City Council, 1964-67, 1968-74; mem., Cambridgeshire County Council, 1974-78; Board mem., Peterborough Development Corp., 1976-78; House of Lords, 1978-; Baroness-in-Waiting (Government Whip), 1978-79; Opposition Whip and Education Spokesman, 1979-85; Opposition Dep. Chief Whip, 1983-87; Opposition Front Bench Spokesman on the Environment, 1985-87, and on Education and Science, 1987-; *interests:* education, environment, Home affairs; *professional career:* JP, 1965-; *honours and awards:* Hon. Fellow, Newnham College, Cambridge, 1986 and Anglia Polytechnic, 1989; *recreations:* walking, swimming, theatre; *private address:* 50 Highsett, Cambridge CB2 1NZ, UK; *office address:* Baroness David, House of Lords, London SW1A 0PW.

DAVIDSON, Inger Margareta; Swedish, Secretary General of the Christian Democratic Party; *born:* 2 December 1944, Enskede, Sweden; *parents:* Ernst Winblad and Kerstin Winblad (née Erlandsson); *married:* Hans G E Davidson, 1968; *children:* Johan, Joakim, Jens; *religion:* Christian; *languages:* English, German; *education:* teacher training college, Stockholm, teaching diploma; 1966-68; Univ. of Stockholm, education and sociology; *party:* Kristdemokratiska Samhällspártiet (KdS, Christian Democratic Party), 1966; *political career:* political sec., KdS, 1987-88; party sec., KdS, 1989-; *professional career:* secondary school teacher, 1968-87; *office address:* Ms Inger Davidson, Kristdemokratiska Samhällspartiet, Mälargt. 7, POB 451, 101 29 Stockholm, Sweden.

DAVIDSON, Jo Ann; American, Ohio State Representative; *party:* Republican Party; *political career:* Ohio State Rep., District 34; Minority Whip; Mem., Finance, Ethics and Standards and Rules Cttees., Ohio House of Reps; *memberships:* National Women's Political Caucus; *clubs:* Ohio CofC; *office address:* Ms Jo Ann Davidson, 6870 E. Livingston Avenue, Apt B Reynoldsburg, Ohio 43068, USA.

DAVIES, Sonja M.L.; New Zealander, Member of Parliament; *born:* 11 November 1923, Wallaceville, New Zealand; *parents:* Gerald Dempsey and Gwladys Ilmavile; *married:* Charles Edward Mercer Davies, 1946; *public role of spouse:* National Councillor New Zealand Federation of Labour; *children:* Penelope Anne, Mark Timothy; *religion:* Agnostic; *languages:* English; *education:* King Edward Technical College, Victoria Univ., Wellington, New Zealand; *party:* Labour Party; *political career:* nine years local govt., Nelson City Council; Dep-Chwn., Nelson Hospital Board; founder, NZ Working Women's Council; co-organiser NZ Working Women's Convention, 1977; she has served on the NZ Federation of Labour Executive, vice-Pres. 1981-87; represented the Federation of Labour at the Working Women's Conference, 1978, and at the Conference on problems of rural workers, 1979; led the NZ delegation to the World Peace Conference, 1986; Justice of the Peace; founder, New Zealand Childcare Assn; *interests:* peace, women's issues, race relations, the environment; *memberships:* adviser New Zealand Childcare Assn; *professional career:* industrial adviser, Wellington Shop Employees' Union; assistant secretary/organiser, NZ Public Service Assoc.; regional representative, NZ Food Processing Union and Wellington Clerical Union; trainee nurse; shop employee; library assistant; *honours and awards:* Order of New Zealand; Honorary Doctor of Laws, Victoria Univ; *publications:* Bread and Roses, 1984; articles in national and international publications; *recreations:* reading, writing, music, theatre, gardening; *private address:* 39 Marine Parade, Eastbourne, New Zealand; *office address:* Ms Sonja Davies, Parliament House, Wellington, New Zealand.

DAVIS, Gloria; American, Member of the New York State Assembly; *born:* 9 February 1938, Bronx, New York, USA; *children:* six; *religion:* Roman Catholic; *education:* Bronx Community College; Fordham Univ; *party:* Democratic Party; *political career:* Mem., New York State Assembly, District 78, 1980-; Chwn., Task Force on Food, Farm and Nutrition Policy, 1989-; Mem., Agriculture and Markets, Banks, Children and Families, Housing and Social Service State Cttees. and Democrat Steering Cttee.; Mem., Community Planning Board; *memberships:* City-Wide Tenants Rights Organisation; City-Wide Parents for Day Care; National Welfare Rights Organisation; Black Elected Officials of New York; *office address:* Ms Gloria Davis, 605 E. 169th Street, Bronx, New York 10456, USA.

DAVIS, Helen Gordon; American, Florida State Senator; *born:* New York City, USA; *married:* Gene Davis; *children:* Stephanie, Karen, Gordon; *education:* Brooklyn College, BA; Univ. of South Florida; *party:* Democratic Party; *political career:* Judicial Chwn., Local Govt Study Commission, Florida, 1963-64; Mem., Tampa Commission on Juvenile Delinquency, 1966-69; Mem., Employment Cttee., Commission of Community Relations, 1966-69; Mem., Mayor's Citizen's Advisory Cttee., Tampa, 1966-69; Mem., Quality Education Commission, 1966-68; Mem., Arts Cncl., Tampa, 1970-74; Mem., Governor's Citizen Cttee. for Court Reform, 1972; Commissioner, Hillsborough County Planning Commission, 1973-74; formerly: Florida State Rep., District 64; Mem., Governor's Citizen Cttee. for Judicial Reform; Vice-

Chwn., Appropriations Cttee.; Co-Chwn., Employee, Pay and Benefits Cttees.; Chwn., Children and Youth Cttee.; Florida House Rep.; currently: Florida State Senator; Vice-Chwn., Economic, Professional and Utilities Regulation Cttee; memberships: League of Women Voters; honours and awards: Univ. of South Florida Young Democrats Humanitarian Award, 1974; NDW Diana Award, 1975; Woman of Achievement in the Arts, 1975; Tampa Human Relations Award, 1977; Woman of the Year in Politics, Soroptomist, 1978; Humanitarian Award, Judeo-Christian Clinics, 1984; Leadership Citation, Florida Cncl. of Churches, 1985; Legislator of the Year Award, Florida Nurses Assn., 1986; Award of Appreciation, Florida Child Wefare and National Cncl. of Juvenile Judges, 1986; Outstanding Political Woman of the 80's, Hillsborough County Democratic Womens Club; publications: Admin. of Justice in Florida, 1971; Florida Juries, 1972; You're Under Arrest, 1973; clubs: PTA; Temple guild Sisterhood; Tampa Symphony Guild; Athena Society; Florida Women's Alliance; private address: 45 Adalia, Tampa, Florida 33606, USA; office address: Mrs Helen Gordon Davis, 178 E. Davis Blvd., Tampa, Florida 33606, USA.

DAVIS WAGNON, Joan; American, Kansas State Representative; born: 17 October 1940, Texarkana, Arkansas, USA; parents: Jack Davis and Louise Davis (née Lucas); married: William O. Wagnon, 1964; public role of spouse: college professor; children: Jack, William III; religion: Methodist; languages: Spanish; education: Hendrix College, Conway, Arkansas, BA, 1962; Univ. of Missouri, Columbia, M.Ed, 1968; party: Democratic Party; political career: Commissioner, Topeka Housing Auth., Kansas, 1973; Mem., SRS Review Commission. Kansas Legislature, 1980-83; Mem., Govt. Cncl. on Fitness; Chwn., Taxation Cttee., Mem., Federal and State Affairs Cttee., Mem., Economic Cttee.; Mem., Permanency Planning Commission, Kansas Supreme Court; Child Support Commission, Kansas Supreme Court; National Conference of State Legislatures Cncl. on Children and Families; former Mem., Attorney General's Health Planning Review Commission and SRS Review Commission; Kansas State Rep., District 55, 1983-; interests: taxation, health, social service; memberships: Exec. Dir., Topeka YWCA, 1977-; professional career: research Asst., Univ. of Arkansas Medical School, Little Rock, 1962-64; Senior Research Asst., Univ. Medical School, Columbia, Missouri, 1964-68; teacher, Northern Hills Jr. High School, Topeka, Kansas, 1968-69 and J.S. Kendall School, Belmont, Mass., 1970-71; Cllr., Youth Corp., Topeka, 1973-74; Exec. Dir., YWCA, 1977-; honours and awards: Service to Education Award, National Education Assn., Topeka, 1979; Women Helping Women, Soroptimist, 1980; clubs: Golden City Forum; Downtown Rotary Club, Nonoso, Delta Kappa Gamma; recreations: sailing, boating; private address: 1606 Boswell, Topeka, Kansas 66604, USA; office address: Mrs Joan Davis Wagnon, YWCA 225 W. 12th, Topeka, Kansas 66612, USA.

DE ASSIS, Auricélia Freitas; Brazilian, Federal Deputy; born: 28 September 1958, Altamira; parents: Aureo Déo de Freitas and Lindanny Teixeira de Freitas; married: Narciso Mendes de Assis; children: Patricia, Narciso; party: Partido Democrático Social (PDS, Social Democrat Party); political career: Federal Deputy for Acre, 1991-95; professional career: Dir., Construction, Mendes Carlos Ltda, 1975-86 and Manager of Industry and Commerce, 1980-86; office address: Ms Auricélia de Assis, Chamber of Deputies, Praça dos 3 Poderes, Ed. Principal, 70160 Brasilia, DF, Brazil; phone: (61) 225 2885.

DEBERRY, Lois; American, Tennessee State Representative; married: Charles Traughber; education: LeMoyne-Owen College, BA; State Technical Institute, Certificate in Real Estate; party: Democratic Party; political career: Tennessee State Rep., District 91; professional career: educator; office address: Ms Lois Deberry, 2429 Verdun Street, Memphis, Tennessee 38114, USA.

DEBONO, Giovanna; Maltese, Member of Parliament; office address: Mrs Giovanna Debono, House of Representatives, The Palace, Valetta, Malta; phone: 222294.

DE FREITAS, Rosilda; Brazilian, Federal Deputy; born: 23 January 1949, Caratinga; parents: Waldemar Antonio de Freitas and Maria Lourdes Teles de Freitas; married: Hugo Borges Jr; children: Gabriel, Julia Maria; party: Partido da Social Democracia Brasileira (PSDB, Social Democratic Party of Brasil); political career: State Deputy, Espirito Santo, 1983-87; Federal Deputy for Espirito Santo, 1987-91 and 1991-95; professional career: professor and journalist; office address: Ms Rosilda de Freitas, Chamber of Deputies, Praça dos 3 Poderes, Ed. Principal, 70160 Brasilia, DF, Brazil; phone: (61) 225 2885.

DÉGLISE, Elisabeth; Swiss, Member of the Nationalrat; born: 20 December 1931, Freiberg; children: one; education: senior education, Freiberg girls' school; party: Parti Démocrate-Chrétien Suisse (Christlichdemokratische Volkspartei der Schweiz, Christian Democratic Party of Switzerland); political career: Mem., district Cncl. of Villarsel-sur-Marly, 1983-; Deputy for Canton of Freiberg, 1971-87, Pres., Great Cncl. of Freiberg, 1986; Mem. of the Nationalrat, 1987-; office address: Mme. Elisabeth Déglise, Nationalrat/Conseil National, Secretariat-General, Parlamentsgebäude, 3003 Berne, Switzerland; phone: Berne 619711.

de GRAAFF-NAUTA, Dieuwke; Dutch, Secretary of State for Home Affairs; *born:* 22 May 1930, Sneek; *children:* two; *political career:* Mem., Friesland Provincial Cncl., 1962; CHU Rep., Sneek Municipal Cncl., 1966-1978; Alderman, Sneek, with responsibility for education, public health and the environment, 1970-78; leader, Anti-Revolutionary Party (ARP), Christian Historical Union (CHU) and Catholic People's Party (KVP), later to become the Christian Democratic Alliance, on the Friesland Provincial Cncl., 1970-82; Mem., CDA Presidium, 1980-82; Mem., Friesland Provincial Exec., Friesland, with responsibility for general affairs, inter-provincial co-operation, admin. organisation, supervision of municipal authorities, planning and co-ordination and information, 1982-; Chwn., Waddenzee Provinces Steering Cttee. and Dep. Chwn., Co-ordinating Board for the Waddenzee Area and Mem., Exec. Cttee., Northern Provinces; State Sec., Home Affairs, July 1986 and 1989-; *memberships:* Christian Historical Union (CHU), 1962; *professional career:* primary school teacher, Parrega, 1949-51; secondary school teacher, Utrecht, 1952-54; *office address:* Mevr. Dieuwke de Graaff-Nauta, Erste Kamer der Staten Generaal, Binnenhof 22, Postbus 20017, The Hague, The Netherlands.

DE HAUTECLOCQUE, Nicole; French, Senator; *born:* 10 March 1913, Commercy, Meuse, France; *parents:* Ernest de Saint-Denis and Madeleine de Saint-Denis (née Delisle); *married:* Pierre de Hauteclocque; *children:* Brigitte (decd.); *education:* Hulst School, Paris; baccalauréat; *party:* UNR; Rassemblement pour la République (PRP, Rally for the Republic); *political career:* Town Councillor, Paris, 1947-65 and since 1968; Vice-President of the District Council, 1949-50; Vice-President of the Town Council, 1954-55 and 1962-63; Deputy, UNR, later RPR, Seine (18th constituency: 15th arrondissement) 1962-86; President of Council of Paris, 1972-73; Deputy Mayor of Paris, since 1977; member of the Central Cttee. and Political Office of RPR, since 1977; Senator, RPR, Paris, 1986-; *honours and awards:* Chevalier of the Legion of Honour; Military Cross 39-45; Rosette de la Résistance; Médaille de la France libre; *recreations:* riding, golf, skiing, swimming; *private address:* 53 avenue du Maréchal Lyautey, 75016 Paris, France; *office address:* Mme. Nicole de Hauteclocque, Sénat de la République Française, Palais du Luxembourg, 75291 Paris Cedex 06, France.

de JONG, Drs. Mechtild; Dutch, Member of the Second Chamber; *born:* 1 April 1939, Maastricht, The Netherlands; *parents:* J.G.Y. de Jong and HMM. de Jong (née ten Doesschate); *married:* K.J.W.H. Deen (second marriage), 1987; *children:* Joerk, Katja, Dosja, Tom, Fedde, Pieter; *religion:* Roman Catholic; *languages:* Dutch, English, French, German; *education:* gymnasium B, 1956; Univ. of Utrecht, biology doctorate, 1962; *party:* Catholic People's Party (KVP), 1966; Christen-Democratisch Appel (CDA, Christian Democratic Appeal), 1985-; *political career:* Chwn., CDA, Delft, 1984-91; Mem., CDA Central Cttee., 1987-91; Mem., Second Chamber, 1989-; Vice-Chwn., KVP, 1966-78; Mem., KVP Central Cttee., 1974-78; *interests:* environment, city and rural planning, nature conservation; *professional career:* cancer researcher, Univ. of Nymegen, 1964-65; High School Teacher, 1966-71; Govt. Adviser, 1974-89; Board, Santa Clara Hospital, Rotterdam, 1989; Board, Bird Protection, 1987; *publications:* Island Theory and Rural Planning in Holland, Spredningsokologi, Denmark, 1984; Ein beschouwing vaumit physiologie en ecologie vandemens over staden landschap, 1986; *recreations:* pianist in quartets; *private address:* Vlamingstraat 86, 2611 LA, Delft, The Netherlands; *office address:* Drs. Mechtild de Jong, Tweede Kamer der Staten-Generaal, Binnenhof 1A, Postbus 20018, The Hague, The Netherlands.

DEL PAPA, Frankie Sue; American, Attorney-General of Nevada; *education:* Univ. of Nevada, BA, 1971; George Washington Univ., National Law Centre, JD, 1974; *party:* Democratic Party; *political career:* Sec.-of-State, Nevada, 1987; currently Attorney-General, Nevada; *memberships:* Sierra Arts Foundation, 1980-; advisory Cttee., Trust for Public Land, 1985-; advisory Cttee., Univ. of Nevada, College of Arts and Science, 1980-81 and Truckee Meadows Community College, 1980-86; Nevada Women's Fund; *professional career:* Assc., Lesley B. Grey, Law Office, Reno., 1975-78; partner, Thornton and Del Papa, 1979-84; private law practice, Reno, 1984-87; *office address:* Ms Frankie Del Papa, Capitol Cpmplex, Carson City, Nevada 89710, USA.

del ROSARIO SINTES ULLOA, Maria; Colombian, Minister of Agriculture; *party:* Partido Social Conservador (PSC, Conservative Party); *office address:* Ms Maria del Rosario Sintes Ulloa, Ministry of Agriculture, Carrera 10 No. 20-30 Piso 2, Bogotá DE, Colombia.

DELRUELLE-GHOBERT, Dr. Janine; Belgian, Senator; *born:* 24 April 1931, Ghent, Belgium; *parents:* Jean Gnobert and Hélène Verbhere; *married:* Jacques Delruelle, 1957; *public role of spouse:* Consul; *religion:* Catholic; *languages:* French, Flemish, English; *education:* Free Univ. of Brussels, Dr. of Law, 1950-55, candidate of Political and Diplomatic Sciences; *party:* Parti Réformateur Libéral (PRL, Liberal Party, French Speaking); *political career:* co-opted Senator, 1981-85 and 1985-87; Pres., Senate PRL Group, 1984-; Senator, Liège, 1987-; mem. of PRL Exec. and Exec. Cttee.; mem. of Senate Commissions, Walloon Regional Cncl. and Cncl. of French Community; Honorary Pres. ONE, Office of Childcare; Pres., Belgian Cttee. Freedom from

Hunger Campaign (F.A.O.); Pres., Liège European District for Social Integration of Handicapped People; *interests:* childcare, housing, co-operation and development; *recreations:* swimming, walking; *private address:* 25 A, Au Thier, 4940 Trooz (Foret), Belgium; *office address:* Dr. Janine Delruelle-Ghobert, Senate, Palais de la Nation, Place de a Nation 1, 1000 Brussels, Belgium.

DELVAUX-STEHRES, Mady; Luxembourgeios, Secretary of State for Social Security and for Youth; *born:* 11 October 1950, Luxembourg City, Luxembourg; *children:* three; *education:* Rumelange Primary School; Hubert-Clement Girls High School, Esch-sur-Alzette; University Preparatory Classes, Luxembourg; University of Paris-Sorbonne, masters degree in classics; *party:* Parti Ouvrier Socialiste Luxembourgeois (POSL, Luxembourg Socialist Workers Party), 1974; *political career:* Communal Councillor, Luxembourg City, 1987; Deputy for Centre constituency, head of list; Secretary of State for Health; Secretary of State for Social Security; Secretary of State for Physical Education and Sport; Secretary of State for Youth; member of management Cttee. of Socialist Workers Party, 1984-; *office address:* Mme. Mady Delvaux-Stehres, Ministère de la Sécurité Sociale, L-2936, Luxembourg.

DE MEESTER-DEMEYER, Wivina; Belgian, Secretary of State for Finance; *born:* 13 December 1943, Alost; *children:* four; *education:* RUG, Agricultural Engineer, 1967; RUG, qualified Secondary School Teacher, 1972; *party:* Christelijke Volkspartij (CVP, Christian Social Party); *political career:* Deputy, 1974-; Local Cllr., 1983-; Sec. of State for Public Health and Policy for Disabled, 1985-88; Sec. of State for Finance, Sep. 1988-; *professional career:* Development Engineer, Building Firm; Professor of Bio-Chemistry, MSTO-Gent, Sint-Geertrui; co-founder of Monikenheide centre for Short Stays; Dir., Monikenheide Centre, 1973-84; co-founder of Activity Centre for mentally handicapped, Monnikenbos; *private address:* Monnikendreef 5, 2153 Zoersel, Belgium; *office address:* Ms Wivina De Meester-Demeyer, 18 rue de la Loi, 1000 Brussels, Belgium.

DE MENEZES, Etevalda Grassi; Brazilian, Federal Deputy; *born:* 13 March 1948, Rio Bananal, Espirito Santo; *parents:* Domingos Grassi and Idalina Elias Grassi; *married:* Nyder Barbosa de Menezes; *children:* Nyder, Etny Adriano; *education:* law, 1983-88; *party:* Partido do Movimento Democrático Brasileira (PMDB, Party of the Brazlian Democratic Movement); *political career:* Federal Deputy for Espirito Santo, 1991-95; *professional career:* Parly. Sec; *office address:* Ms Etevalda de Menezes, Chamber of Deputies, Praça dos 3 Poderes, Ed. Principal, 70160 Brasilia, DF, Brazil; *phone:* (61) 225 2885.

DEMPWOLF, Gertrud; German, Member of the Bundestag; *born:* 3 February 1936, Mönchengladbach, West Germany; *children:* one d; *religion:* Catholic; *education:* dental asst. trainee; *party:* Christlich Demokratische Union (CDU, Christian Democratic Union), 1970; *political career:* mem. of Bundestag, 1984-; *professional career:* farmer; mem. of supervisory board, District Housing Assn., Osterode; mem. of Rural Women's Assn., Osterode, 1965-; *office address:* Frau Gertrud Dempwolf, Bundeshaus, 5300 Bonn 1, West Germany.

DEN HERTOG, Johanna Agatha; Canadian, former President of the New Democratic Party, 1987-89; *born:* 19 August 1952, Rijswijk, Netherlands; *parents:* Willem den Hertog and Ann den Hertog (née Smits); *married:* Ronald Kirk Johnson, 1985; *children:* Alexander, Kirstin; *languages:* English, French, Dutch, German; *education:* N. Gill Univ., Montreal, Canada, Pol.Sci. and Anthropology (Hons.), 1970-72; *party:* New Democratic Party of Canada (NDP), 1975; *political career:* Chwn., Policy Review Cttee., NDP, British Columbia (BC), 1983-85; First Vice-Pres., NDP, BC, 1984-85; candidate, Federal Election, NDP, Vancouver Centre, 1984 and 1988; Pres. NDP, National, 1987-89; Pres., NDP, Canada, 1989-91; *interests:* federal and provincial; *memberships:* OTEU; Board of Dirs., Canadian Centre for Arms Control, 1985-; *professional career:* Communications Dir., Telecommunications Workers Union, 1981-87; Exec. Asst. to Pres., Telecommunications Workers Union, 1987-; National Commissioner, Citizens Inquiry into Peace and Security, 1990-; *publications:* two articles in Socialist International Affairs, 1985-87; *recreations:* camping, travel, languages, hiking; *office address:* Ms Johanna den Hertog, New Democratic Party, 200 Albert Street, Suite 600, Ottawa, Ontario K2P 1R9, Canada; *phone:* (613) 236 3613; *fax:* (613) 230 9950.

DENINGTON, Baroness (cr. 1978, Life Peer) Evelyn Joyce Denington; British, Member of the House of Lords; *born:* 9 August 1907; *parents:* the late Philip Bursill; *married:* Cecil Dallas Denington, 1935; *education:* LCC Schools; Blackheath High School; Bedford College for Women; *party:* Labour Party; *political career:* Gen. Sec., Nat. Assn. of Labour Teachers, 1938-47; mem., St. Pancras Borough Council, 1945-59, and Chmn. of various Cttees.; mem., London County Council, 1946-65; Chmn., New and Expanding Towns Cttee., mem., Stevenage Development Corp., 1950-80, and Chmn., 1966-80; mem., Central Housing Advisory Cttee., 1955-73; mem., Greater London Council, 1964-77, and Chmn., 1975-76; mem., South East Economic Planning Cncl., 1966-79, and Dep. Chmn., 1971-79; Dep. Leader, Labour Opposition, Greater London Council, 1967-73; Chmn., Housing Cttee.; Chmn., Transport Cttee.; House of Lords, 1978-; *professional career:* architectural journalist, 1927-31; teacher, 1933-50; mem., various housing assns; *honours* *and awards:* Freeman, City of London; Hon. MRTPI; Hon. FRIBA; CBE, 1966; DBE, 1974; *recreations:* gardening, music, reading, travel; *private address:* Flat 3, 29 Brunswick Square, Hove BN3 1EJ; *office address:* Baroness Denington, House of Lords, London SW1A 0PW.

DENYS, Marie-José; French, Member of the European Parliament; *born:* 15 March 1950; *party:* Parti Socialiste (PS, Socialist Party); *political career:* regional government; *professional career:* Dir., French National School of Music and Dance; *private address:* 22 quai Maubec, 17000 La Rochelle, France; *office address:* Mme. Marie-José Denys, European Parliament, Centre Européen, Plateau de Kirchberg, BP 2929, Luxembourg; *phone:* Luxembourg 43001.

DEORI, Omem Moyong; Indian, Member of the Rajya Sabha; *born:* 2 July 1943, Pasighat, East Siang District, Arunachal Pradesh; *parents:* Kuttik Moyong; *married:* T.S. Deori, 1962; *children:* three s., two d; *education:* St. Mary's College, Shillong, BA; *party:* Congress Party; *political career:* Mem., Arunachal Pradesh Social Welfare Advisory Board, 1963, Vice Chmn., 1975-79, Chmn., 1979-84; Chmn., Public Implementation Cttee. in Daporijo and Tezu, 1974; organised State Level Seminar on Women, 1975; Mem., Telecommunications Board, North-East region; Mem., Implementation Cttee. for commemoration of the 40th Anniversary of India's Independence and Pandit Jawaharlal Nehru Centenary; Mem. of the Rajya Sabha, 1984-; Mem., Cttee. on Subordinate Legislation, Rajya Sabha, 1988-; *interests:* welfare of women, children and youth; *memberships:* National Childrens' Board, New Delhi; *honours and awards:* Gold Medal for social work, Administrator of the Union Territory, 1975; PADMASHREE for social service, 1984; *recreations:* gardening, horticulture, travelling; *private address:* P. Sector - 4, Itanagar, Arunachal Pradesh; *office address:* Shrimati Omem Deori, Rajya Sabha, Parliament House, New Dehli 110 011, India; *phone:* (11) 389977; 389997.

de PADILLA, María Luisa Beltranena; Guatemala, Minister of Education and Culture; *office address:* Ms María Luisa Beltranena de Padilla, Ministry of Education and Culture, Palacio Nacional, Guatemala City, Guatemala; *phone:* (02) 21212: 20162.

DE PANAFIEU, Françoise Marie-Thérèse; French, Deputy; *born:* 12 December 1948, Moyeuvre, Moselle, France; *parents:* François Missoffe and Hélène Missoffe (née de Mitry); *married:* Guy de Panafieu, 1970; *children:* Thierry, Charlotte, Marc; *education:* Institute, la Tour; sociology degree, University of Paris; diploma, Paris Chamber of Commerce and Industry; *party:* Rassemblement pour la République (RPR, Rally for the Republic); *political career:* adviser to Deputy for 17th arrondissement of Paris, 1974-79; councillor, Paris (17th arrondissement), 1979-80; Deputy mayor, Paris, responsible for extra curricular matters, 1980-83; councillor, Paris (16th arrondissement), 1983; Deputy mayor, Paris, responsible for culture, 1983-; Deputy, Paris, 1986-; *professional career:* executive, personnel recruitment company, 1970-73; *private address:* 5 Square de l'Avenue-du-Bois, 75116 Paris, France; *office address:* Mme. Françoise de Panafieu, L'Assemblée Nationale, 126 rue de L'Université, 75355 Paris, France.

de ST. JORRE, Danielle; Seychelles, Minister of Planning and External Affairs; *office address:* Ms Danielle de St. Jorre, Ministry of Planning and External Affairs, PO Box 656, Victoria, Mahe, Seychelles.

DETIEGE, Leona Maria; Belgian, Secretary of State for Pensions; *born:* 26 November 1942, Antwerp, Belgium; *parents:* A Frans Detiége and Clementina Detiége (née Claes); *children:* Maya; *languages:* Dutch, French, English, German; *education:* College of Governmental Commerce, Antwerp, Bachelor Commercial and Financial Science, 1960-64, then Agrégation (qualified teacher) in Secondary School Education; *party:* Socialistische Partij (SP, Socialist Party); *political career:* Administrative Sec. and Assistant Cllr., Research Service for Ministry of Economic Affairs, dealing with problems of employment in industrial sectors, 1964-77; special Adviser, Cabinet of Economic Affairs for Ministers Leburton, Cools, Simonet and Claes, 1970-74; assigned to Planning Office, 1972-77; Provincial Cllr., Antwerp, 1974-77; Alderman, Antwerp, 1977-82; Deputy, Antwerp,1977-; mem. Interparliamentary Council of Benelux, until 1988; Sec. of State for Pensions, May 1988-; *professional career:* President, Belgian CIRIEC, until May 1988; Vice-President, Belgian COOP; President, OIVO (a consumer association), until May 1988; President, Flemish Opera; Nat. Pres. Socialist Women; Head Master, Adult Education Centre, IEVG Antwerp; *private address:* Cornelius Broeckxstraat 11, 2030 Antwerp, Belgium; *office address:* Ms Leona Detiège, 10 rue de l'Industrie, 1040 Brussels, Belgium.

DEWARE, Mabel Margaret; Canadian, Senator; *born:* 9 August 1926, Moncton, New Brunswick, Canada; *married:* Ralph Deware; *children:* Kimberly, Joanne, Peter, Michael; *party:* Progressive Conservative; *political career:* elected to New Brunswick Legislature, 1978, 1982; Minister of Labour and Manpower, 1978-82; Minister of Community Colleges, 1983-85; Minister of Advanced Education, 1985-87; Chairperson, Canadian Delegation to Geneva on Education; Govt. appointed delegate, Int. Conference on Decade for Women, Copenhagen; delegate, World Conference on Labour Issues, Paris; *memberships:* former Pres., YWCA Moncton; Mem., Moncton Family YMCA

65

Board of Dirs; *professional career:* Mem., Moncton team winners of Canadian Ladies Curling Championship, 1963; included in New Brunswick Hall of Fame, 1976; Canadian Hall of Fame, as Curler/Builder, 1987; *honours and awards:* Queen's Medal, for contribution to sports, 1982; Elmer Freytag Memorial Award, 1983, first woman to win this annual curling award; *clubs:* Dir., Silver Broom Cttee., Moncton World Curling Championship, 1980; *office address:* The Honourable Senator Mabel Deware, Senate, Parliament Buildings, Wellington Street, Ottawa, Ontario K1A OA4, Canada; *phone:* (613) 992 4416.

D'HONDT-VAN OPDENBOSCH, Paula; Belgian, Senator; *born:* 27 August 1926, Kerksken; *education:* Catholic Social School Brussels, social assistant, 1947; *party:* Christelijke Volkspartij (CVP, Christian Social Party); *political career:* member and militant supporter since its foundation, CVP party, 1945-; local councillor, Kerksken, 1952-64; alderman, Kerksken, 1964-76; provincial Senator, East Flanders, 1974-80; Senator (succession), 1980-88; Senator (directly elected), 1981-; Parliamentary Under Secretary, PTT (Post, Telegraph and Telephones), 1981-88; Minister of Public Works, 1988-89; Royal Commissioner for Migrant Policy 1989-; *professional career:* mem. Catholic Workers Wives (KAV), 1947-48; social assistant, NMBS, Aalst-Oudenaarde, 1948-74; *private address:* Ferdinand van Hoeymissenstraat 7, 9451 Haaltert (Kerksken), Belgium; *office address:* Ms Paula D'Hondt-van Opdenbosch, Senate, Palais de la Nation, Place de a Nation 1, 1000 Brussels, Belgium.

DIAZ, Annalisa; Italian, Deputy; *born:* 19 January 1935, Cagliari, Italy; *children:* two; *education:* Degree in Jurisprudence; *party:* Independent Left Parly. Group; *political career:* mem. Regional Directorate, Co-operative league of Sardinia; Deputy, Cagliari-Sassari-Nuoro-Oristano, on PCI lists as Independent, mem. Cttee. on Public and Private Work; *professional career:* Researcher, Study Centres on the position of Women, 'La Tarantola' Co-operative, Cagliari; *office address:* Ms Annalisa Diaz, Camera dei Deputati, Montecitorio, 00186 Rome, Italy.

DIERNER-AEPPLI, Verena; Swiss, Member of the Nationalrat; *born:* 27 March 1949, Zürich, Switzerland; *children:* two; *education:* graduate, business school; *party:* Grüne Partei der Schweiz (Green Party of Switzerland); *political career:* Mem. of the Nationalrat for Buch a. Irel, Canton of Zürich, 1987-; *professional career:* primary school teacher; *office address:* Frau Verena Dierner-Aeppli, Nationalrat/Conseil National, Secretariat-General, Parlamentsgebäude, 3003 Berne, Switzerland; *phone:* Berne 619711.

DIEULANGARD, Marie-Madeleine Jeanne Colette; French, Deputy; *born:* 19 July 1936, Saint-Nazaire, Loire-Inférieure, France; *married:* Bernard Dieulangard, 1961; *children:* two; *party:* Parti Socialiste (PS, Socialist Party); *political career:* Town Councillor, 1977, Deputy Mayor, 1983-, of Saint-Nazaire; Deputy for Loire-Atlantique, 8th constituency, 1988-; *professional career:* medical secretary; *recreations:* music, family; *office address:* Mme. Marie-Madeleine Dieulangard, L'Assemblée Nationale, 126 rue de L'Université, 75355, Paris, France; *phone:* Paris 40 63 60 00; *fax:* Paris 42 60 99 03.

DIEZ DE RIVERA ICAZA, Carmen; Spanish, Member of the European Parliament; *born:* 29 August 1942, Madrid, Spain; *education:* Univ. of Madrid, International Section, licentiate of political sicence; Univ. of Madrid, diploma in hispanic studies; Madrid Central School of Languages, diploma in French; studies in Oxford, UK, Paris, France and Switzerland in English, French and German; *party:* Partido Socialista Obrero Español (PSOE, Spanish Socialist Workers' Party); *political career:* dir., Cabinet of the Pres. of the Government, 1976-77; MEP, Socialist Group, 1987, re-elected 1989-; mem., Commissions for the environment, public health, consumer protection and petitions in the European Parliament; founder mem. joint European environmental pressure group, 1988-; *professional career:* employee, Revista de Occidente, philosophical magazine; employee, Studies and Publications Society; superior teaching prof., three courses of lectures, Costa de Marfil, Afrcia (with French co-operation); head of services of international relations and UER, for RTVE; *honours and awards:* award of the Friends of the Earth Federation for working for the environment in the European Parliament; *publications:* Nueves Aires para Europa, V Torria, 1989; *clubs:* Peace Movement; Movement for Disarmament and Freedom; Commission for the Provision of Aid to Refugees; *office address:* Ms Carmen Diez de Rivera Icaza, European Parliament, Centre Européen, Plateau de Kirchberg, BP 2929, Luxembourg.

DIGNANI GRIMALDI, Vanda; Italian, Deputy; *born:* 25 July 1930, San Severino, Macerata, Italy; *education:* Degree; *party:* Partito Democratico della Sinistra (PDS, Party of the Democratic Left); *political career:* Pres. of provincial section, Italian Blind Union; Councillor, Macerata; Deputy, Parliament, Ancona-Pesaro-Macerata-Ascoli Piceno, 1983; mem. Cttee. on Internal Affairs; re-elected Deputy, 1987; mem. Committee on Social Affairs; *professional career:* Teacher; *office address:* Ms Vanda Dignani Grimaldi, Camera dei Deputati, Montecitorio, 00186 Rome, Italy.

DI PRISCO, Elisabetta; Italian, Deputy; *born:* 26 March 1950, Verona, Italy; *party:* Partito Democratico della Sinistra (PDS, Party of the Democratic Left); *political career:* Head of Women's Cttee. PCI; mem. Regional Cttee., PCI; Deputy, Verona-Padua-Vicenza-Rovigo, 1987; mem. Cttee. on Culture, Science and Teaching; *professional career:* Lecturer, Fine Arts, Verona; scene painter; *office address:* Ms Elisabetta Di Prisco, Camera dei Deputati, Montecitorio, 00186 Rome, Italy.

DIXON, Sharon Pratt; American, Mayor of Washington DC; *born:* 30 January 1944, Washington DC, USA; *parents:* Carlisle Edward Pratt and Mildred Pratt (née Petticord); *children:* Aimee Arrington, Drew Arrington; *education:* Howard Univ., BA 1965, JD, 1968; *party:* Democratic Party; *political career:* Mem., Democratic National Cttee., 1971-; Chwn., Eastern Regional Caucus, 1981; Co-Chwn., Rules Cttee.; Mem., Ad Hoc Credentials Cttee. and Judicial Cncl., Democratic National Convention, 1980; Mayor Washington DC, 1990-; *memberships:* National Women's Political Caucus; American Bar Assn; *professional career:* Assc., Pratt and Queen, 1971-; *office address:* Ms Sharon Pratt Dixon, 8227 W Beach Terrace NW, Washington DC 200112, USA.

DOBBIE, Dorothy; Canadian, Member of the House of Commons and Parliamentary Secretary to the Minister of Indian Affairs and northern Development; *office address:* Ms Dorothy Dobbie, House of Commons, Parliament Buildings, Wellington Street, Ottawa, Ontario K1A OA6, Canada; *phone:* (613) 957 3744; *fax:* 952 0874.

DOBIELINSKA-ELISZEWSKA, Teresa Katarzyna; Polish, Vice-Marshal of the Sejm (Deputy Speaker); *born:* 22 April 1941, Radomsko; *children:* two s; *education:* secondary school, Poznán; Faculty of Medicine, Medical Academy; *party:* Stronnictwo Demokratyczne (SD, Democratic Party), 1969-; *political career:* Deputy Chairperson, Voivodship Cttee. of Democratic Party, Olsztyn; elected mem. of Central Cttee. then Presidium of Democratic Party, 14th Democratic Party; 9th term Sejm deputy; *professional career:* Cancer specialist, Olsztyn, 1965, became Head of Oncology Ward, Olsztyn Municipal Hospital; *office address:* Teresa Katarzyna Dobielinska-Eliszewska, Sejm PRI, ul. Wiejska 4/6/8, 00-489 Warsaw, Poland; *phone:* (22) 28 70 01; 28 40 31.

DOBRIN, Tamara Maria; Romanian, Deputy to the Grand National Assembly; *party:* Romanian Communist Party (RCP); *political career:* Vice-Chairperson, Nat. Cncl. of Socialist Democracy and Unity Front, 1968-; Vice-Chairperson, State Cttee. for Culture and Art, Nat. Cncl. for Socialist Culture and Education, 1971-; candidate Mem., RCP Central Cttee., 1974-76; Mem., State Cncl., 1975-; full Mem., RCP Central Cttee., 1976-; Vice-Chairperson,

Women's Nat. Cncl., 1978-; Chairperson, Exec. Bureau of the Nat. Cncl. of Socialist Democracy and Unity Front, 1979-; Deputy, Grand Nat. Assembly, 1975-; *professional career:* lecturer, Univ. Institute for Modelling Art, 1963; Pro-Rector, Bucharest Univ., 1968; Prof., Bucharest Univ., 1975-; Vice-Chairperson, Red Cross Nat. Cncl., 1978-; *honours and awards:* 25th Anniversary of the Homeland Liberation, 1969; *office address:* Ms Tamara Maria Dobrin, Marea Adunare Nationala, Aleea Marii Adunari Nationale, Bucharest, Romania; *phone:* 16 21 50.

DODUNEKOVA, Penka Mihaylova (Ivanova); Bulgarian, Chairperson of the Bulgarian Communist Party Central Auditing Commission; *born:* 1930, Gabrovo district, Bulgaria; *party:* Bulgarian Communist Party (BCP); *political career:* Mem., Komsomol Central Cttee., 1954-63; official in various offices, Gabrovo Komsomol organizations, 1961; Mem., Central Cncl. of Bulgarian Trade Unions, 1961-; Mem., Gabrovo District Cttee., BCP, 1962-72, Sec., 1962-65; Chairperson, Gabrovo District Cncl. of Trade Unions, 1970-72; Sec., Central Cncl. of Bulgarian Trade Unions, 1972; Chairperson, BCP Central Auditing Commission, 1980-; *office address:* Ms Penka Dodunekova, Central Cncl. Bulgarian Trade Unions, Sofia pl. D. Blagoev 1, Bulgaria.

DOELMAN-PEL, Ali; Dutch, Member of the Second Chamber; *born:* 9 September 1932, Dordrecht, Netherlands; *education:* HBS (secondary school); Social Academy, child protection; *party:* Christen Democratisch Appel (CDA, Christian Democratic Appeal); *political career:* Mem. of town council, Hoogezand, 1974-86; Pres., CDA-group, Hoogezand town council, 1978-82; active Mem., of Hoogezand town-council, Cttees. on social affairs, ethnic minorities and the elderly, 1982-86; former Mem., Provincial States of Groningen; Mem., of Second Chamber, 1986-; *interests:* social affairs, emancipation, welfare work; *professional career:* social worker, specialized in child protection; *private address:* Beethovensingel 12, 9603 AV Hoogezand, the Netherlands; *office address:* Mevr. Ali Doelman-Pel, Tweede Kamer der Staten-Generaal, Binnenhof 1A, Postbus 20018, The Hague, Netherlands.

DOHNAL, Johanna; Austrian, Federal Minister for Women's Affairs; *born:* 14 February 1939, Vienna, Austria; *children:* two; *party:* Sozialistische Partei Österreichs (SPÖ, Socialist Party of Austria); *political career:* Mem., Wiener Kinderfreunde (Vienna Children's Friends); Mem., Vienna 14th Municipal District Cncl., 1969-79; Mem., Vienna Provincial Govt. and Municipal Cncl., 1973-79; Vienna SPÖ Exec. Official dealing with Women's Affairs, 1972-79; state Sec., Federal Chancellery, 1979-90; Federal Minister for Women's Affairs, Federal Chancellery, 1990-; set up a visitors' service for lonely elderly people; co-founder of Vienna Frauhaus (Women's House), help and refuge centre for maltreated women; *interests:* women's problems, questions of family policy, consumer protection; *professional career:* apprentice clerk in industrial firm before entering politics; *office address:* Ms Johanna Dohnal, Nationalrat, Dr. Carl Renner Ring 3, 1017 Vienna, Austria.

DOI, Takako; Japanese, Member of the House of Representatives and Chairman of the Japan Socialist Party; *born:* 30 November 1928; *education:* Doshisha Univ., Graduate School; *party:* Japan Socialist Party (JSP); *political career:* former Vice-Chairperson, JSP; eighth time elected, for Hyogo 2; JSP Chairperson, 1990-; *professional career:* lecturer, Doishisha Univ; *office address:* Ms Takako Doi, Japan Socialist Party, 1-8-1 Nagata-cho, Chiyoda-ku, Tokyo, Japan; *phone:* (03) 580 1171.

DOLE, Elizabeth Hanford; American, former Secretary at the US Department of Labour; *born:* 1936, Salisbury, North Carolina, USA; *married:* Robert J. Dole, 1975; *education:* Duke Univ., BA (Hons.), 1958; Oxford Univ., England, 1959; Harvard Univ., MA, 1960, JD, 1965; *party:* Republican Party; *political career:* Assc. Dir., Legislative Affairs and Exec. Dir., President's Cttee. for Consumer Interests, 1968-71; Dep. Dir., Office of Consumer Affairs, White House, 1971-73; Commissioner, Federal Trade Commission, Washington DC, 1973-79; Chwn., Voters for Reagan-Bush, 1980; Dir., Human Service Group, Office of Exec. Branch Management, 1980; Asst. to Pres. Reagan for Public Liaison, 1981-83; Sec., US Dept. of Transport, 1983-87; Mem., Robert Dole for Pres. Campaign, 1987-88; Sec., US Dept. of Labour, 1989-90; *memberships:* Washington Opera Board; Nominating Cttee., American Stock Exchange, 1972; Trustee, Duke Univ., 1974-; Hon. Chwn., Board of Overseers, Comprehensive Cancer Centre, 1988-; Mem., Harvard Law School Assn. Cncl.; Visiting Cttee., John F. Kennedy School of Govt., Harvard Univ., 1988-; Board of Dirs., Wolf Trap Foundation for Performing Arts; American Bar Assn; *professional career:* Attorney, Washington DC, 1967-68; *honours and awards:* Arthur S. Fleming Award for Outstanding Govt. Service, 1972-; Humanitarian Award, National Commission Against Drunk Driving, 1988; *clubs:* Phi Beta Kappa; Pi sigma Alpha; Pi Sigma Alpha; *office address:* Mrs Elizabeth Dole, US Dept. of Labour, 200 Constitution Avenue NW, Washington DC, 20210, USA.

DOMEIJ, Åsa Elisabeth; Swedish, Member of the Riksdag; *born:* 29 April 1962, Örnsköldsvik, Sweden; *parents:* Karl Ivar Domeij and Ingrid Elisabeth Domeij (née Söderholm); *languages:* English, Spanish, German; *education:* Continuation School, Science Studies, Örnsköldsvik, 1978-81; Agricultural College of Sweden,

M.Sc. in Agriculture, 1981-87; *party:* Miljöpartiet de Gröna (Green Party), 1983; *political career:* member of the Agricultural and Environmental Committees; Deputy member of the Tax Cttee.; member of the survey on revising the Law on Environmental Protection; MP, 1988-; *interests:* environmental and agricultural matters, International co-operation in environmental affairs; *professional career:* Province Agricultural Expert for the Finnmark Province Agricultural Office in Norway; *clubs:* Swedish Society for the Protection of the Environment; Norwegian Society for the Protection of the Environment; Greenpeace; *private address:* Fågelsångsrägen 21, 89171 Örnsköldsvik, Sweden; *office address:* Ms Åsa Domeij, Riksdag, Fack, S-100 12 Stockholm, Sweden.

DOMOTO, Akiko; Japanese, Member of the House of Councillors; *born:* 31 July 1932; *education:* Tokyo Women's Christian Univ; *party:* Japan Socialist Party (JSP); *political career:* elected for National, 1990; Mem., House of Cllrs. Cttee. on Foreign Affairs and the Budget, 1990-; *professional career:* Dir, Tokyo Broadcasting System; *office address:* Ms Akiko Domoto, House of Councillors, 1-7-1 Nagata-cho, Tokyo 100, Japan; *phone:* (03) 5813111.

DONAWA-McDAVIDSON, Muriel; Trinidad and Tobago, Member of the house of Representatives; *party:* People's National Movement (PNM); *political career:* one of three Mems. of PNM to survive Party's defeat in polls, 1986; active in politics for 34 years; *office address:* Ms Mureil Donawa-McDavidson, House of Representatives, Red House, St. Vincent Street, Port-of-Spain, Trinidad and Tobago; *phone:* (62) 32971/76.

DORLHAC DE BORNE, Hélène; French, former Secretary of State for the Family; *born:* 4 October 1935, Sumène, Gard, France; *parents:* Louis Roujon and Madeleine Roujon (née Gilly); *married:* Jacques Dorlhac de Borne, 1957; *children:* Corinne, Jean, Michel; *education:* Montpelier High School; Faculty of Medicine, Montpelier, doctor of medicine; *political career:* President of Gard Federation of Independent Republicans, 1973-; Sec. of State to Minister of Justice (prison conditions), 1974-76; Councillor of State Extraordinary, 1984; Sec. of State to Minister of Solidarity, Health and Social, responsible for Family Affairs, 1988; *professional career:* industrial doctor, Inter-company Medical Service, Nimes, 1967-; senior industrial medicine inspector; *recreations:* reading, travel; *office address:* Mme. Hélène Dorlhac de Borne, Ministry of Solidarity Health Social Protectiont, 127 rue de Grenelle, 75700 Paris, France.

DORMANN, Rosemarie; Swiss, Member of the Nationalrat; *born:* 27 March 1947, Luzern, Switzerland; *parents:* Viktor Dormann and Martha Dormann-Rast; *religion:* Catholic; *languages:* French, Italian;

education: primary school; secondary school; school of commerce; Florence/Italy, language study, 1969; Evening School of Social Work, Luzern, 1969-73; Diploma of Social Work; *party:* Christlichdemokratische Volkspartei der Schweiz (Christian Democratic Party); *political career:* local social worker, Littau, Jan. 1972-Aug. 75; part-time judge, lower district court, Hochdorf, since 1973; employed at Guardianship Office of Sursee and Hochdorf, Sempach, since 1975; public guardian, Guardianship Office of Sursee and Hochdorf, Sempach, since Jan. 1981; Member of Nationalrat; *professional career:* helped out at parents' agricultural co-operative and grocery; *private address:* Bertiswilstraße 70, 6023 Rothernburg, Switzerland; *office address:* Frau Rosemarie Dormann, Nationalrat/Conseil National, Secretariat-General, Parlamentsgebäude, 3003 Berne, Switzerland.

DORON, Sarah; Israeli, Member of the Knesset; *born:* 1925, Lithuania; *party:* Likud; *political career:* Tel Aviv, Yafo City Cncl.; Minister without Portfolio, 1983-84; Mem., Knesset; *office address:* Ms Sarah Doron, Knesset, Hakirya, Jerusalem 91000, Israel; *phone:* (02) 661211.

DOS SANTOS, Maria Odete; Portuguese, Deputy; *born:* 26 April 1941, Guarda, Portugal; *education:* Licenciate of Law; *party:* Partido Comunista Portugues (PCP, Portuguese Communist Party); *political career:* Mem., Administrative Cttee., Setúbal Town Council, 1974-76; Mem., Setúbal Municipal Assembly, 1979-; Deputy, Assembly of the Republic, 1980-; *professional career:* Lawyer; *office address:* Ms Maria dos Santos, Assembléia da República, Palacia de S Bento, 1296 Lisboa Codex, Portugal.

DROMBERG, Kaarina (Ritva Kaarina); Finnish, Member of the Eduskunta; *born:* 22 May 1942, Elimäki, Finland; *parents:* Väinö Hakula and Rakel Elisabet Hakula (née Koskinen); *married:* Jarl Ingmar Dromberg, 1964; *children:* Susanne, Riti; *education:* Commercial College, 1965; Commercial English Exam., 1977; Civil Defence Course, Military Academy, 1985; *party:* Kausallinen Kokoomus (KoK, National Coalition Party); *political career:* Mem., Vantaa City Cncl., 1981; mem. of Eduskunta, 1983-; Exec. Cttee., Advisory Cttee of Uusimaa MPs, 1984; Admin. Board, Delegation on Co-operation, Metropolitan District, 1985; Central Cncl., Helsinki District Planning Assn., 1985; Delegation of Central foundation for Science, 1986; Chmn., South-Vantaa Kokoomus Women Registered Assn.; Kokoomus Womens Registered Assn. of Uusimaa, Council of Consumers; *professional career:* Correspondent, Oy Ford Ab, 1965-78; Marketing Secretary, 1979-83; *honours and awards:* Medal for Merit, Central Chamber of Commerce; *recreations:*

theatre, travel, yoga; *office address:* Ms Kaarina Dromberg, Eduskunta, 00102 Helsinki, Finland.

DUDKIEWICZ, Anna Teresa; Polish, Member of the Sejm; *office address:* Ms Anna Teresa Dudkiewicz, Sejm PRI, ul. Wiejska 4/6/8, 00-489 Warsaw, Poland; *phone:* (22) 28 70 01; 28 40 31.

DUDKO, Tamara Nikolaevna; Soviet, Member of the Council of the Union; *born:* 1945, Belorussian; *party:* Communist Party of the Soviet Union; *political career:* Chwn., Partizansky Raiispolkom, Minsk, Belorussian SSR; elected from the Soviet Women's Cttee. to the Cncl. of the Union; Mem., CPD Drafting Commission; Mem., Supreme Soviet Cttees. on Soviets of People's Deputies, Development and Govt. and Self Govt; *professional career:* engineer; *office address:* Ms Tamara Nikolaevna Dudko, Council of the Union, Kremlin, Moscow, USSR.

DUNN, Jennifer Blackburn; American, Chwn., Washington State Republican Party; *born:* 29 July 1941, Seattle, Washington, USA; *parents:* John Charles Blackburn and Helen Blackburn (née Gorton); *children:* Bryant, Reagan; *education:* Univ. of Washington, 1960-62; Stanford Univ., BA, 1963; *party:* Republican Party; *political career:* Delegate, Republican Nat. Convention, 1980, 1984, 1988; Chwn., Washington State Republican Party, 1981-; US Delegate, 30th Commission on the Status of Women, Vienna, Austria; Delegate, Conservative Party Conference, Blackpool, UK, 1985; Leader, Republican Party Delegation to Kvomongtroy Nat. Congress, Taiwan, 1988; *office address:* Ms Jennifer Dunn, 37 Tatoosh Key, Bellevue, Washington 98006, USA.

DUNN, Hon. Dame Lydia; Hong Kong, Member of the Executive Council; *born:* 29 February 1940, Hong Kong; *married:* Michael David Thomas; *religion:* Catholic; *education:* St. Paul's Convent School, Hong Kong; Univ. of California, Berkeley, BS, Business Administration; Chinese Univ. of Hong Kong, LLD; *political career:* Chmn., Hong Kong Trade Development Council; Deputy Chmn., Executive Cttee., Commonwealth Parly. Assn., Hong Kong Branch; mem., General Cttee., Hong Kong Assn., United Kingdom; mem., ICAC Complaints Cttee.; Chmn., Hong Kong/Japan Business Co-operation Cttee.; mem., Hong Kong / United States Economic Co-operation Cttee.; mem., Council of the Trade Policy Research Centre, London; mem., International Council of the Asia Society; *professional career:* Executive Dir., Swire Pacific Ltd.; Chmn., Swire & Maclaine Ltd.; Chmn., Swire Loxley Ltd.; Dir., John Swire & Sons (HK) Ltd.; Dir., Cathay Pacific Airways Ltd.; Dir., Hong Kong and Shanghai Banking Co.; mem., Volvo International Advisory Board; Chmn., Camberley Enterprises Ltd.; Chmn., Swire Marketing Ltd; *honours* *and awards:* DBE, Justice of the Peace; *office address:* The Hon. Dame Lydia Dunn, Office of the Executive Council, Government Secretariat, Lower Albert Road, Hong Kong.

DUNWOODY, Hon. Gwyneth Patricia; British, Member of Parliament; *born:* 12 December 1930; *parents:* the late Morgan Phillips and Baroness Phillips of Fulham; *married:* Dr. John Elliot Orr Dunwoody, 1954; *children:* two s., one d; *party:* Labour Party; *political career:* Member of Parliament for Exeter, 1966-70, for Crewe, 1974-83 and for Crewe and Nantwich, 1983-; Parliamentary Sec., to Bd. of Trade, 1967-70; Member of the European Parliament, 1975-79, Vice-Chmn., Social Affairs Cttee., Opposition Front Bench Spokesman on Foreign and Commonwealth Affairs, 1979-80, on Health Service Affairs, 1980-83, and on Parliamentary Campaigning and Information, 1983-84; Opposition Spokesman on Transport, 1984-85; *interests:* transport; health service; the Arts; Middle East; *professional career:* Dir., Film Production Assn. of Great Britain, 1970-74; *recreations:* music; reading; *office address:* The Hon. Mrs Gwyneth Dunwoody, House of Commons, London SW1A OAA.

DUPLESSIS, Suzanne (Marie Pauline Suzanne); Canadian, Member of the House of Commons and Parliamentary Secretary to the Minister for External Relations and International Development and for the Minister of State for Indian Affairs Northern Development; *born:* 30 June 1940, Chicoutimi, Canada; *parents:* Jean-Julien Fortin and Pearl Tremblay; *married:* Maurice Duplessis, 1959; *public role of spouse:* Lawyer; *children:* Jean-Maurice, Claude; *education:* Ecole des Beaux Arts, Quebec City; Cégep de Sainte-Foy; Laval Univ., certificate in educational psychology; Laval Univ., BA visual arts; *party:* Conservative Party, 1976; *political career:* Parly. Sec. to the minister of External relations and International Development and Minister of State for Indian Affairs and Northern Development, since 1991; Parly. Sec. to the Minister of Science, June 1990-May 1991; Parly. Sec. to the Minister of State for Science and Technology, June 1987-June 1990; Sec. to the Conservative Party Caucus, 1984-85; Vice-Pres., Canada-France Inter-Parly. Assn.; Mem., Special Cttee. reviewing bilateral trade with the US and Strategic Defence Initiative (SDI), 1985; Vice-Chwn., Canadian Group of the Inter-Parly. Union; Vice-Chwn., Standing Cttee. on Research, Science and Technology; Vice-Chwn., Caucus Cttee. on Science and Technology; Vice-Chwn., Caucus Cttee. on Defence; Mem., Caucus Cttee. on Official Languages; on Regulations and other Statutory Instruments; Mem., Canadian Delegation to the Francophone Summits, Paris and Quebec City; Chwn., various legislative Cttees.; MP for Louis-Hébert, since 1984-; Alderman for city of Sainte-Foy, 1981-84; First Vice-Pres., Quebec Progressive

Conservative Assn., 1979-85; Chwn., YES Cttee. for Louis-Hérbert; *memberships:* mem., Laval Alumni Assn., 1970-, Pres., since, 1989; Exec., Louis-Fréchette Regional; School Union; Area Chwn., Red Cross Blood Drive, 1980; Board of Dirs., Fondation de l'Opéra de Québec, 1983-; Board of Dirs., Alzheimer Society; Board of Directors of the Société Rousseau-Falardeau; Member of the Chamber of Commerce and of the Community Development Cttee.; Mem., Transport Section of the Development Cttee; *professional career:* playground co-ordinator, 1966; teacher, Plastic Arts, Louis-Fréchette Regional School; *clubs:* Pres., Mont-Tourbillon Golf Club, 1978-80; Treasurer, Canadian Ladies Golf Assn., Quebec, 1979; Altrusa Club; Richelieu Club; *office address:* Mrs Suzanne Duplessis, House of Commons, Parliament Buildings, Wellington Street, Ottawa, Ontario K1A OA6, Canada; *phone:* (613) 957 3744; *fax:* 952 0874.

DURISOVA, Irena; Czechoslovakian, Member of the Slovak National Council; *born:* 26 March 1918, Pitvarov, Bratislava, Bulgaria; *party:* Komunistická Strana Ceskoslovenska (KSC, Communist party of Czechoslovakia); *political career:* Mem., illegal CP, Slovakia, 1942; Mem., illegal Regional Cttee., CP, Slovakia, Hnusta, 1942-45; took part in Slovak Rising, 1944; Chairperson, Banská Bystrica Regional Cttee., CP of Slovakia, 1949-52; Deputy to Slovak Nat. Cttee., 1948-; Mem., Central Cttee., CP of Slovakia, 1950-55; Deputy Chairman, Slovak Nat. Cncl., 1950-60; Mem., Cncl. of World Union of Democratic Women, 1950-; Chairperson, Cttee. of Czechoslovak Cttee. of Defenders of Peace (CSVOM), 1952-58; Mem., Central Cttee., CSSR, 1954-58; Mem., Presidium, Slovak Cttee. of Defenders of Peace, 1955-58; Dep. Chairperson, Slovak Elections Commission for Elections to Nat. Cttee., 1957; Mem., Central Cttee., Slovak Nat. Front, 1957-; Mem., Presidium, Slovak Nat. Cncl., 1960-64; Mem., Control and Auditing Commission at Central Cttee., CP of Slovakia, 1962-; Mem., State Population Commission, 1963-68; Mem., Slovak Elections Commission, 1964; Mem., Commission for Trade of Slovak Nat. Cncl., 1964-68; Chairperson, Slovak Cttee. of Czechoslovak Union of Women (CSSZ), 1967-69; Mem., Presidium and Dep. Chairperson, Central Cttee., CSSZ, 1967-69; Mem., Slovak Elections Commissions, 1968; Mem., Presidium of Slovak Nat. Cncl., 1969-81; Mem., Chamber of Nations Federal Assembly CSSR, 1969-; Chairperson, Central Cttee. of Slovak Union of Women (SZZ), 1969-; Mem., Slovak Nat. Cncl., 1981-; *professional career:* worked in Textile co-operative, Rimavská Sobota, 1946-48; *honours and awards:* Order of February 25th 2nd Grade, 1949; for Services in the Reconstruction, 1955; for Services - 10 Years People's Militia, 1958; Order of Labour, 1968; *office address:* Ms Irena Durisova, Slavenská národná rada, Októbrové nám. 12, 800 00 Bratislava, Czechoslovakia; *phone:* (07) 311500.

DURY, Raymonde; Belgian, Vice-President of the Socialist Group of the European Parliament; *born:* 22 July 1947, Haine St. Paul; *parents:* M. Dury and Mme. Dury (née Ducaju); *children:* Marie, Georges Antoine, Guillaume; *languages:* French, English, German; *education:* Free Univ. of Brussels, Sociology graduate, 1970; *party:* Socialist Party; *political career:* Press attaché, Socialist Group of European Parliament, 1976-82; former Mem., Superior Cncl. for Consumption, the family; former Mem., Administration Cncl. for Advanced Institue, La Cambre; Mem., Admin. Cncl., ULB; Mem., European Parliament, 1982-; Pres., Interfederal Commission of Socialist Party Women, 1985-89; Mem., Community Cncl., Jette, 1989-; Mem., Bureau, Socialist Party; Vice-Pres., Socialist Group, European Parliament, Mem., Political Commission, Intitutional Commission, Commission for women's Rights; Dep. Mem., Commission for Co-operation and Development; *interests:* women in politics, social issues, constitutional issues; *professional career:* sociologist, Nat. Secretariat of Socialist Women of Foresight, 1970-76; Pres., Socialist Women of Foresight of Jette; *publications:* Femmes et Nouvelles Technologies, edition Labor, 1986; articles in newspapers; *recreations:* classical music, opera, books; *office address:* Mevr. Raymonde Dury, European Parliament, Centre Européen, Plateau de Kirchberg, BP 2929, Luxembourg; *phone:* Luxembourg 43001.

DYBKJÆR, Lone; Danish, Member of the Folketinget; *born:* 23 May 1940, Frederiksberg, Denmark; *parents:* Kristian Vincents and Else V. F. Vincents (née Jensen); *married:* Ib Dybkjaer; *children:* Lotte, Mette; *languages:* Danish, German, English, some French; *education:* Master of Chemical Engineering, 1958-64; *party:* Radikale Venstre (Radical Social Liberal Party); *political career:* member of Folketinget, 1973-77, 1979-; Spokesman for Radikale Venstre on Environmental Policy, Energy Policy, the Labour Market and Foreign Policy Foreign Politics, 1979; Chairman of the Board for Energy, 1984-87; Chairman of the Board for Technology, 1984-88; Minister for the Environment, 1988-90; *professional career:* engineer, Danish Academy of Technological Sciences, 1964-66; engineer, Medical Engineering Cttee., 1966-70; Head of Secretariat of Information at the Technical University of Denmark, 1970-74; consultant, Academy of Technological Science, 1977, 1978-80; *honours and awards:* Europa Preis für Denkmalpflege (Europa Prize for Maintenance of Memorials), 1991; *private address:* Urbansgade 5, 2100 Copenhagen O, Denmark; *office address:* Ms Lone Dybkjær, Folketing, Christiansborg, 1240 Copenhagen K, Denmark.

DYNOWSKA, Anna; Polish, Member of the Sejm; *office address:* Ms Anna Dynowska, Sejm PRI, ul. Wiejska 4/6/8, 00-489 Warsaw, Poland; *phone:* (22) 28 70 01; 28 40 31.

E

EADS, M. Adela; American, Connecticut State Senator; *born:* Brooklyn, New York, USA; *education:* Sweet Briar College; *party:* Republican Party; *political career:* former Connecticut State Rep.; currently State Senator, District 30; ranking Mem., Education Cttee.; Asst. Republican Leader; Mem. Banks, Legislation Management, Program Revue Investigations Cttees; *office address:* Ms M. Adela Eads, 160 Macedonia Road, Kent, Connecticut 06757, USA.

ECLEO, Hon. Glenda B.; Filipino, Congresswoman; *born:* 10 May 1937, Iligan City; *parents:* the late Roberto Buray Sr. and Rufina Oliveros; *married:* Ruben E. Ecleo Sr., 1956; *public role of spouse:* undefeated Mayor of Dinagat, Surigao del Norte, Most Outstanding Mayor of the Philippines, 1980, President and Founder, Philippine Benevolent Missionaries Association Inc; *children:* Ruben Jr., Glorigen, Gracelyn, Benglen, Alan I, Alan II, Geraldine, Gwendolyn; *religion:* Roman Catholic; *languages:* Pilipino, Visayan, English; *education:* Univ. of the Visayas, BS, Education; Cebu State College, Masters, Educational Management, Doctor of Education; *party:* Laban Ng Demokratikong Pilipino (LDP); *political career:* former Senior Provincial Board Mem., Surigao del Norte, Congresswoman; *interests:* legislation on education, rural development, local development, local government, health, social services, family relations and population; *memberships:* Pres. and Founder, Don Jose Ecleo Memorial Educational Foundation; Founder and former Pres., PBMA Professionals League; Pres., PBMA Women's League; *professional career:* educator; *honours and awards:* awards and citations from: The Sovereign Order of the Knights of Malta; Asian International Institute of Professional Development; Cebu State College; Philippine Media Practitioners' Association; Asia-Pacific Youth Outreach Development, Inc.; Philippine Educational Youth Development; Asian Experimental Fellowship of the Philippines; Community District Leadership Foundation; Lion's Int. District 301-E, Philippines; Univ. of the Philippines; *publications:* Privilege and Sponsorship Speeches published in various national newspapers such as the Manila Bulletin and Philippine Daily Inquirer; *recreations:* swimming, exercising, sight-seeing, travelling; *private address:* San Jose, Surigao del Norte, Philippines; *office address:* The Hon. Ms Glenda Ecleo, 106 Swallow Drive Corner Flicker's Street, Green Meadows Subdivision, Quezon City, Philippines 1100.

ECOCHARD, Jeanine; French, Deputy; *born:* 14 September 1939, Nice, Alpes-Maritimes, France; *party:* Parti Socialiste (PS, Socialist Party); *political career:* Town Councillor for Marseilles, 1983; Regional Councillor, 1979; Federal Sec. of Socialist Party, 1985-; Deputy for Bouches-du-Rhône, 5th constituency, 1988-; *professional career:* civil servant; *office address:* Mme. Jeanine Ecochard, L'Assemblée Nationale, 126 rue de L'Université, 75355 Paris, France.

E COSTA, Oliveira; Portuguese, Secretary of State attatched to the Minister of Parliamentary Affairs; *office address:* Ms Oliveira e Costa, Ministry of Parliamentary Affairs, Rua da Imprensa a, Estrela 8, 1200 Lisbon, Portugal; *phone:* (01) 670953.

EDELEN, Mary Beaty; American, South Dakota State Representative; *born:* 9 December 1944, Vermillion, South Dakota, USA; *parents:* Donald William Beaty and Marjorie Louise Beaty (née Heckel); *married:* Joseph R; *children:* Audra Angelica, Anthony Callaghan, Jarrod Arthur; *religion:* United Church of Christ; *education:* Cottey College, 1963-64; Black Hills State College, South Dakota, 1965; Univ. of South Dakota, Vermillion, BA, 1967; Trinity Univ., Texas, MA, 1971; *party:* Republican Party; *political career:* South Dakota State Rep., District 13, 1972-81, 1983-; *professional career:* lecturer, Univ. of South Dakota, 1969-71; instructor, Yankton College, 1974-75; *office address:* Ms Mary Edelen, 311 Canby Street, Vermillion, South Dakota 57069, USA.

EDERER, Brigitte; Austrian, Member of the Nationalrat; *born:* 27 February 1956, Vienna, Austria; *education:* Vienna XXI High School, matura 1974; Vienna Univ., political economics, magisterium 1980; *party:* Sozialistische Partei Österreichs (SPÖ, Socialist Party of Austria); *political career:* official of the Young Socialists, 1970-81, including a period as Vice-Chmn.; sectional Chmn. of the Vienna/Leopoldstadt SPÖ, 1981-; Nationalrat member for Vienna, 1983-; *professional career:* employee of the Chamber of Labour, 1977-; *office address:* Frau Brigitte Ederer, Nationalrat, Dr. Karl Renner Ring 3, 1017 Vienna, Austria.

EID, Ursula; German, Member of the Bundestag; *born:* 18 May 1949, Landau/Palatinate, West Germany; *education:* Landau High School leaving examination, 1969; Univ. Hohenheim, Landbouwhogeschool Wageningen/Netherlands, Oregon State Univ./USA, Domestic Science Studies, 1969-76; degree, 1975; *party:* Die Grünen (Green Party), 1980; *political career:* mem. of cttee. for Economic Cooperation and Submarine Investigation Cttee., Bundestag; mem. of Bundestag (Baden-Württemberg list), 1985-; mem. of ÖTV trade union (Public Services, Transport and Traffic); *interests:* Work in development politics since 1976; *professional career:* research asst., Inst. for Domestic and Consumer Economics, Univ. Hohenheim, 1976-; *office address:* Frau Ursula Eid, Bundeshaus, 5300 Bonn 1, West Germany.

EJSMONT, Krystyna Stefania; Polish, Member of the Sejm; *born:* 15 February 1934, Grodno, at present USSR; *parents:* Stefan Jurowski and Leokadia Jurowska (née Lozowska); *married:* Czeslaw Ejsmont, 1952; *children:* Janina, Leszek; *religion:* Roman Catholic; *languages:* Polish, Russian; *education:* medical nursery, Lodz Medical College, 1950-54; *party:* not affiliated at present; former Mem., Polish Worker's Party; *political career:* MP, 1989-; *memberships:* Polish Assn. of Medical Nurses; *professional career:* ward supervisor, Lodz, 1954-62; general hospital nurse, Lodz, 1962-70; general nurse, Lodz, 1970-87; semi-retirement and Vice-Gen. Nurse, Lodz, 1987-; *honours and awards:* Silver and Golden Labour Crosses, Polish Govt., 1974 and 1978; Great Labour Cross, 1989; various professional awards and medals; *publications:* articles in medical magazines; *clubs:* MP's Labour Club; *recreations:* house-keepking, reading, theatre, opera; *private address:* Lodz, Olimpijska Str. 7/13, Poland; *office address:* Ms Krystyna Ejsmont, Sejm PRI, ul. Wiejska 4/6/8, 00-489 Warsaw, Poland; *phone:* (22) 28 70 01; 28 40 31.

ELIZABETH II, Queen of Great Britain and Northern Ireland and of Her other Realms and Territories (succeeded to the Throne, 6 February 1952); Elizabeth Alexandra Mary; British, Her Majesty Queen Elizabeth II; *born:* 21 April 1926, London, UK; *parents:* HRH Prince Albert Duke of York, later HM King George VI and Duchess of York, now HM Queen Elizabeth the Queen Mother; *married:* HRH Prince Philip, Duke of Edinburgh, 1947; *children:* Prince Charles Philip Arthur George, Prince of Wales; Princess Anne Elizabeth Alice Louise, Princess Royal; Prince Andrew Albert Christian Edward, Duke of York; Prince Edward Antony Richard Louis; *political career:* succeeded to The Throne following Her father's death, 6. Feb. 1952; *office address:* Her Majesty Queen Elizabeth II, Private Office, Buckingham Palace, London SW1.

ELLES, Baroness (cr. 1972, Life Peer) Diana Louie Elles; British, Member of the House of Lords; *born:* 19 July 1921, Bedford, UK; *parents:* Col. Stewart Newcombe and Elisabeth Newcombe (née Chaki); *married:* Neil Elles, 1945; *children:* Rosamund, James; *religion:* Anglican; *languages:* French, Italian; *education:* schools in London, Paris and Florence; University College, London, BA, 1941; *party:* Conservative Party; *political career:* House of Lords, 1972-; Chmn., Cons. Int. Office, 1973-79; UK delegate, European Parliament, 1973-75; mem., UN Sub-Commission on Discrimination and Minorities, 1974-75; Member of European Parliament, 1979-89; Vice-Pres., 1982-87; Chmn., Legal Affairs Cttee., 1987-89; Mem., European Communities Select Cttee., House of Lords, 1990-; *interests:* Foreign affairs; European Community Law; *professional career:* barrister, 1956-; UK Vice-Pres., Assn. of European Lawyers, 1987-; counsel, Van Bael and Bellis, Brussels, 1989-; *honours and awards:* Life Peerage, 1972; *publications:* Human Rights of Aliens, 1978; Report on European Political Co-operation, 1981; Perceptions of European Parliament, 1983; Single European Act, 1989; *clubs:* Int. Law Assn; Royal Inst. of Int. Affairs; *recreations:* music, languages; *private address:* 75 Ashley Gardens, London SW1, UK; *office address:* Baroness Elles, House of Lords, London SW1A 0PW.

ELLIOT OF HARWOOD, Baroness (cr. 1958, Life Peer) Katharine Elliot; British, Member of the House of Lords; *born:* 15 January 1903; *parents:* Sir Charles Tennant Bt. and Margurite Lady Tennant; *married:* the late Rt. Hon. Walter Elliot MC, MP, 1934; *public role of spouse:* Minister of Agriculture, 1934-36; Sec. of State for Social Services, 1936-38; Minister of Health and Local Govt., 1938-41; *religion:* Protestant; *languages:* French; *education:* private school education; *party:* Conservative Party; *political career:* mem., Women's Consultative Cttee., Min. of Labour and Nat. Service, 1941- 51, 1958-69; mem., Markham Commission on the Women's Services, 1942; councillor, Roxburghshire County Council, 1946-75; mem., Home Office Advisory Cttee. on Treatment of Offenders, 1946-64; Chmn., Women's Nat. Advisory Cttee., Conservative Party, 1954-57; UK Delegate to UN General Assembly, 1954, 1956, 1957; Chmn., Nat. Union of Cons. and Unionist Assns., 1957; House of Lords, 1958-; Chmn., Consumer Cncl., 1963-68; mem., EEC Agricultural Cttee., House of Lords; Joint Pres., UN Assn., 1985; Pres., Anglo-Israeli Association, 1978-90; *interests:* social services, local government, agriculture; *professional career:* farmer; mem., King George V Jubilee Trust, 1936-68; trustee, Carnegie UK Trust 1937-85; Chmn., Nat. Assn. of Mixed Clubs and Girls Clubs, 1939-49; Chmn., Advisory Cncl. For Child Care Scotland, 1957-66; JP, 1968; *honours and awards:* CBE 1946; DBE, 1958; Hon. LLD, Glasgow Univ., 1959 *clubs:* Anglo-Israel Assn. (Pres.); Pres., United Nations Association (Great Britain); *recreations:* foxhunting golf, music; *private address:* Harwood, Bonchester Bridge, Hawick, Roxburghshire, UK; *office address:* Baroness Elliot of Harwood, House of Lords, London SW1A 0PW.

ELLIS, Phyllis Mary; British, Member of the European Parliament; *born:* 20 January 1939, Penisarwaun Caernarfon, Wales, UK; *parents:* William Thomas Ellis and Ellen Elizabeth Ellis (née Jones); *religion:* Calvinistic Methodist; *languages:* Welsh, English, French; *education:* Ysgol Gynradd Penisarwaun; Ysgol Brynrefail; Coleg Santes Fair Bangor; *party:* Plaid Cymru; *political career:* Sec., Plaid Cymru, Rhanbarth Arfon, 1967-; Sec., Gwynedd Talaith, 1979-; Women's Pres., Plaid Cymru, 1972-83; Community Cllr., 1973-; Deputy Treasurer, Plaid Cymru, 1983-; *interests:* Welsh literature and drama, local history; *professional career:* headteacher, 1960-89; *private address:* Rhosfair, Penisarwaun, Caernarfon, LL55 3PG, Wales; *office address:* Ms Phyllis Ellis, European Parliament, Centre Européen, Plateau de Kirchberg, BP 2929, Luxembourg.

ELMALAN, Mireille C.; French, Member of the European Parliament; *born:* 8 January 1949; *party:* Parti Communiste Français (PCF, French Communist Party); *political career:* Mem., PCF Central Cttee.; MEP, 1989-; *private address:* 28 allée de la Clavelière, 693100 Pierre-Benite, France; *office address:* Mme. Mireille C. Elmalan, European Parliament, Centre Européen, Plateau de Kirchberg, BP 2929, Luxembourg; *phone:* Luxembourg 43001.

ELSTNER, Helga; German, President of Hamburg; *education:* Univ. Frankfurt, 1947; *political career:* Min. Dir., Federal Ministry of Youth, Family and Health Affairs (Head of Dept. of Nutrition, Veterinary Medicine, Consumer Protection), 1971-76; Senator for Health Affairs, Hamburg, 1976- now retired; Dep. Mayor, 1978-; Pres., Bürgerschaft Hamburg, 1987-; mem. Economics and Social Cttee., EC, Brussels; *professional career:* mem. of presidency, German Cttee. of Standards; *office address:* Frau Helga Elstner, The Diet, Ratshausmarkt 1, D-2 Hamburg 1, West Germany.

EPPENBERGER, Susi; Swiss, Member of the Nationalrat; *born:* 18 October 1931, Herisau, Switzerland; *children:* three; *education:* business diploma; *party:* Freisinnig-Demokratische Partei der Schweiz (FDP, Liberal Democratic Party of Switzerland); *political career:* Mem. of the St. Gallen Cantonal Cncl., 1979-; Mem. of the Nationalrat for Nesslau, Canton of St. Gallen, 1979-; *professional career:* housewife; former secretary; business woman; *office address:* Susi Eppenberger, Nationalrat/Conseil National, Secretariat-General, Parlamentsgebäude, 3003 Berne, Switzerland; *phone:* Berne 619711.

ERNST DE LA GRAETE, Brigitte; Belgian, Member of the European Parliament; *born:* 23 April 1957, Liège, Belgium; *parents:* Ulric Ernst de la Graete and Anne Ernst de la Graete (née Tomson), 1985; *children:* Bertrand, Grégoire; *languages:* French, English, Dutch; *education:* Liège Univ., bachelor of law, 1975-80; Louvain Univ., bachelor of sociology, 1978-80; *party:* Ecolo (Ecologist Party), 1981; Les Verts Européens (European Greens); *political career:* alderman, participation, youth and sports, Liège, 1983-88; member of town council, Liège, 1988-89; member European Parliament, 1989-; *interests:* ecology, third world, political refugees, participation of women in politics, education; *professional career:* Assistant, law faculty (commercial, economical law), Univ. of Liège, 1980-82; *publications:* L'arrêt Adoui et Cornuaille et ses conséquences sur la libre circulation des personnes, 1983; *clubs:* Amnesty International, Aves, Greenpeace, Natural and Ornithologic Reserves of Belgium; *office address:* Ms Brigitte Ernst de la Graete, European Parliament, Rue Belliard 97-113, 1047 Brussels, Belgium.

ERR, Lydie Clementine Nicole; Luxembourgeios, Member of the Chamber of Deputies; *born:* 23 April 1949, Petange, Luxembourg; *languages:* French, German, English, Italian, Spanish; *education:* Girls' High School, Luxembourg, 1962-69, University entrance examination; University of Strasbourg, 1969-74, first degree in law; Strasbourg Institute of Advanced European Studies, 1974-75, diploma; *party:* Parti Ouvrier Socialiste (Socialist Workers Party), 1980; *political career:* Vice-Chmn. of Parliament, 1989-; Chmn. of Foreign Affairs Committee; ex-Chmn. of Legal Committee; Vice-Chmn. of Socialist Workers Party group; National Chmn. of Socialist Women; National Chmn. of Socialist Lawyers; member of Supervision Cttee. of Socialist Workers Party; ex-member of Environment Committee; ex-member of Letting Lease Committee; member of Constitution Committee; member of Public Security Committee; member of Legal Committee; member of Bureau of Chamber of Deputies; *interests:* environment, equality between the sexes, third and fourth world; *professional career:* barrister, Luxembourg, 1976-; solicitor, Luxembourg, 1979-; *clubs:* Michel Delvaux Circle; *office address:* Mme. Lydie Err, Chambre des Députés, rue du Marché aux Herbes, Luxembourg-Ville, Luxembourg.

EU, March Fong; American, Secretary-of-State for California; *born:* Oakdale, California; *parents:* Yuen Kong and Shiu Kong; *married:* Henry Eu, 1974; *children:* Matthew Fong, Suyin Fong, Henry, Adeline, Yvonne, Conroy, Alaric; *religion:* Unitarian; *languages:* Chinese, Spanish; *education:* Univ. of California, Berkeley, BS; Mills College, MEd; Stanford Univ., Ed.D., 1954; post-grad. study, Columbia Univ. and California State College; *party:* Democratic Party;

political career: Mem., Alameda County Board of Education, California, 1956-66, Pres., 1961-62; California State Assemblywoman, 15th District, 1967-74; delegate and Asst. Sec., Californian Delegation to the Democrat National Convention, 1968; Sec.-of-State, California, 1975-; *interests:* voter participation, crime victims assistance, crime prevention, campaign reform; *memberships:* life Mem., American Dental Hygienists Assn.; Southern California Dental Assn.; League of Women Voters; *professional career:* lecturer in Medical Health, Mills College, Oakland California; supervisor, Dental Health Education, Alameda County Schools; Dental Hygienist, Oakland Public Schools; Chair, Dental Hygiene Div., Univ. of California Medical Health Centre, San Francisco; professor of Health Education; consultant specialist in education, San Joaquin and Santa Clara County Schools; dental hygienist, WWII; *honours and awards:* Hon. LLD, Western State Univ., 1975; Hon. LLD, Univ. of San Diego, 1977; Hon. LLB, Western State Univ. and Lincoln Univ.; Phoebe Apperson Hearst Distinguished Bay Area Woman of the Year, 1967; Loyalty Day Area, VFW, 1970; Merit Citation, California Adult Education Administration, 1970; Outstanding Woman Award, National Womens' Political Caucus, 1980; Woman of Achievement, 1983; Woman of Achievemnet, various chapters of the National Federation of Business and Professional Women; One of America's 100 Most Important Women, Ladies Home Journal, 1988; numerous service, educational and industrial awards for public service; *publications:* The Sons of Chang; *clubs:* Business and Professional Women's Club; Ebell Club; Chinese American Citizens Alliance; Hadassah; AAUW; *recreations:* Chinese brush painting, gardening; *office address:* Mrs March Fong Eu, 1230 J Street, Sacramento, California 95814, USA.

EWART-BIGGS, Baroness (cr. 1981, Life Peer) Felicity Jane Ewart-Biggs; British, Member of the House of Lords; *born:* 22 August 1929; *parents:* the late Basil Fitzherbert Randall and Rena Randall; *married:* the late Christopher Ewart-Biggs, 1960; *children:* one s., two d; *religion:* Church of England; *languages:* French, German; *education:* Downe House School, Cold Ash, Newbury, Berks; *party:* Labour Party; *political career:* Pres., UNICEF-UK; House of Lords, 1981-; Opposition Front Bench Spokesman on Home Affairs, 1984-; on Overseas Development, 1987-, on Consumer Affairs, 1987-, on Foreign Affairs, 1988-; mem., Select Cttee. on Murder and Life Imprisonment, 1988-89; Mem., British-Irish Inter-Parly. Body; Opposition Whip, 1988-; *interests:* Anglo-Irish relations, penal affairs, social issues relating to the family, young people and children; *professional career:* lived in Algiers, Brussels,

Paris and Dublin during husband's service overseas (HM Diplomatic Service), 1960-76; established Christopher Ewart-Biggs Memorial Literary Prize; *honours and awards:* Hon. D.Litt., New Univ. of Ulster, 1978; *publications:* Pay Pack And Follow, 1984; Lady In The Lords, 1988; *recreations:* travel, discussion; *private address:* 63A Abingdon Villas, London W8 6XA, United Kingdom; *office address:* Baroness Ewart-Biggs, House of Lords, London SW1A 0PW.

EWING, Margaret Anne; British, Member of Parliament; *born:* 1 September 1945, Lanark, Scotland, UK; *parents:* John McAdam and Margaret Jamieson Cuthbert McAdam (née Lamb); *married:* Fergus Stewart Ewing, 1983; *public role of spouse:* solicitor; SNP NEC member, PPC Inverness Nairn Louaber; *religion:* Christian; *languages:* French, German; *education:* Univ. of Glasgow, MA, history, English, 1967; Univ. of Strathclyde, BA, economic history, 1973; *party:* Scottish National Party, 1965; *political career:* mem., Nat. Exec., Scottish National Party, 1974-; Member of Parliament, 1974-79, 1987-; Leader, SNP Parly. Group, 1987-; *interests:* Scottish self-government, education, social services; *professional career:* teacher; social services administrator; freelance journalist; *recreations:* gardening, reading; *private address:* Burns Cottage, Tulloch's Brae, Lossiemouth IV31 6QY, Scotland, UK; *office address:* Mrs Margaret Ewing, House of Commons, London SW1A OAA.

EWING, Winifred Margaret; British, Member of the European Parliament; *born:* 10 July 1929, Glasgow, Scotland, UK; *parents:* George Woodburn and Christina Bell Woodburn (née Anderson); *married:* Stewart Martin Ewing, 1956; *children:* Fergus, Annabelle, Terence; *religion:* Presbyterian; *languages:* Gaelic, German, Dutch, French, Spanish; *education:* Queen's Park School; Glasgow Univ., LLB, MA, 1952; *party:* Scottish National Party, 1949; *political career:* MP for Hamilton, 1967-70; MP for Moray and Nairn, 1974-79; Member of European Parliament for the Highlands and Islands of Scotland, 1975-; Pres., Scottish National Party, 1988-; *interests:* fishing, farming, rural and environment, transport and tourism, animal welfare; *memberships:* Law Society of Scotland, Notary Public; *professional career:* solicitor, 1952-; Pres., Glasgow Bar Assn., 1971-72; *honours and awards:* Citizen of Avignon, FR, 1986; Fellow of the Royal Society of Arts; *clubs:* Highland Club; Law Soc. of Scotland; *private address:* 52 Queen's Drive, Glasgow G42 8DD, Scotland, UK; *office address:* Ms Winifred Ewing, European Parliament, Office 3032 Belliard I, 97/113 Rue Belliard, 1047 Brussels, Belgium.

F

FAATZ, Jeanne Ryan; American, Colorado State Representative; *born:* 30 July 1941, Cumberland, Maryland, USA; *parents:* Charles Keith Ryan and Elizabeth Ryan (née McIntyre); *children:* Kristin, Susan; *education:* Univ. of Indiana, 1958-61; Univ. of Illinois, 1962; Univ. of Colorado, MA, 1985; *party:* Republican Party; *political career:* Committeewoman, Denver Rep. Precinct 121, 1971-78; currently Colorado State Rep.; Asst. Majority Leader; Chwn., Highway Legislation Review Cttee.; Mem., Transportation Cttee; *interests:* rapid transit, victims rights, education, consumer issues; *memberships:* Ft. Logan Mental Health Centre Citizens Advisory Board; Harvey Park Improvement Assn; *professional career:* teacher, Urbana Public School, 1963-66, Cherry Creek School, Englewood, Colorado, 1966-67; Sec. to Senate Majority Leader, 1976-78; speech instructor, Metropolitan State College, 1985-; *honours and awards:* Denver Post Gallery of Fame, 1976; Gates Fellowship to Harvard/John F. Kennedy School of Govt., 1984; Woman of the Year in Transportation, 1986; *recreations:* aerobics, walking, theatre, music; *office address:* Ms Jeanne Faatz, 2903 South Quitman Street, Denver, Colorado 80236, USA.

FACCIO, Adele; Italian, Deputy; *born:* 13 November 1920, Pontebba, Udine, Italy; *children:* Dario; *education:* Genoa University, Degree in Letters, 1943; *party:* European Federalist parly. Group; *political career:* Anti-Franco activist, Spain, 1948-52; Imprisoned, Florence for operating abortions in CISA clinics (Information centres for Sterilization and Abortion); Pres. Radical Party; Pres. Women's Liberation Movement, aligned to PR (Radical Party); Deputy, Parliament, Milan-Pavia, 1976; Vice-Pres. Radical Group in Parliament; Reserve Representative, Council of Europe, 1976; re-elected Deputy, 1979; mem. Cttee. on Public Works; re-elected Deputy, 1987; mem. Cttee. on Agriculture; *interests:* civil rights, refugees from Third World to Italy; sexual rights, animal rights, environment, culture, school, health homeopathy, Ayurveda; *professional career:* Assistant, Genoa University, Chair of Romance Philology 1944-48; on Editorial board of 'Underground', 'Discanto', 'Canguro' and 'Via Femminile' magazines; Founded CISA (Centre for Information on Sterilization and Abortion) Milan, 1959; writer; *office address:* Ms Adele Faccio, Camera dei Deputati, Montecitorio, 00186 Rome, Italy.

FACHIN SCHIAVI, Silvana; Italian, Deputy; *born:* 10 July 1938, Mediis, Udine, Italy; *education:* 'Luigi Bocconi', University, Milan, Degree in Foreign Literature, 1960; *party:* Partito Democratico della Sinistra (PDS, Party of the Democratic Left); *political career:* Deputy, Parliament, Udine-Belluno-Gorizia-Pordenone, 1987; mem. Cttee. on Social Affairs; *professional career:* Teacher of English, Language and Literature, Province of Udine; Teaches Didactics of Modern Languages, University of Udine; from 1971; Mem. Regional Pedagogic Centre; Head of LEND Section (Language and New Didactics), Udine; Regional President of ANILS (Nat. Association of Foreign Language Teachers) and of ANILS section, Udine; Mem. Committee of IRRSAE, Friuli, Venezia Giulia (Language teaching); Mem. Committee for the standardisation of written dialect of Friuli; Mem. editorial committee of monthly 'In Uaite'; Co-founder of CLAV (Audiovisual Linguistic Centre), University of Udine; Writer of articles, studies and columns on linguistic education in various magazines. Mem. research group, University of Udine on the 'Training of foreign language teachers in the EEC'; Currently engaged on 'Pilot scheme in bilingual education - Friuli dialect/Italian'; *publications:* Various books, articles, studies on language teaching; Research on The Formation of foreign language teaching in the EEC, published by CNR fund; Books etc on bi-lingual education; *clubs:* Fulbright scholarship to USA, 1969; British Council scholar, 1977, London; *office address:* Camera dei Deputati, Montecitorio, 00186 Rome, Italy.

FAIRBAIRN, Joyce; Canadian, Senator; *born:* 6 November 1939, Lethbridge, Alberta; *married:* Michael Gillan, 1967; *education:* Univ. of Alberta, Edmonton, BA English, 1960; Carleton Univ., Ottawa, BA Journalism, 1961; *party:* Liberal; *political career:* Senator, 1984-; Mem., Senate Cttees. on Foreign Affairs, Standing Rules and Orders, Legal and Constitutional Affairs, Special Cttee. on Terrorism and Public Safety; Special Senate Cttee. on Youth, Deputy Chairperson, Cttee. on Agriculture and Forestry; *professional career:* journalist; *office address:* Hon. Senator Joyce Fairbairn, Senate, Parliament Buildings, Wellington Street, Ottawa, Ontario K1A OA4, Canada; *phone:* (613) 992 4416.

FAITHFULL, Baroness (cr. 1975, Life Peer) Lucy; British, Member of the House of Lords; *born:* 26 December 1910; *parents:* the late Sydney Leigh Faithfull (Decd. 1916); *religion:* Church of England; *education:* Bournemouth High School; *party:* Conservative Party; *political career:* House of Lords, 1976-; fmr. mem., Swan Cttee.; Mem., Fisher Cttee.; Chmn., Cttee. on New Approaches to Juvenile Crime, 1982-; Chmn., All Party Parly. Group for Children, 1982-; *interests:* law and order, juvenile delinquency, prison population, child and family care, race relations, Nat. Trust, charity law; *memberships:* Vice-Pres., Barnardos; Hon. Mem., Cncl., NSPCC; Hon. Mem., British Paediatric Assn.; Trustee, Gracewell Clinic, Birmingham, UK; *professional career:* Sub-Warden, Birmingham Settlement, 1933-35; London County Council Education Dept., 1935-40; Regional Welfare Officer, Min. of Health, 1940-48; Inspector, Children's Dept., Home Office, 1948-58; Children's Officer, Oxford City, 1958-70; Dir. of Social Services, Oxford City, 1970-74; Cncl. mem., Dr. Barnardo's; Governor, Bessel Leigh School of Maladjusted Children; Governor, Caldecott Community, Kent; *honours and awards:* OBE, 1970; Hon. MA, Oxford Univ., 1973; Hon. D.Litt., Warwick Univ., 1978; *clubs:* Nat. Inst. of Social Work (Fmr. Cncl.); Nat. Adoption Socy. (Pres.); British Assn. of Adoption and Fostering (Vice-Pres.); Nat. Children's Bureau (Pres.); *private address:* 303 Woodstock Road, Oxford, OX2 7NY, UK; *office address:* Baroness Faithfull, House of Lords, London SW1A 0PW.

FALCUCCI, Franca; Italian, Senator; *born:* 22 March 1926, Rome, Italy; *party:* Partito della Democrazia Cristiana (DC, Christian Democrat Party), 1944; *political career:* Trade Unionist; Nat. Delegate Womens' Movement, DC, 1964-77; Political Vice-Sec., DC, 1975-76; Pres. European Womens' Union, DC, from 1978; World Vice-Pres., DC Women from 1978; elected Senator, Rome VII, 1968-; mem. Cttee. on Justice; Vice-Pres. Cttee. on Public Instruction and Fine Art; Under-Sec. of State for Public Instruction in II, IV and Vth Andreotti govt.; Confirmed as Under-Sec. of State for Public Instruction in 1st and 2nd Cossiga govt., in Forlani govt. and in 1st and 2nd Spadolini govt.; Minister for Public Instruction in 5th Fanfani govt.; Confirmed as Minister for Public Instruction in 1st and 2nd Craxi govt. and 6th Fanfani govt.; re-elected Senator, 1987; mem. Cttee. on Foreign Affairs, Emigration; *professional career:* lecturer in History and Philosophy, State Lyceums; journalist; *office address:* Ms Franca Falcucci, Senato della Repubblica, Palazzo Madama, 00100 Rome, Italy.

FALKENDER, Baroness (cr. 1974, Life Peer) Marcia Matilda Falkender; British, Member of the House of Lords; *born:* 10 March 1932, Long Buckby, UK; *parents:* Harry Field and Dorothy Field (née Cowley); *married:* George Edmund Charles Williams, 1955; *children:* two s; *religion:* Church of England; *languages:* French; *education:* High School for Girls, Northampton; Queen Mary College, London Univ., BA, history, 1954; *party:* Labour Party; *political career:* Private Sec. to Gen. Sec., Labour Party, 1954-56; Private and Political Sec. to Harold Wilson, 1956-83; Mem., Film Industry Working Party, 1975; Mem., Film Indistry Action Cttee., 1977-; House of Lords, 1974-; *interests:* film industry; *professional career:* mem., Terry Film Cttee., 1974-76; Int. Action Cttee. on the Film Industry, 1976-85; The British Screen Advisory Cttee., 1983-; Dir., Peckham Building Soc., 1986-91; Dir., South London Investment Corp., 1986; lay governor, Queen Mary and Westfield College, London Univ., 1987-; Chmn., Can Vasback Productions, 1989-91; columnist, Mail on Sunday, 1983-88; *honours and awards:* CBE, 1970; *publications:* Inside No. 10, 1972; Perspective on No. 10, 1983; *clubs:* Reform Club; *recreations:* film, New Age, gardening; *private address:* 3 Wyndham Mews, Upper Montagu St., London W1H 1RS, UK; *office address:* Baroness Falkender, House of Lords, London SW1A 0PW.

FALKMER, Karin Gunnel; Swedish, Member of the Riksdag; *born:* 16 August 1936, Malmö, Skåne, Sweden; *parents:* John Pontus Arthur Nilsson and Emmy Gunhild Nilsson (née Lundstedt); *married:* Lars Gunner Falkmer, 1958; *children:* Göran, Charlotte, Niklas; *religion:* Protestant, Ch. of Sweden; *languages:* English and German; *education:* Higher School Certificate, 1955, Exam for the Gymnastics and Sports High School in Stockholm, 1958; Special Teacher Education, 1980-81; *party:* Moderata Samlingspartiet (Moderate Party), 1960; *political career:* Chairwoman of the Moderate Assoc. in Skinnskatteberg, 1985-; Member of the Board of NTS, 1988-; MP, 1987-; *interests:* trade and industrial affairs; *professional career:* physical training master, 1959-87; *clubs:* Swedish Society of PT Masters; The Orienteering Club 'Hedströmmen'; The Fitness Club 'Royal'; The Astley Gallery's Art Society; The Skinnskatteberg Chamber Music Society; *office address:* Ms Karin Falkmer, Riksdag, Fack, S-100 12 Stockholm, Sweden.

FAN HSU, Hon. Rita Lai-Tai; Hong Kong, Member of the Legislative Council; *born:* 20 September 1945, Shanghai, China; *married:* Fan Sheung-tak, Stephen; *children:* two; *education:* Univ. of Hong Kong, B.Sc. Gen.; Univ. of Hong Kong, Certificate in Personnel Management; Univ. of Hong Kong, M.Soc.Sc., Psychology; *political career:* Chmn., Board of Education; mem., Education Commission; Council mem., Family Planning Assn. of Hong Kong; Honorary Adviser, Hong Kong Subsidised Secondary Schools Council; mem., Ho Tung Technical School for Girls Advisory Cttee.; Associate Director, Academic Services and Continuing Education, Hong Kong Polytechnic; *memberships:* Hong Kong Psychological Society; British Psychological Society; *honours and awards:*

OBE, Justice of the Peace; *office address:* The Hon. Ms Rita Fan Hsu, The Legislative Council, Government House, Hong Kong.

FANKHAUSER, Angeline; Swiss, Member of the Nationalrat; *born:* 25 July 1936, La Rippe, VD, Switzerland; *children:* two; *education:* teacher training; *party:* Sozialdemokratische Volkspartei der Schweiz (SDP, Social Democratic Party of Switzerland); *political career:* Mem. of the Binningen district Cncl., (Legislative branch) 1972-83; Mem. of the Binningen borough Cncl., 1976-83; Mem. of the Nationalrat for Binningen, Canton of Basel-Land, 1983-; *professional career:* teacher, adult education lecturer, School for Social Work Studies, Dept. of Education; *office address:* Frau Angeline Fankhauser, Nationalrat/Conseil National, Secretariat-General, Parlamentsgebäude, 3003 Berne, Switzerland; *phone:* Berne 619711.

FAREMO, Grete; Norwegian, Minister of Development Co-operation; *born:* 16 June 1955, Arendal; *parents:* Osmund Faremo and Tora Faremo; *married:* Magne Lindholm (Co-habitant); *public role of spouse:* Director of the Norwegian Labour Party; *children:* Oda; *languages:* English, German; *education:* LLB, 1978; *party:* Norwegian Labour Party; *political career:* Minister of Development Co-operation, Nov. 1990-; *memberships:* Board Mem., Labour Party Forum for Art and Culture; *professional career:* served in Ministry of Finance for one year and NORAD, the Directorate for Development Co-operation, for four years; appointed Head of Div., Ministry of Development Co-operation, 1984; Cultural Dir., Aker Brygge (business, shopping and leisure complex), Oslo, 1986; *private address:* Theresesgt. 7B, 0358 Oslo, Norway; *office address:* Ms Grete Faremo, Ministry of Foreign Affairs, 7 Juniplassen 1, P.O. Box 8114 Dep, 0032 Oslo 1, Norway; *phone:* (02) 34 36 00; *fax:* 412286.

FASSE, Annette; German, former Member of the Bundestag; *born:* 6 September 1947, Imsum/Kreis Cuxhaven, West Germany; *children:* two; *religion:* Protestant; *education:* secondary school; College for Nursery School Teachers, Bremerhaven; qualification as state registered nursery school teacher; *party:* Sozialdemokratische Partei Deutschlands (SPD, Social Democratic Party of Germany), since 1972; *political career:* member of local association, SPD, Langen; member of district association, SPD, Cuxhaven; member of county Exec. board, SPD, Niedersachsen; member of district assembly, Cuxhaven; mem. of Bundestag, party list of Niedersachsen, 1987; *professional career:* nursery school teacher and head teacher; teacher, special school for physically handicapped children, district authority Lüneburg; member of Arbeiterwohlfahrt (AWO, Labour Welfare Organization); member of Gewerkschaft; *private*

address: 2857 Langen-Imsum, West Germany; *office address:* Frau Annette Fasse .

FATIN, Hon. Wendy Frances; Australian, Minister for Local Government and Minister assisting the Prime Minister for the Status of Women; *born:* 10 April 1941, Harvey, Western Australia; *parents:* Jim Fimmel and Nell Fimmel; *children:* one s., one d; *education:* registered nurse, Western Australia; Bachelor of Applied Science (Nursing) (WAIT); Fellow of the College of Nursing, Australia; *party:* Australian Labor Party; *political career:* Sec., Labor Party, Subiaco Branch, 1977; State Pres., Labor Women's Organisation, 1977; Sec. Labor Party, Maylands Branch, 1982; Mem., Labor Party State Executive, Western Australia, 1982-83; Mem., Labor Party Administrative Cttee., Western Australia, 1983-84; elected for Canning, Western Australia, 1983-84, then Brand, 1984-; Conferences, Delegations and Visits: Mem., Observer Delegation to 6th Working Cttee. and Gen. Assembly, Association of South-East Asian Nations Inter-Parly. organisation, Singapore, 1983; Mem., Parly. Delegation, China, 1985; Mem., Joint Party Delegation on Agricultural and Trade Matters, USA and Canada, 1987; Mem., Labor Party Administrative Cttee., Western Australia, 1983-84; Delegate, Labor Party National Conference, 1984 and 1986; Mem., Labor Party National Policy Cttees. on Social Policy and Economic Policy, 1985; Committee Service: Mem. of the House of Representatives Standing Cttee. for Expenditure, 1985-87; for Community Affairs, 1987-; for Employment, Education and Training, 1987-; Mem., Labor Party National Policy Cttee. on the Status of Women, 1987-; Minister for Local Government, 1990-; Minister assisting the Prime Minister for the Status of Women, 1990-; *professional career:* adviser to the Minister for Repatriation and the Minister for Social Security, 1974-75; political research assistant; founder mem., Women's Electoral Lobby, Australia; *recreations:* reading, classical music, gardening; *office address:* The Hon. Ms Wendy Fatin, Parliament House, Canberra, ACT 2600, Australia.

FEGHALI, Jandira; Brazilian, Federal Deputy; *born:* 17 May 1957, Curitiba; *parents:* Albert Feghali and Nilza Mussalem Feghali; *education:* UERJ, Rio de Janeiro, medicine, 1974-79; *party:* Partido Communista do Brasil (PCDB, Communist Party of Brasil, pro-Albanian); *political career:* State Deputy, 1987-91; Federal Deputy for Rio de Janeiro, 1991-95; founder, Women's Union of Rio de Janeiro; *professional career:* doctor in residence, UERJ Clinic, 1980-81 and Bonsucesso-Inamps General Hospital, 1981-82; cardio-pediatrician, Rio de Janeiro; Pres., Nat. Assn. of Medical Residents, 1983-84; Dir., Doctors' Union, Rio de Janeiro, 1984-86; Dir., Assn. of Hospital Functionaries of the Bonsucesso-Inamps General Hospital, 1985-86; Fiscal Cllr., Doctors'

Union, Rio de Janeiro, 1987-89; *office address:* Ms Jandira Feghali, Chamber of Deputies, Praça dos 3 Poderes, Ed. Principal, 70160 Brasilia, DF, Brazil; *phone:* (61) 225 2885.

FEKTER, Dr. Maria Theresia; Austrian, State Secretary for Building and Tourism; *born:* 1956; *children:* one d; *education:* graduate of law and commerce; *party:* Österreichische Volkspartei (ÖVP, Austrian People's Party); *political career:* town Cllr., Attenang-Puckheim, for five years; Mem. of the Nationalrat, 1990-; Leader, ÖVP Parly. Group; State Sec. for Building and Tourism, Ministry of Economic Affairs; *professional career:* Manager, family building firm, Upper Austria; *office address:* Dr. Maria Fekter, Federal Ministry for Economic Affairs, Bundesministerium fuer wirtshaftliche Angelegenheiten, Stubenring 1, A-1014, Vienna, Austria.

FELDGRILL-ZANKEL, Ruth; Austrian, Federal Minister of the Environment, Youth and Family Affairs; *born:* 15 September 1942, Kapfenberg, Styria, Austria; *children:* one s; *education:* secondary education, Bruck an der Mur, Styria; school leaving exam., 1960; North Phoenix High School, Phoenix Arizona, 1960-61; College of Commerce, Vienna, 1961-65; *party:* Österreichische Volkspartei (ÖVP, Austrian People's Party); *political career:* press spokesperson, Styrian provincial headquarters, ÖVP, until 1987; Mem., ÖVP leadership, Graz municipal Branch, 1984; Chairperson, Styrian provincial Women's Section, Austrian Federation of Workers and Employees (ÖAAB), 1987; City Cllr., Graz, 1987, responsible for questions connected with tourism, real-estate, veterinary medicine, market affairs and trade; Mem., ÖVP Federal Party Leadership, 1989-; Dep. Party Chairperson, Styrian provincial ÖVP, 1989; Federal Minister of the Environment, Youth and Family Affairs, 1991-; *professional career:* Viennese advisory institute for the siting of establishments, 1961-65; Journalist, Südost-Tagespost, Graz, 1968-70; journalist, municipal information service, Graz; *office address:* Ms Ruth Feldgrill-Zankel, Ministry of the Environment, Youth and the Family, Radetzkystrasse 2, A-1030 Vienna, Austria.

FENNER, Dame Peggy Edith, DBE, 1986; British, Member of Parliament; *born:* 12 November 1922; *married:* Bernard S. Fenner, 1940; *children:* one d; *education:* L.C.C. School, Brockley; *party:* Conservative Party; *political career:* mem., Sevenoaks Urban District Council, 1957-71, Chmn., 1962-63; mem., West Kent Divisional Exec., 1963-72; contested Newcastle-under-Lyme, 1966; Parliamentary Sec. to the Minister of Agriculture, Fisheries and Food, 1972-79; mem., British Delegation to the European Parliament, 1974; mem., Select Cttee.s on Public Expenditure and the

Civil List; Parliamentary Sec., Agriculture, 1981-86; Fellow, Industry and Parliament Trust; UK Delegate, Council of Europe and Western Union; mem., Select Cttee. on Member Interests; MP for Rochester and Chatham, 1970-74, 1979-83; MP for Medway, 1983-; *private address:* 12 Star Hill, Rochester, Kent, UK; *office address:* Dame Peggy Fenner, House of Commons, London SW1A OAA.

FERNANDEZ, Matilde; Spanish, Minister for Social Welfare; *office address:* Ms Matilde Fernandez, Ministry for Social Affairs, José Abascal 39, Madrid 28071, Spain.

FERNEX, Solange; French, Member of the European Parliament; *born:* 15 April 1934; *party:* Verts (Green); *political career:* Municipal Govt., 1977-; MEP, 1989-; *office address:* Mme. Solange Fernex, European Parliament, Centre Européen, Plateau de Kirchberg, BP 2929, Luxembourg; *phone:* Luxembourg 43001.

FERRAGUTI VALLERINI, Isa; Italian, Senator; *born:* 2 December 1942, Carpi, Modena, Italy; *party:* Partito Democratico della Sinistra (PDS, Party of the Democratic Left); *political career:* mem. Women's Cttee., PCI, 1970-75; Regional Head, Women's section, Emilia-Romagna, 1976-1980; mem. Regional Council; Head of Health and Social Security; Confirmed 1985, Vice-Pres. of Cttee. on Health; and Deputy Head of PCI Council group; elected Senator, Carpi, 1987; Sec. Presidency of the Senate; mem. Cttee. on Labour and Social Security; *professional career:* factory worker; *office address:* Ms Isa Ferraguti Vallerini, Senato della Repubblica, Palazzo Madama, 00100 Rome, Italy.

FERRARO, Geraldine; American, former Member of the House of Representatives; *born:* 26 August 1935, Newburgh, New York, USA; *parents:* Dominick Ferraro and Antonetta Ferraro (née Corrieri); *married:* John Zaccaro, 1960; *children:* Donna, John, Laura; *religion:* Roman Catholic; *education:* Marymount College, BA, 1956; Fordham Univ. School of Law, 1960; *party:* Democratic Party; *political career:* Mem., House of Reps., New York District 9, 1979-85; Democrat Nominee for Vice-Pres., 1984; candidate for US Senate (NY), 1992; *memberships:* Board of National Democrat Inst.; International Inst. for Women Political Leaders; Board of Dirs.: Inst. of Business Ethics, New York; New York Easter Seal Society Inc., New York; ROCK (Reclaim Our City's Kids) Foundation; National Democratic Inst. for International Affairs; Pension Rights Centre, Washington DC; Sight Savers Int., Washington DC; Board of Visitors, Fordham Univ. School of Law, New York; Board of Advocates, Planned Parenthood Federation of America, New York; Vice-Pres. and Dir., P. Zaccaro Co. Inc., New York; Co-founder, Centre for National Independence in Politics (CNIP); *professional career:* private law practice, 1961-

74; Asst. District Attorney, Queens County, 1974-78; *honours and awards:* Hon. Degrees: Marymount Manhattan College, 1982; NYU Law School, 1984; Hunter College, 1985; Plattsburgh College, 1985; College of Boca Raton, 1989; Virginia State Univ., 1989; Briarcliffe College of Business, 1990; Distinguished Service Award, Potsdam College, 1991; *publications:* Ferraro, My Story, 1985; *private address:* 22 Deepdene Road, Forest Hills, New York 13375, USA; *office address:* Ms Geraldine Ferraro, 108-18 Queens Blvd., Forest Hills, New York 13375, USA.

FERREIRA, Maria Luísa Lourenço; Portuguese, Deputy; *born:* 19 January 1936, Coimbra, Portugal; *education:* Primary Teachers' Training Course; *party:* Partido Social Democrata (PSD, Social Democratic Party); *political career:* Deputy, Assembly of the Republic, 1987-; *professional career:* former Primary School Teacher; Co-ordinator of Adult Education, Ansiao; *office address:* Ms Maria Ferreira, Assembléia da República, Palacia de S Bento, 1296 Lisboa Codex, Portugal.

FERRER, Concepció; Spanish, Member of the European Parliament; *born:* 27 January 1938, Ripoll, Spain; *parents:* Miguel Ferrer Griera and María Casals Jofre; *married:* Pedro Mateo Castiñeira, 1960; *children:* Maria, Pere, Eva, Blanca, Manuel; *religion:* Catholic; *languages:* French; *education:* Univ. of Barcelona, licentiate of Romance languages, 1955-60; Univ. of Strasbourg, specialisation courses, 1958-59; *party:* Unió Democràtica de Catalunya (UDC, Catalan Democratic Union Party); *political career:* mem. City Council of Figueres, 1979-80; Deputy, Regional Parliament of Catalonia, and mem. Commission of Culture, 1980-87; Vice-Pres., Parliament of Catalonia, 1980-84; MEP, 1987-; Vice-Pres., delegation for relations with South America; mem. Political Commission, Insitutional Commission, Petitions Cttee; *interests:* construction process of European politics, development of democracy and consolidation in Latin America; *publications:* Una Europa amb ànima, Avui, 1987; Prioridades para la Presidencia Española, La Vanguardia, 1989; La CEE y sus fracasos, La Vanguardia, 1988; El Parlamento Europeo, Motor de Europa, Grup del PPE en el Parlamento Europeo, 1989; Nacionalisme i Europeisme - l'Europa que volem, 1990; *office address:* Ms Concepció Ferrer, European Parliament, Centre Européen, Plateau de Kirchberg, BP 2929, Luxembourg.

FETZ, Anita; Swiss, Member of the Nationalrat; *born:* 19 March 1957, Basel, Switzerland; *parents:* Anton Fetz and Gerda (née Dietrich); *languages:* French, English; *education:* Secondary school, school leaving certificate type B, 1968-76; University of Basel, graduate in History and German, 1977-83; *party:* Organisationen der Schweiz Organisations Progressistes Suisses -

(Progressive Organisation of Switzerland) and Green Party, 1981-; *political career:* cantonal parliament, Basel, 1984-89; mem. of Nationalrat, Basel, 1985-; *interests:* women's issues, genetic engineering, educational issues, employment and social security; *professional career:* teacher, secondary school level, Basel, 1984-85; self employed instructress and adviser, at Femmedia, an Organisation handling material aimed specifically at women, in Basel, 1985-; *publications:* Strukturwandel der Gesellschaft und Veränderung der Frauenrolle, published by Swiss Academic Council, 1988; Gene. Frauen und Millionen. Ein Diskussionbeitrag zur Gen-und Reproduktionstechnologien, published by Rotpunktverlag, Zurich, 1988; *clubs:* Organisation for Womens Issues, OFRA; Swiss Union of feminist Science; European Women's Management Development Network; *private address:* Femmedia, Klosterberg 19, 4051 Basel, Switzerland; *office address:* Frau Anita Fetz, Nationalrat/Conseil National, Secretariat-General, Parlamentsgebäude, 3003 Berne, Switzerland.

FIEDLER, Bobbi; American, former Member of the House of Representatives; *born:* 22 April 1937, Santa Monica, California; *education:* Santa Monica City College; Santa Monica Technical School; *party:* Republican Party; *political career:* Member of the House of Reps. for District 21, California, 1981-86; Mem., Budget Cttee., 1981-86; Mem., joint Economic Study Exec. Cttee.; Mem., Republican Exec. Cttee. on Cttees. and Republican Study Exec. Cttee; *memberships:* Business and Professional Women's Assn.; founder Mem., Conservative Opportunity Society; *honours and awards:* Hon. LLD, West Coast College of Law; Newsmaker of the Year, Los Angeles Daily News; Most Prominent Woman in Southern California, Los Angeles Herald Examiner; Anita S. Perlman Award, B'nai B'rith Youth Organisation; *clubs:* Navy League; Hadassah; B'nai B'rith Youth Organisation; *office address:* Ms Bobbi Fiedler, 1702 Malden Street, Northridge, California 91325, USA.

FILIPAS, Magdalena; Romanian, Deputy to the Grand National Assembly; *education:* Polytechnic Institute, Bucharest; *party:* Romanian Communist Party (RCP); *political career:* Mem., Exec. Cttee. of Women Nation Council, 1966; candidate Mem., Bucharest City RCP Cttee., 1968; Dep. Chairperson, Light Industry Trade Unions Exec. Cttee., 1971-76; candidate Mem., RCP Central Cttee., 1972-73; Mem., Supreme Cncl. for Economic and Social Development, 1973; full Mem., RCP Central Cttee., 1973-84; Mem., Central Cncl. Workers' Control Economic and Social Activity, 1973-82; Mem., Central Auditing Commission, RCP Central Cttee., 1978-81; first Dep. Minister of Light Industry, 1979-82; Dep. to the Nat. Assembly, 1980-; Dep. Chairperson, Commission for Foreign Policy and International Economic Co-operation, Grand Nat.

Assembly, 1980-85; *professional career:* engineer of light industry; Dir., Crinul factory, Bucharest, 1970; Dir. Gen., Bucharest Cotton Industrial Central, 1978-81; Ambassador to the Philippines, 1982-; *office address:* Ms Magdalena Filipas, Marea Adunare Nationala, Aleea Marii Adunari Nationale, Bucharest, Romania; *phone:* 16 21 50.

FILIPPINI, Giovanna; Italian, Deputy; *born:* 17 January 1952, Cattolica, Forli, Italy; *party:* Partito Democratico della Sinistra (PDS, Party of the Democratic Left); *political career:* Deputy, Parliament, Bologna-Ferrara-Ravenna-Forli, 1983, re-elected 1987; mem. Cttee. on Internal Affairs; mem. Election Body; mem. Cttee. on Production, Commerce and Tourism; *office address:* Ms Giovanna Filippini, Camera dei Deputati, Montecitorio, 00186 Rome, Italy.

FILIPPINI, Rosa; Italian, Deputy; *born:* 3 November 1954, Naples; *party:* Federazione Nazionale per Le Liste Verdi (Green Party); *political career:* Radical activist 1971-79; co-founded, with Mario Signorino, Italian section of Friends of the Earth; Pres., Italian section, Friends of the Earth, 1983-87; Promoter of Green Lists until 1983 administrative election campaign; Councillor, Rome, 1985; Co-promoter of Nat. referendum against hunting; Directed Cttee. for gathering signatures, Nat. referendum against hunting; elected Deputy, Genova-Imperia-La Spezia-Savona, 1987; Vice-Pres. of Green Parliamentary group; mem. Cttee. for Justice; mem. Regulatory Body; *office address:* Ms Rosa Filippini, Camera dei Deputati, Montecitorio, 00186 Rome, Italy.

FINCATO, Dott. Laura; Italian, Deputy; *born:* 12 July 1950, Vicenza, Italy; *education:* University of Padua, Degree in Philosophy; *party:* Partito Socialista Italiano (PSI, Italian Socialist Party), 1975; *political career:* Councillor, Vicenza, 1975; re-elected Councillor, 1980; mem. Central Cttee., PSI, from 1980; mem. Nat. Leadership, PSI, from 1981; Head of Educational Organisation and Participation Section; Deputy, Verona-Padua-Vicenza-Rovigo, 1983, re-elected 1987; Vice-Pres. of Cttee. on Teaching and Fine Art; mem. Cttee. on Culture, Science and Teaching; *professional career:* grammar school teacher; *office address:* Dott. Laura Fincato, Camera dei Deputati, Montecitorio, 00186 Rome, Italy.

FINNBOGADOTTIR, Vigdis; Icelandic, President of Iceland; *born:* 15 April 1930, Reykjavik, Iceland; *parents:* Finnbogi Rútur Thorvaldsson and Sigrídur Eiríksdóttir; *children:* Astrídur (adopted); *languages:* English, French, Danish, Swedish; *education:* Menntaskólinn Junior College, 1949; University of Grenoble, French/Drama; Sorbonne, Paris, French/Drama; University of Iceland, English/Education; *political career:* member, Advisory

Cttee. on Cultural Affairs, Nordic council, 1976, Chmn., 1978; Pres. of Iceland, 1980, re-elected 1984-; *interests:* theatre; *professional career:* french teacher, Reykjavik; tourist guide, leader, Guide Training Programme, Icelandic Travel Bureau; Dir., Reykjavik Theatre Company, 1972-80; French drama teacher, University of Iceland; member, Grima Theatre Group; lecturer on Icelandic Culture; presenter, Icelandic State Television; Chairman, Alliance Francaise; *office address:* Ms Vigdis Finnbogadóttir, Presidential Palace, Reykjavík, Iceland.

FINNEY, Joan; American, Governor of Kansas; *born:* 12 February 1925, Topeka, Kansas, USA; *parents:* Leonard McInnoy and Mary McInnoy (née Sands); *married:* Spencer W. Finney Jr., 1957; *children:* Sally, Dick, Mary; *religion:* Catholic; *education:* Kansas City Conservatory of Music, 1946; College of St. Teresa, Kansas, 1950; Washburn Univ., BA; *party:* Democratic Party; *political career:* Asst., US Senator Frank Carlson, Kansas, 1953-1969; State Treasurer, Kansas, 1974-1982; Chwn., Pooled Money Investment Board; currently Gov., Kansas; *memberships:* National Federation of Democratic Women; American Legion; National Assn. of Auditors; League of Women Voters; State Treasurer's Assn.; National Assn. of Unclaimed Property Administration; Women's Political Caucus; Nat. Assn. of Auditors Political Caucus; *professional career:* Governor of Kansas; *honours and awards:* Women of the Year, Topeka Chapter, National Federation of Business and Professional Women's Club; *private address:* 4519 S W 33rd Street Terrace, Topeka, Kansas 66614, USA; *office address:* Mrs Joan Finney, 900 Jackson Suite 201, Topeka, Kansas 66612-1235, USA.

FINOCCHIARO FIDELBO, Annamaria; Italian, Deputy; *born:* 31 March 1955, Modica, Ragusa, Italy; *education:* Degree in Jurisprudence; *party:* Partito Democratico della Sinistra (PDS, Party of the Democratic Left); *political career:* Sec. Association for Democratic Magistrature, East Sicily Section; Deputy, Catania-Messina-Siracuse-Ragusa-Enna, 1987; mem. Cttee. on Justice; mem. leadership Cttee. of Communist parliamentary group; *office address:* Ms Annamaria Finocchiaro Fidelbo, Camera dei Deputati, Montecitorio, 00186 Rome, Italy.

FISHER OF REDNAL, Baroness (cr. 1974, Life Peer) Doris Mary Gertrude Fisher; British, Member of the House of Lords; *born:* 13 September 1919; *parents:* the late Frederick Satchwell; *married:* the late Joseph Fisher, 1939; *children:* two d; *education:* Birmingham schools; Fircroft College; *party:* Labour Party; *political career:* Fmr. mem., Birmingham City Council; Fmr. Chmn., Housing Cttee.; Nat. Pres., Women's Coop Guild, 1961-62; Member of Parliament, 1970-74; House of Lords, 1974-; Fmr. mem. Warrington New

Town Development Corp.; Member of European Parliament, 1975; mem., New Towns Staff Commission, 1976; Opposition Whip, 1983-84; Opposition Spokesman on the Environment, 1983-84; *interests:* housing, local government; *professional career:* JP, 1961-; mem., Gen. Medical Cncl., 1974; Chmn., Baskerville Special School, 1981-; Warden, Birmingham Assay Office, 1981-; Pres., Birmingham Royal Inst. of Blind, 1982; *private address:* 60 Jacoby Place, Priory Road, Edgbaston, Birmingham, UK; *office address:* Baroness Fisher of Rednal, House of Lords, London SW1A 0PW.

FLAHERTY, Mary Diana; Irish, Member of the Dáil Éireann; *born:* 17 May 1953, Dublin, Ireland; *parents:* Thomas Flaherty and Lucy Flaherty (née McManamon); *married:* Alexis Fitzgerald, 1982; *public role of spouse:* former Lord Mayor, Senator amd Member of the Dáil; *children:* Oliver, Nicholas; *religion:* Roman Catholic; *languages:* French, German; *education:* University College, Dublin, BA, Higher Diploma in Education, 1975; *party:* Fine Gael, 1978; *political career:* elected to Dublin City Council, 1979, 1985; elected, Member of The Dáil, 1981, 1982, 1987, 1989; Minister of State, Dept. of Social Welfare, 1982; Opposition Junior Spokesperson for Health, 1987; Opposition Junior Spokesperson for Development Co-operation, 1988; Front Bench Spokesperson for Social Welfare, 1989-91; currently, spokeswoman on Energy; *interests:* development issues, foreign affairs, poverty, childcare, law; *professional career:* secondary school teacher, 1974-81; *publications:* Towards A Policy On Development Co-operation, 1989; *clubs:* An Taisce, Irish Anti-Apartheid Movement, Assn. of Western European Parliamentarians Against Apartheid (AWEPAA), Cambodian Solidarity Group, Irish Council for Soviet Jewry; *recreations:* gardening, cycling; *private address:* 2 Richmond Place, Dublin 6, Ireland; *office address:* Ms Mary Flaherty, Dáil Éireann, Lenister House, Kildare Street, Dublin 2, Ireland.

FLEETWOOD, Baroness Elisabeth Alma Fredrike Swantesdotter; Swedish, Member of the Riksdag; *parents:* Swante Miles Fleetwood and Stina Fredrika Fleetwood (née Flink), 1953; *public role of spouse:* Managing Dir., Road Transport Empolyers' Assn; *children:* Fredrik, Caroline; *religion:* Protestant; *languages:* English, German; *education:* University of Uppsala, English/German, 1946-50; University of Stockholm, MA, History, 1950-52; *party:* Moderata Samlingspartiet (Moderate Party), 1964; *political career:* Member, Stockholm City Council, 1973-79; mem. of Riksdag for Stockholm, 1979-; *interests:* education, constitution, universities; *memberships:* Vice-President of the Group for Political Prisoners in Ethiopia; President of the Moderate Women's Association, Stockholm; board member, Moderate Women's Association of Sweden; Vice-Pres., Swedish Cancer Society; *professional career:*

secondary school teacher, 1960-79; board member, University of Stockholm; Vice-President, Swedish Cancer Society; *honours and awards:* Honorary Engineer of the Stockholm Technical Institute, 1987; *recreations:* outdoor life, literature, culture; *private address:* Bältgatan 3, 11459 Stockholm, Sweden; *office address:* Baroness Elisabeth Alma Fredrike Swantesdotter Fleetwood, Riksdag, Fack, S-100 12 Stockholm, Sweden.

FLEMMING, Marilies; Austrian, Federal Minister of the Environment, Youth and Family and Head of the Austrian Women's Movement; *born:* 1933, Wiener Neustadt, Lower Austria; *children:* two; *education:* LLB and Dr. of Law; courses in drama; language courses in Paris and at Univ. of Cambridge, UK; *party:* Österriechische Volkpartei (ÖVP, Austrian People's Party); *political career:* Viennese Provincial Cncl., Cttee. for Social Affairs and Health, Cultural Cttee., 1978-; Sec.-Gen., Austrian Women's Movement, affiliated to ÖVP, 1977-84, Head, 1984-; Chairperson, Austrian Division of the European Women's Union; Chairperson, Christian-Democrat Women's Union; Chairperson, Austrian Women's Assn.; Minister for Environmental, Youth Affairs and Family, Cabinet of Minister Vranitzky, 1987-; *professional career:* Austrian Academic Assn; *office address:* Ms Marilies Flemming, Nationalrat, Dr. Carl Renner Ring 3, 1017 Vienna, Austria.

FLESCH, Colette; Luxembourgeios, Director-General, Directorate-General X, Commission of the European Communities; *born:* 16 April 1937, Dudelange; *party:* Demokratesch Partei (DP, Democratic Party); *political career:* MP, Luxembourg 1969-80, 1984-89; former Minister of Foreign Affairs, Trade, Co-operation and Justice; Pres., DP; Mayor, Luxembourg 1970-80; MEP, 1969-70, 1979-80, 1984-85, 1989-90; Dir.-Gen., Directorate-Gen. X (Information, Communication and Culture), Commission of the European Communities; *office address:* Ms Colette Flesch, Directorate-General X, Commission of the European Communities, 200 rue de la Loi, 1049 Brussels, Belgium.

FLINNER, Dora; German, former Member of the Bundestag; *born:* 19 February 1940, Heilbronn/Neckar, West Germany; *children:* three; *religion:* Protestant; *education:* elementary school; *party:* Die Grünen (Green Party), 1984-; *political career:* municipal councillor, Boxberg, resigned 1987; local councillor, Boxberg-Bobstadt, 1980-; member of Bundestag, 1984; party list of Baden-Wüttemberg, 1987; *professional career:* practical training as farmer; farmer in small family farm; member of county women's association; member of executive board, Bundschuh-Genossenschaft (peasants' boot co-operative), Boxberg; *private address:* 6973 Boxberg-Bobstadt, West Germany; *office address:* Frau Dora Flinner .

FLUCSA, Maria; Romanian, Deputy to the Grand National Assembly; *party:* Romanian Communist Party (RCP); *political career:* Mem., RCP Central Cttee., 1984-; first Dep. Minister of Light Industy, 1984-87; Dep., Grand Nat. Assembly, Arad district, 1985-; Minister of Light Industry, 1987-; *office address:* Ms Maria Flucsa, Marea Adunare Nationala, Aleea Marii Adunari Nationale, Bucharest, Romania; *phone:* 16 21 50.

FLYNN CURRIE, Barbara; American, Illinois State Representative; *born:* 3 May 1940, LaCrosse, Wisconsin, USA; *parents:* Francis Thomas Flynn Jr. and Elsie Rose Flynn (née Gobel); *married:* David Park Currie, 1959; *public role of spouse:* former Chwn., Illinois Pollution Control Board; Edward H. Levi Distinguished Service Professor of Law, Univ. of Chicago; *children:* Stephen, Margaret; *education:* Univ. of Chicago, Illinois, AB, 1968, AM, 1973; *party:* Democratic Party; *political career:* Illinois State Rep., District 26, 1979-; Chwn., Revenue Cttee.; Mem., Appropriations for Human Services, Energy, Environment and Natural Resources Cttees; *memberships:* National Order of Women Legislators; American Civil Liberties Union; Illinois Citizen's Assembly; Illinois Cncl. on Women; Hyde Park Kenwood Community Conference; *professional career:* Instructor, DePaul Univ., 1973-74; Asst. Study Dir., National Opinion Research Centre, 1974-77; *honours and awards:* Honour Award, National Trust Historic Presevation; Legislator of Year, National Assn., Social Workers, 1984; Best Legislator, Independent Voters of Illinois, 1980, 1982, 1984, 1986, 1988; Ethel Parker Award, 1982; Lottie Holman O'Neill and Susan B. Anthony Awards, Illinois Women's Political Caucus; Legislator of the Year, Illinois Nurses Assn., 1984; *publications:* Co-author, Political Attitudes among American Ethnics: A Study in Perceptual Distortion: Ethnicity in the US; *clubs:* YWCA; Hyde Park Neighbourhood Club; *private address:* 5650 S. Harper Avenue, Chicago, Illinois 60637, USA; *office address:* Mrs Barbara Flynn Currie, 410 State House, Springfield, Illinois 62706, USA.

FOLZ-STEINACKER, Sigrid; German, former Member of the Bundestag; *born:* 10 January 1941, Hamburg, West Germany; *children:* one d., four s; *religion:* Protestant; *education:* elementary school; secondary school; private commercial school; *party:* Freie Demokratische Partei (FDP, Free Democratic Party), since 1977; *political career:* dep. chmn., local association, FDP; dep. chmn., district Exec. board, FDP, Oldenburg; member, county Exec. board, FDP, Niedersachsen; member of special Cttee. of county level Youth Policy, FDP; member of special Cttee. at federal level Development Policy, FDP; mem. of Bundestag, party list of Niedersachsen, 1987-90; *professional career:* commercial apprenticeship; commercial clerk; self-employed wholesale trader; sales representative;

now housewife; trick riding attendant; *private address:* 2880 Brake, West Germany; *office address:* Frau Sigrid Folz-Steinacker .

FONG WONG, Hon. Nellie Kut-Man; Hong Kong, Member of the Legislative Council; *born:* 7 February 1949, Hong Kong; *married:* Eddy Fong Ching; *children:* one; *religion:* Baptist; *education:* Belilios Public School; City of London College, UK; *political career:* mem., Town Planning Board, Hong Kong Govt.; mem., Law Reform Commission; Councillor, Urban Council; mem., Wong Tai Sin District Board; mem., Advisory Cttee. on Legal Education, Hong Kong Govt.; Vice-Chmn., Home Affairs Cttee., Hong Kong General Chamber of Commerce; mem., Ethics Cttee., Hong Kong Society of Accountants; Council mem., International Fiscal Assn.; Chmn., Hong Kong Society for the Protection of Children; mem., Standing Commission on Civil Service Salaries and Conditions of Service; *memberships:* FCA; ATII; FHHSA; CPA; *professional career:* partner, Chartered Accountant; *honours and awards:* Justice of the Peace; *office address:* The Hon. Mrs Nellie Fong Wong, The Legislative Council, Government House, Hong Kong.

FONTAINE, Nicole Claude Marie; French, Member of the European Parliament; *born:* 16 January 1942, Grainville-Ymauville, France; *parents:* Jean Garnier and Geneviève Garnier (née Lambert); *married:* Jean-René Fontaine, 1964; *children:* Christine; *education:* Joan of Arc college, public college, Le Havre; doctor of State in public law; graduate, Institute of Political Science, Paris; *party:* Centre des Démocrates Sociaux (CDS, Social Democratic Centre); Parti Populaire Européen (PPE, European People's Party); *political career:* member, economic and social council, 1980; member, European Parliament, 1984-; *interests:* education; *professional career:* teacher; *publications:* 'l'Enseignement privé associé à l'Etat par contrat', 1978; 'l'Ecole libre et l'Etat', 1982; *private address:* 13 rue Pierre-Nicole, 75005 Paris, France; *office address:* Mme. Nicole Fontaine, European Parliament, Centre Européen, Plateau de Kirchberg, BP 2929, Luxembourg.

FONTENELE, Maria Luiza Menezes; Brazilian, Federal Deputy; *born:* 27 November 1942, Quixadá, Ceará; *parents:* Antonino Fontenele and Diva de Menezes Fontenele; *children:* Andrea; *education:* ESS, Fortaleza, social services, 1962-65; Vanderbilt Univ., USA, M.Sc. sociology, 1971-73; *party:* Partido da Social Democracia Brasileira (PSB, Social Democratic Party of Brasil); *political career:* State Deputy, 1979-83 and 1983-85; Mem., Education Cttee., 1981-82; Mem., Cttee. for Agriculture and Cattle, 1983-84; Mem., Environment Cttee., 1984-85; Prefect for Fortaleza, 1986-89; Federal Deputy for Ceará, 1991-95; *professional career:* social worker and professor;

honours and awards: Certificate of Honour and Merit, Joao Ramos PereiraFoundation; Distinguished Reference, Spiritual Order of Brazil,Fortaleza; Outstanding Personality Award, Radio Dragao do Mar,Fortaleza, 1985; Courageous Speech Honour, Diario, Fortaleza; *office address:* Ms Maria Fontenele, Chamber of Deputies, Praça dos 3 Poderes, Ed. Principal, 70160 Brasilia, DF, Brazil; *phone:* (61) 225 2885.

FOOKES, Dame Janet Evelyn, DBE; British, Member of Parliament; *born:* 21 February 1936; *parents:* Lewis Aylmer Fookes and Evelyn Margery Fookes (née Holmes); *religion:* Church of England; *education:* Hastings and St. Leonard's Ladies College; Hastings High School for Girls; Royal Holloway College, London Univ., BA, 1957; *party:* Conservative Party, 1952; *political career:* councillor, County Borough of Hastings, 1960-61, 1963-70; Member of Parliament, 1970-; mem., Services Select Cttee., 1973-74; mem., Expenditure Select Cttee., 1975-79; Chmn., Education, Arts and Home Office Sub-Cttee., 1975-79; mem., Speaker's Panel of Chmn., 1976-; mem., Home Affairs Select Cttee., 1983-; mem., Select Cttee. to Televise Proceedings, 1988-; *interests:* defence, animal welfare, equal opportunities for women, mental health; *memberships:* Royal Society for the Prevention of Cruelty to Animals (Council mem.); Soldiers' Sailors' and Airmens' Families' Assn. (Council Mem.); Stonham Housing Assn. (Council Mem.); Commonwealth War Graves Commission; *professional career:* teacher, 1958-70; adviser, English Tourist Board, 1983-90; *honours and awards:* Dame Commander of the British Empire, 1989; *recreations:* gardening, theatre, keep-fit; *office address:* Dame Janet Fookes, House of Commons, London SW1A 0AA.

FOST, Paulette; French, Senator; *born:* 18 September 1937, Paris, France; *party:* Parti Communiste (PC, Communist Party), 1956; *political career:* cell secretary, section leader, member of Seine-Saint-Denis Federal Cttee., member of Central Cttee., 1976-, of French Communist Party; Departmental Councillor for Seine-Saint-Denis canton, 1973, and 1st Vice-Chmn. of Departmental Council, responsible for environment and immigration, 1976-; Town Councillor and 1st Deputy Mayor of Saint-Ouen, responsible for town planning and housing, 1977-; member of secretariat of National Association of Communist and Republican Representatives, 1977-; Deputy for Seine-Saint-Denis, 1st constituency: Saint-Ouen, 1978-81; Mayor of Saint-Ouen, 1979-; Senator for Seine-Saint-Denis, 1986-; *office address:* Mme. Paulette Fost, Sénat de la République Française, Palais du Luxembourg, 75291 Paris Cedex 06, France.

FOSTER-HEUER, Ann; American, Chair of District of Columbia State Republican Party; *born:* 12 November

1934, New Orleans, Louisiana, USA; *parents:* Edwin Charles Hollins and Alice C. Hollins (née Foster); *married:* Scott Heuer, 1925; *children:* Catherine Ann, Charles Edwin, Amanda Hollins. Scott C; *religion:* Episcopal; *education:* Vassar College, Poughkeepsie, New York, 1952-54; American Univ., Washington DC, BGS, 1980; *party:* Republican Party; *political career:* Chair, Republican Party, Precinct 9, 1968-80; Commissioner, National Capitol Planning Cttee., 1972-74; alternate delegate, Bush Republican Convention, 1980; Co-Chair, Reagan-Bush, Finance Cttee., 1984; Chair, DC State Republican Party, 1984-; mem., Budget Cttee., 1984-88; delegate, Bush Republican National Convention, 1988; Senior Vice-Chair, Bush-Quayle, DC, 1988; *memberships:* Spring Valley/Wesley Heights Citizens' Assn.; Federal City of 100 Cttee., Meridian House International; Wilson House Cncl.; National Symphony; United Way; *clubs:* Women of DC Golf Assn; *office address:* Mrs Ann Foster-Heuer, DC Republican Committee, 440 First Street NW, 4th Floor, Washington DC 20001, USA.

FOUNTOUKIDOU, Parthena; Greek, Member of Parliament; *children:* two s; *party:* Nea Demokratia (ND, New Democracy Party), 1989; *political career:* MP, ND, Pella, 1989; *professional career:* lawyer; *office address:* Vouli, Parliament Building, Syntagma, Greece.

FRANCESE, Angela; Italian, Deputy; *born:* 15 September 1950, Naples, Italy; *party:* Partito Democratico della Sinistra (PDS, Party of the Democratic Left); *political career:* Deputy, Napoli-Caserta, 1979, re-elected 1983 and 1987; mem. Cttee. on Labour and Social Security; Sec. Office of the Presidency; mem. Cttee. public and private work; *office address:* Ms Angela Francese, Camera dei Deputati, Montecitorio, 00186 Rome, Italy.

FRAYSSE-CAZALIS, Jacqueline Paulette Marguerite; French, Senator; *born:* 25 February 1947, Paris, France; *parents:* Louis Fraysse and Elise Fraysse (née Lasserre); *married:* Claude Gauché-Cazalis, 1976; *children:* Gilles, Claire; *education:* Nanterre High School; Faculty of Medicine, Paris, doctor of medicine, diploma in cardiology; *party:* Parti Communiste (PC, Communist Party); *political career:* Town Councillor for Nanterre, 1971; Departmental Councillor for Nanterre North canton, 1976; Deputy for Hauts-de-Seine, 7th constituency: Nanterre, Suresnes, 1978-86; Senator for Hauts-de-Seine, 1986; Mayor of Nanterre, 1988-; *professional career:* medical practitioner; *recreations:* photography, swimming; *office address:* Mme. Jacqueline Fraysse-Cazalis, Sénat de la République Française, Palais du Luxembourg, 75291 Paris Cedex 06, France.

FREDERICK, Virginia Fiester; American, Illinois State Representative; *born:* Rock Island, Illinois, USA;

parents: John Heise and Myrtle Montgomery Heise; *married:* Kenneth Jacob Frederick, 1978; *children:* Sheryl, Alan R., James D. Feister; *religion:* Methodist; *education:* Univ. of Iowa, BA, 1938; Lake Forest College, 1942-43; *party:* Republican Party; *political career:* Ward Caucus Chwn., Lake Forest, 1972-73; Mem., Finance Cttee., 1974-75; Alderman, First Ward, Lake Forrest, 1974-78; Illinois State Rep., District 59, 1979-; Sec., Republican Caucus; Spokesperson, Cttee. on Revenue; Mem., Appropriations I, Public Utilities State Govt. Admin., Children, Alzheimer's Task Force and Long Term Care Task Force Cttees.; Co-Chwn., Citizen's Cncl. on Children; *memberships:* League of Women Voters; American Assn. of Univ. Women; UN Assn; Illinois Conference of Women Legislators; Chicago Cncl. on Foreign Relations; *professional career:* freelance fashion designer, Lake Forest, Illinois, 1952-78; Pres. Mid-America/China Exchange, Kenilworth, Illinois, 1978-80; *honours and awards:* Chicago Area Woman of Achievement, 1978; Lottie Holman Award for First Term Legislator, 1980; Jane Adams Award for Leadership in Women's Issues, Illinois Legislature, 1982; *office address:* Mrs Virginia Frederick, 1540 Greenleaf Avenue, Lake Forest, Illinois 60045, USA.

FREIBERT, Pat; American, Kentucky State Representative; *born:* 8 June 1936; *religion:* Catholic; *education:* West Virginia Technical, BA; *party:* Republican Party; *political career:* Kentucky State Rep., District 78, 1979-; Mem., Kentucky State Republican Party Central Cttee.; Chwn., Platform Cttee., State Convention, 1980; *memberships:* Board Dir., Central Kentucky Blood Centre and Blue Grass Crippled Children's Advisory Cncl.; Bluegrass Assn., Retarded Citizens; Citizens Water Task Force; Regional Forum National Commission for Exellence in Education; PTA; Shadeland Community Assn., Bluegrass Business and Professional Women's Club; Lexington Education Workers Cncl; *honours and awards:* Distinguished Public Service Award, Kentucky Circuit Judges 1980; Lexington Woman of the Year, 1981; *clubs:* Lexington Altrusa Club; *office address:* Mrs Pat Freibert, 659 Tateswood Drive, Lexington, Kentucky 40502, USA.

FREIVALDS, Laila; Swedish, Minister of Justice; *office address:* Ms Laila Freivalds, Riksdag, Fack, S-100 12, Stockholm, Sweden; *phone:* Stockholm 786 4000.

FRERICHS DODERER, Minnette; American, Iowa State Representative; *born:* 16 May 1923, Holland, Iowa, USA; *parents:* John A. Frerichs and Sophie Frerichs (née Sherfield); *married:* Fred H. Doderer, 1944; *public role of spouse:* Mayor of Iowa City; *children:* Dennis H.J., Kay Lynn; *religion:* Methodist; *education:* Univ. of Northern Iowa; Univ. of Iowa, BA, 1948; *party:* Democratic Party; *political career:* Vice-Chwn., Johnson County Democratic Central Cttee., Iowa, 1953-58; Vice-Pres., Iowa Citizens for Fair

Representation, 1960-62; Iowa State Rep., Johnson County, 1964-68 and District 45, 1980-; Chwn., Ways and Means Cttee.; Mem., Cncl. of State Govt. Midwestern Standing Cttee. on Higher Education, 1965-66; Vice-Pres., Iowa Commission on Inter-State Co-operation, 1965-67; delegate Democrat National Convention, 1968 and 1984; Democrat National Committeewoman, 1968-69; Iowa State Senator, 1968-78; Pres. Pro Temp, Iowa State Senate, 1975-76; Chwn., Senate State Govt. Cttee., until 1979; Mem., Democratic National Policy Cncl. of Elected Officers, 1973-76; Iowa State Rep., 1981-; *memberships:* National Society of State Legislators; League of Women Voters; International Women's Year Continuing Cttee.; Iowa Children and Family Service; National Order of Women Legislators; *professional career:* Chwn., Small Business and Commerce Co.; Fellow of Iowa Univ. School of Religion, 1969-; *honours and awards:* Distinguished Service in Iowa General Assembly Award, Iowa State Education Assn., 1969; Iowa Civil Liberties Award, 1978; Iowa Hall of Fame, 1979; Iowa City Education Award., 1986; Women of Courage Award, National Organisation of Women; Wilson Award for Justice, 1989; *recreations:* tennis; *office address:* Mrs Minnette Frerichs Doderer, 2008 Dunlap Court, Iowa City, Iowa 52245, USA.

FRICHOT, Sylvette; Seychelles, Minister of Information, Culture and Youth; *office address:* Ms Sylvette Frichot, Ministry of Information, Culture and Youth, PO Box 648, Mount Fleuri, Seychelles.

FRIEDMAN, Fanny; Swaziland, Minister of Health; *office address:* Ms Fanny Friedman, Ministry of Health, PO Box 5, Mbabane, Swaziland.

FRIESER, Cordula; Austrian, Member of the Nationalrat; *born:* 17 December 1950, Vorderberg/Gailtal, Austria; *education:* High School, Villach, Matura 1968; Univ. of Graz, Social Sciences and Economics, Magisterium 1972; *party:* Österreichische Volkspartei (ÖVP, Austrian People's Party); *political career:* Provincial Cultural Adviser of the Styrian Women's Movement; collaborated on The Styrian Model; Nationalrat Member for Styria, 1986-; *professional career:* private tax consultant; *office address:* Frau Cordula Frieser, Nationalrat, Dr. Karl Renner Ring 3, 1017 Vienna, Austria.

FRIGGEBO, Birgit; Swedish, Member of the Riksdag; *born:* 25 December 1941, Falköping, Sweden; *children:* one s; *education:* Higher School Certificate, Economics, 1960, Stockholm; *party:* Folkpartiet Liberalerna (Liberal Party), 1957; *political career:* Minister of Housing, 1976-82; Party Secretary for the Liberal Party, 1983-85; Member of Riksdag since 1985; Member of the following Committees: Constitutional, Administrative, Secret Police; Various internal working-groups dealing with MP's professional situation; *professional career:* clerk in father's construction and estate agents company, 1960-66; Head of negotiations, Swedens Beneficial Housing Company (SABO), 1969-76; *office address:* Ms Birgit Friggebo, Riksdag, Fack, S-100 12 Stockholm, Sweden.

FRONZA CREPAZ, Lucia; Italian, Deputy; *born:* 26 August 1955, Trent, Italy; *children:* three; *education:* Classical Secondary Schooling, 1974; Padua University, Degree in Medecine and Surgery, 1981; Specialisation in Paediatrics, Verona, 1985; *party:* Partito della Democrazia Cristiana (DC, Christian Democrat Party); *political career:* Youth activist; Peace activist; Campaigner in support of the victims of natural disasters; Deputy, DC, Trent-Bolzano, 1987; mem. Committees on Constitutional Affairs, Presidency of the Council and Internal Affairs; and Social Affairs; *professional career:* former employee, Ambulance Service and Paediatric Consultancies, Trent province; Promoter of Cultural Centre Trentino; *office address:* Ms Lucia Fronza Crepaz, Camera dei Deputati, Montecitorio, 00186 Rome, Italy.

FUCHS, Anke; German, Member of the Bundestag; *born:* 5 July 1937, Hamburg, West Germany; *parents:* Dr. Paul Neuermann; *children:* two; *education:* abitur, 1956; Univ. of Hamburg and Innsbruck, law examinations, Hamburg, 1960, 1964); *party:* Sozialdemokratische Partei Deutschlands (SPD, Social Democratic Party of Germany), 1956; *political career:* mem. of county Exec. board, SPD in Hamburg, 1968; mem. of City Parliament, Hamburg, 1971; Undersecretary with civil service status, Federal Ministry of Employment and Social Affairs, 1977; mem. of Exec. board, Federal Office of Employment, 1978; mem. of Exec. board, SPD, 1979-; parly. undersecretary, Federal Ministry of Employment and Social Affairs, 1980-82; Federal Minister of Youth, Family and Health, Apr.-Oct. 1982; member of presiding board, SPD, 1986-; dep. chmn., SPD parly. group, until Jun. 1987; federal party secretary, SPD, Jun. 1987-; mem. of Bundestag, party list of Nordrhein-Westfalen; *professional career:* lawyer; asst., Deutscher Gewerkschaftsbund (DGB, German Trades Union Confederation), district Nordmark, 1964; mem. of executive board, Industriegewerkschaft Metall (IGM, Metal Worker's Union), 1971; mem. of supervisory board, Klöckner-Werke AG and Ruhr Kohle A.G.; mem. of presiding committee, German Red Cross; mem. of supervisory board Salzgitter and Dep. Chmn. of supervisory board, Steel Works Peine, 1972-77; *private address:* 5300 Bonn 2, West Germany; *office*

address: Frau Anke Fuchs, Bundeshaus, 5300 Bonn 1, West Germany.

FUJITA, Sumi; Japanese, Member of the House of Representatives; *born:* 3 April 1933; *education:* Mikunigaoka High School; *party:* Japan Communist Party (JCP); *political career:* former Mem., Osaka Prefectural Assembly; fifth time elected, for Osaka 5; Mem., House of Reps. Cttee. on Agriculture, Forestry and Fisheries, 1990-; *office address:* Ms Sumi Fujita, House of Representatives, 1-7-1 Nagata-cho, Chiyoda-ku, Tokyo 100, Japan; *phone:* (03) 5815111.

FUMAGALLI CARULLI, Dott. Ombretta (Battistina); Italian, Deputy; *born:* 5 March 1944, Meda, Milan, Italy; *education:* Doctor of Jurisprudence; *party:* Partito della Democrazia Cristiana (DC, Christian Democrat Party); *political career:* Deputy, Milan-Pavia, 1987; mem. Body for the Authorisations to prosecute; mem. Cttee. on Justice; *professional career:* Lecturer; *office address:* Dott. Ombretta Fumagalli Carulli, Camera dei Deputati, Montecitorio, 00186 Rome, Italy.

FURNEY, Linda Jeanne; American, Ohio State Senator; *born:* 11 September 1947, Toledo, Ohio, USA; *parents:* Robert Ross Furney and Jeanne Furney (née Hogan); *education:* Bowling Green State Univ., BS, 1969; *party:* Democratic Party; *political career:* Precinct Person, Democrat Party, Toledo, 1979-; Ohio State Senator, District 11; *memberships:* National Education Assn.; Ohio National Organisation of Women; *office address:* Ms Linda Furney, 1953 Brussels, Toledo, Ohio 43613, USA.

FYFE, Maria; British, Member of Parliament; *born:* 25 November 1938; *parents:* the late James O'Neill and the late Margaret O'Neill (née Lacey); *married:* the late James Fyfe (decd., 1986), 1964; *children:* two s; *education:* Notre Dame High School, Glasgow; Strathclyde University, 1970-75; *party:* Labour Party; *political career:* District Councillor, Glasgow, 1980-87, Vice-Convenor, Finance, 1980-84, Convenor Personnel, 1984-87; mem., Labour Party Scottish Exec., 1981-88; Chairperson, Local Government Cttee., 1985-87; Opposition Spokesperson on Women's Issues, 1988-91; MP for Glasgow Maryhill, 1987-; *interests:* local government, trades unions, employment law, women's rights; *professional career:* Senior Lecturer, Trade Union Studies Unit, Central College of Commerce, Glasgow, 1978-87; *recreations:* reading, theatre, walking; *private address:* Constituency Office, 1508 Maryhill Road, Glasgow G20; *office address:* Mrs Maria Fyfe, House of Commons, London SW1A OAA.

G

GAER, Evdokiya Aleksandrovna; Soviet, Member of the Council of Nationalities; *born:* 1934; *party:* Communist Party of the Soviet Union; *political career:* Mem., Cncl. of Nationalities; Mem., Commissions on Nationality Policy and Inter-ethnic Relations; founding Mem., MDG (Inter-regional Group of Deps.); *interests:* ecology, preservation of the identity of small nations within the USSR; *professional career:* junior scientific Assc., Inst. of History, Archeology and Ethnography, Far Eastern Branch, USSR Academy of Sciences, Vladivostok; *office address:* Ms Evdokiya Aleksandrovna Gaer, Institute of History, Archeology and Ethnography, Far Eastern Branch, USSR Academy of Sciences, 690600 Vladivostock, Ul. Pushkinskaya 89, USSR.

GAINUSE, Alexandrina; Romanian, Deputy to the Grand National Assembly; *born:* 1932; *party:* Romanian Communist Party (RCP); *political career:* First Sec., Bacau RCP District Cttee., 1979082; Chairperson, Bacau district People's Cncl., 1979-82; Mem., RCP Central Cttee., 1979, Mem., Political Exec. Cttee., RCP Central Cttee., 1979-87; Chairperson, Legislative Chamber of People's Cncl., 1979-81; Mem., Nat. Cncl. of Socialist Democracy and Unity Front, 1980-; Dep., Grand Nat. Assembly, Bacau district, 1980-; Calaresi district, 1985; Mem., State Cncl., 1980-82; Vice Chairperson, Exec. Bureau, Nat. Cncl. of Working People, 1981; Dep. Prime Minister, 1982-86; Chairperson, Cncl. for Co-ordinating of the Activities of Supply and Services to the Population, 1982; Chairperson, Higher Health Cncl., 1983-86; Minister of Labour, 1986-87; First Sec., Ialomite RCP district Cttee., Chairperson, Jalomite District People's Cncl., 1987-; *office address:* Ms Alexandrina Gainuse, Marea Adunare Nationala, Aleea Marii Adunari Nationale, Bucharest, Romania; *phone:* 16 21 50.

GANDHI, Maneka; Indian, Minister of State for Environment and Forests; *office address:* Smt. Maneka Gandhi, Ministry of the Environment and Forests, Paryavaran Bhavan, CGO Complex Phase II, Lodi Rd., New Dehli 110 003, India; *phone:* (11) 360721.

GANSEFORTH, Monika; German, Member of the Bundestag; *born:* 15 December 1940, Gleiwitz, Upper Silesia; *children:* two; *religion:* Protestant; *education:* girls' secondary school emphasising modern languages, Peine, Abitur (advanced matriculation examination), 1960; Technical University of Braunschweig, mechanical engineering; Dip.Ing., 1966; *party:* Sozialdemokratische Partei Deutschlands (SPD, Social Democratic Party of Germany), since 1974; *political career:* Chwn., Arbeitsgemeinschaft Sozialdemokratischer Frauen (AsF, Working Group of Social Democratic Women); member of district Exec. board, SPD in Hannover; Mem. of town council, Neustadt am Rübenberge, 1976-86; Mem. of Bundestag, party list of Niedersachsen, since 1987; Mem., Commission for the Protection of the Earth's Atmosphere; *interests:* problems of climate change and promotion of equal rights for women; *professional career:* development and construction engineer, optical electronic industry, Heidelberg, 1966-70; professor of electronic engineering, special subjects control technology and control engineering, Technical College of Higher Education, Hannover, since 1971, member of Arbeiterwohlfahrt (AWO, Labour Welfare Organisation); member of Gewerkschaft Erziehung und Wissenschaft (GEW, Trade Union for Education and Science); *clubs:* independent women's movement; peace groups; Bund für Umwelt und Naturschutz Deutschland (BUND, Society for the Environment and the Conservation of Nature); *private address:* 3057 Neustadt am Rübenberge 1, West Germany; *office address:* Frau Monika Ganseforth, Bundeshaus, 5300 Bonn 1, West Germany.

GARAVAGLIA, Maria Pia; Italian, Under Secretary of State for Health; *born:* 10 August 1947, Cuggiono, Milan, Italy; *education:* Catholic University of the Sacred Heart, Degree in Literature; Higher Institute of Religious Science, Catholic University of the Sacred Heart, Student, Faculty of Political Science; *party:* Partito della Democrazia Cristiana (DC, Christian Democrat Party); *political career:* mem. Prov. Cttee. of DC, Milan; mem. Women's Movement, Provincial Delegate, 1976; mem. Women's Promotionary Group, DC; mem. Regional Women's Consultancy, DC; Assessor for Public Instruction, Health and Social Services, Cuggiono; mem. leadership Consortium for the integration of the handicapped of Mesero; Deputy, Milan-Pavia, 1979-; mem. Cttee. on Hygene and Public Health; mem. Cttee. on Justice; re-elected deputy, 1987; mem. Cttee., Social Affairs; Under Secretary of State at the Ministry of Health; *interests:* problems of invalids; *professional career:* teacher of Letters, Liceo Scientifico;

WHO'S WHO OF WOMEN IN WORLD POLITICS

Council administrator, Cuggiono, Milan; journalist, press agent; voluntary worker for the help and recovery of drug addicts; *office address:* Ms Maria Pia Garavaglia, Ministry of Health, Viale dell'Industria 20, 00144 Rome, Italy.

GARBE, Charlotte; German, former Member of the Bundestag; *born:* 24 March 1929, Eisenach; *parents:* Emil Nimtz and Elsa Ida Nimtz (née Mieth); *married:* Gerhard, 1952; *children:* Ingo; *religion:* Protestant; *party:* Die Grünen (Green Party), 1980; *political career:* Co-Founder, Anti-Nuclear Power Stations Group and mem. since 1968; cttee. mem., Federal Assn. of Citizen's Initiatives mem. of Lantag of Lower Saxony, 1982-86; mem. of Kreistag Holzminden, 1986-87; mem. of Bundestag (Friesland-Wilhelmshaven), Green Party Group 1987-90; *professional career:* housewife; *office address:* Frau Charlotte Garbe, Bundeshaus, 5300 Bonn 1, West Germany.

GARCIA ARIAS, Ludivina; Spanish, Member of the European Parliament; *born:* 13 December 1945, Morelia, Mexico; *education:* degree in philosophy and letters; *party:* Partido Socialista Obrero Español (PSOE, Spanish Socialist Workers' Party); Socialist Group (S); *political career:* mem. Asturias autonomous parliament; Deputy for Asturias, 1982-86; MEP, 1986-; *professional career:* school teacher; *office address:* Ms Ludvina García Arias, European Parliament, Centre Européen, Plateau de Kirchberg, BP 2929, Luxembourg.

GARDNER OF PARKES, Baroness (cr. 1981, Life Peer) Trixie (Rachel Trixie Anne) Parkes; British, Member of the House of Lords; *born:* 17 July 1927; *parents:* the late Hon. J.J. Gregory and Rachel McGirr; *married:* Kevin Anthony Gardner, 1956; *children:* three d; *education:* Monte Sant Angelo College, North Sydney; East Sydney Technical College; Univ. of Sydney, Australia, BDS, dental surgery, 1954; Cordon Bleu de Paris, FR, diploma, 1956; *party:* Conservative Party; *political career:* mem., Inner London Exec. Cncl., Nat. Health Service, 1966-71; mem., Standing Dental Advisory Cttee. for England and Wales, 1968-76; mem., Westminster City Council, 1968-78; Parly. candidate, 1970, 1974; Chmn., London Canals Consultative Cttee., 1970-73; mem., Greater London Council, 1970-73, 1977-86; mem., Inland Waterways Amenity Advisory Cncl., 1971-74; mem., Westminster Kensington and Chelsea Area Health Authority, 1974-81; mem., Industrial Tribunal Panel for London, 1974-; mem., Dept. of Employment Advisory Cttee. on Women's Employment, 1980-89; mem., North Thames Gas Consumer Cncl., 1980-82; House of Lords, 1981-; UK representative, UN Status of Women Commission, 1982-88; mem., London Electricity Board, 1984-90; Lady Mayoress, Westminster, 1987-88; *interests:* transport, housing, health, planning; *professional career:* JP, North Westminster, 1971-; Governor,

Eastman Dental Hospital, 1971- 80; Governor, Nat. Heart Hospital, 1974-90; mem., Gen. Dental Cncl., 1984-86, 1987-91; Pres., War Widow's Assn. of GB, 1984-87; Dir., Gateway Building Soc., 1987-88; Dir., Woolwich Building Soc., 1988-; Vice-Chwn., N.E. Thames Regional Health Authority, 1990-; *clubs:* Inst. of Directors (Fellow); *recreations:* family life, gardening, needlework, travel; *office address:* Baroness Gardner of Parkes, House of Lords, London SW1A 0PW.

GEAR, Sara Moreau; American, Vermont State Representative; *born:* 20 April 1941, Colchester, Vermont, USA; *parents:* Omer Moreau and Dorothy Moreau (née Martell); *married:* Allen Gear, 1963; *children:* Kristen, Amy, Heather; *religion:* Roman Catholic; *education:* Univ. of Vermont, BS, 1963; *party:* Republican Party; *political career:* Vermont State Rep., 1985-; *office address:* Ms Sara Gear, 76 Crescent Beach Drive, Strafford, Vermont 05072, USA.

GEIGER, Michaela; German, Parliamentary Secretary of State for Economic Co-operation; *born:* 29 September 1943, Oberammergau, West Germany; *children:* one s; *religion:* Protestant; *education:* High school leaving examination, 1963; television picture technician training, final examination, Radio operation technique, Nürnberg, 1964; *party:* Christlich Soziale Union (CSU, Christian Social Union), 1971; *political career:* district cttee. CSU Garmisch-Partenkirchen since 1975; dep. district chmn. CSU Upper Bavaria since 1977; municipal councillor, Garmisch-Partenkirchen, 1978-81; mem. of Foreign Affairs cttee. Foreign affairs politician; Speaker, CDU/CSU, Bundestag Group; mem. of Bundestag; head of the Interparliamentary Group of the Federal Republic of Germany; Chaiperson of the German American Parliamentary Group; Parly. Sec. of State for Economic Co-operation; *professional career:* picture technician, Bayerisches Fernsehen, Munich-Freimann, 1964-67; marriage, housewife and cooperation in medium-sized company belonging to spouse, 1967; mem. of supervisory board, Volksbank, Garmisch-Partenkirchen e.G.; in various Youth Work Assns.; district cttee. Women's Union. Garmisch-Partenkirchen, 1974-81; *clubs:* various sports assns., Alp Assn., various local groups; *office address:* Frau Michaela Geiger, Bundeshaus, 5300 Bonn 1, West Germany.

GELDERBLOM-LANKHOUT, Hanneke M.; Dutch, Member of the First Chamber; *born:* 11 February 1936, The Hague, Netherlands; *parents:* F Lankhout and E Lankhout (née Loeb); *married:* J L Gelderblom, BNA, 1960; *religion:* progressive jew; *languages:* Dutch, English, German, French, Italian; *education:* Grammar school; *party:* Democraten '66, 1966; *political career:* Mem. of the First Chamber; Chair, Cttee. for

Development Co-operation; mem. Cttees for Housing, Social Welfare and Health; *professional career:* mem. board, Red Cross Hospital, the Hague; mem. board, NGO; mem. Int. Board, Int. Centre for Peace in the Middle East; mem. board, Cncl. of Christians and Jews; *private address:* Mechelsestr 36, The Hague, 2587X2 The Netherlands; *office address:* Mevr. Hanneke Gelderblom-Lankhout, Eerste Kamer der Staaten-Generaal, Binnenhof 22, Postbus 20017, The Hague, Netherlands.

GELLI, Bianca; Italian, Deputy; *born:* 11 December 1933, Lecce, Italy; *education:* Degree in Medecine and Surgery specialisation in nervous and mental illnesses; *party:* Partito Democratico della Sinistra (PDS, Party of the Democratic Left); *political career:* mem. Federal Cttee., PCI, Lecce; mem. Health Cttee. and Regional Women's Cttee., Deputy, Lecce-Brindisi-Taranto, 1983, re-elected 1987; mem. Cttee. on Health; Vice-Pres. Cttee. on Culture, Science and Teaching; *professional career:* Lecturer; Psychiatry; Head Physician, Dir., Mental Health Service, Province of Taranto-, Professor of Psychology, Lecce University; *office address:* Ms Bianca Gelli, Camera dei Deputati, Montecitorio, 00186 Rome, Italy.

GEMESCU, Virginia; Romanian, Member of the State Council; *political career:* Mem., State Cncl., 1980-; *office address:* Ms Virginia Gemescu, Marea Adunare Nationala, Aleea Marii Adunari Nationale, Bucharest, Romania; *phone:* 16 21 50.

GEOGHEGAN-QUINN, Máire; Irish, Minister for European Affairs; *born:* 5 September 1950, Galway, Ireland; *parents:* John Geoghegan and Barbara Geoghegan (née Folan); *married:* John Quinn, 1973; *children:* Ruairí, Cormac; *religion:* Roman Catholic; *languages:* Irish, English, French; *education:* Teacher Training College, Dublin, 1968-70; *party:* Fianna Fáil; *political career:* elected Mem., Dáil Éirann for West Galway, 1975; Minister of State at Dept. of Industry and and Commerce, 1977-79; Minister for the Gaeltacht, 1979-81; Minister for Youth and Sport, 1982; Minister for European Affairs, 1987-; 1st Chwn., Parly. Women's Cttee., 1982-87; 1st Women Cabinet Minister, 1979-81; National Vice-Pres., Fianna Fáil; *interests:* European Affairs, women's rights, equality issues; *professional career:* Primary School Teacher, Dublin, 1970-73, Galway, 1973-75; *honours and awards:* Gold Medal, Teacher Training College, 1970; *recreations:* reading, walking; *office address:* Máire Goeghegan-Quinn, Seanad Éireann, Lenister House, Kildare Street, Dublin 2, Ireland.

GEO-KARIS, Adeline Jay; American, Illinois State Senator; *born:* 29 March 1918, Tegeas, Greece; *religion:* Greek Orthodox; *education:* Northwestern Univ.; DePaul Univ. College of Law, LLB; *party:* Republican

Party; *political career:* Justice of the Peace and Asst. State's Attorney, Lake County; Illinois State Rep., 1973-79; Illinois State Senator, District 31, 1979-; Mem., Appropriations II, Exec., Judiciary and Citizen's Cncl. on Children Cttees.; Mem., Violent Crime Victims Assistance Commission; Mem., State Senate, Illinois; *professional career:* Attorney; Lt.-Cmdr. (Ret.), Naval Reserves; *honours and awards:* Purple Heart; Americanism Medal, DAR, 1960; Woman of the Year, Daughters of Penelope, 1958; Jane Adams Leadership Award, 1980; *private address:* 2610 Sheridan Road, P.O. Box 33, Zion, Illinois 60099, USA; *office address:* Ms Adeline Geo-Karis, 309F Capitol Bldg., Springfield, Illinois 62706, USA.

GERMAIN CUTLER, Lynn; American, Vice-Chairwoman of the Democrat National Committee of Iowa; *born:* 15 October 1938, Chicago, Illinois, USA; *parents:* Charles T. Germain and Berneice Germain (née Feldman); *married:* Henry Cutler, 1963; *children:* Megan, Jennifer, Allison, Allan; *religion:* Jewish; *education:* Univ. of Illinois, 1955-57; Univ. of Northern Iowa, BA, 1961, MA, 1967; *party:* Democratic Party; *political career:* Precinct Committeewoman, Black Hawk County Democratic Cttee., Iowa, 1964-71; Mem., Exec. Cttee., 1975; Mem., Platform Cttee., Democrat National Convention, 1972; Vice-Chwn., Advisory Commission on Intergovernmental Relations, 1977-; delegate, Democrat Mid-Term Conference, 1978-; Vice-Chwn., Democrat National Conference, 1981; *memberships:* Iowa Women's Political Caucus; Pres., Iowa Assn. of Regional Counties, 1977-; Pres., State Title XX Advisory Cttee., Iowa; League of Women Voters; *professional career:* Mem., Board, National Assn. of Counties, 1977-; Sec., Democratic County Officials, 1978; *honours and awards:* Distinguished Service Award, Waterloo and State of Iowa Jaycees, 1974; Service Award, Rath Packing Co. Employees, 1978; Humanitarian Service Award, Federal Region VII Community Action Dirs., 1979-; Citizen of the Year, Iowa Assn. of Social Workers, 1980; Public Servant of the Year, Waterloo CofC, 1981; *private address:* 705 Prospect Blvd., Waterloo, Iowa 50701, USA; *office address:* Mrs Lynn Germain Cutler, Democrat National Cttee., 20 Ivy Street SE Washington DC, 20003, USA.

GIBEAU, Hon. Marie; Canadian, Member of the House of Commons; *born:* 11 July 1950, Montreal, Canada; *parents:* Philippe Gibeau and Marguerite Delisle; *married:* Jean-Pierre Bordua, 1990; *public role of spouse:* businessman; *children:* expected, Sept. 1991; *religion:* Catholic; *languages:* French, English, Spanish; *education:* Univ. of Montreal, BA, 1969; Univ. of Québec, B.Ped., 1970; Ecole des Hautes Etudes Commerciales, MBA, 1977; *party:* Progressive Conservative Party, 1988; *political career:* Mem., House of Commons; *interests:* international affairs and trade, social and community affairs; *office address:* The

Hon. Ms Marie Gibeau, House of Commons, Parliament Buildings, Wellington Street, Ottawa, Ontario K1A OA6, Canada; *phone:* (613) 957 3744; *fax:* 952 0874.

GIBSON, Mary Jane; American, Massachusetts State Representative; *born:* 7 February 1933, Commerce, Texas, USA; *married:* R.J. Gibson; *religion:* Methodist; *education:* Centenary College, Louisiana, BA; Boston Univ., MED; *party:* Democratic Party; *political career:* Mass. State Rep., District 26; Asst. Majority Whip; *office address:* Mrs Mary Jane Gibson, 30 Bellevue Road, Belmont, MA 02178, USA.

GIBSON, Yvonne; Saint Vincent, Minister of State for Education, Youth and Women's Affairs; *office address:* Ms Yvonne Gibson, Ministry of Youth, Women's Affairs and Sports, Kingstown, Saint Vincent and the Grenadines.

GIL, Irena Urszula; Polish, Member of the Sejm; *office address:* Ms Irena Urszula Gil, Sejm PRI, ul. Wiejska 4/6/8, 00-489 Warsaw, Poland; *phone:* (22) 28 70 01; 28 40 31.

GILES, Patricia Jessie; Australian, Senator; *born:* 16 November 1928, Minlaton, South Australia; *education:* trained nurse in general, midwifery and infant welfare; BA, Western Australia; *party:* Australian Labor Party; *political career:* Delegate, Labor Party State Executive, Western Australia, 1973-; Conferences, Delegations and Visits: Mem., Australian Govt. Delegation to Tribune, Mexico, International Women's Year, 1975; Leader, Australian Govt. Delegation to World Conference for the End of the Decade for Women, Nairobi, 1985; Leader, Australian Delegation to Meeting of Commonwealth Ministers for Women's Affairs, Nairobi, 1985, Zimbabwe, 1987 and Ottawa, 1990; Mem., Labour Party Administrative Cttee., WA, 1976-81; Pres., Curtin Electorate Council, 1978-79; elected to Senate for Western Australia, 1980-; Vice Pres., Labor Party, WA Branch, 1981; Delegate, Labor Party National Status of Women Cttee., 1981 and Convener, 1983 and 1985; Delegate, Labor Party National Conference, 1981, 1982, 1984, 1986 and 1988; WA Delegate to Labor Party National Executive, 1981-89; Committee Service: Mem. of the Senate Legislative and General Purpose Standing Cttee. for Social Welfare, 1981-87; for Education and the Arts, 1981-83; for Legal and Constitutional Affairs, 1987-; Mem. of the Senate Select Cttee. for Private Hospitals and Nursing Homes, 1981-83 and Chairperson, 1983-87; for Television and Equalisation, 1986-87; Mem. of the Senate Estimates Cttee. G, 1981-83; Chairperson of B, 1983-87; F, Mar.-Jun. 1987; D, 1987-; Mem. of the Senate Standing Cttee. for Regulations and Ordinances, 1985-; Mem. of the Joint Statutory Cttee. for Public Accounts, 1987-; Mem. of the Joint Standing Cttee. for

Australian Capital Territory, 1983-85; Mem., Cttee. on Regulations and Ordinances, 1985 and Chair., 1990-; Junior Vice-Pres., Labor Party National Executive, 1983-85; Convener, Labor Party National Platform Cttee. on Social Security and Community Services, 1987; Chairperson, Senate Priveleges Cttee. 1988-; Deputy Chairperson, Cttees., 1987-; Special Adviser to Minister Assisting on Status of Women and on Violence Against Women; *memberships:* Inaugural mem., World Women Parliamentarians for Peace, 1985-; mem., Women for a Meaningful Summit, 1986-; *professional career:* organiser, Hospital Employees Union; mem., Health Education Council of Western Australia, 1971-81; Inaugural Convener, Women's Electoral Lobby, Perth, 1973; Chairperson, Western Australian Cttee. on Discrimination in Employment and Occupation, 1974-76; mem., Western Australian Cttee., Advisory Cttee. on Homeless Persons, 1975-81; mem. Review Cttee., Legal Aid Commission of Western Australia, 1978-81; Chairperson., ACTU Women's Cttee., 1978-81; *office address:* Ms Patricia Giles, Senate, Parliament House, Room M13, Canberra, ACT 2600, Australia; *phone:* (062) 727111.

GINJAAR née Mass, Drs. Nelly Jeanne; Dutch, Member of the Second Education; *born:* 7 May 1931, Rotterdam, The Netherlands; *parents:* Victor Mass and Cornelia Mass (née Van den Broek); *married:* Leendert Ginjaar, 1954; *public role of spouse:* Minister of the Environment, 1977-81; President of VVD; *children:* Willem, Ineke, Petra; *languages:* Dutch, English; *education:* Univ. of Leiden, Chemistry, 1948-56; *party:* VVD (Liberal Party); *political career:* Mem., Second Chamber, Dutch Parly., 1973-82 and 1982-; State Sec. for Education, 1982-89; *interests:* education, emancipation, minorities; *professional career:* chemistry teacher, 1960-73; *honours and awards:* Commander Oranje Nassau, HM Queen, 1989; *recreations:* bridge, gardening, swimming; *private address:* Rooiedal 8, 4320 PZ Burghe, Haarstede, The Netherlands; *office address:* Drs. Nelly Jeanne Ginjaar, Tweede Kamer der Staten-Generaal, Binnenhof 1A, Postbus 20018, The Hague, The Netherlands.

GJELLERUP, Pia; Danish, Member of the Folketing; *born:* 22 August 1959, Copenhagen, Denmark; *languages:* Danish, English; *education:* Copenhagen University, Bachelor of Laws, 1980-85; *party:* Socialdemokratiet (Social Democratic Party); *political career:* member of the Town Council of Frederiksberg, 1982-87; member of the Folketinget, 1987-; *interests:* fiscal policy, housing policy, human rights; *professional career:* Lawyer, Copenhagen, 1989-; *office address:* Ms Pia Gjellerup, Christiansborg, 1240 Copenhagen K, Denmark.

GJESTEBY, Kari; Norwegian, Minister of Justice; *born:* 16 May 1947, Oslo, Norway; *parents:* Omar Anton

Gjesteby and Ingrid Gjesteby (née Thoresen); *married:* Carl Axel Mikael Klingberg; *public role of spouse:* Director in the Norges Bank; *children:* Mariann, Hanna; *religion:* Human-Ethic; *languages:* Norwegian, English; *education:* Norwegian School of Economics and Business Admin., Degree, 1970; *party:* Norwegian Labour Party; *political career:* former Minister of Trade and Shipping; State Sec., Ministry of Church and Education, 1976-78, Ministry of Finance, 1979-81, Ministry of Foreign Affairs, 1986-88; Minister of Justice, Nov. 1990-; *professional career:* First Dep. Gen.-Sec., Nordic Cncl. of Ministers Secretariat; Mem., National Wages Arbitration Board; Dir., Norges Bank, 1990-; *clubs:* Oslo Balloon Club; *office address:* Ms Kari Gjesteby, Minister of Justice and Police, Akersgaten 42, P.O. Box 8005 Dep, 0030 Oslo 1, Norway; *phone:* (02) 34 51 00; *fax:* 349533.

GLOMAZIC-LEKOVIC, Stanka; Yugoslavian, Delegate to the Yugoslav National Assembly; *born:* 23 March 1924, Zabljak, Yugoslavia; *education:* diploma in law; *party:* Communist Party of Yugoslavia (CPY); League of Communists of Yugoslavia (LCY); *political career:* Mem., CPY, 1941-; elected to Central Cttee., 10th Congress of LCY, 1974-; Mem., LCY Central Cttee., 1982-86; Delegate, Yugoslav Nat. Assembly; *honours and awards:* Spomenica, 1941; *office address:* Ms Stanka Glomazic-Lekovic, Savezna Skupstina, Yugoslavia.

GOES, Eva Christina; Swedish, Member of the Riksdag; *born:* 4 July 1947, Umeå, Västerbotten, Sweden; *parents:* Bertil Andersson and Magnhild Andersson (née Slettvoll); *married:* Stefan Goës, 1976; *children:* Roland, Ellinor, Josefin, Jens, Kåre, Anna; *languages:* English, German, French, Spanish; *education:* teacher training college, Umeå, elementary school teacher; *party:* Miljöpartiet de Gröna (Green Party), 1982; *political career:* substitute deputy, Board of Local Government, Härnösand, 1982-88; Cncl. 1985-88; Chairwoman and treasurer, Härnösand Green Party, 1982- 87; regional representative for Västernorrland and mem. Green Party political cttee., 1983-88; auditor for Green Party, 1986-89; spokeswoman for Green Party in Sweden, 1986-88; mem. Riksdag, 1988-; *interests:* peace, energy and environmental affairs; *memberships:* International Women's Assoc. for Peace and Freedom; Popular Campaign Against Nuclear Power and Nuclear Arms; Greenpeace; Swedish Society for Protection of Nature; East Timor Cttee., (PET); *professional career:* elementary school teacher, local education authorities, Umeå, Laxa, Söderhamn, Härnösand, 1968-86; editorial writer, Alternativet, 1983-86; *publications:* Försumbar risk?? radiakdebatt, Morkullan, 1987; En kruka jord, Många ledare; Ingen Är För Liten Att Påverka, in Sydsvenska Dagbladet, 1988; *clubs:* Härnösands Music Choir; *recreations:* music; *office*

address: Ms Eva Goës, Riksdag, Fack, S-100 12 Stockholm, Sweden.

GOLDING, Llin (Llinos); British, Member of Parliament; *parents:* the late Rt. Hon. Ness Edwards MP; *married:* John Golding, 1980; *children:* one s., two d. (from previous marriage); *education:* Caerphilly Girls Grammar School; *party:* Labour Party; *political career:* Member of Parliament for Newcastle-under-Lyme, 1986-; Opposition West Midlands Whip, Legal Affairs, Womens Affairs, Parliamentary Affairs and Home Affairs, Energy and Treasury; Vice Chmn., Parliamentary Labour Party Home Affairs Cttee; Vice-Chmn., All Party Group on Children; former Mem. North Staffs District Health Authority, 1983-87; Sec. Staffs District Trades Cncl., 1976-86; former mem. District Manpower Services Cttee.; former Branch Sec., National Union of Public Employees; *interests:* health services; trade unions; Home Affairs; children's rights; *professional career:* Sec. and Asst. to John Golding MP, former Member of Parliament for Newcastle-under-Lyme; radiographer; *clubs:* Soc. of Radiographers; *private address:* 6, Lancaster Avenue, Newcastle-under-Lyme, Staffs; *office address:* Mrs Llin Golding, House of Commons, London SW1A OAA.

GOMES, Hon. Henriqueta Godinho; Guinea-Bissau,, Minister of Public Health; *party:* Partido Africano da Independência da Guiné e Cabo Verde (PAIGC); *office address:* The Hon. Ms Henriqueta Godinho Gomes, Ministry of Public Health, Bissau, Guinea-Bissau; *phone:* 213632.

GOMES, Socorro (Maria do Socorro Gomes); Brazilian, Federal Deputy; *born:* 12 January 1952, Cristalandia; *parents:* Nelson Coelho dos Santos and Margarida Gomes dos Santos; *children:* Enelson, Marcos José, Fernanda, Dina Walkiria, Julia Margarida; *education:* UFPA, Belém, history, 1985; *party:* Partido Communista do Brasil (PCDB, Communist Party of Brasil, pro-Albanian); *political career:* Exec. Mem., Municipal Council for Women's Rights, 1987-88; Town Cllr., Belém, 1989-91; Federal Deputy for Pará, 1991-95; *professional career:* professor; *office address:* Ms Socorro Gomes, Chamber of Deputies, Praça dos 3 Poderes, Ed. Principal, 70160 Brasilia, DF, Brazil; *phone:* (61) 225 2885.

GOMOLA, Maria; Polish, Member of the Sejm; *office address:* Ms Maria Gomola, Sejm PRI, ul. Wiejska 4/6/8, 00-489 Warsaw, Poland; *phone:* (22) 28 70 01; 28 40 31.

GONZALEZ, Hon. Pacita T.; Filipino, Congresswoman; *born:* 15 October 1940; *parents:* the late Dr. Nestorio Trinidad and Rosario Pulido; *married:* Raul M. Gonzalez, 1961; *public role of spouse:* Tanodbayan Justice, 1986-87; *children:* Raul Jr., Jose

Mari, Dennis, Marigold, Charmaine; *religion:* Roman Catholic; *languages:* Tagalog, English; *education:* Univ. of Sto. Tomas, Doctor of Medicine; passed Medical Bar Examinations, 1962; *party:* Liberal Democrat Party (LDP); *political career:* Congresswoman; Vice Chairperson, House Cttee. on Health; *interests:* public service; *memberships:* Philippine Medical Assn.; Philippine Women's Medical Assn; *professional career:* former Resident-Intern, Dept. of Surgery, Portsmouth General Hospital, Virginia, USA; *clubs:* Union Zambaleña; Valle Verde Country Club; *private address:* E-9 2nd Floor, Virra Mall, San Juan, Metro Manila, The Philippines; *office address:* The Hon. Ms Pacita Gonzalez, House of Representatives, Quezon City, Metro Manila, The Philippines.

GORBACHEVA, Raisa Maksimovna; Soviet, First Lady of the Soviet Union; *born:* 1934, Stavropol; *married:* Mikhail Gorbachev, 1956; *public role of spouse:* President of the USSR; *children:* one d; *education:* Stavropol Teachers' Training College; *memberships:* Pres., Cultural Heritage Commission, 1987-; *professional career:* teacher, Stavropol; sociologist, Stavropol Teacher Training Institute, 1957-61; lecturer, Philosophy; *office address:* Mrs Raisa Gorbacheva, The Kremlin, Moscow, USSR.

GORDILHO, Regina Helena Costa; Brazilian, Federal Deputy; *born:* 12 May 1933, Salvador; *parents:* Almir Campos Gordilho and Virgília Costa Gordilho; *married:* Antonio Loureiro de Almeida; *party:* Partido Democrático Trabalhista (PDT, Centre Left Party); *political career:* Town Cllr. for Rio de Janeiro, 1987-91; Pres., Rio de Janeiro Municipal Chamber, 1989-90; Federal Deputy for Rio de Janeiro, 1991-95; *professional career:* entrepreneur; *office address:* Ms Regina Gordilho, Chamber of Deputies, Praça dos 3 Poderes, Ed. Principal, 70160 Brasilia, DF, Brazil; *phone:* (61) 225 2885.

GORDON, Elaine; American, Florida State Representative; *born:* 1931, New York City, USA; *parents:* Henry Weitzman and Freda Weitzman (née Singerman); *married:* Arthur Pearlman; *children:* Brian, Seth, Pamela; *education:* City College, New York, 1949-50; Miami-Dade Jr. College, Florida, 1965-66; Florida International Univ; *party:* Democratic Party; *political career:* Legislative Aide to Dade County Rep., 1968-69; currently: Mem., Governor's Commission on Aging; Mem., State Commission on Child Support; formerly: Chwn., Task Force on Econ. Discrimination of Women and Governor's Commission on Status of Women; Florida State Rep., Dade County, 1972-; Chwn., Health and Rehabilitative Services Cttee., 1976-78; Dade County Delegate, 1980-81; Mem., State Govt. Issues and Organisation Cttee., Democratic National Conference; Mem., National and Florida Women's Political Caucus; *memberships:* North Miami CofC;

National Organisation of Women; Dade County Business and Professional Women; Women in Govt. Service; National Women's Forum; National Order of Women Legislators; Charter Mem., Florida Feminist Credit Union; *professional career:* Sales and Marketing Exec., 1969-; Consultant, National Centre for Health Service Research; *honours and awards:* Outstanding Representative Award, Florida Assn. for Retarded Citizens, 1976; Person of the Year, City of Miami, 1982; Legislator of the Year, Florida Health Care Assn., 1983; Good Govt. Award, Dade County League of Cities, 1986; Legislator Award, Mental Health Assn., Florida Div., Maxine E. Baker Human Services, 1984; Woman of the Year, Miami Shores Business and Professional Women, 1984-85; Legislators Effectivness Award, Florida Assn., Rehabilitative Facilities Inc., 1983; *publications:* Equal Rights Amendment, Edition of Annals America, Encyclopedia Britannica, 1977; *office address:* Ms Elaine Gordon, 12100 NE 16th Avenue, North Miami, Florida 33161, USA.

GORDON, Hon. Katherine H.; Filipino, Congresswoman; *born:* 1 May 1948, Olongapo City; *married:* Richard Julco Gordon; *public role of spouse:* City Mayor of Olongapo; *children:* Ma. Renee, Victoria, Amanda Olivia, Leonard James, Brian Patrick; *political career:* Congresswoman; *office address:* The Hon. Ms Katherine Gordon, The Congress of the Philippines - House of Representatives, Batasang Pambana Bldg., Quezon City, Manila, The Philippines.

GORDON, Mildred; British, Member of Parliament; *born:* 24 August 1923; *parents:* the late Judah Fellerman and Dora Fellerman; *married:* Nils Kaare Dahl, 1985; *children:* one s. (from previous marriage); *education:* Raines Foundation School, Stepney; Pitman's College of Commerce; Forest Training College, Walthamstow; Emergency Teacher Training College; *party:* Labour Party; *political career:* Member of Parliament for Bow and Poplar, 1987-; Former chair, Policy Committee of London Labour Party; *interests:* education; race relations; women; children's rights; *professional career:* Teacher of English and History, London, 1945-47, 1952-59 and 1964-85; Visiting Teacher, Holloway Prison (typing), 1960-62; *recreations:* making costume jewellery; pottery; *office address:* Mrs Mildred Gordon, House of Commons, London SW1A 0AA.

GORMAN, Teresa Ellen; British, Member of Parliament; *born:* 30 September 1937; *married:* James Daniel Gorman; *children:* one; *education:* Fulham County School; London University, biology graduate; *party:* Conservative Party; *political career:* Conservative Women's National Cttee. mem., 1983-; Cllr., Westminster City Cncl., 1982-86; Member of Parliament for Billericay, 1987-; *interests:* deregulation, removing government interference, health, housing, education, women's issues; *professional career:* teacher and businesswoman; Chwn., Alliance of Small Firms and Self Employed People; Chwn., Amarant Trust, a charity for the health care of Mature Women; *publications:* The Case for Private Enterprise, 1976; Minimum Wage Laws and Small Firms, 1979; Worried to Death, Centre for Policy Studies, London, 1983; Business Still Burdened, CPS, London, 1984; contributed to Trespassing, Social Affairs Unit, 1984; Quangos Just Grow, CPS London, 1985; The Enterprise Culture, Adam Smith Institute, London 1986; Chichesgate, with Michael Ward, 1990; *recreations:* dress making, travel; *office address:* Mrs Teresa Gorman, House of Commons, London SW1A OAA.

GOSSINGAR, Achta Tone; Chad, Minister of Social Affairs and the Promotion of Women; *office address:* Ms Achta Tone Gossingar, Ministry of Social Affairs and the Promotion of Women, N'Djamena, Chad.

GÖTTE, Dr. Rose; German, Member of the Bundestag; *born:* 21 March 1938; *married:* Dr. Klaus, 1961; *children:* three ch; *religion:* Protestant; *languages:* English, French, Latin; *party:* Sozialdemokratische Partei Deutschlands (SPD, Social Democratic Party of Germany); *political career:* mem. of Bundestag; *professional career:* Scientific Researcher (Educational Theory of Pre-School Education); *publications:* Sprache und Speil im Kindergarten, 5th edition, 1984; *office address:* Dr. Rose Götte, Bundeshaus, 5300 Bonn 1, West Germany.

GOURNAY, Marie-Fanny; French, Senator; *born:* 6 March 1926, Hazebrouck, Nord; *party:* Rassemblement pour la République (RPR, Rally for the Republic); *political career:* General Cnclr.; Mayoress of Caestre; Senator, replacing deceased Pierre Carous, 1990-; *office address:* Mme. Marie-Fanny Gournay, Sénat, Palais du Luxembourg, 75291 Paris Cedex 06, France; *phone:* Paris 42 34 20 00; *fax:* Paris 43 29 86 47.

GOYEMIDO, Geneviève; Central African Republic, Minister of Public Health and Social Affairs; *office address:* Ms Geneviève Goyemido, Ministry of Health and Social Affairs, Bangui, Central African Republic.

GRABARKLEWICS MIROSLAWA, Kasimiera; Polish, Member of the Sejm; *office address:* Ms Kasimiera Grabarklewics, Sejm PRI, ul. Wiejska 4/6/8, 00-489 Warsaw, Poland; *phone:* (22) 28 70 01; 28 40 31.

GRABEWSKA, Danuba; Polish, Member of the Sejm; *office address:* Ms Danuba Grabewska, Sejm PRI, ul. Wiejska 4/6/8, 00-489 Warsaw, Poland; *phone:* (22) 28 70 01; 28 40 31.

GRADIN, Anita; Swedish, Minister of Foreign Trade (Ministry of Foreign Affairs); *born:* 12 August 1933, Hörnefors, Västerbotten, Sweden; *parents:* Ossian Gradin and Alfhild Gradin (née Englund); *married:* Bertil Kersfelt; *children:* Catherine; *languages:* English, German; *education:* Stockholm School for Social Work and Public Administration, 1958-60; *party:* Sveriges Socialdemokratiska Arbetarepartiet (SAP, Social Democratic Party), 1948; *political career:* MP, 1968-; mem. Standing Cttees. on Education and Financial Affairs, 1968-82; delegate to Council of Europe, 1968-82; Chairperson, Stockholm district of Nat. Federation of Social Democratic Women, 1968-82, Vice-Chairperson, 1975-; Working Chairperson, Swedish Council for Intercountry Adoptions, 1973-80; Chairperson, Council of Europe Cttee. on Migration, Refugees and Demography, 1978-82; Vice-Pres., Cabinet Minister for Migration and Equality between Women and Men, 1982-86; Vice-Pres. Socialist International, 1983-86, then Pres. 1986-; Cabinet Minister for Foreign Trade, 1986-; delegate to IPU; *professional career:* journalist, Västerbottens Folkblad, 1950-52, Arbetarbladet, Gävle, 1955-58, TCO - tidningen (Civil Service Organisation Newspaper), 1960-63; employee, Swedish Forestry and Log-floating Labour Union, 1952-55; employee, Social Welfare Planning Cttee., Stockholm; Chmn. Swedish Socio-economist Federation, 1970-79; *publications:* Lagstadgad lycka? En bok om lag, samhälle och äktenskap, 1971; Vårdkunskap: Social medicin, 1972; *clubs:* Swedish Assoc. for Graduates from Schools of Social Work and public administration, Chairman, 1979-; delegate and lecturer to International Planned Parenthood Fed.; delegate and lecturer to International Fed. of Social workers; *recreations:* stamp collecting, fishing; *private address:* Svartviksslingen 27, 161 29 Bromma, Sweden; *office address:* Ms Anita Gradin, Riksdag, Fack, S-100 12 Stockholm, Sweden.

GRAENITZ, Ilona; Austrian, Member of the Nationalrat; *born:* 15 March 1943, Vienna, Austria; *parents:* Georg Hauric and Anna Hauric; *children:* Judith Graenitz; *languages:* German, English, French, Italian; *education:* High School, Vienna, matriculated 1961; College of International Trade, Dipl.-Kfm., 1965; teaching qualification for languages at secondary school, 1969; *party:* Sozialdemokratische Partei Österreichs (SPÖ, Socialdemocrat Party), June 1991; *political career:* Local Councillor on Linz Town Council, 1979-86; mem. of Nationalrat for Upper Austria, Dec. 1986-; Mem., Parly. Assembly of the Cncl. of Europe, 1991; *interests:* environmental issues; *professional career:* Employee, Chemie Linz Export Dept., 1966-68; teacher at Linz Polytechnic, 1968-72; currently working freelance in management training, methodological and didactic further training for teachers, and also concerned in the setting up of teaching materials; *office address:* Frau Ilona Graenitz, Nationalrat, Dr. Karl Renner Ring 3, 1017 Vienna, Austria.

GRAH, Claire Therese Elisabeth; Côte D'Ivoire, Minister for the Promotion of Women; *office address:* Mme Claire Therese Elisabeth Grah, Ministre de la Promotion de la Femme, Abidjan, Côte D'Ivoire.

GRAMAGLIA VIANELLO, Dott. Mariella; Italian, Deputy; *born:* 4 May 1949, Ivrea, Turin, Italy; *children:* two; *party:* Independent Left Parly. group; *political career:* Activist, Women's Movement; Deputy, Rome-Viterbo-Latina-Frosinone, as Independent on the PCI lists, 1987; mem. Cttee. on Social Affairs; *professional career:* Professional journalist; Dir. of magazine Manifesto; Parliamentary writer for Lavoro, (Genoa) Dir. of the Magazine, Noi Donne (We Women); *office address:* Dott. Mariella Gramaglia Vianello, Camera dei Deputati, Montecitorio, 00186 Rome, Italy.

GRANT, Mary; Ghana, Acting Minister for Education and Culture; *political career:* Member of the Provisional Nat. Defence Cncl. and acting Minister for Education and Culture, 1989-; *office address:* Ms Mary Grant, Office of the Provisional National Defence Council, The Castle, Osu, Accra, PO Box 1627, Ghana.

GRANZ, Marianne; German, Deputy Member of the Bundesrat; *born:* 7 March 1942, Berlin, Germany; *children:* one d; *religion:* Evangelical; *languages:* German, English, French, Spanish, Russian, Georgisch; *education:* school leaving exam., 1961; Univ. studies, German language, Sport, Philosophy, 1967; *party:* Sozialdemokratische Partei Deutschlands (SPD, Social Democratic Party of Germany), 1972-; *political career:* Leader of Soc. for Friendship and Relations, BRD-USSR; SPD Deputy, Saarland; Minister for Education and Sport, Saarland, 1990-; *interests:* education, women's questions, communication systems, political groups for freedom; *memberships:* Mem., Broadcasting Centre; *professional career:* study supervisor (German and sport), for six years; *office address:* Ms Marianne Granz, Bundesrat, 5300 Bonn 1, Germany.

GREEN, Pauline; British, Member of the European Parliament; *born:* 8 December 1948; *party:* Labour Party; *political career:* MEP for North London, 1989-; *private address:* Gibson House, 800 High Road, Tottenham, London N17 0DH; *office address:* Mrs Pauline Green, European Parliament, Centre Européen, Plateau de Kirchberg, BP 2929, Luxembourg; *phone:* Luxembourg 43001.

GRENDELMEIER, Verena; Swiss, Member of the Nationalrat; *born:* 16 February 1939, Zurich, Switzerland; *parents:* Alois Grendelmeier; *education:* Maturité; Diploma in Teaching; studies in acting and stage direction in Paris and Vienna; *party:* Landesring der Unabhängigen (LdU, Independent Alliance); *political career:* mem. of Cantonal Cncl., Zurich, 1973-79; Vice-President, LdU, 1980-; mem. of Nationalrat,

1983-; *professional career:* assistant director and actress, Berne, FGR, Paris (J.-L. Barrault); film journalist and documentary film director/moderator Swiss-German Radio and TV Corp, Zurich; *publications:* TV documentary films: Im selben Boot - der psychisch Kranke und wir, 1975; script and direction, Gehirn und Verhalten, 1976; Das gläserne Gefängnis, 1980; Austrian documentary, Das verordnete Glück, 1982; *clubs:* Amnesty International, Press Union; Charity Cncl. for Maltreated Women and Children; *recreations:* classical music, theatre, cookery, mountaineering, hiking; *private address:* Witikonerstrasse 468, Zurich, Switzerland; *office address:* Frau Verena Grendelmeier, Nationalrat/Conseil National, Secretariat-General, Parlamentsgebäude, 3003 Berne, Switzerland.

GRIFFITHS, Martha; American, Lieutenant Governor of Michigan; *born:* 29 January 1912, Pierce City, Missouri, USA; *married:* Hicks G. Griffiths; *languages:* Presbyterian; *education:* Univ. of Missouri, BA; Univ. of Michigan, JD; *party:* Democratic Party; *political career:* Michigan State Rep., District 17, 1949-52; Mem., House of Reps. for Michigan, 1955-75; Mem., Ways and Means Cttee., US House of Reps.; Lt.-Gov., Michigan, 1983-; currently: Chwn., Michigan Equal Employment and Business Opportunity Cncl.; Chief Affirmative Action Officer; *memberships:* American, Michigan and Macomb County Bar Assns; *professional career:* judge, Recorders Court, Detroit, Michigan, 1953; law partner, Griffiths and Griffiths; Board Mem., Burroughs, Chrysler, Consumers Power, Greyhound, K-Mart, Verex and National Bank of Detroit; currently, Trustee, Henry Ford Hospital; *honours and awards:* 27 Hon. Degrees from various Univs; *private address:* P.O. Box 407, Romeo, Michigan 48065, USA; *office address:* Mrs Martha Griffiths, Capitol Bldg., Lansing, Michigan 48909, USA.

GROENMAN, Dr. Louise. S.; Dutch, Member of the Second Chamber; *born:* 29 June 1940, Meppel, Netherlands; *education:* gymnasium-A (sec. ed.); masters sociology; *party:* Democraten '66 (D'66, Democrats); *political career:* former Mem., Political Emancipation Activating Centre (PEAC) of D'66,; Mem., Second Chamber, 1981-; *professional career:* sociologist, Regional Opbouworgaan Amstelland en de Meerlanden, 1976-77; Sec., Interdepartmental Pioneering group Youth policies, min. of Culture, Recreation and Social Work; *private address:* Schippersgracht 12, 3603 BC Maarssen, the Netherlands; *office address:* Dr. Louise Groenman, Tweede Kamer der Staaten-Generaal, Binnenhof 1A, Postbus 20018, The Hague, Netherlands.

GROL (née Overling), Anne Catherine; Dutch, Member of the First Chamber; *born:* 20 March 1931, Doetinchem, The Netherlands; *parents:* Antonius Overling and Maria Overling (née Van der Klugt);

married: Wenceslaus Grol, 1961; *public role of spouse:* lecturer; *children:* Furahisha Marianne, Peter Lubango; *religion:* Roman Catholic; *languages:* Dutch, English, German, English, French, Swahili; *education:* Roman Catholic Univ. of Nymegen, Educational Psychology, BA, 1952, MA, 1954; State Examination M.O., English Language and Literature, BA, 1979; *party:* Christian Democrat Party, 1950; *political career:* Mem., Hengelo Town Cncl., 1970-76; Mem., Provincial States Overyssel, 1978-82; Mem., Eersle Kamer (Senate), 1982-; Chwn., Standing Cttee., Antillean and Aruban Affairs; Vice-Chwn., Standing Cttee. on Education; *interests:* education, Antilles Isles and Aruba, external affairs, third world development; *memberships:* Board Mem., Dutch Group of the Inter-Parliamentary Union, (IPU); *professional career:* teacher of child psychology, secondary and adult education, 1954-63; lecturer, teacher training college, Butimba Mwanza, Tanzania, 1963-65; research fellow, Netherlands Univ. Fellowship of International Co-operation, Tanzania, 1965-68; School of Social Work, Hengelo, 1969-84; lecturer, Conservatory of Music, Enschede, 1984-; *publications:* Noodzakelyk denken, Chapter 6, 1963; De samenwerking tassen blank en zwast, 1966; Primary Education in Sukumaland, Chapter 6, 1969; column in Univ. magazine, Twente, 1981-82; *recreations:* reading, traveling; *private address:* Lansinkweq 48, 7553 Al Hengelo, The Netherlands; *office address:* Mevr. Anne Grol, Erste Kamer der Staten Generaal, Binnenhof 22, Postbus 20017, The Hague, The Netherlands.

GRÖNER, Lissy; German, Member of the European Parliament; *born:* 31 May 1954, Langenfeld, West Germany; *married:* Gerhard Gröner; *children:* Myriam, Nicolai; *party:* Sozialdemokratische Partei Deutschlands (SPD, Social Democratic Party of Germany), 1971; *political career:* MEP, June 1989-; *interests:* Women's rights, vocational training in Europe, youth, family and children's rights; *office address:* Frau Lissy Gröner, European Parliament, Rue Belliard MAE 435, B-1040 Brussels 4, Belgium.

GROSSENBACHER-SCHMID, Ruth; Swiss, Member of the Nationalrat; *born:* 13 September 1936, Capetown, South Africa; *parents:* Oskar Schmid and Margrit Gisiger; *married:* Rolf Grossenbacher, 1961; *children:* one; *religion:* Roman Catholic; *languages:* German, English, French; *education:* language teacher's certificate; *party:* Christlichdemokratische Volkspartei (CVP, Christian Democratic People's Party); *political career:* district Cllr., 1973-81; Verfassungsrätin, 1981-86; Pres., CVP Women of Switzerland; Member of the Nationalrat, 1981-, replacing Peter Hänggi; *interests:* promotion of education, social security and welfare, equal rights for women; *professional career:* primary school teacher; English teacher, technical college, Aarau; *recreations:* hiking, travelling; *office address:* Frau Ruth Grossenbacher-Schmid, Nationalrat/Conseil

National, Secretariat-General, Parlamentsgebäude, 3003 Berne, Switzerland; *phone:* Berne 619711.

GROSSO ROMERO, Gloria (Maria Teresa); Italian, Deputy; *born:* 9 April 1936, Colleferro, Rome, Italy; *party:* Federazione Nationale per Le Liste Verdi (Green Party); *political career:* Founder and Nat. Pres. League for the Abolition of Hunting (L.A.C.); First signatory of referendum against hunting; Represented the Green List on the Provincial council of Milan from 1985; achieved end of bird-shooting in the Province; Deputy, Milan-Pavia, 1987; mem. Cttee. on Agriculture; *professional career:* Primary school teacher; *office address:* Ms Gloria Grosso Romero, Camera dei Deputati, Montecitorio, 00186 Rome, Italy.

GROZA, Maria; Romanian, Deputy Minister of Foreign Affairs; *born:* 1 September 1918, Deva, Hundedoara County, Romania; *education:* Academy of Economics, Bucharest; *political career:* Mem., Grand Nat. Assembly, 1965-81, Vice-Pres.; Sec., Nat. Cncl. of Women of Socialist Republic of Romania. 1958-64, Vice-Pres., 1964-80; delegate to numerous Women's international congresses, UNESCO and UN congresses and conferences on social problems in Montreal, 1960; Chairperson, Third Cttee., for social, humanitarian and cultural problems, of the 25th UN General Assembly Session; Mem., Romanian delegation to UN General Assembly, Sessions XVIII, XX-XXIII; Dep. Minister of Foreign Affairs, (Directorate V-Americas, and Directorate for Press, Culture, and Protocol Directorate), 1980-; Vice Chairperson, Organisation for Promotion of Friendship and Collaboration with Other People, 1980-; *professional career:* assistant, Academy of Economics, Bucharest, 1949-55; lecturer, Social Science, 1955-; *publications:* author of several papers on social position of Romanian women and education of youth in Romania; contributor to UNESCO periodical Femmes du Monde Entier (Women of the entire World); *office address:* Ms Maria Groza, Ministry of Foreign Affairs, Piata Victoriei 1, Bucharest, Romania.

GRUDININA, Anna Kornilovna; Soviet, Member of the Council of the Union; *party:* Communist Party of the Soviet Union; *political career:* Mem., Cncl. of the Union; Mem., Supreme Soviet Cttee. on Public Health; *professional career:* Section Chief, Borisoglebsk Central Raion Hospital; *office address:* Ms Anna Kornilovna Grudinina, Council of the Union, Kremlin, Moscow, USSR.

GRUND, Johanna-Christina; German, Member of the European Parliament; *born:* 17 July 1934; *party:* Die Republikaner (Rep, Republican Party); *political career:* MEP, 1989-; *office address:* Ms Johanna-Christina Grund, European Parliament, Centre Européen, Plateau de Kirchberg, BP 2929, Luxembourg; *phone:* Luxembourg 43001.

GRZEDA, Krystyna; Polish, Member of the Sejm; *office address:* Ms Krystyna Grzeda, Sejm PRI, ul. Wiejska 4/6/8, 00-489 Warsaw, Poland; *phone:* (22) 28 70 01; 28 40 31.

GRZESKEWIAK, Alieja; Polish, Senator; *office address:* Ms Alieja Grzeskewiak, Senat, ul. Ogrodowa 6, 00-896 Warsaw, Poland; *phone:* (22) 20 03 71.

GUDILINA, Valentina Grigorevna; Soviet, Member of the Council of the Union; *political career:* Mem., Cncl. of the Union; *professional career:* Dept. Chief, Solnechnogorsk Central Raion Hospital; *office address:* Ms Valentina Grigorevna Gudilina, Council of the Union, Kremlin, Moscow, USSR.

GUIDETTI SERRA, Bianca; Italian, Deputy; *born:* 19 August 1919, Turin, Italy; *education:* Degree in Jurisprudence; *party:* Democrazia Proletaria Parly. group as Independent; *political career:* Active in the Resistance; mem. of Women's Defence Group for Assisting the fighters for liberty; mem. Agitation Committees; Worked as Trade Union organiser, Camera del Lavoro, Turin; deputy, Turin-Novara-Vercelli, 1987 as Independent in the Democrazia Proletaria lists; mem. Cttee. on Justice and the Body for authorizations to prosecute; *professional career:* lawyer, specializing in Trade Union disputes; *publications:* Various books concerning adoption, institutionalised children, women's political participation; Book of the FIAT dispute; *office address:* Ms Bianca Guidetti Serra, Camera dei Deputati, Montecitorio, 00186 Rome, Italy.

GUIGOU, Elisabeth; French, Minister Delegate to the Minister of State, Minister of Foreign Affairs responsible for European Affairs; *born:* 6 August 1946, Marrakesh, Morocco; *parents:* Georges Vallier and Jeanne Vallier (née Flecchia); *married:* Jean-Louis Guigou, 1966; *public role of spouse:* University lecturer; *children:* Edouard; *education:* Lycée Victor-Hugo, Marrakesh; Lycée Descartes, Rabat; Faculty of Arts, Rabat and Montpellier, Faculty of Economic Science, Montpellier; graduated in arts; diploma, advanced studies in American literature; diploma, general univ. studies, economic science; studied at École Nationale d'administration (National School of Administration), 1971-74; *political career:* Financial Attaché, French Embassy in London, 1979-81; Head of Office for European, American and Asian Affairs, under direction of the Treasury, 1981; Technical Adviser to the cabinet of Jacques Delors, Minister of Economy and Finance, 1982; Technical Adviser, 1982-88; researcher to the Pres. of the French Republic, 1988-; Sec.-Gen., Interministerial Cttee. for Questions of European Economic Co-operation, 1985-; Delegate, Interministerial Mission for countries of central and eastern Europe, 1990-; Minister Delegate to the

Minister of State, Minister of Foreign Affairs, responsible for European Affairs; *professional career:* civil servant, Ministry of Finance, under the direction of the Treasury, 1974; civil servant, office of the Treasury, 1974-75, office of Banking, 1976-78, office of Financial Markets, 1978-79; deputy reporter, Finance Commission for the VII Plan, 1975-78; Head of Conference Management, Institute of Political Studies, Paris, 1976; *private address:* 168 bd. du Montparnasse, 75014 Paris, France; *office address:* Mme. Elisabeth Guigou, L'Assemblée Nationale, 126 rue de L'Université, 75355, Paris, France; *phone:* Paris 40 63 60 00; *fax:* Paris 42 60 99 03.

GUIMARAES, Marilu Segatto; Brazilian, Federal Deputy; *born:* 15 October 1951, Campo Grande, Mato Grosso do Sul; *parents:* José Segatto and Lourdes Brandao Segatto; *married:* José Chadid; *children:* Mariucha; *education:* UFMT, Campo Grande, physical education, 1970-74; Catholic Univ. of Mato Grosso, law, 1970-72; *party:* Partido dos Trabalhadores (PT, Independent Labour Party)B; *political career:* State Deputy for Mato Grosso do Sul, 1987-91; Mem., Cttee. for Women's Rights; Pres., Cttee. for Economic and Social Order and Civil Rights, 1989; Pres., Environment Cttee., 1990; Mem., Finance Cttee., 1990-91; Vice-Prefect, Campo Grande, 1989-91; Federal Deputy for Mato Grosso do Sul, 1991-95; *professional career:* professor; journalist; entrepreneur; former Dir., Ballet Arts Assocs., Carnegie Hall; *office address:* Ms Marilu Guimaraes, Chamber of Deputies, Praça dos 3 Poderes, Ed. Principal, 70160 Brasilia, DF, Brazil; *phone:* (61) 225 2885.

GUINTO-JUCO, Hon. Estelita; Filipino, Congresswoman; *born:* 12 May 1930; *parents:* Alfonso M. Juco and Francisca Alvaran Guinto; *education:* St. Paul's College, Manila, B.Sc., Education; *political career:* helped establish the National Commission Concerning Disabled Persons; Sectoral Representative for Women and the Disabled; Mem. of the House of Representatives; *memberships:* Trustee, Ramon Magsaysay Award Foundation; Trustee, Pope Pius XII Catholic Centre; *professional career:* former columnist, We Forum; Editor-in-Chief, The Paulinian; *honours and awards:* Outstanding Paulian Alumna Golden Jubilee Year Award; Recognition Award from the Poetry Society of Japan; *office address:* The Hon. Ms Estelita Guinto-Juco, The Congress of the Philippines - House of Representatives, Batasang Pambansa Bldg., Quezon City, Manila, The Philippines.

GURNSEY, Kitty (Kathleen W.); American, Idaho State Representative; *born:* 23 June 1927, Donnelly, Idaho, USA; *parents:* Robert G. Wallace and Thelma Wallace (née Halferty); *married:* Vern L. Gurnsey; *children:* Kristina, Steve, Scott; *religion:* Presbyterian; *education:* Boise State Univ., BA; *party:* Republican

Party; *political career:* Idaho State Rep., District 19; Chwn., Appropriations and Environmental Cttee.; Co-Chwn., Joint Finance Appropriations Cttee. 1974-; *memberships:* founder Mem., National Organisation of Women Legislators; *office address:* Mrs Kitty Gurnsey, 1111 W. Highland View Drive, Boise, Idaho 83702, USA.

GU XIULIAN; Chinese, Minister of the Chemical Industry; *born:* 1936, Nantong City, Jiangsu Province; *education:* graduate, Shenyang Metallurgical Machinery College; *party:* Chinese Communist Party; *political career:* Cadre, State Council, 1970-73; Vice Minister, State Planning Commission, 1973-82; Vice Chmn., Central Patriotic Sanitation Campaign Cttee., 1981-83; mem. 6th and 7th National People's Congress for Jiangsu; Mem., CCP 12th, 13th Central Cttees., 1982-; Gov., Jiangsu Province, 1983-89; Dep. Sec., Jiangsu Province CCP, 1983-89; *office address:* Gu Xiulian, Ministry of Chemical Industry, Liupukang, Deshengmenwai, Beijing, People's Republic of China; *phone:* 446561.

H

HAAS-BERGER, Ineke (R.M.); Dutch, President of the National Committee for the Chronically Ill; *born:* 22 February 1935, Abcoude, Netherlands; *parents:* J.A. Berger and M.R. Berger-Reyme; *married:* A. Haas, 1956; *children:* one d; *religion:* none; *languages:* Dutch, English, German, French; *education:* gymnasium-A (sec. ed.); State Univ. of Leiden, masters in Dutch law; *party:* Partij van de Arbeid (PvdA, Labour Party); *political career:* Mem., town council, Leek; Pres. women contact of PvdA, region Groningen; Pres., PvdA region Leek; Mem. of regional PvdA board; Mem., Interparlementary Advising Benelux Council; Mem. of Second Chamber, 1971-91; Mem., Cncl. of Europe, until 1991; currently, Pres., National Cttee. for the Chronically Ill; *professional career:* pres. educational work for young women exempt from education, Midden-Zeewisch-Vlaanderen; *private address:* Oldendert 60, 9351 hp Leek, the Netherlands; *office address:* Mevr. Ineke Haas-Berger, Nationale Commissie Chronisch Zieken, Boerha Avelaan 1, postbus 7100, 2701 AC Zoetermeer, the Netherlands.

HAFNER, Ursula; Swiss, Member of the Nationalrat; *born:* 10 June 1943, Schaffhausen; *education:* Dr. Phil; *party:* Sozialdemokratische Volkspartei der Schweiz (SDP, Social Democratic Party of Switzerland); *political career:* Mem., Basel-Land Cantonal Cncl., 1981-; Mem. of the Nationalrat for Schaffhausen, Canton of Basel-Land, 1987-; *professional career:* French lecturer, Canton school, Schaffhausen, Univs. of Zürich, Caen and Aberdeen; *office address:* Frau Ursula Hafner, Nationalrat/Conseil National, Secretariat-General, Parlamentsgebäude, 3003 Berne, Switzerland; *phone:* Berne 619711.

HAGA, Antónia; Hungarian, Member of the Országgyúlés; *party:* Alliance of Free Democrats (SZDSZ); *office address:* Ms Antónia Hága, Országgyúlés, Kossuth L. tér 1-3, Budapest V, Hungary; *phone:* 22 5058; 22 5059.

HAGER, Elizabeth Sears; American, New Hampshire State Representative; *born:* 31 October 1944, Washington DC, USA; *parents:* Hess Thatcher Sears and Elizabeth Grace Sears (née Harper); *married:* Dennis Sterling Hager, 1966; *children:* Annie Elizabeth, Lucie Caroline; *religion:* Episcopal; *education:* Wellesley College, BA, 1966; Tufts Univ., 1966-67; Univ. of New Hampshire, MPA, 1979; *party:* Republican Party; *political career:* New Hampshire State Rep., 1973-76 and 1984-; Vice-Chwn., Appropriations Cttee.; Mem., Rules Cttee.; Mayor, Concord, 1988-90; City Cllr., 1981-90; *memberships:* Concord YMCA; United Way of Merrimack County; *professional career:* fund-raising consultant; *honours and awards:* Outstanding Young Woman of America, 1977; *office address:* Mrs Elizabeth Sears Hager, 5 Auburn Street, Concord, New Hampshire 03301, USA.

HAGLUND, Ann-Cathrine; Swedish, Member of the Riksdag; *born:* 24 August 1937, Orebro; *parents:* Carl Olof Jansson and Signe Erika Jansson (née Wiklund); *married:* Finn Hugo Haglund, 1957; *children:* Anne, Anders, Maria; *religion:* Evangelical Lutheran; *languages:* English, French, German; *education:* MA, language teacher; *party:* Moderata Samlingspartiet (Moderate Party); *political career:* Member, Standing Cttee. on Social Welfare, 1979-88; Member, Standing Cttee. on Education, 1988; Member, National Commission on Aids; member, Medical Responsibility Board; President, Moderate Women's Association, 1981-90; Mem., Swedish Delegation to the General Assembly of the United Nations, 1984 and 1985; Substitute to Council of Europe Assembly, 1989-; Mem. of Riksdag for Örebro, 1979-; Pres., Israel-Sweden Friendship Assn; *interests:* education; *professional career:* language teacher; *clubs:* Red Cross, Amnesty International, Pres., Sweden-Israel Friendship Assn; *private address:* V. Bangatan 24, 692 35 Kumla, Sweden; *office address:* Ms Ann-Cathrine Haglund, Riksdag, Fack, S-100 12 Stockholm, Sweden.

HAINES, Janine; Australian, Senator; *born:* 8 May 1945, Tanunda, SA; *education:* BA, Adelaide; Adelaide Teachers College, Diploma in Teaching; *party:* Australian Democrats; *political career:* Mem., Australian Democrats State Council, South Australia, 1977-79; chosen by Parliament of South Australia to represent that State in the Senate, 1977-78; Publicity Officer, Australian Democrats, South Australia, 1978-81; Mem., Political Co-ordinating Cttee., 1978-81 and 1983-; Mem., Australian Democrats Campaign Cttee., 1978-81; elected to Senate for South Australia, 1980; Temporary Chairperson of Cttees., 1981-86; Committee Service: Mem. of the Senate Select Cttee. for Private Hospitals and Nursing Homes, 1981-87; for

Allegations concerning a Judge, Sep.-Oct. 1984; Mem. of the Senate Standing Cttee. for Scrutiny of Bills, 1982-87; for Standing Orders, 1981-83; for Disputed Returns and Qualifications, 1986-87; for Procedure, 1987-; Mem. of the Senate Legislative and General Purpose Standing Cttee. for Social Welfare, 1983-85; Mem. of Senate Estimates Cttee. B, 1982-83; Mem. of the Joint Select Cttee. for Australia Card, 1985-86; Conferences, Delegations and Visits: Mem., Parly. Delegation to Italy, Spain, Greece and Cyprus, 1983; Mem., Biennial Exchange Visit to New Zealand, 1984; Dep. Leader of the Australian Democrats, 1985-86; Spokesperson for Australian Democrats on Health, Social Security, Finance, Housing and Construction, and Home Affairs, 1985; on Women's Affairs, Housing and Construction, Attorney-General, Health, Social Security, and Community Services, 1985-87; Parly. Leader of the Australian Democrats, 1986-; Spokesman on Prime Minister, and Cabinet, Finance and Treasury, and on Special Minister of State and Women's Affairs, 1987-; *professional career:* maths. and English teacher; *office address:* Ms Janine Haines, Australian Democrats Party, 96 St. Kilda Roak, St. Kilda, Victoria 3182, Australia; *phone:* (03) 537 1611.

HAJAH RAHMAH OSMAN; Malaysian, Member of the House of Representatives; *born:* 12 June 1939, Selangor; *married:* Mr Mustapha Sheikh Ibrahim; *children:* two; *education:* Sekolah Melayu Bukit Istana, Klang, Selangor; Convent School, Kuala Lumpur; London, Diploma in Business Administration; London School of Journalism, Diploma in Journalism; *party:* Barisan Nasional (National Front Coalition Party); *political career:* Senator, 1976; elected MP for Selayang, Selangor, Barisan, 1982; Deputy Minister of Information, 1982-84; Deputy Minister of Transport, 1984-87; re-elected MP for Shah Alam, Selangor, 1986; elected UMNO Supreme Council Mem., 1977; *memberships:* Mem., Executive Cttee., National Council of Women's Organisation, 1968-82; Treasurer, Malaysian Youth Council, 1975-78; former Secretary, Malaysian Parliamentarians Group on Resources, Population and Development; *professional career:* Assistant Information Officer, Asia News Centre, Kuala Lumpur; worked in private sector and finally became Dir. of Companies; *honours and awards:* Companion of The Most Esteemed Order of The Crown of Malaysia; Commander of Setia Sultan Abdul Halim Mu'adzam Shah; Grand Commander of The Most Esteemed Order of The Defender of The Realm; Meritorious Service Medal; *private address:* 40, Jalan 1/6, Shah Alam, 40000 Selangor; *office address:* Ms Hajah Rahmah Osman, Dewan Rakyat, Parliament Building, 50680 Kuala Lumpur, Malaysia; *phone:* (03) 2321955.

HAJDU, Dr. Istvánné; Hungarian, Member of the Országgyűlés; *party:* Independent Smallholders' Party (FKgP); *office address:* Dr. Istvánné Hajdú, Országgyűlés, Kossuth L. tér 1-3, Budapest V, Hungary; *phone:* 22 5058; 22 5059.

HALL, Katie; American, former Senator for Indiana; *born:* 3 April 1938, Mound Bayou, Mississippi, USA; *parents:* Jeff L. Greene (Decd.) and Bessie Mae Green (née Hooper); *married:* John Henry Hall IV, 1957; *children:* Jacquelne Demetris, Junifer Detrice; *religion:* Protestant; *education:* Mississippi Valley State Univ., BS, 1960; Indiana Univ., Bloomington, MS, 1969; *party:* Democratic Party; *political career:* Mem., Cttee. to elect Robert Kennedy President, Gary, Indiana, 1968; Indiana State Rep., 1974-78; Ranking Majority Mem., Affairs of Lake and Marion County Cttee., 1975-78; Indiana State Senator, 1976-82; Vice-Chwn., Lake County Democratic Cttee., 1979-; Sec., Indiana Democratic State Cttee., 1979-; former, US Senator, 1st District, Indiana; currently: Mem., Gary Cncl. for Social Studies; Vice-Chwn., Gary Housing Board of Commissioners; *professional career:* substitute teacher, Gary Public Schools, Indiana, 1961-64; teacher, social studies, Edison School, Gary, 1964-75; *honours and awards:* Outstanding Achievements in Politics Award, Van Buren Baptist Church, 1974; Outstanding Woman in Politics, Gary 1975; Outstanding Achievements in Politics and Education, Mississippi Valley State Univ., 1975; Outstanding Service to Mankind Award, 1975; Outstanding Alumni Award, 1975; *office address:* Mrs Katie Hall, 1937 Madison Street, Gary, Indiana 46407, USA.

HALLER, Gret; Swiss, Member of the Nationalrat; *born:* 1 October 1947, Zürich, Switzerland; *education:* LLB; study at Univ. of Zürich; *party:* Sozialdemokratische Partei der Schweiz (SDP, Social Democratic Party); *political career:* Borough Cllr., Bern; City Cllr., Bern, 1977-84; Mem. of the Nationalrat for Bern, Canton of Bern, 1987-; *professional career:* civil servant (EJPD); own law firm; school Dir., city of Bern, 1985-; *office address:* Frau Gret Haller, Nationalrat/Conseil National, Secretariat-General, Parlamentsgebäude, 3003 Berne, Switzerland; *phone:* Berne 619711.

HALONEN, Tarja Kaarina; Finnish, Minister of Justice; *born:* 24 December 1943, Helsinki, Finland; *parents:* Vieno Olavi Halonen and Lyyli Elina Forss (Previously Halonen) (née Loimola); *education:* Helsinki Univ., B. of Law, 1968; *party:* Suomen Sosialidemokraattinen Puolue (SDP, Finnish Social Democratic Party); *political career:* Mem., Helsinki City Cncl., 1977; mem., Presidential Electorate, 1978 and 1982; mem. of Eduskunta, 1979-; Second Minister of Social Affairs and Health; Minister of Justice, Mar. 1990-; *professional career:* Lawyer, Credit Control Ltd., 1967-68; Social and Organisation Secretary, Student Union of Finland, 1969-70; Lawyer, SAK (Confederation of Finnish Trade Unions), 1970; *office* *address:* Ms Tarja Halonen, Ministry of Justice, Eteläesplanadi 10, 00130 Helsinki, Finland.

HÄMÄLÄINEN, Tuulikki Katriina (Pia); Finnish, Second Minister of Social Affairs and Health; *born:* 25 November 1940, Helsinki, Finland; *parents:* Jaakko Kustaa Ojala and Alma Anna Liisa Ojala (née Hellberg); *children:* Johanna; *education:* Economist, 1964; *party:* Suomen Sosialidemokraattinen Puolue (SDP, Finnish Social Democratic Party); *political career:* Mem., Hyvinkää Town Cncl., 1976; Chmn, 1985; Chmn, City Admin. Board, 1981-84; mem., Presidential Electorate, 1982; mem. of Eduskunta, 1983; mem., SDP Party Cttee, 1984; Vice-Chmn, Admin. Cncl. of the State Fuel Centre, 1984; mem., Finnish Workers Savings Bank Management, 1984; Representative Board of the E-Co-operative Shop EKA, 1984; Second Minister of Social Affairs and Health, 1990-; *professional career:* Sec., State Computer Centre, 1963-65; Broadcaster, Yleisradio (Finnish Broadcasting Co), 1965-83; *office address:* Ms Tuulikki Hämäläinen, Ministry of Social Affairs and Health, Snellmaninkatu 4-6, 00170 Helsinki, Finland.

HAMBRAEUS, Birgitta (Sigrid Birgitta); Swedish, Member of the Riksdag; *born:* 11 April 1930, Västerås, Sweden; *parents:* Erik David Lindblom and Janesie Edström-Lindblom; *married:* Olof Hambraeus, 1959; *children:* Axel, Anders; *religion:* Protestant; *languages:* Swedish, English; *education:* The Sigtuna Foundation Arts Grammar School, Higher School Certificate, 1946-49; Vassar College, N.Y. State, USA, BA; Stockholm University, Fil Kand, 1954; *party:* Centerpartiet (Centre Party), 1964; *political career:* Member of Orsa Town Council, 1965-88; mem., Bank of Sweden's Jubilee Fund, 1985-; mem., Parliamentary Auditors, 1988-; mem., Swedish Disarmament Delegation, 1989-; mem., Foreign Affairs Committee; mem. of the Riksdag, 1971-; *interests:* environment, energy policies, ecologically and socially responsible economics, peace; *professional career:* youth leader, 1954-71; social worker in school, 1964-66; teacher, 1965-71; *clubs:* Right Livelihood Awards Foundation; *private address:* Hamregården Box 25, 79400 Orsa, Sweden; *office address:* Ms Birgitta Hambraeus, Riksdag, Fack, S-100 12 Stockholm, Sweden.

HAMM-BRÜCHER, Dr. Hildegard; German, former Member of the Bundestag; *born:* 11 May 1921, Essen/Ruhr, West Germany; *children:* two; *religion:* Protestant; *education:* Abitur (advanced matriculation examination), 1939; University of München, Diploma of Chemistry, Dr.Phil., 1945; University of Harvard/USA, Scholarship, 1949-50; study trips to USA, Canada, Scandinavia, Soviet Union, China, Israel, Japan; *party:* Freie Demokratische Partei (FDP, Free Democratic Party); *political career:* member of city council, München, 1948-54; member of regional

parliament, Bayern, 1950-66; undersecretary, Hessian Ministry of Culture, 1967-69; undersecretary, Federal Ministry of Education and Science, 1969-72; member of regional parliament, Bayern, 1970-76; Minister of State, Federal Foreign Ministry, Dec. 1976-Sep. 82; former mem. of Bundestag, party list of Bayern; *honours and awards:* Dr.h.c; *clubs:* Foundation Theodor Heuss Prize (chmn.), since 1964; presiding board, German Evangelical Church Convention, since 1975; synod of German Evangelical Church; International PEN Club; board of trustees, Peace Prize of the German Book Trade; governing board, Welle; *private address:* 8000 München 90, West Germany; *office address:* Dr. Hildegard Hamm-Brücher .

HÄMMERLE, Gerlinde; German, Member of the Bundestag; *born:* 5 June 1940, Wolfach/Schwarzwald, Ortenaukreis, West Germany; *religion:* Catholic; *education:* secondary school; technical college for women; college for vocational educationists; *party:* Sozialdemokratische Partei Deutschlands (SPD, Social Democratic Party of Germany), 1967; *political career:* member of district Exec. board, SPD, city of Karlsruhe, since 1971; member of municipal council, city of Karlsruhe, 1971-87; member of Party council, SPD, 1975-77; chwn., local group, SPD, 1976-86; chwn., SPD group in municipal council, Karlsruhe, 1982-87; member of Sozialdemokratische Gemeinschaft für Kommunalpolitik (SGK, Social Democratic Society of Local Government Policy), since 1982; member of county Exec. Cttee., SPD, since 1983; mem. of Bundestag, party list of Baden-Württemberg, since 1987; member of the Board, SPD - Bundestagsfraktion, since 1989; *professional career:* teacher at technical college; vice-principal (Studienesdirektorin), 1985-87; deputy headmistress, Helene Lange School, Karlsruhe, since 1978; member of Gewerkschaft Erziehung und Wissenschaft (GEW, Trade Union for Education and Science); *clubs:* Naturfreunde (Friends of Nature); Vice Chairperson, federal and local Arbeiterwohlfahrt (AWO, Labour Welfare Organisation) Karlsruhe; other local associations; *private address:* 7500 Karlsruhe 21, West Germany; *office address:* Frau Gerlinde Hämmerle, Bundeshaus, 5300 Bonn 1, West Germany.

HANQUET, Dr. Huberte; Belgian, Senator; *born:* 29 August 1926, Liège, Belgium; *religion:* Catholic; *languages:* French; *education:* Catholic Univ., Louvain, Special Degree in Philosophy, 1945-46, then Bachelor of Religious Science and Bachelor of Social and Political Science, 1945-48; Dr. of Political and Social Science, 1972; *party:* Parti Social Chrétien (PSC, Christian Social Party); *political career:* CAP, Liège, 1959-63, then 1970-76; Cllr., Public Centre of Social Welfare, Liège, 1977-85; Senator, Liège, until 1985; Deputy, Liège, 1985-88; co-opted Senator, 1988-; mem. of Senate Commissions and Benelux Interparly. Cncl. and Chairperson of Foreign Affairs Cttee.; Chairperson, Nuclear Security Cttee., North Atlantic Assembly;

Mem., Belgian Cttee. of IPU; mem. of PSC Local Cttee., Liège Town Cttee., Nat. and Liège Cttee. of PSC Women; mem. of Exec. Cttee., Le Grand Liège; Pres., Nat. Cncl. of Belgian Women; *interests:* foreign affairs, development, social and environmental affairs; *professional career:* teacher then principal, Centre of Social Training; mem. of Management Cttee., Medical Centre, Univ. of Liège; Admin., Univ. for Elderly People; Admin., ND Clinic, Bruyères and Saint-Vincent Clinic, Liège; Admin., Revivre Chez Soi; mem. of General Assembly, Remembrance Homes; founder mem., International Foundation for Social Innovation, 1989; *honours and awards:* Knight of the Order of Leopold; Officer of the Order of Leopold; *publications:* Recherche sociologique fondamentale; Étude des budgets; Planning scolaire, planning hospitalier; nombreuses missions, dont 5 à titre d'expert de l'Office européen des Nations Unies; Le travail professionel des femmes et mutations sociales, Edition Vie Ouvrière, Brussels, 1972; *recreations:* jogging; *private address:* 6 B, bte 102, Quai Churchill, 4020 Liège, Belgium; *office address:* Dr. Huberte Hanquet, Senate, Palais de la Nation, Place de a Nation 1, 1000 Brussels, Belgium.

HANSEN, Matilda Anne; American, Wyoming State Representative; *born:* 4 September 1929, Paullina, Iowa, USA; *parents:* Arthur Henderson and Sada Henderson (née Thompson); *married:* Hugh Hansen, 1965; *children:* Eric, Douglas; *religion:* Soc. of Friends; *education:* Univ. of Colorado, Boulder, BA, 1963; Univ. of Wyoming, MA, 1970; *party:* Democratic Party; *political career:* Wyoming State Rep., 1975-; *memberships:* League of Women Voters; *professional career:* Dir., Adult Education, Albany County, Wyoming, 1967-78; public liaison person for adult education, Laramie, Wyoming, 1977-78; Manager, Laramie Plains Civic Center, 1981-83; *office address:* Ms Matilda Hansen, House of Representatives, Capitol Building, Cheyenne, Wyoming 82002, USA.

HANSEN, Dr. Ursula; German, Deputy Member of the Bundesrat; *born:* 9 July 1935; *married:* Vinzenz; *children:* four; *religion:* Catholic; *party:* Christlich Demokratische Union (CDU, Christian Democratic Union), 1970; *political career:* Minister of Social Affairs, Rheinland-Pfalz since 1988; mem. of Landtag, Vice-Pres., Cen. Cttee. of German Catholics, among other honorary positions; mem. of Bundesrat, 1985-; *professional career:* General Practitioner, Prüm/Eifel; *office address:* Dr. Ursula Hansen, Bundesrat, 5300 Bonn 1, West Germany.

HANZALOVA, Drahomíra; Czechoslovakian, Chairperson of the Education and Sciences Employers Trade Union; *born:* 27 December 1931; *education:* gymnasium; College of Veterinary Medicine, Bron, Kosice, 1950-55; Dr. of Veterinary Medicine, 1955; *party:* Komunistická Strana Ceskoslovenska (KSC, Communist party of Czechoslovakia); *political career:* took active part in Slovak Nat. uprising, 1944; Mem., CP CSSR, 1956-; Mem., Central Cncl., Czechoslovak Revolutionary Trade Union Movement, (ROH), 1969-72; Mem., Presidium and Plenum of Central Cncl. of Trade Unions (URO), 1972-82; Mem., Central Cttee., Revolutionary Trade Union Movement, CSSR, 1982-; Sec. and Mem. Secretariat, Revolutionary Trade Union Movement, Chairperson, Women's Cttee., 1974-82; Chairperson, Education and Sciences Employers Trade Union, 1981-; *office address:* Dr. Drahomíra Hanzalova, Central Council of Trade Unions, Nám A. Zápotockého 2, 113 59 Prague 3, Czechoslovakia.

HAO JIANXIU; Chinese, Member of the Chinese Communist Party 13th Central Committee; *born:* 1935, Qingdao City, Shandong Province; *education:* before 1949, one year of primary school; after 1949, middle school; *party:* Chinese Communist Party; *political career:* Mem., National People's Congress, 1st, 2nd and 3rd for Shandong; Mem., Revolutionary Cttee., Qingdao Municipality, 1967-71, Vice-Chairperson, 1971-78; Mem., Standing Cttee., Shandong Province CCP, 1977-78; Mem., CCP 11th, 12th and 13th Central Cttees., 1982-85; Mem., Secretariat, CCP Central Cttee., 1985-87; Vice Minister for the Textile Industry, 1978-81, Minister, 1981-83; Vice Minister, State Planning Commission, 1987-; *memberships:* Exec. Cncl., Women's Federation, 1953-78; Central Cttee., Democratic Youth Federation, 1953; Central Cttee., Communist Youth League, 1964; Vice Chairperson, Trade Union, Shandong Province, 1973-78; Chairperson, Women's Federation, 1975-78, Vice-Chairperson, 1978-83; *professional career:* cotton worker, State Operated Cotton Factory No.6, Qingdao Hao, 1951; introduced new spinning method propagated as the Hao Jianxiu Work Method; appointed Deputy Dir. of No.6 Cotton Factory, 1964; *honours and awards:* National Model Worker in Industry; *office address:* Hao Jianxiu, The Communist Party of China, Beijing, The People's Republic of China.

HAREWOOD-BENN, Hon. Yvonne; Guyanan, Senior Minister in the President's Office; *party:* People's National Congress (PNC); *office address:* The Hon. Ms Yvonne Harewood-Benn, Office of the President, New Garden and South Streets, Georgetown, Guyana; *phone:* (02) 51330.

HARMAN, Harriet Ruth; British, Member of Parliament; *born:* 30 July 1950; *married:* Jack Dromey, 1982; *children:* two s., one d; *education:* St. Paul's School; York University; *party:* Labour Party; *political career:* Legal Officer, National Cncl. for Civil Liberties, 1978-82; Member of Parliament for Peckham, 1982-, sponsored by the Transport and General Worker's Union; Shadow Minister for Social Security, 1984;

Labour Party Spokesperson on Social Services, 1985-87, and on Health, 1987-; *interests:* women; social services; provision for the under 5s; *professional career:* solicitor; *office address:* Ms Harriet Harman, House of Commons, London SW1A OAA.

HARMS, Inger Birgitte; Danish, Member of the Folketing; *born:* 10 August 1942, Esbjerg, Denmark; *parents:* Vagn Harry Lund and Ida Lund (née Nielsen); *children:* Rene, Lena; *religion:* Lutheran; *languages:* Danish, English, German, Swedish, French; *education:* Prairie High School, high school diploma, Iowa, USA, 1959-60; college degree, 1981; *party:* Socialistisk Folkeparti (Socialist People's Party); *political career:* member of the Folketinget, 1981-; member of the Nordic Council, 1981-; member of the Council of Europe 1987; Pres., Group of Communists and allies, 1990, name changed to Unified European Left; *interests:* foreign policy, minorities, agriculture; *memberships:* 5 Mem. Cttee. for cultural affairs in Sydslesvig (Danish Minority in Germany); Mem., Bureau of the Friendship organisation, Soviet Union-Denmark; *private address:* Lojovej 9, 6200 Abenra, Denmark; *office address:* Ms Inger Harms, Christiansborg, 1240 Copenhagen K, Denmark.

HARNIE, Cécile; Belgian, Senator; *born:* 17 April 1945, Halle; *education:* Heilig Hart Instituut (Sacred Heart Institute), Halle, higher secondary technical education; *party:* Anders Gaan Leven (Agalev, Ecologist Party - Flemish speaking); *political career:* active member, Werkgroep Kristelijke Arbeiders partij (work group christian workers party) (WKAP), 1980-85; co-opted Senator, 1988-; *professional career:* school secretary, 1963-67; propagandist, Vrouwelijke Kristelijke Arbeiders Jeugel (young female christian workers) (VKAJ), 1967-71; worker, food industry, 1971-74; propagandist, National VKAJ, 1974-78; education worker, ACV, Brussel-Halle-Vilvoorde, 1978-88; *private address:* Parlementsgalerij 20, bus 6, 1000 Brussel, Belgium; *office address:* Ms Cécile Harnie, Senate, Palais de la Nation, Place de a Nation 1, 1000 Brussels, Belgium.

HARPER, Ruth Bebe; American, Pennsylvania State Representative; *born:* 24 December 1927, Savannah, Georgia, USA; *parents:* Thomas Deloach and Sallie Deloach (née Bryiant); *married:* James Harper, 1950; *children:* Deloris (Decd.), Catherine; *religion:* Baptist; *education:* LaSalle College, 1970-71; Moore College of Art, 1960; Berean Inst., 1962; Philadelphia Univ., 1975; *party:* Democratic Party; *political career:* Pennsylvania State Rep., District 196, 1977-; Chwn., Urban Affairs Cttee; *memberships:* NAACP; American Red Cross; National Cncl. of Negro Women; Coalition of 100 Black Women; *professional career:* owner, Ruth Harper School of Modelling; *private address:* 1427 W.

Erie Avenue, Philadelphia, Pennsylvania 19140, USA; *office address:* Mrs Ruth Harper, State Capitol, Harrisburg, Pennsylvania 17120, USA.

HARPER WOODS, Pauline; American, Chairwoman of the First Congressional District Executive Committee of Georgia; *born:* 20 December 1930, Savannah, Georgia, USA; *parents:* Otis A. Harper Sr. and Ruby Harper (née Daniel); *married:* William C. Woods, 1951; *children:* Deborah Jean, Lisa Dianne; *religion:* Protestant; *education:* grad., Commercial High School, 1948; John Marshall Law School, 1976; *party:* Democratic Party; *political career:* Mem., Georgia State Democrat Party, 1978-; Vice-Chwn., Chatham County Democrat Cttee., 1980-82; Chwn., First Congressional District, Georgia Federation of Democratic Women, 1980-; Chwn., First Congressional District Democrat Exec. Cttee., Georgia, 1982-; Chwn., Chatham County Democratic Cttee., 1986-; *memberships:* Mem., League of Women Voters; *professional career:* Sec., Gene F. Dyar, Attorney-at-Law, 1953-75; US Magistrate, 1975-84; Carlden Gen. Hospital, 1985-; *clubs:* Commerce Club; CofC; Governor's Club; Georgia Assn. of County Chairman; *office address:* Mrs Pauline Harper Woods, 21 Sheriden Circle, Savannah, Georgia 31406, USA.

HARRICH, Holda; Austrian, Member of the Nationalrat; *born:* 26 October 1931, Klagenfurt; *education:* nursing college, Vienna-Lainz, diploma in adult and child nursing; *party:* Die Grüne Alternative (The Green Alternative); *political career:* mem. of the Nationalrat for Kärnten, Upper Austria, Salzburg, Steiermark, Tirol, and Voralberg, January 1989-; *professional career:* nurse, Klagenfurt Provincial Hospital, 1953-85; *office address:* Frau Holda Harrich, Nationalrat, Dr. Karl Renner Ring 3, 1017 Vienna, Austria.

HARTENSTEIN, Dr. Liesel; German, Member of the Bundestag; *born:* 20 September 1928, Steinehaig; *parents:* Hans Rössler and Lina Rössler (née Gräter); *married:* Eberhard, 1951; *children:* Andrea, Hans-Ulrich; *religion:* Protestant; *languages:* French, English; *education:* Univ. Tübingen, Romance Languages and literature, German Studies, Philosophy, History Studies; Ph.D., 1958; *party:* Sozialdemokratische Partei Deutschlands (SPD, Social Democratic Party of Germany); *political career:* municipal councillor, 1968; District councillor, 1971; mem. of Bundestag, 1976-; *interests:* environmental policy; *professional career:* freelance journalist, 1959-64; high school teacher, 1964-76; educational theorist; *publications:* Bücher und Buchbinder im Wandel der Jahrhunderte, 1959; Editor, Facsimile-Querschnitt Kladderadatsch, 1965; work on journal Germanistik; *office address:* Dr. Liesel Hartenstein, Bundeshaus, 5300 Bonn 1, West Germany.

HARTIGAN CAIN, Virginia; American, Member of the Nevada State Democrat Central Committee and First Vice-Chairwoman of the Nevada Democratic Party; *born:* 1 May 1922, Brooklyn, New York, USA; *parents:* James Gerard Hartigan and Virginia Hainza Hartigan (née Williams); *married:* Edmund Joseph Cain, 1944; *public role of spouse:* Member, Board of Directors, Farwest Lab; retired Dean of Education; Trustee, International Cncl. for Education and Teaching; *children:* Edmund J. III, Mary Ellen, James Michael; *religion:* Christian; *languages:* Spanish; *education:* New York Univ., BA, 1943; Univ. of Delaware, M.Ed., 1963; Univ. of Nevada, Reno, 1973; *party:* Democratic Party; *political career:* Mem., Governor's Commission on Status of Women, Nevada, 1968-; Mem., Governor's Advisory Board on Girls Training Schools, 1970-74; Mem., Northern Nevada Co-ordinators of the Nevada State Democrat Central Cttee., 1970-; former Chwn., Information and Training Cttee.; delegate, Democrat National Convention, 1972 and 1980 and Democrat Mid-Term Conference, 1974; Mem., Democratic National Cttee. Commisssion on Platform Accountability; Northern Nevada Co-ordinator, Jimmy Carter Campaign, 1976; Vice-Chwn., Senator Edward Kennedy Campaign, 1980; Mem., Nevada State Central Cttee.; Mem., Democratic National Cttee. Assn. of Staff Democratic Chairmen; Mem., Washoe County Human Services Advisory Board; Mem., Governor's Advisory Commission on Youth, Nevada, 1986-; *memberships:* Mem., Cttee. to Aid Abused Women; United Way; Business and Professional Women; International Family Law Assn.; American Assn. of Univ. Women; National and Nevada Women's Political Caucus; Democrat Women's Club; Children's Defence Fund; Nevada Women's Caucus; Croesus Corp; *professional career:* personnel counselor, Research and Development Labs., US Govt., 1943-46; research Asst., Group Dynamics, Univ. of Delaware, 1956-57; high school teacher, Nevada, 1968-73; National Child Support Enforcement Dir., and Curriculum Dir., National Cncl., Juvenile and Family Court Judges, 1974-1986; consultant; *honours and awards:* Best Legislator Program, Reno Business and Professional Women's Club; Progress Award, Assn. of Continuing Education; Hon. Mention for I Am Your Child, Rocky Mountain Poetry Assn.; Family Law Award, American Bar Assn; *publications:* The Chosen One, (poem); I am your Child, (poem) and numerous articles; *clubs:* Nevada Univ. Women's Club; Investment Club; Caughlin Club; *recreations:* reading, swimming, walking; *office address:* Mrs Virginia Hartigan Cain, 3710 Clover Way, Reno, Nevada 89509, USA.

HART OF SOUTH LANARK, Baroness (cr. 1988, Life Peer) Judith Constance Mary Hart; British, Chairperson of the United Nations Association in the UK; *born:* 1924; *parents:* the late H. Ridehalgh; *married:* Anthony Hart, 1946; *public role of spouse:* Chairperson of the World Disarmament Campaign in the UK; *children:* two s; *education:* Grammar School; London Univ; *party:* Labour Party; *political career:* Parly. candidate, 1951, 1955; Member of Parliament, 1959-87; Joint Under- Sec. of State for Scotland, 1964-66; Minister of State for Commonwealth Relations, 1966-67; Minister of Social Security, 1967; Paymaster-General, 1968-69; Minister of Overseas Development, 1969-70, 1974-75, 1977-79; Prinicipal Opposition Front Bench Spokesman on Overseas Aid, 1970-74, 1979-80; Chmn., Labour Party, 1981-82; House of Lords, 1988-; Chair, United Nations Association, UK; Vice-President, World Universities Service; Vice-President, World Disarmament Campaign (UK); Co-Chair, UN Secretary General's Panel on South Africa, 1987, 1989; *interests:* Third World development, Latin and Central America, disarmament, human rights, industrial policies, Southern Africa; *professional career:* lecturer and research worker in sociology, 1945-49, 1955-57; *honours and awards:* Privy Council, 1967; DBE, 1979; Hon. Fellow, Inst. of Development Studies, Univ. of Sussex; *publications:* Aid And Liberation; *recreations:* gardening, friends, family; *private address:* 3 Ennerdale Rd., Kew Gardens, Richmond-upon-Thames; *office address:* Baroness Hart of South Lanark, House of Lords, London SW1A 0PW.

HARVEY, Elizabeth Robyn; Australian, Member of the House of Representatives; *born:* 19 October 1946, Adelaide, South Australia; *education:* BA, Adelaide; Adelaide Teachers College, Diploma in Teaching (Secondary); *party:* Australian Labor Party; *political career:* Mem., Women's Policy Cttee., (Labor Party) SA., 1979-80 and 1985-86; Mem., Membership Development Cttee. (Labor Party) SA, 1985-86; Mem., National Executive Policy Cttee. on Status of Women, 1986-87; Mem., National Executive Policy Cttee. on External Relations, 1987; elected for Hawker, 1987-; Committee Service: Mem. of the House of Representatives Standing Cttee. for Community Affairs, 1987-; Mem. of the Joint Statutory Cttee. for the Broadcasting of Parly. Proceedings, 1987-; *professional career:* secondary school teacher, electorate officer; *office address:* Ms Elizabeth Harvey, House of Representatives, Parliament House, Room M80, Canberra ACT, 2600, Australia; *phone:* (062) 726383.

HARWOOD, Madeline Bailey; American, Vermont State Representative; *born:* 7 July 1914, Newbury, Vermont, USA; *parents:* George Allen Bailey and Maud Bailey (née Smith); *married:* Clifford Burr Harwood, 1936; *children:* Clifford Jr., Catherine, Richard, Roger; *religion:* Congregational; *education:* Mary Fletcher Hospital School of Nursing, RN, 1936; *party:* Republican Party; *political career:* Vermont State Senator, District 2, 1968-75 and 1977-85; Vermont State Rep., 1989-; *office address:* Ms Madeline Harwood, Box 904, Village View, Manchester Ctr., Vermont 05255, USA.

HASE, Yuriko; Japanese, Member of the House of Representatives; *born:* 25 April 1947; *education:* Ochanomizu Univ; *party:* Japan Socialist Party (JSP); *political career:* former Chairperson, JSP Tokyo Women's Policy Cttee; elected for Tokyo 11, 1990-; Mem., House of Reps. Cttee. on the Environment, 1990-; *professional career:* commentator; *office address:* Ms Yuriko Hase, House of Representatives, 1-7-1 Nagata-cho, Chiyoda-ku, Tokyo 100, Japan; *phone:* (03) 5815111.

HASELBACH, Anna Elizabeth; Austrian, Member of the Bundesrat; *born:* 6 December 1942, Berlin; *education:* general secondary school, matriculation 1961; *party:* Sozialistische Partei Österreichs (SPÖ, Socialist Party of Austria); *political career:* worked in Federal Women's Office, SPÖ, Vienna, 1976-77; mem. of district Exec., SPÖ, Vienna, Brigittenau, and Vice Chairperson, district Women's Cttee.; district councillor, 20th district of Vienna, 1978-87; mem. of Vienna District Council; mem. of Vienna Provincial Assembly, May-December 1987; sent to Bundesrat from Vienna Provincial Assembly, mem. of Bundesrat, 1987-; *professional career:* civil servant, office of Minister of Science and Research, 1977-87, and Dept. of Research, 1987; *office address:* Frau Anna Haselbach, Bundesrat, Dr. Karl Renner Ring 3, 1017 Vienna, Austria.

HASINA WAJED, Sheikh; Bengali, Leader of the Awami League; *parents:* the late Sheikh Mujibur Rahman, murdered 1975; *party:* Awami League; *political career:* led Awami League in first democratic elections for 20 years, but lost to Bangladesh Nationalist Party led by Begum Zia (q.v.), Feb. 1991; *office address:* Sheikh Hasina Wajed, Awami League, 23 Bangabandhy Ave., Dhaka, Bangladesh.

HASSELFELDT, Gerda; German, Federal Minister of Health; *born:* 7 July 1950, Straubing, Lower Bavaria, West Germany; *children:* two; *religion:* Roman Catholic; *education:* grammar school, Abitur (advanced matriculation examination), 1969; Universities of Munich and Regensburg, Diploma in Economics, 1975; *party:* Christlich Soziale Union (CSU, Christian Social Union), 1969; *political career:* active in Exec. Cttee. at local, district, regional and county level, Junge Union (Young Union); junior employee at senior service level, Federal Office of Employment, 1975; district chmn., CSU, 1975-; careers adviser for college leavers and graduates, Employment Office, Deggendorf, 1978-85; mem. of district assembly, Regen, 1978-; dep, district chmn., CSU, Regen, 1979-, then chmn., 1987; mem. of county Exec. Cttee., Women's Union, 1985-; head of careers advisory service, Employment Office, Deggendorf, 1985-; mem. of Bundestag, party list of Bayern, Mar. 1987-, mem. of Cttees. on Empolyment, Social Planning, Education and Science, Petitions Cttee. and Dep. mem. of Cttee. for Youth, Family, Women and Health Affairs; Federal Minister for Regional Planning, Construction and Urban Development, Apr. 1989-; Federal Minister of Health; *private address:* 8370 Regen, West Germany; *office address:* Frau Gerda Hasselfeldt, Ministry for Regional Planning Construction and Urban Development, Deichmannsaue, 5300 Bonn 2, West Germany.

HAWLICEK, Dr. Hilde; Austrian, Federal Minister of Education, the Arts and Sport; *born:* 14 April 1942, Vienna, Austria; *education:* matriculation, 1960; University of Vienna, Ph.D; Viennese Ford Institute, political science; *party:* Sozialistische Partei Österreichs (SPÖ, Socialist Party of Austria); *political career:* mem. of the Bundesrat 1971-76; mem. of the National Council for Vienna, 1976-87; Minister of Education, Art and Sport, 1987-; *professional career:* general secondary school teacher, 1968-71; *clubs:* Austrian Federal Youth Group; *office address:* Dr. Hilde Hawlicek, Federal Ministry of Education the Arts and Sport, Minoritenplatz 5, 1014 Vienna, Austria.

HAYASHI, Toshiko; Japanese, Member of the House of Councillors; *born:* 27 February 1940; *education:* Gunma Univ; *party:* Japan Communist Party; *political career:* elected for National, 1990; Mem., House of Cllrs. Cttee. on Agriculture, Forestry and Fisheries and Special Cttee. on Disasters and Mem., JCP Central Cttee., 1990-; *professional career:* Announcer; *office address:* Ms Toshiko Hayashi, House of Councillors, 1-7-1 Nagata-cho, Tokyo 100, Japan; *phone:* (03) 5813111.

HECTOR, Margaret; Trinidad and Tobago, Minister in the Office of the Prime Minister and Member of Parliament; *born:* 16 August 1950; *children:* two s., two d; *religion:* Spiritual Babtist; *education:* St. Josephy Convent; Institute of Vocational Arts; *party:* National Alliance for Reconstruction (NAR); *political career:* Education Officer, Diego Martin West Constituency, 1982; Assistant Sec./Treasurer, L'Anse Mitan Party Branch, Organisation for National Reconstruction (ONR), 1981-85; elected to Nat. Exec., ONR, as Women's Affairs Officer, 1982; Second Vice-Chairperson, Nat. Exec., ONR, 1983; Women's Affairs Officer, Nat. Exec. ONR Chaguaramas/Point Cumana Electoral District, 1983; Women's Affairs Officer, Nat. Exec., ONR Chairperson for Nat. Organisation for Women, 1984, 1985; Party Organiser, Diego Martin West Constituency, 1986; Education Officer, Deigo Martin West Constituency, 1986; Chairperson, Nat. Organisation for Women; Women's Affairs Officer, Nat. Bureau of Nat. Alliance for Reconstruction (NAR); *interests:* 4H social and cultural group; *professional career:* community social worker; lay preacher; teacher, Valley Baptist Church; Sunday School Superintendent; Catering tutor, Monte Grande Baptist Church; *clubs:*

Advisor and Wardrobe mistress, Point Cumana Best Village Group; ex officio Mem., Guiding Assn.; founding Mem., L'Anse Mitan Village Cncl.; Returning Officer, Tobacco Road Sports Club; Chairperson, L'Anse Mitan Village Cncl; *office address:* The Honourable Margaret Hector, Central Bank Tower, Office of the Prime Minister, Eric Williams Plaza, Independence Sq., Port of Spain, Trinidad and Tobago.

HEDEGAARD, Connie; Danish, Member of the Folketing; *born:* 15 September 1960, Copenhagen, Denmark; *parents:* Knud W. Hedegaard and Elinor Hedegaard; *religion:* Protestant; *languages:* Danish, English, German, French; *education:* Holbaek Private School, 1967-76; Stenhus Grammar School, 1976-79; Copenhagen University, Degree in Literature, 1979-82 and History, 1990; *party:* Konservative Folkeparti (Conservative People's Party); *political career:* member of the Folketinget, 1984-; Speaker for the Board of Defence Politics, 1987-89; Political Speaker for the Conservative People's Party, 1989-; *interests:* cultural politics, defence and security politics, new idea politics, education and labour market; *office address:* Ms Connie Hedegaard, Christiansborg, 1240 Copenhagen K, Denmark.

HEDERMAN, Carmencita; Irish, Member of the Senead Éireann; *born:* 23 October 1939; *children:* five; *education:* Sacred Hearts Convent, Dublin, Ireland and Woldingham, Surrey, UK; Trinity College, Dublin, modern languages and fine arts, MA, 1964; modern languages and fine arts, Sorbonne, Paris, France; scholarship to the Inst. Palladio, Vicenza, Italy; *political career:* alderman, Dublin City Cncl., 1974-; Lord Mayor, Dublin, 1987-88; Mem., Senead Éireann, Aug. 1989-; Mem., Planning and Cultural; Mational Monuments Advisory; Youth and Community; Traffic; Environmental; Protocol and Selection Cttees. of the Dublin Corp; *memberships:* Mem., Advisory Cttee., Hugh Lane Municipal Gallery of Art; Patron, War on Want; The Aids Fund; Ballymun Job Centre Co-op; The Alzheimer Society of Ireland; Clangowes Youth Club Fund raising; Methodist Widow's Home; Irish national Cncl. for Soviet Jewry; Kitalown House Tallaght; Friends of St. Annes Cancer Therapy (FACT); Friends of the National Collections of Ireland; Life Gov., Royal Hospital, Donnbrook; Dir., People in Need Trust; Dir., Board of Dublin City Food Bank; National Trust; Cycle Action Group; Women's Political Assn.; Irish Countrywoman's Assn.; Irish Assn. for Cultural Economic and Social Relations; Chwn., Civic's Inst., St. Brigids Nursery Centre; *honours and awards:* Hon. Doctorate in Laws, Trinity College, Dublin, 1988 and National Univ. of Ireland, 1988; People of the Year Award, 1988; Spirit of Dublin Award, 1988; *office address:* Carmencita Hederman, Seanad Éireann, Lenister House, Kildare Street, Dublin 2, Ireland.

HEIß, Regina; Austrian, Member of the Nationalrat; *born:* 1 June 1960, Zams; *education:* commercial school in Landeck, Master Craftsman's diploma in rural home economics, 1986; *party:* Österreichische Volkspartei (ÖVP, Austrian People's Party); *political career:* girls' consultant, provincial leadership of Young Populists, Tirol, 1983-; Pres. of Young Farmers' Association in Austrian Farmers' Federation, 1985-; Mem. of Nationalrat, for Tirol, 1986-; *professional career:* in the finance department of Landeck town council, 1977-78; clerk at the Tyrolean hydroelectric power station, AG-Kaunertal Power Station; *clubs:* Tyrolean Young Farmers, Farmers' Federation Section, local and regional director, 1981-84, district director, in Landeck, 1981-84, local, district and provincial director, 1984-; *office address:* Frau Regina Heiß, Nationalrat, Dr. Karl Renner Ring 3, 1017 Vienna, Austria.

HEIBERG, Astrid Noklebye; Norwegian, Mayoral candidate; *born:* 14 April 1936, Oslo, Norway; *parents:* Andreas Noklebye and Else Noklebye (née Holt); *married:* Arvid Heiberg, 1963; *children:* Inger, Lise; *languages:* English, German, French; *education:* University, Oslo, doctor, 1962; University, Oslo, Specialist in Psychiatry, 1969; University, Oslo, MD, 1980; *party:* Hoyre (Conservative Party), 1981; *political career:* State Secretary, Social Services Department, 1981-85; Member of Storting, 1985-89; Minister, Consumer and Administration Department, 1986-; leader, Conservative Women's National Federation, 1985-89; running for Mayor of Oslo, 1991; *interests:* social and family politics, equal rights; *professional career:* professor, Oslo University, 1981-; *office address:* Drammensveien 82D, 0271 Oslo 2, Norway.

HEINRICH, Bonnie Miller; American, North Dakota State Senator; *married:* Willis; *children:* one; *education:* Valley City State College; *party:* Democratic Party; *political career:* North Dakota State Senator, District 32, 1977, 1979 and 1983-; Chwn., Education Cttee.; Mem., Human Services and Veterans Affairs Cttees. and Joint Constitutional Revenue Cttee., North Dakota State Senate; *memberships:* North Dakota Education Assn; *professional career:* freelance humour columnist and political consultant; Co-owner Glass Graphics; *office address:* Ms Bonnie Heinrich, 1006 E. Bowen Avenue, Bismark, North Dakota 58504, USA.

HEJMANOWSKA, Stefania; Polish, Senator; *office address:* Ms Stefania Hejmanowska, Senat, ul. Ogrodowa 6, 00-896 Warsaw, Poland; *phone:* (22) 20 03 71.

HELFER, Gloria; Peruvian, Minister of Public Education; *office address:* Ms Gloria Helfer, Ministry of Public Education, Parque Universitario s/n, Lima One, Peru.

HELGADOTTIR, Gudrún; Icelandic, Speaker of Parliament; *born:* 7 September 1935, Hafnarfiördur, Iceland; *parents:* Helgi Gudlaugsson and Ingigerdur Eyjólfsdóttir; *children:* Hördur, Thorvaldur, Helga, Halla; *religion:* Lutheran; *languages:* Icelandic, English, Danish, German, Norwegian, Swedish; *education:* Reykjavik Grammar School, 1951-55; *party:* Althykubandalag (Ab, People's Alliance), 1967; *political career:* Member, Reykjavik Fourth Council, 1978-82; Member, Nordic Council, 1982-88; Mem. of Althingi 1979-; Speaker of Parliament, 1988-; *interests:* Social Affairs, education, arts, foreign affairs; *professional career:* Head of Department, National Institute of Social Rights, 1973-80; author of children's books; *honours and awards:* Best Book of the year, Reykjavik Council, 1974; Torbiörn Egners' Grant, 1979; IBBY Prize, 1989; *publications:* 13 children's books; *clubs:* Writer's Union of Iceland; *private address:* Tringota 43, 101 Reykjavík, Iceland; *office address:* Ms Gudrún Helgadóttir, Althingi, 101 Reykjavík, Iceland.

HELLWIG, Dr. Renate; German, Member of the Bundestag; *born:* 19 February 1940, Beuthen, Upper Schlesien; *education:* Munich, High school leaving examination, 1959; Univ. Munich and Berlin, Law and Economic Science; Junior examinations and Dr. Jur., 1967; *party:* Christlich Demokratische Union (CDU, Christian Democratic Union); *political career:* Personal asst., public relations work, Ministry of Culture, Baden-Württemberg since 1969; mem. of cttee., CDU North Württemberg; mem. of Diet Baden-Württemberg, 1972-75; Sec. of State, Ministry of Social Affairs, Rhineland-Palatinate, 1975-80; mem. of Bundestag since 1980; *office address:* Dr. Renate Hellwig, Bundeshaus, 5300 Bonn 1, West Germany.

HENNELOWA, Józefa; Polish, Member of the Sejm; *office address:* Ms Józefa Hennelowa, Sejm PRl, ul. Wiejska 4/6/8, 00-489 Warsaw, Poland; *phone:* (22) 28 70 01; 28 40 31.

HENRY, Gloria; Trinidad and Tobago, Minister of Education; *born:* 20 April 1946; *parents:* Ralph Springer and Norma Springer; *children:* Kipkem, Moremi, Shawn; *religion:* Christian; *languages:* English; *education:* Mausica Teachers Training College; Univ. of the West Indies, St. Augustin, Trinidad, BA history; *party:* National Alliance for Reconstuction (NAR); *political career:* Mem., Tapia House Movement; became politically active in 1976; MP, Arouca South; Parly. Sec., Ministry of External Trade and Tourism, 1986; Parly. Sec., Ministry of Industry, Enterprise and Tourism, 1987; Minister of Social Development and Family Services, 1988-90; Minister of Education, 1990-; Mem., Exec. of the Inter-American Commission of Women, 1989-90; Mem., Board of Dirs., Inter-American Parly. Group on Population and Development; Mem., Defence Cncl. of Trinidad and Tobago; *interests:* women and development, population and the environment; *professional career:* primary school teacher followed by seven years as a housewife and a career in insurance sales, real estate sales and insurance education admin; *office address:* The Honourable Senator Gloria Henry, Ministry of Education, Alexander St., St. Clair, Port of Spain, Trinidad and Tobago.

HENSEL, Karitas Dagmar; German, former Member of the Bundestag; *born:* 19 April 1946, Haldensleben; *children:* two; *party:* Die Grünen (Green Party); *political career:* mem. of Bundestag, party list of Hessen, 1987-90; dep. chmn., Cttee. for Inter-German Relations; *professional career:* retd. teacher; *private address:* 6102 Pfungstadt, West Germany; *office address:* Frau Karitas Hensel .

HEPTULLA, Dr. Najma; Indian, Member of the Rajya Sabha; *born:* 13 April 1940, Bhopal; *parents:* Yousuf Ali; *married:* Akbar Heptulla; *children:* three d; *education:* M.Sc.; Ph.D; *political career:* Gen. Sec., Bombay Pradesh Congress Cttee.; Sec., Science Forum in Parliament; Mem., MPCC; Mem., All India Haj Advisory Board; Deputy Chmn., Rajya Sabha, 1985-86; *memberships:* Treasurer, Society of Latin America; Pres., Indo-Arab Society; *professional career:* Joint Research Fellow, Council of Scientific and Industrial Research; Senior Fellow, Council of Scientific and Industrial Research; *private address:* Heptulla Park, 2nd Hasanabad Road, Santa Cruz (West), Bombay - 400054, India; *office address:* Dr. Najma Heptulla, 4, Akbar Road, New Delhi -- 110011, India.

HERATH, Ranuka; Sri Lankan, Minister of Health and Women's Affairs; *office address:* Ms Ranuka Herath, Ministry of Health and Women's Affairs, Inland Revenue Building, 11/1 Sir Chittampalam A. Gardinar Mawatha, Colombo 2, Sri Lanka; *phone:* 21121.

HERMAN-MICHIELSENS, Lucienne A.J.I., LL.D; Belgian, Senator; *born:* 13 March 1926, Ghent; *education:* Graduate in Criminology and Notary Profession; *party:* Partij voor Vrijheid en Vooruitgang (PVV, Liberal Party); *political career:* Govt. clerk, asst. adviser and director, Ministry of Public Works, 1951-77; Nat. Chairperson, Nat. Women's Federation, PVV-PLP; town cllr., Ghent, 1971-89; Deputy Chef de Cabinet for Minister of Justice, 1973-77; Co-Pres., International Women's Year, 1975; Vice-Chairperson, PVV, 1974-77; Chairperson, PVV Fraction, 1983-; Senator, 1977-; Chairperson, PVV Women, 1978-80; State Sec. for Flemish Community responsible to Minister for Flemish Community, 1980; Representative at Parly. Assembly, Council of Europe and Western European Union (WEU), 1982-84; Chairperson, Cttee. for Public Health and Living Conditions; Mem., Cttees. for Social Affairs, Justice,

Institutional Reform and Regulation of Parly. Activities; *professional career:* pupil barrister at Bar, Ghent, 1951-53; *honours and awards:* Civilian Medal (First Class), October 1978; Officer, Order of Leopold, 1981, Commander, 1987; Woman of the Year (Knack and Pop Poll HUMO), 1989; *office address:* Mevr. Lucienne Herman-Michielsens, Senaat/Sénat, Palais de la Nation, Palaca de la Nation 1, 1000 Brussels, Belgium; *phone:* Brussels 5133800.

HERMANS, Anna; Belgian, Member of the European Parliament; *born:* 23 September 1944; *party:* Christelijke Volkspartij (CVP, Christian Social Party); *political career:* MEP 1989-; *private address:* Onde Baan 47, 3070 Boutersen, Belgium; *office address:* Mevr. Anna Hermans, European Parliament, Centre Européen, Plateau de Kirchberg, BP 2929, Luxembourg; *phone:* Luxembourg 43001.

HERNANDEZ BALAGUER, Carmen Rosa; Dominican Republic, Administrative Secretary to the Presidency; *party:* Partido Reformista Social Cristiano (PRSC, Christian Social Reform Party); *political career:* Admin. Sec. to the Pres; *office address:* Ms Carmen Rosa Hernández Balaguer, Office of the President, Palacio Nacional, Calle Moisés García, Santo Domingo, Dominican Republic.

HICKS, Maureen Patricia; British, Member of Parliament; *born:* 23 February 1948; *parents:* Ronald Cutler and Norah Cutler; *married:* Keith Henwood Hicks, 1973; *children:* one s., one d; *religion:* Roman Catholic; *education:* Ashley Secondary School; Brokenhurst Grammar School; Furzedown College of Eucation, London; *party:* Conservative Party; *political career:* Cllr., Stratford District Cncl., 1978-83, Chmn., Tourism Cttee., Vice-Chmn., Stratford Tourism Marketing Group, Vice-Chmn., Amenities Cttee.; Member of Parliament for Wolverhampton North East, 1987-; mem., Conservative Backbench Cttee. on Tourism; mem., Commons Select Cttee on Education, Science and the Arts, 1988-90; appointed Private Sec. to the Rt. Hon. Earl of Caithness, Minister of State and The Hon. Mark Lennox-Boyd MP; *interests:* education; tourism; inner cities; law and order; *professional career:* teacher, 1969; manager, Marks and Spencer plc., 1970-74; Asst. Area Education Officer for North West Surrey, 1974-76; Dir., Stratford Motor Museum, 1976-82; at present, part-timer lecturer in Tourism and Retail Management; mem., Exec. of the Heart of England Tourist Board; School Governor., mem., management team, Stratford Citizens Advice Bureau; *clubs:* Royal Overseas Club; *recreations:* amateur dramatics; golf; *office address:* Mrs Maureen Hicks, House of Commons, London SW1A OAA.

HIDA, Miyoko; Japanese, Member of the House of Councillors; *born:* 1 March 1941; *education:*

Pharmaceutical College; *party:* Japan Socialist Party (JSP); *political career:* elected for National, 1990; Mem., House of Cllrs. Cttee. on Foreign Affairs and Special Cttee. on Okinawa and Northern Problems, 1990-; *professional career:* Children's Tales Writer; Pharmacist; *office address:* Ms Miyoko Hida, House of Councillors, 1-7-1 Nagata-cho, Tokyo 100, Japan; *phone:* (03) 5813111.

HILDEN, Jytte; Danish, Member of the Folketing; *born:* 12 September 1942, Copenhagen, Denmark; *parents:* Jorgen Jensen and Gudrun Schmeltzer Andersen; *married:* Mogens Lykketoft, 1987; *children:* Ida, Ulla Jacob, Eva; *religion:* Protestant; *languages:* Danish, English, German, French; *education:* Rungsted Grammar School, 1960; Bachelor of Science/Chemistry, 1966; *party:* Socialdemokratiet (Social Democratic Party), 1973; *political career:* member of the Folketinget, 1971-81 and 1984-; responsible for questions in the social sector; *interests:* environmental politics, technology politics and social politics; *publications:* Strikke Klubben published by Gyldendal in 1987; Anno 2001 published by AOF in 1985; *office address:* Ms Jytte Hilden, Christiansborg, 1240 Copenhagen K, Denmark.

HILL, Margaret; American, Republican National Committeewoman for Indiana; *born:* 23 February 1924, Indianapolis, Indiana, USA; *parents:* Marvin E. Curle and Florence Curle (née Rilling); *married:* Nat U. Hill, 1946; *children:* Dr. Nat U. Jr., Philip C; *religion:* Christian; *education:* Skidmore College; Indiana Univ., Bloomington, AB, 1944; *party:* Republican Party; *political career:* Vice-Chwn., Monroe County Republican Central Cttee., Indiana, 1963-68; Vice-Chwn., 7th District Republican Central Cttee., 1964-82; delegate-at-large and Mem., Rules Cttee., Republican National Convention, 1972; delegate and Mem., Credentials Cttee., 1976; delegate-at-large, Rules Cttee., 1980; delegate-at-large, 1984; Republican National Committeewoman, Indiana, 1972-; delegate-at-large, Republican National Convention, 1988; Vice-Chwn., Arrangements Cttee., 1988; *professional career:* Personnel Dept., Electronic Labs., Indianapolis, 1945-46; currently Treasurer, Hillandale Inc. Family Farm; *honours and awards:* Woman and Boy Award, Boy's Club of Bloomington, 1971; *clubs:* Woman's Dept. Club; Navajo Club; First Christian Church, Bloomington; Pres., Women's Club; *office address:* Mrs Margeret Hill, 4499 N. Kinser Pike, Bloomington, Indiana 47404, USA.

HILLERICH, Imma; German, former Member of the Bundestag; *born:* 23 May 1954, Köln, West Germany; *religion:* Protestant; *education:* Abitur (advanced matriculation examination), 1972; University of Bonn, French, social science, 1972-79; first state examination for teachers, 1979; asst. teacher; second state examination, Duisburg; *party:* Die Grünen (Green Party), 1984-; *political career:* spokesman of Exec. Cttee., district association, Die Grünen, Duisburg, 1984-87; member of regional parliament; expert, Cttee. for urban development and economic growth, Die Grünen council group, town council of Duisburg; mem. of Bundestag, party list of Nordrhein-Westfalen, 1987-90; *professional career:* teacher of politics, French and social science, Mercator secondary school, Duisburg; member of Gewerkschaft Erziehung und Wissenschaft (GEW, Trade Union for Education and Science); *private address:* 4100 Duisburg 1, West Germany; *office address:* Frau Imma Hillerich. .

HILLE VALLE, Kristin; Norwegian, former Minister of the Environment; *born:* 31 December 1944, Hafslo; *children:* two; *education:* National College of Teachers for Home Economics, graduated 1967; Univ. of Trondheim, chemistry; More and Romsdal District College, political science and public administration; *party:* Senterpartiet (SP, Centre Party); *political career:* served on municipal and county councils, and college and county education cttees. in Buskerud County; mem. Centre Party programme cttee., until 1985; second Vice-Chmn., Centre Party, 1987-; Minister of the Environment, Nov. 1989-Oct. 1990; *professional career:* primary school teacher, 1968-72; upper secondary school teacher, 1972-75; rector, Nesbyen Upper Secondary School, 1975-; Chmn., Nat. Cncl. for Upper Secondary Education, 1984-; first woman to hold position of Chief County Education Officer for Oppland County, until Nov. 1989; *office address:* Ms Kristin Hille Valle, Ministry of the Environment, Myntgt. 2, POB 8013 Dep., 0030 Oslo 1, Norway.

HILLIARD HILLMAN, Elsie; American, Member of the Republican National Committee of Pennsylvania; *born:* 9 December 1925, Pittsburgh, Pennsylvania, USA; *parents:* the late Thomas Jones Hilliard and the late Marianna Hilliard; *married:* Henry L. Hillman, 1945; *children:* Juliet, Audrey, Henry Jr., William Talbott; *religion:* Episcopal; *education:* The Ellis School, Pittsburgh; Ethel Walker School, Connecticutt; Westminster Choir College, Princeton, 1944-45; *party:* Republican Party; *political career:* Mem., Republican Leadership Cttee., 1986-; Mem., Presidential Transitional Advisor, Pennsylvania, 1988-; Mem., Republican National Cttee., Pennsylvania; *memberships:* trustee, Westminster Choir College, Princeton; Mem., Urban League; Pittsburgh Symphony Society; Pittsburgh Cancer Inst; *office address:* Mrs Elsie Hilliard Hillman, Morewood Heights, Pittsburgh, Pennsylvania 15213, USA.

HILLS, Carla Anderson; American, Representative for Trade Negotiations; *born:* 3 January 1934, Los Angeles, California, USA; *education:* St. Hilda's College, Oxford Univ., UK, 1954; Stanford Univ., AB, 1955; Yale Univ., USA, LLB, 1958; *party:* Republican Party; *political career:* first woman US trade rep., negotiating such issues as the expansion of US exports, tariff and commodity agreements, intellectual property rights, unfair trade practices and trade involving energy and investments, 1989-; *memberships:* Board of Dirs.: IBM Corp.; Chevron Corp.; American Airlines; Corning Glass Works; *professional career:* Asst. US Attorney, Civil Attorney, Civil Div., Dept. of Justice, California, 1958-61; Asst. Attorney-Gen., Washington DC, 1974-75; Sec., Housing and Urban Development, 1975-77; private law practice, 1978-88; *office address:* Ms Carla Hills, US Trade Representative Office, 600 17th Street NW, Washington DC, 20506, USA.

HIRONAKA, Wakako; Japanese, Member of the House of Councillors; *born:* 11 May 1934, Tokyo, Japan; *education:* Ochanomizu Women's Univ., English BA, 1957; Brandeis Univ., Wien International Scholar, 1958-60, MA in Anthropology, 1968; *party:* Komeito; *political career:* Mem., House of Cllrs., 1986-; Mem., Special Cttee. on Land Problems, Investigation Cttee. on National Life; former Mem., Curriculum Council; elected for National, 1990; Dir., House of Cllrs. Cttee. on Environment and Mem., House of Cllrs. Cttee. on Commerce and Industry, 1990-; *professional career:* Mem., Int. Group for the Study of Women, 1978-; Mem., Board of Dirs., Avon Products Co., 1982-; Pres., Japan Double-Reed Inc., 1984-86; Mem., Board of Dirs., Year 1200 Kyoto Anniversary Cttee., 1985-86; *honours and awards:* Hon. Doctorate, Brandeis Univ., 1987; *publications:* Between Two Cultures, Bunka Shuppan, 1979; Woman, Her Work and Family, Kodansha, 1981; What Values Should We Leave for the Future Generations?, two-volume series, interviews of distinguished world leaders) Sochisha, 1982; What America wants from Japan - Voices from the American Congress, PHP Institute, 1988; Politics is Unexpectedly Interesting, Tokyu Agency, 1989; translated works of other writers - Shifting Gears, George and Nina O'Neill, Kawade Shobo-shinsha, 1975; Japan as Number One, Erza Vogel with A. Kimoto, 1979; The Doctor's Wife, Sawako Ariyoshi with A.S. Kostant, Kodansha International, 1978; Ameyuki-san, Tomoko Yamazaki, Kodansha International, 1986; Kinu to Bushi, Samurai and Silk, Haru M. Reischauer, Bungei Shunju, 1987; *office address:* Ms Wakako Hironaka, House of Councillors, 1-7-1 Nagata-cho, Tokyo 100, Japan; *phone:* (03) 5813111.

HJELM-WALLÉN, Lena; Swedish, Minister for International Development Co-operation; *born:* 14 January 1943, Sala, Sweden; *parents:* Gustav Hjelm and Elly Hjelm (née Johannson); *education:* Uppsala Univ. M. Phil., 1965; Teacher Training College, 1966; *party:* Sveriges Socialdemokratiska Arbetarepartiet (SAP, Swedish Social Democratic Party); *political career:* Member of Riksdag since 1969; (in Second Chamber for

Västmanland, 1969-70); Deputy member of Constitution Cttee., 1969-70; Cultural Affairs committee, 1971-73; and Labour Market Cttee., 1979-82; Member of the Administration of Justice Cttee., 1971-73; mem., Education Cttee., 1976-78, and 1979-82; UN delegate, 1980 and 1981; Member of Select Parliamentary Cttee., 1978-82; Cabinet Minister without Portfolio, 1973-76; Cabinet Minister and Minister of Education, 1982-85; Minister at the Ministry of Foreign Affairs (Development Cooperation), since Oct 1985; Member of the Public Section Select Cttee., 1977-82; Member of County Education Board in Västmanland, 1977-82; mem., Swedish UNESCO Council, 1980-82; Chairman of Mass Movement Council for Foreign Aid, since 1986; Member of Drafting Cttee. of 1968 for Church and State, 1968-72; Expert on Family Law Cttee., 1969-74; mem., Crime Commission, 1973; mem., Drafting Cttee. for Secondary Schools, 1977-81; mem., Delegation for better school Environment and follow up of Reform Decision concerning Primary Schools, 1979-80; Vice-Chairman of Child and Youth Delegation, 1983-86; Chairman, 1986; Board member of Social Democratic Youth Club in Sala, chairman, 1967-70; Chairman of Social Democratic Women's circle in Västmanland county, 1972-74; Member of the Executive Cttee. of the Young Social Democrats in Västmanland County; chairman, 1967-70; Member of Union Board, 1970-72; Member of Social Democratic Labour Party District in Västmanland County, since 1970, Chairman since 1986; Deputy of Social Democratic Labour Party Executive Cttee., since 1987; Member of School Board in Sala, 1968-73; *professional career:* Secondary School Teacher in Borlänge, 1965, and in Sala, 1965-68; *private address:* Syréngatan 9, 73300 Sala, Sweden; *office address:* Ms Lena Hjelm-Wallén, Ministry of Foreign Affairs, Gustav Adofstorg 1, POB 16121, 103 33 Stockholm, Sweden.

HLALELE, Anna Matlelima; Lesotho, Minister of State for Youth and Women's Affairs; *office address:* Ms Anna Matlelima Hlalele, Ministry of Youth and Women's Affairs, PO Box 527, Maseru 100, Lesotho.

HLAVAC, Dr. Elisabeth; Austrian, Member of the Nationalrat; *born:* 25 February 1952, Vienna, Austria; *parents:* Herbert Hlavec and Edith Hlavec; *languages:* German, English, Czech; *education:* grammar school (science oriented), matriculation, 1970; University of Vienna, jurisprudence, Dr. of Law, 1976; *party:* Sozialistische Partei Österreichs (SPÖ, Socialist Party of Austria); *political career:* district councillor, Vienna, Döbling, 1978-88; district women's Chairperson, SPÖ, Döbling, 1985, and district Vice Party Chairperson, 1985; mem. of Vienna Women's Cttee., SPÖ, 1986; Women's Vice Chairperson, SPÖ Vienna, 1988 and mem. of provincial Party Exec., 1988; member of the Federal Party Exec., 1989-; sent to Bundesrat from Vienna Provincial Assembly, Mem. of Bundesrat from

April 1988 to Dec. 1989; member of the Nationalrat, Dec. 1989-; *interests:* law reform, transport, the environment, women's issues; *professional career:* entered civil service, 1975; *recreations:* cultural interest; *office address:* Dr. Elisabeth Hlavac, Nationalrat, Dr. Karl Renner Ring 3, 1017 Vienna, Austria.

HOCHOVA, Dagmar; Czechoslovakian, Member of the Narodni Rada (Czech National Council); *born:* 10 March 1926; *party:* Civic Forum; *office address:* Ms Dagmar Hochova, Ceská národní rada, Snemovní 4, 110 00 Praha 1, Czechoslovakia; *phone:* (02) 2105.

HÖDL, Eleonore; Austrian, Member of the Bundesrat; *born:* 7/04/44 Deutschlandsberg, Steiermark, Austria; *education:* grammar school (science orientated), matriculation, 1963; Academy of Commerce, Graz, matriculation 1964; University of Graz, Dr. of Law, 1968; *party:* Sozialistische Partei Österreichs (SPÖ, Socialist Party of Austria); *political career:* town councillor, Graz, 1973-76; sent to Bundesrat from Steiermark Provincial Asembly, Mem. of Bundesrat since 1986; *professional career:* practical work experience in court, 1968-69; employee, Sattler Textile Works, Graz Thondorf, 1969-71; employee, Workers' Pensions Insurance Institute, Graz, since 1971; *office address:* Frau Eleonore Hödl, Bundesrat, Dr. Karl Renner Ring 3, 1017 Vienna, Austria.

HODOSAN, Róza; Hungarian, Member of the Országgyülés; *party:* Alliance of Free Democrats (SZDSZ); *office address:* Ms Róza Hodosán, Országgyülés, Kossuth L. tér 1-3, Budapest V, Hungary; *phone:* 22 5058; 22 5059.

HOEGH, Annelise; Norwegian, Member of the Storting; *born:* 26 July 1948, Oslo, Norway; *parents:* Anders Hoegh and Tove Hoegh (née Bothner-By); *married:* Jo Benkow, 1985; *public role of spouse:* Speaker of the Norwegian Parliament; *languages:* English; *education:* University, Olso, Cand. Philol.(MA), History, English, History of Ideas; *party:* Hoyre (Conservative), 1975; *political career:* Mem., Conservative Party's Political Advisory Board, 1976-83; Mem., Standing Cttee. on Health, Social Security and Pensions, Storting, 1981-1989, Spokesman for Conservative Party on Health, Social Security and Pensions, 1985-89; Vice-Chmn., Conservative Party in Oslo, 1988-; Mem., Standing Cttee. on Foreign Affairs, 1989-91; Deputy Leader of Conservative Party Group in Parliament, 1989-91; Chwn., Standing Cttee. on Consumer Affairs and Govt. Admin., 1991-; *professional career:* Research Assistant, North Atlantic Assembly, Brussels, 1977; Junior Executive, Ministry of Foreign Affairs, 1977-78; Research Executive, Federation of Norwegian Professionals Association, 1978-81; mem., Executive Board of Norwegian Association of Women's Rights, 1980-84; mem. of

Board of Control, society of Conserving Stocks and Shares, Norway, 1980-81; *publications:* Parliamentary Elections in Jarlsberg og Larvik Counties, 1814-32, Main History Paper, 1976; The Welfare State, 1982; Women's Rights and Conservatism, (co-author), 1978; Where is the Conservative Party Heading? (co-author), 1984; *private address:* Elisenbergveien 8, 0265 Oslo 2, Norway; *office address:* Ms Annelise Hoegh, Storting, Karl Johansg. 22, 0026 Oslo 1, Norway.

HOFF, Magdalene; German, Member of the European Parliament; *born:* 29 December 1940; *party:* Sozialdemokratische Partei Deutschlands (SPD, Social Democratic Party); *political career:* local govt.; MEP, 1979-; *private address:* Riegestr 8, 5800 Hagen, Germany; *office address:* Ms Magdalene Hoff, European Parliament, Centre Européen, Plateau de Kirchberg, BP 2929, Luxembourg; *phone:* Luxembourg 43001.

HOFROVA, Jarmila; Czechoslovakian, Member of the Narodni Rada (Czech National Council); *born:* 29 June 1958; *party:* Komunistická Strana Ceskoslovenska (KSC, Communist party of Czechoslovakia); *office address:* Ms Jarmila Hofrova, Ceská národní rada, Snemovní 4, 110 00 Praha 1, Czechoslovakia; *phone:* (02) 2105.

HO HON; Cambodian, Minister for Industry; *office address:* Mrs Ho Hon, Ministry of Industry, Phnom Penh, Kampuchea; *phone:* 23477.

HOLLINGER, Paula Colodny; American, Maryland State Senator; *born:* 30 December 1940, Washington DC, USA; *parents:* the late Samuel Colodny and the late Ethel Colodny; *married:* Paul Hollinger, 1962; *children:* Ilene, Marcy, David; *religion:* Jewish; *education:* Mt. Sinai School of Nursing, RN Dip., 1961; *party:* Democratic Party; *political career:* Statewide Health Co-ordination Cncl.; delegate Democrat National Convention, 1976; Mem., Governor's Commission on Violence and Extremism; Vice Pres., Women's Legislative Caucus, 1983, Pres., 1986-88; Maryland State Senator, District 11; Mem., Economic and Environmental Affairs Cttee., 1983, Mem., Joint Cttee., on Health Care Cost Containment, Joint Cttee. on Federal Relations, Maryland State Senate; Chwn., Science and Technology and Resource Planning Commissions, National Conference State Legislature; *memberships:* Chancellor's Health Commission on Status of Women, Univ. of Maryland; National Conference of State Legislators; Independent Democratic Alliance; *professional career:* Head Nurse, Mt. Sinai Hospital Surgery Intensive Care Unit, New York City, 1962-63; clinical instructor in psychiatric nursing, Tuskegee Inst., 1969-70; myasthenia gravis specialist, Univ. of Maryland Hospital, 1971-73; camp nurse, Timber Ridge Camping Reservation, 1974-77;

public health School Nurse, Dept. of Health, Baltimore County, Maryland, 1974-78; *honours and awards:* Murry Guggenheim Award for Excellence in Nursing, Mt. Sinai Hospital School of Nursing; Legislator of the Year, Maryland Nurses Assn., 1984; Outstanding Contribution to Education, Belt County Teacher's Assn., 1984; Dedication to Health and Environment, Central Maryland Health System Agency, 1985; Legislator of the Year, Maryland Psychological Assn., 1987; *office address:* Mrs Paula Colodny Hollinger, 3708 Lanamer Road, Randallstown, Maryland 21133, USA.

HOLMBERG, Joyce; American, Illinois State Representative; *born:* Rockford, Illinois, USA; *married:* Eugene Holmberg; *children:* two; *education:* Northern Illinois Univ., BS; Alfred Adler Inst., Chicago, MA; *party:* Democratic Party; *political career:* Illinois State Rep., District 34, 1983-; Chwn., Local Govt. Cttee.; Vice-Chwn., Elementary and Secondary Education Cttee.; Mem., Appropriations II, Higher Education, Citizen's Cncl. on Women Cttees.; Mem., Scientific Advisory Cncl.; Mem., Illinois State Senate; *private address:* 716 Coolidge Place, Rockford, Illinois 61103, USA; *office address:* Mrs Joyce Holmberg, 825 N. Main Street, Rockford, Illinois 61103, USA.

HOLMES, Eleanor; American, Member of the House of Representatives; *born:* Washington DC, USA; *married:* Edward W. Norton; *public role of spouse:* attorney in private practice; *children:* Katherine, John; *religion:* Episcopal; *education:* Monroe Elementary School; Banneker Junior High School; Dunbar High School, DC; Antioch College; Yale Univ., LLB, MA American studies; *party:* Democratic Party; *political career:* former Human Rights Commissioner, New York City; Chairperson, EEOC, 1977-81; Member of Congress, from District of Columbia,1990-; Mem., House Cttee. on the District of Columbia; *memberships:* Mem., Board of Governors, Washington DC Bar Assn.; Mem., Board: Community Foundation of Greater Washington; Martin Luthter King Jr. Centre for Social Change; Southern Christian Leadership Conference; Nat. Women's Political Caucus Advisory Board; *professional career:* admitted to the bar, 1964; law clerk, Federal District Court, Judge A. Leon Higginbotham, 3rd Circuit, 1964-65; assistant legal Dir., American Civil Liberties Union, 1965-70; adjunct Assistant Prof., New York Univ. Law School, 1970-71; Exec. Assistant, Mayor, New York City, 1971-74; Prof., Georgetown Univ. Law Centre, 1982-90; *honours and awards:* numerous honourary degrees; *office address:* Ms Eleanor Holmes, House of Representatives, Capitol Building, Washington DC, 20515, USA; *phone:* (202) 225-8040.

HONAN née Barwow, Trás; Irish, Member of the Seanad Éireann; *born:* 4 January 1930, Tipperary,

Ireland; *parents:* Matthew Barwow and Carrie Barwow (née Ryan); *married:* the late Dermot Patrick Honan, 1956; *public role of spouse:* former Senator and business man; *children:* T.V. Honan (s.), Ann Honan Croke (d.); *religion:* Catholic; *languages:* English, Irish, French; *education:* St. Leo's Carlow Convent of Mercy, Carlow, Ireland; *party:* Fianna Fáil, 1951; *political career:* former Speaker of the Senate; elected six times to the Upper House Admin. Panel; first women elected to Irish Senate and currently holder of the Defence Portfolio in the Upper House; Senator, 1977-; *interests:* local govt., health, education; *memberships:* Chwn., Clare Mentally Handicapped, 1966-; *professional career:* family business; *clubs:* Ennis Golf Club; Drumoland Castle Golf Club; *recreations:* golk, swimming, walking; *private address:* Heatherlea, Cusack Road, Ennis, County Clare, Ireland; *office address:* Ms Trás Honan, Seanad Éireann, Lenister House, Kildare Street, Dublin 2, Ireland.

HOOPER, Baroness (cr. 1985, Life Peer) Gloria Dorothy Hooper; British, Parliamentary Under-Secretary of State for Health; *born:* 25 May 1939; *parents:* the late Frederick Hooper; *religion:* Roman Catholic; *languages:* Spanish, French; *education:* La Sainte Union Convent; Royal Ballet School; Univ. of Southampton; Universidad Central, Ecuador; *party:* Conservative Party; *political career:* Member of European Parliament, 1979-84; Vice-Chmn., Cttee. on Environment, Public Health and Consumer Protection; Dep. Chief Whip, European Democratic Group; House of Lords, 1985-; Baroness-in-Waiting (Government Whip), 1985-87; Parly. Under-Sec. of State, Dept. of Education and Science, 1987-88, Dept. of Energy, 1988-89; Parly. Under Sec. of State for Health, 1989-; *interests:* EC, Latin America, inner city regeneration; *memberships:* Law Society; *professional career:* asst. to Chief Registrar, John Lewis Partnership; editor, Current Law, Sweet and Maxwell; Information Officer, Winchester City Council; asst. solicitor, Taylor and Humbert; legal adviser, Slater Walker France SA; partner, Taylor Garrett, 1974-84; *publications:* Law of International Trade, Casebook on Company Law; *clubs:* Royal Socy. of Arts (Fellow); Royal Geographical Socy. (Fellow); Industry and Parliament Trust (Fellow); *recreations:* theatre, travel; *office address:* Baroness Hooper, Department of Health, Richmond House, 79 Whitehall, London SW1A 2NS.

HORN AF RANTZIEN, Anna Brita Sofia; Swedish, Member of the Riksdag; *born:* 11 February 1924; *parents:* Olof Wilhelm Arrhenius and Eva Anna Amalia Arrhenius (née Nordenskiöld); *married:* the late Henning Rudolf Henrik Horn af Rantzien (Decd. 1960), 1945; *children:* Carl, Christer, Catharina, Claes, Samuel (Decd. 1974); *religion:* Lutheran; *languages:* English, German, French; *education:* Sthlms University, Fil. Kand., botany, genetics, psychology, art, 1943-47; Fil. Mag., zoology, geology, geography,

1960-62; *party:* Miljöpartiet de Gröna (Green Party), 1982; *political career:* Member, Swedish Association of Environmental Care; member, Municipal Civil Defence Committee; Member, Health and Environment Committee; mem. of Riksdag, 1988-; *interests:* environmental politics, countryside development, Third World development; *professional career:* science teacher, Stockholm, 1962-66; Producer, Educational Programmes, Swedish Broadcasting Corporation, 1965-81; editor, writer on science and environmental issues; *publications:* Min Bit på Jorden, 1983; Kärngårdar, 1987; Vågar du ga med; *clubs:* Amnesty International, Greenpeace, centre for Ecological Techniques, Future in our Hands Group; *private address:* Lilla Fredsberg, 17171 Solna, Sweden; *office address:* Ms Anna Horn af Rantzien, Riksdag, Fack, S-100 12, Stockholm, Sweden; *phone:* Stockholm 786 4000.

HORNBLOWER, Augusta; American, Massachusetts State Representative; *born:* 6 June 1948, Boston, Mass., USA; *parents:* Henry Hornblower and Dorothy Hornblower (née Shapard); *religion:* Episcopal; *education:* Babson College, BS, 1971; *party:* Republican Party; *political career:* Mem., Mass. Notary Public Commission, 1974-; Mem., Watertown Bicentennial Commission and Watertown Historical Commission, 1975-78; alternate delegate, Republican National Convention, 1976; Vice-Chwn., Mass., Republican Finance Cttee., 1978-80; Mgr., Energy Conservation Program, Mass. Exec. Office of Energy Resources, 1979-83; Chwn., 5th District Caucus for Republican Delegate Selection, 1980; delegate to Japan, American Cncl. of Young Political Leaders, 1980; Pres. and Founder, Lavima Baron Papalia PAC, 1980-; State Fellow, National Governor's Assn. of Energy and Environment Cttee., 1982-83; Senior Staff Evaluator, NATO Civil-Military Exercise, Washington DC, 1983; Mem., Groton Republican Town Cttee., 1984-; Mass. State Rep., 1985-; Mem., Joint Cttees. on Election Laws and Taxation and Special Commission on Tax Reform; *memberships:* Development Cttee., Society for the Preservation of New England Antiquities, 1975-78; Plymouth Plantation; Schwamb Mill Preservation Trust; Mass. Legislator's Assn.; American Legislative Exchange Cncl.; National Conference of State Legislators; Women's Republican Club; *professional career:* investigator, Div. of Minimum Wages, Mass. Dept. of Labour and Industries, 1969; partner, the Crepe Record, 1972; museum curator, Abraham Browne House, Watertown, 1975-78; registered Rep., New York Stock Exchange and National Assn. of Securities Dealers, 1973-77; Account Exec., HC Wainwright and Co., Boston, 1973-77; Mem., Cttee., on Development and Public Affairs, Babson College Corp. Board, 1977-82; fundraiser and Consultant, American Tax Reform Foundation, Washington DC, 1981-84; *honours and awards:* outstanding Young Woman of the Year, Mass. Federation of Republican Women, 1972;

Paul Revere Patriot Award, 1965; Thomas E. Wetherbee Award, Minuteman Chapter, Ducks Unlimited, 1988; *private address:* Rocky's Point, Groton, MA 01450, USA; *office address:* Ms Augusta Hornblower, Rm. 26 State House, Boston, MA 02133, USA.

HORNE, Louise; Trinidad and Tobago, Senator; *education:* Univ. graduate; teacher training college; *party:* independent; *political career:* Senator, 1976-; *professional career:* teacher; *office address:* Ms Louise Horne, Senate, Red House, St. Vincent Street, Port-of-Spain, Trinidad and Tobago; *phone:* (62) 32971/76.

HORVATH, Waltraud; Austrian,; *born:* 7 February 1957, Linz, Austria; *education:* general secondary school, matriculation; Johannes Kepler University, Linz, social science, MSc; *party:* Sozialistische Partei Österreichs (SPÖ, Socialist Party of Austria); *political career:* various functions in Socialist Youth Organization, mem. of Nationalrat, for Upper Austria, since 1986; *professional career:* social scientist, employee of SPÖ, district organization, Linz, 1980-86; *clubs:* various associations; *office address:* Ms Waltraud Horvath, Nationalrat, Dr. Carl Renner Ring 3, 1017 Vienna, Austria.

HUBERT, Elisabeth (Michèle Adélaïde Marie); French, Deputy; *born:* 26 May 1956, Lude, Sarthe, France; *parents:* Auguste Hubert and Germaine Hubert (née Guibert); *education:* Saint-Dominique Institute, Saint-Herblain; Univ. of Nantes, Faculty of Medicine; Doctor of medicine; *party:* Rassemblement pour la République (RPR, Rally for the Republic); *political career:* Town Councillor, Nantes, since 1983; Deputy, RPR, Loire-Atlantique, 1986, re-elected 1988; Sec. of the Commission of Social and Cultural Affairs of the National Assembly; *professional career:* doctor in Nantes, since 1982; *office address:* Mme. Elisabeth Hubert, L'Assemblée Nationale, 126 rue de L'Université, 75355 Paris, France.

HUBINEK, Dr. Marga; Austrian, Member of the Nationalrat; *born:* 20 May 1926, Vienna, Austria; *education:* Secondary school, matriculation, 1944; University of Vienna, Ph.D, 1949; *party:* Österreichische Volkspartei (ÖVP, Austrian People's Party); *political career:* worked in Austrian Association of College Students, Austrian Women's Movement, Austrian Federation of Academics, and in Austrian Workers' and Employees' Federation; district councillor, Vienna, 1959-70; mem. of Vienna Provincial Assembly, 1959-70; mem. of Nationalrat, for Vienna, since 1970; second Chairperson of Nationalrat; district Councillor, Breitenfurt bei Wien, since 1978; *professional career:* senior official, Foundation of Viennese Businessmen, since 1952; *honours and awards:* Great Golden Award for services to Austria;

Great Golden Award for services to the Federal Province of Lower Austria; *office address:* Dr. Marga Hubinek, Nationalrat, Dr. Karl Renner Ring 3, 1017 Vienna, Austria.

HULL, Jane Dee; American, Arizona State Representative; *born:* 8 August 1935, Kansas City, USA; *parents:* Justin Bowerstock and Mildred Bowerstock (née Swenson); *married:* Terrance W. Hull, 1953; *children:* Jeanette (d.), Robin (d.), Jeffrey (s.), Michael (s.); *religion:* Catholic; *education:* Univ. of Kansas, BS (Hons.); *party:* Republican Party; *political career:* Arizona State Rep.; former Chair, Govt. Operations and Realignment Cttees; former Chair, Joint Legislative Cttee. on Corporate Commissions; Mem., National Resources, Energy, Public Inst. and Education Commissions; Mem., Govt. Operations Cttee.; Majority Whip; Speaker in the House; Co-Chair, Russ Williams for Governor Cttee., 1974; Chair, County Realignment Cttee.; founder Chair and Sec., Republican Forum; Vice-Chair, Republican Legislative Campaign Cttee., 1980; *memberships:* Florence Crittenden Board; Freedom Found; Vis Nurses Auxillary; Maricopa and Arizona State Medical Auxillary; *private address:* 10458 N Ninth Street, Phoenix, Arizona 85020, USA; *office address:* Ms Jane Hull, 1700 W Washington, Phoenix, Arizona 85007, USA.

HULL, Zenda; American, Member of the Republican National Cttee., Utah; *religion:* Latter Day Saints; *party:* Republican Party; *political career:* Mem., Republican Nat. Cttee., 1983-; *honours and awards:* Republican Woman of the Year, 1985; *office address:* Ms Zenda Hull, 1112 Vista View Drive, Salt Lake City, Utah 84108, USA.

HUMPHREYS, Priscilla Faith; American, Member of the Republican National Cttee., West Virginia; *born:* 28 April 1912, Huntingdon, West Virginia, USA; *parents:* James Edward Cobb and Bertie Cobb (née Esque); *married:* Irvin Wendell Humphreys (née 1936); *children:* David Wendell, Bertie Anne, John Edward; *religion:* Baptist; *education:* Marshall Univ; *party:* Republican Party; *political career:* Mem., Republican Nat. Cttee., West Virginia; *office address:* Ms Priscilla Humphreys, 1546 16th Street, Huntingdon, West Virginia 25701, USA.

HUNTER, Lynn; Canadian, Member of the House of Commons; *born:* 1947, Comox; *children:* Paul, Megan; *education:* Univ. Victoria, distinction in political science and Canadian history, 1985; *party:* New Democrats; *political career:* PR Co-ordinator, Gretchen Brewin successful mayoralty campaign, Victoria, 1985; campaigned for several New Democrats; elected first woman MP from Vancouver Island, 1988; New Democrat Associate Critic for the Environment

(International); Mem., Environment Cttee., Mem., Special Joint Cttee. on the Process for Amending the Constitution of Canada; Sec.-Treasurer, Caucus; *memberships:* Univ. of Victoria, Vice-Pres., Cttee. on Women's Studies; *publications:* The Native Indian Franchise in British Columbia, thesis published through Univ. of Victoria History Dept; *private address:* 208-771 Vernon Avenue, Victoria B.C., V8X 1A7, Canada; *office address:* Ms Lynn Hunter, 760 Confederation Bldg., House of Commons, Ottawa K1A OA6, Canada.

HÜRLAND-BÜNING, Agnes; German, Parliamentary Secretary of State for Defence; *born:* 17 May 1926, Dorsten, West Germany; *children:* four; *religion:* Catholic; *education:* Nursing care placement; Westphalia Welfare School; *party:* Christlich Demokratische Union (CDU, Christian Democratic Union), 1964; *political career:* Federal Authority for Labour; mem. of council, Dorsten 1969-; mem. of Bundestag, 1972-; Parliamentary Sec., CDU/CSU-Bundestag Group to 1987 (mem. of Coucil of Elders); Parliamentary Sec. of State, Federal Ministry of Defence, 1987-; *professional career:* labour and war service; rehabilitation adviser; *office address:* Frau Agnes Hürland-Büning, Ministry of Defence, Postfach 1328, Hardthöhe, 53 Bonn 1, West Germany.

HURSKAINEN-LEPPÄNEN, Sinikka (Ulla Sinikka); Finnish, Member of the Eduskunta; *born:* 22 March 1951, Kuusankoski, Finland; *parents:* Tauno Olavi Hurskainen and Airi Sisko Hurskainen (née Kumpulainen); *married:* Urpo Olavi Leppänen, 1984; *children:* Ida; *languages:* English, Swedish; *education:* Tampere Univ., Sociologist, 1973-76; Studies in Geneva, 1975; *party:* Suomen Sosialidemokraattinen Puolue (SDP, Finnish Social Democratic Party), 1969; *political career:* Councillor, Imatra Town Council, 1979; Youth Cttee., Kyme Province, 1979-82; Councillor, Kuusankoski Town Council, 1973-78;

mem. of Eduskunta, 1983-; Board of Pohjola Liikenne (transport co.), 1984; *interests:* social politics, traffic; *professional career:* Head, Finno-American Society Nursery School, 1977-78; Compensation Processor, Imatra Labour Exchange, 1978-80; Nordic Employment Agency, 1980-82; Planner, 1982-83; *publications:* Kuusankosken nuorisotutkimus, 1977; *office address:* Ms Sinikka Hurskainen-Leppänen, Eduskunta, 00102 Helsinki, Finland.

HUSSAIN, Syeda Abida; Pakistani, Adviser to the Prime Minister on Population Welfare (full Minister status); *political career:* Member of Parliament; Adviser to the Prime Minister, Nawaz Sharif, on Population Welfare, with full Ministerial status, May 1991-; *office address:* Syeda Abida Hussain, Prime Minister's Secretariat, Islamabad, Pakistan.

HYLTON-FOSTER, Baroness (cr. 1965, Life Peer) Audrey Pellew Hylton-Foster; British, Member of the House of Lords; *born:* 19 May 1908; *parents:* the late Viscount Ruffside and the late Viscountess Ruffside; *married:* the late Rt. Hon. Sir Harry Hylton-Foster, 1931; *public role of spouse:* Speaker, House of Commons, 1959-65; *religion:* Church of England; *education:* St. George's Ascot; Ivy House, Wimbledon; *party:* Independent; *political career:* House of Lords, 1965-; Convener, Cross Bench Peers, 1974-; *interests:* social welfare, environment; *professional career:* Dir., Chelsea Division, British Red Cross Soc. (BRCS), 1950-60; Pres., County of London Branch, BRCS, 1960-74; Pres., Prevention of Blindness Research Fund, 1965-76; mem., Exec. Cttee., BRCS, 1966-76; Pres. and Chmn., London Branch, BRCS, 1974-83; Cncl. mem., BRCS, 1977-81; mem., Nat. BRCS HQ Consultative Panel, 1984; *honours and awards:* D.B.E; *recreations:* fishing, gardening; *private address:* The Coach House, Tanhurst, Holmbury St. Mary, Dorking, Surrey RH5 6LU, United Kingdom; *office address:* Baroness Hylton-Foster, House of Lords, London SW1A 0PW.

I

INUI, Harumi; Japanese, Member of the House of Councillors; *born:* 18 October 1934; *education:* Tokushima Univ; *party:* Rengo; *political career:* former Subhead of Tokushima Prefectural Govt.; elected for Tokushima, 1990; Dir., House of Cllrs. Special Cttee. on National Livelihood and Mem., House of Cllrs. Cttee. on Social and Labour Affirs, 1990-; *office address:* Ms Harumi Inui, House of Councillors, 1-7-1 Nagata-cho, Tokyo 100, Japan; *phone:* (03) 5813111.

IOTTI, Dott. Leonilde; Italian, President of the Chamber of Deputies; *born:* 10 April 1920, Reggio Emilia, Italy; *children:* Marisa (adopted); *education:* Catholic University of Milan, Degree in Letters; *party:* Partito Democratico della Sinistra (PDS, Party of the Democratic Left); *political career:* Founded and led, Women's Defence Group during the Resistance; Deputy on the Constituent Assembly, responsible, with the Cttee. of 75 for drafting the Italian Constitution; One of 5 remaining members of the Constituent Assembly still, and uninterruptedly, in office elected Deputy, 1948-; Mem., Nat. Presidency, Italian Women's Union; Mem., Central Cttee. of PCI, 1956; Head of Nat. Women's Section, 1961; Mem., Directorate, PCI, 1962; Promoter of the first motion to revise the Agreement between State and Catholic Church, reached under fascism; Vice-President of PCI Parly. group; Former Secretary of PCI Parly. group; Vice-President, Assembly of Montecitorio; elected to European Parliament, 1969-79; Pres., Cttee. on Constitutional Affairs; President of the Chamber of Deputies, 1979; Confirmed as Pres., Chamber of Deputies; Invited by the President of the Republic to explore ways of resolving the crisis at the end of the 9th Legislature, the first woman, and the first communist to be so invited; successfully reformed the divorce laws while President of the Chamber of Deputies in the 2nd Craxi government; confirmed as Pres., Chamber of Deputies, 1987; *professional career:* teacher, Technical Institute, Reggio Emilia; *office address:* Dott. Leonilde Lotti, Camera dei Deputati, Montecitorio, 00186 Rome, Italy.

IP, Hon. Dr. Henrietta Man-Hing; Hong Kong, Member of the Legislative Council; *born:* 7 December 1947, Hong Kong; *education:* Univ. of Liverpool, UK, M.B.Ch.B; London, Diploma in Child Health; Chinese Univ. of Hong Kong, Diploma in Management for Executive Development; *political career:* Mem., Legislative Cncl; *memberships:* Royal College of Physicians; Royal College of Surgeons; Vice Patron, Hong Kong Assn. for the Mentally Handicapped; Chmn., Advisory Cttee. on Travel Agents; Chmn., Advisory Cttee. on Health Sciences, Hong Kong Polytechnic; Chmn., The Hong Kong Childhealth Foundation; Vice Chmn., Land Development Corp.; Board Dir., United Christian Medical Service; *professional career:* paediatrician; *honours and awards:* OBE, Justice of the Peace; *office address:* The Hon. Dr. Henrietta Ip, The Legislative Council, Government House, Hong Kong.

ISAAC-SIBILLE, Bernadette; French, Deputy; *born:* 30 March 1930, Lyon, France; *parents:* Albert Sibille and Lucile Sibille (née Martin-Monchovet); *married:* Alain Isaac, 1956; *children:* Franck, Cyrille, Serge, Laurence; *religion:* Roman Catholic; *languages:* English; *education:* Belmont School; Institute of the Ladies of Nazareth; Catholic University, Lyon; Univ. of Lyon, degree in classics; *party:* Union Centriste (UC, Centrist Union); *political career:* town councillor, later Deputy Mayor of Lyon, 1977-83; Mayor of 5th arrondissement, Lyon, 1983-; councillor of the urban community, Lyon, 1983-; District Councillor, Rhône, 1985-; Deputy, UDC, 1988-; Vice-Pres., General Council of Rhône; *interests:* family, arts, social work; *professional career:* former teacher, Secondary Schools of Saint-Just and Edouard Herriot, Lyon, 1959-65; *honours and awards:* Chevalier of the National Order of Merit; Family Medal; *clubs:* several; *recreations:* piano; *private address:* 25 rue François Genin, 69005 Lyon, France; *office address:* Mme. Bernadette Isaac-Sibille, L'Assemblée Nationale, 126 rue de L'Université, 75355 Paris, France.

ISHII, Michiko; Japanese, Member of the House of Councillors; *born:* 5 February 1933; *education:* Tokyo College of Pharmacy; *party:* Liberal Democratic Party (LDP); *political career:* former Parly. Dep. Minister for Labour and for the Environment; former Dep. Dir., LDP Environment Div.; second time elected, National, Miyazawa faction; Mem., House of Cllrs. Cttee. on Education, 1990-; *office address:* Ms Michiko Ishii, House of Councillors, 1-7-1 Nagata-cho, Tokyo 100, Japan; *phone:* (03) 5813111.

ISOHOOKANA-ASUNMAA, Tytti; Finnish, Minister of Culture; *party:* Keskustapuolue (KP, Centre Party); *office address:* Ms Tytti Isohookana-Asunmaa, c/o Prime Minister's Office, Aleksanterinkatu 3D, 00170 Helsinki, Finland.

ISRAELSSON, Karin Birgitta; Swedish, Member of the Riksdag; *born:* 27 October 1941; *parents:* Johan Hilding Lindgren and Elsa Margareta Lindgren (née Andersson); *married:* Bengt Erland Israelsson, 1967; *children:* Björn, Maria; *religion:* Protestant, Ch. of Sweden; *languages:* English; *education:* Matron School, 1959-60; Lower School Certificate, Jörn, 1959; Examined Nurse, 1965; District Nurse Education, Stockholm, 1967; *party:* Centerpartiet (Centre Party), 1966; *political career:* Chairwoman of the Sorsele Vestry, 1976-79; mem. survey into the situation of Homosexuals in Society, 1977-84; mem. cttee. on Family Finances, 1979-83; mem. Abortion Cttee. of 1980, 1980-83; Deputy member of the Social Affairs Cttee., 1986-88, 1979-80, 1982-85; Full member of the Social Affairs Cttee., 1981-82; Member of the Social Insurance Cttee. 1982-; Member of the Board for Social Affairs, 1984-; Expert in the survey on the Unborn Child 1985-; Chairwoman of the Sorsele Local Government Council, 1985-; Deputy member of the Board of the Centre Party; MP, 1979-; *interests:* health care; alcohol policies; children and elderly care; immigration and refugees; *memberships:* KSAN - The Women Organisations' Co-operative Council for alcohol and drugs-matters (KSAN) ordförande, 1988; MHF, sober version of the A.A., EFS, Ganghås IF; Red Cross; The Blue Ribbon Movement; DKSN De Kristna Samfundens nykterhetsrötelse ordförande, 1989-; Försäkringsbolaget Ansvars Styrelse; *professional career:* District Nurse, Gargnäs in the Admin. Province of Västerbotten, Sweden, 1965-; *publications:* Basic Safety, a New Pensions System, in Centerpressen, 1989; *private address:* Box 3, 2073 Gargnäs, Sweden; *office address:* Ms Karin Israelsson, Riksdag, Fack, S-100 12 Stockholm, Sweden.

ITHANA, Pendukini; Namibian, Minister of Youth and Sports; *political career:* Minister of Youth and Sports, 1990-; *office address:* Ms Ithana Pendukini, Ministry of Youth and Sport, Windhoek, Namibia.

ITO, Hideko; Japanese, Member of the House of Representatives; *born:* 15 August 1943; *education:* Tohoku Univ; *party:* Japan Socialist Party (JSP); *political career:* elected for Hokkaido 1, 1990-; Mem., House of Reps. Cttee on Social and Labour Affairs and Special Cttee. on Okinawa and Northern Problems, 1990-; *office address:* Ms Hideko Ito, House of Representatives, 1-7-1 Nagata-cho, Chiyoda-ku, Tokyo 100, Japan; *phone:* (03) 5815111.

ITOHISA, Yaeko; Japanese, Member of the House of Councillors; *born:* 23 March 1932; *education:* Chiba Univ; *party:* Japan Socialist Party (JSP); *political career:* former Chmn., House of Cllrs. Cttee. on Communications and Dir., Chiba Prefectural Teachers' Union; second time elected for Chiba; Dir., House of Cllrs. Cttee. on Social and Labour Affairs, 1990-; *office address:* Ms Yaeko Itohisa, House of Councillors, 1-7-1 Nagata-cho, Tokyo 100, Japan; *phone:* (03) 5813111.

IZEBOUD, Dr. Pieternella Johanna; Dutch, Chair of the Communist Party of the Netherlands; *born:* 12 May 1949, Koudekerken; *parents:* Pieter Dingeman Izeboud and Kornelia Izeboud (née Davidse); *languages:* Dutch, English, German; *education:* Free University of Amsterdam, Industrial Sociology, 1966-75; *party:* Communistische Partij van Nederland (CPN, Communist Party of the Netherlands), 1972; *political career:* active Mem. CPN, 1979-86; Chmn. CPN, 1982-; Deputy member of Cttee. Equal Rights; Mem. of Central Appeal for Emancipation, district North-Holland, 1986-; *interests:* emancipation of women, international politics, policies of trades unions; *professional career:* scientific collaborator, Free University, 1975-76; scientific collaborator, University of Amsterdam, 1977-79; *office address:* Dr. Pieternella Izeboud, Communistische Partij van Nederland, Hoogte Kadijk 145, 1018 BH Amsterdam, POB 20165, 1000 HD Amsterdam, The Netherlands.

IZQUIERDO ARIJA, María del Pilar; Spanish, Deputy; *born:* 2 December 1935, Palencia, Spain; *education:* degree in humanities; *party:* former mem. Alianza Popular (AP, Popular Alliance); Partido Popular (PP, People's Party); *political career:* local Pres., AP; Deputy, AP, Zamora, 1986-89; re-elected, PP, 1989-; *office address:* Ms María Izquierdo Arija, Congreso de los Diputados, Fernán Flor 1, Madrid 14, Spain.

IZQUIERDO ROJO, María; Spanish, Member of the European Parliament; *born:* 13 November 1946, Oviedo; *education:* Univ. of Oviedo, doctorate in Romance philology; *party:* Partido Socialista Obrero Español (PSOE, Spanish Socialist Workers' Party); Socialist Group (S); *political career:* mem. PSOE Fed. Exec., 1979; Deputy for Granada, 1977-82; Sec. of State for the Autonomous Communities, 1982-87; MEP, 1989-; *professional career:* former associate prof. of Spanish language, Univ. of Granada; *office address:* Ms María Izquierdo Rojo, European Parliament, Centre Européen, Plateau de Kirchberg, BP 2929, Luxembourg.

J

JAARSMA-BUIJSERD, Drs. Ria (Maria) F.; Dutch, Member of the First Chamber; *born:* 19 June 1942, Amsterdam, Netherlands; *married:* Piet Jaarsma, 1966; *languages:* English, German; *education:* higher professional school, 1959; dutch teaching certificate, 1962; diplomas in editing, bookstore keeping, 1963; Graphic School, 1964; continued professional training editing, 1969; continued graphic training, 1970; marketing and management trainings, 1971; pedagogic teaching certificate, 1979; University of Amsterdam, drs. educational research andrology, 1986; *party:* Partij van de Arbeid (PvdA, Labour Party), 1967; *political career:* Pres. PvdA group, town council, 1974-75; Mem. Provincial States North- Holland, 1975-87; Mem. First Chamber 1987-; *interests:* educational policy, women's emancipation, social policy, Labour market policy; *memberships:* Pres., Board Regional Public Labour Provision Organisation, 1991-; *professional career:* pres., Stichting Uitgeverij NVSH, 1964-67; pres., Moussault's Uitgeverij Ltd., 1967-71; owner of independent and private business; editing, research, advice etc., 1971-; Executive Council Club for Research in Education; club centre for educational research of UvA; helping committee national pillar for creative work with Women; Pres., board General Higher School Amsterdam; club board magazine Education for Adults; *publications:* Equal Opportunities?, 1979; Education and the equality of opportunity for girls and women, 1982; A long way, 1985; Recurrent Education in Western Europe, 1986; EG-projekt; Teacher supply, with particular reference to shortage and surpluses and strategies for overcoming discrepancies, 1989-90; Severed Connections? On Poverty and Pauperization in the Netherlands, 1990; *private address:* Vreelandseweg 56, 1394 BN Nederhorst den Berg, the Netherlands; *office address:* Drs. Ria Jaarsma, Eerste Kamer der Staten-Generaal, Binnenhof 22, Postbus 20017, The Hague, Netherlands.

JÄÄTTEENMÄKI, Anneli Tuulikki; Finnish, Member of the Eduskunta; *born:* 11 February 1955, Lapua, Finland; *parents:* Oiva Jaakoppi Jäätteenmäki and Anna Irja Jäätteenmäki (née Latvala); *religion:* Lutheran; *languages:* English, Swedish; *education:* Helsinki Univ., Master of Laws, 1974-80; *party:* Suomen Keskusta (Finnish Centre Party); *political career:* Political Sec., Council of State Secretariate, 1984; Legislation Sec., KP Parly. Group, 1986; MP, 1987-; Central Cncl. and Admin. Board, Pohjola-Norden; Central Cncl., District Planning Assn., Vaasa Province; mem., Int. Advisory Cttee. on Human Rights; Chmn., Advisory Cttee. on Correctional Treatment of Prisoners; Chmn., Advisory Cttee., Equal Rights; men., Admin. Board, Veikkaus Oy.; mem., Admin. Board, Democratic Lawyers; mem., Advisory Cttee., Assn. of Local Broadcasting; Admin. Board, Assn. of Human Rights and Civil Liberties; *professional career:* Political Sec. Dept. of Foreign Affairs, Municipal Labour Market Organisation, 1982; Municipal Legal Adviser, Lapua; *recreations:* sport; *office address:* Ms Anneli Jäätteenmäki, Eduskunta, 00102 Helsinki, Finland.

JACKSON, Dr. Caroline Frances; British, Member of the European Parliament; *born:* 5 November 1946; *parents:* G.H. Harvey and D.C. Harvey; *married:* Robert Victor Jackson, 1975; *public role of spouse:* MP and Parliamentary Under-Secretary of State for Employment; *children:* one s. (decd.); *religion:* Church of England; *languages:* French, German, Italian; *education:* School of St. Clare, Penzance, St Hugh's and Nuffield Colleges, Oxford, MA, D Phil; Elizabeth Wordsworth Research Fellow, St Hugh's College, Oxford, 1972; *party:* Conservative Party; European Democratic Group (ED); *political career:* Head, London Office, European Democratic Group, 1979-84; MEP for Wiltshire, 1984-; *professional career:* member, National Consumer Council, 1982-84; Dir., Peugeot Talbot UK Ltd., 1987-; *publications:* A Student's Guide to Europe, 1988; Europe's Environment - A Conservative Approach, 1989; *recreations:* walking, painting, tennis, golf; *office address:* Dr. Caroline Jackson, 74 Carlisle Mansions, Carlisle Place, London SW1P 1HZ, UK.

JACOBSON, Judith Helen; American, Montana State Senator; *born:* 26 February 1939, South Bend, Indiana, USA; *parents:* Robert Marcene Haxton and Leah Haxton (née Alexander); *married:* John Raymond Jacobson, 1963; *children:* JoDee, Eric, Wendy; *religion:* Lutheran; *education:* Univ. of Wisconsin, 1957-60; *party:* Democratic Party; *political career:* delegate, National Conference of State Legislators; Montana State Senator, District 36, 1981; Mem., State Human Resources Cttee.; Chwn., Public Health, Welfare and Safety, Cttee. on Cttees. and Audit State Cttees.; former Vice-Chwn., Finance and Claims Cttee.; State Senate Democratic Whip, 1987; Mem., Montana State Senate;

memberships: Easter Seal Society; Montana Medical Auxillary; *office address:* Mrs Judith Jacobson, 330 Blacktail Canyon Road, Butte, Montana 59701, USA.

JACQ, Marie; French, Deputy; *born:* 28 July 1919, Henvic, Finistère, France; *parents:* Adrien Kerrien and Jeanne Kerrien (née Herrec); *married:* Marcel Jacq, 1938; *children:* Monique, Yvan; *education:* Gobelins School; Ecole primarie supérieure Faure, Le Havre; certificate of higher education; *party:* Parti Socialiste (PS, Socialist Party); *political career:* Mayor of Henvic, since 1965; Deputy, PS, Finistère (4th constituency: Morlaix), since 1978; member of commission for control of Fonds d'orientation et de régularisation des marchés agricoles (Forma, Fund for the guidance and regularisation of agricultural markets), since 1978; member of the office of the socialist group; Vice-President of National Assembly, 1981-82; member of commission for cultural, family and social affairs; member of parliamentary delegation for demographic problems; *professional career:* secretary in a building firm; *honours and awards:* Chevalier des Palmes académiques (decoration for services to education in France); *office address:* Mme. Marie Jacq, L'Assemblée Nationale, 126 rue de L'Université, 75355 Paris, France.

JACQUAINT, Huguette Germaine; French, Deputy; *born:* 12 October 1942, Aubervilliers, Seine-Saint-Denis, France; *parents:* Eugène Guénard and Pauline Guénard (née Zilligen); *married:* Claude Jacquaint, 1960; *party:* Parti Communiste Français (PCF, French Communist Party); *political career:* Town Councillor, La Courneuve, since 1977; Deputy Mayor of La Courneuve, since 1977; replaced Jack Ralite as Deputy, PCF, Seine-Saint-Denis (3rd constituency: La Courneuve), 1981; elected Deputy, PCF, Seine-Saint-Denis, 1986, re-elected 1988; *professional career:* unskilled worker; *office address:* Mme. Huguette Jacquaint, L'Assemblée Nationale, 126 rue de L'Université, 75355 Paris, France.

JAGGI, Yvette; Swiss, Member of the Ständerat; *born:* 11 February 1941, Lausanne, Switzerland; *education:* BA Humanities; Univ. of Lausanne, Ph.D Political Science; *party:* Parti Socialiste Suisse (Socialist Party of Switzerland); *political career:* borough Cllr., for Lausanne, 1981-86; city Cllr., Financial Dir., 1986-; Mem. of the Nationalrat, 1979-87; Mem. of the Ständerat for Lausanne, Canton of Vaud, 1987-; *professional career:* economist; lecturer, Univ. of Lausanne; *office address:* Mme. Yvette Jaggi, Ständerat/Conseil d'Etat, Secretariat-General, Parlamentsgebäude, 3003 Berne, Switzerland; *phone:* Berne 619711.

JAKAB, Róbertné; Hungarian, Member of the Országgyülés; *party:* Hungarian Socialist Party (MSZP); *office address:* Ms Róbertné Jakab, Országgyülés, Kossuth L. tér 1-3, Budapest V, Hungary; *phone:* 22 5058; 22 5059.

JAKOBSEN, Carolyn Anne; Australian, Member of the House of Representatives; *born:* 11 September 1947, Auckland, New Zealand; *party:* Australian Labor Party; *political career:* Mem., Labor Party Administrative Cttee. (WA), 1983-; former Electorate Council Pres., Branch Pres., and Branch Sec.; Delegate, Labor Party State Conference (WA); elected for Cowan, Western Australia, 1984-; Committee Service: Mem. of the House of Representatives Standing Cttee. for Libraries, 1985-; for Employment, Education and Training, 1987-; Mem. of the Joint Select Cttee. for Electoral Reform, 1985-87; for Video Material, 1985-; Mem. of the Joint Standing Cttee. for Electoral Matters, 1987-; *professional career:* electorate sec.; ministerial officer; *office address:* Ms Carolyn Jakobsen, House of Representatives, Parliament House, Room M80, Canberra ACT, 2600, Australia; *phone:* (062) 726383.

JANU, Dr. Ivana; Czechoslovakian, Member of the Narodni Rada (Czech National Council); *born:* 13 March 1946; *party:* KDU (Christian Democratic Union); *office address:* Dr. Janu Ivana, Ceská národní rada, Snemovní 4, 110 00 Praha 1, Czechoslovakia; *phone:* (02) 2105.

JAROSOVA, Marie; Czechoslovakian, Member of the Central Committee of the Communist Party of Czechoslovakia; *born:* 13 February 1920, Lidice, Czechoslovakia; *education:* elementary and intermediate school; *party:* Komunistická Strana Ceskoslovenska (KSC, Communist party of Czechoslovakia); *political career:* arrested, Lidice, 1942, interned in Ravensbruck concentration camp, 1942-45; Mem., CP SSR, 1945-; Mem. of Staff, Lidice Village Nat. Cttee., 1945-60, Chairperson, 1960-; Mem., Czechoslovak Cttee. of Defenders of Peace (CSVOM), 1962-68; candidate Mem., Exec. Cncl. of World Federation of Sponsor Cities, 1962-; Mem., Central Auditing Commission of Czechoslovak Union of Youth (CSM), 1963-68; Chairperson, Central Cttee., Czech Union of Women, 1969-; candidate Mem., World Union of Democratic Women, 1970-; Mem., Czech Nat. Cncl., 1969-71; Mem., Chamber of Nations of Federal Assembly CSSR, 1971; Mem., Central Elections Commission of National Front CSSR, 1971; Dep., Czech Nat. Cncl., 1971-; Mem., Presidium, Czech Nat. Cncl., 1971-; Dep. Chairperson, 1973-; Mem., Central Cttee., Czechoslovak Union of Fighters Against Fascism (CSSPB), 1973-; Mem., Presidium, Central Cttee., Nat. Front CSR, 1974-; Chairperson, Nat. Minorities Cttee. of Czech Nat. Cncl., 1977-; Dep. Chairperson, Czechoslovak Soc. for Int. Relations and Czechoslovak Foreign Institute, 1977; candidate Mem., CP CSSR Central Cttee., 1981-, full Mem., 1986-;

honours and awards: Czechoslovak Peace Prize, 1967; Lidice 1942 Medal, 1967; For Services in Reconstruction, 1970; *office address:* Ms Marie Jarosova, Communist Party of Czechoslovakia, Nábr. Ludríka Svobody 12, 125, 11, Prague 1, Czechoslovakia.

JAROSU URSZULA, Wanda; Polish, Member of the Sejm; *office address:* Ms Wanda Jarosu Urszula, Sejm PRl, ul. Wiejska 4/6/8, 00-489 Warsaw, Poland; *phone:* (22) 28 70 01; 28 40 31.

JAYALALITHO JAYARAM; Indian, Member of the Rajya Sabha; *born:* 24 February 1948, Mysore City; *parents:* the late R. Jayaram; *languages:* English, Tamil, Kannada, Telugu, Hindi, Malayalam; *education:* Stella Maris College, Madras; *party:* All India Anna Dravida Munnetia Kazhagam (AIADMK); *political career:* Propaganda Sec., AIADMK, 1983; Mem. of the Rajya Sabha, 1984; Deputy Leader, AIADMK Group in the Rajya Sabha; *professional career:* former film actress and singer; *honours and awards:* awarded Kalaimamani title, 1971-72; *publications:* Manathai Thotta Malargal; Ennangal; Uravin Kaithigal; Ovuthike Sontham; Nenjile Oru Kanal; Nee Insi Naan Illai; *clubs:* Patron and mem., Tamil Nadu Cricket Association; *recreations:* horse riding, chess, swimming, throwball, basketball, cricket, reading, music; *private address:* Vedo Nilayam, 36, Poes Garden, Madras - 600086; *office address:* Shrimati Jayalalitho Jayaram, Rajya Sabha, Parliament House, New Dehli 110 011, India; *phone:* (11) 389977; 389997.

JEANPRETRE, Francine; Swiss, Member of the Nationalrat; *born:* 6 July 1946, Neuchâtel, Switzerland; *children:* two; *education:* secondary education, La Chaux-de-Fonds gymnasium; Univs. of Neuchâtel, Lausanne, LLB; *party:* Parti Socialiste Suisse (Sozialdemokratische Partei der Schweiz, Social Democratic Party of Switzerland); *political career:* district Cllr. for Morges, 1980-81; city Cllr., (urbanism and construction policy) Morges, 1982-; Mem. of the Nationalrat for Morges, Canton of Vaud, 1987-; *office address:* Mme. Francine Jeanprêtre, Nationalrat/Conseil National, Secretariat-General, Parlamentsgebäude, 3003 Berne, Switzerland; *phone:* Berne 619711.

JEGER, Baroness (cr. 1979, Life Peer) Lena May Jeger; British, Member of the House of Lords; *born:* 19 November 1915; *parents:* Charles Chivers; *married:* the late Dr. Santo Jeger; *education:* Southgate County School; Birkbeck College, BA; *party:* Labour Party; *political career:* mem., London County Council, 1951-54; Member of Parliament, 1953-59, 1964-79; mem., Lab. Nat. Exec. Cncl., 1960-61, 1968-80; UK representative, UN Status of Women Commission, 1967; Chmn., Working Party on Sewage Disposal;

mem., Consultative Assembly of Council of Europe and WEU, 1969-71; Chmn., Labour Party, 1979-80; House of Lords, 1979-; Opposition Spokesman on Health, 1983-86, Social Security, 1983-; *professional career:* fmr. Min. of Information and Foreign Office; Asst. Editor, British Ally, Moscow, USSR; staff writer, Guardian, 1959-64; *private address:* 9 Cumberland Terrace, Regents Park, London, NW1, UK; *office address:* Baroness Jeger, House of Lords, London SW1A 0PW.

JENKINS, Jean Alice; Australian, Senator; *born:* 16 March 1938, Bristol, United Kingdom; *education:* Reading Univ., UK; BA (Hons.); *party:* Australian Democrats; *political career:* Australian Democrats State Spokesperson (WA) on Education, 1981-83 and on Ethnic Affairs, 1983-86; Convenor, Australian Democrats Stirling Branch, 1983-85; Australian Democrats State Ombudsman (WA), 1986-87; elected to Senate for Western Australia, 1987-; Committee Service: Mem. of the Senate Legislative and General Purpose Standing Cttee. for Community Affairs, 1987-; Mem. of the Joint Select Cttee. for Video Material, 1987-; Spokesperson for Australian Democrats on Immigration, Local Govt., Ethnic Affairs, Arts, Sport, Tourism and Territories, 1987-; *professional career:* language teacher, Italy and England; language examiner, Univ. of Cambridge, UK; technical and further education (TAFE) lecturer; senior lecturer in Modern Languages and Interpreting/Translating; Head, Dept. of English, Languages and Social Studies, Perth Technical College, Western Australia; *office address:* Ms Jean Jenkins, Senate, Parliament House, Room M13, Canberra, ACT 2600, Australia; *phone:* (062) 727111.

JENKINS MILLER, Janet; American, Republican National Committeewoman for Idaho; *born:* 9 August 1937, Salt Lake City, Utah, USA; *parents:* Preston Arent Jenkins and Donna Jenkins (née Vincent); *married:* Donald Burnes Miller, 1955; *children:* Donald Curtis, Brad Preston, Barbara Lynn, Scott Andrew; *religion:* Protestant; *education:* Univ. of Utah, BS, 1958; San Diego State Univ., California, 1962-63; Boise State Univ., Idaho, 1967-68 and 1982-82; *party:* Republican Party; *political career:* Pres. Ada County Republican Women's Club, Idaho, 1975-77; Chwn., Ada County Republican Central Cttee., 1977-81; Chwn., Govt. Affairs Cttee., Idaho Arthritis Foundation, 1980-83 and 1988-; Chwn., Legislative Affairs, St. Alphonsus Hospital Auxiliary, 1981-84; Republican National Committeewoman, Idaho, 1981-; Mem., Rules Cttee; *memberships:* Mem., Advisory Cttee. on Alternatives to Juvenile Justice, 4th District Juvenile Court, 1982-83; Idaho Certified Public Accountants Auxillary, Pres., 1975-56; Idaho Historians Auxillary; Idaho Arthritis Foundation; St. Alphonsus Hospital Auxillary; Human Resources Assn. of Treasure County; *professional career:* Co-owner and Ores., Employment Security Inc; *clubs:* Boise CofC; Los

Viajeres Motorcycle Club; *office address:* Mrs Janet Jenkins Miller, 5707 Randolph Drive, Boise, Idaho 83705, USA.

JENSEN, Kirsten Maria; Danish, Member of the European Parliament; *born:* 11 March 1961, Esbønderup; *education:* journalism, 1982-86; *party:* Socialdemokratiet (Social Democratic Party); *political career:* Vice-Chairman, Danish Social Democratic Youth (DSU), 1982-86; President, International Socialist Youth (IUSY), 1983-85; Chairman, International Centre for Danish Workers Movement (AIC), 1986-89; MEP, 1989-, Socialist Group; *interests:* environment, employment, Eastern Europe; *professional career:* journalist; *office address:* Ms Kirsten Jensen, European Parliament, Centre Européen, Plateau de Kirchberg, BP 2929, Luxembourg.

JERVOLINO RUSSO, Rosa; Italian, Minister Without Portfolio for Social Affairs; *born:* 17 September 1936, Naples, Italy; *education:* University of Rome, Degree in Jurisprudence (with max. honours); Teaching qualification, Economics and Law; *party:* Partito della Democrazia Cristiana (DC, Christian Democrat Party), 1954; *political career:* Nat. Vice-Pres., Centro Italiano Femminile (CIF, Italian Women's Centre), 1968-78; Nat. Councillor, mem. of Presidency, CIF; mem. Nat. Exec. Women's Movement, DC, 1968-78; Nat. Vice-Delegate, DC, 1978; Nat. Councillor, DC; mem. Regional Cttee., DC, and Exec. of Women's Movement, DC, Region of Lazio, 1963-; Nat. Leader of Family Office, DC, 1974; mem. Leadership of Women's Movement in European Popular Party; Administrative Councillor, RAI, 1975; Head of DC Group, RAI; elected to Senate, Rome, 1979-; mem. Committees on Justice, Hygiene and Health, Cttee. of Inquiry and Regional Affairs; mem. Leadership Cttee. of DC Parly. Group, then Pres., 1985-; mem. Cttee. on Hygiene and Health; mem. Parliamentary Supervisory Committee on Radio-TV Services; former Head of Sub-Cttee. on supervision of Radio-TV Services, 1985; Minister for Special Affairs, 1989-; *professional career:* laywer; employee, Study Office of National Council of Economics and Labour (CNEL), 1961-68; employee, Legislative Office, Ministry of Budget and Economic Planning; writer on several newspapers and magazines; mem. of editorial team of CIF Cronache ed. Opinioni (monthly); mem. editorial team, Donna e Società; Sec. Association, Maria Montessori for the religious education of children; *honours and awards:* thesis immediately published and received National Prize for the best thesis on women's position; *office address:* Ms Rosa Jervolino Russo, Office of the Minister for Social Affairs, Presidenza del Consiglio dei Ministri, Piazza Colonna, Rome, Italy.

JOANNY, Claire; French, Member of the European Parliament; *born:* 28 September 1951, Crozon, France; *education:* engineering, IDN, 1973; IUP, Créteil, urbanism 1978; *party:* Les Verts (Green Party); *political career:* city Cllr., Dunkerque, 1983-85; regional delegate, CNIR, with Marguerite-Marie Dinguirard, 1989-; Mem. of the European Parliament; *interests:* ecology, the environment; *memberships:* Friends of the Earth; Confédération écologiste (Ecologist Federation); *office address:* Mme. Claire Joanny, European Parliament, Centre Européen, Plateau de Kirchberg, BP 2929, Luxembourg; *phone:* Luxembourg 43001.

JOHNSON, Eddie Bernice; American, Texas State Senator; *born:* 3 December 1935, Waco, Texas, USA; *children:* Desmond Kirk; *religion:* Baptist; *education:* Texas Christian Univ., BS; Southern Methodist Univ., MPH; Bishop College, LLD; Jarvis Christian College, LLD; *party:* Democratic Party; *political career:* Texas State Rep., 1972-77; Delegate, Democrat Nat. Convention, 1976-84; Vice-Chwn., State Democratic Party, 1976-77; Texas State Senator, District 23, 1987-; *memberships:* Goals for Dallas; American Red Cross; Charter 100; NAACP; Women's Issues Network Board; *professional career:* Vice-Pres., business; *honours and awards:* Outstanding Community Service Award, NAACP, 1983; Outstanding Citizenship Award, Nat. Confederation of Christians and Jews, 1985; *office address:* Ms Eddie Johnson, 6305 Elder Grove Road, Dallas, Texas 75232, USA.

JOHNSON, Janis; Canadian, Senator; *born:* 1946, Winnipeg; *children:* Stefan; *religion:* Icelandic Lutheran Church; *education:* Univ. of Manitoba, BA Political Science; *party:* Progressive Conservatives; *political career:* Dir., Progressive Party of Canada, 1983, first woman to hold this position; Chairperson, Status of Women Cttee.; Chairperson, Public Relations Cttee.; *professional career:* lecturer, Faculty of Continuing Education, Univ. of Manitoba; Consultant, Winnipeg; Mem., Board of Dirs., Canadian Nat. Railways; former Mem., Board of Regents, Univ. of Winnipeg; Mem., Board of Dirs., Manitoba Special Olympics; Mem., Manitoba Coalition on Maternal and Child Health; Mem., Rockcliffe Park School Parent Support Cttee; *clubs:* River Heights Community Club; *office address:* The Honourable Senator Janis Johnson, Senate, Parliament Buildings, Wellington Street, Ottawa, Ontario K1A OA4, Canada; *phone:* (613) 992 4416.

JOHNSON, Jennifer Ursula; Trinidad and Tobago, Minister of Youth, Sport, Culture and the Creative Arts; *born:* 17 February 1946; *children:* three; *religion:* Pentecostal Assemblies of the West Indies; *education:* Dip., Management Studies, UWI; Certificate in Personnel Management and Industrial Relations, UWI; *party:* ACDC/DLP; *political career:* Parly. Rep. for Princes Town; Mem., ACDC/DCL amd Mem., Strategy

Cttee., Democratic Action Congress (party headed by Trinidad and Tobago's Prime Minister, ANR Robinson); candidate, 1976 election for San Fernando East Constituency, 1971-76; Platform Speaker, candidates contesting Borough Cncl. election for the Alliance/ONR Accomodation, 1983; *interests:* youth development; *recreations:* keep fit, reading; *office address:* The Honourable Mrs Jennifer Johnson, Ministry of Youth, Sports, Culture and the Creative Arts, 69 Eastern main Road, Laventille, Trinidad and Tobago.

JOHNSON, Nancy L.; American, Member of the House of Representatives; *born:* 5 January 1935, Chicago, Illinois, USA; *parents:* the late Noble W. Lee and Gertrude Lee (née Smith); *married:* Theodore Johnson, 1958; *children:* Lindsey, Althea, Caroline; *religion:* Unitarian; *education:* grad., Univ. of Chicago, Radcliffe College, 1957; Univ. of London, UK; *party:* Republican Party; *political career:* Connecticut State Rep., 1976-82; Ranking Minority mem., Appropriations, Finance, Education, State Planning and Development, Govt. Admin. and Policy, Human Rights and opportunities Cttees.; Mem., House of Reps. for Connecticut State District 6, 1983-; Mem., Veterans Affairs Cttee.; Mem., Select Cttee. on Children, Youth and Families; former Mem., Cttee. on Ways and Means and House of Reps. Research Cttee.; Mem., Republican 98th Congressional Class, 92 Group; Mem., Northeast-Northwest Congressional Coalition, Mem., Caucus for Women's Issues Cttee.; Mem., Human Rights Caucus; Co-Chair, Conservative Task Force; *memberships:* Vistors Board, US Coast Guard Academy; *honours and awards:* United Way Outstanding Volunteer, 1976; *publications:* Co-editor, National Industrial Planning; Solution on Illusion; *private address:* 141 South mountain Drive, New Britain, Connecticut 06052, USA; *office address:* Mrs Nancy Johnson, 119 Cannon House Office Bldg., Washington DC, 20515-0706, USA.

JOHNSON, Hon. Urmia; Guyanan, Minister of Regional Planning; *party:* People's National Congress (PNC); *office address:* The Hon. Ms Urmia Johnson, Ministry of Regional Planning, One Water and Cornhill Streets, Stabroek, Georgetown, Guyana; *phone:* 56590.

JOHNSTON, Rita; Canadian, Premier of British Columbia; *office address:* Ms Rita Johnston, Legislative Buildings, Victoria, BC V8V 1X4, Canada.

JONES, Delna; American, Oregon State Representative; *born:* 4 September 1940, Phoenix, Arizona, USA; *parents:* Robert Stiefel and Clara Steifel (née Hayes); *married:* Robert Jones, 1962; *children:* Lorraine Thomson; *education:* Phoenix College, Arizona; Cerritos College, California; *party:* Republican Party; *political career:* Oregon State Rep., District 6;

Mem., Education Cttee., 1983-; *professional career:* Dir., Econ. Development, Pac Northwest Bell, 1985-; *office address:* Mrs Delna Jones, 1625 SW Pheasant Drive, Aloha, Oregon 97006, USA.

JONES, Myra Lee; American, Arkansas State Representative; *born:* 8 March 1936, Belle Fourche, South Dakota; *parents:* Ernest William Gutshe and Edith Gutshe (née Payne); *children:* Melissa Christine, Michael Patrick; *religion:* Catholic; *education:* Oberline College, Ohio, BME; Drake Univ., Des Moines, Iowa, MME, 1963; *party:* Democratic Party; *political career:* City Dir., Little Rock, Arkansas, 1977-84; Vice-Mayor, Little Rock, 1981-84; Arkansas State Representative, District 60, 1985-; *memberships:* Business and Professional Women Organisation; American Assn. of Univ. Women; League of Women Voters; *professional career:* Teacher, Des Moines Public School, 1957-63; Buckbee Public School, Rockford, Illinois, 1095-66; Gen.-Mgr., Dairy Queen Restaurants, Little Rock and Jacksonville, Arkansas, 1970-73; owner, The Hunter, 1974-89; Mem., Board of Dirs., Arkla Inc., 1981-89; *clubs:* Greater Little Rock CofC; *office address:* Ms Myra Jones, P.O. Box 518, Monticello, Arkansas 71655, USA.

JORRITSMA-LEBBINK, Annemarie; Dutch, Member of the Second Chamber; *born:* 1 June 1950, Hengelo, Gelderland, Netherlands; *parents:* Berend-Jan Lebbink and Maria Wilhelmina Lebbink (née Tulp); *married:* Gerlof Jorritsma, 1971; *children:* Maayke, Minke; *religion:* baptist; *languages:* French, German, English, Spanish; *education:* Baudartius College, Zutphen, 1962-67; Tourism Training College, Breda, 1967-68; Unfinished part-time course to obtain teaching diploma in French, 1975-78; *party:* Volkspartij voor Vrijheid en Democratie (VVD, People's Party for Freedom and Democracy), 1973; *political career:* Mem. of town council, Bolsward, 1978-89; Mem. of Second Chamber, 1982-; member of committees on Traffic and Water, Education, Emancipation, Housing and Spatial Order; Mem., Cttee. for controlling building; Mem., special Cttee. Waddenzee; Deputy Mem., Cttee. on Social Affairs and Cttee. on Agriculture; *interests:* traffic and transport policies; *professional career:* organisational function in travel agency, Wolvega, 1969-71; secretary to Export Manager, Bk-Beccon-Edy, Dieren, 1971-74; *office address:* Mevr. Annemarie Jorritsma-Lebbink, Tweede Kamer der Staaten-Generaal, Binnenhof 1A, Postbus 20018, The Hague, Netherlands.

JOSHI, Sudha Vijay; Indian, Member of the Rajya Sabha; *born:* 10 June 1940, Bombay; *parents:* Vishwanath Rangrao Chitnis; *married:* Vijay Chintaman Joshi, 1964; *children:* one s., one d; *education:* Univ. of Bombay, BA; *party:* Congress Party; *political career:* Convener, Bombay Pradesh Mahila Congress, 1978-; Gen. Sec., Lokmanya Seva Sangh Vile

Parle, 1981-83; Sec., All India Mahila Congress, 1984-; Mem. of the Rajya Sabha, 1984-; Party Observer for Assembly and Parly. elections in Punjab, 1985, in Haryana and Nagaland, 1987 and in Meghalaya, 1988; Convener, Bombay North West District of Mahila Congress; Dir., National Federation of Labour Co-operatives and Chairperson of its Women's Wing; Special Invitee, Executive Cttee. of Congress Party in Parliament; *professional career:* Dir., Maharashtra Tourism Development Corporation, 1982-85; *recreations:* reading; *private address:* 1/5, Shivanand Play Ground Cross Road, Vile Parle (E), Bombay - 400057; *office address:* Shrimati Sudha Joshi, Rajya Sabha, Parliament House, New Dehli 110 011, India; *phone:* (11) 389977; 389997.

JOUPPILA, Dr. Riitta Marie Kaarina; Finnish, Member of the Eduskunta; *born:* 30 May 1940, Kuopio, Finland; *parents:* Iivari Rudolf Liukko and Maire Matilda Liukko (née Oinonen); *married:* Pentti Iisakki Jouppila, 1964; *children:* Kaisa, Ulla, Hanna; *education:* Oulu Univ., Lic. Med., 1966; MD & Surgery, 1977; *party:* Kansallinen Kokoomus (Kok, National Coalition Party); *political career:* Mem., Oulu Parish Cncl., 1979; mem., Oulu Town Cncl., 1980; mem. of Eduskunta, 1983-; Chmn., Kokoomus Women, North-Pohjanmaa District, (1984; Representative North-Pohjanmaa District Planning Assn., 1985; Vice-Chmn., Kokoomus Women's Assn., 1986; *professional career:* Asst. Doctor, Oulu Univ. Central Hospital, 1966-67; Asst. Dr, Anasthetics Dept., 1968-72; Specialist, 1973-83; Health Officer, Kuusamo Municipality, 1968; Lecturer in Anaesthesiology, Oulu Univ., 1978; *publications:* The effect of Segmental Epidural Analgesia on Metabolic and Hormonal Changes during Labour (Doctoral Thesis), 1977; numerous articles in scientific publications; *recreations:* literature, theatre; *office address:* Dr. Riitta Jouppila, Eduskunta, 00102 Helsinki, Finland.

JUAN MILLET, Maria Celeste Lidia; Spanish, Deputy; *born:* 16 June 1953, Valencia, Spain; *education:* degree in economic science; *party:* Partido Socialista Obrero Español (PSOE, Spanish Socialist Workers' Party), 1974; *political career:* Women's participation delegate on PSPV-PSOE Exec. Cttee., Valencia autonomous government; Deputy, PSOE, Valencia, 1986-89, re-elected 1989-; mem. Cttee. on Economy, Commerce and Finance, Cortes; *office address:* Ms María Juan Millett, Congreso de los Diputados, Fernán Flor 1, Madrid 14, Spain.

JUCA, Tereza (Maria Tereza Surita); Brazilian, Federal Deputy; *born:* 14 August 1956, Sao Manoel; *parents:* Antonio Saenz Surita and Aurélia Saenz Surita; *married:* Romero Jucá Filho; *children:* Luciana, Ana Paula, Rodrigo, Mariana; *education:* Faculty of Tourism of Morumbi, Sao Paulo, tourism, 1975-79; *party:* Partido Democrático Social (PDS, Social Democrat Party); *political career:* Federal Deputy for Roraima, 1991-95; *professional career:* public functionary; *office address:* Ms Tereza Jucá, Chamber of Deputies, Praça dos 3 Poderes, Ed. Principal, 70160 Brasilia, DF, Brazil; *phone:* (61) 225 2885.

JUNKER, Karin; German, Member of the European Parliament; *born:* 24 December 1940; *party:* Sozialdemokratische Partei Deutschlands (SPD, Social Democratic Party); *political career:* Vice-Chairperson, Social Democratic Women's Trade Union; MEP, 1989-; *office address:* Ms Karin Junker, European Parliament, Centre Européen, Plateau de Kirchberg, BP 2929, Luxembourg; *phone:* Luxembourg 43001.

JURKOVIC, Danica; Yugoslavian, Deputy to National Assembly; *born:* 1925, Ljubljana, Yugoslavia; *education:* studies economics; *party:* League of Communists of Yugoslavia (LCY), 1945-; *political career:* elected to Central Cttee., 10th Congress of LCY, 1974; Dep., Yugoslav Nat. Assembly; Dep. Dir., Institute for Productivity of Labour of Socialist Republic Slovenia; *office address:* Ms Danica Jurkoviæc, Savezna Skupstina, Yugoslavia.

K

KABRHELOVA, Marie; Czechoslovakian, Member of the Presidium of the Czech Federal Assembly; *born:* 4 May 1925, Opatov, Jihlava district, Czechoslovakia; *education:* Higher Party School, Central Cttee. CP CSSR, Prague, 1963-69; *party:* Komunistická Strana Ceskoslovenska (KSC, Communist party of Czechoslovakia); *political career:* Mem., Jihlava Regional Cttee., CP CSSR, Jihlava Regional Cttee. of Women's Cncl., Mem., CSSR-USSR Friendship Union, 1946-48; Mem., Jihlava Regional Trade Union Cncl., 1947-48; Dep. Chairperson, Regional Action Cttee., Nat. Front, Jihlava, 1948; Mem. of Staff, Prague Regional Trade Union Cncl., 1949-50; Mem., Central Cncl., CSSR Trade Unions, (URO), 1949-52, Mem., Presidium, 1950-52; Mem. and Sec., Cultural Commission of Central Nat. Cttee., Prague, 1953-56; Mem., Central Cttee., CP CSSR, 1962-63; Dep. Chairperson and Mem. of the Presidium, Central Cttee. of Trade Union of Workers in Consumer Goods Industry, 1966-68; Chairperson, Federal Cttee., Trade Union of Workers in Textile, Clothing and Leather Industry, 1969-; Dep. Minister of Labour and Social Welfare, CSR, 1969-71; Mem., Presidium Central Cttee., Czech Union of Women, Mem., CSSR Cncl. of Women, 1969-74; Mem., Presidium, Sec., Central Cncl. of CSSR Revolutionary Trade Union Movement, (ROH), 1971-72; Mem., Central Control and Auditing Commission, CP CSSR, 1971-76; Mem., Central Cttee., Mem., Secretariat, CP CSSR, 1976-; Sec. and Chairperson, Women's Commission, Central Cncl. of Trade Unions (URO), 1972-74; Chairperson, CSSR Union of Women, 1974-; Mem., Cncl. and Mem., Bureau of Int. Democratic Women's Union and Mem., World Peace Cncl., 1974; Mem., Presidium, Central Cttee., Nat. Front, 1974-; Dep., Chamber of Nations, CSSR Federal Assembly, 1976-; *professional career:* apprentice dressmaker; *honours and awards:* Order of Labour, 1973; Order of Victorious February, 1975; Eugéne Cottonové Medal, 1983; Order of the Republic, 1985; Order of the Brotherhood (USSR), 1985; *office address:* Ms Marie Kabrhelova, Federální Shromázdení, Vinohradská 1, 110 02 Prague 1, Czechoslovaia; *phone:* (02) 2103.

KAFAROVA, Elmira Mikail kyzy; Soviet, Member of the Council of Nationalities; *born:* 1934, Azerbaijn, USSR; *education:* higher education in philosophy; *party:* Communist Party of The Soviet Union; *political career:* Chwn., Presidium, Azerbaijan SSR Supreme Soviet, Baku; Mem., Cncl. of Nationalities; formerly: Komsomol First Sec.; Minister of Education; Minister of Foreign Affairs and Dep.-Chwn., Azerbaijan SSR Cncl. of Ministers; currently: Dep.-Chwn., USSR Supreme Soviet Presidium; Mem., Supreme Soviet Cttee. on International Affairs; *office address:* Ms Elmira Mikail kyzy Kafarova, Council of Nationalities, Kremlin, Moscow, USSR.

KAILASHPATI; Indian, Member of the Rajya Sabha; *born:* 19 December 1913, Lucknow; *parents:* the late Chhanni Das Chaudhary; *married:* the late Ram Dulare, 1955; *education:* Lucknow; *party:* Congress Party; *political career:* Convenor, District Women Congress, 1971; Convenor, Young Women Congress, Uttar Pradesh, 1972-74; Convenor, Women Youth Congress, Uttar Pradesh, 1973-76; Mem., Uttar Pradesh Legislative Assembly, 1974-77; Mem., Lok Sabha, 1980-84; Mem., Uttar Pradesh Congress Party Working Cttee., 1982-84; Sec., Uttar Pradesh Congress Party Cttee., 1985-88; elected to the Rajya Sabha, 1985, re-elected, 1988; Gen. Sec., All India Mahila Congress; Joint Sec., All India Mahila Congress; Joint Sec., All India Congress Cttee.; *interests:* agriculture, welfare of women, Harijans and the poor; *recreations:* social service; *private address:* Raniganj, Kailash Bhawan, Subhash Marg, Lucknow, Uttar Pradesh; *office address:* Shrimati Kailashpati, Rajya Sabha, Parliament House, New Dehli 110 011, India; *phone:* (11) 389977; 389997.

KAINZ, Hedda; Austrian, Member of the Bundesrat; *born:* 17 June 1942, Linz, Austria; *education:* vocational school; *party:* Sozialistische Partei Österreichs (SPÖ, Socialist Party of Austria); *political career:* various functions in Union of Private Sector Employees, 1970; mem. of General Assembly of Chamber of Workers and Employees for Upper Austria, 1974; mem. of the Exec., Chamber of Workers and Employees for Upper Austria, 1979-; Chairperson of provincial Women's Cttee., Austrian Federation of Trade Unions, Upper Austria, and mem. of Praesidium of provincial Exec., 1987; sent to Bundesrat from Upper Austrian Provincial Assembly, Mem. of Bundesrat, 1988-; *professional career:* apprentice chemical lab technician, nitrogen factory, 1957; lab technician in pharmaceutical field, 1961-; mem. of works' council, Linz Chemicals Joint Stock Company, 1968; employee, CL Pharma Joint Stock Company, 1988-; Chairperson of works' council,

CL Pharma Joint Stock Company, 1988-; *office address:* Frau Hedda Kainz, Bundesrat, Dr. Karl Renner Ring 3, 1017 Vienna, Austria.

KALAYCIOGLU, Göksel; Turkish, Member of the National Assembly; *office address:* Ms Göksel Kalaycioglu, National Assembly, TBNN, Ankara, Turkey.

KALDI, Meropi; Greek, Member of Parliament; *party:* Nea Demokratia (ND, New Democracy Party), 1989; *political career:* MP, ND, Preveza, 1989; *professional career:* architect; *office address:* Vouli, Parliament Building, Syntagma, Greece.

KALIK, Barbara Faith; American, Member of the New Jersey State Assembly; *born:* 8 November 1936, Bronx, New York, USA; *parents:* Albert Benowitz and Lydia Benowitz (née Cohen); *children:* Darcie Lynn, Andrew Jay, Lance Jon; *religion:* Jewish; *education:* City College of New York, 1953-55; *party:* Democratic Party; *political career:* Mayor, Willingboro, 1974 and 1977; Mem., National Democrat Policy Cncl.; Chwn., Assembly Revenue, Finance and Appropriations Cttee., 1984-85; Co-Chwn., Joint Appropriations Cttee; Chwn., State Govt. Cttee., Election Civil Service Cttee. and Pensions Cttee.; Mem., Economic and Industrial Strategy Cttees.; Currently, Assc. Assembly Leader and Chwn., Task Force on Equitable Management of Revenues and Expenditures; Mem., New Jersey State Assembly, District 7, 1978-; *memberships:* Willingboro Planning and Welfare Board; Mem., Historical Commission; Steering Cttee. of NJ State Bi-partisan Coalition for Women's Appointments; former Pres., Burlington County Chamber of Commerce; Advisory Cttee. of the Special Service School District of Burlington County; Mem., Board of Dirs., Burlington County College; Hon. Chwn., Burlington County March of Dimes Birth Defect Foundation; *professional career:* Pres., Jolie Travel Centre, 1973-; *honours and awards:* Woman of the Year, Willingboro Women's Club; Outstanding Woman of the Year, New Jersey Business and Professional Women; Honoured for Contributions to preserve, enhance and protect The New Jersey Pinelands, Sponsors of NJ Celebrates the Pinelands, Feb. 1991; Public Affairs Award, Planned Parenthood, Apr. 1991; Woman of Achievement in the Legislative Branch of State Govt., Women's Political Caucus of New Jersey, May 1991; *clubs:* Beth Torah Sisterhood; Burlington County CofC; Mt. Larel Ballet Co; *office address:* Ms Barbara Kalik, 13 Radford Place, Willingboro, New Jersey 08046, USA.

KALOUSOVA, Eva; Czechoslovakian, Member of the Narodni Rada (Czech National Council); *born:* 20 September 1941; *party:* Civic Forum; *office address:* Ms Eva Kalousová, Ceská národní rada, Snemovní 4, 110 00 Praha 1, Czechoslovakia; *phone:* (02) 2105.

KAMP, Drs. Margreet; Dutch, Member of the Second Chamber; *born:* 22 June 1942, Borne; *languages:* Dutch, English, French, German; *education:* Higher Professional School, State diploma A; Social Academy; social sciences, doctorandus; *party:* Volkspartij voor Vrijheid en Democratie (VVD, People's Party for Freedom and Democracy); *political career:* VVD committees : Pres. national overall Cttee. for Health and Welfare, Cttee. for social development; Mem. of Second Chamber, 1982-; Second Chamber committees : Welfare and Culture, Public Health, Social Affairs and Agriculture; *publications:* Cherchez La Femme, SMO, 1990; *recreations:* walking, tennis; *office address:* Drs. Margreet Kamp, Tweede Kamer der Staaten-Generaal, Binnenhof 1A, Postbus 20018, The Hague, Netherlands.

KANTURKOVA, Eva; Czechoslovakian, Member of the Narodni Rada (National Council); *born:* 11 May 1930; *party:* Civic Forum; *office address:* Ms Eva Kanturková, Ceská národní rada, Snemovní 4, 110 00 Praha 1, Czechoslovakia; *phone:* (02) 2105.

KAPTUR, Angela; American, Member of the House of Representatives; *born:* 17 June 1946, Toledo, Ohio, USA; *parents:* Stephen Jacob Kaptur and Anastasia Delores Kaptur (née Rogowski); *religion:* Roman Catholic; *education:* Univ. of Wisconsin, BA, 1964-68; Univ. of Michigan, MS, 1973-74; Massachusetts Inst. of Technology, 1982-; *party:* Democratic Party; *political career:* Mem., US House of Reps., 9th District, Ohio, 1983-; Mem., Banking, Finance, Urban Affairs and Budget Cttees., US House of Reps; *memberships:* American Planning Assn; *private address:* 1841 Dority Road, Toledo, Ohio 43615, USA; *office address:* Ms Angela Kaptur, 1228 Longworth House Office Bldg., Washington DC 20515, USA.

KARI, Hilda; Solomon Islander, Member of Parliament; *born:* 29 April 1949, Bouna Village, Guadalcanal Province; *parents:* the late Ishmael Avui and the late Elizabeth Votaia; *married:* Solomon Kari, 1973; *public role of spouse:* police officer; *children:* four; *religion:* Rhema Family Church; *languages:* Longu dialect, Pidgin English, English; *education:* secondary education in Sydney, New South Wales; *party:* People's Alliance Party; *political career:* Mem. of Parliament, 1990-; *interests:* conservation, steering development to a sustainable level; *professional career:* administration, public service; *clubs:* christian gatherings and activities; *private address:* Kolo'ale House; *office address:* Ms Hilda Kari, PO Box 845, Honiara, Solomon Islands.

KARITA, Teiko; Japanese, Member of the House of Councillors; *born:* 21 May 1932; *education:* Tokyo Gakugei Univ; *party:* Komeito (Clean Government Party); *political career:* second time elected for National; Dir., House of Cllrs. Cttee. on Audit and Dir.,

Komeito Women's Bureau, 1990-; *memberships:* Adviser, Japan Housewives Co-operative Assn; *office address:* Ms Teiko Karita, House of Councillors, 1-7-1 Nagata-cho, Tokyo 100, Japan; *phone:* (03) 5813111.

KARL, Elfriede; Austrian, Member of the Nationalrat; *born:* 14 September 1933, Salzburg, Austria; *party:* Sozialistische Partei Österreichs (SPÖ, Socialist Party of Austria); *political career:* Sec. of State, Federal Chancellery, 1971-79; mem. of Nationalrat, for Salzburg, 1974-83 and since 1984; Sec. of State, Ministry of Finance, 1979-83; Minister of Environment, Youth and Family, May 1983-September 1984; Sec. to Nationalrat; *professional career:* Commercial training, 1947-50, commercial diploma; saleswoman; shorthand typist, Salzburg Provincial leadership, Union of Construction Workers and Lumberjacks, 1953-60; attended Vienna Chamber of Workers and Employees Social Academy; employee, Dept. of Economics, Salzburg Chamber of Workers and Employees, since 1961, and Sec. to this Chamber, since 1968; *honours and awards:* Great Silver Award of the Riband for Services to Austria; Great Cross of the Italian Order of Service; *office address:* Frau Elfriede Karl, Nationalrat, Dr. Karl Renner Ring 3, 1017 Vienna, Austria.

KARLSSON, Irmtraut; Austrian, Member of the Bundesrat; *born:* 4 May 1944, Windschau, Czechoslovakia; *parents:* Gerhard Marsch and Theresia Marsch (née Schneider); *married:* Lars-Gösta Karlsson, 1982; *children:* Martin; *languages:* English; *education:* University of Vienna, Ph.D in psychology; Institute of Advanced Studies, Vienna, diploma in sociology; *party:* Sozialistische Partei Österreichs (SPÖ, Socialist Party of Austria), 1969; *political career:* Gen.-Sec., Socialist International Women (SIW), 1980-85; Sec. to the SPÖ Federal Women's Association, 1985-; mem. of the Bundesrat, 1987-; *publications:* Verwaltete Kinder, Jugend und Volk, 1976; 75 Years And Still Going Strong, 1982; Das Gebrochene Tabu, 1988; Studienzirkel, 1988; Johanna ist Fünfzig, 1989; *office address:* Frau Irmtraut Karlsson, Bundesrat, Dr. Karl Renner Ring 3, 1017 Vienna, Austria.

KARPAN, Kathleen Marie; American, Secretary of State, Wyoming; *born:* 1 September 1942, Rock Springs, Wyoming, USA; *parents:* Thomas Michael Karpan and Pauline Karpan (née Taucher); *religion:* Roman Catholic; *education:* Univ. of Wyoming, Laramie, BS, 1964, MA, 1975; Univ. of Oregon, Eugene, JD, 1978; *party:* Democratic Party; *political career:* Sec. of State, Wyoming, 1987-; *memberships:* Wyoming and Washington DC Bar Assns.; Nat. Assn. of Secs. of State; *office address:* Ms Kathleen Karpan, State Capitol, Cheyenne, Wyoming 82002, USA.

KARWATZKI, Irmgard; German, Member of the Bundestag; *born:* 15 December 1940, Duisburg, West Germany; *education:* business training, 1955-58; College of Social Work, 1963-66; State recognition, 1967; *party:* Christlich Demokratische Union (CDU, Christian Democratic Union), 1960; *political career:* mem. of council, Duisburg, 1975-; mem. of Bundestag, 1976-; Parliamentary Sec. of State, Federal Ministry of Youth, Family and Health Affairs, 1982-87; Minister of Education and Science, 1987-; mayor, Duisburg; *professional career:* business employee, 1958-63; diocese asst., Assn. of Catholic Youth, Essen, 1967-71; Asst., Catholic College of Higher Education, North Rhine-Westphalia, 1971-76; social worker; *private address:* 4100 Duisburg, Germany; *office address:* Frau Irmgard Karwatzki, Bundeshaus, 5300 Bonn 1, West Germany.

KASSEBAUM, Nancy; American, Member of the House of Representatives; *born:* 29 July 1932, Topeka, Kansas, USA; *parents:* Alfred Landon and Theo Landon; *children:* John, Linda, Richard, William; *religion:* Episcopal; *education:* Univ. Kansas, BA, 1954; Univ. of Michigan, MA, 1956; *party:* Republican Party; *political career:* Mem., Kansas Govt. Ethics Commission and Humanities Cttee.; US Senator, Kansas, 1978-, Mem., Budget, Science, Transport and Foreign Relations Cttees.; currently Chwn., Aviation and African Affairs Sub-Cttees., 1979-, Mem., Banking, Housing, and Urban Affairs, Foreign Relations, Labour and Human Resources Senate Cttees.; Mem., Special Senate Cttee. on Aging; Mem., National Republican Senate Cttee.; Mem., Exec. Cttee., Congress Caucus on Women's Issues; Mem., Military Reform and Senate Rural Health Caucus; *memberships:* Kansas Press Women's Assn.; Women's Assn. of Institutional Logopedics; *professional career:* Dir. and Vice-Pres., KFH Radio, Wichita, Kansas; *office address:* Ms Nancy Kassebaum, SR-302 Russell, Senate Office Bldg., Washington DC, 20510-1602, USA.

KASURINEN, Anna-Liisa; Finnish, Member of Parliament; *born:* 8 May 1940, Kivijärvi, Finland; *parents:* Otto Oksanen and Ida Johanna Oksanen (née Autio); *married:* Lauri Kasurinen, 1989; *children:* Petri, Anna-Mari, Mika-Petteri; *religion:* Evangelical-Lutheran; *languages:* Finnish; *education:* Tampere, Psychiatric Nurse, 1964; Registered Nurse, 1968; *party:* Suomen Sosialidemokraattinen Puolue, (SDP, Finnish Social Democratic Party); *political career:* Mem., Kotka Town Cncl., 1972; mem., Central Admin. Board, Assn. of Nursing, 1976-79; SDP Party Cncl., 1978; mem., Presidential Electorate, 1978, 1982, 1988; Mem. of Eduskunta, 1979-; 2nd Vice-Chmn., Kotka Town Cncl., 1981; Minister of Education, 1987-91; *professional career:* Psychiatric Nurse, Pitkäniemi Hospital, 1964-66; Registered Nurse, Kotka Central Hospital, 1969; *office address:* Ms Anna-Liisa Kasurinen, Eduskunta, 00102 Helsinki, Finland.

KASUYA, Terumi; Japanese, Member of the House of Councillors; *born:* 19 April 1924; *education:* Tokyo Women's Normal School; *party:* Japan Socialist Party (JSP); *office address:* Ms Terumi Kasuya, House of Councillors, 1-7-1 Nagata-cho, Tokyo 100, Japan; *phone:* (03) 5813111.

KATZ, Vera; American, Oregon State Representative; *born:* 3 August 1933, Dusseldorf, Germany; *parents:* Lazar Pistrak and Raissa Pistrak (née Goodman); *married:* Melvin Katz, 1954; *children:* Jesse; *education:* Brooklyn College, BA, 1954; *party:* Democratic Party; *political career:* Oregon State Rep., Ditrict 8, 1972-, District 10, 1983-; Speaker, 1985-91; *professional career:* Dir. of Development, Portland Community College; *honours and awards:* Outstanding Legislator Award, 1977; *office address:* Ms Vera Katz, 2068 Johnson NW, Portland, Oregon 97209, USA.

KAUL, Sheila; Indian, Member of the Lok Sabha; *born:* Lucknow, Uttar Pradesh; *parents:* Rajeswar Nath Kaul and Saraswati Kaul; *married:* Kalias Nath Kaul; *children:* two s., one d; *party:* Congress Party; *political career:* Minister of State for Education and Culture and Social Welfare, GOI, 1980-84; re-elected to Lok Sabha, 1989; *private address:* 16, Gokhale Marg, Lucknow, U.P; *office address:* Shrimati Sheila Kaul, Lok Sabha, Parliament House, New Dehli 110 011, India; *phone:* (11) 381825; 377102.

KELLETT-BOWMAN, Dame Elaine (Mary Elaine), OBE; British, Member of Parliament; *born:* 8 July 1924, Lancashire, UK; *parents:* Walter Kay; *married:* Edward Thomas Kellett-Bowman, JP, MEP, 1971; *children:* Charles, Anthony, John, Frances-Anne, St. John, Alistair, Dominic, Melanie; *religion:* Church of England; *languages:* French; *education:* Queen Mary School, Lytham; The Mount, York; St. Anne's College, Oxford, Welfare diploma; *party:* Conservative Party, 1945; *political career:* mem., Union of European Women, 1956-; delegate to Luxembourg, 1958; alderman, Camden Borough Council, 1968-72; Vice-Chmn., Housing Cttee., 1968; Chmn., Welfare Cttee., 1969; Member of Parliament, 1970-; Member of European Parliament, 1975-84; *interests:* health, agriculture, education; *professional career:* called to the bar, Middle Temple, 1964; lay mem., Press Cncl., 1964-68; *honours and awards:* No.1 Country Housewife, 1960; Christal Mac Millan Law Prize, 1963; DBE, 1988; *office address:* Dame Edith Kellet-Bowman, House of Commons, London SW1A OAA.

KELLY, Hon. Ros; Australian, Minister for the Arts, Sport, the Environment and for Tourism and Territories; *born:* 25 January 1948, Sydney, Australia; *education:* St. Ursula's College, Kingsgrove; Univ. of Sydney, BA degree and Diploma of Education; *party:* Australian Labor Party; *political career:* Consultant and Mem., ACT Consumer Affairs Council, 1974-79; Mem., Legal Aid Commission, 1976-79; Mem., ACT Legislative Assembly; elected for Canberra, 1980-; Chairman, Joint Cttee. on the ACT; Mem., Parly. Public Accounts Cttee.; Parly. Expenditure Cttee.; Sec., Federal Labor Party Parly. Caucus, 1981-87; Minister for Defence and Personnel, 1987-89; Minister for Telecommunications and Aviation Support 1989-90; Minister for Arts, Sport, the Environment, Tourism and Territories, 1990-; *professional career:* teacher, 1969-74; *office address:* The Hon. Mr. Ros Kelly, Department of the Arts, Sport, the Environment, Tourism and Territories, Tobruk House, 15 Moore St., Canberra City, ACT 2601, Australia; *phone:* (062) 689411.

KEMPKA, Doreta; Polish, Member of the Sejm; *office address:* Ms Doreta Kempka, Sejm PRI, ul. Wiejska 4/6/8, 00-489 Warsaw, Poland; *phone:* (22) 28 70 01; 28 40 31.

KENNEDY-MORGAN, Juanita; American, Executive Secretary, Organisational and Regional Director of the National Black Women's Political Leadership Caucus; *born:* Birmingham, Alabama, USA; *parents:* William Kennedy and Viola Kennedy; *married:* William R. Morgan, 1945; *public role of spouse:* World War Two veteran; *religion:* United Methodist; *education:* Alabama State Teacher's College, Montgomery, Alabama; Teacher's College, Washington DC, BS, 1962; Terrell Law School, Washington DC, LLB, 1969; Washington DC Teacher's College, Cert. in Civil Defence; Washington Urban League, Cert. in Leadership Development; Federal City College (now Univ. of the District of Columbia), Cert. in Arbitration and Mediation of Community Disputes and Conflict Management; George Washington Univ., Washington DC, History of Christianity; Howard Univ., Washington DC, Present Day History; *political career:* first became politically active as a federal employee successfully campaigning to Pres. Franklin Roosevelt and Pres. Harry Truman against segregation in Treasury Dept., Restaurants, Cafeterias and locker rooms, dismissed as the result of such action and successfully fought a legal battle against the govt. of five years duration, eventually winning reinstatement with five years back pay; Chwn., Decorations Cttee., Dollars for Democrats, 1962-63; Chwn., Voter Registration, Asbury United Methodist Church, 1964; Alternate Delegate, Nat. Convention, Reeves Lanahan ticket, 1964; has worked closely with her brother Kenneth Kennedy in community work throughout DC area; Pres., Woodridge Civic Assn., 1967-68; Mem., Board of Dirs., League of Women Voters; Mem., Board of Dirs., Northeast Community Organization for the Preservation of our Residential Properties; Mem.-at-Large, Women's Auxilliary, Board of Child Care, United Methodist Church; Mem., Black Caucus Group of the Middle Atlantic Convocation for the United Methodist Church; Life Mem., Nat. Cncl. of Negro

Women; Exec. Dir., Organizational and Regional Dir., Nat. Black Women's Political Leadership Caucus, 1974-; Cllr., Ward 5, DC City Cncl., 1977; voter registration co-ordinator, Academy of Educational Development Int. Div., 1987; Chwn., Cttee. on Re-building the Black Family, NAACP; *interests:* aging, discrimination, voter registration; *memberships:* Coalition of Black Organisations, 1990-; Mem., board of Dirs., Kiwakis Club NE; *professional career:* Real Estate Broker, Ultra Realty Service, 1952-89; former teacher, Congress Heights Elementary School, Anacostia Community Project, Washington DC; *honours and awards:* Outstanding Grass Roots Awardee, Woodridge Civic Assn; *clubs:* Greek Organisation; Hon. Mem., Sigma Gamma Rho-Sor; *private address:* 630 11th Court West, Birmingham, Alabama 35204, USA; *office address:* Ms Juanita Kennedy-Morgan, 3005 Bladensburg Road NE NO 217, Washington DC 20018, USA.

KENNELLY, Barbara B.; American, Member of the House of Representatives; *born:* 10 July 1936, Hartford. Connecticut, USA; *parents:* John Moran Bailey and Barbara Bailey (née Leary); *married:* James J. Kennelly, 1959; *children:* Eleanor, Barbara, Louise, John; *religion:* Catholic; *education:* Trinty College, Washington DC, BA, 1958; Harvard Radcliffe School of Business Admin., 1959; Trinity College, Hartford, Connecticut, MA, 1971; *party:* Democratic Party; *political career:* Vice-Chair, Hartford Cttee. on Aging, 1971-75; Mem., Hartford Court of Common Council, 1975-79; Chair, Education, Public Safety and Zoning Cttees.; Sec.-of-State for Connecticut, 1979-82; Dir., Hartford Architecture Conservancy, 1979-82; Mem., House of Representatives for District 1 Connecticut, 1982-; Mem., House Ways and Means Cttee.; Mem., Select Revenue Measures and Human Resources Sub-Cttees.; Mem., Select Permanent Cttee. on Intelligence; Chwn., Sub-Cttee. on Legislation; Mem., Cttee. on Organisation Study and Review; *memberships:* Congress Caucus for Women's Issues Exec. Cttee.; Vice-Chair, Northeast-Midwest Congress Coalition; Mem., Arms Control and Foreign Policy Caucus Steering Cttee.; Mem., Board of Trustees, Trinity College; *honours and awards:* Hon. Degrees, Sacred Heart Univ., 1981, Mount Holyoke College, 1984, Hartford Univ., 1985 and St. Mary's College, Notre Dame, 1986; *private address:* One Corporate Center, 11th Floor, Hartford, CT 06103, USA; *office address:* Rep. Barbara B. Kennelly, 201 Cannon House Office Bldg., Washington DC 20515-0701, USA.

KEPPELHOFF-WIECHERT, Hedwig; German, Member of the European Parliament; *born:* 31 May 1939; *party:* Christlich Demokratische Union Deutschlands (CDU, Christian Democratic Union); *political career:* Chairperson, Deutschen Landfrauenverbandes (German Federation of Women in Agriculture); MEP, 1989-; *private address:* Postfach 1237, 4280 Borken, Germany; *office address:* Ms Hedwig Keppelhoff-Wiechert, European Parliament, Centre Européen, Plateau de Kirchberg, BP 2929, Luxembourg; *phone:* Luxembourg 43001.

KERNOT, Cheryl; Australian, Senator; *born:* 5 December 1948, Maitland, New South Wales; *education:* Newcastle, BA; Newcastle CAE, Dip. Ed; *party:* Australian Democrats; *political career:* Policy Co-ordiantor, Australian Democrats, 1981, Assistant State Sec., (Qld.), 1983, State Sec., 1984, State Pres., 1984-89, Rep., Young Political Leaders' Exchange to USA, 1986, Dep. Nat. Pres., 1988-90; Senator for Queensland, 1990-; Mem., Senate Legislative Cttee. and General Purpose Standing Cttee.; Mem., Joint Standing Cttee. on Electoral Matters and Mem., Select Cttee. on Community Standards Relevant to the Supply of Services Utilising Telecommunications Technologies; Mem., Cttee. on Transport, Communications and Infrastructure and Cttee. on Electoral Matters, 1990-; Spokesperson for Australian Democrats on Transport and Communications, Aboriginal Affairs and Consumer Affairs; Spokesperson on Territories, Northern Australia, 1990-; *professional career:* secondary school teacher; freelance radio producer; electorate officer; *clubs:* qualified cricket umpire; *private address:* 145 Melbourne Street, South Brisbane, Queensland 4101, Australia; *office address:* Ms Cheryl Kernot, Suite S1-33 Telelift 20.8, Parliament House, Canberra, ACT 2600, Australia.

KESTELŸN-SIERENS, Marie-Paule; Belgian, Member of the Chamber of Representatives; *born:* 28 May 1945, Poperinge; *married:* Paul Kestelŷn; *education:* Catholic University Leuven, B.Sc applied economic sciences, 1963-67; *party:* Christelijke Volkspartij (CVP, Christian Social Party); *political career:* member of Chamber of Reps., Brugge district, 1988-; member, Chamber of Reps. commissions on finance, industry, agriculture and small businesses; member, chamber of Reps. advisory Cttee. for european affairs; member, Flemish council commissions on economy, employment and energy, foreign and external affairs; member, CVP district Cttee. and district office; *professional career:* Regional Development Authority (GOM) West Flanders, 1976-86; attaché cabinet of the attache cabinet of the community minister for external relations, 1986-88; *clubs:* Soroptimists International; *private address:* Bisschopsdreef 40, 8310 Brugge, Belgium; *office address:* Ms Marie-Paule Kestelŷn-Sierens, Kamer van Volksvertegenwoordigers, Palais de la Nation, Place de la Nation 2, 1000 Brussels, Belgium.

KHAPARDE, Saroj; Indian, Member of the Rajya Sabha; *born:* 15 August 1941, Bombay; *parents:* Purushottan Khaparde; *education:* BA; *party:* Congress Party; *political career:* Vice Pres., Maha Congress

129

Cttee.; Mem., Rajya Sabha 1972-; attended International Women's Conferences in Berlin, 1972, and in Copenhagen, 1981; Minister of State for Health and Family Welfare, 1986-88; Minister of State for Health, 1988-89; Minister of State for Textiles, 1989; Mem., various Parly. Cttees; *recreations:* travelling, knitting, reading, social work; *private address:* Gandhikuti, Dr. Ambedkar Road, Nagpur 44017, India; *office address:* Shrimati Saroj Khaparde, 100 South Avenue, New Delhi -- 110011, India.

KHATUN, Kumari Sayeeda; Indian, Member of the Rajya Sabha; *born:* 15 January 1944, Balaghat, Madhya Pradesh; *parents:* Muqeem Ahmed Khan; *education:* Nagpur Univ.; Kamla Nehru Mahila College, Balaghat; Saguar Univ.; Law College, Waraseoni, Balaghat; Jabalpur Univ.; MA, Geography, LLB, B.Ed; *party:* Congress Party; *political career:* Mem. of the Rajya Sabha, 1986-; Vice Pres., Balaghat District Congress Cttee.; Convenor, Shikshak Congress, Madhya Pradesh; Organising Sec., All India Quami Ekta; Mem., All India Mahila Congress; *memberships:* Patron, Muslim Education Society, Jabalpur, Madhya Pradesh; mem., Indian Medical Council; *clubs:* Vice Pres., Kamla Nehru Mahila Club, Balaghat; *private address:* Ward No.7, Balaghat, Madhya Pradesh, India; *office address:* Shrimati Kumari Khatun, Rajya Sabha, Parliament House, New Dehli 110 011, India; *phone:* (11) 389977; 389997.

KIAUSCH, Elisabeth; German, Deputy Member of the Bundesrat; *born:* 19 January 1933; *party:* Sozialdemokratische Partei Deutschlands (SPD, Social Democratic Party of Germany); *political career:* mem. of Bürgerschaft, Hamburg, 1987-; Senator for Finance, SPD, 1987-88; Senator for the Senate Offices and the Senate Chancellery, Hamburg, 1988-; mem. of Bundesrat, 1987-; *office address:* Frau Elisabeth Kiausch, Bundesrat, 5300 Bonn 1, West Germany.

KIERINASZEK-LAMLA, W.; Polish, Member of the Sejm; *office address:* Ms W. Kierinaszek-Lamla, Sejm PRI, ul. Wiejska 4/6/8, 00-489 Warsaw, Poland; *phone:* (22) 28 70 01; 28 40 31.

KIHIRA, Teiko; Japanese, Member of the House of Councillors; *born:* 2 February 1928; *education:* The Univ. of Sacred Heart; *party:* Independent; *political career:* former Vice-Pres. of Japan Women Electors' Assn.; elected for Kumamoto, 1990; Mem., House of Cllrs. Cttee on Judicial Affairs, 1990-; *office address:* Ms Teiko Kihira, House of Councillors, 1-7-1 Nagata-cho, Tokyo 100, Japan; *phone:* (03) 5813111.

KING, Hon. Annette Faye; New Zealander, former Member of Parliament; *born:* 13 September 1947, Murchison; *children:* one; *education:* Murchison District High School; Naimea College, graduated a dental nurse, 1967, post graduate diploma, advanced dentistry, 1981; Waikato Univ., BA degree, political science and history, 1981; *party:* Labour Party; *political career:* joined Labour party, 1972; branch secretary and chairperson; LEC secretary; delegate to annual and regional conferences; vice-Pres., State Dental Nurse's Institute, 1981-84; mem., central cttee. of the Public Service Assn. (dental nurse's occupational group), 1983-84; elected to parliament for Horowhenna, 1984-87; chairperson: Parly. Select Cttee. on Social Services; a sub-Cttee. on Social Welfare; re-elected to Parliament 1987-; mem.: House Select Cttee; Caucus Cttee. on Women, Social Services and Community Affairs; Minister of Employment, Minister of Immigration and Minister of Youth Affairs, 1989-90; Under-Secretary for Social Welfare, Employment and Youth Affairs; helped establish the Social Welfare District Executive Cttees.; representative for the Minister on the Social Welfare Commission; considerable involvement with the following institutions: Rehabilitation League Review, Social Welfare organisations, Regional Employment and Access Councils, Community Resource Centre Assn., Enterprise Agencies, community based Employment Network and the Student Job Search Organisation; chairperson, working party to establish the Local Employment and Enterprise Development Programme; mem., Tourism 2000 Task Force Cttee; *professional career:* school dental nurse, 1965-70 and 1973-82; dental tutor, 1982-84; *office address:* The Hon. Ms Annette King, House of Representatives, POB 18041, Wellington, New Zealand; *phone:* (04) 719199; *fax:* (04) 4990704.

KIRALY, Izabella B.; Hungarian, Member of the Országgyülés; *party:* Hungarian Democratic Forum (MDF); *office address:* Ms Izabella Király, Országgyülés, Kossuth L. tér 1-3, Budapest V, Hungary; *phone:* 22 5058; 22 5059.

KIRCHEVA, Dr. Elena Peikova; Bulgarian, Member of the Grand National Assembly; *born:* 18 September 1949, Lom, Bulgaria; *parents:* Petko Dimitrov Kirchev and Maria Alexandrova Kircheva (née Kadieva); *married:* (divorced), 1980; *children:* Simeon; *religion:* East-Orthodox; *languages:* Bulgarian, German, Russian; *education:* High School, Lom; Kl. Ohridsky Univ., Sofia, Law, 1967-71; *party:* Agrarian Party, 1981-; *political career:* Mem. of the Grand Nat. Assembly; Mem., Board of Dirs., Agrarian Party, 1990-; Dep. Chairperson, Constitution Commission in 7th Great Nat. Assembly, 1990-; Mem., Grand Nat. Assembly Cttee. on Kuwait, 1991; *interests:* integrity and unity of Agrarian Party, representation of Bulgaria in Cncl. of Europe; *memberships:* Board of Dirs., Nat. Academic Endowment/Foundation; Board of Foreign Relief Ageny; *professional career:* junior lecturer in law, 1976-80; senior lecturer in law, 1980-85; chief assistant in law, Univ. of Nat. and World Economy, 1985-90; *publications:* Stand und Entwicklung des

Sozialversicherungsrechts in Bulgarien - Studie mit einem Versuch des Rechtsvergleiches der sozialen Sicherung in Bulgarien mit der deutschen sozialen Sicherung nach den sozialen Lagen - in Südosteuropa Mitteilungen, No. 1, 1989; Ausgewählte Probleme des neuen bulgarischen Arbeitsgesetzbuches von 1986 - Studie im Jahrbuch für Ostrecht, Band XXVIII, 1987, Munich; Das bulgarische Arbeitsgesetzbuch von 1986 - Studie in : WGO Monatshefte für Osteuropäisches Recht, Heidelberg, 1988; das Recht auf bezahlten Jahresurlaub in Bulgarien, article in magazine Das Recht der Arbeit (the right to work), Vienna, 1990; *recreations:* sauna, cosmetics, massage; *private address:* Sofia 1404, 128 Georgi Avramov Str. apt. 49, Bulgaria; *office address:* Dr. Elena Peikova Kircheva, Narodno Sobranie, 3 National Assembly Square, Sofia 1000, Bulgaria; *phone:* 85-01.

KIRK, Jenny N.; New Zealander, former Member of Parliament; *born:* 1945; *party:* Labour Party; *political career:* Electorate Secretary, Glenfield; mem., National Organisation for Women; founding mem., North Shore Labour Women's Collective; MP, Labour, Birkenhead; *professional career:* Secretary, Sunnybrae School Cttee.; secretary, Onepoto Playcentre; Journalist; *private address:* 25 Hillcrest Avenue Northcote, Auckland 9, New Zealand; *office address:* Ms Jenny Kirk, House of Representatives, POB 18041, Wellington, New Zealand; *phone:* (04) 719199; *fax:* (04) 4990704.

KIRNER, Hon. Joan; Australian, Premier of Victoria, Minister for Ethnic Affairs and Minister resposible for Women's Affairs; *office address:* The Hon. Ms. Joan Kirner, Legislative Council and Assembly of Victoria, Parliament House, Spring Street, Melbourne 3002, Australia; *phone:* (03) 651 8911; *fax:* (03) 650 7245.

KLEVELAND, Åse; Norwegian, Minister of Cultural Affairs; *born:* 18 March 1949, Stockholm; *married:* Oddvar Bull Tuhus (Co-habitant); *public role of spouse:* film director; *party:* Norwegian Labour Party; *political career:* Sec., then leader, Norwegian Musicians' Union, 1979-83 and 1983-87; Minister of Cultural Affairs, Nov. 1990; *professional career:* popular singer during 60s and 70s (represented Norway in the Eurovision Song Contest); television presenter; Mgr., Tusenfryd Amusement Park; due to take over as Olympic Cultural Dir. before ministerial appointment; *office address:* Ms Åse Kleveland, Ministry of Culture and Scientific Affairs, Akersgaten 42, P.O. Box 8030 Dep, 0032 Oslo 1, Norway; *phone:* (02) 34 90 90; *fax:* 349550.

KNIGHT, Dame Jill (Joan Christabel Jill), DBE; British, Member of Parliament; *born:* 1927; *married:* the late James Montague Knight; 1947; *children:* two s; *languages:* some French; *education:* King Edward Grammar School, Birmingham; *party:* Conservative Party; *political career:* councillor, Northampton County Borough Council, 1956-66; Parly. candidate, 1959, 1964; Member of Parliament, 1966-; mem., Western European Union and Council of Europe, 1977-88; Chmn., Cons. Parly. Cttee. for Health; Chmn., Lords and Commons All-Party Family and Child Protecton Group; fmr. Sec. and Vice-Chmn., 1922 Cttee.; fmr. mem., Pres. Cttee., Western European Union; Pres., West Midlands Area Conservative Political Centre, 1980-83; Chmn., WEU Parly. and Public Relations Cttee., 1984-88; *interests:* health, social security, education, European affairs; *memberships:* National Deaf Children's Society (Pres., Birmingham); Psoriasis Assn. (Pres., Birmingham); Limbless Ex-Service Men's Assn. (Vice-Pres.); National Union of Townswomen's Guilds (Vice-Pres.); Quinton Operatic Socy. (Patron), 1991-; Pres., Birmingham Central Branch Arthritis Care; *professional career:* Company Dir., Computech International; *honours and awards:* MBE, 1964; DBE, 1985; *recreations:* tapestry, theatre, antiques; *office address:* Dame Jill Knight, House of Commons, London SW1A OAA.

KNOWLES, Susan Christine; Australian, Senator; *born:* 10 April 1951, Brisbane, Queensland, Australia; *party:* Liberal Party; *political career:* life Mem., Young Liberal Movement; State Pres., Young Liberal Movement (WA), 1977-81; Mem., State Executive 1977-85; Mem., State Council, (WA), 1977-; State Vice-Pres., (WA), 1981-83; State Campaign Chairperson (WA), 1982-85; Senior Vice-Pres., Liberal Party (WA), 1983-85; elected to Senate for Western Australia, 1984-; Committee Service: Mem. of the Senate Standing Cttee. for the House, 1985-; Mem. of the Senate Legislative and General Purpose Standing Cttee. for Education and the Arts, 1985-87; for Community Affairs, 1987-; Conferences, Delegations and Visits: attended Commonwealth Parly. Association Annual Group Discussion, London and Isle of Man, 1985; Mem., Australian Political Exchange Delegation, Canada, 1985; Deputy Opposition Whip in the Senate, 1987-; *professional career:* sales/marketing manager; *office address:* Ms Susan Knowles, PO Box 930, West Perth, Western Australia, 6005.

KOCHANOWSKA, Anna; Polish, Member of the Democratic Party Central Committee; *born:* Plock, Poland; *education:* studies at State Higher School of Fine Arts; Film and Theatre school; *party:* Democratic Party of Poland; *political career:* Mem., cultural Commission, Municipal People's Cncl.; Mem., Presidium, Democratic Party Voivodship Cttee., Olsztyn, 1962, Chairperson, 1981; Mem., Central Advisory Group for Cultural Affairs, Democratic Party, Voivodship Cttee., Olsztyn, 1962, Chaiperson, 1981; Mem., Central Advisory Group for Cultural Affairs, Democratic Party Central Cttee., Deputy for Sejm, 1972-80; *professional career:* Theatre Inspector, Central Theatres Administration; Literary Dir., Theatres in Olsztyn, Bialystok and Grudziadz; Mem. of Staff,

Polish Radio, Bydgoszcz, 1956-60, Olsztyn, 1960-81; Chairperson, Intelligentsia Club, Bydgoszcz; *honours and awards:* Gold Cross of Merit; Merited Cultural Leader; Gold Badge for Services to Warmai and Mazury Region; First Prize, Co-ordination Commission, Ministry of Culture and Art; *office address:* Ms Anna Kochanowska, Democratic Party of Poland Central Cttee., 00--21 Warsaw, UL. Rutkowskiego 9, Poland.

KOCK-PETERSEN, Elsebeth; Danish, Member of the Folketinget; *born:* 15 January 1949, Copenhagen, Denmark; *parents:* Ejnar Larsen and Mia Larsen; *education:* Norre Gymnasium, 1967; Copenhagen Univ. bachelor of laws, 1973; *party:* Venstre (Liberal Party), 1975; *political career:* principal in Ministry of Foreign Affairs, 1979-; member of the committee of Danish Liberal Party for Youth, Copenhagen-Frederiksberg, 1965-70; Member of Folketinget, 1975-; Minister of Ecclesiastical Affairs, 1982-84; Minister for Social Affairs, 1984-85; Minister of Health, 1988-91; *professional career:* mem. cttee for SJL Bank, 1986-; *clubs:* member of the committee for the Mission for Homeless People; *private address:* Trondhjemsgade 15, 2100 Copenhagen O, Denmark; *office address:* Ms Elsebeth Kock-Petersen, Ministry of Health, Amaliegade 13, Copenhagen K, Denmark.

KOEFOED, Ingerlise; Danish, Member of the Folketing; *born:* 9 February 1922, Copenhagen, Denmark; *parents:* Aage Nielsen and Esther Hansen; *married:* Flemming Koefoed, 1949; *children:* Torsten, Niels, Martin, Ole; *religion:* Protestant; *languages:* Danish, English, German, French, Swedish; *education:* School for Library Education, 1958-61; *party:* Socialistisk Folkeparti (Socialist People's Party), 1972; *political career:* member of the Folketinget, 1979-; member of the Municipal Council in Lyngby-Taarbaek; member of the Boards for Finance, Culture and Research, 1979; Minister of the Board for Cultural Politics, 1981; *interests:* cultural politics, financial policy, rural politics, policy regarding youth and children, research in medecine, ethics and morals, information about technology; *professional career:* Librarian in Lyngby 1968-76; Librarian Consultant in the Library Inspection Society 1976-89; Literature Reviewer on the Politiken 1972-; *honours and awards:* Dossingprisen, Library League, 1983; Klods Hans Prisen, Ibby, 1986; Uglen, Forfatterforeningen, 1989; *publications:* Bureau for Women Trine og Josefine published by Artakon in 1964; Sommer hos Morfar published by Jespersen in 1968; Vi er en del af jer selv published by Aschehoug in 1978; Kulturcentre published by Bibliotekscentralen in 1967; several articles and feature articles in different newspapers; *clubs:* Association for preservation of Natural Amenities in Denmark; *recreations:* art, media, literature, music, theatre, dance; *private address:* Gadevangen 11, 2800 Lyngby, Denmark; *office address:*

Ms Ingerlise Koefoed, Christiansborg, 1240 Copenhagen K, Denmark.

KOLAROVA, Daniela; Czechoslovakian, Member of the Narodni Rada (Czech National Council); *born:* 21 September 1946; *party:* Civic Forum; *office address:* Ms Daniela Kolarova, Ceská národní rada, Snemovní 4, 110 00 Praha 1, Czechoslovakia; *phone:* (02) 2105.

KONECNY, Theodora; Austrian, Member of the Bundesrat; *born:* 24 December 1924; *education:* Women's College of Commercial Professions; training college for nursery school teachers, state examinations; *party:* Sozialistische Partei Österreichs (SPÖ, Socialist Party of Austria); *political career:* Chairperson of Female Nursery School Teachers' Group, Austrian Association of Socialist Teachers, Lower Austria; district councillor, Angern an der March, 1960-68 and since 1980; district Women's Chairperson, district Vice-Chairperson, and Vice-Chairperson, SPÖ Directive Cttee., Lower Austria, since 1968; sent to Bundesrat from Lower Austrian Provincial Assembly, mem. of Bundesrat, since 1983; *professional career:* Nursery school inspector; Pres., Lower Austrian provincial social association; People's Aid; district Chairperson, People's Aid, Gänserndorf; mem. of Commission for the Penal System, Vienna Provincial Criminal Court; Federal-Vice-Chairperson, Specialist Commission for Nursery School Teachers, and Children's Home Wardens, since 1980; *honours and awards:* Golden Award for Services for the Federal Province of Lower Austria; *office address:* Frau Theodora Konecny, Bundesrat, Dr. Karl Renner Ring 3, 1017 Vienna, Austria.

KONSTANTINOVA, Dr. Elka Georgeiva; Bulgarian, Member of the Grand National Assembly; *born:* 25 May 1932, Sofia, Bulgaria; *parents:* Georgi Konstantinov Gogov and Vassilka Konstantinova (née Mincheva Chakirova); *children:* Vassil; *religion:* Christian Orthodox; *languages:* Bulgarian, French, Polish, Russian; *education:* St. Joseph French College, Sofia; Sofia Univ., MA Bulgarian philology; Prof., Bulgarian Literature; *party:* Radical Democratic Party, 1989; *political career:* Pres., Radical Democratic Party; MP, 1990-; Chwn., Parly. Cttee. for Science and Education; *interests:* liberal ideologies; *professional career:* senior research Assc., higher Inst. of Pedagogy, Shumen, 1958-90; prof. in literature, Bulgarian Academy of Sciences, Sofia, 1990; *publications:* five Bulgarian language publications, 1974-87; *private address:* Levski Blvd. 47-B, Sofia 1000, Bulgaria; *office address:* Dr. Elka Georgeiva Konstantinova, Narodno Sobranie, 3 National Assembly Square, Sofia 1000, Bulgaria; *phone:* 85-01.

KONYA, Imréné; Hungarian, Member of the Országgyúlés; *office address:* Ms Imréné Kónya,

132

Országgyúlés, Kossuth L. tér 1-3, Budapest V, Hungary; *phone:* 22 5058; 22 5059.

KOPYLOVA, Aleksandra Vasilevna; Soviet, Member of the Council of the Union; *party:* Communist Party of the Soviet Union; *political career:* Mem., Cncl. of the Union; Mem., Supreme Soviet Ctees. on Science, Public Education, Culture and Upbringing; *professional career:* Chief, Public Health Dept., Mtsenk Gorispolkom; *office address:* Ms Aleksandra Vasilevna Kopylova, Council of the Union, Kremlin, Moscow, USSR.

KORINKOVA, Kvetoslava; Czechoslovakian, Federal Minister of Control; *party:* unaffiliated; *office address:* Mrs Kvetoslava Korínková, Urad predsedníctva vlády CSFR, Nábr. kpt. Jarose 4, 125 09 Praha 1, Czechoslovakia.

KORITAROVA, Rosa (Smirna) Vasileva; Bulgarian, Deputy Chairperson of the Bulgarian Women's Commitee; *born:* 28 March 1921, Gorna Dzhumaya (now Blagoevgrad); *party:* Bulgarian Communist Party (BCP); *political career:* Mem., Young Communist League, 1936; Mem., BCP, 1040; imprisoned, 1943; partisan, 1944; various posts in BCP City Cttees., Dupnitsa, Sofia; Sec., Plovdiv City BCP Cttee., 1950-52; Mem. of Staff, Sofia City BCP Cttee., 1952-59; Sec., Kyustendil District Party Cttee., 1959-61; Sec., Central Cncl. of Trade Unions, 1961-66, Pres., 1967-70, Vice-Pres., 1971; Deputy, Nat. Assembly, 1962-79, Mem., Presidium, 1966-71; Mem., BCP Central Cttee., 1962-71; Mem., Secretariat of BCP Central Cttee., 1968-71; Ambassador to Switzerland, 1972-76; Deputy Chairperson, Bulgarian Women's Cttee., 1979; *office address:* Ms Rosa Koritarova, Bulgarian Women's Committee, Blvd. Patriyarkh Ertimii 82, Sofia, Bulgaria.

KORNBLITH KOPP, Nancy; American, Maryland State Representative and Speaker Pro Tem; *born:* 7 December 1943, Coral Gables, Florida, USA; *parents:* Lester Kornblith Jr. and Barbara Kornblith (née Levy); *married:* Robert Evans Kopp, 1969; *children:* Emily Frances, Robert E; *education:* Wellesley College, BA, 1965; Univ. of Chicago, MA, 1968, Ph.D. work 1968-; *party:* Democratic Party; *political career:* staff Asst., US House Education Sub-Cttee., 1969-71; staff Asst., Maryland House Delegation, 1971-74; Maryland State Delegate, District 16, 1975-; Chwn., House Appropriations Sub-Cttee., 1979-; Asst. Majority Leader, 1987-; Mem., Exec. Cttee., National Conference of State Legislators; Mem., Exec. Cttee., Southern Regional Education Board; *memberships:* American Political Science Assn; *professional career:* teacher, Univ. of Illinois, Chicago, 1968-69; *honours and awards:* Hon. Degree, D.Litt., Hood College; Merriam Fellowship, Univ. of Chicago, 1967-71;

Young Woman of the Year, Maryland, 1978; Fellow, Univ. of Baltimore; *private address:* 6301 Dahlonega Road, Bethesda, Maryland 20816, USA; *office address:* Mrs Nancy Kornblith Kopp, Rm. 313 House Office Bldg., House of Delegates, Annapolis, Maryland 21401, USA.

KORNSSLEWICZ, Alicja Jézeía; Polish, Member of the Sejm; *office address:* Ms Alicja Jézeía Kornsslewicz, Sejm PRI, ul. Wiejska 4/6/8, 00-489 Warsaw, Poland; *phone:* (22) 28 70 01; 28 40 31.

KORODI, Mária; Hungarian, Member of the Országgyúlés; *party:* Alliance of Free Democrats (SZDSZ); *office address:* Ms Mária Kóródi, Országgyúlés, Kossuth L. tér 1-3, Budapest V, Hungary; *phone:* 22 5058; 22 5059.

KOROSEC, Ingrid; Austrian, Member of the Nationalrat; *born:* 22 November 1940, Böheimkirchen, Lower Austria; *education:* commercial school, academy of commerce, matriculation; studied economics; *party:* Österreichische Volkspartei (ÖVP, Austrian People's Party); *political career:* Women's Chairperson, Christian Group, Union of Private Sector Employees, 1978- and Vice Chairperson, Christian Group, Union of Private Sector Employees, 1983-; district councillor, Vienna, 1983-86; mem. of Vienna Provincial Assembly, 1983-86; Federal Women's Chairperson, Austrian Workers' and Employees' Federation, 1984- and Federal Chairperson for Employees, 1986-; district chairperson, Austrian Women's Movement, 1984-; mem. of Nationalrat, for Burgenland, Lower Austria and Vienna, 1986-; *professional career:* employee, ADEG, St. Pölten, 1956,- and head of electronic data processing, 1961-; Chairperson works' council, ADEG headquarters, Vienna, 1976-; Chairperson, central works council, ADEG Austria, 1982-; senior official, Chamber of Workers and Employees for Vienna; *office address:* Frau Ingrid Korosec, Nationalrat, Dr. Karl Renner Ring 3, 1017 Vienna, Austria.

KOSA, Magdolna; Hungarian, Member of the Országgyúlés (Parliament); *born:* 4 November 1940, Budapest, Hungary; *parents:* Dr. Kovacs Ferenc and Kelemen Terézia; *married:* Dr. Kosa Levente, 1961; *children:* Judit, Eszter; *languages:* Hungarian, French; *education:* Kossuth Lajos Univ., Debrecen, Hungarian and French language and literature, 1959-61; Eötvös Lorand Univ., Budapest, Language and Literature, MA, 1961-60; *party:* MSzMP (Hungarian Socialist Workers' Party), 1967-89; MSzP, (Hungarian Socialist Party), since 1989; *political career:* Sec., Teachers Trade Union, 1977-85; Sec., Trade Union Federation, 1985-90; Mem., Parliament, 1990-; *interests:* syndicalism, social Politics; *professional career:* secondary school teacher and literary historian, 1964-77; *publications:* many (at Least 50) articles on press-history and comparative literary history, 1967-79; articles on the system and working of trade unions, 1980-90; *office address:* Ms Magdolna Kosa, Országgyülés, Kossuth L. tér 1-3, Budapest V, Hungary; *phone:* 22 5058; 22 5059.

KOSANE, Dr. Kovács Magda; Hungarian, Member of the Országgyülés; *party:* Hungarian Socialist Party (MSZP); *office address:* Dr. Kovács Magda Kósáné, Országgyülés, Kossuth L. tér 1-3, Budapest V, Hungary; *phone:* 22 5058; 22 5059.

KRAUZ, Stanislawa; Polish, Member of the Sejm; *office address:* Ms Stanislawa Krauz, Sejm PRI, ul. Wiejska 4/6/8, 00-489 Warsaw, Poland; *phone:* (22) 28 70 01; 28 40 31.

KREJCOVA, Zdenka; Czechoslovakian, Member of the Narodni Rada (Czech National Council); *born:* 17 May 1942; *party:* Civic Forum; *office address:* Ms Zdenka Krejcova, Ceská národní rada, Snemovní 4, 110 00 Praha 1, Czechoslovakia; *phone:* (02) 2105.

KRISTAN, Anica; Yugoslavian, Member of the Central Committee of the League of Communists of Yugoslavia; *born:* 1934; *party:* League of Communists of Yugoslavia (LCY); *political career:* Mem., Central Cttee., LCY; *office address:* Ms Anica Kristan, LCY (CPY) Central Committee, Novi Beograd, Bul. Lenjina 6, Yugoslavia.

KRYUCHENKOVA, Nadezhda Aleksandrovna; Soviet, Member of the Council of the Union; *party:* Communist Party of the Soviet Union; *political career:* Mem., Cncl. of the Union; Mem., Congress of People's Deps. Drafting Commission; Mem., Supreme Soviet Cttees. on Science, Public Education, Culture and Upringing; *professional career:* secondary school teacher, School No. 2, Inzhavino Workers Settlement; *office address:* Ms Nadezhda Aleksandrovna Kryuchenkova, Council of the Union, Kremlin, Moscow, USSR.

KRZYZANOWSKA, Ms Olga; Polish, Vice-Marshal of the Sejm (Deputy Speaker); *born:* 10 September 1929, Warsaw; *parents:* father, officer during war, Home Army Commander, Vilna Region, died in Mokotów prison, Warsaw and mother, physician; *public role of spouse:* husband, independent researcher, Polish Acad. of Sciences; *children:* one d; *education:* Faculty of Medicine, Medical Acad., Gdansk; *party:* Solidarnosc (Solidarity); *political career:* Mem., Medical Service Workers Nat. Co-ordinating Commission, Solidartiy Trade Union; *professional career:* Doctor in Voivodship Hospital, Gdansk and Medical Acad., Gdansk; industrial health worker, Gdansk shipyard, 1963-; *office address:* Olga Krzyzanowska, Sejm PRI, ul. Wiejska 4/6/8, 00-489 Warsaw, Poland; *phone:* (22) 28 70 01; 28 40 31.

KUBOTA, Manae; Japanese, Member of the House of Councillors; *born:* 6 October 1924; *education:* Keio Univ; *party:* Japan Socialist Party (JSP); *political career:* former Manager, Prime Minister's Office; Second time elected for National; JSP Vice-Chairperson, Dir., House of Cllrs. Special Cttee. on Environment and Dir., JSP Women's Bureau, 1990-; *office address:* Ms Manae Kubota, House of Councillors, 1-7-1 Nagata-cho, Tokyo 100, Japan; *phone:* (03) 5813111.

KUC BOZENNA, Marianna; Polish, Member of the Sejm; *office address:* Ms Marianna Kuc Bozenna, Sejm PRI, ul. Wiejska 4/6/8, 00-489 Warsaw, Poland; *phone:* (22) 28 70 01; 28 40 31.

KULLMANN FIVE, Kaci; Norwegian, Leader of Hoyre; *born:* 13 April 1951, Oslo, Norway; *parents:* Kjell Kullmann and Anne-Lise Kullmann (née Heiberg); *married:* Carsten O. Five, 1972; *children:* Christina, Christian; *religion:* Protestant; *languages:* English, French; *education:* University, Oslo, Graduate in Politics, 1970-77; University, Oslo, Political Science, French, Public Law, 1979-80; *party:* Hoyre (Conservative), 1968; *political career:* mem. of the Borough Board, Barum, 1975-81; Chairperson of Young Conservative National Federation, 1977-79; Vice-Chairperson of Hoyre, 1982-88; vice-leader of Hoyre Parliamentary Group, 1985-89; mem. of the Stortings Finance Cttee., 1981-85; mem. of the Stortings Foreign Affairs Cttee., 1985-89; Minister of Trade and Shipping, 1989-Oct. 1990; leader, Hoyre Apr. 1991-; *interests:* environment, equal rights, economic politics, foreign affairs, safety and security politics, European integration; *professional career* consultant, Norwegian Employers' Association, 1980-81; *office address:* Ms Kaci Kullmann Five, Ministry of Trade and Shipping, Victoria Terrasse 7, POB 8113 Dep. 0032, Oslo 1, Norway.

KUMARANATUNGA, Chandrika B.; Sri Lankan Leader of the United Socialist Alliance; *office address:* Ms Chandrika Kumaranatunga, United Socialist Alliance (USA).

KUNIN, Madeleine May; American, Governor of Vermont; *born:* 28 September 1933, Zurich, Switzerland; *parents:* Ferdinand May and René May (née Bloch); *married:* Arthur Kunin, 1959; *children:* Peter, Julia, Adam, Daniel; *religion:* Jewish; *education:* Univ. of Massachusetts, BA, 1956; Columbia Univ. School of Journalism, MS, 1957; Univ. of Vermont MA, 1967; *party:* Democratic Party; *political career:* Vermont State Rep., 1973-78; Lt.-Gov., Vermont 1978-82; Gov., Vermont, 1984-; *professional career:* reporter, Burlington Free Press, 1957-58; instructor Trinity College, 1971-72; writer, 1972-; radio show host, WJOY, Burlington, Vermont, 1983-; *honours and awards:* Hon. Degrees: Middlebury College; Norwich

Univ.; St. Michael's College; Marlboro College; Univ. of Massachusetts; Green Mountain College; *publications:* The Big Green Bear, Barre Publications, 1976; articles; *office address:* Ms Madeleine Kunin, Office of the Governor, 109 State Street, Montpelier, Vermont 05602, USA.

KUO, Shirley; Taiwan, Minister of State and Chair of the Council for Economic Planning and Development; *born:* 25 January 1930, Taiwan; *married:* Nieh Wenya; *children:* three d; *education:* National Taiwan Univ., BA; Kobe Univ., Japan, Dr. of Econ; *political career:* Minister of Finance, 1988-90; Vice Chair, EPC, Exec. Yuan, 1973-77; Vice Chair then Chair, Cncl. for Economic Planning and Development, 1990-; Minister of State, 1990-; *professional career:* lecturer and Assoc. Prof., National Taiwan Univ.; Prof., National Taiwan Univ., 1966-89; Dep. Gov., Central Bank of China, 1979-88; *publications:* The Taiwan Economy in Transition; Growth with Equity; The Taiwan Sucess Story; Macroeconomics; Microeconomics; *private address:* 11th Floor -1, 539 Tunhua South Road, Taipei, Taiwan; *office address:* Ms Shirley Kuo, Office of the Executive Yuan, Chunghsiao E. Road, Section One, No. 1, Taipei, 105, Taiwan; *phone:* (02) 391-5231; *fax:* (02) 3948727.

KURATOWSKA, Zofia; Polish, Vice-Marshal of the Senate (Deputy Speaker); *born:* 1932; *children:* one s; *education:* Faculty of Medicine, Medical Academy, Warsaw; *party:* Solidarnosc (Solidarity), 1980-; *political career:* Mem., Nat. Co-ordinating Commission, Solidarity Trade Union of Health Service Workers; Chairperson, Lech Walesa's Civic Cttee. Health Commission; Co-Chairperson, team for health at the round table; Senator for Nowy Sacz Voivodship; *professional career:* Physician in haematology; Asst. Prof., Medical Centre of Postgraduate Education; Ed., Books of Independent Medical Thought (underground circulation); work for Primatial Cttee. for Aid to Imprisoned Persons and their Families, 1981-; Pres., Social Solidarity Foundation; *publications:* about 140 scientific papers, numerous articles in Catholic magazines; *office address:* Mrs. Zofia Kuratowska, Sejm PRI, ul. Wiejska 4/6/8, 00-489 Warsaw, Poland; *phone:* (22) 28 70 01; 28 40 31.

KUS, Janina; Polish, Member of the Sejm; *office address:* Ms Janina Kus, Sejm PRI, ul. Wiejska 4/6/8, 00-489 Warsaw, Poland; *phone:* (22) 28 70 01; 28 40 31.

KUSAKABE, Kiyoko; Japanese, Member of the House of Councillors; *born:* 2 November 1935; *education:* London Univ; *party:* Japan Socialist Party (JSP); *political career:* elected for National, 1990; Mem., House of Cllrs. Cttee. on Social and Labour Affairs and Special Cttee. on National Livelihood, 1990-;

professional career: Researcher of Social Welfare Systems; *office address:* Ms Kiyoko Kusakabe, House of Councillors, 1-7-1 Nagata-cho, Tokyo 100, Japan; *phone:* (03) 5813111.

KUSHNER, Linda; American, Rhode Island State Representative; *born:* 27 March 1939; *religion:* Jewish; *education:* Brandeis Univ., Boston, BA, 1960; Boston Univ., M.Ed., 1961; *party:* Democratic Party; *political career:* Rhode Island State Rep., District 4, 1983-; *memberships:* Women's Political Caucus; Rhode Island Bar Assn., League of Women Voters; *professional career:* attorney; *office address:* Mr Linda Kushner, 560 Lloyd Avenue, Providence, Rhode Island 02906, USA.

KUTSUNUGI, Dr. Takeko; Japanese, Member of the House of Councillors; *born:* 7 July 1922; *education:* Osaka Women's Medical College; *party:* Japan Communist Party; *political career:* third time elected for Osaka; Mem., House of Cllrs. Cttee. on Social and Labour Affairs and Special Cttee. on Environment and Mem., JCP Central Cttee., 1990-; *professional career:* Doctor; *office address:* Dr. Takeko Kutsunugi, House of Councillors, 1-7-1 Nagata-cho, Tokyo 100, Japan; *phone:* (03) 5813111.

KUUSKOSKI-VIKATMAA, Eeva Maija Kaarina; Finnish, Minister of Social Affairs and Health; *born:* 4 October 1946, Aura, Finland; *parents:* Timo Mauri Kuuskoski and Kirsti Mirjam Kuuskoski (née Haapanen); *married:* Juha Ville Vikatmaa, 1973; *children:* Katri (decd.); *education:* Lic. Med., 1972; Specialist in Paediatrics, 1982; *party:* Suomen Keskusta (Finnish Centre Party); *political career:* Mem., Turku City Cncl., 1973-80; Admin. Board of Student Health Care Foundation, 1975-81; mem., Presidential Electorate, 1978; mem. of Eduskunta, 1979-; Minister, Health and Social Security, 1983-87; *professional career:* Ilomantsi Health Centre Dr., 1972; Asst., Turku Univ. Public Health Studies Inst., 1973; Turku Health Centre Dr., 1973; Asst. Dr., Helsinki Univ. Central Hospital (Paediatrics Clinic), 1976-80; *clubs:* Chmn, Assn. of Finnish Operas, 1985; *office address:* Ms Eeva Kuuskoski-Vikatmaa, Ministry of Social Affairs and Health, Snellmaninkatu 4-6, 00170 Helsinki, Finland.

KWIETNIEWSKA, Anna Jolanta; Polish, Member of the Sejm; *office address:* Ms Anna Jolanta Kwietniewska, Sejm PRI, ul. Wiejska 4/6/8, 00-489 Warsaw, Poland; *phone:* (22) 28 70 01; 28 40 31.

KYNSOK, Anna Maria; Polish, Member of the Sejm; *office address:* Ms Anna Maria Knysok, Sejm PRI, ul. Wiejska 4/6/8, 00-489 Warsaw, Poland; *phone:* (22) 28 70 01; 28 40 31.

L

LABARIA, Hon. Violeta T.; Filipino, Congresswoman; *born:* 29 April 1934; *parents:* the late Guillermo B. Tabios and the late Basilia R. Nazareno; *married:* Pompey N. Labaria; *children:* Paolo, Valia Gemma, Peter; *education:* Univ. of Sto. Tomas, B.Sc., Biology; Southwestern Univ., Doctor of Medicine; *political career:* Congresswoman; *professional career:* formerly: Resident Physician, Bukidnon National Hospital; Retainer Physician, Development Bank of the Philippines and Social Security System, Bukidnon; School Physician, San Isidro College, Malaybalay; Mem. of the Board, Bukidnon Provincial Medicare Cncl; *office address:* The Hon. Ms Violeta Labaria, The Congress of the Philippines - House of Representatives, Batasang Pambansa Bldg., Quezon City, Manila, The Philippines.

LABUDA, Barbara; Polish, Member of the Sejm; *office address:* Ms Barbara Labuda, Sejm PRI, ul. Wiejska 4/6/8, 00-489 Warsaw, Poland; *phone:* (22) 28 70 01; 28 40 31.

LAFAYETTE, Rene; American, Rhode Island State Representative; *born:* 2 May 1961, Woonsocket, Rhode Island, USA; *education:* Providence College, BA, 1963; *party:* Democratic Party; *political career:* Rhode Island State Rep., District 65, 1984-; *office address:* Ms Rene Lafayette, 85 LeBrun Avenue, Woonsocket, Rhode Island 02895, USA.

LAGOVA, Hana; Czechoslovakian, Member of the Narodni Rada (Czech National Council); *party:* Komunistická Strana Ceskoslovenska (KSC, Communist party of Czechoslovakia); *office address:* Ms Hana Lagová, Ceská národní rada, Snemovní 4, 110 00 Praha 1, Czechoslovakia; *phone:* (02) 2105.

LAKATOS, Józsefné; Hungarian, Member of the Országgyülés; *party:* Independent Smallholders' Party (FKgP); *office address:* Ms Józsefné Lakatos, Országgyülés, Kossuth L. tér 1-3, Budapest V, Hungary; *phone:* 22 5058; 22 5059.

LALLA, Diallo; Mali, Minister of Employment and Civil Service; *office address:* Ms Diallo Lalla, Ministry of Employment and the Civil Service, BP 80, Bamako, Mali.

LALLIAM, Nafissa; Algerian, Minister of Health; *born:* Algiers; *children:* two; *political career:* Minister of Health; *professional career:* Prof., Fac. of Medecine; Head of Gynaecology, Hospital of Parnet, Algiers; *office address:* Mrs Nafissa Lalliam, Ministry of Health, 128 Ave. Mohammed Gacem, Algiers.

LAM, Hon. Peggy; Hong Kong, Member of the Legislative Council; *born:* 2 May 1928, Shanghai, China; *married:* Gilbert Lam Kwong-Kui; *children:* one; *religion:* Christian; *education:* Shanghai Univ., BA; American Univ., Fellowship in Family Planning; *political career:* mem., 7th Chinese People's Political Consultative Conference; *memberships:* Hon. Adviser, Shenzhen Family Planning Assn. of China; Hon. Vice Pres., Hong Kong Girl Guides Assn.; Hon. Sec., Hong Kong Juvenile Care Centre; Founder and Vice Pres., Hong Kong Sex Educatin Assn.; School Supervisor and Board Chmn., Shanghai Alumni Primary School; Mem., Kwan Fong Charitable Foundation Advisory Centre; *professional career:* Company Dir.; Lay Assessor, Magistrates' Court; *honours and awards:* MBE, Justice of the Peace; *office address:* The Hon. Mrs Peggy Lam, The Legislative Council, Government House, Hong Kong.

LAMBERT BARTON, Nelda Ann; American, Vice-Chairwoman of the Republican National Committee for Kentucky; *born:* 12 May 1929, Providence, Kentucky, USA; *parents:* Eulis Grant Lambert and Rubie Lois Lambert (née West); *children:* William Grant (Decd.), Barbara Lynn, Harold Bryan Jr., Stephen Lambert, Suzanne; *religion:* Protestant; *education:* Western Kentucky Univ., 1947-49; Norton Memorial Infirmary School of Medical Technology, 1950; *party:* Republican Party; *political career:* 5th District Gov., Kentucky Federation of Republican Women, 1963-67; Mem., American and Kentucky Education, Medical and Political Action Cttees., 1963-; Republican, District Campaign Chwn., 1967-; Whitley County Campaign Chwn., 1968; Chwn., Whitley County Republican Cttee., 1968-72; Mem., Kentucky State Republican Central Cttee., 1968-; Republican National Committeewoman, Kentucky, 1968-; Conference Chwn., Kentucky National Republican Women's Conference, DC, 1969; Mem., Advisors Cncl., Corbin, Kentucky, 1969-70; Mem., DO Cttee., Republican National Cttee., 1969-72; Mem., Rule 29,

1973-75, Exec. Cttee., 1976-80 and Rules Cttee., 1977-; Co-Chwn., Urban Renewal and Community Development Agency, Corbin, 1970-73; Mem., Republican National Cttee. Adivisory Cncl. General Govt., 1977-; Mem., Republican National Site Selection Cttee., 1981-82; Mem., Federal Cncl. on Aging, 1982-87; Vice-Chwn., Republican National Cttee., 1984-; Sec. and Treasurer, National Republican Inst. for Internal Affairs, 1984-86; Kentucky Co-Chwn. and 5th District Chwn., Bush for President Campaign, National Steering Cttee., 1987-; *memberships:* Pres., Corbin Republican Women's Club, 1968; Second Vice-Pres., Kentucky Federation Republican Women's Club, 1968-70; Advisory Cttee., Assn. of Degree Nursing Program, Cumberland College, 1973-; Board Mem., Univ. of Kentucky Centre for Aging Foundation, 1987; Women's Auxillery to Southern and Kentucky Medical Assns.; Women's Auxillary to Whitley County Medical Society; Business and Professional Women Assn; *professional career:* medical technologist, 1950-53; Pres., Health Systems Inc., Corbin, Kentucky; Pres., Barton and Asscs. Inc., Hazard Nursing Home Inc., Barbourville Nursing Home Inc., Corbin Nursing Nursing Home Inc., Harlan Nursing Home Inc., and Knott County Nuring Home Inc.; Dir. and Mem., Exec. Cttee., Greensburg Deposit Bank, 1987-; Chwn., Green County Bancorp Inc., 1987; *honours and awards:* Kentucky College, 1968; PTA Life Mem. Award; Kentucky Republican Woman of the Year, 1968-69; Better Life Award, Kentucky Assn. of Health Care Facilities, 1981; State Woman of Achievement, Kentucky Business and Professional Women's Club, 1982 and 1983; Medal of Honour Cumberland College, 1988; *office address:* Ms Nelda Lambert Barton, 1311 Seventh Street Road, Corbin, Kentucky 40701, USA.

LANDRY, Monique; Canadian, Minister of State for Indian Affairs and Northern Development; *born:* 25 December 1937, Montreal, Canada; *married:* Jean-Guy Landry; *children:* four; *education:* Univ. of Montreal; *party:* Progressive Conservative Party (PCP); *political career:* Mem. of House of Commons, 1984-; Mem. of several Inter-Parl. Assns.; former Parl. Sec. to the Sec. of State and the Minister of Int. Trade; Minister for Indian Affairs and Northern Development 1986-; former Mem., Standing Cttee. on Communications and Culture, joint Cttee. on Official Languages Policy and Programs and the Standing Cttee. on Finance, Trade and Economic Affairs, Canada-Europe Parl. Assn., Canada-France Inter-Parl. Assn., Canada-NATO Parl. Assn; *office address:* Ms Monique Landry, CIDA, 200 du Portage, 12th Floor, Hull, Quebec, Canada.

LANGFORD, Lorraine; American, Nebraska State Senator; *born:* 1 November 1923, Monroe, Nebraska, USA; *married:* Jack Langford, 1946; *children:* three; *education:* Univ. of Nebraska; Univ. of Southern California; *political career:* Nebraska State Senator; Mem., State Senate Appropriations Cttee;

memberships: National Board of Republican Women; *office address:* Mrs Lorraine Langford, 1717 W. 26th Street, Kearney, Nebraska 68847, USA.

LANGOWSKA, Grazyna Miroslawa; Polish, Member of the Sejm; *office address:* Ms Grazyna Miroslawa Langowska, Sejm PRI, ul. Wiejska 4/6/8, 00-489 Warsaw, Poland; *phone:* (22) 28 70 01; 28 40 31.

LANING-BOERSEMA, Dr. Frouwke J.; Dutch, Member of the Second Chamber; *born:* 5 July 1937, Groningen, Netherlands; *education:* State Univ. Groningen, medicine; *party:* Christen Democratisch Appel (CDA, Christian Democratic Appeal); *politica. career:* Mem. party council, CDA, 1977-82; Mem. of Second Chamber, 1982-; *professional career:* General Practitioner; pres. Regional Discussion menta Handicapped in Noord-Holland, Association's Heeren-Loo (caring for mentally handicapped persons); *clubs.* pres. Regional Discussion Mental Handicapped in Noord-Holland, Association 's Heeren-Loo (caring for mentally handicapped persons); *private address* Plantsoenstraat 11, 1781 JP Den Helder, the Netherlands; *office address:* Dr. Frouwke Laning-Boersema, Tweede Kamer der Staaten-Generaal, Binnenhof 1A, Postbus 20018, The Hague Netherlands.

LARIMER, Janet McMaster; American, Member o the Republican National Cttee., Wyoming; *born:* 2 April 1942, Youngstown, Ohio, USA; *parents:* Pau Douglas McMaster and Jessie McMaster (née Hunter) *married:* Jack Austin Larimer, 1966; *children:* Dougla Austin, Amy Elizabeth; *religion:* Methodist; *education* Bowling Green State Univ., Ohio, BS, 1964; *party* Republican Party; *political career:* Mem., Republicar Nat. Cttee., Wyoming, 1988-; *professional career* teacher, Ohio, 1964-71; *office address:* Ms Jane Larimer, P.O. Box 610, Teton Village, Wyoming 83025 USA.

LARSEN, Ester; Danish, Minister for Health; *party* Venstre (Liberal Party)); *office address:* Ministry o Health, Amaliegade 13, 1256 Copenhagen K, Denmark

LATASI, Naama; , Minister of Health, Education an Community Services; *office address:* Ms Naama Latas Ministry of Social Services, Vaiaku, Funafuti atoll Tuvalu; *phone:* 774 4800 tv comm.

LAU, Hon. Miriam Kin-Yee; Hong Kong, Member o the Legislative Council; *born:* 27 April 1947, China *married:* Alfred Lau Tit-Hon; *children:* one; *religion* Catholic; *education:* Univ. of Hong Kong, BA (Hons.) *political career:* Mem., Legislative Cncl; *membership.* Hon. Sec., Hong Kong Federation of Women Lawyer Mem., Regional Cncl. of Hong Kong; Mem., Lega

Practitioners Disciplinary Cttee; *professional career:* Solicitor of Supreme Courts of Hong Kong and England; Barrister and Solicitor of Supreme Court of Victoria; Notary Public, Hong Kong; *clubs:* Zonta Club of Kowloon; *office address:* The Hon. Mrs Miriam Lau, The Legislative Council, Government House, Hong Kong.

LAUDONIU, Diamanta; Romanian, Secretary of the Leading Committee of the National Council for Science and Technology; *party:* Romanian Communist Party (RCP); *political career:* candidate Mem., RCP Central Cttee., 1979-84; Mem., Bureau of the Bucharest Municipal Party Cttee., 1984; full Mem., RCP Central Cttee., 1984-; Vice-Chairperson, Women's Nat. Cncl., 1985-; Mem., State Cncl., 1985-; Mem., Exec. Bureau, Nat. Cncl. of Working People, 1986-; *professional career:* chemical engineer; Sec., Basic Party Organisation, Institute for Chemical Research, 1967; Dir., Enterprise for Research and Production of Semi-conductors, 1982; *honours and awards:* Order of Labour Second Class, 1967; Order of Labour, First Class, 1983; *office address:* Ms Diamanta Laudoniu, National Council for Science and Technology, Piata Victoriei nr. 1, Bucharest, Romania.

LAURA, Maria (Maria Laura Sales Pinheiro); Brazilian, Federal Deputy for the Federal District Deputy for the Federal District, 1991-95; *born:* 20 August 1941, Jaguaribe; *parents:* Ataliba Pinheiro and Eglantina Sales Pinheiro; *married:* Paulo Henrique Veiga; *children:* Alexandre, Manuela, Augusto, Henrique; *education:* UFC, Fortaleza, social services, 1962-65; UFPE, Recife, post-grad. studies in sociology; *party:* Partido dos Trabalhadores (PT, Independent Labour Party); *political career:* politically active since 1960s, participated in the resistance movement against military govts.; former welfare assistant, Sec. for Health, Ceara State; prof., Federal Univ. of Caera, 1967 and Univ. of Brasilia, 1989; Pres., Union of Public Service Workers of the Federal District; Federal Deputy for the Federal District, 1991-95; *professional career:* professor, welfare assistant and sociologist; *office address:* Ms Maria Laura, Chamber of Deputies, Praça dos 3 Poderes, Ed. Principal, 70160 Brasilia, DF, Brazil; *phone:* (61) 225 2885.

LAUREL-TRINIDAD, Hon. Milagros; Filipino, Congresswoman; *born:* 5 July 1941, Manila, The Philippines; *parents:* Jose B. Laurel Jr; *married:* Noel Trinidad; *children:* Patricia Marie, Noel Gerard, Michael Frederick; *education:* Maryknoll College, AB Major, Business Administration; *political career:* Congresswoman; *interests:* tourism, social services, youth development; *office address:* The Hon. Ms Milagros Laurel-Trinidad, The Congress of the Philippines - House of Representatives, Batasang Pambansa Bldg., Quezon City, Manila, The Philippines.

LAURIEN, Dr. Hanna-Renate; German, President of the Berlin Parliament; *born:* 15 April 1928, Danzig; *parents:* Dr. Helmut Laurien and Charlotte Laurien (née Feuerabend); *religion:* Catholic; *languages:* English, some French; *education:* High School leaving examination, 1946; Berlin, German Studies, British Studies, Slavic Studies, Philosophy; Berlin, Degree and Ph.D., 1951; *party:* Christlich Demokratische Union (CDU, Christian Democratic Union); *political career:* candidate, Bundestag, 1969; Secretary of State, Rhineland-Palatinate, 1971-76; Minister of Culture, Rhineland-Palatinate, 1976-81; Senator, Berlin, 1981-89; Mayor and Dep. Governing Mayor, Berlin, 1986-89; Senator for School, Vocational Training and Sports, Berlin; Dep. Federal Chmn., CDU; Pres. of the Berlin Parliament, 1991-; *professional career:* Schools service to 1957; Section Dir. for German; Dir., Königin-Luise School, Cologne; Chmn., Assn. of Rhine School Directors, 1967-70; *honours and awards:* Hermann-Vop Prize, German Orchestra Assn., 1979; Grand Cross of the Order of Merit of the Federal Republic of Germany, 1981; *publications:* Berufliche Bildung, 1973; Der Kampf um die Köpfe in: Neue Bildungspolitik; Co-Editor, Klingende Anthologie Fernsehserie: Der Weg zum Abitur, 1969; Nicht Ja und nicht Amen, 1984; Pastoral für Randchristen, 1985 Gedankengänge, 1988; *recreations:* theology, literature, cooking; *private address:* Dillgesstr. 4, 1 Berlin 46, Germany; *office address:* Dr. Hanna-Renate Laurien, Rathaus Schoneburg, 1 Berlin 62, Germany.

LAURILA, Ritva Tellervo (neé Toivonen); Finnish, Member of the Eduskunta; *born:* 13 April 1932, Helsinki, Finland; *parents:* Erik Olavi Toivonen and Anni Alina Toivonen (née Ring); *married:* The late Erkki Olavi Laurila, 1962; *children:* Tero, Erja; *education:* Helsinki Univ., M.A., 1953; Further Studies at the Univ. of Missouri, USA, 1955-56; *party:* Kansallinen Kokoomus (KoK, National Coalition Party); *political career:* Mem., Helsinki City Cncl., 1973-; Chmn., Helsinki City Hospital Board, 1973-78; mem., Metropolitan District Deleg. for Co-operation, 1973-80; Advisory Cttee., State Police Dept., 1974-87; Chmn., Kokoomus Party Group, 1987-90; Chmn., Lastenlinna Hospital Exec. Cttee., 1977-; mem., Helsinki City Theatre Admin. Board., 1977-, Chmn., 1982-85, Vice-Chmn., 1985-; mem. of Eduskunta, 1978-; mem., Admin. Cncl., Helsinki Co-op., 1978-, Vice-Chmn., 1980-; mem., Group of Representatives, Helsinki Telephone Co., 1979-; Admin. Cncl., Yleisradio, 1979-; Parly. Law Cttee. for Radio and TV, 1980-84; Admin. Cncl., SKOP (Bank), 1981-; mem., Presidential Electorate, 1982 and 1988; Chmn., Assn. of Kokoomus Women, 1986-; *professional career:* Journalist, Ilta-Sanomat (newspaper), 1952 and 1954-55; Teacher of Finnish and History, Apollo Co-ed.

Grammar School, 1953-55; PR-officer, SPR (Finnish Red Cross), 1959-61; Journalist, Sub-Editor, Man. Editor and Editor-in-Chief, Kotilääkäri (Magazine on Health Care), 1961-79; *office address:* Ms Ritva Laurila, Eduskunta, 00102 Helsinki, Finland.

LAURISTIN, Marju; Soviet, Member of the Council of the Union; *born:* 1940, Estonia; *education:* grad., Tartu State Univ., Philology; *party:* Communist Party of the Soviet Union; *political career:* active in Estonian New Left Movement during 1960's; founding Mem. and leading theoretician, Popular Front of Estonia; Mem., Supreme Soviet Exec. Cttee.; Mem., Congress of People's Deps. Drafting Commission and the Commission on the Molotov-Ribbentrop Pact; Mem., Cncl. of the Union's Commissions on Labour, Prices and Social Policy; Mem., MDG (Inter-regional Group of Deps.); *interests:* Estonian sovereignty and economic independence; *professional career:* head of Journalism Dept., Tartu State Univ., Estonia; *office address:* Ms Marju Lauristin, Tartu State University, 202400 Estonian SSR, Tartu, Ülikooli 18, Estonia, USSR.

LAUSTSEN, Agnete; Danish, Minister of Housing; *born:* 25 September 1935, Copenhagen, Denmark; *parents:* Otto Laustsen and Else Laustsen; *education:* N. Zahles School, 1954; Copenhagen Univ., Bachelor of Laws, 1961; *party:* Konservative Folkeparti (Conservative Party), 1979; *political career:* Sec. then Prinicipal, Ministry of the Interior; Chairman of the board for social politics, parliament, 1983-87; candidate of the party in Raadhuskredsen, 1964, in Christioanshavn, 1971, in Hvidovre, 1973; President of the Danish section of European Union of Women, 1972; member of Nordic Council, 1983; Minister of Health, 1987-88; Minister of Housing and Building, 1988-; *professional career:* office manager to the Consumers' Ombudsman, 1977-; *publications:* several feature articles in Danish and foreign newpapers and magazines; *clubs:* Chairman of Council for Students, studying political science and law, 1958-60; council for Union of Lawyers, 1958-60; committee for the Culture Foundation of Copenhagen City Council, 1970-; committee of Museum of Thorvaldsen, 1972-80; committee for Ny Carlsberg Glyptotek, 1986-87; President of the Danish section in the European Women's Union and member of the union's presidium, 1975-81; *private address:* Frederiksholms Kanal 20, 1220 Copenhagen K, Denmark; *office address:* Ms Agnete Laustsen, Ministry of Housing, H. C. Andersens Boulevard 40, 1553 Copenhagen V, Denmark.

LAVOIE-ROUX, Thérèse; Canadian, Senator; *born:* 12 March 1928, Rivière-du-Loup; *married:* Lucien Lavoie-Roux; *children:* Françoise, Elisabeth, Jacques, Claude; *education:* Univ. of Montreal, BA, 1984, MA, 1951; *party:* Progressive Conservatives; *political career:* Mem., Quebec Nat. Assembly, 1976, 1981, 1985;

Minister of Health and Social Services, Bourassa Cabinet, 1985-89; *professional career:* social worker, Montreal Children's Hospital; therapist; Prof. and Lecturer, Univ. of Montreal; Board Mem. and Chairperson, Home Care Cttee., Montreal Assn. for the Mentally Retarded; former Treasurer, Quebec Assn. of Social Workers; former Dir., Institute Beausejour for Emotionally Disturbed Children; former Dir., Cncl. on Social Work and American Assn. on Mental Deficiency and Quebec Cncl. for Exceptional Children; Pres., Catholic School Board of Montreal; *honours and awards:* Woman of Achievement, Montreal YWCA, 1975; Edouard-Montpetit medal, 1987; *office address:* The Honourable Senator Thérèse Lavoie-Roux, Senate, Parliament Buildings, Wellington Street, Ottawa, Ontario K1A OA4, Canada; *phone:* (613) 992 4416.

LAWSON, Véronique; Benin, Minister of Public Health; *office address:* Ms Véronique Lawson, Ministry of Public Health, BP 882 and 883, Cotonou, Benin.

LAZAR, Maria; Romanian, Vice Chairperson of the Grand National Assembly; *party:* Romanian Communist Party (RCP); *political career:* Sec., Buzau County Party Cttee., in charge of Propoganda, and Vice-Chair, County People's Cncl., 1979-85; candidate Mem., RCP Central Cttee., 1984; First Vice-Chair, Buzau County People's Cncl., 1985; Vice-Chair, Grand Nat. Assembly, 1985-; *office address:* Ms Maria Lazar, Marea Adunare Nationala, Aleea Marii Adunari Nationale, Bucharest, Romania; *phone:* 16 21 50.

LECUIR, Marie-France; French, Deputy; *born:* 2 May 1941, Fécamp, Seine-Inférieure, France; *parents:* Léopold Soublin and Jeanne Soublin (née Cazenave); *married:* Jean Lecuir, 1962; *children:* Claire, Gilles; *education:* School at Fécamp and Paris; Sorbonne, Paris, qualified in French language and literature; secondary school teaching certificate; *party:* Parti Socialiste Unifié (PSU, Unified Socialist Party); Parti Socialiste (PS, Socialist Party); *political career:* SGEN-CFDT Trade Unionist, 1966-81; founder of the consumers' union of Pontoise, 1970; General Councillor of the Val-d'Oise, 1976-82; Town Councillor of Pontoise, 1977-82; member of the management committee and the executive board of the PS, 1979-87; elected Socialist Deputy of the Val-d'Oise, 1981, re-elected 1986 and 1988; Vice-President of the cultural, family and social affairs commission, 1981-83; Reporter of the employment budget at the National Assembly, 1982-86, 1988-91; Regional Councillor of l'Ile-de-France, 1981-86; Sec. of the National Assembly, 1986-; Mayoress of Domont, 1989; Pres., Intercommunal Union 'Plaine de France Ouest'; *professional career:* secondary school teacher at Pontoise secondary school, 1966-70 and Pontoise school, 1970-81; *private address:* 2 allée du Cheval Gris,

95330 Domont, France; *office address:* Mme. Marie-France Lecuir, Mairie du Domont, 95330 France.

LEEMANN, Ursula; Swiss, Member of the Nationalrat; *born:* 7 October 1936, Winterthur, Switzerland; *education:* MSc; *party:* Sozialdemokratische Partei der Schweiz (SDP, Social Democratic Party of Switzerland); *political career:* Mem. of the Zürich Cantonal Cncl., 1978-91; Mem. of the Nationalrat for Esslingen, replacing Dr. Hansjörg Braunschweig, Canton of Zürich, Jan. 1991-; *professional career:* biologist; *office address:* Frau Ursula Leemann, Nationalrat/Conseil National, Secretariat-General, Parlamentsgebäude, 3003 Berne, Switzerland; *phone:* Berne 619711.

LEES, Meg Heather; Australian, Senator; *born:* 19 October 1948, Burwood, New South Wales; *education:* Adelaide CAE, B.Ed.; Sydney Teacher's College, Dip. P.E; *party:* Australian Democrats; *political career:* Sec., Australian Democrats Mt. Gambier Branch, 1982-85; Branch Rep., State Cncl., Australian Democrats, 1983-86; Policy Convenor, Australian Democrats, South Australia, 1986-87, Vice-Pres., 1986-87, State Pres., 1987-89; Senator to Parliament of South Australia, under Section 15, 1990-; Mem., Senate Legislative Cttee. and General Purpose Standing Community Affairs, 1990-; Spokesperson for Australian Democrats on Arts, Sport, Tourism and Territories; Spokesperson Australian Democrats for Status of Women, 1990, for Social Security, including Retirement Income, for Community Services, including Aged Care, and for Sport and Tourism, 1990-; *professional career:* teacher; Cllr., Australian Conservation Foundation; *office address:* Ms Meg Lees, Senate, Parliament House, Room M13, Canberra, ACT 2600, Australia; *phone:* (062) 727111.

LEFLEROVA, Helena; Czechoslovakian, Member of the Presidium of the Federal Assembly CSSR; *born:* 12 October 1921, Bustehrad, Czechoslovakia; *education:* external studies, Law Faculty, Charles Univ., Prague, 1953-57; *party:* Komunistická Strana Ceskoslovenska (KSC, Communist party of Czechoslovakia); *political career:* prisoner in Nazi concentration camp, Ravensbrück, 1942-45; Chairperson, Lidice Village Nat. Cttee., 1945-48; Deputy, Nat. Assembly, 1948-; Chairperson, Lidice Village CP CSSR Cttee., 1948-54; Mem., Prague-West District Nat. Cttee., 1949-54; Staff Mem., Prague CP CSSR Regional Cttee., 1949-56; Presidium Mem, CSSR Defenders of Peace, 1951-58; Dep. Chairperson, Cttee. for Planting a Rose Garden of Friendship and Peace Between Nations in Lidice, 1952-; Dep. Chairperson, Czechoslovak Group of Interparliamentary Union, 1954-60; Mem., UNO Women's Rights Commission, 1957-; Mem., CP CSSR Central Cttee., 1958-81; Chairperson, Czechoslovak-British Parly. Group, 1958-; Chief of Section and

Presidium, Nat. Front Central Cttee., 1960-68; Chairperson, Foreign Policy Cttee., Nat. Assembly, 1960-64; Mem., Union of Fighters Against Fascism Central Cttee., 1962-69; Chairperson, CSSR Women's Cttee., 1963-67; Mem., Mid-Czech CP CSSR Regional Cttee., 1964-68; Dep. Chairperson, Presidium of Nat. Assembly, 1964-68; Dep. Chairperson, Mem. of Bureau of World Union of Democratic Women, 1964-; Mem., Legal Commission, CP CSSR Central Cttee., 1965-69; Chairperson, Presidium Mem., Union of Czechoslovak Women Central Cttee., 1967-68; Mem., Presidium of Federal Assembly, 1981; Mem., Chamber of People of Federal Assembly CSSR, 1981-85; *professional career:* worked in Lidice, 1940-42; *honours and awards:* for Merit - 10 years People's Militia First Class, 1958; Order of the Republic, 1961; Commemoration Medal, 20th Anniversary of the Liberation of the CSSR, 1965; *office address:* Ms Helena Leflerova, Federální Shromázdení, Vinohradská 1, 110 02 Prague 1, Czechoslovaia; *phone:* (02) 2103.

LEMKE-SCHULTE, Eva-Maria; German, Deputy Member of the Bundesrat; *born:* 16 OCTOBER 1948; *party:* Sozialdemokratische Partei Deutschlands (SPD, Social Democratic Party of Germany); *political career:* mem. of Bürgerschaft, Bremen since 1979; Senator for Environmental Protection since 1984; Senator for Environmental Protection and Town Development, Free and Hanseatic City of Bremen; mem. of Bundesrat, 1984-; *office address:* Frau Eva-Maria Lemke-Schulte, Bundesrat, 5300 Bonn 1, West Germany.

LENZ, Marlene; German, Member of the European Parliament; *born:* 4 July 1932, Berlin, Germany; *parents:* Dr. Otto Lenz and Marieliese Lenz (née Pohl); *religion:* Roman Catholic; *languages:* English, French; *education:* Secondary education, matriculation, Munich; Studies in Heidelberg, 1951-53; *party:* Christlich Demokratische Union (CDU, Christian Democratic Union), 1957; Parti Populaire Européen (PPE, European People's Party); *political career:* Mem., Cabinet of Jean Rey, Commission of the EC, 1957; Mem., CDU Women's Association, Bonn, 1963-72; Sec.-Gen., European Union of Women, 1967-73, Pres. of Political Cttee., 1981-; scientific assistant, Bundestag research cttee. on Women and Society, 1977-79; co-founder, Christian Union of Democratic Women, 1978, current mem. of management cttee.; Pres., CDU/CSU European Women Section, 1979-; MEP, 1979-, Pres., Cttee. for Women's Rights, European Parl., 1984-87; *interests:* human rights, Latin America, women's issues; *professional career:* contributor/associate, various European organisations in Paris and Bonn, 1954-56; *honours and awards:* Bundesverdienstkreuz (First Class), 1990; *publications:* Der Weg der Frau in die Politik, 6 editions, Konrad-Adenauer-Stiftung, 1988; *private address:* Burgstraße 102, 5300 Bonn 2, Germany; *office address:* Frau Marlene Lenz, European

141

Parliament, Centre Européen, Plateau de Kirchberg, BP 2929, Luxembourg.

LERKSAMRAN, Lalita; Thai, Member of the House of Representatives; *office address:* Ms Lalita Lerksamran, House of Representatives, U-Thong Nai Road, Bangkok 10300, Thailand; *phone:* (02) 2826181 to 99.

LESTOR, Joan; British, Member of Parliament; *born:* 13 November 1931; *parents:* the late Charles Lestor and Etty Lestor; *children:* one s., one d. (adopted); *education:* Teacher Training College; London University; *party:* Labour Party; *political career:* Member of Parliament for Eton and Slough, 1966-83, and for Eccles, 1987-; Parliamentary Under Sec., Dept. of Education and Science, 1969-70; Under Sec. of State, Foreign and Commonwealth Office, 1974-75; Under Sec. of State, Dept. of Education and Science, 1975-76; mem., Labour Party National Exec. Cttee., 1968; Labour Party Chmn., 1977-78; Head, Lambeth London Borough Cncl. Police Unit, 1984-85; Dir., Trade Unions Child Care Project, 1986-87; Opposition Spokesperson for Development and Co-operation, 1988-; *interests:* education; employment; foreign affairs; race relations; *professional career:* Teacher, 1952-59; ran kindergarten, 1959-68; Chmn., Defence for Children International, UK Branch; *recreations:* playing with children; studying animals; theatre; *office address:* Ms Joan Lestor, House of Commons, London SW1A OAA.

LEUNG, Hon. Wai-Tung; Hong Kong, Member of the Legislative Council; *born:* --/01/46 Hong Kong; *married:* Leong Mai; *education:* Belilios Public School; Univ. of Hong Kong, BA (Hons.), Geography and Geology; Univ. of Hong Kong, M. Phil., Urban Geography; *political career:* mem., Hong Kong Housing Authority; mem., Special Cttee. on Clearance of Kowloon Walled City; mem., Land Development Corporation; Adviser, Education Cttee., Hong Kong Institute of Planners; mem., Broadcasting Authority; *professional career:* lecturer, Department of Geography and Geology, Univ. of Hong Kong; *office address:* The Hon. Ms Wai-Tung Leung, The Legislative Council, Government House, Hong Kong.

LEUTENEGGER-OBERHOLZER, Susanne; Swiss, Member of the Nationalrat; *born:* Chur, Graubünden, Switzerland; *parents:* Jean Leutenegger and Gertrud (née Mayrhuber); *married:* Beat Oberholzer; *education:* Schools in Chur; Univ. of Basel, Political Economy; *political career:* Cllr., Allschwill Residents Cncl., 1980-84; Constitutional Cllr., Basel-Landschaft's Cantonal Cncl., 1979-84; Cllr., Cantonal Cncl., 1983; mem. of Nationalrat, 1987-; *professional career:* Economic Editor, 'National Zeitung'; Departmental Director, Wholesale Distribution, 1973-76; *private address:* Parkallee 30, 4123 Allschwil, Switzerland; *office*

address: Frau Susanne Leutenegger-Oberholzer, Nationalrat/Conseil National, Secretariat-General, Parlamentsgebäude, 3003 Berne, Switzerland.

LEVI BALDINI, Natalia (Natalia Ginsburg); Italian, Deputy; *born:* 14 July 1916, Palermo; *party:* Independent Left Parly. Group; *political career:* Deputy, Turin-Novara-Vercelli, 1983, as independent on PCI lists; mem. Cttee. on Affairs of the Presidency of the Council, Internal and Religious Affairs; Public Organisations; re-elected Deputy, Perugia-Terni-Rieti, 1987; mem. Cttee. on Environment, Land and Public Works; *professional career:* writer, journalist, editorial consultant; *publications:* numerous novels; *office address:* Ms Natalia Levi Baldini, Camera dei Deputati, Montecitorio, 00186 Rome, Italy.

LEYSEN, Anna; Belgian, Member of the Chamber of Representatives; *born:* 16 May 1942, Turnhout; *education:* Handelshogeschool (commercial university), Antwerp, BSc commercial and consular sciences, 1960-64; *party:* Christelijke Volkspartij (CVP, Christian Social Party); *political career:* alderman of education, research, development cooperation and economy, Turnhout, 1977-82; alderman of education, town and country planning, planning, building and development policy, development cooperation and self development, Turnhout, 1983-88; Deputy for Turnhout district, 1988-; local councillor, chair of CVP party in the council, Turnhout, 1988-; member, Chamber of Reps. commissions on education, scientific policy and culture, public health, the environment and families, employment and social policy, naturalisation; member, Flemish council commissions on education, welfare, culture, the media; district chair, CVP Vrouw en Maatschappij (women and society); *professional career:* teacher, handelsvakken (commercial subjects), Sint-Lutgardisinstituut (Saint Lutgard Institute), Turnhout, 1964-86; deputy chair, Centrum voor Informatie van de Provincies Antwerpen en Limburg (CIPAL) (Centre for Information for the Provinces Antwerp and Limburg), 1980-; *private address:* de Merodelei 30-40, 2300 Turnhout, Belgium; *office address:* Ms Anna Leysen, Kamer van Volksvertegenwoordigers, Palais de la Nation, Place de la Nation 2, 1000 Brussels, Belgium.

LIAO WENHAI; Chinese, Alternate Member of the Chinese Communist Party 13th Central Committee; *party:* Chinese Communist Party; *political career:* Alternate mem., Chinese CCP 13th Central Cttee., 1987-; *professional career:* Vice-Pres., PLA General Hospital, 1986-; Major-General, 1988-; *office address:* Liao Wenhai, The Communist Party of China, Beijing, The People's Republic of China.

LIENEMANN, Marie-Noëlle Thérèse; French, Deputy; *born:* 12 July 1951, Belfort; *parents:* Pierre Lienemann and Françoise Lienemann (née Géhant);

married: Patrice Finel, 1976; *children:* Marianne, Olivier; *education:* Belfort Girls' College; Fustel-de-Coulanges College, Massy; Lakanal College, Sceaux; Fénelon College, Paris; Higher School of Technical Education; Univ. of Paris-Orsay; Higher diploma in Physical Chemistry; Certificate of Teaching Skills in Second Degrees in Physical Sciences; *party:* Parti Socialiste (PS, Socialist Party); *political career:* National Sec., Socialist Students, 1973; Deputy Mayor of Massy, 1977-; member of Management Cttee., 1978, Executive Office, 1981 and Deputy National Sec., 1983, Socialist Party; County Councillor, Essonne, 1979-; MEP, Socialists for Europe Group, 1984-88; elected Socialist Deputy for Essonne, 1988; *professional career:* Physics teacher, 1978-83; *publications:* Pour réussir à gauche, 1983 (co-author under the pseudonym of Les Gracques); *recreations:* Knitting, cinema; *private address:* 2 bis rue des Anglais, 91300 Massy, France; *office address:* Mme. Marie-Noëlle Lienemann, L'Assemblée Nationale, 126 rue de L'Université, 75355 Paris, France.

LIEVANO de MARQUEZ, Mirna; El Salvador, Minister for Planning and Co-ordination of Economic and Social Development; *office address:* Ms Mirna Lievano de Marquez, Ministry of Planning, Casa Presidencial, San Salvador, El Salvador.

LI HUIFEN; Chinese, Alternate Member of the Chinese Communist Party 13th Central Committee; *born:* 1941; *education:* Qinghua Univ; *party:* Chinese Communist Party; *political career:* Alternate mem., Chinese CCP 12th and 13th Central Cttees., 1982-; Vice-Mayor, Tianjin Municipality, 1988-; *professional career:* Deputy Manager and Chief Engineer, Tianjin Radio Equipment Joint Company, 1982-; *office address:* Li Huifen, The Communist Party of China, Beijing, The People's Republic of China.

LI LANQING; Chinese, Vice Minister of Foreign Economic Relations and Trade; *born:* 1932; *education:* Fudan Univ., Business Administration; *party:* Chinese Communist Party; *political career:* Dir., Administration of Foreign Capital, Min. of Foreign Economic Relations and Trade, 1981-83; Vice-Mayor, Tianjin Municipality, 1983-86; Vice-Minister, Min., of Foreign Economic Relations and Trade, 1986-; Alternate mem., Chinese CCP 13th Central Cttee., 1987-; *office address:* Li Lanqing, Ministry of Foreign Economic Relations and Trade, 2 Changan East Road, Beijing, People's Republic of China; *phone:* 553031; 556631.

LIM, Narzalina; Filipino, Minister of Tourism; *office address:* Ms Narzalina Lim, Department of Tourism, DOT Building, T.M. Kalaw St, Rizal Park, POB 3451, Metro Manila, The Philippines.

LINDSTROM, Beth; American, Executive Director of the Massachusetts Republican State Committee; *born:* 26 August 1961, West Palm Beach, Florida, USA; *parents:* Richard Carl Lindstrom and Vesta Louise Lindstrom (née Helgesen); *married:* Raymond Martin Murphy, 1989; *public role of spouse:* Attorney; *religion:* Congregational; *languages:* English; *education:* Univ. of Connecticut, BA communication science, 1983; *party:* Republican Party, 1979; *political career:* Sec., Massachusetts Federation of Republican Women, 1988-90; Sec., Convention Planning Cttee., 1988; delegate liaison National Convention, 1990; State Party Convention Planner, 1990; Mem., State Party Targeting Cttee., 1990; Exec. Dir., Massachusetts Republican State Cttee; *memberships:* Massachusetts Women's Political Caucus; *recreations:* skiing, golf; *office address:* Ms Beth Lindstrom, #9 Galem Street, Suite 329, Watertown 02172, Massachusetts, USA.

LINFOOT SHANNON, Marylin; American, Member of the Republican National Committee of Oregon; *born:* 7 September 1941, La Grande, Oregon, USA; *parents:* Delmer Burl Linfoot and Ruth Linfoot (née Kube); *married:* Albert Allen Shannon, 1964; *children:* Delmer Allen, William Linfoot, Christine Alisa; *religion:* Assembly of God; *education:* Northwest College, 1959-60; Central Washington Univ., BA, 1972; *party:* Republican Party; *political career:* precinct Cttee. Mem., Clackamas County and Kittitas County Republican Central Cttees., 1978-; Mem., Oregon State Republican Central and Exec. Cttees., 1984-; Chwn., Marion County Republican Central Cttee., 1986-; Mem., Republican National Cttee., Oregon, 1988-; *professional career:* owner/designer, Make-N-Take Pattern Co., 1982; Field Rep., US CofC; *private address:* 231 NE Ginsberg Drive, Estacada, Oregon 97023, USA; *office address:* Mrs Marylin Linfoot Shannon, 3603 Aldous Avenue S, Salem, Oregon 97302, USA.

LIN LIYUN; Chinese, Member of the Chinese Communist Party 13th Central Committee; *born:* 1933, Taiwan, Taizhong City; *party:* Chinese Communist Party; *political career:* Mem., 4th, 5th, 6th, 7th National People's Congress for Taiwan; Mem., Standing Cttee.; Mem., CCP 10th, 11th, 12th, 13th Central Cttees., 1973-; *office address:* Lin Liyun, The Communist Party of China, Beijing, The People's Republic of China.

LINZIN-VANDERSPEETEN, Anne-Marie; Belgian, Secretary of State for Europe 1992; *born:* 5 January 1949, Huy; *education:* Univ. of Liège, Economic Science, 1968-71; *political career:* Deputy Mayor, Ben-Ahin, 1971-76; Minister of Economic Affairs, 1972-73; mem. of Simonet's Cabinet, Commission for Community, 1973-77; mem. of Cabinet of Foreign Affairs, 1977-79; MEP, 1979-88; Deputy Mayor of Huy, 1980-82; Mayor of Huy, 1983; mem. of Walloon Cttee. for Union of Towns; Sec. of State for Europe

1992, May 1988-; *professional career:* Trainee, FNRS, 1971; lecturer, University of Liège; mem. of Permanent Executive, Provincial Society of Industrialisation, Liège; *office address:* Mme. Anne-Marie Linzin-Vanderspeeten, 61 rue de la Régence, 1000 Brussels, Belgium.

LI SHUZHENG; Chinese, Alternate Member of the Chinese Communist Party 13th Central Committee; *born:* 1930; *party:* Chinese Communist Party; *political career:* Deputy Dir., Foreign Relations Dept., Communist Youth League, 1962-67; Alternate Sec., Communist Youth League, 1964-67; Sec., Women's Federation, 1978-80; bureau dir., International Liaison Dept., Chinese CCP Central Cttee., 1980-81; Deputy Dir., International Liaison Dept., Chinese Central Cttee., 1981-; Alternate mem., Chinese CCP 12th and 13th Central Cttees., 1982-; *office address:* Li Shuzheng, The Communist Party of China, Beijing, The People's Republic of China.

LISZCZ, Prof. Teresa; Polish, Secretary of State at the Chancellery of the President; *born:* 26 May 1944, Choiny, Poland; *parents:* Leon Malinowski and Janina Augustyniak (née Pezda); *married:* Leszek Jan Liszcz, 1970; *public role of spouse:* law adviser to Solidarity; *religion:* Roman Catholic; *languages:* Polish, German, Russian; *education:* Marie Curie Sklodowska (MCS) Univ., Lublin, Poland, Master of Law, 1968, Ph.D., Law, 1974; *party:* Porozumienie Centrum (Centre Alliance); *political career:* parliament Dep., 1989; Sec.-of-State at the Chancellery of the Pres., 1991-; *interests:* constitutional social rights, village community problems; *memberships:* Lubelskie Towarzystwo Naukowe, (Lublin Scientific Assn.); *professional career:* prof. of law, Univ. of Lodz, 1987; *honours and awards:* Zloty Krzyz Zaslugi, (Golden Cross of Merit), 1989; *private address:* 20-631 Lublin, Pana Balcera 1 Apt. 201, Poland; *office address:* Prof. Teresa Liszcz, Sejm PRI, ul. Wiejska 4/6/8, 00-489 Warsaw, Poland; *phone:* (22) 28 70 01; 28 40 31.

LITVAJOVA, Dr. Elena; Czechoslovakian, Deputy to Slovak National Council; *born:* 8 June 1924, Uhrovec, Topolcany district, Czechoslovakia; *education:* Higher School of Political Sciences of Central Cttee. of CP CSSR; Dr. of Political Science, 1967; *party:* Komunistická Strana Ceskoslovenska (KSC, Communist party of Czechoslovakia); *political career:* illegal party activist, 1943-44; took part in Slovak Uprising as Mem. Jan Zizka von Trocnov Partisan Brigade and Vpred (Forward) Partisan Brigade, 1944-45; Dep. Chairperson, Constitutional Law Cttee., People's Chamber of Federal Assembly CSSR, 1969-71; Chairperson, Central Cttee., Slovak Union of Women, 1970-; Mem., Presidium of Central Cttee., Slovak Nat. Front, 1972-; Mem., Central Cttee. and of Presidium, CP of Slovakia, 1971-; Dep., Slovak Nat. Cncl., 1971-,

Mem., Presidium, 1971-; First Dep. Chairperson, Czechoslovak Union of Women, 1974-, Mem., Presidium and Sec., 1979-; *professional career:* factory worker, 1942-43; *honours and awards:* Order of 25th February Second Class, 1949; Order of Slovak Nat. Uprising Second Class, 1949; CSSR Medal for Bravery in the Face of the Enemy 1949; CSSR Military Medal for Merit, 1950; USSR Medal for Victory over Germany, 1951; For Services in the Reconstruction, 1955; For Merit 10 Years People's Militia, 1958; Order of Labour, 1969; USSR Order of Red Star, 1970; Order of Victorious February, 1973; Medal for Victory over Fascism First Class, 1974; Order of the Republic, 1984; Order of the Red Star (USSR), 1970; *office address:* Dr. Elena Litvajova, Slavenská národná rada, Októbrové nám. 12, 800 00 Bratislava, Czechoslovakia; *phone:* (07) 311500.

LIU YUJIE; Chinese, Alternate Member of the Chinese Communist Party 13th Central Committee; *party:* Chinese Communist Party; *political career:* Sec., Communist Youth League, Henan Province, 1979-85; Alternate mem., Chinese CCP 12th and 13th Central Cttees., 1982-; Vice-Governor, Henan Province, 1986-; *office address:* Liu Yujie, The Communist Party of China, Beijing, The People's Republic of China.

LLEWELYN-DAVIES OF HASTOE, Baroness (cr. 1967, Life Peer) Patricia Liewwlyn-Davies; British, Member of the House of Lords; *born:* 16 July 1915; *parents:* the late Charles Percy Parry; *married:* Richard Llewelyn-Davies, 1943; *children:* three d; *education:* Liverpool College, Huyton; Girton College, Cambridge; *party:* Labour Party; *political career:* Parly. candidate, 1951-60; Sec., Lab. Parly. Assn., 1960; House of Lords, 1967-; Baroness-in-Waiting, 1969; Chief Opposition Whip, 1973-74; Government Chief Whip and Capt. Hon. Corps. of Gentlemen at Arms, 1974-79; PC, 1975-; Chmn., Women's Nat. Commission, 1976-79; Opposition Chief Whip, 1979-82; Principal Dep. Chmn. of Cttees., 1982-86; Chmn., EC Select Cttee., 1982-86; *professional career:* Civil servant, 1940-51; mem., Board of Governors, Great Ormond Street Hospital for Sick Children, 1955-67, and Chmn., 1967-69; Dir., Africa Educational Trust, 1960-69, and trustee, 1969-74; Chmn., Women's Nat. Cancer Control Campaign, 1972-74; *honours and awards:* Hon. Fellow, Girton College, Cambridge, 1978; *private address:* Flat 15, 9-11 Belsize Grove, London NW3 4UU, UK; *office address:* Baroness Llewelyn-Davies of Hartoe, House of Lords, London SW1A 0PW.

LLORCA VILAPLANA, Carmen; Spanish, Member of the European Parliament; *born:* 29 November 1921, Alcoy/Alicante, Spain; *education:* Complutense Univ. Madrid, doctorate in history; *party:* European People's Party (PPE, Christian Democratic Group); *political career:* Deputy for Madrid, 1982-86; MEP, 1986-;

professional career: prof. of contemporary history, Complutense Univ. of Madrid; dir., National Office of Tourism in Milan, Italy; first woman Pres., Athenaeum of Madrid; *honours and awards:* Lady's Ribbon of Civil Merit; Order of Arts and Letters, France; *publications:* El Mascal Bazaine en Madrid, 1950; Isabel II y su tiempo, 1956; Emilio Castelar precursor de la democracia Cristiana, 1966; El sistema, 1970; Diario de un viaje a la China de Mao, 1978; las mughres de los dictadores, 1978; Llamadme Evita, 1980; Los Discursos de la Corona en las Cortes, 1983; Del apertivismo al cambio: mi testimonio, 1985; Parlamentarismo español, 1986; *office address:* Ms CArmen Llorca Vilaplana, European Parliament, Centre Européen, Plateau de Kirchberg, BP 2929, Luxembourg.

LLOYD, Marilyn; American, US Representative for Tennessee; *born:* 3 January 1929, Fort Smith, Arkansas, USA; *married:* Dr. Robert Fowler, 1991; *public role of spouse:* retired Surgeon General and Colonel, Tennessee National Guard; *children:* Morty, Nancy, Mari, Travis; *religion:* Church of Christ; *education:* Shorter College; *party:* Democratic Party; *political career:* US Rep., District 3, Tennessee, 1975-; Mem., Congressional Textile Caucus; *professional career:* former owner WTTI Radio Station; *office address:* Ms Marilyn Lloyd, 2266 Rayburn House Office Building, Washington DC, 20515, USA.

LLOYD-JONES, Jean; American, Iowa State Senator; *born:* 14 October 1929, Washington DC, USA; *parents:* John Hall and Lucille Hall (née Thurston); *married:* Richard Lloyd Jones, 1951; *children:* Richard A., Mary, John D, Jeffrey; *education:* Univ. of New Mexico, 1946-49; Northwestern Univ., Illinois, BS, 1951; Univ. Iowa, MA, 1971; *party:* Democratic Party; *political career:* Iowa State Rep., District 46; Asst. Majority Leader, 1983-85; Chwn., Govt. Cttee, 1985; currently, Iowa State Senator, District 23; *memberships:* Iowa League of Women Voters, Pres., 1972-76, Civil Liberties Union; Iowa Railroad Passengers Assn.; National Organisation for Women; UN Assn.; Iowa Peace Inst; *office address:* Mrs Jean Lloyd-Jones, State Capitol, Des Moines, Iowa 50319, USA.

LOBREGAT, Hon. Ma. Clara L.; Filipino, Congresswoman; *born:* 26 April 1921, Zamboanga City; *parents:* the late Pablo Lorenzo and the late Luisa Rafois; *married:* the late Celso Tito Lobregat; *children:* six; *education:* Pilar College, Maryknoll; St. Scholastica's College; *political career:* Delegate to the 19th Constitutional Convention; Congresswoman; *interests:* coconut farmers and their dependents; *memberships:* Pres., Philippine Coconut Producers Federation; Governor, Philippine National Red Cross; *clubs:* ZONTA Club of Manila; *office address:* The Hon. Ms Clara Lobregat, The Congress of the Philippines -

House of Representatives, Batasan Pambansa Bldg., Quezon City, Manila, The Philippines.

LOCKWOOD, Baroness (cr. 1978, Life Peer) Betty Lockwood; British, Member of the House of Lords; *born:* 22 January 1924; *parents:* the late Arthur Lockwood; *married:* Lieut.-Col. Cedric Hall, 1978; *education:* East Borough Girls School, Dewsbury; Ruskin College, Oxford; *party:* Labour Party; *political career:* Asst. Agent, Reading Labour Party, 1948-50; Sec.-Agent, Gillingham Labour Party, 1950-52; Women's Officer, Lab. Yorkshire Region, 1952-67; Chief Women's Officer and Asst. Nat. Agent, Labour Party, 1967-75; Chmn., Equal Opportunities Commission, 1975-83; House of Lords, 1978-; Chmn., European Advisory Cttee. on Equal Opportunities for Women and Men, 1982-83; mem., Cncl. of Advertising Standards Authority, 1983-; *interests:* sex equality, industrial training, links between education and training, higher education; *memberships:* Board Mem., Leeds Development Corporation; *professional career:* Pres. Birkbeck College, Univ. of London, 1983-89; Cncl. mem., Univ. of Bradford, 1983, and Pro-Chancellor, 1987-; Cncl. mem., Univ. of Leeds, 1985-; Pres., Hillcroft College, 1987; *honours and awards:* Hon. D. Litt., Bradford, 1981; Hon. Doctor of Law, Strathclyde Univ., 1985; Hon. Fellow, UMIST, 1986; Birkbeck College, 1987; Dep. Lieut., West Yorkshire, 1987; *clubs:* Industry and Parliament Trust (Fellow); Soroptomist Int; *recreations:* enjoying the Yorkshire Dales; *private address:* 6 Sycamore Drive, Addingham, nr. Ilkley, West Yorkshire, LS29 0NY, UK; *office address:* Baroness Lockwood, House of Lords, London SW1A 0PW.

LOHOUES-OBLE, Jacqueline; Côte D'Ivoire, Minister of Justice and Keeper of the Seals; *office address:* Mme Jacqueline Lohoues-Oble, Ministry of Justice, Boulevard Angoulvant, Bloc Ministériel, B.P. V-107, Abidjan, Côte D'Ivoire; *phone:* 32 08 88.

LONG, Jill; American, Member of the House of Representatives; *born:* 15 July 1952; *religion:* Methodist; *education:* Valparaiso Univ., BS; Indiana Univ., MBA, Ph.D; *party:* Democratic Party; *political career:* Mem., House of Reps., Indiana, District 4, 1989; *office address:* Ms Jill Long, 1632 Longworth House Office Bldg., Washington DC, 20515-1404, USA.

LÖÖW, Maj-Lis; Swedish, Minister with special responsibility for Immigration (Ministry of Labour); *born:* 13 August 1936, Eskilstuna, Sweden; *parents:* Einar Lindskog and Heldine Lindskog (née Nilsson); *education:* general certificate of secondary education, 1957; *party:* Sveriges Socialdemokratiske Arbetarepartiet (SAP, Swedish Social Democratic Labour Party); *political career:* Board mem. Södermanlands County Council, 1971-79; substitute

MP, 1976; MP, 1979-; mem. cttees for Taxation, Foreign Affairs, 1979-88; Vice-Chmn., Culture Cttee., 1988-89; Chmn. Social Democratic Women's Section, Södermanlands County, 1979-82; Chairperson, Social Democratic Women's Federation, 1981-; mem. SAP board, 1978-81; mem. Advisory Cncl. on Foreign Affairs, 1983-89; mem. Parly. Social Democratic Board, 1985-89; Minister with special responsibility for Immigration, Ministry of Labour, 1989-; *professional career:* employment in hotel and tourist industry, 1958-74; employment agent in Eskilstuna, 1974-79; *private address:* Ryborgsvägen 24, 647 00 Mariefrèd, Sweden; *office address:* Ms Maj-Lis Lööw, Riksdag, Fack, S-100 12 Stockholm, Sweden.

LOPEZ-GORDIENKO, Mercedes; Costa Rican, Minister of Culture; *education:* Licentiate in Philosophy; *political career:* Minister of Culture, 1990-; *memberships:* founder, Students' Assn. of the School of Philosophy; *professional career:* prof. of secondary education; *office address:* Ms Mercedes Lopez-Gordienko, Ministry of Culture, Apartado 10227, San José 1000, Costa Rica.

LORET DE RANGE, Aura; Venezuelan, Minister of Women's Affairs; *office address:* Ms Aura Loret de Range, Cámara de Diputados, Congreso Nacional, Palacio Legislativo, Caracas 1010, Venezuela; *phone:* (02) 483-3347.

LOUVO, Anna-Kaarina; Finnish, Member of the Eduskunta; *born:* 14 October 1937, Kauhava, Finland; *parents:* Eero Jaakko Vähäpassi and Helmi Margareeta Vähäpassi (née Huhtinen); *married:* Jarmo Tapio Louvo, 1956; *children:* Arno, Päivi, Tuuli; *education:* Helsinki Univ., B.D.Sc., 1959; Lic.D.Sc., 1961; Specialist in D.Sc., 1977; Studies in Sweden, 1975; *party:* Kansallinen Kokoomus (Kok, National Coalition Party); *political career:* Mem., Anjala Municipal Cncl., 1972-74; MP, 1979-; mem., Presidential Electorate, 1982; Kouvola City Cncl., 1981-; *professional career:* School Dentist, Kurikka Municipality, 1961-65; School Dentist, Kinnula Municipality, 1965-67; School and Health Centre Dentist, Anjala, 1967-74; Health Centre Dentist, Anjalakoski, 1975-76; School and Health Centre Dentist, Kouvola-Valkeala, 1976-; *publications:* Articles in Dentistry Journals; *recreations:* Piano, tennis, gardening; *office address:* Ms Anna-Kaarina Louvo, Eduskunta, 00102 Helsinki, Finland.

LOWEY, Nita; American, Member of the House of Representatives; *born:* 5 July 1937; *religion:* Jewish; *education:* Mt. Holyoke College, BA; *party:* Republican Party; *political career:* Asst. Sec.-of-State, New York, 1985-87; Mem., House of Reps., District 20, New York, 1989-; Mem., Education, Labour, Merchant Marine and Fisheries Cttees. and Mem., Select Cttee. on Narcotics Abuse and Control, US House of Reps.; Mem., Exec. Cttee., Democrat Study Group; Mem., Long Island Sound Caucus and Congressional Caucus on Womens Issues; *office address:* Ms Nita Lowey, 325 Cannon House Office Bldg., Washington DC, 20515-3220, USA.

LUBEWAKA, Teresa; Polish, Member of the Sejm; *office address:* Ms Teresa Lubewaka, Sejm PRI, ul. Wiejska 4/6/8, 00-489 Warsaw, Poland; *phone:* (22) 28 70 01; 28 40 31.

LUC, Hélène; French, Senator; *born:* 13 March 1932, Saint-Etienne, Loire, France; *parents:* Sabatino Del Cucina; *married:* Louis Luc, 1955; *children:* Nadine Serge; *party:* Parti Communiste Français (PCF, French Communist Party); *political career:* Departmental Sec., Young Communists; National Sec., Union of Young French Women, 1953; County Councillor, Choisy-le Roi, 1967-; Vice-Chmn., Val-de-Marne County Council; member of Regional Council, Ile-de- France, 1976-77; Communist Senator, Val-de-Marne, 1977-; member of PCF directorate, Val-de-Marne; member of Senate Cultural Affairs Committee; Vice- President, 1978, President, 1979 of Senate Communist Group; *office address:* Mme. Hélène Luc, Sénat de la République Française, Palais du Luxembourg, 75291 Paris Cedex 06, France.

LUDROVSKA, Dr. Marta; Czechoslovakian, Member of the Secretariat of the Slovak Trade Union Council; *born:* 12 March 1931; *education:* secondary school studies completed, 1951; Prague College of Political and Economic Sciences; Law Faculty, Comenius Univ., Bratislava, 1951-55; external postgraduate studies, Economic Law, Faculty of Comemius Univ., Bratislava, 1967; *political career:* head of Organisation Section, West Slovak Regional Nat. Cttee., 1963-68; Mem., West Slovak Regional Nat. Cttee., 1966-71; Mem., Cttee. of Czechoslovak Lawyers, 1967-; Sec., Slovak Union of Women, 1968-69, Mem., Presidium, 1969-; Gen. Sec., CSSR Cncl. of Women, 1969-70; Chairperson, Slovak Cttee. of Trade Union of State Employees, 1970-75; Mem., Slovak Trade Union Cncl., (SOR) 1972-, Sec., the Mem. of Presidium and Mem. Secretariat, 1974-; co-opted Mem., Central Cncl. of Trade Unions (URO), 1975-; Mem., Central Control and Audit Commission, CP CSSR, 1981-; *professional career:* tax consultant, Bratislava Regional Nat. Cttee., 1955-57; chief arbitrator, Bratislava State District Court of Arbitration, 1957-63; *office address:* Dr. Marta Ludrovska, Slovak Trade Union Council, Odborárskae Nám. 3,, 897 17 Bratislava, Czechoslovakia.

LUKASSER, Therese; Austrian, Member of the Bundesrat; *born:* 11 September 1932, St. Jakob in Defereggen; *education:* grammar school (classically oriented); teacher training college; teaching proficiency certificate for primary school teaching, 1955; teaching certificate for secondary school teaching, 1971; University of Innsbruck, pedagogy and political science, 1987-; *party:* Österreichische Volkspartei (ÖVP, Austrian People's Party); *political career:* district leader, Austrian Women's Movement, Tirol, and provincial deputy leader, and Women's Movement candidate in Provincial Assembly elections, 1984; senior district councillor, Matrei, Osttirol, 1980-86; mem. of Tirol Provincial Assembly, November 1988-April 1989; sent to Bundesrat from Tirol Provincial Assembly, Mem. of Bundesrat, 1989-; *professional career:* primary school teacher for 18 years; secondary school teacher for 17 years; involvement in further education for teachers and in adult education; joined Austrian Federation of Trade Unions, Compulsory School Teachers' Section, 1952; mem. of ÖVP Austrian Workers' and Employees' Federation, 1961; mem. of Women's Movement, 1975-; mem. of staff, Provincial Schools Inspectorate, 1979-89; mem. of departmental committee of staff council; *office address:* Frau Therese Lukasser, Bundesrat, Dr. Karl Renner Ring 3, 1017 Vienna, Austria.

LULLING, Astrid; Luxembourgeios, Member of the European Parliament; *born:* 11 June 1929; *party:* Parti Chrétien Social (PCS, Christian Social Party); *political career:* MP, Luxembourg, 1965-89; MEP, 1965-; *private address:* 28 rue Chemin Vert, 3878 Schifflange, Luxembourg; *office address:* Ms Astrid Lulling, European Parliament, Centre Européen, Plateau de Kirchberg, BP 2929, Luxembourg.

LUNDBLAD, Grethe; Swedish, Member of the Riksdag; *born:* 3 April 1925, Copenhagen, Denmark; *parents:* Johan Emanuel Hansen and Thyra Mathilde Hansen (née Eriksen); *children:* Ingrid, Thomas; *religion:* Church of Sweden; *languages:* English; *education:* Social Univ., Lund, Sweden, 1948-51; *party:* Sveriges Socialdemokratiska Arbetarepartiet (SAP, Social Democratic Party); *political career:* mem. local authority Board, 1962-70; mem. County Council, 1966-73; MP, 1969-; mem. Presidium, Nordic Council, 1985-; Obligate in UN, 1979, 1982, 1985; *office address:* Ms Grethe Lundblad, Riksdag, Fack, S-100 12 Stockholm, Sweden.

LUNDHOLT, Anne Birgitte; Danish, Minister of Industry; *party:* Det Konservative Folkeparti (Conservative People's Party); *office address:* Ms Anne Lundholt, Ministry of Industry, Slotsholmsgade 12, 1216 Copenhagen K, Denmark.

LYONS TERHES, Hon. Joyce; American, Chairwoman of the Maryland Republican Party; *born:* 21 June 1940, Calvert County, Maryland, USA; *parents:* Arthur Gorman Lyons and Mildred Ward Lyons; *religion:* Catholic; *languages:* English; *education:* Mary Washington College, Univ. of Virginia, BA history, 1962; *party:* Republican Party; *political career:* Chwn. Maryland Republican Party; Commissioner, Calvert County Board of Commissioners, 1986-; *memberships:* founder Mem., Dunkirk Area Concerned Citizens Assn.; Calvert County Chamber of Commerce; Calvert County League of Republican Women; League of Women Voters; former Pres., Alpha Delta Kappa (The Honourary Society of Women Educators); *honours and awards:* Outstanding Service to Calvert County, Commission for Women, 1985; Outstanding Educator Prince George's County Chamber of Commerce, 1985 and Prince George's County Board of Education, 1972; *publications:* co-authored social-studies text books; *clubs:* Ferry Landing Woods Civic Assn.; Ferry Landing Woods Garden Club; Calvert County Republican Club; *office address:* The Hon. Ms Joyce Lyons Terhes, 1623 Forest Drive, Suite 400, Annapolis 21403, Maryland, USA.

M

MACLEOD OF BORVE, Baroness (cr. 1971, Life Peer) Evelyn Hester Macleod; British, Member of the House of Lords; *born:* 19 February 1915; *parents:* Rev. Gervase Blois and Hon. Mrs Blois; *married:* the late Rt. Hon. Iain Macleod (killed by enemy action, 1937), 1941; *children:* one s., one d; *religion:* Church of England; *languages:* French; *education:* Lawnside; *party:* Conservative Party; *political career:* Dep. Lieut., Greater London, 1977; mem. House of Lords; *interests:* Law and Order, family, road traffic; *professional career:* JP, Middlesex, 1953; Co-Founder and Pres., 'Crisis at Christmas', 1967-; Mem., Independent Broadcasting Authority, 1971-75; Chmn., Nat. Gas Consumers Council, 1972-77; Pres., Nat. Assn. of Widows, 1972-; Pres., Nat. League of Hospital Friends, 1985-86; Mem., Parole Board, 1977-81; Governor, Queenswood Sch., 1978-86; *private address:* Luckings Farm, Coleshill, Amersham, Bucks., United Kingdom; *office address:* Baroness Macleod of Borve, House of Lords, London SW1A 0PW.

MAEHATA, Sachiko; Japanese, Member of the House of Councillors; *born:* 16 August 1937; *education:* Graduate School of Chukyo Univ; *party:* Japan Socialist Party (JSP); *political career:* former Vice-Chairperson, JSP Aichi Prefectural HQ; elected for Aichi, 1990; Mem., House of Cllrs. Cttee. on Finance and Special Cttee. on National Livelihood, 1990-; *office address:* Ms Sachiko Maehata, House of Councillors, 1-7-1 Nagata-cho, Tokyo 100, Japan; *phone:* (03) 5813111.

MAES, Nelly; Belgian, Member of the Chamber of Representatives; *born:* 25 February 1941, Sinaai; *children:* three; *languages:* Dutch, French, English, German; *education:* Onze-Lieve-Vrouw Presentatie, Sint-Niklaas, teaching qualification, Dutch history and teaching certificate for lower secondary education; *party:* Volksunie (VU, People's Union); *political career:* local councillor, St. Niklaas, 1970-; Deputy for St. Niklaas district, 1971-78; Senator, 1981-85; Deputy for St. Niklaas district, 1985-; secretary, office of Chamber of Reps., 1988-; member, Chamber of Reps. advisory Cttee. on European affairs; member, Chamber of Reps. commission on foreign relations; member, Flemish council commission on education; member, party council commission; mem. VU women; First Alderman, St. Niklaas, alderman for Culture, education, youth, agriculture, development co-operation and emancipation, 1989-; *professional career:* teacher, until 1970; advisory committee, Vlaams-Arabische Vereniging (Flemish-arabic society); member, political commission of the National womens council; chair, Vlaams International Centrum, (flemish international centre); advisory council, VVOB; *private address:* Sint-Jansplein 15, 2700 Sint-Niklaas, Belgium; *office address:* Ms Nelly Maes, Kamer van Volksvertegenwoordigers, Palais de la Nation, Place de la Nation 2, 1000 Brussels, Belgium.

MAHISHI, Dr. Sarojini; Indian, Member of the Rajya Sabha; *born:* 3 March 1927, Dharwar; *parents:* Bindurao Mahishi; *education:* R.L. Law College, Belgaum; Bombay Univ.; Karnataka Univ.; Vikram Univ., MA, LLB, Ph.D; *party:* Janata; *political career:* Mem., Lok Sabha, 1962-77; Mem., Panel of Chmn., Lok Sabha, for three years; Parly. Secretary attached to the Prime Minister's office, 1965-66; Deputy Minister attached to the Prime Minister's office, 1967-69; Deputy Minister for Tourism and Civil Aviation, 1969-71; Minister of State for Tourism and Civil Aviation, 1971-74; Minister of State for Law, Justice and Company Affairs, 1974-76; Mem. of the Rajya Sabha, 1983-; nominated to the Panel of Vice Chmn., Rajya Sabha, 1984-85; Pres., Dharwar District Women's Assn; *professional career:* Assistant Professor of Law, Karnataka Univ., for six years; Professor, Law College, Dharwar; Editor, Veeramata and Samaj Kalyan; mem., Karnataka Univ. Senate; *honours and awards:* Honorary Doctor of Literature; Mysore State Sahitya Akademi Award; *publications:* 25 books in Kannada, Hindi and English including: The Art of Indian Embroidery; Atithi Satkar; Muruthama; Home Science; Muruthama Darshanam; Yeh Hamare; Navilu Inchara; *recreations:* reading, writing, embroidery, tailoring, badminton; *private address:* Ram Nagar, Hosyallapur Road, Dharwar, Karnataka, India; *office address:* Dr. Sarojini Mahishi, Rajya Sabha, Parliament House, New Dehli 110 011, India; *phone:* (11) 389977; 389997.

MAHON, Alice; British, Member of Parliament; *born:* 28 September 1937; *parents:* the late Thomas Edward Reginald Bottomley and the late Edna Bottomley; *married:* Tony Mahon; *children:* two s; *education:* Bradford University, BA(Hons.) 1980; *party:* Labour Party; *political career:* Activist, National Union of

Public Employees; Cllr., Calderdale Cncl., 1982; Mem., Calderdale District Health Authority; Member of Parliament for Halifax, 1987-; *interests:* employment; local government; trade unions; *professional career:* nursing auxiliary, National Health Service; lecturer, Trade Union Studies, Bradford College; *recreations:* family; *office address:* Mrs Alice Mahon, House of Commons, London SW1A OAA.

MAIBAUM, Gepa; German, Member of the European Parliament; *born:* 21 December 1935; *party:* Sozialdemokratische Partei Deutschlands (SPD, Social Democratic Party); *political career:* Municipal Cncllr., Cologne, 1975-89, Mayor 1984-89; MEP, 1989-; *office address:* Ms Gepa Maibaum, European Parliament, Centre Européen, Plateau de Kirchberg, BP 2929, Luxembourg; *phone:* Luxembourg 43001.

MAIJ-WEGGEN, Hanja (Johanna Rika Hermanna); Dutch, Minister of Transport and Public Works; *born:* 29 December 1943, Emmen, Netherlands; *children:* two; *education:* nurses training, Amstelveen; Amsterdam Univ., major in Social and Community Studies; *political career:* Mem., European Parly., 1979; Vice-Chwn., European People's Party and party spokeswoman on social affairs and employment; Mem., Dutch delegation to the UN, 1977; Mem., Joint African, Caribbean and Pacific States - European Community Assembly; Minister of Transport and Public Works, Nov. 1989-; *memberships:* former Mem., Party Cncl., Anti-Revolutionary Party (ARP) and Christian Democratic Alliance (CDA); former Mem., ARP research Cncl. and CDA Women's Cncl; *professional career:* health care teacher, Amstelveen and Apeldoorn; *office address:* Mevr. Hanja Maij-Weggen, Ministry of Transport and Public Works, Plesmanweg 1, POB 20901, 2500 EX The Hague, The Netherlands.

MAINARDI FAVA, Anna; Italian, Deputy; *born:* 10 July 1933, Salsomaggiore Terme, Parma, Italy; *party:* Partito Democratico della Sinistra (PDS, Party of the Democratic Left); *political career:* Mayor of Salsomaggiore Terme; mem. Regional Cttee., Fidenza; mem. Leadership Cttee. of Section; mem. Regional and National Cttee. of PCI; Deputy, Parma-Modena-Piacenza-Reggio Calabria-1983, re-elected 1987; mem. Cttee. on Health; mem. Cttee. on Social Affairs; *office address:* Ms Anna Mainardi Fava, Camera dei Deputati, Montecitorio, 00186 Rome, Italy.

MAKINDA, Anna; Tanzanian, Minister of Social Development, Women and Development; *office address:* Ms Anna Makinda, Office of the Prime Minister and First Vice-President, PO Box 3021, Dar-es-Salaam, Tanzania.

MÄKIPÄÄ, Lea Kaarina; Finnish, Member of the Eduskunta; *born:* 6 May 1947, Kihniö, Finland; *parents:*

Lauri Mäkipää and Tyyne Mäkipää (née Hakola); *education:* Commercial Coll., 1968; *party:* Suomen Maaseudun Puolue, SMP (Finnish Rural Party); *political career:* Cllr., Kihniö Municipal Cncl., 1981-; Social Welfare Cttee., 1981-; mem., Parish Cncl., 1982-; MP, 1983-; Admin. Cncl., Kihniö Co-op. Bank, 1985-; *professional career:* Accountant 1976-83; *office address:* Ms Lea Mäkipää, Eduskunta, 00102 Helsinki, Finland.

MALCUEWAKA, Teresa; Polish, Member of the Sejm; *office address:* Ms Teresa Malcuewaka, Sejm PRI, ul. Wiejska 4/6/8, 00-489 Warsaw, Poland; *phone:* (22) 28 70 01; 28 40 31.

MALENAKOVA, Jarmila; Czechoslovakian, Member of the Narodni Rada (Czech National Council); *born:* 29 March 1937; *party:* Civic Forum; *office address:* Ms Jarmila Malenakova, Ceská národní rada, Snemovní 4, 110 00 Praha 1, Czechoslovakia; *phone:* (02) 2105.

MAMMONE GROSSI, Natia; Italian, Deputy; *born:* 20 September 1954, Sora, Frosinone, Italy; *education:* Classical secondary education; *party:* Partito Democratico della Sinistra (PDS, Party of the Democratic Left); *political career:* Sec. Communist Federation, Frosinone; mem. Central Cttee., PCI; Councillor, and Head of PCI Group, Frosinone; re-elected Deputy 1987, Rome-Viterbo-Latina-Frosinone; mem. Cttee. on Foreign and Community Affairs; *office address:* Ms Natia Mammone Grossi, Camera dei Deputati, Montecitorio, 00186 Rome, Italy.

MANDEL, Dr. Ruth Blumenstock; American, Director of the Center for the American Woman and Politics, (CAWP); *born:* 29 August 1938, Vienna, Austria; *married:* Barrett John Mandel (first), Jeffrey Lucker, 1991; *children:* Maud; *languages:* English, German; *education:* Brooklyn College, BA English Literature, 1956-60; Univ. of Connecticut, MA English/American Literature, 1960-62, Ph.D., 1969; *political career:* writes and speaks widely about women and leadership with particular emphasis on women as political candidates, women in office, women's political networks and the 'Gender Gap'; as a political analyst and observer of emerging trends, Mandel appears frequently on television and radio programmes and is often called upon as a speaker and lecturer; *memberships:* co-founder, Public Leadership Education Network; Rutgers Univ. Faculty of Arts and Sciences; Co-Chwn., Advisory Cttee., Inst. for Research on Women, 1982-; Research Cncl. Advisory Panels on the Social Sciences, 1982-85; President's Commission on the Arts, Humanities and Social Sciences in an Era of High Technology, 1983-84; Provost's Cttee. on Political Oppression, 1985; Women's Studies Advisory Board, Laurie, NJ, 1986-; Provost's Budget and Planning Cttee., 1988-90; Faculty Cncl. Budget and Planning Cttee., 1990-; Univ. Faculty Budget Cttee., 1990-;

Presidential Search Cttee., 1990; *professional career:* instructor (part-time), Univ. of Connecticut, 1960-66; lecturer, Univ. of Pittsburgh, 1968-70; Asst. Prof., Rider College, 1970-71; Asst. Prof., Rutgers Univ., 1973, Assc. Prof., 1978, Prof., 1985; educational co-ordinator, Center for the American Woman and Politics (CAWP), Rutgers Univ., 1971, Dir. of Educational Programs and Admin., 1971, Dir., 1973-; *honours and awards:* Baccalaureate Speaker, Douglass College, Rutgers Univ., 1981; Convocation Speaker, Chatham College, 1982; Douglass Medal for distinguished service to undergraduate students, June 1989; *publications:* In the Running: The New Woman Candidate, Ticknor & Fields, 1981; The Political Woman in The American Woman, 1988-89; No Striving for Glory, essay in Frontiers, Vol. XI, 1987 and numerous other articles and essays; *private address:* 46 Cameron Court, Princeton, New Jersey 08540, USA; *office address:* Dr. Ruth Mandel, Center for the American Woman and Politics, Eagleton Inst. of Politics, New Brunswick, New Jersey 08901, USA.

MANDELA, (Nomzano) Winnie; South African, South African Politician; *born:* 1934, Bizana, Pondoland, Transkei; *married:* Nelson Mandela, 1958; *public role of spouse:* Deputy Leader of the African National Congress; *party:* African National Congress (ANC); *political career:* campaigned actively for the ANC until its banning, 1960; campaigned on behalf of her husband during his 26 years imprisonment for political activities, 1964-90; held in solitary confinement, 1969-70; named a banned person, by authorities, 1976; *honours and awards:* Third World Prize, 1985; *private address:* Soweto, Transvaal, South Africa; *office address:* Ms Winnie Mandela, 3rd Floor, Munich Re Centre, 54 Sauer St, Johannesburg 200, South Africa.

MANIERI, Maria Rosaria; Italian, Senator; *born:* 30 May 1943, Nardò, Lecce; *party:* Partito Socialista Italiano (PSI, Italian Socialist Party), 1972; *political career:* Councillor, Nardò from 1975; currently Deputy Mayor and Assessor for Public Instruction, Culture and Sport; elected Senator, Gallipoli-Galatina, 1987; Sec. Presidency of the Senate; mem. Cttee. on Public Instruction, Cultural Heritage; *professional career:* Associate Prof. Moral Philosophy, Faculty of Letters, Lecce University; writer on modern humanism, women's position in technological society, moral and political issues, ethical socialism; *publications:* 'Donna e capitale', Milan, 1977; 'Bisogni e politica', oltre Hegel e oltre Marx', 1984, Bari; *office address:* Ms Maria Manieri, Senato della Repubblica, Palazzo Madama, 00100 Rome, Italy.

MÄNNLE, Ursula; German, Member of the Bundestag; *born:* 7 January 1944, Ludwigshafen, West Germany; *religion:* Catholic; *education:* Abitur (advanced matriculation examination), 1964; Universities of München and Regensburg, sociology, modern history, political science; MA, 1969; *party:* Christlich Soziale Union (CSU, Christian Social Union), since 1964; *political career:* dep. federal chmn., Junge Union (Young Union), 1973-77; member of State Exec. Cttee., CSU, since 1974; State chmn., Women's Union, CSU, 1981-1991; mem. of Bundestag, party list of Bayern; *professional career:* research asst., Academy of Political Education, Tutzing, 1970-76; professor of political science, Catholic Foundation College of Higher Education München, division Benediktbeuern; member of presiding board, German Catholic Women's Association; vice-president, World Union of Catholic Women's Organisation, Europe; member of Federation of Women Academics; member of Association of Teachers in Technical Colleges of Higher Education; *private address:* 8132 Tutzing, West Germany; *office address:* Frau Ursula Männle, Bundeshaus, 5300 Bonn 1, West Germany.

MAR, Countess of (31st in line from Rundri, 1st Earl of Mar, 1115) Margaret; British, Member of the House of Lords; *born:* 19 September 1940; *parents:* 30th Earl of Mar; *married:* J.H. Jenkin, MA (Cantab), FRCO, 1982; *children:* one d. (first marriage); *party:* Independent; *political career:* holder of Premier Earldom of Scotland; mem. House of Lords; *interests:* Communications, Adult Educ., Unemployment, Forestry, NHS; *professional career:* Clerical Officer, Civil Service, 1959-63; Sales, Superintendent, P.O./BT, 1969-82; Lay Governor, The King's Sch., Gloucester, 1984-87; Patron, Dispensing Doctors Assn., 1985; Lay Mem., Immigration Appeal Tribunal, 1985; Mem., English Advisory Cttee. for Telecommunications, 1985-86; Patron, Worcester Branch, Nat. Back Pain Assn., 1987; Pres., Avanti, 1987-; *private address:* St. Michael's Farm, Great Witley, Worcester WR6 6JB, UK; *office address:* Countess Margaret of Mar, House of Lords, London SW1A 0PW.

MARCHIORO, Karen Louise; American, Chairwoman of the Washington State Democratic Party; *born:* 19 September 1933, Jacksonville, Illinois, USA; *parents:* Morris Byus and Frances Byus (née Hankins); *married:* Thomas Marchioro, 1956; *children:* Thomas, Kevin, Ann, Stephen, Joan, Katherine, Gregory; *religion:* Catholic; *education:* St. Louis Univ., BS; *party:* Democratic Party; *political career:* Chwn., Washington State Democratic Party; Chwn., Western Regional Caucus; Mem., Democratic Nat. Cttee., Washington; *memberships:* League of Women Voters; UN Assn; *office address:* Ms Karen Marchioro, 1701 Smith Tower, Seattle, Washington 98104, USA.

MARGOLIS, Gwen; American, Florida State Senator; *born:* 4 October 1934, Philadelphia, Pennsylvania, USA; *parents:* Joseph Liedman and Rose Liedman; *children:* Edward, Ira, Karen, Robin; *religion:* Jewish;

education: Temple Univ., 1952-54; Univ. of Tampa; Dade Jr. College; *party:* Democratic Party; *political career:* Florida State Rep., 1974-80; former Mem., Governor's Tax Reform Commission; Chwn., Dade County Legislative Delegation, 1978-79; Florida State Senator, District 37, 1980-; *memberships:* Miami Board of Realtors; South Florida Planning and Zoning Assn. and Women's Cncl. of Realtors; League of Women Voters; Florida Anti-Defamation League; Business and Professional Women's Assn; *professional career:* realtor and appraiser; *honours and awards:* Outstanding Woman in Politics, Business and Professional Women's Assn., 1974; Humanitarian of the Year, City of Hope, 1974 and 1979; Woman of the Year, North miami CofC, 1980; Legislative Friend of the Arts Award, Governor of Florida, 1982; Gwen Cherry Award, National Organisation of Women, 1984; *clubs:* North Miami Beach CofC; Gold Coast CofC; *private address:* 19355 Turnberry Way, North Miami Beach, Florida 33181, USA; *office address:* Ms Gwen Margolis, 13899 Biscayne Blvd., North Miami Beach, Florida 33181, USA.

MARGRETHE II, H.M. The Queen; Danish, Queen of Denmark; *born:* 16 April 1940; *parents:* the late Frederik IX and Queen Ingrid; *married:* Count Henri de Laborde de Monpezat (now Prince Henrik of Denmark), 1967; *children:* two s; *education:* Univ. of Copenhagen; The Sorbonne, Paris; London School of Economics; *political career:* succeeded to the throne, 1972; undertaken many official visits abroad with her husband; *professional career:* illustrator; *honours and awards:* Hon. LLD, Cambridge, 1975, London, 1980; Hon. Dr., Univ. of Iceland, 1986; K.G., 1979; Medal of the Headmastership, Univ. of Paris, 1987; *publications:* (Trans.) All Men are Mortal, with Prince Henrik, 1981; The Valley, 1988; The Fields, 1989; The Forest (Trans.), 1989; illustrated The Lord of the Rings, Tolkein, 1977-78; illustrated Norse Legends as Told by Jorgen Stegelmann, 1979; *office address:* H.M. Queen Margrethe II, Amalienborg Palace, Copenhagen, Denmark.

MARIAMA, Maillele; Niger, Secretary of State for National Education; *office address:* Ms Maillele Mariama, Ministry of National Education, Niamey, Niger.

MARIETA, Beth; American, Alabama State Representative; *born:* 2 November 1950, Pensacola, Florida, USA; *parents:* Don E. Marieta and Doris Marieta (née Murphy); *education:* Univ. of South Alabama, BA, 1973; Univ. of Alabama, JD, 1977; *party:* Democratic Party; *political career:* Alabama State Rep., 1983-; Chair, Sunset Cttee.; Mem., Judiciary, Natural Resources, Highway Safety and Permanent Study Cttee. on Judiciary; currently Mem., Child Support Commission; Alabama House Rep; *memberships:*

American Cncl. of Young Political Leaders; Alabama Bar Assn. Cttee. on Appellate Court Restructure; Alabama Mobile Bar Assn.; Alabama Trial Lawyers Assn.; Mem., Board of Dirs., Volunteers of America Mobile Chapter; Mem., Board of Dirs., Deep South Girl Scout Cncl; *professional career:* Attorney, Whiddon, Hanley and Marietta; *private address:* 5259 Dog River Road, East Theodore, Alabama 36582, USA; *office address:* Ms Beth Marieta, 557 Church Street, Mobile, Alabama 36602, USA.

MARIN-MOSKOVITZ, Gilberte; French, Deputy; *born:* 22 June 1937, Belfort, Territoire de Belfort, France; *parents:* Louis Marin and Victoire Marin (née Biehler); *married:* Jean-Paul Moskovitz, 1976; *party:* Parti Socialiste (PS, Socialist Party); *political career:* Municipal Councillor, Belfort, 1977; County Councillor, Belfort-Sud, 1982; elected Socialist Deputy for Belfort (2nd constituency), 1988; Deputy Mayor, Belfort, 1989-; *professional career:* secretary; *office address:* Mme. Gilberte Marin-Moskovitz, L'Assemblée Nationale, 126 rue de L'Université, 75355 Paris, France.

MARINUCCI MARIANI, Elena; Italian, Senator; *born:* 18 August 1928, Aquila, Italy; *children:* two; *education:* Degree in Jurisprudence; *party:* Partito Socialista Italiano (PSI, Italian Socialist Party); *political career:* mem., Italian League for Divorce (LID); Organiser of petition for abortion, Aquila, 1975; mem., Women's Liberation Movement (MLD); mem. Rome Women's Legal Collective; mem. Editorial Collective of EFFE (magazine); Founded Women's League for Socialism, 1977; Organised, with a group of Doctors and health-workers, 'Co-ordination for the application of law 194', mem. Central Cttee., PSI, 1981; mem. Nat. Leadership, PSI; Head of 'Women's Issues' section; Founder mem., Leadership Cttee. of CRODI (Centre for the requalification and employment of Italian Women); Active mem. Leadership Cttee., Italy, of European Movement; and Nat. Cttee. of European Left; mem. Italian Delegation of UN Delegation for Women, Copenhagen and Nairobi; Representative of PSI on Women's Socialist International; elected Senator, Aquila-Sulmona, 1983; mem. Cttee. on Justice; Reserve mem. on Committee for prosecution procedure; re-elected Senator, 1987; Under-Sec. for Health, in Goria govt. and in the Andreotti govt., April 1989-; *professional career:* Lecturer, Law and Economics, Technical Institutes; Writer, for various newspapers and magazines; Director of 'Quaderni delle donne socialiste'; *clubs:* Assoziazione per la Salute della Donna; *office address:* Ms Elena Marinucci Mariani, Senato della Repubblica, Palazzo Madama, 00100 Rome, Italy.

MARKOWITSCH, Helga; Austrian, Member of the Bundesrat; *born:* 17 November 1944, Brunn am

Gebirge; *education:* commercial school; *party:* Sozialistische Partei Österreichs (SPÖ, Socialist Party of Austria); *political career:* provincial Party Sec., SPÖ, Lower austria, 1960-64; local and district Women's consultant, SPÖ; mem. of provincial Exec., SPÖ, Lower Austria; district Vice Chairperson, SPÖ, Mödling; mem. of all local, district and provincial committees, SPÖ, Mödling; mem. of Federal Women's Cttee., SPÖ; Chamber of Workers and Employees for Lower Austria, Mödling, 1964-72; district councillor, Brunn am Gebirge, 1979-; Exec. mem. of district council responsible for, canals, water, lighting, children's playgrounds, parks and the green belt; sent to Federal Council from Lower Austrian Provincial Assembly, mem. of Bundesrat, 1987-; *professional career:* clerk; Gierlinger, Brunn am Gebirge, 1979-80; association, Safe Energy-Safe Future, 1982-87; *office address:* Frau Helga Markowitsch, Bundesrat, Dr. Karl Renner Ring 3, 1017 Vienna, Austria.

MARONEY, Jane P.; American, Delaware State Representative; *born:* 29 July 1923, Boston, Mass., USA; *parents:* John H. Perkins and Mary Perkins (née Boland); *married:* John Walker Maroney, 1956; *children:* Jane, John W. Jr; *education:* Radcliffe College, 1940-41; *party:* Republican Party; *political career:* Delaware State Rep., 12th District, 1979-82, District 10, 1983-; Co-Chair Cttee. on Children; Chair Human Resources Cttee.; Mem., Substance Abuse Cttee.; currently, Delaware State Rep.; Mem., National Conference State Legislature, 1982-; Chair, Advisory Cttee. on Children and Youth; Mem., Federal Budget and Human Resources Cttee., 1985-; Chair, Eastern Regional Conference, Cncl. of State Govts; *memberships:* Rockwood museum Advisory Cttee.; Chair Co-ordinating Cncl.for Handicapped Children of Delaware; Junior League of Wilmington; League of Women Voters; New Castle County Medical Society Auxillary; Delaware Hospice; *honours and awards:* Outstanding Citizen Award, Academy of Paediatrics 1985; World of People Award, Girl Scouts, 1983; Outstanding Service Award, March of Dimes, 1983; *clubs:* YWCA; Delaware Women's Agenda; *office address:* Mrs Jane Maroney, 4605 Concord Turnpike, Wilmington, Delaware 19803, USA.

MARSDEN, Lorna R.; Canadian, Senator; *born:* 6 March 1942, Sidney, BC; *married:* Edward Harvey; *education:* Univ. of Toronto; Princeton Univ; *party:* Liberal; *political career:* Senator, for Toronto, Taddle Creek, Ontario, 1984-; Chairperson, Social Affairs Cttee. of Senate, Mem., Science and Technology Cttee. and Cttee. for Nat. Finance; *interests:* status of women, social and economic policy, research and development; *office address:* Ms Lorna Marsden, Senate, Parliament Buildings, Wellington Street, Ottawa, Ontario K1A OA4, Canada; *phone:* (613) 992 4416.

MARSHALL, Mary Aydelotte; American, Virginia State Delegate; *born:* 14 June 1921, Cook County, Illinois, USA; *parents:* John Andrew Rice and Nell Aydelotte Rice; *married:* Roger Duryea Marshall; *children:* Nell, Jenny, Alice; *religion:* Congregational; *education:* Swarthmore College, BA (highest honours); *party:* Democratic Party; *political career:* Virginia State Delegate, District 48, 1966-70 and 1972-; Vice-chwn., State-Federal assembly, Nat. Conference on State Legislature, 1980- and Mem., Exec. Cttee., 1982-; *memberships:* Mem., Virginia Library Board; Women's Roundtable; Phi Beta Kappa; *office address:* Ms Mary Marshall, 2256 N. Wakefield Street, Arlington, Virginia 22207, USA.

MARTENSSON, Ingela Birgitta; Swedish, Member of the Riksdag; *born:* 18 August 1939, Ström, Sweden; *parents:* Hans Sigfrid Mårtensson and Märta Margareta Mårtensson; *children:* Suzan, Yasemin, Mårten; *languages:* English, German, French; *education:* Gothenburg University, Degree in Science and Philosophy, 1969; *party:* Folkpartiet Liberalerna (Liberal Party), 1976; *political career:* Chairwoman of the Frölunda House of Culture, 1978-82; Local Government Councillor, 1979-82; Chairwoman of the Lib. Party's Peace Council, 1986-90; Deputy member of the Constitutional Affairs Cttee., 1985-; Dep. mem. of the Financial Cttee., 1988; Lay Assessor and Chairwoman of the Service panel, 1987-88; Member of the Legislative Cttee. concerning Terrorism, 1989-; mem., Liberal Party's Parliamentary Groups Trust Council; Chairwoman of the Gothenburg Student Housing Foundation, 1980-82; mem. of Riksdag for Gothenburg, 1985-; *interests:* peace and cultural affairs; computer technology; *professional career:* air hostess, Scandinavian Airlines, 1960-63; teacher of Sociology, 1969-77; Survey Secretary, Gothenburg City Secretariate, 1977-; mem., Governing Board of Gothenburg Univ., 1981; *publications:* Scholars in the Industry, The Sociological Faculty of Gothenburg University, 1975; *clubs:* Chairperson of the Swedish Section, WILP, 1990-; Clipped Wings (former Air-hostesses); the Assn. Statistics and Planning; *private address:* PL 1096, 13085 Branno, Sweden; *office address:* Ms Ingela Mårtensson, Riksdag, Fack, S-100 12 Stockholm, Sweden.

MARTIN, Lynn Morley; American, Secretary of Labour; *born:* 26 December 1939, Evanston, Illinois, USA; *party:* Republican Party; *political career:* US Rep., District 16, Illinois, 1981; Sec., for Labour, 1991-; *professional career:* teacher, 1966-69; *office address:* Ms Lynn Martin, Department of Labour, 200 Constitution Avenue NW, Washington DC, 20210, USA.

MARTIN, Hon. Shirley; Canadian, Minister of State for Transport; *party:* Progressive Conservative Party (PCP); *office address:* The Hon. Ms Shirley Martin,

Department of Transport, Place de Ville, Transport Canada Building, 330 Sparks Stret, Ottowa K1A OR5; *phone:* (613) 990 2309; *fax:* (613) 996 9622.

MARTIN, Simone; French, Member of the European Parliament; *born:* 14 April 1943, Tourcoing, (Nord), France; *parents:* Raoul Motte and Odette Lejeune; *married:* André Martin, 1963; *public role of spouse:* Mayor of Thonnance les Moulins; *children:* Florence, Xavier, Jérome; *education:* state nursing diploma; *party:* Parti Républican (PR, Republican Party); *political career:* MEP; *interests:* agriculture, economics, the environment; *office address:* Mme. Simone Martin, European Parliament, Centre Européen, Plateau de Kirchberg, BP 2929, Luxembourg; *phone:* Luxembourg 43001.

MARTINI, Dott. Maria Eletta; Italian, Deputy; *born:* 24 July 1922, Lucca, Italy; *education:* Doctor of Letters; *party:* Partito della Democrazia Cristiana (DC, Christian Democrat Party); *political career:* Deputy, Pisa-Livorno-Lucca-Massa Carrara, 1963; mem. Cttee. on Labour and Social Security; mem. Cttee. on Justice; re-elected Deputy 1968; mem. Cttee. on Justice; mem. Leadership Cttee. of Parly. group; Co-ordinator of minorities, Divorce law and unified text for proposed reform of Family Law, approved 1971; re-elected Deputy, 1972; Sec. Cttee. on Justice; re-elected Deputy, 1976; Pres. Cttee. on Hygene and Health; Vice-Pres. Chamber, and Pres. of Cttee. for Documentation, from 1978; Pres. Cttee. for problems of population, Presidency of the council of ministers; re-elected Deputy, 1979; Confirmed as Vice-Pres. of Chamber; elected Senator, Viareggio, 1983; mem. Cttee. on Foreign Affairs; Council for the Affairs of the European Community; and mem. supervisory Cttee. on the radio-television services; Vice-Pres. parliamentary Cttee. on the phenomenon of the Mafia; re-elected Deputy, 1987; mem. Cttee. on Foreign and Community Affairs; *professional career:* Journalist; *office address:* Dott. Maria Eletta Martini, Camera dei Deputati, Montecitorio, 00186 Rome, Italy.

MARVANOVA, Hana; Czechoslovakian, Member of the Narodni Rada (Czech National Council); *born:* 26 November 1962; *party:* Civic Forum; *office address:* Ms Hana Marvanová, Ceská národní rada, Snemovní 4, 110 00 Praha 1, Czechoslovakia; *phone:* (02) 2105.

MASATOVA, Milada; Czechoslovakian, Member of the Narodni Rada (Czech National Council); *born:* 26 March 1945; *party:* Civic Forum; *office address:* Ms Milada Masatová, Ceská národní rada, Snemovní 4, 110 00 Praha 1, Czechoslovakia; *phone:* (02) 2105.

MASDIT, Supatra; Thai, Member of the House of Representatives; *education:* Univ. of Hawaii, MA journalism, 1976-78; Chulalongkorn Univ., graduated

in journalism; *party:* Democrat Party; *political career:* elected for Nakhou Si Thammarat, 1979-; she has since become: Democrat Party spokesperson; chairman, Parly. Cttee. on House Affairs in the House of Representatives; former Minister of the Prime Minister's Office; *professional career:* lecturer, Kasetsart Univ; *office address:* Ms Supatra Masdit, House of Representatives, U-Thong Nai Road, Bangkok 10300, Thailand; *phone:* (02) 2826181 to 99.

MASHAM OF ILTON, Baroness (cr. 1970, Life Peer) Susan Lilian Primrose Cunliffe-Lister; British, Member of the House of Lords; *born:* 14 April 1935; *parents:* the late Sir Ronald Sinclair; *married:* Lord Masham, now 2nd Earl of Swinton, 1959; *children:* one s., one d; *education:* Heathfield School, Ascot; London Polytechnic; *party:* Independent; *political career:* Chmn., Home Office Crime Prevention Working Group on Young People and alcohol; Mem. All Party Disablement Cttee; Vice Chmn. All Party Drug Misuse Cttee.; All Party Aids Cttee; All Party Penal Affairs Group; All Party Children's Group; mem. House of Lords; *interests:* Health and Disability Problems; Penal Affairs; Drug Abuse Matters; *professional career:* Pres., North Yorkshire Red Cross, 1963-; Pres., Yorkshire Assn for disabled; on the Board of Visitors, Youth Custody Centre, Wetherby; Pres., Spinal Injuries Assn.; Mem., Peterlee and Newton Aycliffe Corp., 1973-85; Pres., Chartered Soc. of Physiotherapy, 1975-82, Vice-Pres., 1982; Vice-Pres., Disabled Drivers Assn.; Patron, Disablement Income. Income Group; Vice-Pres., Action for Dysphasic Adults (DIA); Trustee, Spinal Research Trust; Mem., Winston Churchill Trust; Patron, Yorkshire Faculty of Gen. Practitioners; Yorkshire Regional Health Authority; fmr. Mem., Volunteer Centre; Vice-Pres., The Hospital Saving Assn.; Chmn., Board of Directors, Phoenix House; Pres., Papworth and Enham Village Settlements; Vice-Pres., Assn. of Occupational Therapists; *honours and awards:* Hon. Degree MA, York Univ., 1985; Hon. Degree, Master of Arts, Open Univ.; Hon. Degree, Master of Law, Leeds Univ.; Hon. Fellowship, Royal Coll. of Gen. Practioners; *recreations:* breeding Highland Ponies; *private address:* Dykes Hill House, Masham, Nr. Ripon, North Yorkshire, UK; *office address:* Baroness Masham of Ilton, House of Lords, London SW1A 0PW.

MASINI, Dott. Nadia; Italian, Deputy; *born:* 13 November 1949, Padua, Italy; *education:* Degree in Letters; *party:* Partito Democratico della Sinistra (PDS, Party of the Democratic Left); *political career:* mem. organisations of the Communist Federation of Forli; Head of School Committee; Councillor, Forlì, from 1975; Assessor of Higher Education, and Professional training; then Assessor of Public Instruction, 1979; Deputy Mayor, Forlì, 1985-86; Deputy, Bologna-Ferrara-Ravenna-Forlii, 1987; mem. Cttee. on Culture, Science and Teaching; *professional career:* Teacher;

office address: Dott. Nadia Masini, Camera dei Deputati, Montecitorio, 00186 Rome, Italy.

MASLAROVA, Emiliya; Bulgarian, Minister of Social Welfare; *political career:* Minister of Social Welfare, 1990; *office address:* Ms Emiliya Maslarova, c/o Ministry of Public Health and Social Welfare, 1000 Sofia, pl. Lenina 5, Bulgaria.

MASLOFF, Sophie; American, Mayor of Pittsburgh; *born:* 23 December 1917, Pittsburgh, Pennsylvania, USA; *parents:* Louis Friedman and Jennie Friedman; *married:* Jack Masloff, 1939; *children:* Linda; *religion:* Jewish; *education:* Duquesne Univ.; Univ. of Pittsburgh; *party:* Democratic Party; *political career:* Mem., Democrat Cable Television Sub-Cttee., 1980-; Pittsburgh City Cllr., 1980-; Mayor, Pittsburgh, 1988-; *memberships:* Sec., Alleghany County Women's Guild, Pittsburgh, 1940-; Sec., Pennsylvania Federation of Democrat Women, 1967-; Board of Dirs., Municipal Employees Pension Board; Board of Mgrs., Firemen's Relief and Pension Board; Mem., Pittsburgh Police Pension Board; *professional career:* chief investigator, Allegheny County Court, Pittsburgh, 1940-; *office address:* Mrs Sophie Masloff, 414 Grant Street, Pittsburgh, Pennsylvania 15219, USA.

MATHIASEN, Lissa; Danish, Member of the Folketing; *born:* 8 August 1948, Gadstrup, Denmark; *parents:* Johannes Olsen and Tove Olsen; *married:* Alex Klug, 1984; *children:* Camilla, Louise, Rikke; *education:* primary and lower secondary school, 7 years; *party:* Social Democratic Party, 1967; *political career:* Mem. of the Folketing, 1978-; *interests:* labour market, industry, housing conditions, administration of justice; *private address:* Adalsvg 47, 2720 Vanlose, Denmark; *office address:* Ms Lissa Mathiasen, Folketing, Christiansborg, 1240 Copenhagen K, Denmark.

MATTHÄUS-MAIER, Ingrid; German, Member of the Bundestag; *born:* 9 September 1945, Werlte; *parents:* Heinz-Günther Matthäus and Helmtraud (née v. Hagen); *married:* Robert Maier, 1974; *children:* one d., one s; *languages:* French, English; *party:* Freie Demokratische Partei (FDP, Free Democratic Party) to 1982; Sozialdemokratische Partei Deutschlands (SPD, Social Democratic Party of Germany), 1982-; *political career:* Federal chmn., Young Democrats, 1972; mem. of Land and Federal cttee., 1974-; mem. of Bundestat SPD North Rhine-Westphalia list, 1976-; SPD Group cttee., 1982-; chmn., Second Investigation Cttee. of the German Bundestag on the Investigation of Nuclear Scandals, 1988-; *professional career:* Judge; *private address:* 5205 Sankt Augustin, Germany; *office address:* Frau Ingrid Matthäus-Maier, Bundeshaus, 5300 Bonn 1, West Germany.

MATUSIAK, Romualda; Polish, Member of the Sejm; *office address:* Ms Romualda Matusiak, Sejm PRI, ul. Wiejska 4/6/8, 00-489 Warsaw, Poland; *phone:* (22) 28 70 01; 28 40 31.

MAUCH, Ursula; Swiss, Member of the Nationalrat; *born:* 29 March 1935, Oftringen, Switzerland; *children:* three; *party:* Sozialdemokratische Volkspartei der Schweiz (SDP, Social Democratic Party of Switzerland); *political career:* Mem. of the Aargau Canton Great Cncl., 1974-80; Mem. of the Nationalrat for Oberlunkhofen, Canton of Aargau, 1979-; Pres. of the SDP; *professional career:* Chemist (HTL, Technikum Winterthur); *office address:* Frau Ursula Mauch, Nationalrat/Conseil National, Secretariat-General, Parlamentsgebäude, 3003 Berne, Switzerland; *phone:* Berne 619711.

MAYENCE-GOOSSENS, Jacqueline; Belgian, Senator; *born:* 14 September 1932, Aarschot; *married:* Philippe Mayence, 1958; *children:* three; *religion:* Catholic; *languages:* French, English, Dutch; *education:* UCL, graduate in political science and diplomacy; *party:* Parti Reformateur Liberal (PRL, Liberal Party, French Speaking); *political career:* District Cllr., for PRL, Charleroi, 1976-; Senator, for PRL district of Charleroi-Thuin, 1978-; State Sec., for Ministry of Development Co-operation, 1981-83; Minister for Housing and Computing for Wallonia region, 1983-85; mem. of Senate Commissions for Foreign affairs, Foreign Trade, Development Co-operation, Public Health; Deputy Campaigns Officer for the Senate Environmental Commission; mem. of the Wallonia Regional Cncl; *interests:* international problems, ethics and the role of women; *honours and awards:* Commander of the Order of Leopold; Grand Cross of the Order of the Sun of Peru; *clubs:* Montgomery club; *private address:* 30, Rue Haies Germaine, 6032 Mont-sur-Marchienne; *office address:* Mme. Jacqueline Mayence-Goossens, Senate, Palais de la Nation, Place de a Nation 1, 1000 Brussels, Belgium.

MAYER, Sylvie; French, Member of the European Parliament; *born:* 13 October 1946; *party:* Parti Communiste Français (PCF, French Communist Party); *political career:* MEP, 1989-; *office address:* Mme. Sylvie Mayer, c/o Comité Central du PCF, 2 place Colonel Fabien, 75940 Paris Cedex 19, France.

MAZALOVA, Gerta; Czechoslovakian, Member of the Narodni Rada (Czech National Council); *party:* HSD; *office address:* Ms Gerta Mazalová, Ceská národní rada, Snemovní 4, 110 00 Praha 1, Czechoslovakia; *phone:* (02) 2105.

MAZIDAH BINTI HJ ZAKARIA; Malaysian, Senator; *political career:* Senator, Parliament Malaysia, 1986-; *professional career:* Chmn., Sungei Wang Plaza

Sdn. Bhd; *office address:* Ms Mazidah Binti Hj Zakaria, Sungei Wang Plaza Sdn. Bhd., President House, Parkroyal Hotel, Jalan Sultan, 5000 Kuala Lumpur.

MAZZUCONI, Dott. Daniela; Italian, Deputy; *born:* 16 May 1953, Milan, Italy; *education:* Doctor, Classics; *party:* Partito della Democrazia Cristiana (DC, Christian Democrat Party); *political career:* Mayor of Usmate Velate; Deputy, Milan-Pavia, 1987; mem. Cttee. on Constitutional Affairs, Presidency of the Council and Internal Affairs; *professional career:* Teacher; *office address:* Dott. Daniela Muzzuconi, Camera dei Deputati, Montecitorio, 00186 Rome, Italy.

MBA, Lucie; Gabon, Secretary of State for Foreign Affairs, Co-operation and Francophone Affairs; *office address:* Ms Lucie Mba, Ministry of Foreign Affairs and Co-operation, BP 2245, Libreville, Répubique Gabonaise.

McCUNE-DAVIS, Debbie; American, Arizona State Representative; *born:* 12 August 1951, McKeesport, Pennsylvania, USA; *parents:* Harry Valentine Ponte and Ernestine Ponte (Née Skrabak); *married:* William McCune; *children:* Cara Lynn, Michael Eric, Courteney Elizabeth; *education:* Glendale Community College, AA, 1971; Arizona State Univ., BS, 1975; *party:* Democratic Party; *political career:* Arizona State Rep., District 20, 1979-; Mem., Banking and Insurance, Commerce and Environmental Cttees; *professional career:* community relations specialist; *private address:* 4817 North 54th Drive, Phoenix, Arizona 85007, USA; *office address:* Ms Debbie McCune-Davis, 1700 West Washington, Phoenix, Arizona 85007, USA.

McDOUGALL, Barbara Jean; Canadian, Secretary of State for External Affairs; *born:* 1937, Toronto, Canada; *parents:* Robert James Leaman and Margaret Jean Leaman (née Dryden); *languages:* English, French; *education:* Univ. of Toronto; *party:* Progressive Conservative; *political career:* Govt. Affairs and Financial Consultant, 1982-83; Campaign Manageress for the Hon. David Crombie, Fed. elections, 1979, 1980; Pres., Rosedale Progressive Conservative Assn., 1981-82; Minister of State for Finance, 1984-86; Minister for Privatisation and Regulatory Affairs, 1987-88; Minister for Employment and Immigration, 1988-91; Sec.-of-State for External Affairs, 1991-; *memberships:* former Chairperson, Community Occupational Therapy Assn.; Salvation Army Red Shield Appeal; former Dir., Second Mile Club, Toronto; *professional career:* business journalist, writer for TV; former Vice-Pres., Dominion Securities Ames Ltd., AE Ames and Co. Ltd.; former Investment Analyst, Odium Brown Ltd., Vancouver; Exec. Dir., Canadian Cncl. of Financial Analysts, 1982, 1983; *office address:* Ms Barbara McDougall, House of Commons, Parliament Buildings, Wellington Street, Ottawa, Ontario K1A OA6, Canada; *phone:* (613) 957 3744; *fax:* 952 0874.

McELDERRY, Betty; American, Chairwoman of the Oklahoma State Election Board; *born:* Sulpher, Oklahoma, USA; *parents:* Michael Suchy and Virgie Suchy (née Franks); *married:* Neil McElderry, 1958; *public role of spouse:* Chairman of Purcell Municipal Hospital and Purcell Planning Commission; *children:* Neil III, Michael E; *religion:* Methodist; *education:* Univ. of Oklahoma, BA, 1961, MA, 1964, doctoral 1981; *party:* Democratic Party; *political career:* Chwn., Oklahoma State Election Board, 1983-; Chwn., Oklahoma State Democrat Party, 1987-; Mem., Credentials Cttee., Democratic National Cttee; *memberships:* American Assn. of Univ. Women; League of Women Voters; National Education Assn; *honours and awards:* Outstanding Democratic Women, (Oklahoma), 1980; *publications:* The ABC's of School Finance; Clothing and Textile Practice of HE Alumni; *recreations:* reading; *office address:* Mrs Betty McElderry, 1304 N. 9th Purcell, Oklahoma 73080, USA.

MCFARLAND, Dr. Gwen Nation; American, Member of the Tennessee State Democratic Cttee; *born:* 4 July 1930, Lawrenceburg, Tennessee, USA; *parents:* James Luther Nation and Martha Nation (née Owens); *married:* George Henry McFarland, 1947; *children:* Anthony Joel, Joni Elizabeth; *religion:* Episcopalian; *education:* George Peabody College, BA, 1952, MA, 1963, Ph.D., 1970; YMCA Law School, 1980; *party:* Democratic Party; *political career:* Mem., Tennessee State Democratic Cttee., 1974-; *memberships:* United Teaching Profession; Assn. of Supervision and Curriculum Development; Assn. of Teacher Educators; Pres., Nashville Urban League, 1976-; *professional career:* teacher, 1952-80; attorney, Cheatham and Palermo, 1980-; *office address:* Dr. Gwen McFarland, 43 Music Square, W. Nashville, Tennessee 37203, USA.

MCFARLANE OF LLANDAFF, Baroness (cr. 1979, Life Peer) Jean Kennedy McFarlane; British, Member of the House of Lords; *born:* 1 April 1926; *parents:* Dr. James McFarlane; *education:* Howell's School, Llandaff; Bedford and Birkbeck Colls., Univ. of London, MA, B.Sc. (Soc.); FRCN, SRN, SCM, HV Tut. Cert; *party:* Independent; *political career:* mem. House of Lords; *professional career:* Staff Nurse, St. Bartholomew's Hospital, London, 1950-51; Health Visitor, Cardiff City 1953-59; Tutor, Royal Coll. of Nursing, London, 1960-62; Education Officer, Royal Coll. of Nursing, Birmingham 1962-66; Research Project Leader, Royal College of Nursing, London, 1967-69; Dir. of Education, RCN, London, 1969-71; Sr. Lecturer in Nursing, Univ. of Manchester, 1971-74; Prof. and Head of Dept. of Nursing, Univ. of Manchester, 1974-; Mem. of Commonwealth War

Graves Commission; *honours and awards:* Hon. M.Sc. (Manch.); Hon. D.Sc. (Ulster); *clubs:* VAD Club, Sloane Club, Royal Commonwealth Soc; *private address:* 5 Dovercourt Avenue, Heaton Mersey, Stockport SK4 3QB, UK; *office address:* Baroness Mcfarlane of Llandaff, House of Lords, London SW1A 0PW.

MCHUGH, Jeannette; Australian, Member of the House of Representatives; *born:* 18 December 1934, Kandos, NSW, Australia; *education:* Sydney, BA; *party:* Australian Labor Party; *political career:* Delegate, Labor Party NSW Annual Conference, NSW Council and NSW Labor Women's Cttee., 1970-; Mem., Labor Party State Policy Cttees. on Sport and Recreation, 1974-75 and on Social Security, Welfare and Repatriation, 1976-81; Mem., Labor Party National Policy Cttes. on Industrial Development, Minerals and Energy, and Science and Technology, 1982-83; elected for Phillip, NSW, 1983-; Mem., Advisory Council for Inter-Govt. Relations, 1983-86; Committee Service: Mem. of the House of Representatives Standing Cttee. for Environment and Conservation, 1985-87; for Environment, Recreation and the Arts, 1987-; for Community Affairs, 1987-; Mem., Labor Party National Policy Cttee. on Social Security and Community Services, 1987-; *professional career:* housewife; teacher of modern languages; former mem., NSW Women's Advisory Council; former lay mem., NSW Solicitors Statutory Cttee; *office address:* Ms Jeannette McHugh, House of Representatives, Parliament House, Room M80, Canberra ACT, 2600, Australia; *phone:* (062) 726383.

MCINTOSH, Anne Caroline Ballingall; British, Member of the European Parliament; *born:* 20 September 1954, Edinburgh, Scotland; *parents:* Dr. Alastair Ballingall McIntosh and Grete-Lise (née Thomsen); *religion:* Church of England; *languages:* French, Danish, Spanish, German; *education:* Harrogate College, Yorkshire, 1964-73; University of Edinburgh, LLB (Hons.), Scottish, European and International law, 1973-77; University of Aarhus, Denmark, 1977-79; *party:* Conservative Party; *political career:* Parliamentary Candidate, Wokingham, 1987; Deputy Whip, Spokesman on Rules of Procedure, European Democratic Group; MEP for North-East Essex, 1989-, ED, European Democratic Group; *interests:* transport, tourism, legal affairs, Poland, East Germany, Scandinavia; *professional career:* Administrative Trainee, Commission of the European Communities, 1978; Advocate, European Community, 1982-83; Secretariat member, European Democratic Group European Parliament, 1983-89; Legal Advisor, Didier and Associates, Brussels, 1979-80; admitted to the Scottish Bar, 1982; *publications:* EEC Competition Rules and Maritime Transport, 1980; Lloyds Maritime and Commercial Law Review; *private address:* 78 Maldon Road, Colchester, Essex, CO3 3AL; *office address:* Ms Anne McIntosh, European Parliament,

Centre Européen, Plateau de Kirchberg, BP 2929 Luxembourg.

McINTOSH SLAUGHTER, Louise; American, Member of the House of Representatives; *born:* 1 August 1929, Lynch, Kentucky, USA; *parents:* Oscar Lewis McIntosh and Grace McIntosh (née Byers); *married:* Robert Bruce Slaughter Jr., 1956; *children* Megan Rae, Amy Louise, Emily Robin; *religion* Episcopal; *education:* Univ. of Kentucky, BS, 1951, MS 1953; *party:* Democratic Party; *political career:* Mem., New York State Assembly, District 130, 1983-86; Mem., House of Reps., District 30, New York, 1987-; Mem., Select Cttee. on Aging, Govt. Operations, Public Works and Transport Cttees., US House of Reps; *memberships:* League of Women Voters; *office address:* Mrs Louise McIntosh Slaughter, 1707 Longworth House Office Bldg., Washington DC, 20515, USA.

McLANE, Susan; American, New Hamshire State Senator; *born:* 28 September 1929, Boston, Mass., USA; *parents:* Lloyd Kellock Neidlinger and Marion Ruth Neidlinger (née Walker); *married:* Malcolm McLane, 1948; *public role of spouse:* Mayor of Concord, New Hampshire, 1968-74; *children:* Susan B., Donald W., Deborah, Alan, Ann Lloyd; *religion:* Protestant; *languages:* French; *education:* Mt. Holyoke College, 1947-48; *party:* Republican Party; *political career:* New Hampshire State Rep., 1969-80; New Hampshire State Senator, District 15, 1980-; Chwn., Ways and Means Cttee; *interests:* human services, environment; *honours and awards:* Eastern Women's Ski Champion, 1948; Hon. Degrees: LLD, New England College, 1983 and Franklin Pierce College, 1988; Fellowship, Kennedy School of Govt., Harvard Univ; *clubs:* Audubon, N.E. Ski Museum; *recreations:* skiing; *office address:* Sen. Susan McLane, 205 Mountain Road, Concord, New Hampshire 03301, USA.

McLAUGHLIN, Audrey; Canadian, Leader of the New Democratic Party; *born:* 7 November 1936, Dutton, Ontario, Canada; *parents:* W.M. Brown and Margaret Brown; *married:* Don McLaughlin, 1954; *children:* two; *education:* Univ. of Toronto, MA Social Work, 1967; *party:* New Democratic Party; *political career:* delegate, leadership convention, 1975; managed Roger Kimmerly's campaign, Yukon, 1981 and Justice Minister, 1985; first Mem., New Democratic party to represent Yukon, House of Commons, 1987; Chair., Parly. Caucus, Jan. 1989; Finance Critic for New Democratic Party 1989; Leader, New Democratic Party, Dec. 1989-; *professional career:* co-owner of mink farm, Ontario; teacher of English, Western Africa; social worker, Metro Toronto Children's Aid Soc.; owner, consulting firm; Exec. Dir., Canadian Mental Health Assn., 1975; volunteer for Canadian Crossroads Int.; helping women start small businesses, Barbados, 1986; *office address:* Ms Audrey McLaughlin, Office of the Leader of the New Democratic Party, Rm. 531-C, Centre Block, House of Commons, Ottawa, Ontario K1A OAL, Canada.

McPHAIL, Evelyn; American, Chairwoman of the Mississippi State Republican Party; *born:* 9 June 1930, Meridian, Mississippi, USA; *parents:* Richard W. Williams and Alline Williams (née Dove); *married:* John Robert McPhail, 1949; *children:* John Robert Jr., Janet, Frances; *religion:* Presbyterian; *education:* Mississippi Univ. for Women; Univ. of Southern Mississippi; *party:* Republican Party; *political career:* Mem., Republican National Cttee. of Miss.; delegate, Republican National Convention, 1980, 1984 and 1988, Chwn, 1988; Mem., State Steering Cttee., Reagan for Pres.; Mem., Presidential Scholars Cttee.; Mem., Arrangements Cttee., Republican National Convention Rules Cttee., 1984; Chwn., Miss. State Republican Party; *memberships:* Order of Amaranth; Mem., Board of Dirs., Magnolia Chapter, March of Dimes and Palmer Children's Home; *professional career:* owner, EMCO Service Co; *clubs:* CofC; Republican Women's Club; Alpha Zeta; *office address:* Mrs Evelyn McPhail, 5574 Diamondhead Drive, East Bay, Saint Louis, MS 39520, USA.

MEBRAK-ZAIDI, Nora; French, Member of the European Parliament; *born:* 1965; *party:* Parti Socialiste (PS, Socialist Party); *political career:* MEP, 1989-; *private address:* 7 rue Marconi, 25200 Bethoncourt, France; *office address:* Mme. Nora Mebrak-Zaidi, European Parliament, Centre Européen, Plateau de Kirchberg, BP 2929, Luxembourg; *phone:* Luxembourg 43001.

MEIER, Josi J.; Swiss, Member of the Ständerat; *education:* Univ. of Geneva, Bachelor of Law; *political career:* Great Cncl., Canton Lucerne, 1971-76; mem. of Nationalrat, 1971-83; mem. of Ständerat, 1983-; *professional career:* lawyer, Troller, Meier and Hitz, Lucerne; mem. of International Assn. for Protection of Industrial Property; military rank, Officer in Red Cross Unit; *publications:* contributor, Wahlen Cttee. Report (revision of Federal Constitution); *clubs:* Soroptimist Club, Professional and Business Women's Club, Swiss Lawyers' Assn., Swiss Law Club; *private address:* Schweizerhofquai 2, 6004 Lucerne, Switzerland; *office address:* Frau Josi Meier, Ständerat, Secretariat-General, Parlamentsgebäude, 3003 Berne, Switzerland.

MERKOURI, Melina; Greek, Member of Parliament; *party:* Panelliniou Socialistikou Kinema (PASOK, Panhellenic Socialist Movement); *political career:* MP, B' Piraeus, 1977-81; MP of State, 1985; MP of State, 1989; Alternate member of the Exec. office of PASOK; Minister of Culture, 1981-89; *professional career:* actress; *office address:* Vouli, Parliament Building, Syntagma, Greece.

MESSNER, Evelyn; Austrian, People's Attorney of the Republic of Austria; *born:* 10 November 1938, Vienna, Austria; *education:* grammar school (classically oriented), matriculation, 1956; University of Vienna, Magisterium in teaching of German and physical education, 1963; *party:* Sozialistische Partei Österreichs (SPÖ, Socialist Party of Austria), 1963; *political career:* town councillor, Oberwart, 1977-; district women's Chmn., SPÖ, Oberwart, 1985-; mem. of Nationalrat, for Burgenland, 1986-; Peoples Attorney of the Republic of Austria, July 1989-; *professional career:* teacher at Federal Technical College for the Clothing Trade, Oberwart, 1961-; Principal, Federal College of Economic Women's Professions, Oberwart, 1970-; *office address:* Frau Evelyn Messner, Nationalrat, Dr. Carl Renner Ring 3, 1017 Vienna, Austria.

MEYER, Natalie; American, Secretary-of-State for Colorado; *born:* 20 May 1930, Henderson, North Carolina, USA; *parents:* Ranie Thomas Clayton and Mary Clayton (née Johnson); *married:* Harold Lee Meyer, 1951; *children:* Mary Elizabeth, Rebecca Leigh, Amy Louise; *religion:* Lutheran; *education:* Univ. of Northern Iowa, BA, 1951; *party:* Republican Party; *political career:* Committeewoman, Arapahoe County Rep. Cttee., Colorado, 1960-83, Vice-Chair, 1967-74; campaign Mgr. for Congressman Bill Armstrong, 1974; political Dir., Colorado, 1980; Legislative Dir., Colorado State Republican Party, 1980-81; Presidential Appointee, 19-Member delegation to observe Philippine elections, 1986; Leader, State Leadership Initiative delegation to USSR (trade, business and cultural focus), 1989; Sec.-of-State, Colorado, 1983-; *interests:* good govt., Republican Cttees; *memberships:* Women in State Govt.; National Assn. of Secs.-of-State; Colorado and International Women's Forum; Cncl. of State Govts./Chwn., Strategic Planning for State Govts. Sub-Cttee; *professional career:* teacher, Jefferson County School, Colorado, 1951-57; Principal and teacher, Ascension Lutheran Midweek School, 1966-78; leasing Dir., Von Frelick Assn., Colorado, 1972; *honours and awards:* Hon. Lifetime Mem., Colorado Cttee. of Elected Officials for Soviet Jewry; Hon. Mem., Lion's Club; *publications:* article published in Lutheran Witness, 1989; *recreations:* golf, bridge, reading; *office address:* Mrs Natalie Meyer, Colorado Secretary of State, 1560 Broadway, Suite 20, Denver 200, Colorado, USA.

MEYERS, Jan; American, Member of the House of Representatives; *born:* 20 July 1928, Lincoln, Nebraska, USA; *married:* Louis Dutch Meyers; *children:* Valerie, Philip; *religion:* Methodist; *education:* Univ. of Nebraska, BA, 1951; William Woods College, AA, 1968; *party:* Republican Party; *political career:* City Councilwoman, 1967-72; Kansas State Senator, District 8, 1972-84; Chwn., Public Health and Welfare Cttee., Kansas State Senate; Member of the House of Reps., District 3, Kansas, 1985-; Mem., Small Business, and Foreign Affairs Cttees.; Mem., House Republican Research Exec. Cttee.; Mem., Regulatory Reform Task Force and Environment and Energy Study Conference Exec. Cttee.; Mem., 92 Group; Mem., Congress Caucus for Women's Issues Exec. Cttee.; Mem., Congress Human Rights Caucus, Export Task Force, Congressional Grace Caucus, Congressional Competitiveness Caucus, Military Reform Caucus; *private address:* 8408 W. 90th Overland Park, Kansas 66212, USA; *office address:* Mrs Jan Meyers, 315 Cannon House Office Bldg., Washington DC, 20515-1603, USA.

MICHAUX-CHEVRY, Lucette Adrien; French, Deputy; *born:* 5 March 1929, Saint-Claude, Guadeloupe; *parents:* Edouard Chevry and Florentine Chevry (née Labry); *married:* Emile Michaux; *children:* Octave, Marie-Luce; *education:* Gerville-Reache College, Basse-Terre, Guadeloupe; Faculty of Law, Paris; Bachelor of Law; *party:* Rassemblement pour la République (RPR, Rally for the Republic); *political career:* Municipal Councillor, Saint-Claude, Guadeloupe, 1957-62; County Councillor for Guadeloupe (Saint-Claude-Gorbeyre), 1976-; and Chairwoman of County Council, 1982-85; Regional Councillor, Guadeloupe, 1983-; elected RPR Deputy for Guadeloupe, 1986; handed over her seat to Edouard Chammougon; Sec. of State to the Prime Minister, in charge of the French-speaking countries, 1986-88; Mayor of Gourbeyre, 1987-; elected RPR Deputy for Guadeloupe, 1988; *professional career:* Solicitor, Basse-Terre, Guadeloupe, 1955-; *office address:* Mme. Lucette Michaux-Chevry, L'Assemblée Nationale, 126 rue de L'Université, 75355 Paris, France.

MICHELMAN, Kate; American, Executive Director of the National Abortion Rights Action League (NARAL); *children:* three d; *political career:* Exec. Dir., NARAL, 1985; led successful fight to block Robert Bork's appointment to US Supreme Court, 1987; *professional career:* prior to appointment at NARAL she distinguished herself in developmental child psychology and reproductive health; developed and implemented a multi-disciplinary diagnostic therapeutic treatment programme for developmentally disabled pre-school children and their families, 1978; Dir., Planned Parenthood, Harrisburg, Penn., 1980-85; activist, lobbyist and fundraiser; *honours and awards:* One of One Hundred most Powerful Women in Washington, Washingtonian Magazine; *office address:* Ms Kate Michelman, 1101 14TH Street NW, Washington DC 20005, USA.

MICHIE, Ray (Janet); British, Member of Parliament; *born:* 4 February 1934, Scotland, UK; *parents:* Lord and Lady Bannerman of Kildonan; *married:* Dr. Iain Michie, 1957; *children:* Fiona, Joanne, Deirdre; *religion:* Church of Scotland; *education:* Lansdowne House, Edinburgh; College of Speech Therapists, Edinburgh, MCST; *party:* Scottish Liberal Party, 1950; Scottish Liberal Democrats, 1988; *political career:* Member of Parliament, 1987-; Parly. Spokesman on Transport, Scottish Affairs and Women's Issues, 1987-88; former Vice-Chwn., Scottish liberal Party; Joint Chwn., Parly. Working Group on the United Nations Convention on the Rights of the Child; Joint Vice-Chwn., Parly. Group on the Whisky Industry; *interests:* Constitutional reform, Scottish home rule; *memberships:* Campaign for Scottish Assembly; NFU Scotland; Rural Forum; Scottish Crofters Union; An Comunn Gaidhealach; Vice-Pres., College of Speech and Language Therapists; Hon. Assc., National Cncl. of Women of Great Britain; *professional career:* speech therapist; *clubs:* Nat. Liberal Club; Scottish Liberal Club; *recreations:* golf; rugby; swimming; gardening; *private address:* 5 Stafford Street, Oban, Argyll, PA34 5NJ; *office address:* Mrs Ray Michie, House of Commons, London SW1A OAA.

MIDZIC, Fatima; Yugoslavian, Member of the Central Committee of the League of Communists of Yugoslavia; *born:* 1929; *religion:* Muslim; *party:* League of Communists of Yugoslavia (LCY); *political career:* Mem., Central Cttee., LCY, 1982-; *office address:* Ms Fatima Midzic, League of Communists of Yugoslavia, Novi Beograd bul. Lenjina 6, Yugoslavia.

MIGLIASSO, Teresa; Italian, Deputy; *born:* 25 March 1942, Turin, Italy; *party:* Partito Democratico della Sinistra (PDS, Party of the Democratic Left); *political career:* Assessor for Public Assistance, Turin; mem. Fed. Cttee., PCI; Deputy, Turin-Novara-Vercelli, 1983, re-elected 1987; mem. Cttee. on Internal Affairs; mem. Cttee. on Public and Private Work; *professional career:* Accountant; *office address:* Ms Teresa Migliasso, Camera dei Deputati, Montecitorio, 00186 Rome, Italy.

MIGNON, Hélène; French, Deputy; *born:* 2 June 1934, Toulouse, Haute-Garonne, France; *married:* Jean-Marie Mignon, 1962; *party:* Parti Socialiste (PS, Socialist Party); *political career:* Member of Managing Cttee., Socialist Party; Municipal Councillor, Muret, 1973; member of Haute-Garonne County Council, 1979, re-elected 1985; elected Socialist Deputy for Haute-Garonne (6th constituency), 1988; *professional career:* Doctor; *office address:* Mme. Hélène Mignon, L'Assemblée Nationale, 126 rue de L'Université, 75355 Paris, France.

MIKULSKI, Barbara Ann; American, Senator; *born:* 20 July 1964, Baltimore, Maryland, USA; *parents:* William Mikulski and Christine Mikulski (née Kutz); *religion:* Catholic; *education:* Mt. St. Agnes College, BA, 1958; Univ. of Maryland, MSW, 1965; *party:* Democratic Party; *political career:* political worker, John F.

Kennedy for Pres., 1960; Co-ordinator, 1st District, Joseph D. Tydings for Senator, Baltimore, 1970; city councilwoman, Baltimore, 1971-76; special adviser to R. Sargent Shriver, 1972; Chwn., Commission for Delegate Selection and Party Structure, Democrat National Cttee., 1973; Mem., Govt. Commission on Structure and Governance Education; Mem., House of Reps. for Maryland, 3rd District, 1977-87; Mem., Energy, Commerce, Merchant Marine and Fisheries Cttees.; Mem., Health and Environment, Commerce, Transport and Tourism, Coast Guard and Navigation, Merchant Marine and Panama Canal Sub-Cttees.; Chwn., Oceanography Sub-Cttee.; delegate, Democrat National Convention, 1980; Mem., Democrat National Cttee.; Maryland; National Co-Chwn., Mondale-Ferraro Campaign, 1984; US Senator, Maryland, 1986-; Mem., Appropriations, Labour and Human Resources, Small Business Senate Cttees.; currently: Dep. Majority Whip; Mem., Democrat Senators Campaign Cttee.; Mem., Exec. Cttee., Congressional Caucus for Women's Issues; Mem., Exec. Board, Federal Govt. Service Task Force; Board Mem., National Urban Coalition; *memberships:* League of Women Voters; Women's Political Caucus; Catalyst Inc; *professional career:* teacher, Vista Training Centre, Mt. St. Mary's Seminary, Baltimore; administrator, Dept. of Social Service, Baltimore Health and Welfare Cncl.; prof., sociology, Loyola College, Maryland, 1972-76; currently, author and lecturer; *honours and awards:* Hon. Degrees.: LLD, Goucher College, 1973; DHL, Pratt Inst. of Planning and Architecture, 1974; National Citizen of the Year, Buffalo American-Political Eagle, New York State, 1973; Woman of the Year, Business and Professional Women's Club, Baltimore, 1973; Outstanding Alumnus, Univ. of Maryland School of Social Work, 1973 and Loyola College, 1974; National Fellowship Award, Philadelphia Fellowship Commission, 1974; *publications:* Who Speaks for Ethnic America?, New York Times; Growing Up Ethnic Means Learning Who You Are, Redbook Magazine; numerous other articles; *private address:* 616 S. Ann Street, Baltimore, Maryland 21231, USA; *office address:* Ms Barbara Ann Mikulski, SH-320, Hart Senate Office Bldg., Washington DC 20510-2003, USA.

MILES-LAGRANGE, Vicki; American, Oklahoma State Senator; *born:* 30 September 1953, Oklahoma City, Oklahoma, USA; *parents:* Charles Miles and Mary Miles (née Greenard); *married:* Jacques LaGrange; *religion:* Baptist; *education:* Vasser College, BA, 1974; Howard Univ., LLB, 1977; *party:* Republican Party; *political career:* Oklahoma State Senator, District 48, 1987-; *professional career:* attorney; *office address:* Mrs Vicki Miles-LaGrange, 4020 N. Lincoln, No. 204, Oklahoma City, Oklahoma 73105, USA.

MILLER, Louise; American, Washington State Representative; *born:* 28 December 1936, Redding, California, USA; *parents:* John Wesley Haydock and

Claribel Haydock (née Pomeroy); *married:* Stafford W. Miller, 1960; *children:* Claribel Rebecca, Geoffrey Stafford; *education:* San Jose State Univ., BA, 1966; Univ. of Washington,1967-70; *party:* Republican Party; *political career:* Washington State Rep., District 45, 1983-; Mem., High Level Nuclear Waste Board and Washington State Arts Commission, 1983-; *memberships:* CofC; American Assn. of Univ. Women; King County Rep.Club; Washington Women; American Assn. of Business and Professional Women; *professional career:* teacher, Seattle, 1966-72; admin. asst., King County, 1976-81; private music teacher, 1966-83; *office address:* Ms Louise Miller, 17005 191st Avenue, NE Woodnville, Washington 98072, USA.

MINOZZI, Rosanna; Italian, Deputy; *born:* 18 June 1942, Dire-Daua, Ethiopia; *education:* Classical secondary education; *party:* Partito Democratico della Sinistra (PDS, Party of the Democratic Left); *political career:* mem. Leadership Cttee. of Communist Federation; Deputy, Florence Pistoia, 1983, re-elected 1987; mem. Cttee., teaching, re-elected Deputy, 1987; Sec. Cttee. on Production, Trade and Tourism; *office address:* Ms Rosanna Minozzi, Camera dei Deputati, Montecitorio, 00186 Rome, Italy.

MIRANDA DE LAGE, Ana; Spanish, Member of the European Parliament; *born:* San Sebastián, Spain; *party:* Partido Socialista Obrero Español (PSOE, Spanish Socialist Workers' Party), 1975; Socialist Group (S); *political career:* Chief of Cabinet at the Ministry of the Interior, 1978; Senator for the Basque Country Autonomous Community, 1984-87; MEP, 1986-; *professional career:* former exec. sec., Hospital of Diseases for the Chest, San Sebastián; *office address:* Ms Ana Miranda de Lage, European Parliament, Centre Européen, Plateau de Kirchberg, BP 2929, Luxembourg.

MISSOFFE, Hélène; French, Senator; *born:* 15 June 1927, Paris, France; *parents:* Comte Emmanuel de Mitry and Comtesse Marguerite de Mitry (née de Wendel); *married:* François Missoffe, 1948; *children:* Françoise, Chantal, Patricia, Elisabeth, Olivier, Isabelle, Brigitte, Alain; *religion:* Catholic; *languages:* French, English; *party:* Rassemblement pour la République (RPR, Rally for the Republic); *political career:* RPR Deputy for Paris (17th arondissement, Epinettes, Batignolles), 1974-77 and 1978-86; Councillor for Paris, former National Sec., UDR; Sec. of State to the Minister of Health and Social Security, 1977-78; Vice-Chmn., Ile-de-France Regional Council, 1981-86; elected Deputy for Val d'Oise, 1986; handed over her seat to Jean Bardet; elected RPR Senator for Val d'Oise, 1986; *private address:* 38 rue Boileau, 75016 Paris, France; *office address:* Mme. Hélène Missoffe, Sénat de la République Française, Palais du Luxembourg, 75291 Paris Cedex 06, France.

MITCHAM, Hon. Constance; St. Christopher and Nevis, Minister of Health and Women's Affairs; *born:* 19 November 1947, Sandy Point, Saint Kitts; *parents:* Rosina Augusta Mitcham (née Benjamin); *religion:* Methodist; *languages:* English, French; *education:* London Univ., LLB (Hons.), 1968-71; Inns of Court, School of Law, London, UK, Barrister-at-Law, 1971-72; *party:* People's Action Movement; *political career:* acting Minister of Education, 1986, 1987, 1989; acting Minister of Tourism and Labour, 1987; Minister of Women's Affairs, 1984-89; currently Third Vice-Pres., St. Kitts People's Action Movement; Minister of Health and Women's Affairs, 1989-; *interests:* research and history of political parties; *memberships:* former Pres., St. Kitts-Nevis Bar Assn; *professional career:* election supervisor, British Virgin Islands, 1973; Senior Partner, Mitcham & Benjamin Legal Firm; Chief-Magistrate, British Virgin Islands, 1972-75; First Pres., Eastern Caribbean Girl Guides Cncl., 1975-78; *honours and awards:* International Woman of the Year, Business and Professional Women's Club, 1975; *publications:* editor, People's Action Movement 25th Aniversary Historical Magazine, 1990; International Business in St. Kitts & Nevis, Inner Temple Yearbook, 1991; *clubs:* Business and Professional Women's Club; *recreations:* walking, exercise, gardening; *private address:* P.O. Box 440, Franklands Estate, St. Kitts; *office address:* The Hon. Ms Constance Mitcham, Ministry of Health and Women's Affairs, Government Headquarters, PO Box 186, St. Kitts, State of Saint Christopher and Nevis.

MITSUISHI, Hisae; Japanese, Member of the House of Councillors; *born:* 21 September 1927; *party:* Japan Socialist Party (JSP); *political career:* former Vice-Chairperson, JSP Mie Prefectural HQ; elected for National, 1990; Mem., House of Cllrs. Cttee. on the Cabinet and Special Cttee. on National Livelihood, 1990-; *office address:* Ms Hisae Mitsuishi, House of Councillors, 1-7-1 Nagata-cho, Tokyo 100, Japan; *phone:* (03) 5813111.

MIXCO REYNA, Miriam Eleana; El Salvador, Member of the Legislative Assembly; *office address:* Mrs Miriam Mixco Reyna, Asamblea Nacional Constituyente, San Salvador, El Salvador; *phone:* 21 72 01.

MØLLER, Grethe Fenger; Danish, Member of the Folketing; *born:* 1941; *education:* Hamline Univ., Minnesota, USA, 1961-62; law, 1969; *party:* Conservative Party; *political career:* Dep. Chairperson, Danish Women Soc. Youth Section; Mem., Danish Women's Soc. Exec. Cttee., 1967-81, Chairperson, 1974-81; Head of the Nat. Secretariat, The United Nations Women's Year, 1975; Mem., Board of Nat. Cncl. of Women in Denmark, 1971-76; Mem. of the Folketing, 1977; Minister of Labour, 1982-86; Political Spokesperson, until 1987; Chairperson., Legal Cttee. of

Folketing; Chairperson, Danish Delegation of North Atlantic Assembly, one of two female Mems. in the Military Cttee.; Vice-Chairperson, Political-Economic Cttee.; Mem., Special Cttee. on Danish Security Policy; Mem., Frederiksberg Town Cncl., 1974-82; Chairperson, Social Cttee. and house rent Cttee.; Chairperson, Danish Delegation in Nairobi, 1985; Chairperson, Cttee. working out the Danish Govt.'s Nat. Plan of Action after Nairobi Conference; Chairperson, Danish Equal Status Cncl.; Mem., Conservative Party Exec. Cttee., 1975-; *professional career:* employed in Dept. of Labour and Social Affairs, 1969-75; employed in Secretariat, Danish Equal Status Cncl., 1976-79, Chairperson, 1987; employed, Secretariat of the Danish Equal Status Cncl., 1976-79; participated in three UN Women's Conferences; *publications:* books and articles, headed many seminars on women in politics; *office address:* Ms Grethe Møller, Folketing, Christiansborg, 1240 Copenhagen K, Denmark.

MOERPRATOMO, A. Sulasikin; Indonesian, Minister of State for Women's Affairs; *born:* 18 April 1927, Jakarta; *religion:* Islam; *education:* faculty of letters, Univ. of Indonesia, Jakarta; UN Asia Institute of Training on Social Development and Planning; *political career:* secretary and later vice chairperson, Women's Organisation PERWARI, 1953-56; UNICEF programme officer, 1958-83; chairperson, provincial board of 'PERISCA POSTEL' (Assn. of Women in the Department of Posts and Telecommunications), 1962-72; secretary to the Education Standing Cttee. of the central board of PERWARI, 1962-67; chairperson, Public Information Standing Cttee. of the Federation of Kindergarten Teacher's Assn., 1965-67; presidium, National Commission on the Status of Women, 1975-78; posts held between 1978-88: general chairperson, Executive Board of KOWANI (Indonesian Women's Congress), Jakarta; Mem., Working Team for the Role of Women; first Pres., ASEAN Confederation of Women's Organisations, 1981-83; Mem., Resource Team for the Role of Women in Comprehensive Child Development Programme, 1982-84; Mem., House of Representatives, 1982-87; Mem., People's Consultative Assembly, 1983-92; chairperson, Central Board of GOLKAR (Functional Group), 1983-88; honorary adviser to National Activity Motivating Team of the Family Welfare Movement, 1983-88; vice chairperson, Central Board of Himpunan Wanita Karya, 1987-92; Minister of State for Women's Affairs in Fifth Development Cabinet, 1988-; *professional career:* teacher, Taman Siswa elementary and high school, 1945-52; *office address:* Ms A. Moerpratomo, Office of the Minister of State for the Role of Women, Jalan Merdeka Barat 15, Jakarta Pusat 10110, Indonesia; *phone:* (021) 3805563.

MOFFARD, Rose; American, Governor of Arizona; *born:* 10 June 1922, Globe, Arizona, USA; *education:*

Phoenix College; US Defence Industrial College; *party:* Democratic Party; *political career:* Sec.-of-State, Arizona, 1978 and 1982-; Gov., Arizona, 1990-; *memberships:* Hon. Mem., Glendale Optimist International; Board mem., National Cncl. for Alcoholism; *honours and awards:* Humanitarian of the Year, Cystic Fibrosis Foundation; Public Service Award, Arizona Retarded Citizens; Distinguished Public Service and Dedicated Humanitarian Award, St. Jude's Children's Research Hospital; Arizona Heritage Award, American Red Cross, 1987; *clubs:* Fraternal Order of Eagles; *office address:* Ms Rose Moffard, Office of the Governor, 1700 West Washington Street, Phoenix, Arizona 85007, USA.

MOGAMI, Cynthia; Botswana, General-Secretary of the Botswana Commercial and General Workers' Union; *office address:* Ms Cynthia Mogami, Botswana Commercial and General Workers' Union, P.O. Box 62, Gaborone, Botswana.

MOIR (née PUTT), Margaret; New Zealander, Member of Parliament; *born:* 9 September 1941, Kimberley, Rep. of South Africa; *parents:* Frederick Charles Putt and Dorothy Mary Putt (née Harvey); *married:* Derek Raymond Moir, 1963; *children:* Glenn, Christian, Tracey, Susan; *religion:* Anglican; *education:* Alexandra Grammar School, Singapore; *party:* National Party, 1978; *political career:* Mem., Westland County Cncl., 1980-89; West-Coast United Cncl., 1980-89; Westland District Cncl., 1989-90; West Coast Regional Cncl., 1989-90; West Coast Regional Development Cncl., 1984-90; MP for West Coast, 1990-; *interests:* local govt., resource use, primary production; *honours and awards:* 1990 Medal, Minister of Local Govt., 1990; *recreations:* people, television, reading, walking; *office address:* Mrs Margaret Moir, House of Representatives, POB 18041, Wellington, New Zealand; *phone:* (04) 719199; *fax:* (04) 4990704.

MOLINARI, Susan; American, Member of the House of Representatives; *born:* 27 March 1958, Staten Island, New York, USA; *parents:* Guy Molinari and Marguerite Wing; *education:* State Univ., New York-Albany, BA, 1980, MA 1982; *party:* Republican Party; *political career:* Mem., New York City Cncl., District 1, 1986-; Minority Leader, 1986-; Mem., Standards and Ethics, Priveleges and Elections, Fiance and Environmental Protection Cttees.; currently, Mem., US House of Reps; *office address:* Ms Susan Molinari, 250 Broadway 24th Floor, New York City, New York 10007, USA.

MOLTISANTI, Maria Luisa; Italian, Senator; *born:* 29 November 1939, Ispica, Ragusa, Italy; *religion:* Catholic; *education:* Teaching Diploma, Higher Institute of Physical Education, Palermo; *party:* Movimento Sociale Italiano - Destra Nazionale (Italian Social Movement); *political career:* Asst. to Senator, Fatner, 1958-64; Vice-Pres., Catholic Action; mem; *professional career:* Dir., Agricultural firm; Winner of Chair and Professor of Physical; *publications:* 'Rigidità articolare post-traumatica-Terapia Rieducativa', 1972; *office address:* Ms Maria Moltisanti, Senato della Repubblica, Palazzo Madama, 00100 Rome, Italy.

MOMPATI, Ruth; South African, Member of the National Executive Committee of the African National Congress; *born:* 14 September 1925, Huhudi, (Vryburg), South Africa; *children:* two; *party:* African National Congress (ANC); *political career:* participated in Defiance Campaign, 1952, raised funds for more than 8000 people arrested during campaign; involved in Women's marches of 1956; left country temporarily, 1962, feared for her safety after arrests took place during her absence, ten years later her children joined her in exile; worked for ANC, Dar-es-Salaam, Morocco; Sec., to Oliver Tambo, ANC Pres., Lusaka; South African Delegate, Women's International Democratic Federation, Berlin, 1976-79; ANC Chief Rep., London; Mem., ANC Nat. Exec. Cttee., portfolio of head of the ANC board of religious affairs; involved in Women's Section of ANC, internal policy Commission and served on political and military Cncl.; following unbanning of ANC, formed part of team which helped talks with South African Govt. reps., Groote Schuur, Cape Town, 1990; *professional career:* Sec., Legal Practice of Oliver Tambo and Nelson Mandela, until Mandela arrested and firm forced to close; Gen. Sec., Theatre Company until 1962; *office address:* Ms Ruth Mompati, Parliament, Cape Town, South Africa; *phone:* (012) 403-2911.

MONTANARI FORNARI, Nanda; Italian, Deputy; *born:* 17 February 1934, Piacenza, Italy; *party:* Partito Democratico della Sinistra (PDS, Party of the Democratic Left); *political career:* Prov. Assessor and Council Assessor, Piacenza; Vice-Pres. USL; mem. Federal Cttee. and Leadership Cttee. of PCI; Deputy, Parma-Modena-Piacenza-Reggio Emilia-1983; mem. Cttee. on Hygene and Health; re-elected Deputy 1987; mem. Cttee. on social affairs; *professional career:* Hospital Director; *office address:* Ms Nanda Montanari, Camera dei Deputati, Montecitorio, 00186 Rome, Italy.

MONTECCHI, Elena; Italian, Deputy; *born:* 30 September 1954, Reggio Emilia, Italy; *party:* Partito Democratico della Sinistra (PDS, Party of the Democratic Left); *political career:* Deputy, Parma-Modena-Piacenza-Reggio Emilia, 1987; mem. Cttee. on Agriculture; mem. Leadership Cttee. of parliamentary group; *professional career:* Teacher; Party functionary; *office address:* Ms Elena Montecchi, Camera dei Deputati, Montecitorio, 00186 Rome, Italy.

MOORE, Gwen; American, California State Assemblywoman; *born:* Detroit, Michigan, USA; *married:* Ronald Dobson; *children:* Ronald II; *education:* California State Univ., Los Angeles, BA; currently studying at Univ. Southern California; *party:* Democratic Party; *political career:* California State Assemblywoman, District 49, 1978-; Majority Whip; Chair, Utilities and Commerce Cttee.; currently Mem., Finance and Insurance, Health, Local Govt., Govt. Efficiency and Consumer Protection Cttees.; currently Mem., Commission on California State Govt. Organisation and Economics; delegate, Democrat National Convention, 1980 and 1984; Western Regional Chair, National Black Caucus State Legislature; currently regional Vice-Chair, National Caucus State Legislature; Mem., National Organisation of Black Elected Legislative Women; *memberships:* Los Angeles Community College District Board of Trustees, 1975; California Elected Womens' Assn.; United Negro College Fund; Los Angeles Coalition of 100 Black Women; California Black Legislative Caucus; Democratic Women's Forum; National Women's Political Caucus; *professional career:* formerly Dir., Public Affairs and Personnel, Community Action Centre, Los Angeles; teacher, Compton Community College; *honours and awards:* Golden Shopping Cart Award for Legislator of the Year, National Alliance of Supermarket Shoppers, 1975; National Caucus of Black State Legislator Award, 1984; California State Package Store and Tavern Owners Assn. Award, 1984; Meritorious Award for Outstanding Service, Women for Good Govt.; Newsmaker of the Year, National Assn. of Media Women, 1983; *clubs:* CofC; YWCA; *private address:* 3754 Lockland Drive, Los Angeles, California 90008, USA; *office address:* Ms Gwen Moore, State Capitol Room 2117, Sacramento, California 95814, USA.

MOORE, Martha Christine; American, Vice-Chairwoman of the Republican National Committee of Ohio; *born:* Cambridge, Ohio, USA; *parents:* Charles Ellis Moore and Nannie Belle Moore (née Hammond); *religion:* Protestant-Presbyterian; *languages:* English; *education:* Wellesley College, Wellesley, Mass., 1936-37; Muskingum Collegem New Concord, Ohio, AB, Speech 1937-40; Ohio State Univ., Columbus Ohio, MA, Gen. Speech, 1948-52; Columbia Univ., New York, 1959; *party:* Republican Party; *political career:* Mem., State Women's Cttee., 18th District, Ohio, 1950-, 15th District, 1950 and 1966, 17th, 1966 and 1972, 18th, 1972-; Vice-Chwn., Republican State Party, 1968-; Mem., Republican national Cttee., 1968-; Vice-Chwn., Republican National Cttee., 1984-; *professional career:* professor, Muskingum College, New Concord, Ohio, 1948-87; *honours and awards:* Outstanding Women Award, American Assn. of Univ. Women, 1972; Mem., Hall of Fame, Guernsey County Historical Society, Ohio, 1987; Distinguished Alumni Award, Muskingum College, 1986; *clubs:* Univ. Club, Columbus, Ohio; Capitol Hill Club, Washington DC; Women's National Republican Club; *office address:* Miss Martha Moore, 50 Oakland Boulevard, Cambridge, Ohio 43725, USA.

MORA, Dr. Christiane Marie-Lys; French, Deputy; *born:* 14 November 1938, Talence, Gironde, France; *parents:* Etienne Mora and Marie Mora (née Verten); *education:* Communal School, Bouscat; Camille Jullian College, Bordeaux; Fénélon College, Paris; Ecole Normale Supérieure; Sorbonne; doctorate; agrégée in history and geography; *party:* Parti Socialiste (PS, Socialist Party); *political career:* Municipal Councillor, Bléré (Indre-et-Loire); National Socialist Party Delegate for the Environment, then for Energy; member of Socialist Party National Secretariat, in charge of communications and publicity; Socialist Deputy for Indre-et-Loire (Loches-Amboise), 1981-; *professional career:* teacher at Baltzac State School, Tours, 1962-63; Insitute of Political Studies, Bordeaux, 1964-70; Univ. of Bordeaux, 1963-81; F. Rabelais Univ., Tours, 1975-81; Head of Lectures in Contemporary History, Univ. of Bordeaux; member of Historical and Economic Study Centre, Univ. of Lyon II; Assn of Contemporary Historians; *publications:* Saint Simon, 1977; Les Chambres d'Agriculture en France 1924-1940 (doctoral thesis); *private address:* Le-Haut-Village, 37150 Bléré, France; *office address:* Dr. Christiane Mora, L'Assemblée Nationale, 126 rue de L'Université, 75355 Paris, France.

MOREAU, Louise; French, Deputy; *born:* 29 January 1921, Grenoble, Isère, France; *parents:* Pierre-François Mont-Reynaud and Marie-Pierrette Mont-Reynaud (née Lan franchi); *married:* the late Pierre Moreau; *children:* Richard; *education:* science graduate; *party:* Union pour la Démocratie Française (UDF, Union for French Democracy); *political career:* representative of the Provisional Government, USA, 1945; delegate to San Francisco Conference, 1945; secretary-general, first congress of Europe-Africa Interparliamentary Association, 1959; Mayor, Mandelieu-la-Napoule, 1971-; Deputy for Alpes-Maritimes, 1978-; MEP, 1979-84; Deputy chairman, National Assembly, 1984-85; Deputy chairman, UDF group, National Assembly, 1986; Chmn., Parly. France-Brazil Friendship Group., 1986; Deputy chairman, Parly. France-USA Friendship Group., 1986; Cttee. member, French association for the Atlantic Community; Cttee. member, French delegation to the European Movement; *professional career:* Company directorships; *honours and awards:* office of the legion of Honour; 39-45 War Cross; Rosette of the Resistance; *clubs:* Polo Club, Paris; Circle of the Stirrup; *recreations:* golf, riding, sailing; *private address:* 66 Avenue Henri Martin, 75116 Paris, France; Esfrala, 747 Avenue des Pins, 06210 Mandelieu-la-Napoule, France; *office address:* Mme. Louise Morean, L'Assemblée Nationale, 126 rue de L'Université, 75355 Paris, France.

MORENO IRUEGAS, María de los Angeles; Mexican, Minister of Fisheries; *party:* Partido Revolucionario Institucional (PRI, Institutional Revolutionary Party); *office address:* Ms María de los Angeles Moreno Iruegas, c/o Ministry of Agriculture, Wisma Tani, Jalan Sultan Salahuddin, 50624 Kuala Lumpur, Malaysia.

MORF, Doris; Swiss, Member of the Nationalrat; *born:* 17 September 1927; *children:* three; *education:* Univ. Zürich; *party:* Sozialdemokratische Partei der Schweiz (Social Democratic Party of Switzerland); *political career:* Pres., Parly. group on Culture; distict Cllr., 1970-77; Mem. of the Nationalrat for Zürich, 1975-; *office address:* Frau Doris Morf, Nationalrat/Conseil National, Secretariat-General, Parlamentsgebäude, 3003 Berne, Switzerland; *phone:* Berne 619711.

MORGANTI, Dttssa. Fausta Simona; San Marino, Deputy for Education and Culture; *party:* Partito Democratico Progressista (PDP, Democratic Progressive Party); *office address:* Dttssa. Fausta Simona Morganti, Ministry of Education and Culture, Contrada Omerelli, 47031 San Marino.

MORI, Nobuko; Japanese, Member of the House of Councillors; *born:* 23 April 1932; *education:* Okayama Univ; *party:* Japan Socialist Party (JSP); *political career:* former Vice-Chairperson, JSP Okayama Prefectural HQ and Vice-Pres. of Okayama Prefectural Teachers' Union; elected for Okayama, 1990; Mem., House of Cllrs. Cttee. on Education, 1990-; *office address:* Ms Nobuko Mori, House of Councillors, 1-7-1 Nagata-cho, Tokyo 100, Japan; *phone:* (03) 5813111.

MORIYAMA, Mayumi; Japanese, Member of the House of Councillors; *born:* 7 November 1927; *education:* Tokyo Univ; *party:* Liberal Democratic Party (LDP); *political career:* former Parly. Dep. Minister for Foreign Affairs; former Chief Cabinet Sec.; second time elected, for Tochigi, Komoto faction, 1990-; Mem., House of Cllrs. Cttee. on Education, 1990-; *office address:* Ms Mayumi Moriyama, House of Councillors, 1-7-1 Nagata-cho, Tokyo 100, Japan; *phone:* (03) 5813111.

MORO, Maria Fida; Italian, Senator; *born:* 17 December 1946, Rome, Italy; *children:* one s; *education:* Degree in Political Science; *party:* Partito della Democrazia Cristiana (DC, Christian Democrat Party); *political career:* elected Senator, Britonto, 1987; mem. Cttee. on Justice; *professional career:* Professional Journalist from 1971; Writer on magazine: 'Discussione'; *publications:* 'La casa dei Cento Natali'; 'Un Dio Simpatico'; 'In viaggio con mio; *office address:* Ms Maria Moro, Senato della Repubblica, Palazzo Madama, 00100 Rome, Italy.

MORSE, Maryanne; American, Secretary of the Florida State Republican Executive Committee; *born:* 23 July 1944, Madison, Wisconsin, USA; *parents:* Herbert Hipp and Winifred Hipp (née Williams); *married:* Guy A. Morse, 1967; *education:* Rollins College, BS, 1980; *party:* Republican Party; *political career:* Vice-Chwn., Seminole County Republican Cttee., Florida, 1974-80; Committeewoman, 1979, Chwn., 1980; voter turn-out Chwn. and Co-ordinator, 1974; Co-Chwn., Florida Federation of Young Republicans, 1975-78; alternate delegate, Republican National Convention, 1976; campaign Co-ordinator, 1976, 1978 and 1982; Sec., Florida State Republican Exec. Cttee., 1980-; campaign Mgr., 1982, 1984 and 1986; *professional career:* book-keeper, Motor Securities Corp., 1966-68; comptroller, Whitaker, Koepke and Asscs. and Whitaker Oil and Gas Properties, 1968-82; Vice-Pres., Whitaker Energy Inc., 1978-82; *honours and awards:* Campaign Leadership Award, 1980; Outstanding Achievement Award, Florida Young Republicans, 1975; Bronze Hardcharger Award, National Young Republicans, 1976; Outstanding Woman of Seminole County, Seminole Singers, 1977; *clubs:* Greater Seminole County CofC; *office address:* Mrs Maryanne Morse, 1370 Dunhill Drive, Longwood, Florida 32750, USA.

MOSEROVA, Dr. Jaroslava, DrSc; Czechoslovakian, Member of the Narodni Rada (Czech National Council); *born:* 17 January 1930; *party:* Civic Forum; *office address:* Dr. Jaroslava Moserová, Ceská národní rada, Snemovní 4, 110 00 Praha 1, Czechoslovakia; *phone:* (02) 2105.

MOSINYI, Hon. Ester; Botswana, Member of the National Assembly; *office address:* The Hon. Ms Ester Mosinyi, National Assembly, P.O. Box 240, Gaborone, Botswana; *phone:* 355681/85.

MOTTER, Klara; Austrian, Member of the Nationalrat; *born:* 1 October 1935, Lindau, West Germany; *education:* commercial training; *party:* Freiheitliche Partei Österreichs (FPÖ, Freedom Party of Austria); *political career:* mem. of the Provincial Assembly, Vorarlberg, 1976-79; Federal Vice-Chmn., FPÖ, 1982-; Mem. of the Nationalrat, for Kärnten, Upper Austria, Salzburg, Steiermark, Tirol and Vorarlberg, 1986-; *professional career:* dental nurse; *office address:* Frau Klara Motter, Nationalrat, Dr. Karl Renner Ring 3, 1017 Vienna, Austria.

MOUMOUNI, Aissata; Niger, Minister of Social and Women's Affairs; *office address:* Ms Aissata Moumouni, Ministry of Public Health, Social Services, and Women's Conditions, Niamey, Niger.

MOUNTBATTEN OF BURMA, Countess (2nd in line, UK, cr. 1947) Patricia Edwina Victoria Knatchbull,

CBE; CD; JP; DL; D.St.J; British, Member of the House of Lords; *born:* 14 February 1924; *parents:* 1st Earl Mountbatten of Burma and Edwina Ashley (d. of 1st Baron Mount Temple); *married:* 7th Baron Brabourne, 1946; *public role of spouse:* Film and Television Producer and Chairman of Thames Television; *children:* five s. (one decd.), two d; *religion:* Christian; *languages:* French, German; *education:* Malta; England; New York; *party:* Cross-Bencher; *political career:* JP, Kent, 1971; DL, County of Kent, 1973; Vice Lord Lieut., 1984; mem., House of Lords, 1979-; *professional career:* Wren and Third Officer, WRNS, 1943-46; App. Col.-in-Chief of Princess Patricia's Canadian Light Infantry, 1974; Dep. Vice-Chmn., NSPCC; Vice-Pres., British Red Cross Soc., Family Planning Assn., Nat. Childbirth Trust; Soldiers', Sailors' and Airmen's Families Assn.; Royal Life Saving Soc.; Shaftesbury Soc.; Royal Coll. of Nursing; Royal Nat. Coll. for the Blind; Nat. Soc. for Cancer Relief; Chmn., Sir Ernest Cassel Educational Trust; Pres., Shaftesbury Homes and Arethusa; Friends of Cassel Hospital; SOS Children's Villages (UK); Hon. Pres., Soc. for Nautical Research and British Maritime Charitable Foundation; Patron Legion of Frontiersmen of the Cmmw. and the Commando Assn.; Vice-Patron, Burma Star Assn., Pres., Kent Branch of Save the Children Fund, and Kent Marriage Guidance Council; Vice-Pres., Kent Voluntary Service Council; Patron, East Kent Hospice, and Kent Council on Drug Addiction; Governor, Ashford School, Kent; mem. of Council of Caldecott Community, Kent; *honours and awards:* CBE; CD; JP; D.St.J; *private address:* Newhouse, Mersham, Ashford, Kent TN25 6NQ; *office address:* Countess Mountbatten of Burma, House of Lords, London SW1A 0PW.

MOUSSAVOU MISSAMBO, Paulette; Gabon, Minister for the Civil Service and Administrative Reform; *office address:* Ms Paulette Moussavou Missambo, Ministry of Finance, Budget and Participation, BP 165, Libreville, République Gabonaise.

MOWLAM, Dr. Marjorie; British, Member of Parliament; *born:* 18 September 1949, Watford, Herts., UK; *parents:* the late Frank William Mowlam and Bettina Mary Mowlam; *education:* Coundon Court Comprehensive School, Coventry; Durham University, BA, 1968-71; Iowa University, USA, MA, PhD, 1973-77; *party:* Labour Party, 1969; *political career:* Member of Parliament for Redcar, 1987-, COHSE sponsored MP; mem., Transport and General Worker's Union; Opposition Spokesperson on Northern Ireland, 1988-89; mem., National Labour Party NEC Sub. Cttee. on Energy; Shadow Cabinet Spokesperson for City and Corporate Affairs in Trade and Industry Team; *professional career:* research assistant to Tony Benn, MP, 1971-72 to Alvin Toffler, 1972-73; Lecturer, Univ. of Wisconsin, 1976-77; Lecturer, Florida State Univ., 1977-78; Lecturer, Newcastle University, 1979-83;

Senior Administrator, Northern College, Barnsley, 1984-87; *recreations:* swimming, travel, walking, watching football, jigsaws; *office address:* Dr. Marjorie Mowlam, House of Commons, London SW1A OAA.

MUCHINGURI, O.C.Z; Zimbabwe, Member of the House of Assembly and Deputy Minister of Political Affairs; *office address:* Ms O.C.Z. Muchinguri, House of Assembly, P.O. Box 8055, Causeway, Harare, Zimbabwe; *phone:* 2141.

MUJURU, Hon. Joyce; Zimbabwe, Minister of Community Development and Co-operatives; *office address:* The Hon. Ms Joyce Mujuru, Ministry of Community Development and Co-operatives, Chaminuka Building, Private Bag 7735, Causeway, Harare, Zimbabwe; *phone:* 793671.

MUKHERJEE, Geeta; Indian, Member of the Lok Sabha; *born:* 8 January 1924; *parents:* Kumar Roy Chowdhary; *married:* Biswanath Mukherjee; *party:* Communist Party of India (Marxist); *political career:* Mem., WB state council of Communist Party of India, 1947-; Joint Sec., AISF, 1948; Mem., Secretariat of the Women's International Democracy, 1958; Mem., executive Cttee. of National Federation of Indian Women, 1965; Mem., WB Assembly, 1967-77; Mem., WB Cttee. of All India Kisan Sabha; Mem. of Lok Sabha; *interests:* women's employment, illiteracy; *publications:* Bharat Upakatha; Chotoder Ravindranath; He Atit Katha Kao; *private address:* 18 Bow Street, Block-D, Flat 12, Calcutta-700012, India; *office address:* Shrimati Geeta Mukherjee, Lok Sabha, Parliament House, New Dehli 110 011, India; *phone:* (11) 381825; 377102.

MUKHERJEE, Kanak; Indian, Member of the Rajya Sabha; *born:* 30 December 1921, Jessore Town, Bangladesh; *parents:* the late Satish Chandra Dasgupta; *married:* Saroj Kumar Mukherjee, 1942; *children:* one s; *education:* Bethune College and Women's College, Univ. of Calcutta; David Hare Teachers' Training College, Calcutta, MA, BT; *party:* Communist Party of India (Marxist); *political career:* arrested, 1939-40; lived underground, 1941-42; organised Mahila Samiti and relief work, 1943-45; Mem., Communist Party of India, 1943-64; imprisoned and detained under PD Act, 1950-51, and under DIR, 1962-63; Mem., Communist Party of India (Marxist), 1964-; Alderman, Calcutta Corporation, 1969-71; elected to the Rajya Sabha, 1978, re-elected, 1984; nominated to the Panel of Vice Chmn., Rajya Sabha, 1985-86 and 1986-87; State Cttee. Mem., Communist Party of India (Marxist); *professional career:* editor, Gharebaire, 1957-66; editor, EKSATHI, 1968-; mem., Paschim Bengal Bangala Academy; lecturer in English, Women's College, Calcutta, until 1981; Pres., Governing Body, Women's teacher Training College, Hasting House, Calcutta;

publications: Raudra Dhara; Karagar; Sapath Nilam; Saurya Uthbe Bole; Rakta Golaper Kanta; Brinita Hin; Ujan; Bandi Phalgun; Fire Paoya; Desh Rakshar Dak; Women's Education Series; Chin Bharmaner Diary Theke; Chin Theke Phere; Ekti Samaj Tantrik Deshe Kayek Din; Nari O Samaj; Nirbachita Kavita; Navi, Atit, Bartaman and Bhabiswat; Marx-Engels-Lenin-Stalin on Women's Questions; Nirbachita Galpa; Marx leader Aloke; Pragati Sahityer Dhara Beye; *recreations:* literary writing, journalism, reading; *private address:* Village Bahadurpur, P.O. Eral, District Burdwan, West Bengal, India; *office address:* Shrimati Kanak Mukherjee, Rajya Sabha, Parliament House, New Dehli 110 011, India; *phone:* (11) 389977; 389997.

MUPANGA, Joyce; Ugandan, Minister of State for Women's Development; *office address:* Ms Joyce Mupanga, Office of the Prime Minister, P.O. Box 341, Kampala, Uganda.

MURESAN, Ana; Romanian, Minister of Domestic Trade; *party:* Romanian Communist Party (RCP); *political career:* candidate Mem., Bucharest City Party Cttee., 1962; Mem., Dep. Sec., Party Cttee. of Trade Unions, Ministry of Domestic Trade and Bucharest City Trade enterprises, 1966-71; Chairperson, Trade Union for Trade and Co-operation and Mem., General Cncl., Romanian Trade Unions, 1971-78; Mem., Nat. Cncl., Socialist Unity Front, 1974-; Vice-Chairperson, Cncl. of the Romanian Cncl. on Socialist Culture and Education, 1978-; full Mem., RCP Central Cttee., candidate Mem., Political Exec. Cttee., RCP Central Cttee., 1979-; Vice Chairperson, Nat. Cncl. of Socialist Democracy and Unity Front, 1980-; Dep., Grand National Assembly, Toplita district, 1980-85, Braila South district, 1985-; Minister of Domestic Trade, 1985-; *office address:* Ms Ana Muresan, Marea Adunare Nationala, Aleea Marii Adunari Nationale, Bucharest, Romania; *phone:* 16 21 50.

MUSCARDINI, Cristiana; Italian, Member of the European Parliament; *born:* 6 November 1948, Cannobio, Novara, Italy; *party:* Movimento Sociale Italiano-Destra Nazionale (MSI-DN, Italian Social Movement-National Right); *political career:* municipal cnclr., mIlan; mem. central cttee., MSI-DN, and women's regional sec., Lombardy; Deputy, Jun 1983-, mem. of Commissions on Health and Hygiene; *professional career:* contributor to Candido; mem. Nat. Cncl. of Italian Writers' TU; journalist; *publications:* Potere animale; Una notte di florido; L'algognotico; *private address:* Via P. Sottocorno 5, I-20122 Milan, Italy; *office address:* Ms Cristiana Muscardini, European Parliament, Centre Européen, Plateau de Kirchberg, BP 2929, Luxembourg.

MUSTONE, Amelia P.; American, Connecticut State Senator; *born:* 16 July 1928, Salem, Mass., USA; *parents:* Udo A. Poppey and Alberta Poppey (née Durand); *married:* John Mustone, 1950; *children:* John, Lisa, Paul, Mary Ellen, Anastasia, Jessica; *religion:* Roman Catholic; *education:* Goddard College, Vermont, BA; *party:* Democratic Party; *political career:* Connecticut State Senator, District 13, 1979-; Dep. Majority Leader, 1983 and 1987; Dep. Minority Leader, 1985; *memberships:* Pres., Board of Education, Meriden, Connecticut, 1974-78; Mem., Cncl. on State Govts.; Vice-Chair New England Board of Higher Education; Mem., Connecticut Student Loan Foundation; Meriden League of Women Voters; Hon. Mem., Latin American Society; *private address:* 119 Lambert Avenue, Meriden, Connecticut 06450, USA; *office address:* Mrs Amelia Mustone, 34 Tunxis Circle, Meriden, Connecticut 06450, USA.

MUTSCH, Lydia; Luxembourgeios, Member of the Chamber of Deputies; *born:* 17 August 1961, Dudelange, Luxembourg; *parents:* Antoine Mutsch and Antoinette Mutsch (née Baum); *languages:* French, German, English, Spanish; *education:* Hubert Clement High School, Esch-sur-Alzette, 1974-80, modern languages option; University of Göttingen, West Germany, Faculty of Political and Social Sciences, 1980-85; degree in social sciences; *party:* Parti Ouvrier Socialiste Luxembourgeois (POSL, Luxembourg Socialist Workers Party), 1985; *political career:* member of Communal Council for Esch-sur-Alzette and spokesman for Socialist Group; Chmn. of Environment Committee; International Secretary of Young Luxembourg Socialists (JSL); Deputy; Vice-Chmn. of Cttee. for Middle Classes and Tourism; member of Foreign Affairs Committee; member of Sport and Youth Committee; member of Economic Cttee.; member of Control Commission of IUSY (International Union of Socialist Youth); *interests:* foreign affairs, economics, environment (particularly at community level); *professional career:* freelance journalist, 1983-86; advertising consultant, 1986-87; manager of advertising agency, 1987-89; *private address:* 1 rue St Jean, L-4153 Esch-sur-Alzette, Luxembourg; *office address:* Mme. Lydia Mutsch, Chambre des Députés, rue du Marché aux Herbes, Luxembourg-Ville, Luxembourg.

MUYUNDA, Mavis; Zambian, Minister of Water, Lands and Natural Resources; *party:* United National Independence Party (UNIP); *office address:* Mrs Mavis Muyunda, United National Independence Party, Freedom House, POB 30302 Lusaka, Zambia.

MYRICK, Sue; American, Mayor of Charlotte, North Carolina; *born:* 1 August 1941, Tiffin, Ohio, USA; *married:* Ed Myrick; *party:* Republican Party; *political career:* Mayor, Charlotte, North Carolina, 1987-; Mem., Board of Dirs., North Carolina Highway Safety Foundation; Mem., Pres. Bush's Affordable Housing

Commission; Co-Chwn., Task Force on Hunger and Homelessness, US Conference of Mayors; Trustee, US Conference of Mayors; Mem., Strengthening America Commission; former Mem., Republican National Cttee; *memberships:* Board of Dirs., Sister Cities International and North Carolina Inst. of Political Leadership; Handicapped Organised Women, National Board; Lay Leader and Speaker, Methodist Church; founder, Charitable Outreach Society (COS); *clubs:* Providence Country Club; *office address:* Mrs Sue Myrick, 310 W. 8th Street, Charlotte, North Carolina, 28202, USA.

N

NABHOLZ-HAIDEGGER, Zollikon; Swiss, Member of the Nationalrat; *born:* 31 December 1944, Solothurn, Switzerland; *children:* two; *education:* Dr. of Law; *party:* Freisinnig-Demokratische Partei der Schweiz (Liberal Democratic Party of Switzerland); *political career:* Pres., Commission for Women's Affairs, 1980-; Mem. of the Nationalrat for Zollikon, Canton of Zürich, 1987-; *professional career:* lawyer; *office address:* Frau Zollikon Nabholz-Haidegger, Nationalrat/Conseil National, Secretariat-General, Parlamentsgebäude, 3003 Berne, Switzerland; *phone:* Berne 619711.

NAE, Elena; Romanian, Deputy to the Grand National Assembly; *born:* 1928; *party:* Romanian Communist Party (RCP); *political career:* Chairperson, Trade Union Cttee., Bucharest Cloth and Knitting Factory, 1964-78; candidate Mem., Exec. Cttee. and Mem. Central Cncl., Gen. Federation of Trade Unions, 1965-79; Mem., Bucharest Municipal Cncl. of Socialist Democracy and Unity Front, 1968-; Mem., Central Cttee., Communist Youth, 1971-74; candidate Mem., RCP Central Cttee., 1974-79; Vice Chairperson, Cttee. of Light Industry's Trade Union, Chairperson, 1976-79; Dep., Grand Nat. Assembly, Ilfov district, 1977; Vice Chairperson, Workers Nat. Cncl., 1977-; Chairperson, Women's Commission of Central Cncl. of Trade Unions, 1978-79; First Sec., Bucharest Municipal RCP, Sector 6 Cttee., Mayoress, 1979-84; Mem., RCP Central Cttee., candidate Mem., Political Exec. Cttee., 1979; Dep., Grand Nat. Assembly, Bucharest Municipality, 1980; Vice Chairperson, GNA Commission for Health, Labour, Social Welfare and Environmental Protection, 1980; First Sec., Sibiu RCP District Cttee. and Chairperson, District People's Cncl., 1984-87; Dep., Grand Nat. Assembly, Sibiu district, 1985-; *office address:* Ms Elena Nae, Marea Adunare Nationala, Aleea Marii Adunari Nationale, Bucharest, Romania; *phone:* 16 21 50.

NAGEL, Mónica; Costa Rican, Vice-Minister of Justice; *office address:* Ms Mónica Nagel, Ministry of Justice, Apartado 5685, San José 1000, Costa Rica.

NAGYNE, G.; Hungarian, Member of the Országgyülés; *party:* Hungarian Democratic Forum (MDF); *office address:* Ms G. Nagyné, Országgyülés, Kossuth L. tér 1-3, Budapest V, Hungary; *phone:* 22 5058; 22 5059.

NAKANISHI, Tamako; Japanese, Member of the House of Councillors; *born:* 19 March 1919; *education:* Tsuda College; *party:* Komeito (Clean Government Party); *political career:* former Deputy Dir. of ILO Tokyo Branch; second time elected for National; Chmn., House of Cllrs. Special Cttee. on Science and Technology and Mem., House of Cllrs. Cttee. on Foreign Affairs, 1990-; *office address:* Ms Tamako Nakanishi, House of Councillors, 1-7-1 Nagata-cho, Tokyo 100, Japan; *phone:* (03) 5813111.

NAMAZOVA, Adila Avaz kyzy; Soviet, Member of the Council of Nationalities; *party:* Communist Party of the Soviet Union; *political career:* Mem., Cncl. of Nationalities; Mem., Supreme Soviet Cttees. on Women's Affairs, Family Protection, Motherhood and Childhood; *professional career:* faculty chief, Azerbaijan Medical Inst., Baku; *office address:* Ms Adila Avaz kyzy Namazova, Council of Nationalities, Kremlin, Moscow, USSR.

NAMIR, Ora; Israeli, Chairperson of the Knesset Select Committee on Labour and Welfare; *born:* 1933, Hadera; *party:* Ma'arach (Israeli Labour Party); *political career:* Mem., Knesset; chwn., Prime Minister's Select Cttee. on the Status of Women; *office address:* Ms Ora Namir, Knesset, Hakirya, Jerusalem 91000, Israel; *phone:* (02) 661211.

NAPSIAH BTE OMAR, Dato'; Malaysian, Minister at the National Unity and Social Development Ministry; *born:* 21 April 1943, Kuala Pilah, Negeri Sembilan; *education:* Tunku Khursiah School, Kuala Pilah; Tunku Mohamad School, Kuala Pilah; Telopea Park High School, Canberra, Australia, 1961-63; Australian National Univ., Canberra, B.Sc., Zoology and Botany, 1963-66; Cornell Univ., Ithica, New York, M.Sc., Nutrition and Education, 1969-72; *political career:* elected MP for Kuala Pilah, Negeri Sembilan, Barisan, 1982, re-elected 1986; Deputy Federal Minister of Housing and Local Govt.; 1982-87; Minister of Public Enterprises, 1988-; Mem., Supreme Council UMNO, 1988-; Deputy Chief, Wanita UMNO, 1988-; Chmn., Wanita UMNO Movement, Negeri Sembilan, 1988-; Chief, Wanita UMNO, Kuala Pilah Division, 1988-; *memberships:* founder and Vice-President, Australian Overseas Student Assn., Canberra, 1963-65; cttee. mem., Life, Family Planning, Selangor and Federal

Territory; Chairman, Kuala Pilah District Cooperative Development; Cttee. Mem., National Cooperative Development; *professional career:* Administrative Officer, Department of Settlers Development, FELDA Kuala Lumpur, 1967-69; Lecturer, College of Agriculture Malaysia, Serdang, Selangor, 1972; Coordinator, Home and Nutrition Technology Department, Univ. Pertanian Malaysia (UPM), 1972-73, promoted to Acting Head of Department, 1973-76; promoted to Head of Human Development Studies Department, 1978-80 Associate Professor, 1981-82; concurrently, Head, 4th UPM College Accomodation, 1974-82; resigned as Associate Professor to enter politics, 1982; *honours and awards:* Commander of The Order of Negeri Sembilan; First Woman MP to come from Negeri Sembilan; *clubs:* President, Federal Territory Girl Guides; *private address:* Kementerian Perusahaan Awam, Tingkat 3 Wisma PKNS, Jalan Raja Laut, 50652 Kuala Lumpur; *office address:* Dato' Napsiah Bte Omar, Ministry of National and Rural Development, Banguan Bank Rakayat, 1st Floor, Jalan Tangsi, 50606 Kuala Lumpur, Malaysia; *phone:* (03) 2910255.

NARAYAN, Irene Jai; Fijian, Minister for Indian Affairs; *born:* 23 February 1932; *parents:* George Hamilton and Violet Hannah Hamilton; *married:* Jai Narayan, 1954; *public role of spouse:* Principal of Indian College, Suva; served on Boundaries Commission, 1971-86; *children:* three s., one d; *religion:* Hindu; *languages:* English, Urdu, Hindi; *education:* Christ Church Convent; Methodist High School; Isabella Thoburn College; Lucknow Univ. BA, LT; Banaras Hindu Univ., India, MA; *party:* Alliance Party; *political career:* elected to Legislative Council, 1966; Mem., Fiji's Legislative Council delegation in London to discuss framing a constitution, 1970; elected to House of Representatives as a Federation candidate, 1972, re-elected 1977 and 1982; Opposition Whip, 1977-82; Opposition Spokesperson on Finance, 1977-82; Deputy Leader of the Opposition, 1979-85; Fijian representative at the Commonwealth Parly. Assn. conferences in Australia, 1969, and in Jamaica, 1978; Minister for Indian Affairs, Oct. 1987, re-appointed Dec. 1989; *professional career:* Principal, D.A.V. Girls College, Suva, 1956-62; Head of English Dept., M.G.M. High School, 1963-71; *private address:* 11 Mataritosuva Street, Suva, Fiji; *office address:* Ms Irene Narayan, Ministry of Indian Affairs, Suva, Fiji.

NATARAJAN, Jayanthi; Indian, Member of the Rajya Sabha; *born:* 7 June 1954, Madras; *parents:* C R Sundararajan; *married:* V.K.Natarajan; *education:* BA; BL; *political career:* Mem., Rajya Sabha, 1986-; Mem., Cttee. of Privilegism, Rajya Sabha; Mem., Social Welfare Board, 1988-; engaged in social work in All India Womens' Conference and legal aid for the poor; *professional career:* advocate; *private address:* 'Badri', 47, Warren Road, Mylapore, Madras 600004; *office*

address: Shrimati Jayanthl Natarajan, Ab-8, Pandara Road, New Delhi -- 1.

NCUBE, Sister Bernard; South African, President of the Federation of Transvaal Women; *born:* 9 March 1935, Pietersburg, Transvaal, South Africa; *parents:* Benedict Ncube and Anna Ncube; *religion:* Catholic; *education:* Sacred Heart Primary School, Germiston; St Thomas' School, Heidelberg; St Mary's Teacher Training College, Lesotho; *party:* United Democratic Front (UDF); *political career:* involved in launch of Federation of Transvaal Women, Pres., 1984-; arrested and detained on several occasions, three months solitary confinement, 1986; charged with sedition, subversion and assault, together with 13 members of Krugersdop Residents' Organisations (KRO), case against them collapsed when the state failed to supply details of the charges, 1988; travelled to USA with UDF delegation, met Pres. George Bush, 1989; *interests:* emancipation of women and the oppressed; *professional career:* teacher, Catholic schools, Johannesburg, St. Peters, Dobonsville, St. Angelas, 1955; field worker, South African Catholic Bishops' Conference, 1980-87; worker, Institute of Contextual Theology, 1987; *office address:* Sister Bernard Ncube, Parliament, Cape Town, South Africa; *phone:* (012) 403-2911.

NDIAYE, Ndioro; Senegalese, Minister-Delegate for Women and Child Affairs; *office address:* Ms Ndioro Ndiaye, Assemblee National, Place Tascher, Dakar, Senegal; *phone:* 23 10 99; 21 16 29.

NEIERTZ, Véronique; French, Secretary of State for Women's Rights; *born:* 6 November 1942, Paris, France; *parents:* Michel Dillard and Hélène Dillard (née Querenet); *married:* Patricke Neiertz, 1965; *children:* Nicolas Aurélie Julien; *education:* National Institute for Information Science of the National Centre for Arts and Crafts; Ecole des Hautes Etudes Commerciales Jeunes Filles, graduate; *party:* Parti Socialiste (PS, Socialist Party); *political career:* Head of Socialist Party's Central Office for political, economic and social Information, 1972-79; contributor to Unité, 1976-79; member, Socialist Party's executive bureau, 1979-84; national secretary, Socialist Party's women's rights, 1979-81, then for international relations, 1981; Deputy, Seine Saint-Denis, 1981, re-elected 1986 and 1988; Sec., National Assembly's foreign affairs commission, 1981-86; regional councillor, Ile de France, 1981-86; Deputy mayor, Boudy, 1983-; chairman, French section of Interparliamentary Franco-Canadian Association, 1981-86; Deputy chairman, Parly. France-Québec friendship group, 1981-; chairman, National Noise Council, 1982-86; spokesperson, National Assembly's socialist group, 1983-86; Deputy chairman, Parly. France-USSR friendship group, 1986-; Deputy chairman, National Assembly's socialist group, 1986; chairman, National Assembly's research group into apartheid, 1988; Sec. of State, Ministry of the Economy, Finance and the Budget, responsible for Consumer Protection, 1988; Secretary of State for Women's Rights; *professional career:* lecturer, University of Madagascar, 1967-70; *publications:* Véridique histoire d'un septennat peu ordinaire, 1987; *recreations:* mountain sports, tennis; *office address:* Mme. Veronique Neiertz, Secretariat of State for Women's Rights, 31 rue Le Peletier, 75009 Paris, France.

NEIMAN, Joan; Canadian, Senator; *born:* 1920, Winnipeg, Man; *married:* Clemes Michael (Neiman), 1953; *children:* Dallis, Patricia, David; *education:* Mount Allison Univ., New Brunswick; Osgoode Hall Law School; *party:* Liberal; *political career:* Senator for Peel, Ontario, 1972-; Mem., Senate Cttees. on Foreign Affairs, Nat. Defence and Chairperson Cttees. on Legal and Constitutional Affairs; *professional career:* lawyer; *office address:* Honarary Senator Joan Neiman, Senate, Parliament Buildings, Wellington Street, Ottawa, Ontario K1A OA4, Canada; *phone:* (613) 992 4416.

NÉLIS, Denise; Belgian, Senator; *born:* 14 August 1927, Woluwe-Saint-Pierre; *education:* Brussels School of Social work, 1945-48; *party:* Ecolo (Ecologist Party - French Speaking); *political career:* Head of government Cttee. on Health; Trade Unionist, 1947-86; Regional Sec., Ecolo. Charleroi, 1987; Pres., Ecolo. Federal Cttee. on Health, 1987; Senator for Charleroi-Thuin, 1988-; Pres. of Ecolo - FDF Section of Wallonia Regional Cncl., 1988-; Researcher for Senate Commission on Social Affairs; mem. of Senate Commission for Internal Affairs; mem. of Cncl. for French Community; *professional career:* Head of Youth Assn. of Belgian Coast, 1947-49; Social Worker, at Intercom sa, Charleroi, 1950-86; *private address:* rue des Mésanges 12, batiment 7, 6110 Montigny-le-Tilleul; *office address:* Mme. Denise Nélis, Senate, Palais de la Nation, Place de a Nation 1, 1000 Brussels, Belgium.

NEMCOVA, Helena; Czechoslovakian, Member of the Narodni Rada (Czech National Council); *born:* 17 January 1922; *party:* Civic Forum; *office address:* Ms Helena Nemcova, Ceská národní rada, Snemovní 4, 110 00 Praha 1, Czechoslovakia; *phone:* (02) 2105.

NENNA D'ANTONIO, Anna; Italian, Deputy; *born:* 2 August 1927, San Vito Chietino, Chieti; *education:* Degree in Letters; *party:* Democrazia Cristiana (DC, Christian Democratic Party); *political career:* Council Assessor, Provincial and Regional Councillor, Abruzzo; Abruzzo Regional Council, 1970-83; Assessor for Industry, Trade and Crafts, 1972-74; Assessor for Health, Hygene and Ecology, 1977-80; Pres. Regional Authority of Abruzzo, 1980-83; Deputy Vice-Pres., DC, Southern Regional Cttee., at the Ministry for extraordinary interventions in the South; Deputy, Parliament, Aquila-Pescara-Chieti-Teramo, 1983;

Head of DC group, on Bicameral Cttee. on Regional Questions; mem. Cttee. on Affairs of the Presidency of the Council and of Internal Affairs; mem. Nat. Council of DC; Nat. Dir., USL, for the DC; re-elected Deputy, 1987; mem. Cttee. on Social Affairs; *professional career:* Teacher (Lyceum, Gymnasium); *office address:* Ms Anna Nenna D'Antonio, Camera dei Deputati, Montecitorio, 00186 Rome, Italy.

NERALIC-MILIVOJEVIC, Nevenka; Yugoslavian, Member of the Federal Chamber; *political career:* Mem., Federal Chamber, 1982-; Mem., Federal Exec. Cncl., Minister Without Portfolio, 1986; Pres., Housing Questions Commission, 1986-; Pres., Human Environmental and Urban Planning Commission, 1986; *office address:* Ms Nevenka Neralic-Milivojevic, Savezna Skupstina, Yugoslavia.

NERI, Adelaide (Antonia Adelaide de Rocha); Brazilian, Federal Deputy; *born:* 16 December 1940, Taraucá; *parents:* Vicente Crescencio da Rocha and Rosa Nachado da Rocha; *married:* Raimundo Nonato de Paiva Neri; *children:* Vicente José, Marlon José, Missilene Maria, Maria do Socorro, Jacqueline Maria, André Augosto; *education:* UFAC, Rio Branco, literature, 1980-84; *party:* Partido do Movimento Democrático Brasileira (PMDB, Party of the Brazlian Democratic Movement); *political career:* Federal Deputy for Acre, 1991-95; *professional career:* Dir., Dept. of Supplementary Teaching, Sec. of Education and Culture, 1983-90; *office address:* Ms Adelaide Neri, Chamber of Deputies, Praça dos 3 Poderes, Ed. Principal, 70160 Brasilia, DF, Brazil; *phone:* (61) 225 2885.

NESPOLO, Carla Federica; Italian, Senator; *born:* 4 March 1943, Novara, Italy; *education:* Degree in Philosophy; *party:* Partito Democratico della Sinistra (PDS, Party of the Democratic Left); *political career:* Provincial Councillor and Assessor for Public Instruction, Alessandria; *professional career:* Teacher; *office address:* Ms Carla Nespolo, Senato della Repubblica, Palazzo Madama, 00100 Rome, Italy.

NETELENBOS, Tineke; Dutch, Member of the Second Chamber; *born:* 15 February 1944, Wormerveer, Netherlands; *married:* J.C. Netelenbos, 1967; *public role of spouse:* medical doctor; *children:* two; *languages:* English, German; *education:* MULO, HBO (sec. ed.); *party:* Partij van de Arbeid (PvdA, Labour Party); *political career:* Mem. of town council, Haarlemmermeer; second secretary PvdA party board; Mem. directing department Haarlemmermeer and region Noord-Holland; Pres. region Noord-Holland south; Mem. PvdA party board; Mem. Second Chamber, 1987-; *professional career:* teacher LHNO and MBO schools; branch trainer, adult education; *recreations:* mountaineering; *private address:* Florence

Nightingalestraat 124, 1231 EE Hoofddorp, the Netherlands; *office address:* Mevr. Tineke Netelenbos, Tweede Kamer der Staaten-Generaal, Binnenhof 1A, Postbus 20018, The Hague, Netherlands.

NEWMAN, Jocelyn Margaret; Australian, Senator; *born:* 8 July 1937, Melbourne, Victoria, Australia; *married:* K.E. Newman, 1961; *public role of spouse:* Former Federal Minister, 1975-83; *children:* one s., one d; *religion:* Church of England; *education:* LLB, Melbourne; *party:* Liberal Party; *political career:* chosen by Parliament of Tasmania to represent Tasmania in the Senate, 1986 and elected, 1987-, re-elected 1990-; Committee Service: Mem. of the Senate Standing Cttee. for the Scrutiny of Bills, 1986-87; Mem. of the Senate Legislative and General Purpose Standing Cttee. for Education and Arts, 1986-87; for Foreign Affairs, Defence and Trade, 1987-90; Mem. of the Senate Select Cttee. for the Education of Gifted and Talented Children, 1987-88; Mem. of the Senate Estimates Cttee. D, 1986-87; E, 1987-88; B, 1988-; *memberships:* Law Society of Tasmania; founding mem., Women's Shelters in Hobart and Launceston; former State Executive, National Trust (Tas.); former Dep. Chairperson, Association of Independent Schools of Tasmania; *professional career:* barrister and solicitor; heritage developer; hotelier; *office address:* Ms Jocelyn Newman, 11 Elphin Road, Launceston 7250, Tasmania.

NEYTS-UYTTERBROECK, Anne-Marie; Belgian, Member of the Chamber of Representatives; *born:* 17 June 1944, Ixelles, Belgium; *education:* VUB, Bachelor of Latin Philology; qualified Secondary School Teacher; VUB, Bachelor of Journalism and Communications; *party:* Partij vor Vrijheid en Vooruitgang (PVV, Liberal Party, Dutch Wing); *political career:* Press Attaché to Minister of Justice Merman Vander-poorten, 1973-75; Leader of Deputy Cabinet for Deputy Governor, Brabant; Pres., PVV Brussels-Town, 1977-85; Co-Pres., Second Congress of Flemish Brussels Citizens, 1979-81; mem. of PVV Permanent Exec., 1980-81; Deputy, 1981-; secretary of state for Brussels Region, 1981-85; Vice-Pres. then Pres., PVV women, until 1982; Local Cllr., Brussels-Town, 1983; mem. of Permanent Cttee. of European Liberals and Democrats LDE, 1983-; Pres., PVV, 1985-; *professional career:* Teacher of French, Royal Secondary School, Zaventem, 1963-73; *private address:* L. Lepagestraat 24, 1000 Brussel, Belgium; *office address:* Ms Anne-Marie Neyts-Uytterbroeck, Kamer van Volksvertegenwoordigers, Palais de la Nation, Place de la Nation 2, 1000 Brussels, Belgium.

NGUYEN THI BINH; Vietnamese, Vice Chair of the Council of State and President of the Vietnamese Women's Union; *born:* 1927; *education:* school in Saigon; *party:* Vietnamese Women's Union; *political career:* student political leader in Saigon; organised

(with Nguyen Huu Tho, qv) first anti-American demonstration, 1950; imprisoned by French Authorities, 1951-54; Vice-Pres., S. Vietnamese Cttee. for Solidarity with the American People; Vice-Pres., Union of Women for the Liberation of S. Vietnam; Mem., Central Cttee., Nat. Liberation Front (NLF); appointed NLF spokesperson to four party peace talks, Paris, 1968; Minister for Foreign Affairs, Provisional Revolutionary Govt. of S. Vietnam, 1969-76; Minister of Education, Socialist Republic of Vietnam, 1976-87; Vice-Pres., Vietnamese Women's Union, 1976-; *office address:* Mme. Nguyen Thi Binh, Vietnamese Women's Union, 39 Hang Chuoi, Hanoi, Viet-Nam.

NICHOLSON, Emma Harriet; British, Member of Parliament; *born:* 16 October 1941; *parents:* Sir Godfrey Nicholson and the late Lady Katharine Lindsay Nicholson; *married:* Sir Michael Harris Caine, 1987; *public role of spouse:* Chairman of Booker PLC, Commonwealth Scholarships Commission and The Royal African Society, United Kingdom Overseas Council for Student Affairs; *religion:* Church of England, Methodist; *languages:* French; *education:* Portsdown Lodge School, Bexhill; St. Mary's School, Wantage; Royal Academy of Music, London, LRAM, ARCM; *party:* Conservative Party; *political career:* Mem., Select Cttee. on Employment, 1990; Mem., Medical Research Cncl., 1991; Mem., European Union of Women, 1983; founder and joint Chwn., All Party Parly. Group for Romanian Children, 1990; Mem., All Party Group on Aids, 1990; Mem., Steering Cttee., The Conservative Cncl. on Eastern Europe, 1987; Exec. Mem., Inter-Parly. Union (IPU), 1990; Mem., 300 Group, 1985; Vice-Chwn., Conservative Party with special responsibility for Women, 1983-87; Chwn., Conservative Backbench Environment Cttee.; MP for Devon West and Torridge, 1987-; Vice-Pres., Assn. of District Cncls., 1991; Mem., British-Turkish Parly. Group, 1987; Mem., Franco-British Parly. Group, 1987; Treas., British Caribbean All Party Group, 1987; Mem., British-Argentinian Parly. Group, 1990; Mem., Hansard Society Cncl., 1990; Mem., PITCOM (Parly. Information Technology Cttee.) Cncl., 1988; Fellow, Industry and Parly. Trust (IBM) 1990; Mem., Conservative Friends of Israel, 1987; Mem., Tory Green Initiative, 1990; *memberships:* Vice-Pres., Devon Young Farmers Club; Patron, Devon HIV/AIDS Trust; Hon. Mem., Business and Professional Women's Assn.; Royal Assn. in Aid of Deaf People; Prince of Wales Advisory Trust on Disability; Royal Academy of Music Appeal Cttee.; Fellow, Royal Society of Arts; Patron, CRUSAID; Chwn., Friends of the Duke of Edinburgh Award Scheme; Dep. Chwn., Duke of Edinburgh's 30th Anniversary Tribute Project and International Proct '87; Patron, Suzy Lamplugh Trust; Gov., Mary Hare Grammar School; Dir., Cities in Schools; Patron, British Deaf Accord and Women into Information Technology Foundation; Friend, Societe des Amies d'Enfance, Poland; Patron, National Assn. of

Deafened People and Sense South West, the National Deaf, Blind and Rubella Assn.; Pres., British Tinnitus Foundation; Trustee, Covent Garden Cancer Research Trust, The Little Foundation and Motor Neurone Disease Assn.; Vice-Patron, The Child Psychotherapy Trust; Vice-Moderator, Movement for the Ordination of Women; Friend, Parkhurst Society; Trustee, Shelter; Chwn., ADAPT (Access for Disabled People to Arts Premises Today); Mem., Forum UK; Centre for Policy Studies; Royal Inst. for International Affairs; Royal Horticultural Society; *professional career:* computer programmer, instructor and systems analyst, ICI, 1963-66; computer consultant, John Tyzack & Partners, 1967-69; Computer and Gen. Management Consultant, McLintock, Mann and Whinney Murray, 1969-73; Dir. of Fundraising, Save the Children Fund, 1977-85, Pres., Hatherleigh Branch; Pres., Plymouth and West Devon Cassette Talking Newspaper; Board mem., Stichting Redt De Kinderen (Nederland); Mem., Comité d'Honneur Sauvez Les Enfants (France), 1982-88; *publications:* various articles and pamphlets; *clubs:* The Reform Club; St. Stephen's Constitutional Club; *recreations:* music, walking; *office address:* Miss Emma Nicholson, House of Commons, London SW1A OAA.

NICHOLSON, Pamela; Trinidad and Tobago, Minister of Settlement and Public Utilities; *born:* 21 January 1945; *religion:* Christian; *education:* Charlotteville Methodist Bishop's High School, Tobago; Elizabeth College, Tobago; Univ. West Indies, BA, General, History, Sociology, English, 1976; *party:* Democratic Action Congress (DAC); *political career:* entered politics, 1970; Mem. of DAC since it's institutionalisation; Mem. of Parliament for Tobago East, 1981-86; Mem. of Parliament for Tobago West, Mem. of the Govt. Office; Minister of Settlement and Public Utilities; *professional career:* Sec. and Mem., Board of the Carnbee/Mt. Pleasant Village Cncl.; organized nursery school, Community Centre of Mt. Pleasant Village; *recreations:* table tennis, football; *office address:* The Honourable Pamela Nicholson MP, Ministry of Settlement and Public Utilities, 16-18 Sackville St., Port of Spain, Trinidad and Tobago.

NICKELS, Christa; German, former Member of the Bundestag; *born:* 29 July 1952, Setterich, Nordrhein-Westfalen, West Germany; *children:* two; *religion:* Roman Catholic; *education:* Ursuline grammar school for girls emphasising modern languages, Geilenkirchen, Abitur (advanced matriculation examination), 1971; *party:* Die Grünen (Green Party), founder member, 1979; *political career:* co-founder, district association Heinsberg, Die Grünen, 1980; spokeswoman of district association Heinsberg, Die Grünen, for two years; parly. secretary, Die Grünen, 1983-84; member of women's Exec. Cttee., Die Grünen parly. group, 1984-85; former mem. of Bundestag, party list of Nordrhein-Westfalen; *professional career:* training as nurse, 1971-74; full-time housewife, for two years; night nurse,

intensive care unit of internal medecine, 1977-, on leave 1983; member of Gewerkschaft Öffentliche Dienste, Transport und Verkehr (ÖTV, Trade Union for Public and Transport Services); *clubs:* Pax Christi; *private address:* 5130 Geilenkirchen, West Germany; *office address:* Frau Christa Nickels .

NICOL, Baroness (cr. 1983, Life Peer) Olive Mary Wendy Nicol; British, Member of the House of Lords; *born:* 21 March 1923; *parents:* the late James Rowe-Hunter and Harriet Rowe-Hunter; *married:* Alexander Douglas Ian Nicol CBE, 1947; *children:* two s., one d; *education:* Cahir Sch., Eire; *party:* Labour Party; *political career:* JP, Cambridge, 1972-86; Camb. City Council, 1972-82, Dep. Mayor, 1974, Chmn., Environment Cttee., 1978-82, Careers Service Consultative Panel, 1978-81; mem., House of Lords, 1982; Opp. Dep. Chief Whip, 1987-89; Opp. Front Bench Spokesman on Environment, 1987-; *interests:* local govt., strategic planning, employment, commerce, conservation and environment; *memberships:* FRSA; FRGS; *professional career:* Inland Revenue, 1942-44; Admiralty, 1944-48; United Charities, 1967-86; Co-operative Board, 1976-85, Pres., 1981-85; various Sch. Governing Bodies and other public service areas, including Granta Housing Assn; *recreations:* reading, walking, talking; *office address:* Baroness Nicol, House of Lords, London SW1A 0PW.

NIEHUIS, Dr. Edith; German, Member of the Bundestag; *born:* 2 August 1950, Gölriehenfeld; *children:* two; *religion:* Protestant (Lutheran); *languages:* English; *education:* Abitur (advanced matriculation examination), 1969; Universities of Oldenburg and Göttingen; first state examination for elementary school teachers, 1972; College of Education, Niedersachsen, Diplompädagogin (Diploma of Education), 1977; University of Göttingen, Dr. Phil. (Doctor of Philosophy), 1983; *party:* Sozialdemokratische Partei Deutschlands (SPD, Social Democratic Party of Germany), 1972; *political career:* sub-district chmn., Working Group of Social Democratic Women, since 1990-; member of district Exec. Cttee., SPD in Hannover since 1987-; dep. sub-district chmn., SPD in Northeim/Einbeck, since 1983; mem. of Bundestag for Northeim-Osterode, since 1987; Pres., Cttee. on Women and Youth in the Bundestag; *professional career:* education officer, rural adult education, 1973; scientific employee, Parity Education Establishment, 1973-76; education officer, Residential Adult Education College Jägerei Hustedt, 1976-79; education officer, Residential Adult Education College Mariaspring, 1980-87; member of Working Group New Education; member of Gewerkschaft Erziehung and Wissenschaft (GEW, Trade Union for Education and Science); *publications:* numerous; *clubs:* German Red Cross; Arbeiterwohlfahrt (AWO, Labour Welfare Organisation); *private address:* 3412 Nörten-

Hardenberg, West Germany; *office address:* Dr. Edith Niehuis, Bundeshaus, 5300 Bonn 1, West Germany.

NISHIOKA, Ruriko; Japanese, Member of the House of Councillors; *born:* 22 July 1934; *education:* Tosa High School; *party:* Japan Socialist Party (JSP); *political career:* former Vice-Chairperson, JSP Kochi Prefectural HQ and Chief Secretary of Kochi Division of Japan Broadcasting Labour Union; elected for Kochi, 1990; Mem., House of Cllrs. Cttee. on Education, 1990-; *office address:* Ms Ruriko Nishioka, House of Councillors, 1-7-1 Nagata-cho, Tokyo 100, Japan; *phone:* (03) 5813111.

N'JIE, Louise; Gambia, Minister for Health and Social Welfare; *office address:* Ms Louise N'Jie, Ministry of Health and Social Welfare, MacCarthy Square, Banjul, Republic of Gambia.

NORBERG, Gudrun; Swedish, Member of the Riksdag; *born:* 30 May 1938, Glanshammar, Sweden; *parents:* Erik Larsson and Aina Larsson; *married:* Karl Erik Norberg, 1965; *children:* Ulrica, Gabriel; *religion:* Protestant, Church of Sweden; *languages:* a little English and German; *education:* Lower School Certificate, Örebro Praktiskc Realskola, Örebro, 1951-55; *party:* Folkpartiet Liberalerna (Liberal Party), 1968; *political career:* Deputy Chairwoman of the Delegation for non-military resistance; Member of the board of the Transport Council; Chairwoman of Folkpartiet Provincial Assoc. in the Admin. Province of Örebro; Chairwoman in the Glanshammar Local Folkpartiet; MP, 1985-; *interests:* trade and industry; energy affairs, artisan matters; retail trade matters; *clubs:* Blue Ribbon-Movement, MHF, Red Cross, White Ribbon, Swedish Soc. for Protection of the Environment; *office address:* Ms Gudrun Norberg, Riksdag, Fack, S-100 12 Stockholm, Sweden.

NORDBO, Eldrid; Norwegian, Minister of Trade and Shipping; *born:* 12 August 1942, Skien; *married:* Bjorn Skogstad Aamo; *public role of spouse:* Special Adviser; *education:* Degree in Political Science, 1968; *political career:* Minister of Trade and Shipping, Nov. 1990; *professional career:* junior Exec. Officer, Ministry of Health and Social Affairs, until 1970; Private Sec. to the Minister of Health and Social Affairs, 1971; Municipal policy Cllr. for Health and Social Affairs, Oslo, 1972-79; Analyst, International League of the Red Cross, Geneva, 1979-81; Special Advisor, Ministry of the Environment, 1989-90; *office address:* Ms Eldrid Nordbo, Office of the Prime Minister, Akersgaten 42, P.O. Box 8001 Dep, 0030 Oslo 1, Norway; *phone:* (02) 34 90 90; *fax:* 349500.

NOVOA CARCACIA, María del Pilar; Spanish, Deputy; *born:* 13 April 1957, Toldaria, Orense, Spain; *education:* degree in social work; *party:* Partido Socialista Obrero Español (PSOE, Spanish Socialist Workers' Party); *political career:* Dept. of Education of Galicia autonomous government; Deputy, PSOE, Orense, 1986-89, re-elected 1989-; mem. Cttee. on Social Policy and Employment, Cortes; *office address:* Ms María Novoa Carcacia, Congreso de los Diputados, Fernán Flor 1, Madrid 14, Spain.

NUCCI MAURO, Anna Maria; Italian, Deputy; *born:* 1 May 1943, Cervinara, Avellino; *education:* Degree in Philosophy; *party:* Democrazia Cristiana (DC, Christian Democratic Party); *political career:* Dir. of SPES-Training and Culture of Cosenza; Deputy, Catanzaro-Cosenza-Reggio Calabria, 1983; mem. Cttee., Finance and Treasury; re-elected Deputy, 1987; Under-Secretary for Public Instruction in Goria govt; *professional career:* Lecturer in Italian and History in State Institutes (Lower level); *office address:* Ms Anna Nucci Mauro, Camera dei Deputati, Montecitorio, 00186 Rome, Italy.

O

OAKAR, Mary Rose; American, Member of the House of Representatives; *born:* 5 March 1940, Cleveland, Ohio, USA; *parents:* Joseph Oakar and Margaret Oakar (née Ellison); *education:* Ursuline College, BA, 1962; John Carroll Univ., MA, 1966; Academy of Drama, London, UK; Westham Adult College, Warwickshire, England, UK; Columbia Univ., New York, USA; *party:* Democratic Party; *political career:* Mem., US House of Reps., Ohio, District 20, 1977-; Mem., Banking, Finance, Urban Affairs Cttee.,; Mem., Select Cttee. on Aging, Post Office and Civil Service, House Admin. and Joint Library Cttees., US House of Reps; *memberships:* trustee, Society for Crippled Children; *clubs:* YWCA; *office address:* Ms Mary Oakar, Rayburn House Office Bldg., Washington DC, 20515, USA.

OBERNDORF, Meyera E.; American, Mayor of Virginia Beach, Virginia; *married:* Roger L; *children:* Marcie, Heide; *religion:* Jewish; *education:* Old Dominion Univ., BS, 1964; *political career:* City Cllr., Virginia Beach, 1976-86, the Vice-Mayor, 1986-88 and Mayor, 1988-; *private address:* 5404 Challedon Drive, Virginia Beach, Virginia 23462, USA; *office address:* Ms Meyera Oberndorf, Municipal Center, Virginia Beach, Virginia 23456-9002, USA.

O'CONNOR, Maureen Frances; American, Mayor of San Diego; *born:* 14 July 1946, San Diego, California,, USA; *parents:* Jerome O'Connor and Frances O'Connor; *married:* Robert Peterson, 1977; *religion:* Roman Catholic; *education:* San Diego State Univ., California, BA, 1970; *party:* Democratic Party; *political career:* City Councilwoman, San Diego, 1971-79; Mem., Metropolitan Transit Development Board, 1976-81; Mem., Port Commission, 1979-85; Mayor, San Diego, 1986-; *professional career:* teacher and Cllr., Rosary High School, 1970-71; *office address:* Ms Maureen O'Connor, 202 C Street, San Diego, California 92101, USA.

O'CONNOR, Sandra Day; American, Associate Justice to the US Supreme Court; *born:* 26 March 1930, El Paso, Texas, USA; *parents:* Harry A. Day and Ada Mae Day (née Wilkey); *married:* John Jay O'Connor III, 1952; *children:* Scott, Brian, Jay; *religion:* Episcopal; *education:* Stanford Univ., BA, 1950, LLB, 1952; *political career:* Dep. County Attorney, San Mateo County, California, 1952-53; civilian attorney,

Frankfurt, Germany, 1954-57; referee, Juvenile Court, 1962-65; Chair, Visitors Board, Maricopa County Juvenile Detention home, 1963-64; Mem., Maricopa County Board of Adjustments and Appeals, 1963-64; Asst. Attorney-General, Arizona, 1965-69; Mem., Arizona Personnel Commission, 1968-69; Arizona State Senator, 1969-75; Chair, State, County and Municipal Affairs Cttee., 1972-73; Senate Majority Leader, 1972 and 1975; Mem., Legislative Cncl., Probate Code Commission and Arizona Advisory Cncl. on Inter-Govt. Relations; Chair, Cttee. to Re-organise the Lower Courts, Arizona Supreme Court, 1974-75; judge, Maricopa County Superior Court, 1975-79; Arizona Court of Appeals, 1979-81; Vice-Chair Select Law Enforcement Revue Commission, 1979-80; Assc. Justice, US Supreme Court, 1981-; *memberships:* Mem., Editorial Board, Stanford Univ., Law Revue; Mem., Phoenix Community Cncl., Arizona Academy, 1970-75; Mem., Advisory Board, Phoenix Salvation Army, 1975-81; trustee, Stanford Univ., 1976-80; National Assn. of Women Judges; America, Arizona, California and Maricopa County Bar Assns.; Smithsonian Assn; *professional career:* attorney in private practice, Phoenix, Arizona, 1959-65; Pres., Heard Museum, Phoenix, 1968-74, trustee, 1980-81; *honours and awards:* Women of the Year, Phoenix Advert Club, 1973; Distinguished Achievement Award, Arizona State Univ., 1980; Distinguished Service Award, National Conference of Christians and Jews, 1975; *clubs:* Soroptimists; Order of Coif; *office address:* Mrs Sandra O'Connor, US Supreme Court One, First Street NE, Washington DC 20543, USA.

ODDY, Christine Margaret; British, Member of the European Parliament; *born:* 20 September 1955; *party:* Labour Party; *political career:* MEP for Midlands Central, 1989-; *private address:* 3 Copthall House, Station Square, Coventry CV1 2FZ; *office address:* Ms Christine Oddy, European Parliament, Centre Européen, Plateau de Kirchberg, BP 2929, Luxembourg; *phone:* Luxembourg 43001.

ODENDAHL, Doris Frieda; German, Member of the Bundestag; *born:* 30 June 1933, Stuttgart, West Germany; *children:* one d; *education:* Business training; *party:* Sozialdemokratische Partei Deutschlands (SPD, Social Democratic Party of Germany), 1969; *political career:* mem. of Bundestag (Baden-Württemberg list);

town councillor, Böblingen/Sindelfingen, 1971-83; chwn., SPD-District Assn., Böblingen since 1981; *professional career:* admin. asst. for sales, Personnel and accounts; trips abroad; self- employed, textiles retail trade, 1967-81; admin. asst., Business Advisory Inst. since 1981; *clubs:* AWO, OTV; *office address:* Frau Doris Odendahl, Bundeshaus, 5300 Bonn 1, West Germany.

ODIE-ALI, Hon. Stella; Guyanan, Minister of Home Affairs; *party:* People's National Congress (PNC); *office address:* The Hon. Ms Stella Odie-Ali, Ministry of Home Affairs, 6 Brickdam, Stabroek, Georgetown, Guyana; *phone:* (02) 56221; 62444; 62445.

ODIO BENITO, Elizabeth; Costa Rican, Minister of Justice; *education:* Licentiate in Law and qualified Notary; *political career:* Solicitor General of the Republic, 1978; Minister of Justice, 1978-82 and 1990-; *professional career:* prof., Catholic Univ; *office address:* Ms Elizabeth Odio Benito, Ministry of Justice, Apartado 5685, San José 1000, Costa Rica.

OESTERLE-SCHWERIN, Jutta; German, former Member of the Bundesrat; *born:* 25 February 1941, Jerusalem, Israel; *children:* two; *languages:* German, Hebrew; *education:* school in Israel; State Academy of Visual Art, Stuttgart; qualification as interior designer; *party:* Sozialdemokratische Partei Deutschlands (SPD, Social Democratic Party of Germany), 1974-80, resignation because of NATO Twin Track Decision; Die Grünen (Green Party), 1983-; *political career:* active in the Easter March, Opponents of Nuclear Weapons, since 1962; member of Association of German Socialist Students, 1962 until its dissolution; active in the Women's Movement and Day-Nursery Movement, 1970-74; member of SPD group, municipal council, Ulm, 1975-80; member of Die Grüne group, municipal council, Ulm, 1984-87; spokeswoman of Die Grüne group; mem. of Bundestag, party list of Baden-Württemberg, since 1987; mem. of the Lesbians Assn. (Lesbenring); Political Cllr., 1991-; *professional career:* self-employed interior designer, Ulm, 1979-; *publications:* various publications on feminist and lesbian politics; *clubs:* Speaker, Lesbenring (Lesbians Assn.); *private address:* 7900 Ulm, West Germany; *office address:* Frau Jutta Oesterle-Schwerin, Bundeshaus, 5300 Bonn 1, West Germany.

OFFENBECK, Dr. Jolanda; Austrian, Member of the Nationalrat; *born:* 1 September 1930, Graz, Austria; *education:* secondary school; college of further education, Dr. of Law, 1954; *party:* Sozialistische Partei Österreichs (SPÖ, Socialist Party of Austria); *political career:* mem. of SPÖ, Party Exec. for Province of Steiermark, 1968; mem. of Federal Council, 1970-73; mem. of SPÖ Federal Party Exec., 1974-; Deputy Chairperson, Socialist Reps. and Federal Council

Members Group, 1979-; Federal Pres., Socliast Women of Austria, 1981-; SPÖ Deputy Federal Party Chairperson, 1981-; mem. of SPÖ Party Exec. Cttee., 1981-; mem. of Nationalrat for Steiermark, 1973-; *professional career:* Chairperson, Steiermark Provincial Women's Cttee., 1975; *honours and awards:* Great Golden Award, for services to Austria; Great Silver Award, for services to Austria; *office address:* Dr. Jolanda Offenbeck, Nationalrat, Dr. Karl Renner Ring 3, 1017 Vienna, Austria.

OFUCHI, Kinuko; Japanese, Member of the House of Councillors; *born:* 12 November 1944; *education:* High School; *party:* Japan Socialist Party (JSP); *political career:* elected for Niigata; Mem., House of Cllrs. Cttee. on Commerce and Industry and on Audit and Special Cttee. on Disasters, 1990-; *professional career:* Housewife; *office address:* Ms Kinuko Ofuchi, House of Councillors, 1-7-1 Nagata-cho, Tokyo 100, Japan; *phone:* (03) 5813111.

OGASAWARA, Sadako; Japanese, Member of the House of Councillors; *born:* 20 April 1920; *education:* Sapporo Women's High School; *party:* Japan Communist Party; *political career:* former Chairperson, House of Cllrs. Cttee. on Discipline; fourth time elected for Hokkaido; Mem., House of Cllrs. Cttee. on Discipline and Vice-Chairperson, JCP Presidium, 1990-; *office address:* Ms Sadako Ogasawara, House of Councillors, 1-7-1 Nagata-cho, Tokyo 100, Japan; *phone:* (03) 5813111.

OGOT, Grace; Kenyan, Assistant Minister for Culture and Social Services; *office address:* Ms Grace Ogot, Minister of Culture, and Social Services, Reinsurance Plaza, Taifa Road, P.O Box 30547, NAIROBI., KENYA; *phone:* (02)339650.

OKAZAKI, Hiromi; Japanese, Member of the House of Representatives; *born:* 12 June 1951; *education:* Akashi - Minami High School; *party:* Independent; *political career:* former Dir. of Hyogo Prefectural Govt. Workers' Union; elected for Hyogo 1, 1990; Mem., House of Reps. Cttee. on Social and Labour Affairs, 1990-; *office address:* Ms Hiromi Okazaki, House of Representatives, 1-7-1 Nagata-cho, Chiyoda-ku, Tokyo 100, Japan; *phone:* (03) 5815111.

OKAZAKI, Tomiko; Japanese, Member of the House of Representatives; *born:* 10 February 1944; *education:* Fukushima Women's High School; *party:* Japan Socialist Party (JSP); *political career* elected for Miyagi 1, 1990; Dir., JSP Women's Bureau, 1990-; *professional career:* Announcer of a Commercial Broadcasting Corporation; *office address:* Ms Tomiko Okazaki, House of Representatives, 1-7-1 Nagata-cho, Chiyoda-ku, Tokyo 100, Japan; *phone:* (03) 5815111.

OKUNU, L.M.; Nigerian, Deputy Governor of the Lagos State; *office address:* Mrs L.M. Okunu, Office of the Governor of Lagos State, State House, Lagos State, Nigeria.

OLESEN, Aase; Danish, Member of the Folketinget; *born:* 24 September 1934, Horsens, Denmark; *parents:* Eigill Larsen and Erna Larsen (née Nielsen); *married:* Tormod Olesen, 1954; *children:* Mads, Mette; *languages:* Danish, English; *education:* Copenhagen, 1952; Embrupborg College of education, qualified teacher, 1956; *party:* Radikale Venstre (Radical Liberal Party), 1969; *political career:* Sec. for the County of Frederiksborg, 1969-71; Second Chairman of the Board of Organisation, 1970-72; Chairman of the Political Club in Helsinge, 1970-74; Sec. to the chairman of the municipal council in the party, 1972- 73; Town Councillor in Helsinge, 1974-75; member of the Folketing, 1974-: Minister for Social Affairs; *interests:* social and fiscal policy; *professional career:* teacher, Horskolen, 1956-58; *office address:* Ms Aase Olesen, Minstry of Social Affairs, Slotsholmsgade 6, 1216 Copenhagen K, Denmark.

ONDO, Purificaçion Angue; Equatorial Guinea, Minister Delegate for Women's Development; *office address:* Ms Purificaçion Angue Ondo, Ministry for the Promotion of Women, Malabo, Equatorial Guinea.

ONGARO BASAGLIA, Franca; Italian, Senator; *born:* 5 September 1928, Venice; *party:* Sinistra Independente, (Independent Left Parly. Group); *political career:* elected Senator, Venice, 1983-; mem. Cttee. on Hygiene and Health; *professional career:* writer; journalist (dailies and magazines); co-founder, with F. Basaglia, of Movement for Renewal of Italian Psychiatry; *publications:* 'Salute/Malattia' (Enciclopaedia Einaudi, 1982); 'Una Voce-Rifflessioni sulla donna', 1982; 'Manicomio Perché', 1982; 'Mujer, locura y sociedad', Mexico, 1983; Edited: 'Scritti' I and II of F. Basaglia, 1981/82; with F. Basaglia: 'Morire di classe', 1969; 'La maggioranza deviante', 1971; 'La violencia en la marginalidad', Buenos Aires, 1975; 'Crimini di pace', 1975; with M. G. Giannichedda, 'Psichiatria, tossicodipendenze, perizia', 1987; *office address:* Ms Franca Ongaro Basaglia, Senato della Repubblica, Palazzo Madama, 00100 Rome, Italy.

ONKELINX, Laurette; Belgian, Member of the Chamber of Representatives; *born:* 2 October 1958, Ougrée; *parents:* Gaston Onkelinx and Germaine Onkelinx (née Ali Bakir); *married:* Abbés Guenned, 1987; *religion:* agnostic; *languages:* French, English; *education:* Univ. of Liège, Bachelor of Law, 1976-81; *party:* Parti Socialiste (PS, Socialist Party), 1974; *political career:* Deputy, 1987-; Cncl. of French Community, March 1989-; Vice-Pres. of PS Group in the Chamber of Reps., October 1989-; Pres. Interfederal Commission of Socialist Women; *interests:* justice institutional reforms, social emancipation, consumei protection, protection of the environment; *professiona, career:* Barrister, Liège, 1981-; Teacher ol Administrative, Science (Social Law), 1982-85; President, Medical Home, Ougrée; President, Medical Service Village (for disabled); Vice-President, Cttee. foi Protection of Youth; *private address:* Rue du 1er. Mai 2-74, 4200 Ougrée, Belgium; *office address:* Mme. Laurette Onkelinx, Kamer van Volksvertegenwoordigers, Palais de la Nation, Place de la Nation 2, 1000 Brussels, Belgium.

ONO, Kiyoko; Japanese, Member of the House of Councillors; *born:* 4 February 1936; *education:* Tokyo Univ. of Education; *party:* Liberal Democratic Party (LDP); *political career:* elected for Tokyo, Watanabe, 1990; Dir., House of Cllrs. Cttee. on Social and Labour Affairs and Mem., House of Cllrs. Cttee. on the Budget, 1990-; *memberships:* Mem., Japan Olympic Cttee; *office address:* Ms Kiyoko Ono, House of Councillors, 1-7-1 Nagata-cho, Tokyo 100, Japan; *phone:* (03) 5813111.

ONO, Yuriko; Japanese, Member of the House of Representatives; *born:* 20 January 1942; *education:* Kyoto Univ; *party:* Komeito (Clean Government Party); *political career:* former Deputy Dir., Komeito Tokyo Metropolitan Women's Bureau; elected for Tokyo 7, 1990; Mem., House of Reps. Cttee. on Social and Labour Affairs, 1990-; *professional career:* Pharmacist; *office address:* Ms Yuriko Ono, House of Representatives, 1-7-1 Nagata-cho, Chiyoda-ku, Tokyo 100, Japan; *phone:* (03) 5815111.

ONUR, Leyla; German, Member of the European Parliament; *born:* 8 January 1945; *party:* Sozialdemokratische Partei Deutschlands (SPD, Social Democratic Party); *political career:* MEP, 1989-; *private address:* Schloß Straße 8, 3300 Braunschweig, Germany; *office address:* Ms Leyla Onur, European Parliament, Centre Européen, Plateau de Kirchberg, BP 2929, Luxembourg; *phone:* Luxembourg 43001.

ORAON, Smt Sumati; Indian, Member of the Lok Sabha; *born:* 15 February 1935, Simdega Village, District Gumla, Bihar; *parents:* Teju Bhagat; *children:* one s., three d; *party:* Congress Party; *political career:* Pres., Mahila Cell, Akhil Bhartiya Adivasi Vikas Parishad; Mem. of Lok Sabha, 1982-; Deputy Minister for Welfare, GOI, 1988-89; *office address:* Shrimati Smt Oraon, Lok Sabha, Parliament House, New Dehli 110 011, India; *phone:* (11) 381825; 377102.

ORBETZOVA, Prof. Dr. Verbka Tzekova; Bulgarian, Member of the Grand National Assembly and President of the Medical Education Sub-Commission; *born:* 4 December 1938, Byala Slatina, Bulgaria; *parents:* Tzeko peev Dankov and Maria Todorova Dankova (née

Ivanova); *married:* Mitko Angelov Orbetzov, 1972; *children:* Angel, Maria; *languages:* Bulgarian, French, English, Russian; *education:* Medical Univ., Sofia, Med. Sci., 1969, Dr.Med. Sci., 1979; Post Grad. Medical Inst., Sofia; Inst. of Experimental Medicine, Lenigrad (now St. Petersburg), USSR; *party:* Bulgarian Socialist Party (BSP); *political career:* Sec., School Youth Organisation, DKMS B.Slatiba, 1955-56; Sec., Student Youth Organisation, Sofia, 1956-62; chief, Union of Youth Scientists, Medical Univ. Sofia, 1976-78; Sec., BSP Cttee., Medical Univ., Sofia, 1974-81; Mem., BSP Central Cttee., 1990-91; MP, 1990-91; Pres., Sub-Commission on Medical Education, 1990-; *interests:* human rights, inter.-Parly. relations, social politics, health, science, education, political strategy; *memberships:* Union of Bulgarian Scientists; Biochemical Biophysical Society; *professional career:* research fellow, Bulgarian Academy of Science, 1969-76; Assc. Prof., Medical Academy-2, 1976-84, Prof., 1984-; Chief of Central Clinical Laboratory, Medical Academy-2, 1984-; *honours and awards:* Golden Medal, Ministry of Education, 1956; Excellent Worker, Ministry of Health, 1986; *publications:* Co-enzyme Alterations in Rats with Experimental Hypertension, 1976; The Influence of Nicotinic Acid Treatment on the Synthesis of Cholesterol and Fatty Acids in a Rat Liver, 1976; Metabolism of Low Density Lipoproteins in Human Fibroblasts Culture, 1979; Chamges in ECG, Plasma and Myocardial Lipids in Experimental Myocardial Hypertrophy in Rats, 1988; *clubs:* Socialist Physicians Club; *recreations:* extrasensorics and untraditional medicine, writing poetry; *private address:* Sofia 1505, bul. Chr. Habaktchiev 41, 2, B, Bulgaria; *office address:* Prof. Dr. Verbka Tzekova Orbetsova, Narodno Sobranie, 3 National Assembly Square, Sofia 1000, Bulgaria; *phone:* 85-01.

O'REGAN, Katherine Victoria; New Zealander, Minister of Consumer Affairs; *born:* 1946, Hamilton; *children:* two; *education:* Te Mata Primary School; Hamilton Girls' High School; *party:* National Party, 1974; *political career:* Deputy Chairman, Hamilton Airport Authority; mem., Waipa County Council, 1977-84; mem., Council Executive/Planning Cttee., Waipa Health and Social Welfare Co-ordinating Cttee. and served on the Noxious Weeds and Pest Destruction Cttee.; active in National Party in Raglan and Waikato electorates; contested Waikato seat, 1981, and won Waipa seat, 1984; spokesperson, Consumer Affairs and Post Office; introduced Private Mems.' Bill seeking recognition of children with specific learning disabilities; served on parliamentary Select Cttee. on Justice and Law Reform, and Social Services (specialising on health); mem., Commonwealth Parly. Assn. tour of Australia, 1985; mem., New Zealand Delegation to China, 1985; visited Indonesia, South Korea and Japan on a Speakers Tour, 1986; MP for Waipa; Opposition Spokeswoman on Women's Affairs and Statistics and Associate Spokeswoman on Health;

Minister of Consumer Affairs with additional responsibility as Associate Minister of Women's Affairs and Associate Minister of Health, Nov. 1990-; *memberships:* advisory status to the Federation of Specific Learning Disabilities Associations of New Zealand; *professional career:* nursing, Waikato Hospital, 1965; *honours and awards:* Justice of the Peace; *recreations:* reading, art, music and tennis; *private address:* 57 Gibson Lane Te Awamutu, New Zealand; *office address:* Ms Katherine O'Regan, Ministry of Consumer Affairs, Private Bag, Wellington, New Zealand; *phone:* (04) 742750.

ORLANDI, Dott. Nicoleta; Italian, Deputy; *born:* 31 January 1961, Avezzano l'Aquila, Italy; *education:* Degree in Jurisprudence; *political career:* Councillor, Avezzano; mem. Exec. FGCI; Deputy, Aquila-Pescara-Chieti-Teramo, 1987; mem. Cttee. on Justice; *office address:* Dott. Nicoleta Orlandi, Camera dei Deputati, Montecitorio, 00186 Rome, Italy.

O'ROURKE, Mary; Irish, Minister for Education; *born:* 31 May 1937, Athlone, Ireland; *parents:* P.J. Lenihan; *married:* Edna O'Rourke; *children:* two s; *education:* St. Peter's Convent; Univ. College Dublin; St. Patrick's College, Maynooth, Co. Kildare; *party:* Fianna Fáil; *political career:* mem. Westmeath County Cncl., 1979-; mem., Dáil Éireann, 1982-; Minister for Education, 1987-; *professional career:* former secondary school teacher; *private address:* Aisling, Arcadia, Athlone, Co. Westmeath, Ireland; *office address:* Department of Education, Marlborough Street, Dublin 1, Ireland.

OSMAN, Amal Abd ar-Rahim; Egyptian, Minister of Social Insurance and Social Affairs; *political career:* Mem., most Political and Social Conferences; Minister of Social Insurance and Social Affairs, 1978-; *publications:* works on criminal law; *office address:* Ms Amal Abd ar-Rahim Osman, Ministry of Social Insurance, 3 Sharia El Alfi, Cairo, Egypt.

OSMOS, Dr. Mária; Hungarian, Member of the Országgyűlés; *party:* Hungarian Socialist Party (MSZP); *office address:* Dr. Mária Osmos, Országgyűlés, Kossuth L. tér 1-3, Budapest V, Hungary; *phone:* 22 5058; 22 5059.

OTAKA, Yoshiko; Japanese, Member of the House of Councillors; *born:* 12 February 1920; *education:* High School; *party:* Liberal Democratic Party (LDP); *political career:* former Chairperson, House of Cllrs. Special Cttee. on Okinawa and Northern Problems; third time elected for National, Independent; Acting Dir., LDP Foreign Affairs Division and Mem., House of Cllrs. Cttee. on Foreign Affairs, 1990-; *office address:* Ms Yoshiko Otaka, House of Councillors, 1-7-1 Nagata-cho, Tokyo 100, Japan; *phone:* (03) 5813111.

OTTOLINA, Rhona; Venezuelan, Co-leader of the Derecha Emergente de Venezuela; *party:* Derecha Emergente de Venezuela (DEV); *office address:* Ms Rhona Ottolina, Derecha Emergente de Venezuela, Caracas, Venezuela.

OWEN, Nora; Irish, Deputy Spokesperson on Foreign Affairs; *born:* 22 June 1945, Dublin, Ireland; *parents:* James O'Mahony and Katherine O'Mahony (née Collins); *married:* Brian Joseph Owen, 1968; *children:* Vincent, Richard, Edward; *religion:* Roman Catholic; *languages:* English, Irish, French; *education:* Univ. College, Dublin, B.Sc., chemistry/biochemistry, diploma in microbiology; *party:* Fine Gael, 1973; *political career:* Chwn., Joint Parly. Cttee. on Overseas Development, 1981-87; Mem., EC Secondary Legislation Parly. Cttee., 1989-91; Mem., Dublin County Cncl., 1979-; *interests:* foreign affairs particularly development and third world issues, local govt., European community; *memberships:* Irish Cncl. of the European Movement; British-Irish Parly. Body; Exec. Mem., Assn. of Western European Parlimentarians Against Apartheid; *professional career:* quality control chemist, Linson Ltd., 1965-68; research chemist, Linson Ltd., 1968-72; Personal Asst. to MEP, Dublin, 1987-89; *clubs:* sports and leisure complex, Portnarnock; Old Malahide Historical Society; *private address:* 17 Ard na Mara, Malahide, Dublin, Ireland; *office address:* Dep. Nora Owen, Seanad Éireann, Lenister House, Kildare Street, Dublin 2, Ireland.

OYANGEN, Gunhild; Norwegian, Minister of Agriculture; *born:* 31 October 1947, Levanger, Norway; *parents:* Kåre Utnes and Hildur Bergljot Nilsen; *married:* Egil Oyangen; *public role of spouse:* Member of the Storting; *children:* three; *religion:* Lutheran; *languages:* Norwegian, English, German; *education:* Univ. of Trondheim, MA, 1975; *party:* Norwegian Labour Party; *political career:* former Leader, Agdenes Labour Party; Board Mem., Sor Trondelag Labour Partyu Women's Cttee.; Mem., Labour Party Exec. Board; Mem., Labour Party Special Cttee. on Agriculture; Mem., Storting, 1989-; Dep. Chair, Standing Cttee. on Agriculture, 1989-90; Minister of Agriculture, Nov. 1990-; *professional career:* former teacher and farmer; *private address:* 7136 Lensvik, Norway; *office address:* Ms Gunhild Oyangen, Ministry of Agriculture, Akersgaten 42, P.O. Box 8007 Dep, 0030 Oslo 1, Norway; *phone:* (02) 34 90 90; *fax:* 349555.

OZAL, Semra; Turkish, Head of the Motherland Party for Istanbul Province; *married:* Turgut Ozal; *party:* Motherland Party; *political career:* founder, Foundation for the Strengthening and Recognition of the Turkish Woman; Head, Motherland Party, Istanbul Province; *recreations:* smoking cigars, whisky, collecting antique revolvers; *office address:* Ms Semra Ozal, Motherland Party, Istanbul, Turkey.

P

PACCOLAT, Monique; Swiss, Member of the Nationalrat; *born:* 12 February 1954, Collonges, Switzerland; *education:* teacher training college, Sion; Univ. of Lausanne, Faculty of Social Science and Politics; *party:* Parti-Démocrate-Chrétien Suisse (Christlichdemokratische Volkspartei der Schweiz, Social Democratic People's Party of Switzerland); *political career:* Deputy for Canton of le Valais, 1977, Pres. of Great Cncl., 1986-87; Mem. of the Nationalrat for Collonges, Canton of le Valais, 1987-; *professional career:* responsible for implementing training courses; *office address:* Mme. Monique Paccolat, Nationalrat/Conseil National, Secretariat-General, Parlamentsgebäude, 3003 Berne, Switzerland; *phone:* Berne 619711.

PACK, Doris; German, Member of the European Parliament; *born:* 18 March 1942, Schiffweiler; *children:* two; *religion:* Catholic; *education:* High school leaving examination, 1962; Teacher training college, Saarbrücken; Teaching examinations, 1965 and 1967; *party:* Christlich Demokratische Union (CDU, Christian Democratic Union), 1962; *political career:* mem. of municipal council, Bübingen, 1969-74; mem. of town council, Saarbrücken, 1974-76; mem. of Bundestag (Saarland list) 1974-83 and 1985-89; mem of the Parliamentary Assembly of the European Council and member of the European Parliament, 1989-; *professional career:* school service, Ottweiler and Bübingen; director of school (Rektorin); *office address:* Frau Doris Pack, European Parliament, Centre Européen, Plateau de Kirchberg, BP 2929, Luxembourg.

PADRON QUERO, Marisela; Venezuelan, Minister of Family Affairs; *office address:* Ms Marisela Padrón Quero, Ministry of Family Affairs, Torre Oeste, Piso 39-41, Parque Central, Caracas 1010, Venezuela; *phone:* (02) 574-8111; 574-8211.

PAHADIA, Shanti; Indian, Member of the Rajya Sabha; *born:* 1 August 1936, Village Rasidpur, Tehsil Mahuva, District Sawai Madhopur; *parents:* the late Sona Ramji; *married:* Jagannath Pahadia, 1950; *children:* two s., five d; *party:* Congress Party; *political career:* Mem., Legislative Assembly, Rajasthan, May-Oct. 1980; Mem. of the Rajya Sabha, 1984-; Mem., Mahila Sangathan; Mem., Mahila Vidyapeeth, Bhusavar, District Bharatpur, Rajasthan; *interests:* rural development, social welfare; *memberships:* National Consumers' Co-operative Federation; *recreations:* discussion, embroidery, weaving; *private address:* Bhusavar, District Bharatpur, Rajasthan; *office address:* Shrimati Shanti Pahadia, Rajya Sabha, Parliament House, New Dehli 110 011, India; *phone:* (11) 389977; 389997.

PAINE, Marylin J.; American, acting Executive Director of Alaska State Republican Party; *born:* 9 December 1931, Michigan, USA; *parents:* John Kaan Jensen and Mildred Jensen (née Gott); *married:* Luther Leraan Paine, 1963; *children:* Marcus, Susan, Brent, John, Lindsay; *religion:* Lutheran; *education:* Edward W. Sparrow Hospital, RN, 1952; *party:* Republican Party; *political career:* District Chair, Republican Party Cttee., Alaska, 1980-84; Republican National Committeewomen, Alaska, 1980-84; Mem., Exec. Board, Alaska State Central Republican Cttee., 1984; delegate, Republican National Convention, 1984 and 1988; acting Exec. Dir., Alaska State Republican Party; *memberships:* Anchorage Municipal Library Advisory Board; Alaskan Federation of Republican Women; Commissioner, Anchorage Health and Human Services; *professional career:* office manager and bookkeeper; dental office; *honours and awards:* Republican Woman of the Year, 1986; *office address:* Ms Marylin Paine, 1100 Hillcrest Drive, Anchorage, Alaska 99503, USA.

PAISCHER, Edith-Maria; Austrian, Member of the Bundesrat; *born:* 24 May 1929, Mauerkirchen; *parents:* Hans Brunner and Olga Brunner (née Kathrein); *married:* Leopold Paischer, 1956; *children:* Gerhard-Maximilian; *education:* primary school and secondary school, 1936-44; *party:* Sozialistische Partei Österreichs (SPÖ, Socialist Party of Austria), 1946; *political career:* town councillor, Branau, 1973-79; First Deputy Mayoress, Branau, 1979-82; mem. of Bundesrat, 1982-; district Chairperson, SPÖ Women's Association; district Vice-Chmn. SPÖ, Branau; *interests:* social, family, youth and environmental policies, the health service; *professional career:* mem. of the Federal Women's Cttee.; mem. of provincial Women's Praesidium, Upper Austria; mem. of provincial Women's Cttee.; secretary, SPÖ, 1946-82; *honours and awards:* Victor Adler Plaque, SPÖ, 1989; *private* *address:* 5261 Uttendorf/H, Dir. Mayrstr. 68, Branau, Austria; *office address:* Frau Edith-Maria Paischer, Bundesrat, Dr. Karl Renner Ring 3, 1017 Vienna, Austria.

PAKKINEN, Saara-Maria; Finnish, First Deputy Speaker of the Eduskunta; *born:* 4 October 1941, Pori, Finland; *parents:* Viljo Vihtori Yli-Kerttula and Elvi Maria Yli-Kerttula (née Pekkonen); *married:* Rauli Pertti Paakkinen, 1978; *children:* Lennart, Eva Maria; *religion:* Lutheran; *languages:* Finnish, Swedish, English; *education:* Pori, Graduate of Commercial College, 1962; *party:* Suomen Sosialidemokraattinen Puolue (SDP, Finnish Social Democratic Party); *political career:* Mem., Tuusula Municipal Cncl., 1973; Chmn., Social Affairs Cttee, Ibid., 1973-80 and Vice-Chmn., 1981-83; mem. of Eduskunta, 1979; mem., Central Cttee., Central Assn. of Nuoret Kotkat, 1978 and Chmn., 1981; Chmn., 1985 Int. Year of the Youth Cttee; *interests:* children all over the world, foreign policy, international affairs; *professional career:* Clerical Asst., Nat. Board of Public Roads and Waterways, 1962-67; Office Administrator, Assn. of Civil Servants, Nat. Board of Public Roads and Waterways, 1967-71; Organisation Sec., Helsinki Local Govt. Officers and Clerical Employees Registered Assn., 1971-75; Editor, Ahjo, and Metal Workers' Union; Chairperson, STETE 1975; *office address:* Ms Saara-Maria Paakkinen, Eduskunta, 00102 Helsinki, Finland.

PALLI-PETRALIA, Fani; Greek, Under Secretary of State for Culture; *children:* four; *party:* Nea Demokratia (ND, New Democracy Party); *political career:* MP, Nov. 1985; MP, Nea Demokratia (ND, New Democracy Party), B' Athens, 1989; responsible for the women's section of ND; Under Sec. of State for Culture, 1990-; *professional career:* lawyer; *office address:* Ministry of Culture, Odos Aristidou 14, 101 86 Athens, Greece.

PANDEY, Manorama; Indian, Member of the Rajya Sabha; *born:* 23 July 1932, Buxar; *parents:* the late Pt. Rama Kant Pandey; *married:* J.N. Pandey, 1954; *children:* three s; *education:* Banaras Hindu Univ., MA, LLB and BA, vocal music; *party:* Congress Party; *political career:* Mem., Bihar Legislative Assembly, 1957-77; Parly. Sec., Finance and General Administration, Bihar, 1961-66; Deputy Minister, Information and Home, Bihar, 1972; State Minister, Education, Information and Home, Bihar, 1972-74; Mem. of the Rajya Sabha, 1980-; *professional career:* Chmn., Bihar State Finance Corp., 1977-78; *recreations:* sport, gardening; *private address:* Nehru Nagar, Patna - 800013, India; *office address:* Shrimati Manorama Pandey, 32 Dr. Rajendra Prasad Road, New Delhi 1, India.

PAPANDREOU, Dr. Vasso; Greek, Member of the European Commission; *born:* 1944; *education:* Economic Univ. of Athens, B.Sc., 1969; Univ. of London, M.Sc., economics, 1971; Univ. of Reading, Ph.D., economics, 1980; *party:* Panellinion Socialistikon Kinema (PASOK, Panhellenic Socialist Movement), founding Mem., 1974-; *political career:* founder Mem. and Mem., Central Cttee. PASOK, 1974-; MP, 1984-89; Dep. Minister for Industry, Energy and Technology, 1985-86; Alternate Minister for Industry, Energy and Technology, 1986-87; Alternate Minister for Trade, 1988-89; EC Commissioner, responsible for Employment, Industrial Relations and Social Affairs, 1989-; *memberships:* Dir., Hellenic Organisation for the Small and Medium Size Enterprises, 1981-85; Mem., Board of Dirs., Commercial Bank of Greece, 1982-85; *professional career:* economics tutor, Exeter Univ., UK, 1971-73; research Asst., Oxford Univ., 1973-74; lecturer, Economic Univ. of Athens, Greece, 1981-85; Small and Medium-Sized Businesses, Athens; mem. Admin. Cncl., Greek Commercial Bank; *publications:* Multinational Companies in Less Developed Countries: The Case for Greece, Gutenburg Publications Co., 1981; several papers and articles on economic and political subjects; *office address:* Dr. Vasso Papandreou, Commission of the European Communities, 200 rue de la Loi, 1049 Brussels, Belgium.

PAPON, Christiane; French, Secretary of the National Assembly; *born:* 3 September 1924, Vienna, Austria; *parents:* Alexandre Eraud and Marie-Louise Eraud (née Garnier); *married:* Jean-Pierre Papon, 1954; *languages:* French, English; *education:* secondary school, Nantes; Jeanne de Chantal and Chavagnes institutions, Nantes; Faculty of Law, University of Paris; Doctorate in Legal History and Civil Law; Diploma from the Institute of Political Studies, Paris; qualified lawyer; *party:* Rassemblement pour La République (RPR, Rally for the Republic); *political career:* Official, Neuilly section, 1972 and President of the Association Femme-Avenir, 1975-88; Member of the central committee, 1976- and Member of the political council of Rassemblement pour La République; Vice-Chairman of Carrefour du gaullisme, 1976-; Municipal councillor, Neuilly-sur-Seine, 1977-; Deputy, Val-de-Marne, 1986-; President of the Femme-Avenir movement, 1975-88; MEP, 1987-89; Sec. of the National Assembly, 1988-; *interests:* economics, foreign affairs, women's participation in society; *professional career:* lawyer, Paris, 1948-53; press attaché at the Ministry of Foreign Affairs, 1953-54; journalist, Radiodiffusion Française, 1956-58; Director of the social affairs service and of the workforce, 1958-78 and Director of general services, 1978-83 of the Federation of electrical, Electronic and computer Industries; *honours and awards:* Knight of the Legion of Honour; Employment Medal (Médaille du Travail); *publications:* Participation of Women in French Society; *clubs:* Racing Club of France;

recreations: music, art, tennis, swimming; *private address:* 1 bis Boulevard de la Saussaye, 92200, Neuilly-sur-Seine, France; *office address:* Mme. Christiane Papon, L'Assemblée Nationale, 126 rue de L'Université, 75355 Paris, France.

PAPON, Monique Geneviève Elizabeth; French, Deputy; *born:* 5 October 1934, Gentilly, Seine, France; *parents:* Pierre Cloquet and Suzanne Cloquet (née Berthe); *married:* Yves Papon, 1954; *children:* Marie-Catherine, Jean-Marc, Anne-Claire, Xavier; *education:* Courses at Chapuis, Sorbonne and the Catholic Faculty of Paris; degree in literature; *party:* Union pour la Démocratie Française (UDF, Union for French Democracy); Union Centriste (UC, Centrist Union); *political career:* Departmental Delegate of the UDF, 1978-; General Councillor, Nantes, Loire-Atlantique, 1979-; Deputy Mayor, Nantes, 1983-; Chmn., Bureau for the Elderly and Retired, 1983-; Chmn. of Community Centre for Social Action, 1983-; member of the Political Bureau, 1984-, and President of the Departmental Federation, Loire-Atlantique, 1984-; Deputy, Loire-Atlantique, 1986-; *professional career:* French teacher at the Paviot School, Nantes 1967-80; *private address:* 61 Boulevard du Maréchal-Joffre, 92340, Bourg-la-Reine, France 14 Boulevard de Launay, 44100, Nantes, France; *office address:* Mme. Monique Papon, L'Assemblée Nationale, 126 rue de L'Université, 75355 Paris, France.

PARADIS, Judy; American, Maine State Representative; *born:* 17 January 1944, Ste. Agathe, Maine, USA; *parents:* Laurence Ayotte and Irene Ayotte (Albert); *married:* Ross Paradis, 1970; *public role of spouse:* teacher of Latin, English and French at Madawaska High School; *religion:* Roman Catholic; *languages:* French, English; *education:* Univ. of Maine, Fort Kent, BS; Univ. of Maine, Orono, advanced studies; *party:* Democratic Party; *political career:* Maine State Rep., District 150; Mem., Democratic State Cttee.; Vice-Chwn., Aroostock County Democratic Cttee; *memberships:* Optimists; American Assn. of Univ. Women; Business and Professional Women's Club; *professional career:* French teacher; *honours and awards:* Distinguished Legislator, NCSL, 1990; 1991 Toll Fellow; *publications:* columnist, St. John Valley Times; *recreations:* tennis, cross country skiing; *private address:* P.O. Box 296, Frenchville, Maine 04745, USA; *office address:* Mrs Judy Paradis, RFD 1 Box 1009, Madawaska, Maine 04756, USA.

PARTIK-PABLÉ, Dr. Helene; Austrian, Member of the Nationalrat; *born:* 12 August 1939, Vienna, Austria; *education:* commercial school, Federal Grammar School For Working People, Vienna 15, 1964-68; matriculation, 1968; University of Vienna, Dr. of Law, 1973; *party:* Freiheitliche Partei Österreichs (FPÖ, Freedom Party of Austria); *political career:* mem. of Federal Party Exec., FPÖ, and of provincial Party Exec., FPÖ, Vienna; mem. of Nationalrat, for Vienna, 1983-; *professional career:* secretary; book-keeper; judge, 1977; *office address:* Dr. Helene Partik-Pablé, Nationalrat, Dr. Karl Renner Ring 3, 1017 Vienna, Austria.

PASSONI, Irma Rossetto; Brazilian, Federal Deputy; *born:* 5/14/43 Concórdia, Santa Catarina; *parents:* Jady Rossetto and Theresa Slongo Rossetto; *married:* Armelindo Passoni; *children:* Paulo Thiago, Moara; *education:* Sao Paulo, teacher-supervisor, 1971-74; *party:* Partido dos Trabalhadores (PT, Independent Labour Party); *political career:* Sao Paulo State Deputy, 1979-83; Mem., Special Cttee. for Investigation of the Living Conditions of the People of the Ribeira Valley, 1979-80; Mem., Human Rights Cttee., 1979-81; Mem., Education Cttee., 1979-83; Federal Deputy, 1983-87, re-elected 1987-91 and 1991-95; *professional career:* professor; *office address:* Ms Irma Passoni, Chamber of Deputies, Praça dos 3 Poderes, Ed. Principal, 70160 Brasilia, DF, Brazil; *phone:* (61) 225 2885.

PATIL, Pratibha Devisingh; Indian, Member of the Rajya Sabha; *born:* 19 December 1934, Jalgaon, Maha; *parents:* Narayanrao Patil and Gangaji Patil; *married:* D.R. Shekhawat; *children:* one s., one d; *education:* MA; LLB; *political career:* organiser, Women Home Guards, Jalgaon District, 1962; Mem., Maha Assembly, 1962-85; Deputy Minister, 1967-72; Cabinet Minister for Social Welfare, 1972-74; for Public Health and Social Welfare, 1974-75, for Prohibition, Rehabilitation and Cultural Affairs, 1975-76, for Education, 1977-78, for Urban Development and Housing, 1982-83, for Civil Supplies and Social Welfare, 1983-85; Deputy Chmn., Rajya Sabha; Vice Chmn., National Federation for Coop Urban Banks and Credit Society; Chmn., Bhartiya Granin Mahila Sangh, Maha; Mem., Standing Cttee., All India Women's Council; convener, first Women's Conference, Delhi; *private address:* 84, Rajul - B Apartments, 9, Harkness Road, Malabar Hill, Bombay - 400006; *office address:* Shrimati Pratibha Patil, 11, Teen Murti Lane, New Delhi -- 110011.

PATIL, Suryakanta Jayawantrao; Indian, Member of the Rajya Sabha; *born:* 15 August 1948, Waiphana Taluka-Hadgaon, District Nandad, Maharashtra; *parents:* the late Jayawantrao Patil; *married:* R.B. Maske, 1966; *children:* one s., one d; *education:* Marathwada Univ., BA; *party:* Congress Party; *political career:* imprisoned three times during the Janata regime and appeared before the Shah Commission; Pres., Nanded District Congress (Women's Wing), 1971-; Gen. Sec., District Youth Congress, 1972-74; Mem., Nanded Municipal Council, 1974; Founder Mem., Nanded District Congress Party, 1977-78; Mem., Zila Parishad, 1978; Mem., Maharashtra Legislative Assembly, 1980-85; Gen. Sec., M.P. Youth Congress,

1981-85; Mem. of the Rajya Sabha, 1986-; Chmn., Multipurpose Labour Union, Nanded; *interests:* women, labour movement, rural development, improving the conditions of the underpriviledged; *memberships:* Pres., District Journalists' Association, 1980-; *professional career:* Editor, Godawari Times, Marathi; *recreations:* reading, music, swimming, shooting, table tennis, nature; *private address:* Priyadarshini, Kailashnagar, District Nanded, Maharashtra, PIN - 431602, India; *office address:* Shrimati Suryakanta Patil, Rajya Sabha, Parliament House, New Dehli 110 011, India; *phone:* (11) 389977; 389997.

PATTERSON, Elizabeth Johnston; American, US Representative for South Carolina; *born:* 18 November 1939, Columbia, South Carolina, USA; *parents:* Olin Dewitt Johnston and Gladys Johnston (née Atkinson); *married:* Dwight Fleming Patterson, 1967; *children:* Dwight Fleming III, Olin Dewitt Johnston, Catherine Leigh; *religion:* Methodist; *education:* Columbia College, BA, 1961; Univ. of South Carolina, 1961-62 and 1964; *party:* Democratic Party; *political career:* South Carolina State Senator, 1979-86; US Rep., South Carolina, 1986-; *memberships:* Trustee, Wofford College, 1978-; Business and Professional Women; *office address:* Ms Elizabeth Patterson, P.O. Box 5564, Spartanburg, South Carolina 29304, USA.

PATTERSON, Kay Christine Lesley; Australian, Senator; *born:* 21 November 1944, Sydney, NSW, Australia; *education:* Sydney; BA (Hons.), Monash; Ph.D., Diploma in Education; *party:* Liberal Party; *political career:* Hawthorn West Branch Delegate, Liberal Party State Council, 1985-87; Membership officer, 1985-87; Mem. Hawthorn and East Yarra Province Electorate Cttee., 1985-87; Mem. of a number of Policy and Advisory Cttees. of Liberal Party; Vice-Pres. Liberal Party State Council, 1986-87; elected to Senate for Victoria, 1987-; Committee Service: Mem. of the Senate Standing Cttee. for Scrutiny of Bills, 1987-; Mem. of the Senate Legislative and General Purpose Standing Cttee. for Employment, Education and Training, 1987-; *memberships:* mem., Australian Psychological Society; mem., Monash Univ. Council, 1978-; mem., State Council of Girl Guides Association of Victoria, 1974-; *professional career:* small business sec. and office manager, 1961-64; tutor, Faculty of Education, Univ. of Sydney, 1970; senior tutor, Psychology Dept., Monash Univ., 1974-76; lecturer, 1977-83, Senior lecturer, 1983-85; Principal lecturer and Chairpersonperson, 1986-87, at the School of Behavioural Sciences, Lincoln Institute of Health Sciences; Kellog Travelling Fellow and Visiting Fellow, Institute of Gerontology, Univ, of Michigan; Visiting Scholar, Gerontology Centre, Pennsylvania State Univ., 1985; mem. State Executive of Girl Guides Association of Victoria, 1974-85; *office address:* Ms Kay

Patterson, Senate, Parliament House, Room M13, Canberra, ACT 2600, Australia; *phone:* (062) 727111.

PAULINA-MÜRL, Lianne; German, President of the Landtag of Schleswig-Holstein; *born:* 18 September 1944, Bühlau; *education:* Economics; *party:* Sozialdemokratische Partei Deutschlands (SPD, Social Democratic Party of Germany); *political career:* Pres. of the Lantag of Schleswig-Holstin since 1987; *professional career:* Economist; *office address:* Frau Lianne Paulina-Mürl, Landeshaus, D-23 Kiel, West Germany.

PAVLIKOVA, Dr. Jirina; Czechoslovakian, Member of the Narodni Rada (Czech National Council); *party:* Civic Forum; *office address:* Dr. Jirina Pavliková, Ceská národní rada, Snemovní 4, 110 00 Praha 1, Czechoslovakia; *phone:* (02) 2105.

PEACOCK, Elizabeth Joan; British, Member of Parliament; *born:* 4 April 1937; *children:* Jonathan, Nicholas; *education:* St. Monica's Convent, Skipton; *party:* Conservative Party; *political career:* Cons. Election Agent, 1979; Councillor, North Yorkshire County Council, 1981-84; Member of Parliament, for Batley and Spen, 1983-; Sec., Yorkshire Cons. Members' Cttee., 1983-89; mem. Select Cttee. on Employment, 1983-87; Vice-Pres., Yorkshire Area Young Conservatives, 1984-87; Exec. mem., 1922 Cttee., 1987-; mem. Select Cttee. on House of Commons Services, 1988-; mem., Exec. Cttee., UK branch, Commonwealth Parly. Assn.; Chmn., All-Party Parly. Transpennine Group; mem., BBC General Advisory Cncl.; Pres., Yorkshire Cons. Trade Unionists; Pres., Dewsbury 'Kick It' Organisation Against Solvent Abuse; *interests:* health care provision, social welfare, housing, employment matters, education, law and order, voluntary organisations; *professional career:* Asst. Dir., York Council for Voluntary Service, 1979-83; JP, 1982-; Dir., Shilton Investments; magistrate, 1975-; *clubs:* Westminster Dining Club (Joint Chmn.); House of Commons Motor Club (Sec.); Soroptomists Int. of Dewsbury; UK Business and Professional Women's Club; *recreations:* motoring, reading, theatre; *office address:* Mrs Elizabeth Peacock, House of Commons, London SW1A OAA.

PEDRAZZI CIPOLLA, Anna Maria; Italian, Deputy; *born:* 4 November 1944, Cento, Ferrara, Italy; *education:* Lower Secondary School Education; *party:* Partito Democratico della Sinistra (PDS, Party of the Democratic Left); *political career:* Assessor, San Guiliano Council, 1975-; Councillor, Milan, 1975-80; mem. Secretariat of Fed. PCI, Milan, 1980-83; mem. Regional leadership PCI, Lombardy; Deputy, Milan-Pavia, 1983; mem. Cttee. on Justice; re-elected Deputy, 1987; mem. Cttee. on Justice; *professional career:* Clerk; *office address:* Ms Anna Pedrazzi Cipolla, Camera dei Deputati, Montecitorio, 00186 Rome, Italy.

PELAES, Fatima Lucia; Brazilian, Federal Deputy; *born:* 13 December 1959, Macapa, Amapa; *parents:* Marcionila Pelaes; *married:* Silvado da Silva Brito; *children:* Iuri; *education:* UFPA, Belém, sociology, 1978-81; *party:* Partido Da Frente Liberal (PFL, Liberal Alliance); *political career:* Federal Deputy for Amapa, 1991-95; *office address:* Ms Fatima Pelaes, Chamber of Deputies, Praça dos 3 Poderes, Ed. Principal, 70160 Brasilia, DF, Brazil; *phone:* (61) 225 2885.

PELAYO DUQUE, María Dolores; Spanish, Deputy; *born:* 25 November 1943, Santa Cruz de Tenerife, Spain; *married:* Salvador Dorta Reyes, 1970; *children:* two; *languages:* Spanish, French; *education:* Univ. of La Laguna, law degree; *party:* Union Centro Democratico (UCD, Union of the Democratic Centre); Partido Socialista Obrero Español (PSOE, Spanish Socialist Workers' Party); *political career:* delegate in Canary Islands of Spanish Association of Women Jurists; Senator, UCD, Santa Cruz, 1977-79; Deputy, UCD, Santa Cruz, 1979-89, re- elected Deputy, PSOE, Santa Cruz, 1989-; first vice Pres., Cttee. on National Defence; mem., Justice and Labour Committees; first vice Pres., Cttee. on Agriculture, Livestock, and Fishing; Sec., 3a Congreso Diputados; *interests:* women in the judiciary; *professional career:* mem. governing board, Santa Cruz Bar Association; *honours and awards:* numerous; *private address:* San Lucas 48, E-38002, Santa Cruz de Tenerife, Spain; *office address:* Ms María Pelayo Duque, Congreso de los Diputados, Fernán Flor 1, Madrid 14, Spain.

PELLEGATTI, Ivanna; Italian, Deputy; *born:* 16 May 1948, Ficarolo; *party:* Partito Democratico della Sinistra (PDS, Party of the Democratic Left); *political career:* mem. Factory Council; . Mem Provincial Leadership FILLEA-CGIL; mem. Prov. secretariat of FILTEA-CGIL (Textile Union), Alto Polesine region; Sec. Gen. Textile Union, 1981-; mem. Gen. Council of CGIL-Veneto; mem. Gen. Council, National FILTEA; mem. Secretariat CdLT CGIL, 1982-, Rovigo; Prov. Sec CdLT, Rovigo, 1985-; Head of Labour market, and industrial politics; Deputy, Verona-Padua-Vicenza-Rovigo, 1987; mem. Cttee. on Social Affairs; *professional career:* Factory worker, ICAP, Magnanini di Ficarolo; *office address:* Ms Ivanna Pellegatti, Camera dei Deputati, Montecitorio, 00186 Rome, Italy.

PENG PEIYUN; Chinese, Minister in Charge of the State Family Planning Commission; *born:* 1929, Liuyang County, Hunan Province; *parents:* Peng Zhen; *education:* Southwest Associated Univ.; Qinghua Univ; *party:* Communist Party of China; *political career:* Party Sec., Qinghua Univ., 1949-50; Dep. Sec., Univ. Commission under Beijing Govt., 1964-66; Dep. Dir., Beijing Chemical Engineering Inst., 1977-78; Dir., Policy Research Office under Min. of Education, 1979-82; Vice Minister of Education, 1982-85; appointed mem., Standing Cttee., 1983; Vice Minister of State Economic Commission, 1985-88; Minister of the State Family Planning Commission, 1988-; *office address:* Ms Peng Peiyun, State Family Planning Commission, Xizhimen Shuncheng Nan Jie, Beijing, People's Republic of China; *phone:* 668971.

PEREIRA, Hon. Carmen; Guinea-Bissau,, Minister of State for Social Affairs; *party:* Partido Africano da Independênt da Guiné e Cabo Verde (PAIGC); *office address:* The Hon. Ms Carmen Pereira, Ministry of Social Welfare, Bissau, Guinea-Bissau.

PEREIRA, Hon. Francisca; Guinea-Bissau,, Minister of Women's Affairs; *party:* Partido Africano da Independência da Guiné e Cabo Verde (PAIGC); *political career:* Minister of Women's Affairs and Mem., Cncl. of State; *office address:* The Hon. Ms Francisca Pereira, Ministry of Women's Affairs, Bissau, Guinea-Bissau.

PEROVIC, Latinka; Yugoslavian, former Member of the League of Communists' Presidium; *born:* 1933, Kraguijevac, Serbia; *parents:* father, merchant and mother, housewife; *married:* Slobodan Perovic, 1958; *public role of spouse:* retired journalist and lawyer; former editor-in-chief of a publishing house and director of Ekonomska Politika; *children:* two s; *religion:* atheist; *languages:* Russian, French; *education:* Belgrade Univ., Philosophy, 1952, M.Phil., 1958, M.Pol.Sc., 1965, Ph.D., Political Science, 1975; *party:* League of Communists of Yugoslavia (LCY), 1951-74; *political career:* active in Youth and Women's Movements; Mem., Exec. Cttee., League of Communists of Serbia Central Cttee., 1966-68; Exec. Sec., Central Cttee., LCS, 1968-72; Mem., Central Cttee., LCY Presidium, 1969-72; forced to resign, 1972; expelled from LCY, 1974; *professional career:* scientific counselor, Inst. of the Labour Movement History of Serbia; visiting Prof., Novi Sad Univ; *honours and awards:* Medal of Brotherhood and Unity; Medal of Merit for Nation; *publications:* several articles published in historical reviews and textbooks; Mita Cenic's Monograph and His Chosen Texts, 1988; Od Centralizma do Federalizma, (From Centralism to Federalism), 1984; Serb Socialists of the 19th Century, 1985; Memories of Avram Petrovic, 1988; Diary of Pera Todorovic, 1990; Planirana Revolucija, (Planned Revolution- a study and choice of texts of Russian populists), 1988; *private address:* Georgi Dimitrova Street 9/v, Yugoslavia; *office address:* Ms Latinka Perovic, Institut za istoriju radnickog pokreta Srbije, Nemanjina 24, Yugoslavia.

PERY, Nicole; French, Member of the European Parliament; *born:* 15 May 1943, Bayonne, France; *parents:* Jean Duprat and Marie Rose Duprat (née

Duhart); *married:* Albert Péry, 1964; *children:* Nadine, Jean-Marc; *education:* Primary and Secondary Schools, Bayonne; Ecole Normale, Pau; University of Bordeaux, diploma of teaching; *party:* Parti Socialiste, 1971-; *political career:* Member, European Parliament, 1981-; Vice President, European Parliament, 1984; Regional Cllr., Aquitaine; *professional career:* teacher; *recreations:* music, mountain sports; *private address:* Villa Xori-Kanta, rue Massy 40, 64500 Ciboure, France; *office address:* Mme. Nicole Pery, European Parliament, Rue Belliard, 1040 Brussels, Belgium.

PETER, Dr. Brunhilde; German, Member of the Bundesrat; *born:* 4 October 1925, Mainz, West Germany; *children:* three; *religion:* Catholic; *education:* German Theology and Philosophy; Ph.D., 1955; *party:* Sozialdemokratische Partei Deutschlands (SPD, Social Democratic Party of Germany); *political career:* mem. of Kreistag Saarlouis, 1968-70; mem. of Landtag Saarland since 1970; Minister of Labour, Health and Social Affairs and Dep. Minister-Pres. since 1985; mem. of Bundesrat, 1985-; *office address:* Dr. Brunhilde Peter, Bundesrat, 5300 Bonn 1, West Germany.

PETROVA, Dimitrina Gueorguieva; Bulgarian, Member of the Grand National Assembly; *born:* 11 January 1957, Burgas; *parents:* Gueorgui Dimitrov Petrov and Trendafila Sotirova; *married:* Krassimir Ivanov Kanev, 1978; *public role of spouse:* Mem., Co-ordinating Cttee. of the Union of Democratic Forces; *children:* Dafina, Vania; *languages:* Bulgarian, English, Russian, French, German; *education:* English Language School, 1971-76; University of Sofia, philosophy, 1977-81; *party:* ECOGLASNOST (Independent Association), 1989-; *political career:* Int. Contacts Co-ordinator, ECOGLASNOST, 1989-90, Exec. Cttee. mem., 1989-90; mem. of Parliament representing Union of Democratic Forces (UDF), 1990-, mem., Commissions for Human Rights, National Question and Science and Education; Adviser to Bulgarian Pres. on pardoning prisoners, 1990-91; Bulgarian contact with Helsinki's Citizens' Assembly, 1991; *interests:* protection of human rights, stopping the escalation of nationalism in south-eastern Europe, environmental policies; *memberships:* Centre for the Study of Democracy; *professional career:* Asst., Philosophy Faculty, Univ. of Sofia, 1981-87, Chief Asst., 1987-; Mem., Editorial Board, Kritka i Humanizam, Inst. for Social Critique, 1989-; editor, South-East European Quarterly, Centre for the Study of Democracy, Sofia, 1991-, Dir., Women's Studies Programme, 1991-; *publications:* Policy Statement of the Social Movement ECOGLASNOST, 1989; The Utopian Counterpoint in the Critical Theory of Society (Essay), Critics and Critical Theory in Eastern Europe, 1990; Political Pluralism in Bulgaria (Article), New Politics, Vol. 3, No. 3, 1991; Sotsializmat i Utopiite (Article), Kritka i Humanizam, No. 2, 1991; *clubs:* Association of Academic Women, Sofia; *private address:* Zh. K.

Nadezhda 6, Bl. 636B, apt. 85, 1231 Sofia, Bulgaria; *office address:* Ms Dimitrina Gueorguieva Petrova, Narodno Sobranie, 3 National Assembly Square, Sofia 1000, Bulgaria; *phone:* 85-01.

PETTERSEN, Oddrunn; Norwegian, Minister of Fisheries; *born:* 5 March 1937, Hadsel, Finnmark; *parents:* Omar Hansen and Kristine Hansen; *married:* Birger Pettersen, 1961; *languages:* English, German; *education:* Cambridge Univ., UK, English, 1957; Tromso College of Education, Degree, 1961; *party:* Norwegian Labour Party; *political career:* Mayor of Berlevåg, 1976-77; Former Board Mem., Norwegian Assn., Local Authorities; Mem., Storting, 1977-; Mem., Standing Cttee. on Local Govt., the Environment (Chair, 1978-81) on Communications (Leader 1985-86) and on Shipping and Fisheries; Delegate to the UN General Assembly, 1982; Minister of Consumer Affairs and Govt. Admin., Apr.-Oct. 1989; Minister of Fisheries, Nov. 1990-; *interests:* equal rights questions; *professional career:* former teacher and headmistress; *private address:* Nyrudveien, Beilevåg; *office address:* Ms Oddrunn Pettersen, Ministry of Fisheries, Ovre Slottsgaten 2, P.O. Box 8118 Dep, 0032 Oslo 1, Norway; *phone:* (02) 34 90 90; *fax:* 349585.

PHILLIPS, Baroness (UK, cr. 1964, Life Peer) Norah Phillips; British, Member of the House of Lords; *born:* 12 August 1910; *parents:* William Lusher; *married:* Morgan Phillips, 1930; *children:* one s., one d; *religion:* Catholic; *education:* Marist Convent; Hampton Training Coll; *party:* Labour Party; *political career:* Mem., House of Lords, 1964; a Baroness-in-Waiting; Govt. Whip, 1965-70; mem., Home Office Standing Cttee. on Crime Prevention, Consumer Forum; fmrly., HM Lord Lieut. of Greater London, 1978-85; *professional career:* Dir., Assn. for the Prevention of Theft in Shops; Pres., Nat. Assn. of Women's Clubs, Inst. of Shops, Health and Safety Acts Administration, Keep Fit Assn., Assn. for Research into Restricted Growth, Int. Professional Security Assn.; Pre-retirement, Vice-Pres., Nat. Chamber of Trade, Fair Play for Children, Nat. Assn. for Maternal and Child Welfare, Employment Fellowship; fmrly. mem., Advertising Standards Authority, British Standards Inst., Council of Europe, Nat. Consumer Council, Women's Nat. Cmn., Snowdon Working Party; *office address:* Baroness Phillips, House of Lords, London SW1A 0PW.

PIAT, Yann; French, Deputy; *born:* 12 June 1949, Saigon, Vietnam; *parents:* Luce Millet; *married:* Jean Piat, 1977; *children:* Laetitia, Angélique; *religion:* Catholic; *languages:* French, English; *party:* Parti Republicain (PR, Republican Party); independent; *political career:* member, Front National central committee, 1983-, and political bureau, 1984-; Regional Councillor, Provence-Alpes-Côte-d'Azur,

1986-; Deputy, 1986-, re-elected 1988-; excluded from the Front Nationale, 1988; *professional career:* departmental head, Var, 1984-88; secretary of departmental federations of les Landes, 1983-; *publications:* Seule Tout en Haut à Droite, Ed. Fixot; *private address:* 43 Bd Gambetta, 83400 Hyères, France; *office address:* Mme. Yanne Piat, L'Assemblée Nationale, 126 rue de L'Université, 75355 Paris, France.

PIETIKÄINEN, Sirpa Maria; Finnish, Minister of the Environment; *born:* 19 April 1959, Parikkala, Finland; *parents:* Erkki Alexander Pietikäinen and Sylvi Susanna Pietikäinen (née Hirvelä); *education:* B. Sc., (Econ.), 1986; *party:* Kansallinen Kokoomus (Kok, National Coalition Party); *political career:* Education Sec., Kokoomus Youth, South-Häme District, 1976-77 and mem., District Admin. Board and Exec. Cttee., 1977-79; mem., Cttee. for Cultural Policy, South-Häme Kokoomus, 1977 and Chmn., 1980; District Cncl., South-Häme Kokoomus, 1978-80; mem., Representatives of Helsinki Univ. Students Union, 1980-81; mem., Representatives of Helsinki School of Economics Student Union, 1980-81 and mem., of the Admin. Board and Chmn., Sub-Cttee. for Foreign Affairs, 1980; mem., Hämeenlinna town Cncl., 1981; mem., Häme Provincial Union Admin. Board, 1982; mem. of Eduskunta, 1983-; Advisory Cttee., Regional Politics, Häme Province, 1984; mem., Cttee on Int. Year for Peace (1986); Advisory Cttee. Developing Countries, 1986; *recreations:* culture, visual arts, music, theatre; *office address:* Ms Sirpa Pietikäinen, Eduskunta, 00102 Helsinki, Finland.

PIKE, Baroness (UK, cr. 1974, Life Peer) Irene Mervyn Parnicott Pike; British, Member of the House of Lords; *born:* 16 September 1918; *parents:* Samuel Pike; *religion:* Church of England; *education:* Hunmanby Hall; Reading Univ., BA, (Hons.) economics and psychology; *party:* Conservative Party; *political career:* contested Pontefract (Yorks) 1951, and Leek (Staffs) 1955; MP (Cons.), Melton, 1956-74; Asst. Postmaster-Gen., 1959-63; joint Parly. Under-Sec. of State, Home Office, 1963-64; mem., House of Lords, 1974; *interests:* community care, broadcasting; *professional career:* WAAF, 1941-46; Man. Dir., Clokie and Co. Ltd., 1946-62; Dir., Watts, Blake, Bearne, 1964-89; Nat. Chmn., WRVS, 1974-81; Chmn., Broadcasting Complaints Cmn., 1981-86; *honours and awards:* D.B.E; *clubs:* Reform Club; *recreations:* gardening; reading; walking; *private address:* Hownam, nr. Kelso, Roxburgh, Scotland, UK; *office address:* Baroness Pike, House of Lords, London SW1A 0PW.

PINES, Lois G.; American, Massachusetts State Senator; *born:* 1940, Malden, Mass., USA; *married:* Joseph Pines; *children:* two; *education:* Barnard College, BA, 1960; Univ. of Cincinnati Law School, JD, 1963; *party:* Democratic Party; *political career:* Alderma Newton, Mass., 1971-73; Mass. State Rep., 1973-7 candidate for Sec.-of-State, 1978 and Lt. Gov., 198 regional Dir., New England Federal Tra Commission, 1979-81; Mass. State Senator, 198(currently Chwn., Commerce and Labour Cttees.; Mem Banks and Banking and Local Affairs Cttees.; Chwr Commission for Early Childhood Educatio *professional career:* Corp. Tax Attorney, 1964-72; Exe Dir., International Co-ordination Cncl., 1984-8 *private address:* 40 Helene Road, Newton, MA 0216 USA; *office address:* Mrs Lois Pines, State Hous Boston, MA 02133, USA.

PINTO RENDA, Roberta; Italian, Deputy; *born:* December 1948, Rome, Italy; *party:* Parti(Democratico della Sinistra (PDS, Party of th Democratic Left); *political career:* Councillor, Rome from 1976; Assessor for Schools, 1979-82; mem Federal Secretariat, PCI; Mem Fed. Cttee., PCI; Pres. c UISP, Rome; Deputy, Rome-Viterbo-Latina Frosinone, 1987; mem. Cttee. on Culture, Science an Teaching; mem. Leadership Cttee. of Parliamentar group; *professional career:* Teacher; *office address:* M Roberta Pinto Renda, Camera dei Deputat Montecitorio, 00186 Rome, Italy.

PIRCHEGGER, Grete; Austrian, Member of th Bundesrat; *born:* 11 June 1941, Stanz im Mürztal *education:* St. Martin Agricultural Technical College *party:* Österreichische Volkspartei (ÖVP, Austria People's Party); *political career:* district representative of ÖVP Austrian Women's Movement, Steiermark since 1980; mem. of provincial Exec. Cttee., Styrian Farmers' Federation, since 1980, and provincial Vice-chairperson, since 1985; senior official, Provincial Chamber of Agriculture and Forestry, Steiermark, since 1986; sent to Bundesrat from Steiermark Provincial Assembly, mem. of Bundesrat, since 1986; *professiona career:* Community Farmer, Allerheiligen im Mürztal, since 1963; District Farmer, since 1976; Deputy Provincial Farmer since 1986; mem. of Home Economics Advisory Council, since 1964; *office address:* Frau Grete Pirchegger, Bundesrat, Dr. Karl Renner Ring 3, 1017 Vienna, Austria.

PITTELOUD, Françoise; Swiss, Member of the Nationalrat; *born:* 3 August 1951, Martigny, Valais, Switzerland; *parents:* Antoine Pitteloud and Gabrielle Pitteloud (née Tissières); *children:* Annaïk, Cyrian, Moïra; *languages:* French, English, German; *education:* primary schools, Sion, 1958-64; Classical College, Sion, 1965-70; School of Social and Pedagogical Studies, Lausanne, 1976-79, diploma in teaching handicapped children; *party:* Parti Socialiste Suisse (PSS, Swiss Socialist Party), 1974; *political career:* Deputy for Vaud canton, 1981-83; member of Nat. Council, 1983-; member of Social Policy committee; *interests:*

international politics, social policy, education, position of women, policy regarding political asylum and foreign residents; *private address:* Rue du Vallon 10, 1005 Lausaune, Switzerland; *office address:* Frau Françoise Pitteloud, Nationalrat/Conseil National, Secretariat-General, Parlamentsgebäude, 3003 Berne, Switzerland.

PLA PASTOR, Adela; Spanish, Deputy; *born:* Sedavi, Valencia, Spain; *education:* elementary school teaching certificate; *party:* Partido Socialista Obrero Español (PSOE, Spanish Socialist Workers' Party); *political career:* Deputy, PSOE, Valencia, 1982-89, re-elected 1989-; Mem., Cttee. on Education and Culture; mem., Foreign Affairs Cttee; *office address:* Ms Adela Pla Pastor, Congreso de los Diputados, Fernán Flor 1, Madrid 14, Spain.

PLATT OF WRITTLE, Baroness (cr. 1981, Life Peer) Beryl Catherine Platt, CBE; DL; British, Member of the House of Lords; *born:* 18 April 1923; *parents:* the late Ernest Myatt; *married:* Stewart Sydney Platt, 1949; *children:* one s., one d; *religion:* Church of England; *languages:* elementary French, German, Italian; *education:* Westcliff High Sch. for Girls; Girton Coll., Camb; *party:* Conservative and Unionist Party; *political career:* mem., Chelmsford RDC, 1959-74; elected to Essex CC, 1965; Alderman 1969-74; Vice-Chmn., Educ. Cttee., 1969-71, Chmn. 1971-80; Vice-Chmn., CC, 1980-83; mem., House of Lords, 1981; DL, County of Essex, 1983; Mem., House of Lords Select Cttee. on Murder and Life Imprisonment, 1988-89; Mem., House of Lords Select Cttee. on Science and Technology, 1990-; *interests:* educ., engineering industry women's opportunities; *professional career:* technical asst., Hawker Aircraft, 1943-46; technical asst., British European Airways, 1946-49; mem. of Court, Essex Univ., from its establishment; mem. of Court, City Univ., 1969-78; trustee, Homerton Coll., 1970-81; mem., CNAA, 1973-79; TEC, 1973-82; training and educ. for RAF Advisory Cttee., 1976-79; ACC Educ. Cttee. from its establishment to 1980; CLEA, 1976-80; Council NFER, 1975-77; City and Guilds of London Inst. Council, 1974, Vice-Chmn., London Regional Advisory Council for Technological Educ., 1975-81; Burnham Further Educ. Salary Negotiation Cttee., 1975-80; Camb. Univ. Appointment Board, 1975-79; Royal Aeronautical Soc. Educ. Cttee., 1975-77 and 1989-; Pres., Chelmsford Engineering Soc., 1979-80; Engineering Council, 1981-90; Chmn., Equal Opportunities Cmn., 1983-88; mem. of Council, RSA, 1983-88; mem., Careers Research Advisory Council, 1983-; Vice-Pres., UMIST, 1985-; mem. of Court, Brunel Univ., 1985-; Board mem., British Gas, 1988-; mem. of Court Cranfield Inst., 1989-; Mem., Engineering Training Authority, 1990-; *honours and awards:* Hon. D.Sc., City Univ.; Hon. D.Sc., Univ. of Salford; Hon. F.I. Mech. E.; Hon. F.Inst. of Training and Dev.; Fellowship of Royal Aeronautical Soc.; Hon. D.Sc., Cranfield Inst., Hon. D. Univ., Open Univ.;

Hon. D. Eng., Bradford Univ., Hon. D. Univ. of Essex; Hon. F. Polytechnic of Wales; Hon. D., Brunel Univ., 1986; Hon. F., Royal Coll. of Preceptors, 1986; Fellow of the Fellowship of Eng. (F. Eng.), 1987; European Engineer (Eur.Ing.), 1987; Hon. LLD., Camb. Univ., 1988; Hon. F., Girton Coll., 1988; City and Guilds of London Insignia Award, 1988; Hon. Fellow, Manchester Polytechnic, 1989; Hon. Fellow I. Gas E., 1990; Hon. Fellow Inst. of Structural Engineers, 1991; Hon. Fellow Inst. of Civil Engineers, 1991; *clubs:* United Oxford & Cambridge University; *recreations:* reading, gardening, cookery; *office address:* Baroness Platt of Writtle, House of Lords, London SW1A 0PW.

PLAZA, Hon. Charito B.; Filipino, Congresswoman; *born:* 23 November 1957, Butuan City; *married:* Mayor Figurado O. Plaza; *children:* Flavia, Figurado Jr., Frederic, Francois; *education:* Father Urios College, B.Sc., Commerce; *political career:* Congresswoman; *interests:* the underpaid; *office address:* The Hon. Ms Charito Plaza, The Congress of the Philippines - House of Representatives, Batasang Pambansa Bldg., Quezon City, Manila, The Philippines.

POCEK-MATIC, Dr. Mirjana; Yugoslavian, Member of the Central Committee of Croatia League of Communists; *born:* 1932; *education:* Dr. of Economics; *party:* League of Communists of Yugoslavia (LCY), 1959-; *political career:* elected to Central Cttee., LCY, 10th Congress, 1974; Chairperson, Conference for Social Activity of Women of Croatia; Mem., Standing Cttee. of Conference of LCY; Mem., Presidium, Croatia LC, 1982-, Mem., Central Cttee., 1982, 1986-; *office address:* Dr. Mirjana Pocek-Matic, League of Communists of Yugoslavia, Novi Beograd, bul. Lenjina 6, Yugoslavia.

POHJANOKSA, Dr. Aino Siviä; Finnish, Member of the Eduskunta; *born:* 17 March 1936, Rauma, Finland; *parents:* Taavetti Kuosmanen and Bertta Siviä Kuosmanen (née Ketola); *married:* Kimmo Teuvo Arimo Pohjanoksq, 1964; *children:* Iiro, Pauno; *education:* Hämeenlinna, Primary School Teacher, 1958; Jyväskylä, MA (Educ.), 1974; Turku, Ph. D., 1980; *party:* Kansallinen Kokoomus (KoK, National Coalition Party); *political career:* Mem., Rauma Town Cncl., 1977; mem., Turku Univ. Cncl. 1981-83; mem., Rauma Parish Cncl., 1983; mem. of Eduskunta, 1983-; Chmn., Admin. Board, Nat. Cttee. for Education & Culture, 1985; Chmn., Right-Wing Youth Assn., 1986; *professional career:* Primary School Teacher, Karvia, 1958-59; Rauma, 1959-66; Rauma Teachers Training College (Primary School), 1966-74; Lecturer, Summer Univ. of Western Finland, 1971; Lecturer in Education, Tampere Univ., 1982 Head, Rauma Normal School, 1974-78; Lecturer in Didactics, Rauma Teachers Training College (Turku Univ.), 1978 and Head of Dept., 1979-83; *publications:* Visuaalisen, verbaalisen ja taktiilisen luovuuden kehittänusestä alkuopetusikäisillä (Doctoral Thesis), 1980; *office address:* Dr. Aino Pohjanoksa, Eduskunta, 00102 Helsinki, Finland.

POKKA, Hannele (Pirkko Hannele); Finnish, Minister of Justice; *born:* 25 May 1952, Ruovesi, Finland; *parents:* Aino Tellervo Pokka; *education:* M. of Law, 1975; Lic.L., 1978; *party:* Keskustapuolue (KP Centre Party); *political career:* Mem. of Eduskunta 1979-; mem., Presidential Electorate, 1982; Cllr., National Pensions Inst.; Chairperson, Women's Organization of the Centre Party, 1985-; Vice-Chairperson, Finnish Centre Party, 1986-; *professional career:* Lawyer, MTK (Farm Producers Central Assn.), 1976; *office address:* Ms Hannele Pokka, Ministry of Justice, Eteläesplanadi 10, 00130 Helsinki, Finland.

POLFER, Lydie; Luxembourgeios, Member of the Chamber of Deputies; *born:* 22 November 1952, Luxembourg; *married:* Hubert Wurth, 1981; *children:* Nora; *education:* School leaving examinations, Jul. 1972; doctor of law, University of Grenoble, Jun. 1976; Diplôme d'Etudes Aprofondie (DEA, Diploma in Advanced Studies) in European Integration, Centre of University Research into International and European Affairs, Sept. 1977; *party:* Parti Democratique; *political career:* mem. of Luxembourg Parliament, Jun. 1979-85, mem. of Commissions for Foreign Affairs, Justice, Public Works and Constitutional Reform, re-elected, Jun. 1989, mem. of commissions on Justice, Community Affairs, Housing, Urbanism, Constitutional Reform and Foreign Affairs; Elected to District Council for Luxembourg, Oct. 1981 re-elected 1987; Designated in Nov. 1981 by Democratic Party as Mayoress of Luxembourg Jan. 1982; European Parliament, 1985; Mayoress of Luxembourg, 1988-; Council of Europe, mem. of Commissions for legal matters, migrations of refugies and demography and parliamentary and public relations; mem. of Commissions of UEO (Union de L'Europe Occidentale), for General Matters and for Parliamentary relations; *professional career:* mem. of Luxembourg Bar, Feb. 1977-; trainee/researcher for Liberal and Democratic Reformist Group at European Parliament; *office address:* Mme. Lydie Polfer, Chambre des Députés, rue du Marché aux Herbes, Luxembourg-Ville, Luxembourg.

POLI BORTONE, Dott. Adriana; Italian, Deputy; *born:* 25 August 1943, Lecce, Italy; *children:* two; *education:* Degree in Classical Letters; *party:* Marimento Sociale Italiano-Destra Nazionale (MSI-DN, Italian Social Movement-National Right); *political career:* mem. Nat. Secretariat, and Nat. Political Office of MSI-DN; Political Sec for Women's problems from 1981; Councillor, Lecce, 1967; re-elected in subsequent elections; elected Deputy, Lecce-Brindisi-Taranto,

1983; re-elected Deputy, 1987; mem. Cttee. on Teaching and Fine Art; Head of MSI-DN Group, for the special Cttee. on Pensions; in 9th Legislature; mem. Cttee. on Culture Science and Teaching, in 10th Legislature; *professional career:* Associate Professor of Latin Literature, Faculty of Philosophy and Letters, University of Lecce; *office address:* Dott. Adriana Poli Bortone, Camera dei Deputati, Montecitorio, 00186 Rome, Italy.

POLLACK, Anita Jean; British, Member of the European Parliament; *born:* 3 June 1946; *party:* Labour Party; *political career:* Research Asst. to MEP 1981-89; MEP for London South West, 1989-; *private address:* 177 Lavender Hill, London SW11 5TE; *office address:* Mrs Anita Pollack, European Parliament, Centre Européen, Plateau de Kirchberg, BP 2929, Luxembourg; *phone:* Luxembourg 43001.

POLLACK, Lana; American, Michigan State Senator; *born:* 11 October 1942, Ludington, Michigan, USA; *parents:* Abbie Schoenberger and Genevieve Schoenberger (née Siegel); *married:* Henry Pollack, 1963; *children:* Sara (Decd.), John; *religion:* Jewish; *education:* Univ. of Michigan, Ann Arbor, BA, 1965, MA, 1970; American Academy for the Performing Arts, 1976; American Univ., District of Columbia; *party:* Democratic Party; *political career:* Chwn., Ann Arbor Democrat Cttee., 1975-77; Mgr., Campaign for State Senate, 1978, Campaign for 2nd Congressional District, 1980; trustee Ann Arbor Board of Education, 1979-82; Michigan State Senator, District 18, 1983-; Mem., Senate Joint Cttee. on Administration Rules, 1985; Mem., Senate Commission on Crime, Justice and Urban Affairs, 1985; *professional career:* instructor, East Michigan Univ., 1974-76 and Washtenaw Community College, 1975-81; Senior Administrator, John Howard Compound School, Zambia, 1970-71; *publications:* Opposing Out-of-Formula Districts Lobbyist, 1981; 60 Years Later, Michigan Alumnus, 1982; Managing Declining Enrollments, Ann Arbor News, 1982; *office address:* Mrs Lana Pollack, Michigan State Senate, P.O. Box 30036, Lansing, Michigan 48909, USA.

POPIELA, Stanislawa; Polish, Member of the Sejm; *office address:* Ms Stanislawa Popiela, Sejm PRI, ul. Wiejska 4/6/8, 00-489 Warsaw, Poland; *phone:* (22) 28 70 01; 28 40 31.

POPTODUROVA-PETROVA, Rt. Hon. Elena Borislavova; Bulgarian, Member of the Grand National Assembly; *born:* Sofia, Bulgaria; *parents:* Borislav Nikolov Poptodorov and Rada Nikolova Poptodorova (née Piteva); *married:* Georgi Tsvetanov Petrov, 1975; *children:* Georgi; *religion:* Christian Orthodox; *languages:* Bulgarian, English, Italian, French, Russian; *education:* Univ. of Sofia, MA Letters, English and

Italian Language and Literature, 1969-74; *party:* Bulgarian Socialist Party, 1990; *political career:* Mem., of Parl., Yambol Region, 1990-; Mem., Grand Nat. Assembly, 1990-; *interests:* foreign policy, social affairs, local government, women's affairs; *memberships:* Union of Bulgarian Translators; *professional career:* Sec. to Cllr., Ministry of Foreign Affairs, 1975-90; *publications:* articles on European Intergration, 1990-91; *recreations:* skiing, swimming, hiking, aerobics, reading, music; *private address:* Mladosti Bl. 25, Entr. B, Sofia, Bulgaria; *office address:* The Rt. Hon. Ms Elena Borislavova Poptodurova-Petrova, Narodno Sobranie, 3 National Assembly Square, Sofia 1000, Bulgaria; *phone:* 85-01.

POSADA CHAPADO, Her Exellency Rosa María; Spanish, President of the Madrid Autonomous Parliament; *born:* 1940, Madrid, Spain; *education:* Complutence Univ., Madrid, Spain, LLD; firther studies at Strasbourg and Oxford Univ., UK; *party:* Centro Democrático y Social (CDS); *political career:* senate candidate for Madrid; Pol. Sec., Cabinet, 1981; Sec. of State for Information; Pres., Madrid Autonomous Parly. 1987-; *professional career:* lawyer; *office address:* HE Mrs Rosa María Posada Chapado, Asamblea de Madrid, San Bernardo 49, E-28015, Madrid, Spain; *phone:* (91) 2325700.

POWELL, Janet Frances; Australian, Federal Parliamentary Leader of the Australian Democrats; *born:* 29 September 1942, Nhill, Victoria, Australia; *children:* four; *education:* BA, Diploma in Education, Melbourne; *party:* Australian Democrats; *political career:* Convener, Australian Democrats National Rural Policy, 1980-82; Senior Vice-Pres., Australian Democrats, Victoria, 1982-83 and 1983-84; Pres., Australian Democrats, Victoria, 1983-84 and 1984-85; National Dep. Pres., Australian Democrats, 1984-85 and 1985-86; chosen by Parliament to represent Victoria in the Senate, 1986 and elected, 1987-; Temporary Chwn. of Cttees., 1987-88; Spokesperson for Democrats on Social Security, Administrative Services, Consumer Affairs, Primary Industry (from Primary Industry and Energy), Communications (from Transport and Communications), Local Govt., 1987-90; Committee Service: Mem. of the Senate Standing Cttee. for Privileges, 1987-90; for Scrutiny of Bills, 1987-90; Mem. of the Senate Legislative and General Purpose Standing Cttee. for Transport, Communications and Infrastructure, 1987-90; for Legal and Constitutional Affairs, 1987-90; Mem. of the Senate Select Cttee. for Television Equalisation, 1986-87; Leader of Federal Parliament, 1990-; *memberships:* Women's Electoral Lobby; Australian Conservation Foundation; Amnesty International and Amnesty International Parliamentary Group; World Women Parliamentarians for Peace; Inter Parliamentary Union; Commonwealth Parliamentary Association; Friends of the Earth; *professional career:* teacher; *office*

address: Ms Janet Powell, 400 Flinders Street, Melbourne 3000, Australia.

PRADHAM, Sahana; Nepalese, Leader of United Left Front and former Minister of Industry and Commerce; *party:* United Left Front (ULF, Communist Party of Nepal); *political career:* Leader, United Left Front coalition formed in early 1990, as coalition of seven Communist groups; appointed Minister of Industry and Commerce, April 1990; *office address:* Ms Sahana Pradham, United Left Front, Kathmandu, Nepal.

PRAHER, Adelheid; Austrian, Member of the Nationalrat; *born:* 16 October 1933, St. Pölten, Austria; *education:* federal commercial school, St. Pölten; *party:* Sozialistische Partei Österreichs (SPÖ, Socialist Party of Austria); *political career:* Red Falcons, 1946; mem. of Socialist Youth; SPÖ official, 1954-; mem. of provincial Party Exec., SPÖ, Lower Austria, 1972; Pres., district Women's Cttee., SPÖ, St. Pölten; Vice-Chairperson, SPÖ, St. Pölten, 1982-; mem. of District council and Town council, St. Pölten, 1975-82; mem. of Nationalrat, for Lower Austria, 1982-; *professional career:* employee of municipal authority, St. Pölte, 1949; consultant on the schools and nursery schools system, municipal authority, St. Pölten, 1967-; mem. of Schools Inspectorate St. Pölten, 1967-; mem. and reserve mem. of Schools Inspectorate, Province of Lower Austria, 1965-; *office address:* Frau Adelheid Praher, Nationalrat, Dr. Karl Renner Ring 3, 1017 Vienna, Austria.

PRAXMARER, Karin; Austrian, Member of the Nationalrat; *born:* 9 July 1944, Zwettl, Lower Austria; *education:* federal grammar school (science oriented), Wels, matriculation, 1962; University of Vienna, M.Sc. in Philosophy, history teaching and physical education teaching, 1968; *party:* Freiheitliche Partei Österreichs (FPÖ, Freedom Party of Austria); *political career:* provincial womens' speaker, FPÖ, Upper Austria, 1975-; provincial Party Vice-Chmn., FPÖ, Upper Austria, 1982-; district councillor, Grieskirchen, 1985-; mem. of Nationalrat, for Upper Austria, 1986; *professional career:* teacher, upper federal grammar school (science orientated), Grieskirchen, 1967-86; teacher at general secondary school; *office address:* Frau Karin Praxmarer, Nationalrat, Dr. Karl Renner Ring 3, 1017 Vienna, Austria.

PRIETO, María Cynthia; Paraguay, Minister of Health; *office address:* Ms María Cynthia Prieto, Ministry of Public Health and Social Welfare, Avenida Pettirossi Y Brasil, Asunción, Paraguay.

PRIMAROLO, Dawn; British, Member of Parliament; *born:* 2 May 1954; *married:* Thomas Ian Ducat, 1990; *children:* one s; *education:* Thomas Bennett Comprehensive School; Bristol Polytechnic, BA(Hons.)

in Social Science; Bristol University; *party:* Labour Party; *political career:* Cllr., Avon County Cncl., 1985-87; Member of Parliament for Bristol South, 1987-; *interests:* defence, arms conversion, Central and Latin America, the Palestinian question, employment, social security, women's rights; *professional career:* sec. and advice worker, East London Law Centre; sec. working for Avon County Cncl., 1975-78; *office address:* Ms Dawn Primarolo, House of Commons, London SW1A OAA.

PRIOTEASA, Paula; Romanian, Deputy to the Grand National Assembly; *party:* Romanian Communist Party (RCP); *political career:* Vice-Chairperson, Central Cncl. of Workers' Control of Economic and Social Activity, 1980-82; Dep. Minister of Foreign Trade and International Economic Co-operation (responsible for Asia and Oceania), 1982-86; candidate mem., RCP, Central Cttee., 1982-84, full Mem., 1984-; Dep., Grand Nat. Assembly, 1985-; Minister of Food Industry and ·Collection of Agricultural Products, 1986; *office address:* Ms Paula Prioteasa, Marea Adunare Nationala, Aleea Marii Adunari Nationale, Bucharest, Romania; *phone:* 16 21 50.

PRITAN, Amrita; Indian, Member of the Rajya Sabha; *born:* 31 August 1919, Gujranwala, Pakistan; *parents:* Sardar Kartar Singh Hitkari; *children:* one s., one d; *education:* Khalsa School; private College in Lahore; *political career:* Mem., Rajya Sabha, 1986-; represented India at Republic Day Celebrations, Nepal, 1960; participated on Bulgarian Cttee. for Friendship and Cultural Relations with Foreign Countries, 1966; participated in Cultural Exchange Programme of the Govt. of India, in Yugoslavia, Hungary and Romania, 1967; participated in Indo-Yugoslav Cultural Exchange Programme, Yugoslavia, 1972; attended World-Peace Congress, Moscow, 1973; attended International Peace Conference, Moscow, 1987; *professional career:* writer and author; *honours and awards:* Sahitya Akademi Award, 1956; 'Sanman-Patter', Language Department, Punjab Govt., 1958; Man Patter, Bhartiya Mahila Federation, Delhi, 1965; 'PADMA SHREE', 1969; 'Sanman', Vishav Hindi Sanmelan, Nagpur, 1975; National Investment and Finance Award, 1976; 'Souvenir' for distinguished broadcasting, 1978; 'Sanman', Kanada Literary Conference, 1978; 'International Vaptsarove' Award, Republic of Bulgaria, 1979; 'Cyril and Methodius' Award, Republic of Bulgaria, 1980; 'Bhartiya Janapith' Award, 1982; D. Litt. (Honoris Causa) conferred by Viswa Bharti, Delhi, Jabalpur and Punjab Universities; degree of 'Officer dans/order des arts et des letters', French Govt., 1988; *publications:* editor, Punjabi monthly, 1966-; author of more than 50 books, including novels, short stories, poems, prose and her Autobiography 'Rasidi Ticket'; *recreations:* reading; *office address:* Shrimati Amrita Pritan, K-25, Hauz Khas, New Delhi -- 16.

PROCACCI, Dott. Annamaria; Italian, Deputy; *born:* 17 September 1949, Rome, Italy; *education:* Degree in Letters; *party:* Federazione Nationale per Le Liste Verdi (Green Party); *political career:* mem. of LAC (Lega per L'Abolizrone della Caccia-League for the abolition of Hunting; mem. Leadership and Nat. Sec. LAC since 1982; Co-promoter of 2 national referenda on environmental issues, 1980, 1986; mem. Green Party from its inception; mem. Co-ordination Committee; Lazio; Head of Hunting section, Nat. Green Federation; elected Deputy, Rome-Viterbo-Latina-Frosinone, 1987; mem. Cttee. on Culture Science and Teaching; *interests:* environment, anti-hunt, vivisection campaigns, animal rights, ecology; *professional career:* Literature Teacher, Liceo Scientifico Sperimentale, Rome; *office address:* Dott. Annamaria Procacci, Camera dei Deputati, Montecitorio, 00186 Rome, Italy.

PROCOPIO, Margarida; Brazilian, Minister of Social Welfare; *office address:* Ministry of Social Welfare, Esplanada dos Ministérios, Bloco U, 70.065 Brasília, DF, Brazil.

PROSZOWSKA, Joanna; Polish, Member of the Sejm; *office address:* Ms Joanna Proszowska, Sejm PRI, ul. Wiejska 4/6/8, 00-489 Warsaw, Poland; *phone:* (22) 28 70 01; 28 40 31.

PRUSTI, Riitta Anneli; Finnish, Chair of the Confederation of Salaried Employees; *born:* 10 September 1941, Vaasa; *children:* Timo, Johanna; *languages:* Swedish; *party:* Suomen Sosialdemokraattinen Puolue (SDP, Finnish Social Democratic Party); *political career:* Co-pres., Confederation of Salaried Employees in Finland (TVK); *office address:* Ms Riitta Prusti, Toimihenkilö-ja Virkamiesjärjestöjen Keskusliitto, Asemamiehenkatu 4, 00520 Helsinki, Finland.

PUGONOWSKA-JUCHA, Emilia; Polish, Member of the Sejm; *office address:* Ms Emilia Pugonowska-Jucha, Sejm PRI, ul. Wiejska 4/6/8, 00-489 Warsaw, Poland; *phone:* (22) 28 70 01; 28 40 31.

PUOLANNE, Ulla Kaija; Finnish, Second Minister of Finance; *born:* 28 June 1931, Lahti, Finland; *parents:* Eero Eemil Raivo and Maili Matilda Raivo (née Penttilä); *education:* Helsinki, B. Sc. (Econ.), 1954; *party:* Kansallinen Kokoomus (KoK, National Coalition Party); *political career:* Mem., Lahti Town Cncl., 1969-84; Town Admin. Board, Lahti; 1972-75; mem. of Eduskunta, 1975-; mem., Presidential Electorate, 1978 and 1982; Chmn., Kokoomus Parly. Group, 1984; Admin. Cncl., Finnair Oy., 1984; Second Minister of Finance; *professional career:* Correspondent, L.A. Levanto Oy., 1954-56; Correspondent, Rauma-Repola Oy. (Lahti), 1956-59;

Correspondent, Asko Oy., 1959-65; Head of Dept., Asko Oy., 1965-68; Financial Man., Reijo Puolanne & Partners Ltd (Civil Engineering); *honours and awards:* Knight (1st Class) of the Order of the Lion of Finland; *office address:* Ms Ulla Puolanne, Ministry of Finance, Snellmaninkatu 1A, 00170 Helsinki, Finland.

PURCELL, Joan; Grenada, Minister of Tourism, Civil Aviation and Women's Affairs; *office address:* Mrs Joan Purcell, Ministry of Tourism, Civil Aviation and Women's Affairs, Young Street, Grenada; *phone:* (440) 3162; 2737; 2738; 2199.

PUYAT-REYES, Ma. Consuelo; Filipino, Congresswoman; *born:* 26 November 1937, Manila, The Philippines; *parents:* Deogracias J. Puyat and Patria Gil; *married:* Gregorio Reyes; *education:* St. Paul's College, BS (cum laude), Education, AB (cum laude); Centre for Research and Communictions, MS, Business Economics; Alliance Francaise, Buenos Aires, Argentina, French Language; *political career:* Congresswoman; Chairperson, Cttee. on Urban Planning and Development; *interests:* workers' and women's rights, youth and sports development, budgeting, banking; *honours and awards:* Pro-Ecclesia et Pontifical Papal award; *office address:* Ms Ma. Puyat-Reyes, The Congress of the Philippines - House of Representatives, Batasang Pambansa Bldg., Quezon City, Manila, The Philippines.

Q

QUIN, Joyce Gwendolen; British, Member of Parliament; *born:* 26 November 1944, Tynemouth, UK; *parents:* Basil Godfrey Quin and Ida Quin (née Ritson); *languages:* French, Italian; *education:* Univ. of Newcastle-Upon-Tyne, BA, French, 1967; Univ. of London, M.Sc., International politics, 1969; *party:* Labour Party, 1969; *political career:* Member of European Parliament, 1979-89; Member of Parliament, 1987-; party spokesperson on consumer affairs, Feb. 1989-, and on trade, Oct. 1989-; *interests:* industrial policy, regional policy, European Community, women's rights; *professional career:* lecturer, Bath Univ., 1972-76; lecturer, Durham Univ., 1976-79; *honours and awards:* Hon. Fellow, Sunderland Polytechnic, 1986; *clubs:* Fabian Society; Socialist Environment and Resource Assn; *private address:* Old Bank, Swinburne Str., Gateshead NE8 1AN, UK; *office address:* Ms Joyce Quin, House of Commons, London SW1A OAA.

QUINT (née Maagdenberg), Drs. Monique; Dutch, Member of the Second Chamber; *born:* 22 January 1945, Holland; *parents:* Wilhemus Christoffel Andreas Maagdenberg and Adriana Maagdenberg (née Verhagen); *married:* Hendrians Wilhelmus Quint, 1970; *languages:* Dutch, English, German, French; *education:* Univ. of Leiden; *party:* Party van de Arbeid (Social Democrats); *political career:* Mem., Second Chamber; *interests:* development co-operation, social security, women's issues, education, European affairs; *private address:* Oostbroek 18, 6243 CB Geulle, The Netherlands; *office address:* Drs. Monique Quint, Tweede Kamer der Staten-Generaal, Binnenhof 1A, Postbus 20018, The Hague, The Netherlands.

QUISTHOULT-ROWOHL, Godelieve; German, Member of the European Parliament; *born:* 18 June 1947; *party:* Christlich Demokratische Deutschlands (CDU, Christian Democratic Union); *political career:* MEP, 1989-; *private address:* Zingel 30, 3200 Hildesheim, Germany; *office address:* Ms Godelieve Quisthoult-Rowohl, European Parliament, Centre Européen, Plateau de Kirchberg, BP 2929, Luxembourg; *phone:* Luxembourg 43001.

QUISTORP, Eva; German, Member of the European Parliament; *born:* 28 August 1945; *party:* Die Grünen (Green Party); *political career:* MEP, 1989-; *professional career:* theoligian; teacher; *private address:* Hochhaus Tupenfeld, 5300 Bonn 1, Germany; *office address:* Ms Eva Quistorp, European Parliament, Centre Européen, Plateau de Kirchberg, BP 2929, Luxembourg; *phone:* Luxembourg 43001.

R

RAAB, Rosemarie; German, Deputy Member of the Bundesrat; *born:* 12 November 1946, Lübeck; *children:* one; *education:* High School leaving examination; Univ. Hamburg, Sociology, Political Science, History and Social Education; Univ. Hamburg, MA in Sociology and completion of supplementary studies in Social Education, 1973; *party:* Sozialdemokratische Partei Deutschlands (SPD, Social Democratic Party of Germany), 1979; *political career:* mem. of Bürgerschaft, Hamburg, 1982-87; Senator and Pres. of School and Vocational Training Authority since 1987; mem. of Bundesrat since 1987; Senator and Pres. of Youth Authority since 1988; *professional career:* research asst.; Social Worker, Hamburg, Wilhelmsburg; Scientific asst., SPD Bürgerschaft Group; Head of Dept., Social Services, Berufsbildungswerk, Hamburg, 1982-85; *office address:* Frau Rosemarie Raab, Bundesrat, 5300 Bonn 1, West Germany.

RABL-STADLER, Dr. Helga; Austrian, Member of the Nationalrat; *born:* 2 June 1948, Salzburg, Austria; *education:* grammar school for girls (with emphasis on commerce and housekeeping); matriculation; University of Salzburg, Dr. of Law; *party:* Österreichische Volkspartei (ÖVP, Austrian People's Party); *political career:* Mem. of Nationalrat for Salzburg, 1983-; Vice-Pres., Chamber of Industry, Salzburg, 1985-; *professional career:* Correspondent for economic and domestic affairs, editorial offices of Die Presse, Die Wochenpress, and Kurier, 1970-78; Lawyer, Mother's Fashion Shop, Salzburg and Linz, 1978-; mem. of the Board of the Cttee., Institute for Economic Promotion, 1980-; chairperson, local group, Altstadt, Austrian Employers' and Trade People's Federation, Salzburg, 1980-; Chairperson, study group, Woman in Society, within the framework of Model Salzburg 2000; Pres. of Group; Woman in the Business World, Salzburg; *office address:* Dr. Helga Rabl-Stadler, Nationalrat, Dr. Karl Renner Ring 3, 1017 Vienna, Austria.

RADZIWIT, Anna; Polish, Senator; *office address:* Ms Anna Radziwit, Senat, ul. Ogrodowa 6, 00-896 Warsaw, Poland; *phone:* (22) 20 03 71.

RAKESTRAW, Priscilla B.; American, Republican National Committeewoman for Delaware; *party:* Republican Party; *political career:* Republican National Cttee.-Woman, Delaware; Mem., Exec. Cttee., Delaware Republican State arty, 1976-; delegate, Republican National Convention, 1976, 1980, 1984; Mem., Commission on Presidential Scholars, 1982-; *professional career:* Personnel Supervisor, Agricultural Chemicals Dept., EI DuPont DeNemours & Co., Inc; *office address:* Ms Priscilla Rakestraw, 1813 Delaware Avenue, Wilmington, Delaware 19806, USA.

RAKHIMOVA, Bikhodzhal Fatkhitdinovna; Soviet, Member of the Council of Nationalities; *party:* Communist Party of the Soviet Union; *political career:* Party Sec. for Ideology, Leninabad Obkom, Tajik SSR; elected from the Soviet Women's Cttee.; spoke at the Congress of People's Deps. on social issues and called for the Supreme Soviet to establish a state fund to equalise the socio-economic conditions in the Soviet Republics; Mem., Supreme Soviet Cttees. on Women's Affairs, Family Protection, Motherhood and Childhood; Mem., Council of Nationalities and Deputy Premier responsible for Social Policy Issues; *office address:* Ms Bikhodzhal Fatkhitdinovna Rakhomova, Council of Nationalities, Kremlin, Moscow, USSR.

RANDZIO-PLATH, Christa; German, Member of the European Parliament; *born:* 29 October 1940, Ratibor; *married:* Dr. Ronald Randzio, 1975; *languages:* English, French, German, Italian, Spanish; *education:* Univ. education, Kiel, Bonn, Amsterdam, Pescara, Shrapburg, Lausanne, law and sociology, 1961-70; *party:* Sozialdemokratische Partei Deutschlands (SPD, Social Democratic Party of Germany); *political career:* Mem., Hamburg City Parliament, 1986-89; MEP, 1989-; *interests:* economic policies, development, women's rights, external economic relations, environment; *professional career:* journalist, 1970-72; lawyer, 1972-74; tax and duty jurist and author, 1974-89; *publications:* Laßt uns endlich mitregieren; Europa - eine Chance für Frauen; Europa nach der Direktwahl; Europa und die Dritte Welt; Frieden; Frauenweg - Ausweg aus der Krise; Paragraph 218 - Zu Lasten der Frauen; Was geht uns Frauen der Krieg an; numerous articles; *recreations:* reading, ballet, travel; *private address:* Europa-Büro, Kurt-Schumacher-Allee 10, D-2000 Hamburg 1; *office address:* Ms Christa Randzio-Plath, European Parliament, Centre Européen, Plateau de Kirchberg, BP 2929, Luxembourg; *phone:* Luxembourg 43001.

RANGEL, Beatrice; Venezuelan, Secretary-General of the Presidency; *office address:* Ms Beatrice Rangel, Ministry of the Secretariat of the Presidency, Palacio de Miraflores, Caracas, Venezuela.

RASUL, Santanina Tillah; Filipino, Senator; *born:* 4 September 1930, Siasi, Sulu; *married:* Abraham Abubakar; *education:* Laum Tabawan Elementary School, Valedictorian, South Ubian, Tawi-Tawi, 1941; Sulu High School, First Honor, Jolo, Sulu, 1948; Univ. of the Philippines, Bachelor of Arts, Political Science, Cum Laude, 1952; National Defence College of the Philippines, Masters in National Security Administration, 1976; Univ. of the Philippines Doctoral Units in Public Administration; *political career:* Political Career Elected Barrio Councillor, Moore Avenue, Jolo, Sulu, two terms, 1960-61, 1962-63; Technical Assistant Office Staff of the Pres., Malacanana, Manila, 1963-64; Supervising Management Analyst, Department of Finance, Manila, 1964-65; Special Consultant, National Economic Council, Manila, 1966-67; elected Mem. of the Provincial Board of Sulu, 1971-76; Mem., Executive Cttee., League of Provincial Board Mems. of the Philippines to draft proposals resolutions and a position paper for the league for presentation to the Cttee. to Review the Local Govt. Code, 1972; Resource Person Review of the Proposed Local Govt. Code, Local Govt. Center, 1973; Observed and Studied rural development in Muslim countries, Kingdom of Saudi Arabia, Republic of Egypt, 1973; Cultural visit to Egypt as guest of the Supreme Council for Islamic Affairs, 1974; represented Filipino Mothers during the culminating activity of the Southeast Asian and Japanese Youth on the Ship for Southeast Asia, 1974; Cttee. Chairman, Mindanao Executive Development Academy, sponsored First Policy conference on Mindanao, Cagayan de Oro and Manila, Chair, Political Sub-Cttee. which drafted the political solutions to the Mindanao problem and the final position paper, on the Conference, 1975; Head Philippine Delegation, International Seminar work shop on The Muslim Women and their full Potential Rabat, Morocco, 1977; Cultural Visit to Iraq as guest of the Iraqi Ministry of Awkaff and Lord Mayor of Bagdad, 1977; Observation Tour of the United States as guest, US State Department International Visitors Program, 1978; Participant, International Conference of the American Society of Public Administrators, Phoenix, Arizona, 1978; Resource Person, Second MEDA Policy Conference Mindanao, Zamboanga City, 1978; Commissioner representing Muslims and other ethnic minorities, National Commission on the role of Filipino Women, 1978-85; Delegate, representing private sector, UNESCO Regional Literacy Workshop, Udaipur, India, 1979; Alternate Delegate, UN World Conference on Women, 1980; Delegate, Mid-Decade forum on women, 1980; Chair., National Womens Congress, sponsored by the NCRFW to launch its Action program for 1981-85; Resources Person, World Bank -- sponsored seminar for spouses of Finance Secretarys, on Women Involvement, Washington DC, 1983; Head, Philippine Delegation, Southeast Asia and Pacific Regional Conference on 'Muslim women in Development' sponsored by RIEAP and PER/KIM, Malaysia, 1983; one of 7 women Leaders from third world invited as International Participants, Post-Copenhagen Mid-Decade Dialogue with American Women in selected Cities in the United States, 1984; Paper presentor 'A Study of some Philippine ethnic Women and their Status', workshop on Ethnic Identity and the Status of women, Colombo Sri Lanka, 1984; Represented Region IX, (MECS-NHI-sponsored/workshop on Rewriting Philippine History to include viewpoints of Muslims and Other ethnic minorities, sponsored by the Ministry of Education, Culture and National Sports and the National Historical Institute, DAP Tagaytay, 1985; participant and paper writer on the Topic 'Some Facts of the Mindanao Questions', for the Round Table discussion sponsored by Solidarity, 1986; participant and paper writer on the topic 'The Moro National Liberation Front and Philippine Security', for the Round Table Discussion sponsored by the International Security Council, Manila Hotel, 1986; Project Dir., Magbassa Kita, an adult literacy project under the auspices of the Ministry of Education, Culture and Sports, 1986-87; Mem., Textbook Board, Ministry of Education, Culture and Sports, 1986, mem., UNESCO Philippine Commission, representing Non-governmental Organizations, 1986-; Vice-chair of: Education, National Defense and Security, Cultural Communities; special Cttee. on Mindanao Affairs; Chwn., Senate Cttees.: Civil Service and Govt. Reorganization; Cttee. on Women and Family Relations; sub Cttee. on Peace; Mem., Commission on appointments; elected Senator, Republic of the Philippines, 1987; UNESCO General Conference, Mem., Philippine Delegation, Paris, France, 1987; International Conference on Worldwide Education for Women Delegation and Resources Massachusetts, USA, 1987; ILO Conference Mem., Philippine Delegation, Geneva, Switzerland, 1988; Delegate, Afro-Asian Islamic Conference Bandung, Indonesia; Chwn., NCRFW Peace Cttee., tasked with the involvement of women in the promotion of peace; Chair., NCRFW Cttee. to Promote Literacy; *memberships:* President, Sulu Lawyers League Auxilliary, 1971; First President, Jolo Jaycerettes, Jolo, Sulu; President, Jolo Women's Club, responsible for the establishment of the first family planning clinic in Jolo and sponsored family planning seminar; organized and elected first President of the Siasi Women's Club, Siaisi, Sulu; Member, Philippine Muslim Welfare Relief Agency, 1974; Member, Board of Directors and Treasurer's, National Defense College of the Philippines Alumni Association Inc., 1976-78; National President, Muslim Professional and Business Women Association of the Philippines; Member, Philippine

Constitution Association; Member, Board of Editors, National Manpower and Youth Council Publication, 1976; Consultant, Mindanao State Univ., 1976; Project Development Associate, Office of the President, Univ. of the Philippines, 1976; Head, Department of Political Science, National Defence College of the Philippines, 1976-78; Originator and Project Director, Project Magbassa Kita, a pilot Intergrated Adult Education Program for Illiterate Muslims and Others in Region IX, 1978-80, (subsequently adapted as Project Matiya Tanu in Region XII, 1980-83); Member, Board of Directors, Philippine Foundation for the Rehabilitation of the Disabled, 1978-79; Member, Board of Directors, Abilities Unlimited, a corporation assisted by Levi-Straus Philippines to assist the disabled, 1979; Member, representing Muslim Sector, Board of Review for Motion Picture and Television, 1982-85; Program Co-ordinater, lecture series on Islam, 1983, part of the UP Diamond Jubilee Celebration, co-sponsored by the Muslim Porfessional and Business Women Association of the Philippines and UP Asian Center, the UP Institute of Islamic studies, UP, Diliman, 1983; Member, Board of Directors: Mindanao-Sulu Development Foundation and Business and Professional Women Association of the Philippines; Member, Board of Trustees, Philippine Rural Reconstruction Movement; Vice-President for Mindanao, the Fellows of the Asia Foundation, 1986; assisted the late Father Cuthbert Bullman OMI, organize the first Sulu newspaper, the Sulu Star; *professional career:* Public School teacher, 1952-57; Educator; *honours and awards:* Arsenio Larson Award for Best Student Paper in Political Science, 1950-51; PI GAMM MU, International Honor Society, UP Chapter; PHI KAPPA PHI, International Honour Society, UP Chapter, 1952; Most Useful Citizen Award, by Philippine Women's Univ., 1977; Joy of Achievement Award by Soroptimist International, Manila, 1980; Tandano Sora Award for Government and Community Service, 1981; UNESCO Award of Merit, Manila, 1983; Sultan Dipatuan Kudarat Award of Distinction as Oustanding Achiever of Mindanao Sulu; Outstanding Muslim Women Leader, by the Mindanano Information Network for Development and Nationalism Makali, 1985; UNESCO NESIM HABIF AWARD, Asia and the Pacific, third prize, Bangkok, Thailand, 1985; Most Outstanding Alumnus of the National Defence College of the Philippines, 1986; Most Outstanding Alumnus of the National Defence College of the Philippines as Senator, 1987; Gintong Ina Awardee for Government and Public Services, Gintong Ina Foundation, 1988; Family Unit and Individual Achievements Award, Civic Assembly of Women of the Philippines, 1988; *publications:* 'Project Magbassa Kita': A literacy Project that worked case Study discussed at the International Conference on Women in Education, Mount Holyoake College, USA; Magbassa Kita, a Tausag Literacy Primer, Sulu; Amassa Kiram, A Samal Literacy Primer, Tawi-Tawi; Matiya

Tana, Maguindanao literacy Primer, Cotabato; Tayo'y Bumasa, Tagabg Literacy Primer, Articles on the Muslim Women, the Sulu Sultanate, the Sabah Claim, etc, published in magazines and national newspaper; *private address:* 155 Lopez Rizal St, Mandakiyong, Metro Manila, The Philippines; *office address:* Ms Santanina Rasul, The Congress of the Philippines - Senate, Batasang Pambansa Bldg., Quezon City, Manila, The Philippines.

RATAN KUMARI; Indian, Member of the Rajya Sabha; *born:* 13 December 1913; *parents:* the late Seth Govind Das; *married:* the late Laxmi Chand, 1925; *party:* Congress Party; *political career:* elected to the Rajya Sabha, 1976, 1982 and 1988; Mem., General Body of Central Social Welfare Board, 1982-84; *interests:* social service; *professional career:* former Sec., Hitkarini Sabha (educational institution), Pres., 1983-; mem., Board of Trustees of Shahid Smarak; mem., Bharati Sangam (organisation of writers): Trustee, Gopal Lalji Trust; *publications:* Ankur; Ritu Parva; *recreations:* writing, painting, gardening, agriculture; *private address:* 238, Kotwali Ward, Jabalpur, Madhya Pradesh; *office address:* Shrimati Ratan Kumari, Rajya Sabha, Parliament House, New Dehli 110 011, India; *phone:* (11) 389977; 389997.

RATTLEY, Jessie Menifield; American, Mayor of Newport News, Virginia; *born:* 4 May 1929, Birmingham, Alabama, USA; *parents:* the late Alonzo Bedell Menifield and the late Altona Cochran Menifield; *married:* Robert Louis Rattley, 1952; *children:* Florence, Robin; *religion:* Presbyterian; *education:* Hampton Institute, BS, 1951; LaSalle Univ; *party:* Democratic Party; *political career:* Cllr., Newport News, Virginia, 1970-, Vice-Mayor, 1976- then Mayor 1986-; *memberships:* Pres., Peninsula Co-ordinating Cttee.; Hon. Mem., Nat. Assn. of Negro Business and Professional Women's Clubs; life Mem., NAACP, Voter Education Project; *professional career:* Mem., Board of Dirs., Nat. Institute of Public Management; Mem., Advisory Cttee., Institute of Government, Univ. of Virginia, Charlottesville; *office address:* Ms Jessie Rattley, 529 Ivy Avenue, Newport News, Virginia 23607, USA.

RAWLINGS, Patricia Elizabeth; British, Member of the European Parliament; *born:* 27 January 1939; *party:* Conservative Party; *political career:* MEP for Essex South West, 1989-; *office address:* Miss Patricia Rawlings, European Parliament, Centre Européen, Plateau de Kirchberg, BP 2929, Luxembourg; *phone:* Luxembourg 43001.

RAYMUNDO, Hon. Adelisa A.; Filipino, Congresswoman; *born:* 5 July 1934, Caloocan City; *parents:* Pablo B. Almario and Felicidad Ricerra Almario; *married:* Mario R. Raymundo; *children:* two;

education: Maryknoll, B.Sc., Education; Hunter College, New York, USA, Masters, Sociology; *political career:* Pres., Samahang Manggagawang Filipino; Congresswoman; *memberships:* Philippine Sociological University; Philippine Association of Universities; *office address:* The Hon. Ms Adelisa Raymundo, The Congress of the Philippines - House of Representatives, Batasang Pambansa Bldg., Quezon City, Manila, The Philippines.

READ, Imelda Mary; British, Member of the European Parliament; *born:* 8 January 1939, Hillingdon, United Kingdom; *parents:* Robert Alan Hocking and Teresa Mary Hocking (née Breheny); *children:* Michael, Susannah; *education:* Bishopshalt School, Hillingdon, 1950-57; Nottingham University, BA Hons., Politics, 1974-77; *party:* Labour Party, 1969; *political career:* member, National Exec. Council, M.S.F. Union, 1975-; MEP for Leicester, 1989-, Socialist Group; *interests:* women's rights, trade union matters; *publications:* co-author, Against a Rising Tide - Racism, Europe and 1992; *clubs:* Child Poverty Action Group; *recreations:* bee-keeping; *private address:* Labour Euro Office, 81 Great Central Street, Leicester LE1 4ND, United Kingdom; *office address:* Ms Imelda Read, European Parliament, Centre Européen, Plateau de Kirchberg, BP 2929, Luxembourg.

REDING, Viviane; Luxembourgeios, Member of the European Parliament; *born:* 27 April 1951; *party:* Parti Chrétien Social (PCS, Christian Social Party); *political career:* MP, Luxembourg, 1979-89; Pres., Christian Democrat Women; MEP, 1989-; *private address:* c/o Luxemburger Wort, 2 rue Plantin, L-2388 Luxembourg; *office address:* Ms Viviane Reding, European Parliament, Centre Européen, Plateau de Kirchberg, BP 2929, Luxembourg; *phone:* Luxembourg 43001.

REDZIERSKA-TRUSZYNSKA, Dobrochna; Polish, Member of the Sejm; *office address:* Ms Dobrochna Redzierska-Truszynska, Sejm PRI, ul. Wiejska 4/6/8, 00-489 Warsaw, Poland; *phone:* (22) 28 70 01; 28 40 31.

REHN, Elisabeth (Märta Elisabeth); Finnish, Minister of Defence; *born:* 6 April 1935, Helsinki, Finland; *parents:* Andreas Petrus Carlberg and Ruth Leonida Carlberg (née Weurlander); *married:* Ove Harald Rehn, 1955; *public role of spouse:* President of Finnish Football Association; *children:* Veronica, Joakim, Charlotta, Johan; *religion:* Lutheran; *languages:* Swedish, Finnish, English, German; *education:* general certificate of education, 1953; MA, Economics and Business Administration, 1955; Helsinki Swedish School of Economics, diploma in economics, 1957; *party:* Svenska Folkpartiet (SFP, Swedish People's Party); *political career:* Mem. SFP Board in Kauniainen, 1972-79; Mem. Kauniainen City Council, 1973-80; MP, 1979-; Mem. Kauniainen City Board,

1979-80; Chairperson, Kauniainen School Board, 1977-79; Vice Chairperson., SFP for Uusimaa constituency, 1978-79; Mem. SFP Board, Kirkkonummi, 1980-; elector, Presidential election, 1982; Chairperson, SFP, Companies Cttee., 1982-; Mem. SFP working cttee., 1985-; Mem., Advisory Board, Economic Relations between Finland and Developing Countries, 1985-; Chairperson, SFP, Parly. Group, 1987-90; Chairperson, Parly. Cttee. for Ordinary Law, 1983-87; Chairperson, Finnish Cttee. for UNICEF, 1990-; Minister of Defence, 1990-; *interests:* Africa; *memberships:* Chairperson, Working Cttee. of the Nat. Cttees. for UNICEF; Vice chmn. Finnish Red Cross 1982-88; mem., Board of Trustees, World Wildlife Fund, 1982-88; Board mem., UNICEF, 1982 and chmn., 1988-; *professional career:* office manager, Board mem. Renacta Ab Ltd., 1960-79; office manager, Rehn Trading AB, 1978-79; teacher in charge of vocation guidance, 1973-77; Careers officer, Kauinen Comprehensive School, 1973-77; Mem. Board of Trustees, Kirkkonummi Merchant Bank, 1984-, then Chmn., 1988-; mem. Board of Trustees, the Merchant Banks Central Sharebank, 1987-; mem. Board of Trustees, Suomi-Salama Distribution; *honours and awards:* White Rose of Finland, Knight of the First Class, 1989; *clubs:* Vice Chmn. Solvalla Athletic Institute, 1980; *recreations:* environment, nature, sports, fine arts; *office address:* Ms Elisabeth Rehn, Ministry of Defence, PO Box. 31, 00131 Helsinki, Finland.

REICHHARDT, Irmgard; German, Deputy Member of the Bundesrat; *born:* 23 August 1935, Utphe; *children:* two; *education:* Master training in rural home economics; *political career:* Minister of Agriculture, Forestry and Nature Conservation, Hesse, 1987-; Deputy mem. of Bundesrat, 1987-; *professional career:* mem. of Rural Women's Assn., 1953; President, Rural Women's Assn., Hesse, 1973; mem. of Presidency, German Rural Women's Assn., 1976, Vice-President, 1979, President, 1986; mem. of Presidency, Farmers' Assn., Hesse and Farmers' Assn. Germany; Cttee. mem., Farmers' Assn. Hesse; Farming, Holgut Ringelshausen; Trainer, rural home economics; *office address:* Frau Irmgard Reichhardt, Bundesrat, 5300 Bonn 1, West Germany.

REID, Margaret Elizabeth; Australian, Senator; *born:* 28 May 1935, Crystal Brook, South Australia; *education:* LLB, Univ. of Adelaide; *party:* Liberal Party; *political career:* chosen by Parliament to represent the Australian Capital Territory in the Senate, 1981 and elected, 1983-; Committee Service: Mem. of the Senate Estimates Cttee. A, 1981-83; C, 1982-83; F, 1983-87 and 1987-; E, Mar.-Jun., 1987; Mem. of the Joint Standing Cttee. for New Parliament House, 1983-, on the Australia Capitol Territory, 1983-; Chairperson for Australian Capital Territory, 1981-83; Mem. of the Senate Legislative and General Purpose Standing cttee.

for Education and the Arts, 1981-83; Mem. of the Senate Standing Cttee. for Procedure, 1987-; Dep. Govt. Whip in the Senate, 1982-83; Dep. Opposition Whip in the Senate, 1983-87; Conferences, Delegations and Visits: Mem., 74th Inter-Parly. Conference, Ottawa, 1985; Mem., Advisory Council on Australian Archives, 1985-; Opposition Whip in the Senate, 1987-; *professional career:* barrister and solicitor; *honours and awards:* Queen Elizabeth Jubilee Medal, 1977; Order of Polonia Restituta, 1987; *office address:* Ms Margaret Reid, Senate, Parliament House, Room M13, Canberra, ACT 2600, Australia; *phone:* (062) 727111.

REIS, Wanda Mendes; Brazilian, Federal Deputy; *born:* 20 January 1953, Rio de Janeiro; *parents:* Waldemiro Mendes and Abigayr de Souza Mendes; *children:* Jaqueline, Johnson, Jefferson, Jonh; *education:* CERJ, Rio de Janeiro, 1985-87; *party:* Partido do Movimento Democrático Brasileira (PMDB, Party of the Brazlian Democratic Movement); *political career:* Federal Deputy for Rio de Janeiro, 1991-95; *professional career:* programmer; executive secretary; accountant; *office address:* Ms Wanda Reis, Chamber of Deputies, Praça dos 3 Poderes, Ed. Principal, 70160 Brasilia, DF, Brazil; *phone:* (61) 225 2885.

RELL, M. Jodi; American, Connecticut State Representative; *born:* Norfolk, Virginia, USA; *education:* Old Dominion Univ.; West Connecticut State Univ; *party:* Republican Party; *political career:* Connecticut State Rep., District 107, 1985-; Mem., Family and Workplace Cttee. and Finance Revenue and Bonding Cttee; *office address:* Ms M. Jodi Rell, 125 Long Meadow Hill Road, Brookfield, Connecticut 06804, USA.

REMBO, Sonja Marie Hillevi; Swedish, Member of the Riksdag; *born:* 17 January 1933, Gothenburg, Sweden; *parents:* Alvar Rembo and Junis Rembo (née Gregorsson); *religion:* Protestant; *languages:* English, German; *education:* Institute of Commerce, Gothenburg, 1951; *party:* Moderata Samlingspartiet (Moderate Party), 1954; *political career:* mem. Board of the Moderate Party for Gothenburg and Bohus Iän, 1973-83; First Vice-Chmn., 1978-83 mem. Social District Board, Gothenburg, 1974-79; First Vice-Chmn. Conservative Women's Federation, Gothenburg, 1976-81; MP, 1979-; mem. Labour Market Cttee., 1979-85; mem., Nat. Insurance Cttee. 1979-85 and Parly. Salaries Delegation, 1979-85; mem. Parly. Board of Trustees of the Moderate Party, 1985-; mem. War Delegation, 1988-; Chmn., Moderate Party Board for Gothenburg, 1989-; *professional career:* Sec. in various companies, 1951-68; Sec. Swedish Ball Bearings Co. Ltd., Gothenburg, 1968-79; Board mem., Nat Insurance Inspection, 1982-; Board mem., Swedish Delegation for Marine Resources, 1985-90; Board mem., Port of Gothenburg Ltd., 1985-; *private address:*

Sylvestergatan 7, 411 32 Gothenburg, Sweden; *office address:* Ms Sonja Rembo, Riksdag, Fack, S-100 12 Stockholm, Sweden.

RENAU I MANEN, María Dolores; Spanish, Deputy; *born:* 15 November 1935, Barcelona, Spain; *education:* Univ. of Barcelona, degree in Education and Psychology; *party:* Partido Socialista Obrero Español (PSOE, Spanish Socialist Workers' Party); *political career:* Mem. of teaching team of Cornellá City Council, Barcelona; Deputy, PSOE, Barcelona, 1982-86; spokesman for Cttee. on Social Policy and Employment; MEP, 1985-86; Dir. General of Legal Protection of Minors; elected Deputy, PSOE, Cataluña, 1989-; *professional career:* Dir., Flor de Maig School, Barcelona; *private address:* Cea Bermúdez 46, E-28003, Madrid, Spain; *office address:* Ms María Renau i Manen, Congreso de los Diputados, Fernán Flor 1, Madrid 14, Spain.

RENGER, Annemarie; German, Vice President of the Bundestag; *born:* 7 October 1919, Leipzig, East Germany; *children:* one s; *education:* secondary school for girls; *party:* Sozialdemokratische Partei Deutschlands (SPD, Social Democratic Party of Germany), 1945; *political career:* chmn., Kurt Schumacher Society; chmn., German Helsinki Human Rights Committee; private secretary of Dr. Kurt Schumacher, 1945-52; head of office, Exec. Cttee., SPD Berlin, 1946; member of advisory council, Council of Europe and WEU, 1959-66; parly. secretary, SPD parly. group, 1969-72; member of Exec. Cttee., SPD parly. group; Pres. of Bundestag, 1972-76; member of presiding and Exec. Cttee., SPD, until 1973; chmn., federal women's Cttee., SPD, until 1973; Vice-Pres. of Bundestag, since 1976; chmn., German-Israeli group of parliamentarians, since 1976; Federal MP, party list of Nordrhein-Westfalen; member of control commission, SPD, 1979-86; *professional career:* publishing apprenticeship; publishing salesperson; member of Gewerkschaft Handel, Banken und Versicherungen (HBV, Trade Union for Commerce, Banks and Insurance); *honours and awards:* honorary vice-president, European Union Germany; honorary member of presiding board, German Council of the European Movement; honorary president, Central Committee of Democratic Resistance Fighters and Organisations of Persecuted Persons; *clubs:* Friends of Children Movement, before 1933; Workers' Sports Association, before 1933; Workers' Samaritans (president); *private address:* 5300 Bonn, West Germany; *office address:* Frau Annemarie Renger, Bundeshaus, 5300 Bonn 1, West Germany.

REXHA, Lumturi; Albanian, President of the Albanian Women's Union; *party:* Albanian Workers' Party (AWP); *political career:* candidate Mem., AWP Central Cttee., 1981-; Dep., People's Assembly, Tirana constituency district, Presidium Mem., 1982-; Pres., Albanian Women's Union, 1982-; *office address:* Ms Lumturi Rexha, Kuvënd Popullore, Tirana, Albania.

REYES, Hon. Carmencita O.; Filipino, Congresswoman; *parents:* Dr. Ramon J. Ongsiako and Carmen de la Paz; *married:* Edmundo M. Reyes; *public role of spouse:* former Commissioner of Immigration and Deportation; *children:* Violette, Bernadette, Maria del Carmen, Regina Victoria, Edmundo II; *education:* Univ. of Sto. Tomas, B.Sc. (Magna cum Laude); Philippine Women's Univ., Doctorate, Social Work; *political career:* Delegate, 1971 Constitutional Convention; Assemblywoman, Interim Batasang Pambansa; Mem. of Parliament, Regular Batasang Pambansa; Congresswoman; Secretary for Social Services and Development; *office address:* The Hon. Ms Carmencita Reyes, The Congress of the Philippines - House of Representatives, Batasang Pambansa Bldg., Quezon City, Manila, The Philippines.

REYNOLDS, Hon. Margaret; Australian, Minister Assisting the Prime Minister on the Status of Women; *born:* 19 July 1941, Launceston, Tasmania; *education:* Diploma in Special Education, James Cook; BA, Queensland; *party:* Australian Labor Party; *political career:* Alderman, Townsville City Council, 1979-83; Mem., Labor Party State Council, Queensland, 1981-83; North Queensland Labor Party Organiser, 1982-83; Mem., Labor Party National Platform Cttee. on Aboriginal and Islander Affairs, 1983-; Mem., Labor Party National Platform Cttee. on Status of Women, 1983; elected to the Senate for Queensland, 1983-; Committee Service: Mem. of the Senate Standing Cttee. for Libraries, 1983-85; for the House, 1985-87; Mem. of the Senate Legislative and General Purpose Standing Cttee. for Education and the Arts, 1983-87; for Science Technology and the Environment, 1983-85; for Finance and Govt. Operations, 1985-87; for Constitutional and Legal Affairs, Feb.-Jun. 1987; Mem. of the Senate Select Cttee. for Volatile Substance Fumes, Feb.-Dec. 1985; of the Senate Estimates Cttee. E, 1983-85; D, Apr.-Sep. 1985 and 1986-87; Chairperson of F, Mar.-Jun. 1987; Mem. of the Joint Standing Cttee. for Australian Capital Territory, 1983-84; for New Parliament House, 1985-87; Mem. of the Joint Select Cttee. for Video Material, 1985-87; Conferences, Delegations and Visits: Mem. Parly. Delegation to the European Parly. Institutions, Strasbourg and Berlin, 1985; Mem., Labor Party National Platform Cttee. on Foreign Policy, 1986-87; Minister for Local Govt., 1987-; Minister Assisting the Prime Minister on the Status of Women, 1988-; *professional career:* teacher, 1960-76; lecturer, 1977-82; *office address:* The Hon. Ms. Margaret Reynolds, Office of the Prime Minister, 3-5 National Circuit, Barton ACT 2600, Australia; *phone:* (062) 715111.

RHYNE MARVIN, Helen; American, North Carolina State Senator; *born:* 30 November 1917, Gastonia, North Carolina, USA; *parents:* Dane SAmuel Rhyne and Tessie Rhyne (née Hastings); *married:* Ned Irving Marvin, 1941; *children:* Kathryn Andrea Nisbet, Richard Morris, David Rhyne; *religion:* Presbyterian; *education:* Furman Univ., BA, 1938; Louisiana State Univ., MA, 1939; Univ. of Colorado; Univ. of Vermont; Univ. of North Carolina, Chapel Hill; Univ. of Oslo, Norway; *party:* Democratic Party; *political career:* North Carolina State Senator, District 25, 1976-; North Carolina Senate Rep. to National Conference of State Legislators Cttee. on Arts and States; Chwn., Senate Appropriations Cttee. on Justice and Public Safety; Vice-Chwn., Senate Cttee. on Pension and Retirement and Cttee. on Children with Special Needs; Mem., North Carolina Women's Legislative Caucus; *honours and awards:* Valand Award for Outstanding Service in the Field of Mental Health; *office address:* Mrs Helen Rhyne Marvin, 119 Ridge Lane, Gastonia, North Carolina, 28052, USA.

RICHARDS, Ann Willis; American, Governor of Texas; *born:* 1 September 1933, Waco, Texas; *parents:* R. Cecil Willis and Ona Willis; *children:* Cecile, Dan, Clark, Ellen; *education:* Baylor Univ., Waco, BA, 1954; Univ. of Texas, Austin, teaching cert., 1954-55; *party:* Democratic Party; *political career:* admin. asst. to Texas State Rep., 1973-75; Co.-Commissioner, Travis County, Texas, 1977-82; State Treasurer, 1983-90; Gov., 1990-; *memberships:* Nat. Women's Political Caucus; *professional career:* govt. and history teacher, Austin Independent School District, 1955-57; *honours and awards:* Woman of the Year, Women in Communications, 1978; One of Austin's Ten Most Influential Citizens, Austin American-Statesman, 1978; Woman of the Year, Texas Women's Political Caucus, 1981 and 1983; Texan Women's Hall of Fame, 1985; *clubs:* Sierra Club; *office address:* Ms Ann Richards, P.O. Box 12404, Capitol Station, Austin, Texas 78711, USA.

RICHARDSON, Jo; British, Member of Parliament; *born:* 28 August 1923; *parents:* the late J.J. Richardson and Mrs. F.R. Richardson; *religion:* Agnostic; *languages:* English, some French and German; *education:* Southend-on-Sea High School for Girls; *party:* Labour Party; *political career:* former Cncl. Hornsey Borough Cncl., and Alderman, Borough of Hornsey; former Cllr., Hammersmith Borough Cncl.; mem., Labour Party National Exec. Cttee.; Sec., Keep Left Group, Bevan Group and Tribune Group; mem. MSF Trade Union; Vice-Pres., Campaign for Nuclear Disarmament; Member of Parliament for Barking, 1974-; Opposition Spokesperson on Women, 1983-; Chairperson, Labour Party, 1988-90; *interests:* civil liberties; defence; equality for women; *publications:* various articles; *recreations:* cooking, reading; *office* *address:* Ms Jo Richardson, House of Commons, London SW1A OAA.

RICHARDSON, Hon. Ruth Margaret; New Zealander, Minister of Finance; *born:* 1950, Waitotara; *children:* two; *education:* educated at Wanganui and New Plymouth; Univ. of Canterbury, Christchurch, LLB (Hons.); *party:* National Party; *political career:* legal adviser, Law Reform Division, Justice Department, 1972-75; Legal adviser, Federated Farmers, 1975-81; held number of executive positions in National Party; unsuccessful candidate for Tasman, 1978; elected MP for Selwyn, 1981-; appointed to the National Advisory Council on the Employment of Women, 1976; mem., Govt. Cttee. on Women, 1977; served on parliamentary select committee on Education and Science, and the Mems. Services Cttee.; has been Opposition Spokeswoman on education and youth issues; Minister of Finance, with additional responsibility for the Earthquake and War Damage Commission and the National Provident Fund, Nov. 1990-; *professional career:* farmer in her own right since 1972; *private address:* Newtons Road, R.D.5 West Melton, Christchurch, New Zealand; *office address:* The Hon. Ms Ruth Richardson, Ministry of Finance, PO Box 3724, Wellington, New Zealand; *phone:* (04) 722733; *fax:* (04) 730982.

ROA, Hon. Benedicta B.; Filipino, Congresswoman; *born:* 6 May 1929, Cagayan de Oro City; *parents:* Apolonio Bacan and Ubaida Cabañez; *married:* Pedro N. Roa Sr; *public role of spouse:* former City Mayor, Governor and Congressman; *children:* Evelyn, Pedro Jr., Manuel, Emma, Fe Helengrace; *education:* Zamora Music School, Piano and Voice Culture; *political career:* Congresswoman; *memberships:* Chmn.: Rural Improvement Club, Four-H Club, Farmers Association; *professional career:* formerly: Treasurer, P.N. Roa Realty Corporation and Roa Agro Corporation; Business Associate of Roawood Ind. Inc; *clubs:* Congressional Ladies Club, Manila, 1969-72; adviser, Carmen Neighbourhood Association and Liling Roa's Mothers' Club, Cagayan de Oro City; *office address:* The Hon. Ms Benedicta Roa, The Congress of the Philippines - House of Representatives, Batasang Pambansa Bldg., Quezon City, Manila, The Philippines.

ROBERSON, Alexis H.; American, former Director of Department of Employment Services of the Government of District of Colombia; *religion:* Zion Baptist Church, Washington DC; *education:* Howard Univ., Washington DC, BA, 1963, MA in Education and Administration, 1974; Univ. of the District of Columbia, post graduate studies; *political career:* Dep. Dir., DC Dept. of Recreation, Govt. of the District of Columbia, 1980-82, 1983-86; Dir., DC Dept. of Employment Services, Govt. of District of Columbia,

1987-91; Commissioner, Board of Appeals and Review; Commissioner, Commission on Post-secondary Education in the District of Columbia; Govt. Rep., Apprenticeship Cncl., Occupational Safety and Health Board, Private Industry Cncl; *memberships:* Int. Assn. of Industrial Accident Boards and Commissions; The Eastern Assn. of Workers' Compensation Boards and Commissions; The Interstate Conference of Employment Security Administrators; The Nat. Assn. of Labor Officials; The Interstate Labor Standards Administrators; The Nat. Assn. of Crime Victims' Compensation Board; The Nat. Organization of Black Law Enforcement Exec; *professional career:* Mem.: Advisory Cttee. on Client Self-Sufficiency; The Education In Partnership with Technology Corporation; The Institutional Appeals Board; The Mayor's Blue Ribbon Advisory Cttee. on Public Housing; The Mayor's Child Development Co-ordinating Cttee.; The Blue Ribbon Panel on Teenage Pregnancy Prevention; The Juvenile Justice Prevention Initiative Co-ordinating Cttee.; The States Job Training Co-ordinating Cncl.; The United Conference of Mayor's Employment and Training Cncl.; The Univ. of the District of Columbia Intercollegiate Athletic Advisory Board; *honours and awards:* Outstanding Public Service Award, Parent Advisory Board, Dept. of Recreation's Day Care Program, 1986; Excellence in Management Award, Prince Hall Shriners, 1986; Outstanding Young Woman of the Year, 1979; Metro Talent Search, 1983; USA Nat. Guard Award, 1983; Nat. Theatre Award, 1984; Run for the Arts Award, presented by Young Audiences of the District of Columbia, 1984; United Black Fund's Community Service Award, 1985; Dept. of Human Service's Distinguished One-Fund Program Award, 1985; Washington NAACP Highest Leadership Award, 1986; Dept. of Housing and Community Development, Distinguished Public Service Award, 1986; Award for Support of the Arts, Crispus Attucks Museum and Park of the Arts; Cert. of Appreciation, Cncl. of the District of Columbia, 1986; Mayoral Proclamation proclaiming April 10 F. Alexis H. Roberson Day in the district of Columbia, 1987; Leadership Award, DC Recreation Advisory Cttee., 1987; Howard Univ., Distinguished Alumni Award, 1987; Distinguished Public Service Award, United Planning Organization, 1987; Dept. of Recreation's Distinguished Leadership Award, 1988; Distinguished Govt. Service Award, Nat. Coalition of Black Women, 1989; first recipient of Washington Urban League's Distinguished Public Service Award, 1989; *clubs:* The Links Incorporated; The Girl Friends Incorporated; NAACP; The Washington Urban League; *private address:* 6230 Ninth Street, NW, Washington DC 20011, USA; *office address:* Ms Alexis Roberson, House of Representatives, Capitol Building, Washington DC, 20515, USA; *phone:* (202) 225-8040.

ROBERTS, Barbara; American, Governor of Oregon; *born:* 21 December 1936, Corvallis, Oregon, USA;

married: Frank Roberts, 1974; *children:* Mark J. Saunders, Michael S. Saunders; *party:* Democratic Party; *political career:* Sec.-of-State, Oregon, 1985-90; Gov., Oregon, 1990-; *memberships:* National Society of Autistic Children; *office address:* Mrs Barbara Roberts, 11609 NE Klickitat, Portland, Oregon 97220, USA.

ROBERTSON, Brenda; Canadian, Senator; *born:* 23 May 1929, Sussex, Kings County, NB; *married:* Wilmot W. Robertson, 1955; *children:* Leslie, Tracy, Doug; *education:* Sussex High School; Mount Allison Univ., Sackville, NB, B.Sc; *party:* Progressive Conservatives; *political career:* New Brunswick Legislature, 1967, MLA for Albert County, re-elected, 1970; Mem., MLA for Riverview, 1974, 1978, 1982; appointed to Senate for Riverview, New Brunswick, 1984-; *professional career:* home economist, special interest in Sales Management; *honours and awards:* Hon. Degree, Dr. of Humane Letters, Mount St. Vincent Univ., 1973; Hon. Degree, Dr. of Social Science; *office address:* The Honourable Senator Brenda Robertson, Senate, Parliament Buildings, Wellington Street, Ottawa, Ontario K1A 0A4, Canada; *phone:* (613) 992 4416.

ROBINSON, Mary; Irish, President of Ireland; *born:* 21 May 1944, Ballina, County Mayo, Ireland; *married:* Nicholas Robinson, 1970; *public role of spouse:* solicitor; *children:* Tessa, William, Aubrey; *education:* Trinity College, Dublin, BA, 1967, LLB, 1967, MA, 1970; King's Inn, Dublin, Barrister-at-Law, 1967; Harvard Univ., LLM, 1968; *political career:* Mem., Irish Senate, representing Dublin Univ., 1969-89; Mem., Vedel Cttee. (Enlargement of the European Parl.), 1971-72; Chwn., Social Affairs Sub-Cttee., 1977-87 and Legal Affairs Cttee., 1987-89 of the Irish Parly. Joint Cttee. on EC Secondary Legislation, 1973-89; Mem., Dublin City Cncl., 1979-83; Senior Counsel, 1980-90; Mem., Irish Parly. Joint Cttee. on Marital Breakdown, 1983-85; Mem., New Ireland Forum, 1983-84; co-founder, Irish Centre for European Law (ICEL), 1988; Dir. and Chwn., Exec. Cttee., ICEL, 1988-90; President of Ireland, Dec. 1990-; *memberships:* Mem., English Bar, Middle Temple, 1973-Dec. 1990; Editorial Board, Irish Current LAw Statutes Annotated, 1984-Dec. 1990; Pres., Cherish, the Irish Assn. of Single Parents, 1973-90; *professional career:* Reai Prof. of Criminal Law and lecturer in European Law, Trinity College, Dublin, 1969-Dec. 1990; *office address:* Mrs Mary Robinson, Office of the President, Phoenix Park, Dublin 8, Ireland.

ROBSON OF KIDDINGTON, Baroness (cr. 1974, Life Peer) Inga-Stina Robson; British, Member of the House of Lords; *born:* 20 August 1919; *parents:* Erik Arvidsson and Lilly Arvidson (née Danielson); *married:* Lawrence W. Robson (decd. 1982), 1940; *children:* one s., two d; *religion:* Church of England; *languages:* Swedish, German; *education:* in Stockholm, Sweden; *party:*

Liberal Party; Social and Liberal Democrats (SLD); *political career:* past Pres., Lib. Party Organisation; mem., House of Lords, 1974-; *interests:* Europe, health, environment; *professional career:* JP; Chmn., Board of Governors, Queen Charlotte's and Chelsea Hospitals, 1970-84; Chmn., SW Thames Regional Health Authority, 1974-82; mem. of Council, Surrey Univ., 1974; *clubs:* National Liberal Club; *private address:* Kiddington Hall, Woodstock, Oxford, UK; *office address:* Baroness Robson of Kiddington, House of Lords, London SW1A 0PW.

ROCK, Helga; German, former Member of the Bundestag; *born:* 25 February 1951, Siegen, West Germany; *party:* Die Grünen (Green Party); *political career:* speaker of district association, Die Grünen (Green Party), Siegen-Wittgenstein, 1980-84; member of town council, Siegen, 1984-87; member of district assembly, Siegen-Wittgenstein, 1984-87; member of central Cttee., Deutscher Städtetag (German Convention of Municipal Authorities), 1986-87; mem. of Bundestag, Die Grünen party list of Nordrhein-Westfalen, 1987-90; *professional career:* transportation services clerk, Krupp Stahl AG, Siegen; *private address:* 5300 Bonn 1, West Germany; *office address:* Frau Helga Rock, Bundeshaus, 5300 Bonn 1, West Germany.

RODI, Nelly; French, Senator; *born:* 16 February 1918, Saint-Gall, Switzerland; *party:* Rassemblement pour la République (RPR, Rally for the Republic); *political career:* Municipal Councillor, 1965-; Mayor, Aubergenville, 1971-; General Councillor, Yvelines, 1973-; Deputy Chmn., General Council, Yvelines, 1979-; Senator, RPR, Yvelines, 1986-; *professional career:* Midwife; *office address:* Mlle. Nelly Rodi, Sénat de la République Française, Palais du Luxembourg, 75291 Paris Cedex 06, France.

ROE, Marion Audrey; British, Member of Parliament, *born:* 15 July 1936; *parents:* the late William Keyte; *married:* James Kenneth Roe, 1958; *children:* one s., two d; *education:* Bromley High School; Croydon High School; The English School of Languages, Vevey, Switzerland; *party:* Conservative Party; *political career:* Cncl., Bromley London Borough Cncl., 1975-78; Vice Pres., Greater London Young Conservatives Group, 1977-80; mem., Greater London Area Local Govt Advisory Cttee., 1978-82; mem., Greater London Cncl. for Ilford North, 1977; spokesman, Police Cttee., 1982-83; mem., GLC Conservative Leaders' Cttee., 1982-83; Dep. Chief Whip, 1978-82; Vice-Chmn., Cncl. Historic Buildings Cttee., Whip for Planning and Communications Group, Vice-Chmn., General Management Cttee., GLC Rep., General Service Cttee., Assn. of Metropolitan Authorities, 1977-81; UK Representative, Conference of Local and Regional Authorities of Europe; Served on Greater London Cncl., Cttees. for Industry, Employment, Legal Affairs

Policy, Performance Review, Arts, Recreations and the Greater London Manpower Board, 1981-82; Member of Parliament for Broxbourne, 1983-; mem., Select Ctte. on Agriculture, 1984-85; Sec., Conservative Horticulture Cttee., 1983-85; PPS to the Parliamentary Under Sec. of State for Transport, 1985-86; Sec., Party Organisation Cttee., 1985; PPS to the Minister of State for Transport, 1986; PPS to the Sec. of State for Transport, 1986-87; Parliamentary Under Sec. of State, Dept. of the Environment, 1987-88; *interests:* agriculture; environment; horticulture; transport; *professional career:* Mem., London Advisory Cttee., Independent Broadcasting Authority, 1978- 81; mem., Gatwick Airport Consultative Cttee., 1979-81; Governor, St. Peter's Hospitals, London, 1978-82; mem., South East Thames Regional Health Authority, 1980-83; former Governor, St. Olave's School for Boys; mem., BBC General Advisory Cncl., 1986-87; *honours and awards:* Freeman of the City of London; *clubs:* UN Development Fund for Women (Patron); Women's National Cancer Control Campaign (Vice-Pres., 1985); Carlton Club (Assoc. mem.); *recreations:* ballet; opera; *office address:* Mrs Marion Roe, House of Commons, London SW1A OAA.

ROITZSCH, Ingrid; German, Member of Bundestag; *born:* 30 July 1940, Munich, West Germany; *children:* two; *education:* High school leaving examination, 1961; Law and Journalism studies; Univ. Angers, France, one year practical editorial training; *party:* Christlich Demokratische Union (CDU, Christian Democratic Union), 1970; *political career:* mem. of Bundestag; mem. of CDU District cttee., Pinneberg since 1971; civil cttee. mem., Town council, Quickborn, 1970-80; mem. of Kreistag Pinneberg, 1978-80; Land cttee., Schleswig-Holstein since 1979; Federal cttee. CDU-Women's Assn. since 1981; CDU-Land cttee. Schleswig-Holstein since 1981; Parliamentary Sec., CDU/CSU-Group since 1987; *professional career:* Editor, incl. Pinneberg Daily Paper, Hamburg Daily Paper and Die Welt, 1971-80; *office address:* Frau Ingrid Roitzsch, Christlich Demokratische Union, Konrad-Adernauer Haus, Friedrich-Ebert-Allee 73-75, 5300 Bonn, West Germany.

ROJAS, Virginia; Costa Rican, Vice-Minister of Education; *office address:* Ms Virginia Rojas, Ministry of Education, Apartado 10087, San José 1000, Costa Rica.

ROKIATOU SOW, Sow; Mali, President of the Union Nationale des Femmes du Mali; *party:* Union Nationale des Femmes du Mali (UNFM, National Women's Union of Mali); *office address:* Mme. Sow Rokiatou Sow, Union Nationale des Femmes du Mali, Bamako, Mali.

ROMANI CIGNOMI, Daniela; Italian, Deputy; *born:* 9 February 1956, Monterotondo, Rome, Italy; *education:* Classical secondary education; *party:* Partito Democratico della Sinistra (PDS, Party of the Democratic Left); *political career:* Sec. PCI Fed. Tivoli; Councillor, Monterotondo 1975-80; Deputy, Rome-Viterbo-Latina-Frosinone, 1987; mem. Committee on Finance; *professional career:* Party Worker, PCI; *office address:* Ms Daniela Romani Cignomi, Camera dei Deputati, Montecitorio, 00186 Rome, Italy.

RÖNSCH, Hannelore; German, Federal Minister for the Family and Senior Citizens; *party:* Christlich Demokratische Union (CDU, Christian Democratic Union); *political career:* mem. of Bundestag, 1983-; Federal Minister for the Family and Senior Citizens; *office address:* Frau Hannelore Rönsch, Bundeshaus, 5300 Bonn 1, West Germany.

ROOSEN-VAN PELT, Riet (M.) J.J.; Dutch, Member of the Second Chamber; *born:* 1 March 1934, Tilburg, Netherlands; *education:* sec. ed.; middle professional education, home economics; followed many courses on general development, politics, political forming; *party:* Christen Democratisch Appel (CDA, Christian Democratic Appeal); *political career:* Mem. of town council, Schayk, 1974-86; Mem. of Second Chamber, 1986-; *professional career:* Mem. of Board, 6th. Farmers and Gardeners Union; *clubs:* former pres., Cath. Country women the Netherlands; pres. Head Office country women and Cath. women orgainsations Noord-Brabant, Zeeland and Zuid-Gelders rivierengebied; *private address:* Gagelstraat 13, 5374 NHP Schayk, the Netherlands; *office address:* Mevr. Riet Roosen-van Pelt, Tweede Kamer der Staaten-Generaal, Binnenhof 1A, Postbus 20018, The Hague, Netherlands.

ROSCHOVA, Dr. Anna; Czechoslovakian, Member of the Narodni Rada; *born:* 26 May 1951; *party:* Civic Forum; *office address:* Dr. Anna Roschová, Ceská národní rada, Snemovní 4, 110 00 Praha 1, Czechoslovakia; *phone:* (02) 2105.

ROS-LEHTINAN, Ileana Carmen; American, Florida State Senator; *born:* 15 July 1952, Havana, Cuba; *parents:* Enrique Emilio Ros and Amanda Adato Ros; *married:* Dexter Lehtinan; *children:* Katherine Lehtinan, Douglas Lehtinan, Amanda Michelle, Patricia Marie; *religion:* Catholic; *education:* Miami Dade Community College, AA, 1972; Florida International Univ, BA, 1975, MS, 1987; *party:* Republican Party; *political career:* Florida State Rep., District 110, 1982-86; Florida State Senator, District 34, 1986-; *memberships:* Board Mem., AMI Kendall Hosp.; Hon. Pres., Bi-lingual Private School Assn., 1980-; Vice-Pres., Cncl. of Bi-lingual Schools, 1979; National Federation of Business and Professional Women's Club; National Order of Women Legislators;

Coalition of Hispanic American Women; *professional career:* school principal, Eastern Academy, 1978-; *publications:* Themes on Education; *office address:* Mrs Ileana Ros-Lehtinan, 8421B NW 56th Street, Miami, Florida 33166, USA.

ROSSITER, Eileen; Canadian, Senator; *born:* 14 July 1929, Souris, PEI; *married:* the late Linus J Rossiter, 1952; *children:* Philip, Leonard, Kevin, Patricia, Colleen, Mary; *education:* Georgetown and Souris Public Schools, PEI; St. Mary's Convent, Souris, PEI; Prince of Wales College, Charlottetown, PEI; *party:* Progressive Conservative; *political career:* Senator for Prince Edward Island, 1986-; Mem., Senate Cttees. for Internal Economy, Budgets and Administration, Agriculture and Forestry and Fisheries; *professional career:* Realtor; *recreations:* reading, knitting, swimming; *office address:* The Honourable Senator Eileen Rossiter, Senate, Parliament Buildings, Wellington Street, Ottawa, Ontario K1A OA4, Canada; *phone:* (613) 992 4416.

ROSTBØLL, Grethe Fogh; Danish, Minister for Cultural Affairs; *born:* 30 May 1941, Aarhus, Denmark; *parents:* Gustav Fogh and Ellen Marie Fogh (née Brandt); *married:* Torben Rostbøll, 1961; *children:* Martin, Solveig, Benedikte, Christian; *education:* teacher training college, 1965; MA Literary History, 1978; *party:* Conservative Party; *political career:* Mem., Ryslinge Local Cncl., 1966-70; candidate for election, European Parliament, 1979; Conservative candidate, election to the Folketing, 1990; Mem., Programmme Cttee. for Children's Daily Life, 1987-88; Mem., Legislative Cttee. for Folk High Schools, 1985-87; Mem., Cttee. for further education, 1989-90; Minister of Cultural Affairs, 1990-; *memberships:* Mem., Programmee Cttee. adult education in Danmarks Radio, 1982-87; Mem., Board for the Logumkloster Seminary, 1988-90; *professional career:* co-principal and teacher, Ryslinge Folk High School, 1962-90; Mem., Ryslinge Local Cncl., 1966-70; literary and theatre critic, Morgenavisen Jyllandsposten; commentator and columnist, Berlingske Tidende, 1987-90; Chairperson, Soc. for the Advancement of the Danish Language, 1984-90; Dep. Chairperson, Nordic Folk Academy, 1985-90; Chairperson, Board of Midtfyns Grammar School, 1980-86; *publications:* About Seven Gothic Tales, 1980; Family and Future, 1986; contributor to The Personal Freedom and Myths about the Nordic Countries and the EEC and others; editor, The Language and EDP-machines; The Language and the Poets; The Language in the Air; Linguistic Barriers; Language and Sex; *private address:* Troense Strandvej 56, 5700 Svendborg, Denmark; *office address:* Ms Grethe Rostbøll, Ministry for Cultural Affairs and Communications, Nybrogade 2, DK-1203 Copenhagen K, Denmark; *phone:* (01) 33 92 33 70; *fax:* 33 91 33 88.

ROTH, Claudia; German, Member of the European Parliament; *born:* 15 May 1955; *party:* Die Grünen (Green Party); *political career:* Parly. Press spokeswoman for Federal German Greens, 1985-; MEP, 1989-; *professional career:* political theatre and popular music; *private address:* Hochhaus Tulpenfeld, Bundeshaus, 5300 Bonn 1, Germany; *office address:* Ms Claudia Roth, European Parliament, Centre Européen, Plateau de Kirchberg, BP 2929, Luxembourg; *phone:* Luxembourg 43001.

ROUDY, Yvette; French, Deputy; *born:* 10 April 1929; *parents:* Joseph Saldou and Jeanne Saldou (née Dicharry); *married:* Pierre Roudy, 1951; *languages:* English; *education:* Girls' Technical College, Bordeaux, school leaving exam., philosophy; English degree; *party:* Parti Socialiste (PS, Socialist Party), 1965; *political career:* member of the executive board of the Convention of Republican Institutions; member of management committee and National Sec. of Socialist Party, with responsibility for women's issues; Mem., European Parliament, 1979-81; Minister of Women's Rights, 1981-86; Deputy for Calvados, 1986-; Vice-Chmn. of Social Issues Commission of National Assembly, 1988-; National Sec. of Socialist Party with special responsibility for women's rights, 1988-; Mayor of Lisieux, 1989-; Vice-Chmn. of International Socialist; member of executive board of Socialist Party; *honours and awards:* Personality of the Year 1986; *publications:* translations; la Femme Mystifiée by Betty Friedan, 1965; Ma vie by Eleanor Roosevelt, 1967; La Place de la femme dans un monde d'hommes by Elizabeth Jeannewan, 1969; various articles; essays: la Rèussite de la femme, 1969; la Femme en marge, 1975; les Métiers et les conjoints (2nd edition, 1981); A cause d'elles, 1985; *office address:* Mme. Yvette Roudy, L'Assemblée Nationale, 126 rue de L'Université, 75355 Paris, France.

ROUKEMA, Marge; American, Member of the House of Representatives; *born:* 19 September 1929, Newark, New Jersey, USA; *married:* Richard W. Roukema, 1951; *children:* Greg, Todd (Decd.), Meg; *religion:* Protestant; *education:* Montclair State College, BA, 1951; Rutgers Univ., 1975; *party:* Republican Party; *political career:* Vice-Pres., Ridgewood Board of Education, New Jersey, 1970-73; Mem., House of Reps. for District 5, New Jersey, 1981-; Mem., Banking, Finance, Urban Affairs, Education and Labour Cttees., US House of Reps; *memberships:* trustee, Leukemia Society of Northern New Jersey and Family Counseling Service; *professional career:* high school history and Govt. teacher; *clubs:* Distributive Education Clubs of America; *office address:* Mrs Marge Roukema, 226 Cannon House Office Bldg., Washington DC, 20515, USA.

ROYAL, Ségolène; French, Deputy; *born:* 22 September 1953, Dakar, Senegal; *married:* François Hollande; *children:* Thomas, Clémence, Julien; *education:* Lycée, Epinal; university of Nancy; economics degree, Paris institute of political studies; *party:* independent; *political career:* head of mission (social affairs) to the Presidency, 1982-88; adviser to the Paris administrative court; Deputy, socialist, Deux-Sèvres, 1988-; *professional career:* pupil, national management school, 1978-80; *publications:* Le Printemps des grands-parents; *private address:* 30 Boulevard Maillot, 92200 Neuilly-sur-Seine, France; *office address:* Mme. Ségolène Royal, L'Assemblée Nationale, 126 rue de L'Université, 75355 Paris, France.

ROY-ARCELIN, Nicole; Canadian, Member of the House of Commons and Parliamentary Secretary to the Minister of Public Works; *office address:* Mrs Nicole Roy-Arcelin, House of Commons, Parliament Buildings, Wellington Street, Ottawa, Ontario K1A OA6, Canada; *phone:* (613) 957 3744; *fax:* 952 0874.

RUBACH, Peggy; American, Mayor of Mesa; *born:* 7 July 1947, New York, USA; *children:* Kristin, Jon, Matthew; *education:* New York State Univ., BA; Arizona State Univ., College of Law; Harvard Univ., John F. Kennedy School of Government; *political career:* former Mem., Budget Task Force, US Mayors Conference and Public Transport Sub-Cttee.; currently Mem., Admin. and Intergovt. Relations Cttees.; Treasurer, Regional Public Transport Authority; Mayor, Mesa, 1988-; *memberships:* Arizona Board of Education; advisory board, Univ. of Arizona Cancer Centre; *professional career:* Healthcare System Consultant, Lutheran Healthcare Network; Co-Dir.,Kurzwell Reading Machine Project; cost analyst and medical claims administrator, Aetna Life and Casuality; lecturer, New York State Univ; *office address:* Mrs Peggy Rubach, 55 North Centre Street, P.O.Box 1466, Mesa, Arizona 85211-1466, USA.

RUDDOCK, Joan Mary; British, Member of Parliament; *born:* 28 December 1943, Abergavenny, Gwent, UK; *parents:* Kenneth Charles Anthony and Eileen Anthony (née Messenger); *married:* Prof. Keith Ruddock, 1963; *education:* Pontypool Grammar School for Girls; Imperial College of Science and Technology, Univ. of London, B.Sc., ARCS, botany and plant science, 1965; *party:* Labour Party, 1970; *political career:* Member of Parliament, 1987-; mem., British delegation, Council of Europe and WEU, 1988-89; mem., Select Cttee. on Televising House of Commons; Shadow Minister of Transport, 1989-; *interests:* transport, environment, women, foreign affairs; *honours and awards:* Frank Cousins Peace Award, Transport and General Worker's Union, 1984; *publications:* CND Scrapbook, 1987; *clubs:* Campaign for Nuclear Disarmament; Anti-Apartheid; *office*

address: Ms Joan Ruddock, House of Commons, London SW1A OAA.

RUDIN, Anne; American, Mayor of Sacramento; *born:* 27 January 1924, Passaic, New Jersey, USA; *married:* Edward Rudin, 1948; *children:* four; *education:* Temple Univ., BS, 1945; Hospital School of Nursing, RN, 1946; Univ. of Southern California, MPA, 1983; *party:* Democratic Party; *political career:* City Councilwoman, Sacramento, 1971-83; Mem., California State Democratic Central Cttee.; Mayor City of Sacramento, 1983-; *memberships:* World Conference of Mayors for Peace; co-founder and Pres., 1984, California elected Womens' Assn.; League of Women Voters; American Society of Public Admin; *professional career:* Nursing Educator, Temple Univ., 1946-48; Mt. Zion Hospital, San Francisco, 1948-49; *honours and awards:* Woman of Distinction, Sacramento Area Soroptomist Clubs, 1985; Woman of the Year, California State Legislature, 1989; Sacramento Women in History Award for Courage, 1989; *private address:* 1410 Birchwood Lane, Sacramento, California 95822, USA; *office address:* Mrs Anne Rudin, 915 I Street, Sacramento, California 95814, USA.

RUDI UBEDA, Luisa Fernanda; Spanish, Deputy; *born:* 14 December 1950, Seville, Spain; *education:* business expert; *party:* former mem. Alianza Popular (AP, Popular Alliance); Partido Popular (PP, Popular Party); *political career:* regional Secretary, AP, Aragón; mem. of Aragón autonomous parliament, 1983-86; Deputy, AP, Zaragoza, 1986-89; re-elected Deputy, PP, Zaragoza, 1989-; *professional career:* chartered accountant; *private address:* Coso 56, E-50001, Zaragoza, Spain; *office address:* Ms Luisa Rudi Ubeda, Congreso de los Diputados, Fernán Flor 1, Madrid 14, Spain.

RUIZ-GIMENEZ AGUILAR, Guadalupe; Spanish, Member of the European Parliament; *born:* 10 August 1947; *party:* Centro Democrático y Social (CDS, Party of the Democratic and Social Centre); *private address:* Claudio Coella 86, 4 derecha, 28006 Madrid, Spain; *office address:* Ms Guadalupe Ruiz-Giménez Aguilar, European Parliament, Centre Européen, Plateau de Kirchberg, BP 2929, Luxembourg; *phone:* Luxembourg 43001.

RUMBOLD, Rt. Hon. Angela Claire Rosemary, CBE,; British, Minister of State at the Home Office; *born:* 11 August 1932, Bristol, UK; *parents:* Harry Jones and Frances Molly Jones (née O'Neill); *married:* John Marix Rumbold, 1958; *children:* Philip John Marix, Polly-Ann Frances, Matthew John George; *religion:* Church of England; *languages:* French, Spanish; *education:* Perse School for Girls; Cambridge, Notting Hill and Ealing High Schools; King's College, London, LLB, 1952, BA, 1972; *party:* Conservative Party, 1961; *political career:*

205

Councillor, Royal Borough of Kingston-upon-Thames, 1974-82; Chmn., Education Cttee., Policy and Resources Cttee., and Dep. Leader; Member of Parliament, 1982-; PPS to Hon. Nicolas Ridley MP, 1983-85; Parly. Under Sec. of State, Dept. of the Environment, 1985-86; Co-Chmn., Women's National Commission, 1986-; Minister of State, Dept. of Education and Science, 1986-90; Minister of State at the Home Office, Jul. 1990-; *interests:* health, education, environment, finance, women's affairs; *honours and awards:* CBE, 1981; *clubs:* Bow Group; City of London (Freeman); *office address:* The Rt. Hon. Angela Rumbold, Home Office, 50 Queen Anne's Gate, London SW1H 9AT.

RUSANEN, Pirjo Maija; Finnish, Minister of Housing; *born:* 18 December 1940, Mikkeli, Finland; *parents:* Viljo Jalmari Rusanen and Lyyli Ester Rusanen (née Tarkiainen); *education:* B. Sc. (Econ.), 1963; MBA, 1970; *party:* Kansallinen Kokoomus (Kok, National Coalition Party); *political career:* Mem., Mikkeli Town Cncl., 1973-, mem., Mikkeli Town Admin. Board, 1973-80; 2nd. Vice-Chmn., Mikkeli Town Cncl., 1981, then Chmn., 1982-; MP, 1983-; *professional career:* teacher, Commercial College, 1963-83; *office address:* Ms Pirjo Rusanen, Eduskunta, 00102 Helsinki, Finland.

RUST, Bärbel; German, former Member of the Bundestag; *born:* 22 April 1955, Braunschweig, West Germany; *children:* two; *education:* grammar school stressing natural sciences, Abitur (advanced matriculation examination); *party:* Die Grünen (Green Party); *political career:* part-time spokeswoman, emphasis on environmental policy, Die Grünen parly. group; member of budget Cttee., Die Grünen; mem. of Bundestag, party list of Bayern, 1987-90; *professional career:* training as electronics asst., University of Braunschweig; software developer, until 1985; *private address:* 5300 Bonn 3, West Germany; *office address:* Frau Bärbel Rust, Bundeshaus, 5300 Bonn 1, West Germany.

RUZICKOVA, Marie; Czechoslovakian, Member of the Central Committee of the Revolutionary Trade Union Movement; *born:* 13 October 1923, Hornosín, Czechoslovakia; *education:* intermediate school; *party:* Komunistická Strana Ceskoslovenska (KSC, Communist party of Czechoslovakia); *political career:* Chairperson, Works Cncl., Rico Works, Most, 1948-52; Mem., Most District Trade Union Cncl., 1949-52; Mem., Exec. Cttee., Usti and Labem Trade Union Cncl., 1949-57; Chairperson, Usti and labem District Cttee. Trade Union of Textile and Leather Industry Workers, 1952-56; Mem. of Staff, Usti and Labem District Cttee., CP CSSR, 1957-60; Mem. of Staff, North Bohemian Regional Cttee., CP CSSR, 1960-65; Chairperson, Combined Works Cttee., CP CSSR,

Bozená Nemecová Works, Teplice-Sanov, 1960-65; Mem., North Bohemian Regional Cttee., CP CSSR, 1960-64, Mem., Exec. Cttee., 1962-64; Mem., Central Control and Auditing Commission, CP CSSR, 1962-; Mem., Central Commission for People's Control and Statistics, 1963-67; Mem., Commission for Living Standards, Central Cttee. CP CSSR, 1963-68; Chairperson, TU Commission of Central Commission of Central Cttee. of TU of Workers in Knitware Industry, Písek, 1965-69; Mem., Presidium, Central Cttee., TU of Consumer Goods Industry, 1966-68; Mem., Bureau Central Control and Auditing Commission, CP CSSR, for Control and Auditing Work in Bohemia, 1968-71; Sec. and Mem. of Secretariat, Exec. Cttee. and Plenum, Czech Trade Union Cncl., (CROS), 1970-72; co-opted Mem., Plenum of Central Cncl. of CSSR Revolutionary Trade Union Movement (ROH), 1970; Mem., Plenum and Sec., Secretariat of Czech Trade Union Cncl., (COR), 1972-; Mem., Presidium Czech Union of Women, 1974-; Mem., Central Control and Auditing Commission of CP CSSR, 1981-; Presidium Mem., Czech Cncl. of Revolutionary Trade Unions, 1982-; Mem., Central Cttee., Revolutionary Trade Union Movement, 1982-; *professional career:* farm worker; worker in textile factory, Prague and Most; *office address:* Ms Marie Ruzicková, Central Council of Trade Unions, Nám A Zápotockého 2, 113 59 Prague 3, Czechoslovakia.

RYAN, Hon. Susan Maree; Australian, Senator; *born:* 10 October 1942, Sydney, NSW, Australia; *education:* BA, Sydney; MA, ANU; *party:* Australian Labor Party; *political career:* Vice-Pres., Labor Party Belconnen Branch, 1972; Branch Council Delegate, 1973-76; Mem., Australian Capital Territory Legislative Assembly, 1974-75; elected to Senate for Australian Capital Territory, 1975-; Mem., Federal Policy Cttee. on Women (Labor Party), 1976; Committee Service: visited Phnom Penh with USA Congressional Women's Delegation, 1979; Mem., Inter-Parly. Union (IPU) Spring Meeting, Laos, 1982; Mem., 69th IPU Annual Conference, Rome, 1982; Mem., Gen. Assembly UNESCO Conference, Paris, 1983; Mem., Australian Irish Relations Conference, Kilkenny, 1983; official visits to Denmark, Norway and Sweden, 1983; to New Zealand and Thailand, 1985; to ASEAN countries, South Pacific, Papua New Guinea, China and Japan, 1986; to USA, 1987; Mem. of Opposition Shadow Ministry, 1977-83; Spokesperson on Communications, 1977-80; on Arts and Letters, 1977-83; on Women's Affairs, 1979-83; on Media, Mar.-Nov, 1980; on Aboriginal Affairs, 1980-83; Mem., Council of the Australian Institute of Aboriginal Studies, 1981-83; Minister for Education, 1983-87; Minister Assisting the Prime Minister on Status of Women, 1983-88; Special Minister of State, 1987-88; Minister Assisting the Prime Minister on the Bicentennial, 1987-88; Minister Assisting the Minister for Community Services and Health, 1987-88; *interests:* Women's Movement, especially education and employment; *professional career:* school teacher; tutor, Canberra College of Advanced Education; education officer, Secretariat for International Women's Year, 1975; National Executive Officer, Australian Council of State School Organisations, 1973-75; *office address:* The Hon. Ms. Susan Ryan, Senate, Parliament House, Room M13, Canberra, ACT 2600, Australia; *phone:* (062) 727111.

RYDER OF WARSAW, Baroness (cr. 1978, Life Peer) Sue Ryder, OBE; CMG; British, Member of the House of Lords; *born:* 3 July 1923; *parents:* the late Charles Ryder and Elizabeth Ryder; *married:* Group Capt. Leonard Cheshire, VC, OM, DSO, DFC, 1959; *children:* one s., one d; *education:* Benenden School, Kent; *party:* Independent; *political career:* mem., House of Lords, 1978-; *professional career:* FANY and the Polish Section of the highly secret Special Operations Exec., 1939-45; founder and social worker, Sue Ryder Foundation for the Sick and Disabled of all age groups; co-founder, Mission for the Relief of Suffering; *honours and awards:* Officer's Cross, Order of Polonia Restituta (Poland), 1965; Medal of Yugoslav. Flag with Gold Wreath and Diploma, 1971; Hon. LLD, Liverpool Univ. 1973; Golden Order of Merit, Polish People's Republic, 1976; Polish Order of Smile, 1980; Hon. LLD, Exeter Univ., 1980; Hon. LLD., London Univ., 1981; Hon. Degree, Doctor of Letters, Reading Univ., 1982; Hon. Degree, Doctor of Laws, Leeds Univ., 1984; Hon. Doctorate of Civil Law, Kent Univ., 1986; Hon. LLD, Cambridge University, 1989; *publications:* The Morrow Is Theirs, 1975; Child Of My Love, 1986; *clubs:* SOE Club; *private address:* Sue Ryder Foundation, Cavendish, Suffolk, UK; *office address:* Lady Ryder of Warsaw, House of Lords, London SW1A 0PW.

RYSLINKOVA, Dr. Jana, CSc.; Czechoslovakian, Member of the Narodni Rada (Czech National Council); *born:* 10 May 1951; *party:* Civic Forum; *office address:* Dr. Jana Ryslinkova, Ceská národní rada, Snemovní 4, 110 00 Praha 1, Czechoslovakia; *phone:* (02) 2105.

S

SAASTAMOINEN, Ulla Riitta; Finnish, Member of the Eduskunta; *born:* 10 February 1940, Kuopio, Finland; *parents:* Yrjö Lyytikainen and Elisabet (née Tiilikainen); *married:* Jukka Saastamoinen, 1962; *children:* Johanna, Jyri, Silja, Mirja-Maaria; *religion:* Lutheran; *languages:* Finnish, Swedish, German, English, French; *education:* Kuopion Yhteiskoulu Kuopio, 1951-59; Commercial School, Kuopio, 1959-60; University of Helsinki, Master, Political Science, 1960-67; *party:* Kansallinen Kokoomus (Kok, National Coalition Party) 1975; *political career:* member, Kuopio City Council; member, Nordic Council; mem. of Eduskunta, 1987-; *professional career:* Dir., Writers Organization, Suomen Maakuntakirjailijat, 1986-87; *office address:* Ms Ulla Saastamoinen, Eduskunta, 00102 Helsinki, Finland.

SABATOVA, Anna; Czechoslovakian, dissident; *born:* 23 June 1951; *parents:* Jaroslav Sabata; *married:* Petr Uhl; *education:* studied philosophy; *political career:* arrested and sentenced to three years imprisonment, 1971; released 1973; prevented from completing studies; signed declaration of Human Rights Movement, Charter 77, 1977; founding Mem., Assn. for Defence of Unjustly Persecuted VONS; Spokeswoman, Charter 77, 1986-87; signed East European Dissident's Appeal on Hungarian Revolution Anniversary, 1986; *professional career:* clerk; kept up husband's periodical Informace o Charte 77 (Information abour Charter 77) while he was imprisoned, 1979-84; *office address:* Ms Anna Sabatova, Association for the Defence of the Unjustly Persecuted VONS, Czechoslovakia.

SADAUKI, Pamela; Nigerian, Deputy Governor of the State of Kaduna; *office address:* Mrs Pamela Sadauki, Office of the State Governor of Kaduna, State House, Kaduna, Nigeria.

SAFIEVA, Gulrukhsor; Soviet, Member of the Council of Nationalities; *born:* 17 December 1947, Tajikistan, USSR; *parents:* Nabiev Safi and Khalimova Matsura; *married:* Radzhibov Nigmat, 1968; *public role of spouse:* geologist; *children:* Aziz; *religion:* Muslim; *languages:* Russian, Tajik, Dari, Persian, Turkish; *education:* Tajik State Univ., philologist-historian, orientalist; *party:* Communist Party of the Soviet Union; *political career:* Chwn., Tajik SSR Branch of the Soviet Cultural Foundation; Mem., Cncl. of Nationalities; Mem., Supreme Soviet Cttee. on International Affairs; Mem., Supreme Soviet Commission for Deputy Ethics; *interests:* international relations; *memberships:* USSR Cncl. of Writers; USSR Cncl. of Journalists; *professional career:* poet; *honours and awards:* laureate of the Literary Prize VLKSM and the Youth of Tajikistan; *publications:* 32 individual poetry collections; *recreations:* tennis, floriculture, moutain walking, collecting medicinal herbs; *private address:* g. Dyshanbe, ul. Gogolya, D.18/3, KV.7., USSR; *office address:* Ms Gulrukhsor Safieva, Moscow, Kremlin, Verkhovnii, USSR.

SAHLIN, Mona Ingeborg; Swedish, Minister of Labour; *born:* 9 March 1957, Sollefteå, Sweden; *parents:* Hans Andersson and Siv Rentrop; *married:* Bo Sahlin, 1982; *children:* Ann-Sofi, Jenny, Gustav; *languages:* English; *education:* The Södra Latin Continuation School, Civic Sciences Studies, 1973-76; *party:* Sveriges Socialdemokratiska Arbetarepartiet, (SAP, Swedish Social Democratic Labour Party), 1974; *political career:* Government Deputy on the National Sports and Athletics Board; Chairwoman of the State Youth Council and The Working Life Centre; Chairwoman of the Warlerry Life Cttee., 1987; Member of the Executive Cttee. of the Social Democrat's Youth Organisation; MP, 1982-90; Minister of Labour, 1990-; *interests:* youth affairs, labour Market; *professional career:* Secretary of the Nat. Soc. of the Blind, 1976-77; Ombudsman of the Pupil's Assoc., 1977-78; Investigator of the Correspondence School, 1978-80; Secretary of the Union of the State Employees, 1980-82; *clubs:* Union of Retail Workers; *office address:* Ms Mona Sahlin, Ministry of Justice, Rosenbad 4, 103 33 Stockholm, Sweden.

SAIBOLD, Hannelore; German, former Member of the Bundestag; *born:* 1 October 1943, Bankau, Oberschlesien, Poland; *children:* two; *education:* Mittlere Reife (intermediate high school certificate), Passau, 1960; *party:* Die Grünen (Green Party), founder member; *political career:* member of consumer Cttee., Federal Ministry of Nutrition, Agriculture and Forestry; member of advisory Cttee., Consumer Institute Foundation, Berlin; member of advisory Cttee., Working Group of Consumers, Bonn; member of Association for the Conservation of Nature, Bayern; member of citizens' forum, Vilshofen; member of

Research Institute of Peace Policy, Starnberg; member of 'Mothers against Nuclear Power', member of Environmental Institute, München; Action Group of Independent Germans, München, 1977; member of county Exec. Cttee., Die Grünen, Bayern, 1979-82; member of federal Exec. Cttee., Die Grünen, 1980-81; co-operation, Die Grünen parly. group, 1983-87; mem. of Bundestag, party list of Bayern, 1987-90; *professional career:* secretary, housewife, health adviser; *private address:* 8359 Aldersbach-Kriestorf, West Germany; *office address:* Frau Hannelore Saibold, Bundeshaus, 5300 Bonn 1, West Germany.

SAIKI, Patricia; American, Member of the House of Representatives; *born:* 28 May 1930, Hilo, Hawaii; *parents:* Kazuo Fukuda and Shizue Fukuda (née Inoue); *married:* Stanley Mitsuo Saiki, 1954; *children:* Stanley M. Jr., Sandra S., Margaret C., Stuart K., Laura H; *religion:* Episcopal; *education:* Univ. of Hawaii, BS; *party:* Republican Party; *political career:* State Sec., Hawaii State Republican Party, 1964-66; State Vice-Chwn., 1966-68, Chwn., 1983-85; research Asst., State Senate Representatives, 1966-68; delegate, Hawaii Constitutional Convention, 1968; alternate delegate, Republican National Convention, 1968; Hawaii State Rep., 17th District, 1968-70, 9th District, 1970-74; Asst. Republican Floor Leader, Hawaii House of Reps.; Hawaii State Senator, 1974-82; Chwn., Western Interstate Commission for Higher Education, 1978-80; Republican Nominee for Lt-Gov., Hawaii, 1972; Mem., House of Reps. for Hawaii, 1986-; *memberships:* Mem., Pres. Advisory Cncl. on Status of Women; Hawaii Pacific College; Boy Scouts; Western Mental Health Cncl.; Hawaii Special Olympics for Retarded Children; *professional career:* teacher, Punahou School, Kaimuku Intermediate and Kalani High School, 12 years; Dir., AmFac Inc., 1972-88; currently Dir. at Hawaii Airlines; *honours and awards:* Most Promising Legislator, Eagleton Inst., Rutgers Univ., 1970; *office address:* Mrs Patricia Saiki, 784 Elepaio Street, Honolulu 96816, Hawaii.

SAINT CYR, Mona; Swedish, Member of the Riksdag; *born:* 15 February 1934, Stockholm, Sweden; *parents:* Knut Johnsson and Irma Saint Cyr; *married:* Sture Hjalmarsson, 1981; *children:* Sture, Katarina; *religion:* Lutheran; *languages:* German, English, French; *education:* Trenton Teachers College, USA, Nutrition, 1958; Newark Teachers College, USA, Sociology, Education, Psychology, 1958; Linköping High School, Education, 1960; Stockholm High School, German, 1964; Kristinehamm, Military Education, 1956-57; *party:* Moderata Samlingspartiet (Moderate Party), 1948; *political career:* Municipal Posts, since 1960-; Health Inspector in Kinda, 1974-76; Municipal Secretary in Kinda, 1976-85; Secretary for Planning in Kinda, since 1985-; mem., Child Care Board; Chairman of the Municipal Council, 1976-82 and since 1988-; mem., Drafting Cttee. for the Budget; Member of

County Council Health Board and the Direction Cttee., 1970-76; Member of Riksdag since 1979-; mem., Labour Market committee; mem., Consumer Delegation; Member of the Provisional Board; member of Equality Council; Member of the Reference Group for monitoring the Equality Law; Member of the Working Environment Council; *professional career:* journalist in Borås Tidning, 1953-54; Nurse in USA, 1958; journalist in Östgöta Correspondenten, 1954-60; teacher in Kisa, 1961-70; industrial secretary in Längasjönas Paper Factory, 1970-74; *clubs:* Automobile Club; *office address:* Ms Mona Saint Cyr, Riksdag, Fack, S-100 12 Stockholm, Sweden.

SAINZ GARCIA, María Jesús Amparo; Spanish, Deputy; *born:* 1947, Santander, Spain; *education:* philosophy and law degrees; *party:* former mem. Alianza Popular (AP, Popular Alliance); Partido Popular (PP, Popular Party); *political career:* former head of Education and national Pres. Education Cttee. of the AP; Dir. general, Univ. Preparation, autonomous government of Galicia, 1982-86; Council for Education, Galician autonomous government, 1986-; Deputy, PP, Coruña, 1989-; *professional career:* professor of Spanish language and literature and school inspector; *office address:* Ms María Sainz Garcia, Congreso de los Diputados, Fernán Flor 1, Madrid 14, Spain.

SALEMA, Rt. Hon. Dr. Margarida; Portuguese, Member of the European Parliament; *born:* 19 January 1954, Lisbon, Portugal; *parents:* Eduardo Maria De Brito Melo e Castabo e Albuquerque Da Costa Salema and Maria Do Amparo Simoes Be Lima Mello Do Rego Da Costa Salema (née Simoes De Lima Mello Do Rego); *children:* Joana Maria; *religion:* Catholic; *languages:* Portuguese, French, English, German; *education:* grad., Univ. of Lisbon Law School, 1971-76, Masters in Law (political science), 1979-1984; *party:* Portuguese Social Democrat Party (PSD), 1974; *political career:* Mem., Prime Minister's Cabinet of Deputy Ministers, 1980; consultant to the Prime Minister, 1980-82; Mem., UN Cttee. on the Elimination of Discrimination against Women, New York, 1982-88; Mem., National Cncl., PSD, 1988-90; MEP, 1989-94; *interests:* constitutional affairs, legal affairs, human rights, women's affairs; *professional career:* lawyer, Lisbon, 1976-91; Asst. Prof. of Constitutional Law, Lisbon Univ., 1976-80; Asst. Prof. of International Law, 1985-89; *publications:* The Veto in the 1976 Constitution, 1980; The Review of the Constitution and Political Parties, 1980; Veto, Polis Enciclopedia Verbo da Sociedade e do Estado, 1986; Regional Autonomy, Nos Dez Anos da Constituiçaô, 1986; Positive Actions and the Portuguese Law, 1989; *office address:* The Rt. Hon. Dr. Margarida Salema, European Parliament, Centre Européen, Plateau de Kirchberg, BP 2929, Luxembourg; *phone:* Luxembourg 43001.

SALGUERO GROSS, Mercedes Gloria; El Salvador, Member of the Legislative Assembly; *office address:* Mrs Mercedes Salguero Gross, Asamblea Nacional Constituyente, San Salvador, El Salvador; *phone:* 21 72 01.

SALTOUN OF ABERNETHY, Lady (20th in line, Scotland, cr. 1445) Flora Marjory Fraser; British, Member of the House of Lords; *born:* 18 October 1930, Edinburgh, Scotland, UK; *parents:* 19th Lord Saltoun and Dorothy Fraser (née Welby); *married:* Capt. Alexander Ramsay of Mar, 1956; *children:* Katherine, Alice, Elizabeth; *religion:* Episcopal Church of Scotland; *languages:* French; *education:* St. Mary's School, Wantage; Cordon Bleu School of Cookery, diploma, 1950; *party:* Independent; *political career:* Mem., House of Lords, 1979-; *interests:* forestry, Scotland, food, sport; *professional career:* Chief of the Name of Fraser; Mem., Standing Council of Scottish Chiefs; *clubs:* Turf Club; *private address:* Cairnbulg Castle, Fraserburgh, Aberdeenshire, AB4 5TN; *office address:* Lady Saltoun of Abernethy, House of Lords, London SW1A 0PW.

SALVATO, Ersilia; Italian, Senator; *born:* 30 June 1941, Castellammare di Stabia, Naples, Italy; *education:* Degree in Philosophy; *party:* Partito Democratico della Sinistra (PDS, Party of the Democratic Left); *political career:* mem. inter-departmental Leadership, Chamber of Labour, Castellammare; mem. Cttee. on Prov. Schools and Prov. Women's Committee; PCI; mem. Fed. Cttee., Naples PCI; mem. Citizen's Secretariat, PCI Castellammare; elected Deputy, Naples-Caserta, 1976; mem. Cttee. on Justice; elected Senator, Torre del Greco, 1983; mem. Leadership Cttee. of Parly. Group; mem. Parly. Cttee. on the phenomenon of the Mafia; mem. Cttee. on the Interventions in the South; mem. Cttee. on Elections and Parliamentary Immunity; Sec. Cttee. on Justice; re-elected Senator, 1987; Vice-Pres. Cttee. on Justice; *professional career:* Lecturer in Literature, Middle-High Schools; *office address:* Ms Ersilia Salvato, Senato della Repubblica, Palazzo Madama, 00100 Rome, Italy.

SAMUELSSON, Birgit Marianne; Swedish, Member of the Riksdag; *born:* 9 December 1945, Aliugsès, Sweden; *married:* Sven Samuelsson, 1967; *children:* Viktoria, Evelina, Johannes; *religion:* Protestant, Swedish Missionary Society; *languages:* English; *party:* Miljöpartiet de Gröna, (Green Party), 1982; *political career:* Nordic Council; Dep. member of the Foreign and Social Affairs Committees; mem. of the Riksdag; *interests:* environment, social and development aid; *professional career:* Keeper, Älvsborg County Council; *office address:* Ms Birgit Samuelsson, Riksdag, Fack, S-100 12 Stockholm, Sweden.

SANDBAEK, Ulla Margrethe; Danish, Member of the European Parliament; *born:* 1 April 1943; *party:* Folkebevaegelsen mod EF (F mod EF, People's Anti-EC Movement); *political career:* former Minister of Religion; MEP, 1989-; *private address:* Nórrebrogade 18B, 2200 Copenhagen N, Denmark; *office address:* Ms Ulla Sandbaek, European Parliament, Centre Européen, Plateau de Kirchberg, BP 2929, Luxembourg; *phone:* Luxembourg 43001.

SANGIORGIO FESTA, Dott. Maria Luisa; Italian, Deputy; *born:* 23 September 1947, Milan, Italy; *education:* Degree, Bocconi University, 1971; *party:* Partito Democratico della Sinistra (PDS, Party of the Democratic Left); *political career:* Councillor, Milan, from 1970; Assessor for Education, 1977-85; Assessor for Women's position, 1977-85; Deputy, Milan-Pavia, 1987; Sec. Cttee. on Culture, Science and Teaching; *professional career:* Teacher; Sec. 'Casa della Cultura', Milan (Cultural Centre), 1970-; Promoter of 'Milano Donna' - (Woman-Milan); *office address:* Dott. Maria Sangiorgio Festa, Camera dei Deputati, Montecitorio, 00186 Rome, Italy.

SANNA, Anna Filippa; Italian, Deputy; *born:* 6 July 1948, Thiesi, Sassari, Italy; *education:* Higher School Diploma; *party:* Partito Democratico della Sinistra (PDS, Party of the Democratic Left); *political career:* Councillor, Samatzai, Cagliari; mem. Regional Sec, Sardinia; mem. Central Cttee., PCI, (now PDS); elected Deputy, Cagliari-Sassari-Nuoro-Oristano, 1987; mem. Cttee. on Social Affairs; *professional career:* Teacher; *office address:* Ms Anna Sanna, Camera dei Deputati, Montecitorio, 00186 Rome, Italy.

SANTA CLARA GOMES, Maria Teresa Dória; Portuguese, Deputy; *born:* 31 January 1936, Aveiro, Portugal; *education:* Licenciate of Germanic Philology; *party:* Partido Socialista (PS, Socialist Party); *political career:* Secretary of State for Culture, III Constitutional Government; Secretary of State, Prime Minister's Office, 1978-79; Deputy, Assembly of the Republic, 1980-83 and 1987-; *professional career:* mem., Coordinating Council; *publications:* Articles on topical subjects in daily and weekly newspapers; papers given at international conferences published by UNESCO, Council of Europe and United Nations University; *clubs:* GRAAL; IF; Futuribles; *office address:* Ms Maria Santa Clara Gomes, Assembléia da República, Palacia de S Bento, 1296 Lisboa Codex, Portugal.

SANT (née Pace), The Hon. Mrs Carmen; Maltese, Member of Parliament; *born:* 16 June 1945, Birkirkara, Malta; *parents:* the late Joseph Pace and Josephine Pace (née Camilleri); *married:* Lawrence Sant, 1968; *public role of spouse:* Member of Parliament; *languages:* Maltese, English, Italian; *education:* Govt. Primary and Secondary education; *party:* Malta Labour Party, 1982;

political career: Mem., Parl., 1987; *interests:* education, women, children, senior citizens, social services, youth; *professional career:* Clerk, General Workers's Union, 1961-71; *honours and awards:* World Women Parliamentarians for Peace; *publications:* regular fortnightly column in Maltese newspaper, since 1987; *recreations:* reading; *private address:* Tria Ir- Ridott, M' Scala, Malta; *office address:* The Hon. Mrs Carmen Sant, House of Representatives, The Palace, Valeta, Malta; *phone:* 222294.

SANTO, Akiko; Japanese, Director General of the Science and Technology Agency; *born:* 11 May 1942; *education:* Bunka Gakuin; *party:* Liberal Democratic Party (LDP); *political career:* former Parly. Vice-Minister for Environment; third time elected for National, Takeshita faction; Chmn., House of Cllrs. Cttee. on Foreign Affairs and Deputy Chairperson, LDP Public Division and Organization Division, 1990-; Dir.-Gen., Science and Technology Agency, 1991-; *office address:* Ms Akiko Santo, Science and Technology Agency, 2-2 Kasumigaseki, Chiyoda-ku, Tokyo 100, Japan; *phone:* (03) 5815271.

SANTOS, Maria Amélia do Carmo Mota; Portuguese, Member of the European Parliament; *born:* 25 August 1952, Lisbon, Portugal; *education:* Diploma of Education and Arts, National Conservatory, Lisbon; *party:* Os Verdes (The Greens); *political career:* Deputy, Assembly of the Republic, 1985-89; Co-Pres., The Greens Parly. Group; former Mem., Municipal Assembly, Almada; Mem., National Exec. and National Council, The Greens; Alternate Mem., Admin. Council, Assembly of the Republic; MEP, 1989-; *professional career:* Lecturer in Expression and Communication; *office address:* Ms Maria Santos, European Parliament, Centre Européen, Plateau de Kirchberg, BP 2929, Luxembourg.

SARNEY, Roseana Maciera; Brazilian, Federal Deputy; *born:* 1 June 1953, Sao Luis, Maranho; *parents:* José Sarney and Marly Maciera Sarney; *children:* Rafaela, Pedro; *education:* UNB, Brasilia, political science and sociology, 1972-78; *party:* Partido Da Frente Liberal (PFL, Liberal Alliance); *political career:* Special Sec. for Marinho, 1983-84; Federal Deputy for Marinho, 1991-95; *professional career:* professor; *office address:* Ms Roseana Sarney, Chamber of Deputies, Praça dos 3 Poderes, Ed. Principal, 70160 Brasilia, DF, Brazil; *phone:* (61) 225 2885.

SASANO, Teiko; Japanese, Member of the House of Councillors; *born:* 27 May 1933; *education:* Graduate School of Doshisha Univ; *party:* Rengo; *political career:* elected for Kyoto, 1990; Mem., House of Cllrs. Cttee. on Education and Mem., House of Cllrs. Special Cttee. on Election System, 1990-; *professional career:* Professor of Sakai Women's College; *office address:* Ms

Teiko Sasano, House of Councillors, 1-7-1 Nagata-cho, Tokyo 100, Japan; *phone:* (03) 5813111.

SATYA BAHIN; Indian, Member of the Rajya Sabha; *born:* 5 January 1944, Village Dalippur Naraini, P.O. Todar Pur, District Mainpuri, Uttar Pradesh; *parents:* the late Baldev Prasad; *married:* Chandra Prakash Naik, 1957; *children:* five s., one d; *education:* Agra Univ., MA, Sociology; *party:* Congress Party; *political career:* Adhyaksha, Sarva Dharam Sam Bhav; Pres., Scheduled Castes/Scheduled Tribes Women's Welfare Society; Mem., Lok Adalat, Etah; Mem. of the Rajya Sabha, 1988-; *interests:* working for the downtrodden, Harijans, needy children and women; *memberships:* Pres., Press Congress of India; *professional career:* Editor, Jagat Sudhar and Surya Rath; Patron, Amar Jawahar; *private address:* Laxman Sadan, Lalpur, Civil Lines, Etah, Uttar Pradesh; *office address:* Shrimati Satya Bahin, Rajya Sabha, Parliament House, New Dehli 110 011, India; *phone:* (11) 389977; 389997.

SAUVAIGO, Suzanne Liliane Berthe; French, Deputy; *born:* 15 July 1930, Rabat, Morocco; *parents:* Marcel Reynaud and Marie-Jeanne Reynaud (née Commeyras); *married:* Pierre Sauvaigo; *children:* Dominique, Anne; *education:* Lycée, Metz; Lycée, Paris; Lycée, Nice; law degree, university of Nice; *party:* Rassemblement pour la République (RPR, Rally for the Republic); *political career:* general councillor, Alpes-Maritimes, 1983-88; Mayor, Cagnes-sur-Mer, 1984-; Deputy, URC-RPR, Alpes-Maritimes, 1988-; *professional career:* lawyer, Nice, 1952-73; lawyer, Grasse, 1973-; president of the bar, 1983-84; *private address:* Carpe Diem, 39 Avenue des Collettes, 06800 Cagnes-sur-Mer, France; *office address:* Mme. Suzanne Sauvaigo, L'Assemblée Nationale, 126 rue de L'Université, 75355 Paris, France.

SAVITSKAYA, Svetlana Evgenevna; Soviet, Member of the Council of the Union; *born:* 8 August 1948; *education:* grad., Moscow Inst. of Aviation; *party:* Communist Party of the Soviet Union; *political career:* Vice-Pres., Soviet Peace Foundation; Mem., Cncl. of the Union; *professional career:* Cosmonaut, Parachutist and former test pilot; Dep.-Head, Energiya - Scientific Production Assn., Moscow; USSR's second female Cosmonaut and the first women ever to walk in space; *honours and awards:* holder of 18 flying records; *office address:* Ms Svetlana Evgenevna Savitskaya, Council of the Union, Kremlin, Moscow, USSR.

SAVOLAINEN, Lea Tuulikki; Finnish, Member of the Eduskunta; *born:* 4 January 1946, Toijala, Finland; *parents:* Toivo Johannes Seppänen and Anna Marjatta Seppänen (née Siren); *married:* Matti Pekka Juhani Savolainen, 1969; *children:* Harri, Henri; *education:* Registered Nurse, 1969; Specialist Nurse, 1973; Dir. of Nursing, 1978; *party:* Suomen Sosialidemokraattinen

Puolue, (SDP, Finnish Social Democratic Party); *political career:* Mem., Hämeenlinna Town Cncl., 1973; mem., Presidential Electorate, 1978 and 1982; mem. of Eduskunta, 1979-; 2nd Vice-Chmn., Hämeenlinna Town Cncl., 1981; *professional career:* Nurse, Kanta-Häme Central Hospital, 1970-73; Ward Sister, Ronni Institution, 1973-74; Matron, Hämeenlinna District Health Centre, 1977; *office address:* Ms Lea Savolainen, Eduskunta, 00102 Helsinki, Finland.

SAYGIN, Isilay; Turkish, Member of the National Assembly; *office address:* Ms Isilay Saygin, National Assembly, TBNN, Ankara, Turkey.

SAYMANSKA-KWIATKOWSKA, Anna; Polish, Member of the Sejm; *office address:* Ms Anna Saymanska-Kwiatkowska, Sejm PRI, ul. Wiejska 4/6/8, 00-489 Warsaw, Poland; *phone:* (22) 28 70 01; 28 40 31.

SCHICKER, Johanna; Austrian, Member of the Bundesrat; *born:* 15 May 1943, Bruck an der Mur; *education:* secondary school; commercial school; *party:* Sozialistische Partei Österreichs (SPÖ, Socialist Party of Austria); *political career:* district councillor, Niklasdorf, 1975-; Deputy Mayoress of Niklasdorf, since 1985; sent to Bundesrat from Steiermark Provincial Assembly, mem. of Bundesrat, since 1986; Sec. to Bundesrat; *professional career:* industrial employee, Brigl and Bergmeister Joint Stock Company, since 1960, and Chief secretary, since 1966; chief secretary, Leykam Mürztaler Joint Stock Company, 1976-; Secretary, SPö district organisation, Leoben, 1984-; *office address:* Frau Johanna Schicker, Bundesrat, Dr. Karl Renner Ring 3, 1017 Vienna, Austria.

SCHIERHUBER, Agnes; Austrian, Member of the Bundesrat; *born:* 31 May 1946, Reith, Lower Austria; *education:* agricultural vocational school; agricultural technical college for girls, rural home economics; *party:* Österreichische Volkspartei (ÖVP, Austrian People's Party); *political career:* Vice-Chairperson, district Chamber of Farmers, since 1975; mem. of local party leadership, community party leadership, district party leadership and principal district party leadership of ÖVP, Ottenschlag, since 1977; mem. of the Praesidium, Lower Austrian Farmers' Federation, since 1985; senior official, Lower Austrian Provincial Chamber of Agriculture, 1985-87; sent to Bundesrat from Lower Austrian Provincial Assembly, mem. of Bundesrat, since 1986; *professional career:* worked in family business, 1964-67; took over farm, Lugendorf 2, 1967; District Farmer, Ottenschlag, since 1974; mem. of local farmers' council, mem. of community farmers' council and mem. of district farmers' council, since 1975; mem. of provincial farmers' council, since 1980; mem. of Board of Dirs., Raiffeisen Bank, Ottenschlag-Martinsberg, since 1979, and Vice-Chairperson, (of the

Board) since 1980; mem. of the Board of Dirs. Biogenetic Raw Materials Co-operative, 1982-86, and Vice-chairperson of the Co-operative, since 1986; *office address:* Frau Agnes Schierhuber, Bundesrat, Dr. Karl Renner Ring 3, 1017 Vienna, Austria.

SCHILLING, Gertrud; German, former Member of the Bundestag; *born:* 30 March 1949, Solingen-Ohligs; *education:* Abitur (advanced matriculation examination), 1968; University of Frankfurt, eudcation; *party:* Die Grünen (Green Party), 1979; *political career:* member and co-founder of peace initiative Osthessen; member of Easter March Group Hessen; member of citizens' union against toxic waste in Vogelsberg; active in citizens' initiative against nuclear power stations, Hanau, 1978; active in Green List Hessen, 1978; member of district association, Die Grünen, Vogelsberg; member of county Exec. Cttee., Die Grünen, 1980-82; conscientious objector, 1981-; member of regional parliament, Hessen, 1982-85; member of Die Grünen group, regional parliament, Hessen, 1985-87; spokeswoman on domestic policy; mem. of Bundestag, party list of Hessen, 1987-90; *professional career:* teacher, mainly at special and elementary school, since 1972; private teacher, Main-Kinzig-Kreis; personal adviser, Gewerkschaft Erziehungund Wissenschaft (GEW, Trade Union for Education and Science); peace worker, 1981-; member of Child and Youth Employment; member of Education and Meeting Centre Non-violent Action, Wustrow; *clubs:* Amnesty International; Association of Italian Culture, Wiesbaden; VVN Union of Anti-Fascists, Frankfurt; Bund für Umwelt und Naturschutz Deutschland (BUND, Society for the Environment and the Conservation of Nature); Greenpeace; Committee for Children's Rights in Democracy; *private address:* 6479 Schotten-Einartshausen, West Germany; *office address:* Frau Gertrud Schilling, Bundeshaus, 5300 Bonn 1, West Germany.

SCHMIDBAUER, Barbara; German, Member of the European Parliament; *born:* 15 November 1937; *party:* Sozialdemocratishe Partei Deutschlands (SPD, Social Democratic Party of Germany); *political career:* MEP, 1987-; *private address:* Heidelberger Landstraße 77B, 6100 Dramstadt 13, Germany; *office address:* Ms Barbara Schmidbauer, European Parliament, Centre Européen, Plateau de Kirchberg, BP 2929, Luxembourg; *phone:* Luxembourg 43001.

SCHMIDT, Dr. Heide; Austrian, Member of the Bundesrat; *born:* 27 November 1948, Kempten, Allgäu, West Germany; *education:* grammar school (science orientated), matriculation, 1966; University of Vienna, Dr. of Law, 1971; part time study at Economic University of Vienna, teaching certificate for intermediate and upper commercial schools teaching Mag. rer. soc. oec., 1976; *party:* Freiheitliche Partei

Österreichs (FPÖ, Freedom Party of Austria); *political career:* sent to Bundesrat from Vienna Provincial Assembly, mem. of Bundesrat, 1987-; *professional career:* year in court, Vienna Provincial Criminal Court and District Court, Vienna Inner City; Legal Dept., Ministry of Education and Art, 1972-77; personal secretary and legal Dir. in charge of the responsibilities of Gustav Zeillinger, People's lawyer, 1977-83; legal Dir. in charge of the jurisdiction of Helmuth Josseck Dipl-Vw (diploma in economics), people's lawyer; *honours and awards:* Golden Service Award of Austria; *office address:* Dr. Heide Schmidt, Bundesrat, Dr. Karl Renner Ring 3, 1017 Vienna, Austria.

SCHMIDT, Renate; German, Member of the Bundestag; *born:* 1943; *party:* Sozialdemokratische Partei Deutschlands (SPD, Social Democratic Party of Germany); *political career:* MP for Nürnberg North; *professional career:* systems analyst; *private address:* 8500 Nürnberg 30, Germany; *office address:* Ms Renate Schmidt, Bundestag, Bundeshaus, 5300 Bonn 1, Germany.

SCHNEIDER, Claudine Cmarada; American, US Representative for Rhode Island; *born:* 25 March 1947, Pittsburgh, Pennsylvania, USA; *religion:* Catholic; *education:* Windham College, BA, 1969; *party:* Republican Party; *political career:* US Rep., District 2, Rhode Island; Treasurer, Northeast-Midwest Congressional Coalition; Mem., Advisory Board, Nat. Women's Political Caucus; founder and co-chwn., Congressional Competitiveness Caucus; *professional career:* TV producer; *office address:* Ms Claudine Schneider, 1512 Longworth House Office Building, Washington DC, 20515, USA.

SCHNEIDERS, Lolita; American, Wisconsin State Representative; *born:* 3 March 1931, Chicago, Illinois, USA; *parents:* Albert Krell and Eve Krell (née Lis); *married:* Don Schneiders, 1954; *children:* Nancy, Donna, Lita Sue; *religion:* Catholic; *education:* Mundelin College, 1948-50; Wisconsin State Univ., BE, 1952; *party:* Republican Party; *political career:* Wisonsin State Rep., District 97, 1981-; *memberships:* American Assn. of Univ. Women; Business and Professional Women; *professional career:* teacher, Wisconsin, Minnesota and Michigan; Insurance sales, Milwaukee, 1976-78; sales rep., Milwaukee, 1978-80; *office address:* Ms Lolita Schneiders, N. 89 W. 17151, Highland Court, Menomonee Falls, Wisconsin 53051, USA.

SCHOPPE, Waltraud; German, former Member of the Bundestag; *born:* 27 June 1942, Bremen, West Germany; *children:* two; *education:* University of Bremen, first state examination for secondary school teachers, subjects of German and history; *party:* Die Grünen (Green Party), founder member of district

association Diepholz; *political career:* member of citizens' initiative against nuclear power stations, Bremen; former mem. of Bundestag, party list of Niedersachsen; *professional career:* trained educationalist; asst. teacher at secondary school; worked in women's groups; member of Gewerkschaft Erziehung und Wissenschaft (GEW, Trade Union for Education and Science); *private address:* 2830 Bassum 1, West Germany; *office address:* Frau Waltraud Schoppe, Bundeshaus, 5300 Bonn 1, West Germany.

SCHORN, Hildegard; Austrian, Member of the Nationalrat; *born:* 10 January 1947, Vienna, Austria; *education:* agricultural technical college, master craftsman's certificate in rural home economics; *party:* Österreichische Volkspartei (ÖVP, Austrian People's Party); *political career:* mem. of SPÖ local Party Executive, 1980-, mem. of SPÖ district Party Executive 1986-; senior official, district Chamber of Farmers Schwechat, 1985-; mem. of Nationalrat, for Lower Austria, 1987-; *professional career:* district farmer, Schwechat district, 1984-; committee mem. district farmers' council, 1984-; *office address:* Frau Hildegard Schorn, Nationalrat, Dr. Karl Renner Ring 3, 1017 Vienna, Austria.

SCHROEDER, Patricia; American, Member of the US House of Representatives; *born:* 30 July 1940, Portland, Oregon, USA; *parents:* Lee Combs Scott and Bernice Scott (née Lemoin); *married:* James White Schroeder, 1962; *public role of spouse:* attorney; *children:* Scott, Jamie; *religion:* United Church of Christ; *languages:* English; *education:* Univ. of Minnesota, Minneapolis, BA, 1961; Harvard Law School, JD, 1964; *party:* Democratic Party; *political career:* Precinct Committeewoman, Denver County Democratic Cttee., 1968-70; Mem., House of Reps., First District Colorado, 1972-; Mem., Armed Service, Post Office, Civil Service and Judiciary Cttees.; Chwn., Select Cttee. on Children, Youth and Families, 1991; Democratic Whip, 1978-87; Deputy Whip, 1987-; Co-Chwn., Democratic Caucus Task Force on National Security; Mem., Armed Services Cttee., Judiciary Cttee., Cttee. on Post office and Civil Service, US House of Reps.; Co-Chwn., Congressional Caucus for Women's Issues; *interests:* women's economic equity, family issues, women's health issues, defence burdensharing; *memberships:* Mem. American Bar Assn.; League of Women Voters; National Organisation of Women; National Womens' Political Caucus; *professional career:* field attorney, National Labor Relations Board, Colorado, Wyoming and Utah, 1964-66; lecturer and law instructor, Community College, Denver, 1969-70; Univ. of Denver, 1969, Regis College, 1970-72; Hearing Officer, Colorado Dept. of Personnel, 1971-72; legal counsel, Planned Parenthood of Colorado; *honours and awards:* Hon. Doctor of Public Service, Metropolitan State College, Denver, 1983; Commendation for Distinguished Service Against Hunger, Bread for the

World, 1984; 100 Most Influential Women in America, Ladies Home Journal, 1983; Mother of the Year, National Mothers Day Cttee., 1982; Woman of Distinction, American Newswomen Club, 1982; Nine Politicians Who Bring Honour to their Trade, Notre Dame Magazine, 1981; *publications:* Champion of the Great American Family, 1989; *private address:* 1600 Emerson Street, Denver, Colorado 80218, USA; *office address:* Rep. Patricia Schroeder, Rayburn House Office Bldg., Washington DC 20515-0601, USA.

SCHULTE, Brigitte; German, Member of the Bundestag; *born:* 26 September 1943, Treuburg, East Prussia; *religion:* Protestant; *education:* Lüneburg teacher training college, 1963-66; teaching examinations, 1966 and Theology, Political Science and General Education Theory, 1969; *party:* Sozialdemokratische Partei Deutschlands (SPD, Social Democratic Party of Germany), 1970; *political career:* various party posts; mem. of Bundestag since 1976; Pres., Government Hanover; mem. of town council and Kreistag, Hanover; *professional career:* Schools service, Eimbeckhausen and Gehrden since 1966; preschool adviser, 1973-76; *office address:* Frau Brigitte Traupe, Bundeshaus, 5300 Bonn 1, West Germany.

SCHÜTZ, Waltraud; Austrian, Member of the Nationalrat; *born:* 7 February 1957, Linz, Austria; *parents:* Josef Schütz and Anna Schütz (née Schmidjell); *religion:* none; *languages:* German, English; *education:* Univ. of Linz, Mag.rer.soc.oec. (social economy); *party:* Sozialistische Partei Österreichs (SPÖ, Socialist Party of Austria), 1975; *political career:* Sec. for Women, SPÖ; Chairwoman, SPÖ Linz; Mem. of the Nationalrat; *interests:* women's affairs, social justice for all, third world affairs, development co-operation; *office address:* Ms Waltraud Schütz, Nationalrat, Dr. Carl Renner Ring 3, 1017 Vienna, Austria.

SCINDIA, Vijaya Raje; Indian, Member of the Rajya Sabha; *born:* 12 October 1919, Sagar, Madhya Pradesh; *parents:* the late Thakur Mahendra Singhji; *married:* His Highness the late Maharaja Sir Jiwaji Rao Scindia of Gwalior, 1941; *children:* one s., three d; *education:* I.T. College, Lucknow; *party:* Bharatiya Janata Party; *political career:* previously associated with Indian National Congress and Jana Sangh; Mem., Lok Sabha, 1957-62, 1962-67 and 1971-77; Mem., Madhya Pradesh Vidhan Sabha, 1967-71; Mem. of Rajya Sabha, 1978-; Leader, Sanyukta Vidhayak Dal in Madhya Pradesh Vidhan Sabha; *memberships:* India International Centre, New Delhi; *professional career:* Founder Pres., Shishu Mandir and Scindia Kanya Vidyalaya, Gwalior; Pres., Board of Governors: Scindia Kanya Vidyalaya, Gwalior; Madhav Engineering College, Gwalior; Samrat Ashok Technological Institute, Vidisha; Chancellor, Sagar Univ., 1976; *clubs:* Gymkhana Club, Delhi; Willingdon Sports Club,

Bombay; *recreations:* music, art, reading; *private address:* Jeeja Asheesh, Jai Vilas Premises, Gwalior, M.P., India; *office address:* Shrimati Vijaya Scindia, Rajya Sabha, Parliament House, New Dehli 110 011, India; *phone:* (11) 389977; 389997.

SCRIVENER, Christiane; French, Member of the European Commission; *born:* 1 September 1925, Mulhouse; *parents:* Pierre Fries and Louise Fries (née Scheer); *married:* Pierre Scrivener; *children:* Noël; *education:* Grenoble Grammar School; Arts and Law Faculty of Paris, degree in Psychology; Harvard Business School, degree; *party:* Union pour la Démocratie Française (UDF, Union for French Democracy); *political career:* MEP, 1979-; Mem. Nat. Cncl., UDF; EC Commissioner, responsible for Taxation and Customs Union, 1989-; *professional career:* Dir., Assn. for the organization of training in France, 1958-; Dir. of the Agency for industrial and economic technical co-operation, 1969-; member of the board of Assurances Générales de France (AGJ, French General Insurance Company), 1986-89; *honours and awards:* Knight of the Legion of Honour; *publications:* L'Europe, une bataille pour l'avenir, 1984; *clubs:* mem., European Cttee., Harvard Business School; Vice-Pres., advanced management Programme; *recreations:* skiing, tennis; *private address:* 21 av. Robert Schuman, 92100 Boulogne Billancourt, France; *office address:* Mme. Christiane Scrivener, Commission of the European Communities, 200 rue de la Loi, 1049 Brussels, Belgium.

SEDLAKOVA, Emilia; Czechoslovakian, Member of the Chamber of Nations of the Federal Assembly; *born:* 13 December 1926, Vrbová, Czechoslovakia; *education:* apprentice dressmaker, 1941-46; Political School of CP of Slovakia, 1947; Central Party School of Central Cttee. of CP of Slovakia, Bratislava, 1953-55; external studies, Philosophy Faculty, Bratislava Comenius Univ., 1961-66; *party:* Komunistická Strana Ceskoslovenska (KSC, Communist party of Czechoslovakia); *political career:* Mem., Bánovce and Bebravou district Cttee., CP of Slovakia, 1947; Mem., Slovak TU Cncl., (SOR), Sec., Kosice Regional Trade Union Cttee., (KOR), 1947-48; Sec., then Chairperson, Slovak Cttee. of Trade Union of Textile and Leather Industry Workers, 1949-55; Mem. of Staff, Bratislava Town Cttee. of CP of Slovakia, 1949-53; Mem., Slovak TU Cncl., (SOR), 1949-53; Chief Sec., Cttee. of Union of Czechoslovak Women in Slovakia, 1958-60; Assistant to Commander of Slovak Nat. Cncl. for Eduation and Culture, 1960-67; Sec., Commission for Education and Culture, Slovak Nat. Cncl., 1962-67; Mem., Central Cttee. of TU of Education and Culture Workers, 1963-65; Dep. Chairperson, Sec. and Mem., Slovak Cttee., Czechoslovak Women's Union, 1967-69; co-opted Mem., Slovak Nat. Cncl., 1968; Dep. Chairperson, Chief Sec., Slovak Women's Union, 1969; Mem., Chamber of Nations, Federal Assembly CSSR and Mem. of Presidium, 1969-81; *professional career:* lecturer, Chair of History of the CP CSSR, Central Party School, 1955-58; lecturer, Central Cttee. of CP of Slovakia; *office address:* Ms Emilia Sedlakova, Federální Shromázdení, Vinohradská 1, 110 02 Prague 1, Czechoslovaia; *phone:* (02) 2103.

SEDLAKOVA, Mária; Czechoslovakian, Member of the Slovak National Council; *born:* 6 August 1922, Sered, Galanta district; *education:* intermediate school, Sered; Central Party School of Central Cttee., CP of Slovakia, 1952-53; Dept. of Journalism, Komensky Univ., Bratislava; *party:* Komunistická Strana Ceskoslovenska (KSC, Communist party of Czechoslovakia); *political career:* founding Mem., CP CSSR Gozinarov; Mem., Disciplinary Board of Czechoslovak Journalists' Union (SCSN), 1951-54; Chairperson, Pravda CP of Slovakia Organisation, 1951-59; Mem., Presidium, Central Cttee. of Czechoslovak Journalists' Union, 1954-57; Chairperson, Presov Regional Publishing House, 1954-50; Mem., Central Cncl. of TUs, 1955-59; Mem., Central Cttee., SCSN, 1959; Mem., West Slovak Regional Cttee., CP of Slovakia, 1960-; Mem., Exec. Cttee., West Slovak Regional Cttee. of CP of Slovakia, 1964-66; Mem., People's Control Commission, Slovak Nat. Cncl., 1964; Mem., CP CSSR Central Cttee., 1968, Mem., Secretariat, 1968; Mem., Rehabilitation Commission, 1968; Mem., Political Commission, CP CSSR, Central Cttee. for Prepartion of XIV Extraordinary Congress, 1969; Minister of Labour and Social Welfare, SSR, 1969-83; *professional career:* farm worker; construction worker; editor, Pravda, Bratislava, 1949-68, chief editor, 1968-69; *honours and awards:* For Outstanding Work, 1962; Prize of the City of Bratislava, 1951; Czechoslovak Journalists' Prize, 1964; *office address:* Ms Mária Sedlakova, Federální Shromázdení, Vinohradská 1, 110 02 Prague 1, Czechoslovaia; *phone:* (02) 2103.

SEEAR, Baroness (cr. 1971, Life Peer) Beatrice Nancy Seear; British, Member of the House of Lords; *born:* 7 August 1913; *parents:* the late Herbert Charles Seear; *education:* Newnham Coll., Camb.; LSE; *party:* Social and Liberal Democrat (SLD); *political career:* mem., House of Lords, 1971-; Leader of the Lib. Peers, 1984-88, Dep. Leader of the SLD Peers, 1988-; *professional career:* Personnel Mgr., C.J. Clark Ltd., 1936-46; Reader in Personnel Mgt., LSE, 1946-78; fmr. Pres., The Fawcett Soc.; Chmn., Charta Mede Ltd.; Pres. of Council, Tavistock Inst. of Human Relations; mem. of Board of Trustees, Population Services Family Planning Programmes Ltd.; Chmn. of Manpower Services Cmn. Area Manpower Board, Bucks., 1982-86; Chmn., Apex Trust; Hon. Visiting Prof. of Personnel Mgt., City Univ., London, 1980-87; *honours and awards:* Dr. of Laws, h.c., Univ. of Leeds, 1979; Dr. of Letters, h.c., Univ. of Bath, 1982; LLD, Univ. of Exeter, 1989; *clubs:* Nat Council for Carers and Their Elderly

Dependants, Chmn., 1972-88, Pres. 1988-; Royal Cmmw. Soc.; Nat. Lib. Club; *recreations:* gardening, reading, travelling; *private address:* 189B Kennington Road, London SE11 6ST, UK; *office address:* Baroness Seear, House of Lords, London SW1A 0PW.

SEET AI MEE, Dr.; Singaporean, acting Minister of State for Community Development and Education; *born:* 31 March 1943, Malacca; *parents:* the late Ling Ding Ming and Chan Swee Lin; *married:* Dr. Lip Chai Seet, 1967; *children:* one s., one d; *religion:* Methodist; *languages:* English, Malay, Mandarin; *education:* Methodist Girls' School, Malacca High School, Malacca; Univ. of Adelaide, B.Sc. in Biochemistry (First Class Honours), 1965, Univ. of Singapore, Dr. of Philosophy in Clinical Chemistry, 1969; Fellow, Singapore National Institute of Chemistry, 1977; Fellow, Royal Institute of Chemistry, UK, 1978; Fellow, Royal Society of Chemistry, UK, 1980; Fellow, American Institute of Chemists, 1982; *party:* People's Action Party (PAP); *political career:* Mem., Resource Panel, Government Parly. Cttee. for Health and Environment, 1987-88; mem., Cttee. on Education and Training Advisory Council on the Disabled Ministry of Community Development, 1988; MP, PAP, Bukit Gombak, 1988-; appointed Minister of State, Community Development and Education, 1988-; acting Minister of State for Community Development, July 1991-; *memberships:* founder, Vice-President, Quota Club of Singapore, 1980-81, then President, 1981-83; Council mem., Singapore Assn. for the Deaf, 1982-84, then President, 1985-88; Chairman, School Executive Cttee., Blangah Rise Primary School, 1984-88; *professional career:* Tutor, Department of Biochemistry, Faculty of Medicine, Univ. of Malaya, Kuala Lumpur, 1965-66; Biochemist, Department of Pathology, Ministry of Health, Republic of Singapore, 1966-73; Principal Research Fellow, Singapore Institute of Standards and Industrial Research, Republic of Singapore, 1973-77; Private Medical Laboratory Practice, 1978-88; *publications:* author of 23 scientific papers on biochemistry and clinical chemistry; *clubs:* Tanglin Club, Raffles Country Club, Pyramid Club; *office address:* Dr. Seet Ai Mee, Ministry of Community Development, 512 Thomson Road, MCD Building, Singapore 1129.

SEFEROWICZ, Elzbieta Maria; Polish, Member of the Sejm; *office address:* Ms Elzbieta Maria Seferowicz, Sejm PRl, ul. Wiejska 4/6/8, 00-489 Warsaw, Poland; *phone:* (22) 28 70 01; 28 40 31.

SEGALL, Dr. Inge; German, former Member of the Bundestag; *born:* 25 February 1930, Hildesheim, West Germany, 1966; *education:* elementary school, secondary school, Abitur (advanced matriculation examination); Universities of Marburg, München, Kiel and Innsbruck/Austria, economics; University of Kiel, state examination, doctorate ('The Problems of the Regulation of the Money Supply'); *party:* Freie Demokratische Partei (FDP, Free Democratic Party), 1970; *political career:* member of district Exec. Cttee., FDP, 1971-; member of county special Cttee. for economic, financial and fiscal policy, 1971-; dep. chmn., county special Cttee. for economic, financial and fiscal policy, 1973-; member of county Exec. Cttee., 1973-77; member of programme commission for economic policy, election campaign for the elections to the regional parliament, 1974; treasurer, FDP, 1983-; former mem. of Bundestag, party list of Hessen; *professional career:* employed in German textile industry, 1957-63; head of staff, market research, 1957-63; employed in import and export firm, United Kingdom, 1964- 65; housewife, London, United Kingdom, 1966-; *private address:* 6272 Niedernhausen, West Germany; *office address:* Dr. Inge Segall, Bundeshaus, 5300 Bonn 1, West Germany.

SEGMÜLLER, Eva; Swiss, Member of the Nationalrat; *born:* 21 January 1932, Zürich, Switzerland; *children:* three; *education:* classical studies, Zürich; qualified as medical/scientifc secretary/translator; *party:* Christlichdemokratische Volkspartei der Schweiz (CVP, Christian Democratic Party of Switzerland); *political career:* Mem. of the St. Gallen Cantonal Cncl., 1976-80; Pres., CVP, 1987-; Mem. of the Nationalrat for St. Gallen, 1979-; *professional career:* housewife; *office address:* Frau Eva Segmüller, Nationalrat/Conseil National, Secretariat-General, Parlamentsgebäude, 3003 Berne, Switzerland; *phone:* Berne 619711.

SEILER, Hilde; Austrian, Member of the Nationalrat; *born:* 6 April 1931, Vienna, Austria; *education:* vocational school, trained as industrial manager; *party:* Sozialistische Partei Österreichs (SPÖ, Socialist Party of Austria); *political career:* junior official, Union of Private Sector Employees, 1946-55; Sec., Treasurer, district leader and deputy section leader, SPÖ, Vienna, Rudolfsheim, 1950-62; mem. of works' council, Union of Chemical Industry Workers, 1966-69; Sec., Union of Chemical Industry Workers, 1968-73, and Women's Sec., 1968-85; provincial Sec. for Vienna, Union of Chemical Industry Workers, 1971-85; senior official, Chamber of Workers and Employees, Vienna, 1971-, and mem. of the Exec., 1983-; mem. of Praesidium, Austrian Federation of Trade Unions, and mem. of Federal Exec., 1983-; mem. of Commission for Taxes, Austrian Federation of Trade Unions, 1983-; leader of Women's Section Austrian Federation of Trade Unions, 1983-; Vice Pres. of Austrian Federation of Trade Unions, 1983-; mem. of Int. Federation of Free Trade unions; mem. of Nationalrat, for Kärnten, Upper Austria, Salzburg, Steiermark, Tirol and Vorarlberg, 1988-; *professional career:* book-keeper, WITAX; Chairperson, works' council, WITAX, 1955-57; office employee, 1957-68; mem. of the Board of Directors, Workers' Pensions Insurance Institute, 1981-; *office*

address: Frau Hilde Seiler, Nationalrat, Dr. Karl Renner Ring 3, 1017 Vienna, Austria.

SEILER-ALBRING, Ursula; German, Minister of State for Foreign Affairs; *born:* 19 July 1943, Saarbrücken, West Germany; *children:* two; *education:* Univ. Göttingen, Tübingen and Berlin, Sociology, Politics, Psychology and National Law, Sociology degree, 1969; *party:* Freie Demokratische Partei (FDP, Free Democratic Party); *political career:* mem. of Bundestag (Baden-Württemberg list), 1983-; Minister of State for Foreign Affairs; *professional career:* Personnel and Organisational adviser; Steel Industry North Rhine Westphalia (Thyssen Industry GmbH, Düsseldorf, 1969-72; König Brewery, Duisberg, 1972-73; *office address:* Frau Ursula Seiler-Albring, Bundeshaus, 5300 Bonn 1, West Germany.

SELENICA, Eleni; Albanian, Deputy to the People's Assembly; *party:* Albanian Workers' Party (AWP); *political career:* candidate Mem., AWP Central Cttee., 1971-; Dep., People's Assembly, Korce constituency district, 1982-; Presidium Mem., People's Assembly, 1982-; Vice Pres., Supreme Court, 1972-; Vice Pres., Albanian Women's Union, 1978; *office address:* Ms Eleni Selenica, Kuvënd Popullore, Tirana, Albania.

SELLÆG, Wenche Frogn; Norwegian, Member of Parliament; *born:* 12 August 1937, Oslo, Norway; *parents:* Henry Osvald Frogn and Bergljot Magna Frogn (née Osmundsen); *married:* Johan Sellaeg, 1976; *children:* one; *religion:* Lutheran; *languages:* English, German; *education:* Cand. Med, 1963, Specialist Internal Medicine, 1971; DTM&H, London, 1971; *party:* Hoyre (Conservative Party); *political career:* Minister of the Environment, 1981-83; mem. of the Conservative Party's central executive committee since 1981, mem. of the working committee, since 1982; Vice-Chwn. of the board of the Directorate of Labour, 1983-85; Chwn. of the Commission on Working Hours, 1984-85; Minister of Justice, 1985-86; Vice-Chwn. of the Conservative Party, since 1988; Minister of Health and Social Affairs, 1989-Oct. 1990; currently, MP; *professional career:* local medical officer, Vaeroey and Roest, 1965; hospital service in Molde, Oslo, Drammen, Namsos, 1964-75; missionary doctor, Bhutan, 1972; assistant senior medical officer, Namdal Hospital, Namsos, 1975-83; *clubs:* mem. of the national Sport Council; mem. of the Norwegian Cultural Council; mem. of the Norwegian National Council for Museums; mem. of the general council of Den Norske Creditbank; deputy mem. of Norwegian National Commission for UNESCO; mem. of the council of the Norwegian Bible Society; mem. of the board of the Norwegian Confederation of Sport; *private address:* 7863 Overhalla, Norway; *office address:* Ms Wenche Sellæg, Ministry of Health and Social Affairs, Akersgt. 42, POB 8011 Dep., 0030 Oslo 1, Norway.

SENESI LOMBARDI, Giovanna; Italian, Senator; *born:* 17 November 1945; *children:* two; *party:* Partito Democratico della Sinistra (PDS, Party of the Democratic Left); *political career:* Regional Councillor, Lombardy, 1980-85; mem. Cttee. on Planning, Transport, Public Works; mem. Regional Secretariat Lombardy, FILT-CGIL, 1986-87; elected Senator, Vimercate, 1987; Sec. Cttee. on Public Works, Communications; *professional career:* employee, Prov. Fed. Cooperatives and Mutual Associations, Milan, 1963-74; employee, Municipal Tramway authority, Milan, 1975; *office address:* Ms Giovanna Senesi Lombardi, Senato della Repubblica, Palazzo Madama, 00100 Rome, Italy.

SEPSOVA, Dr. Lenka; Czechoslovakian, Member of the Narodni Rada (Czech National Council); *party:* Civic Forum; *office address:* Dr. Lenka Sepsová, Ceská národní rada, Snemovní 4, 110 00 Praha 1, Czechoslovakia; *phone:* (02) 2105.

SERAFINI, Dott. Anna Maria; Italian, Deputy; *born:* 4 March 1953, Piancastagnaio, Siena; *education:* Degree in Philosophy; *party:* Partito Democratico della Sinistra (PDS, Party of the Democratic Left); *political career:* Sec. PCI Fed. Siena; Head of Women's Section; mem. Regional Leadership; Deputy, Siena-Arezzo-Grosseto-1987; mem. Cttee. on Foreign and Community Affairs; *office address:* Dott. Anna Maria Serafini, Camera dei Deputati, Montecitorio, 00186 Rome, Italy.

SEROTA, Baroness (cr. 1967, Life Peer) Beatrice Serota; British, Member of the House of Lords; *born:* 15 October 1919; *married:* Stanley Serota, B.Sc. (Eng.), FICE, 1942; *children:* one s., one d; *education:* John Howard Sch.; LSE, B.Sc. (Econ.); *party:* Labour Party; *political career:* mem., Hampstead BC, 1945-49; mem., LCC for Brixton, 1954-65, Chmn. of Children's Cttee., 1958-65; mem., GLC for Lambeth, Chief Whip, and Vice-Chmn. Inner London Educ. Cttee., 1964-67; mem., House of Lords, 1967; app. Baroness- in-waiting to HM The Queen, 1968; Minister of State for Health (Lab.), 1969- 70; a Dep. Speaker, House of Lords, 1986; Chmn., House of Lords Select Cttee. on the ECs, and Principal Dep. Chmn. of Cttees., 1986-; *professional career:* JP (Inner London Area); civil servant, Min. of Fuel and Power, 1941-46; mem., Advisory Council in Child Care, and Central Training Council in Child Care, 1958-68; mem., Advisory Council on Treatment of Offenders, 1960-64; mem., Royal Cmn. on Penal System, 1964-66; mem., Longford Cttee. on 'Crime - a Challenge to us all', 1964; mem., Latey Cttee. on 'Age of Majority'; mem., Advisory Council on the Penal System, 1966-68, Chmn., 1976-78; mem., Seebohm Cttee. on Organization of the Local Authority Personal Social Services, 1966- 68; mem., Community Relations Cmn., 1971-77; Founder Chmn., Cmn. for Local Administration in England, and Local Cmnr. for

Greater London and the South East, 1974-82; mem., BBC Complaints Cmn., 1975-77; Governor, BBC, 1977-82; Pres., The Volunteer Centre; *recreations:* gardening, crochet, collecting shells; *private address:* The Coach House, 15 Lyndhurst Terrace, London NW3 5QA, UK; *office address:* Baroness Sarota, House of Lords, London SW1A 0PW.

SERRA, Gianna; Italian, Deputy; *born:* 13 August 1950, San Giovanni in Persiceto, Bologna; *party:* Partito Democratico della Sinistra (PDS, Party of the Democratic Left); *political career:* Assessor for the Budget, San Giovanni in Persiceto Council, from 1975; Mayor S. Giovanni in Persiceto, 1979-86; elected Deputy, Bologna-Ferrara- Ravenna-Forli, 1987; mem. Committee on Finance; *professional career:* Accountant; Employee, UDI, Bologna from 1975-76; *office address:* Ms Gianna Serra, Camera dei Deputati, Montecitorio, 00186 Rome, Italy.

SEUSTER, Lisa; German, Member of the Bundestag; *born:* 17 April 1942, Lüdenscheid, West Germany; *children:* three; *religion:* Protestant; *education:* secondary school; *party:* Sozialdemokratische Partei Deutschlands (SPD, Social Democratic Party of Germany), 1974-; *political career:* dep. sub-district chmn., SPD, Märkischer Kreis; member of town council, Lüdenscheid, 1975; chmn., SPD group, town council, Lüdenscheid, until 1984; dep. mayor, Lüdenscheid; mem. of Bundestag for Märkischer Kreis II, 1987-; *professional career:* trained industrial clerk, until 1963; housewife, 1963-; *clubs:* Arbeiterwohlfahrt (AWO, Labour Welfare Organisation), German Association for the Protection of Children; German Red Cross, district association Lüdenscheid; *private address:* 5880 Lüdenscheid, West Germany; *office address:* Frau Lisa Seuster, Bundeshaus, 5300 Bonn 1, West Germany.

SEVERINSEN, Hanne; Danish, Member of the Folketing; *born:* 12 June 1944, Copenhagen, Denmark; *parents:* Erik Severinsen and Else Marie Severinsen (née Madsen); *married:* William McFetrich, 1986; *religion:* Lutheran; *languages:* Danish, English; *education:* Copenhagen University, Degree in History and Social Science Subjects, 1964-73; *party:* Venstre (Liberal Party), 1971; *political career:* member of the Folketinget, 1984-; member of Copenhagen Town Council, 1974- 84; member of Boards for Traffic, Schools, Reconstruction and for Re-building; member the Commission for Women of UN, 1984-88, and vice-president, 1986-88; Member of the Nordic Council, 1984-85; member of the Executive Cttee. for the Danish Liberal Party, 1976-85, and Vice-chairman, 1982-85; party spokesperson and mem. of Parly. Cttees. for the environment, higher education and social questions; mem. Cultural Cttee. and Science and Development Cttee; *interests:* environment; higher education; social questions; *professional career:* senior lecturer in history and social science subjects; Chairman Radio Aadalen, 1988-; *publications:* Author of Ny-Liberalismen - og dens Rodder and several articles and feature articles in different magazines and newspapers; *clubs:* member of Boldhus theatre, 1980-; *office address:* Ms Hanne Severinsen, Christiansborg, 1240 Copenhagen K, Denmark.

SHAFFER, Gail; American, Secretary-of-State for New York; *born:* 1 August 1948, Kingston, New York, USA; *parents:* Robert Schaffer and Marion Schaffer (née Gallagher); *religion:* Presbyterian; *education:* Elmira College, BA, 1970; Univ. of Paris, France, 1968-69; *party:* Democratic Party; *political career:* Sec.-of-State, New York, 1983-; Mem., Capitol District High Technology Cncl; *memberships:* Mem., Centre for Women in Govt; *clubs:* Phi Beta Kappa; *private address:* Indian Trail Road, North Blenheim, NY 12131, USA; *office address:* Ms Gail Schaffer, 162 Washington Avenue, Albany, NY 12231, USA.

SHAHANI, Leticia Ramos; Filipino, Senator; *born:* 30 September 1929, Lingayen, Pangasinan; *parents:* Narciso Ramos; *married:* Ranjee Shahani; *children:* two s., one d; *education:* Wellesley College, Wellesley, Mass., USA, BA, English Literative, 1951; Columbia Univ., New York, USA, MA, Comparative Literature, 1954; Univ. of Paris, France, Ph.d, Comparative Literature and Sociology, 1961; *political career:* Alternate Representative of the Philippines to the United Nations Commission on the Status of Women, 1969, Representative, 1970-74, Rapporteur, 1972, Chwn., 1964.; Mem., Philippine Delegation to the United Nations General Assembly, 1974-79, Alternate Mem., 1980; Philippine Representative to the Third Cttee. of the General Assembly, 1974-79; Pres., Assn. of Awardees of the Outstanding Women of the Philippines, 1974-78; Ambassador to Romania and non-resident Ambassador to Hungary and the German Democratic Republic, 1975-78; Mem., Philippine delegation to the United Nations World Conference on International Women's Year, Mexico, 1975; Commissioner, National Commission on the Role of Filipino Women, Manila, 1975; Mem., Executive Cttee., World Young Women's Christian Assn., 1975-79; Vice-Chwn., Philippine delegation to the Philippine-Romanian Joint Trade Commission, 1976; Vice-Chwn., Philippine delegation to the Philippine-Romanian Scientific and Technological Commission, 1976; Ambassador to Australia, 1978-80; Chwn., Third Cttee. of the United Nations General Assembly, 1978; Chwn., Philippine delegation to the Joint Philippine-Australian Trade Commission, 1978; Philippine Representative, Preparatory Cttee. for the United Nations Conference on the Mid-Decade for Women, 1978-80; Chwn., ASEAN-Camberra Cttee., Jan-Dec. 1979; Vice-Chwn., Philippine delegation to Joint Philippines-Australian Trade Commission, 1979;

Chwn., 1980; Vice-Chwn., Philippine delegation to the World Conference on the United Nations Mid-Decade for Women, 1980; United Nations Assistant Secretary General for Social Development and Humanitarian Affairs, 1981-86; Special Representative of the United Nations Secretary-General, International Year of Disabled Persons, 1981; Secretary-General, World Conference to Review and Appraise the Achievements of the United Nations Decade for Women, 1985; Secretary-General, United Nations Congress on the Prevention of Crime and the Treatment of Offenders, 1985; Undersecretary of Foreign Affairs, 1986-87; Chwn., National Commission on Women; Senator, 1987-; Chwn., Cttee. on Foreign Relations; *professional career:* former Mem. of the Faculty: Univ. of the Philippines; New School for Social Research, New York, USA; International Study and Research Institute, New York, USA; Dean, Graduate School, Lyceum of the Philippines, 1970-75; Pres., National YMCA of the Philippines, 1970-72; William Quasha Professor of International Relations, Graduate School, Lyceum of the Philippines, 1974-75; *honours and awards:* One of the Oustanding Women in the Nation's Service, 1974; Honorary Doctor of Laws, Centro Escolar Univ., 1976; Order of Teodor Vladimirescu, Government of Romania, 1978; Honorary Doctor of Humanities, Silliman Univ., 1983; Most Distinguished Alumnae Achievement Award, Wellesley College, Mass., USA, 1987; *publications:* The Philippines -- The Land and People, 1965; *office address:* Ms Leticia Shahani, The Congress of the Philippines - Senate, Batasang Pambansa Bldg., Quezon City, Manila, The Philippines.

SHARPLES, Baroness (cr. 1973, Life Peer) Pamela Sharples; British, Member of the House of Lords; *born:* 11 February 1923; *parents:* the late Lt.-Cdr. K.W. Newall (retd.); *married:* Robert Douglas Swan, 1983; *children:* two s., two d., (from previous marriage); *religion:* Church of England; *languages:* French; *education:* Southover Manor, Lewes; Florence; *party:* Conservative Party; *political career:* mem., House of Lords, 1973-; *interests:* small businesses, cheque-book journalism, prisoners' wives; *professional career:* WAAF, 1941-46; mem, Review Body on Armed Services Pay, 1979-81; Dir., TVS, 1982; *clubs:* Mid-Ocean Club Bermuda; Royal Cape Golf Club; *recreations:* tennis, golf, walking, gardening; *private address:* Nunswell, Higher Coombe, Shaftesbury, Dorset SP7 9LR, UK; *office address:* Baroness Sharples, House of Lords, London SW1A 0PW.

SHEPHARD, Gillian Patricia; British, Minister of State attatched to the Treasury; *born:* 22 January 1940; *parents:* Reginald Watts and Bertha Watts; *married:* Thomas Shephard, 1975; *children:* two step s; *education:* North Walsham Girls' High School; St. Hilda's College, Oxford University; *party:* Conservative Party; *political career:* Cllr., Norfolk County Cncl.,

1977, Chmn. Social Services and Education Cttees., Dep. Leader of Cncl.; Chmn., West Norfolk Health Authority, 1981-85; Chmn., Norwich Health Authority, 1985-87; Member of Parliament for Norfolk South West, 1987-; Sec., Conservative Backbench Health and Social Services Cttee., 1987; mem., Commons Select Cttee. on Social Services, 1987; Parly. Under Sec. of State for Social Security, 1989-; *interests:* EC; education; health; penal affairs; *professional career:* Education Officer and Schools Inspector, Norfolk County Cncl., 1963-75; Anglia Television, 1975-77; *clubs:* Royal Commonwealth Soc; *recreations:* gardening; France; music; *private address:* The Old Rectory, 63 High Street, North Wold, Thetford, Norfolk, United Kingdom; *office address:* Mrs Gillian Shephard, Her Majesty's Treasury, Parliament Street, London SW1P 3AG, United Kingdom; *phone:* (071) 233 3000.

SHIELDS, Hon. Margaret; New Zealander, Member of New Zealand Labour Party Policy Council; *born:* 18 December 1941, Wellington, New Zealand; *parents:* Blake (Ernest Blake) Porter and Dorothy B. Porter; *married:* Patrick John Shields, 1960; *children:* two D; *languages:* English, working knowledge of French; *education:* Victoria Univ., social science, 1973; *party:* Labour Party, 1969; *political career:* co-founder, National Secretary and Pres., Society for Research on Women, 1966-70; co-covener of 2nd United Women's Convention, 1975; delegate, United Nations International Women's Year Conference, Mexico, 1975; Labour Party candidate for Karori, 1975; Mem., New Zealand Executive, 1975-78; Pres., Labour Women's Council, 1974-75 and 1977-78; Mem., Wellington Hospital Board, 1977-80; Labour Parly. candidate for Kapiti, 1978; Mem., Policy Council, 1979-82; elected to Parliament for Kapiti, 1981-84; Minister of Customs, 1984-87; Associate Minister of Housing; re-elected for Kapiti, 1984-87; New Zealand's first Minister of Consumer Affairs, 1984-87; senior research and executive officer for the Department of Statistics; re-elected for Kapiti, 1987-90; Minister of Women's Affairs, 1987-90; Minister of Statistics, 1987-90; Minister of Consumer Affairs, 1987-90; Minister of Customs, 1988-89; Associate Minister of Education, 1989-90; Minister responsible for the National Library, 1990; Mem.: Social Equity Cabinet Cttee., Honours Appointments Cabinet Cttee.; Travel Cabinet Cttee.; Legislation Cabinet Cttee.; retired from Parliament, 1990, currently Mem., Labour Party Policy Cncl., 1990-93; *memberships:* Mem., Labour Women's Cncl.; Vice-Pres., Socialist International Women; New Zealand Sociological Assn; *professional career:* housewife and part time student before entering politics; nine years in the New Zealand Dept. of Statistics and Research Officer, New Zealand Consumers Inst; *honours and awards:* Winston Churchill Fellow, 1971; *publications:* numerous articles on women's issues and social research; *recreations:* tennis, tramping, ski-ing, music,

drama; *office address:* The Hon. Ms Margaret Shields, #2/32 Hobson Street, Thorndon, Wellington, New Zealand.

SHIMIZU, Kayoko; Japanese, Member of the House of Councillors; *born:* 9 November 1935; *education:* Tokyo Univ; *party:* Liberal Democratic Party (LDP); *political career:* former Subhead, LDP Women's Section and Section Manager, Ministry of Health and Welfare; elected for National, Abe, 1990; Mem., House of Cllrs. Cttee. on Social and Labour Affairs and on Audit, 1990-; *office address:* Ms Kayoko Shimizu, House of Councillors, 1-7-1 Nagata-cho, Tokyo 100, Japan; *phone:* (03) 5813111.

SHIMIZU, Sumiko; Japanese, Member of the House of Councillors; *born:* 1 March 1928; *education:* High School; *party:* Japan Socialist Party (JSP); *political career:* former Chairperson of Japan Women's Conference; elected for National, 1990; Mem., House of Cllrs. Cttee. on Judicial Affairs and Special Cttee. on Environment, 1990-; *office address:* Ms Sumiko Shimizu, House of Councillors, 1-7-1 Nagata-cho, Tokyo 100, Japan; *phone:* (03) 5813111.

SHINOZAKI, Toshiko; Japanese, Member of the House of Councillors; *born:* 12 June 1918; *education:* Nagasaki Women's Normal School; *party:* Japan Socialist Party (JSP); *political career:* former Vice-Chairperson, JSP Nagasaki Prefectural HQ; elected for Nagasaki, 1990; Mem., House of Cllrs. Cttee. on Local Administration and Special Cttee. on Environment, 1990-; *office address:* Ms Toshiko Shinozaki, House of Councillors, 1-7-1 Nagata-cho, Tokyo 100, Japan; *phone:* (03) 5813111.

SHIPLEY, Hon. Jenny; New Zealander, Minister of Social Welfare and Minister of Women's Affairs; *children:* two; *education:* Marlborough Girls' College; Christchurch Teachers' College; Lincoln College; *party:* National Party, 1975; *political career:* held number of executive positions in National Party; community service involvement include, Child Safety Officer, Plunket, 1979-81, Malvern Plunket Executive, 1979-84, Playcentre Pres., 1980-82, Malvern County Councillor, 1983-, Aged Peoples Welfare Cttee., 1983-, Malvern Community Arts Council 1983-, Lincoln College Conference Cttee., 1985-, New Zealand Federated Farmers and School Cttee. membership; mem., Party Policy Co-ordinating Cttee. and since 1985, a Divisional Councillor; MP for Ashburton, 1987-; Minister of Social Affairs and Minister of Women's Affairs, Nov. 1990-; *professional career:* primary school teacher, 1972-76; farmer; *private address:* Racecourse Road Ashburton; *office address:* The Hon. Ms Jenny Shipley, Ministry of Women's Affairs, Private Bag, Wellington, New Zealand; *phone:* (04) 734112; *fax:* (04) 720961.

SHOPE, Gertrude; South African, President of the African National Congress Women's League; *born:* 15 August 1925, Johannesburg, South Africa; *parents:* John Moeketsi and Mary Moeketsi; *married:* Mark Shope; *public role of spouse:* activist in ANC and South African Congress of Trade Unions, detained 1960 and lived as exile in Botswana, Czechoslovakia, Zambia and Nigera, worked for World Federation of Trade Unions, Prague; *children:* two s., one d; *religion:* Methodist; *languages:* English, Tswana, Xhosa, Zulu; *education:* schooling in Salisbury, Southern Rhodesia, 1942-43; St. Hilda's College, Ladysmith, Natal, 1944-45; *party:* African National Congress (ANC); *political career:* joined ANC, 1954-; Chwn., Soweto's Central Western Jabavu branch of the Federation of South African Women (FEDSAW); Transvaal Provincial Sec., FEDSAW until leaving South Africa, 1966; following her husband's arrest, left country to join him in exile in Botswana, 1966; returned to Zambia, after first conference of Women in the External Mission of the ANC, 1981; Head of the ANC Women's section and Mem., ANC Nat. Exec. Cttee., 1981-; elected with her husband, co-convenors, Internal Leadership Core and Task Force, May 1990-; led ANC Women's Section back to South Africa, June 1990; elected Pres., ANC Women's League at the first National Conference, Kimberley, Northern Cape, Apr. 1991-; *interests:* worker's, women's and youth's work conditions, liberation struggle; *professional career:* teacher, Indaleni High School, Richmond, Natal, 1948-51; teacher, Pimville High School, 1951-54 when the system of Bantu Education was introduced; worked in Occupational Therapy Dept., Coronation Hospital; Johannesburg City Cncl., organising women's clubs and assisted the disabled, 1956; volunteer worker, Margaret Ballinger Hospital; *private address:* Apartment 42, Parkleigh Court, 95 Wolmarans Street, Joubert Park, South Africa; *office address:* Ms Gertrude Shope, P.O. Box 61884, Marshalltown, 2107, South Africa.

SHORT, Clare; British, Member of Parliament; *born:* 15 February 1946, Birmingham, UK; *parents:* Frank Short and Joan Short (née O'Loughlin); *married:* Alex Lyon, 1981; *public role of spouse:* MP for York, 1966-83; Minister of State at the Home Office, 1974-76; *education:* Keele Univ., Leeds Univ., BA, political science, 1970; *party:* Labour Party, 1970; *political career:* Member of Parliament, 1983-; mem. Lab. National Exec. Cttee., 1988-; *interests:* women, Northern Ireland, Palestinians, race and immigration, low pay, unemployment; *honours and awards:* Campaigner of the Year, The Spectator, 1990; *publications:* Dear Clare, Hutchinsons Radius, 1991; *clubs:* National Union of Public Employees (sponsored MP); *recreations:* swimming, dog owner; *office address:* Ms Clare Short, House of Commons, London SW1A OAA.

SIDIBÉ, Sy Oumou Louise; Mali, Minister of Public Health, Welfare and Women's Affairs; *party:* Transition Committee for the Salvation of the People (CTSP); *office address:* Mme. Sy Oumou Louise Sidibé, Ministry of Public Health, Welfare and Women's Affairs, Koulouba, Bamako, Mali.

SIELICKA-GRACKA, Maria Teresa; Polish, Member of the Sejm; *office address:* Ms Maria Teresa Sielicka-Gracka, Sejm PRI, ul. Wiejska 4/6/8, 00-489 Warsaw, Poland; *phone:* (22) 28 70 01; 28 40 31.

SIERAKOWSKA, Izabella; Polish, Member of the Sejm; *office address:* Ms Izabella Sierakowska, Sejm PRI, ul. Wiejska 4/6/8, 00-489 Warsaw, Poland; *phone:* (22) 28 70 01; 28 40 31.

SIGURDARDOTTIR, Jóhanna; Icelandic, Minister of Social Affairs; *born:* 4 October 1942; *married:* Porvaldur Steinar Jóhannesson; *party:* Althykuflokkurinn (SDP, Social Democratic Party); *political career:* Cttee. Member, Iceland Air Hostess' Union, 1966-69, Chmn., 1961-66; member, Reykjavik Shop and Office Workers Union, 1976-83; Chmn., Government Cttee. for the Disabled, 1979-83; member, Social Security Board, 1978, Chmn., 1979-80; Minister of Social Affairs; Deputy leader of the SDP; mem. of Althingi for Reykjavik, 1978; *professional career:* stewardess, Loftleidir (Icelandic Airways), 1962-71; clerk, Kassagerd Reykjavikur, 1971-78; *office address:* Ms Jóhanna Sigurdardóttir, Ministry of Social Affairs, Hafnarhúsinu vid Tryggvagötu, 150 Reykjavík, Iceland.

SIMEON, Rosa Elena; Cuban, President of the Cuban Academy of Sciences; *born:* 17 June 1943, Havana, Cuba; *children:* one d; *education:* Marianao High School; Univ. of Havana; *political career:* Dir., National Centre of Agriculture and Health (CENSA), 1985; Pres., Academy of Sciences of Cuba, 1985-; *professional career:* Chief, Dept. of Virology, National Centre of Scientific Research, 1968-73; Chief, Microbiological Div., 1974-76; Prof., School of Veterinary Medecine, 1969-73; National Hospital and National Centre of Scientific Investigations, 1975; National Inst. of Veterinary Medecine, 1977-78 and 1981; *honours and awards:* awards and decorations from Cuba, Czechoslovakia and France; *publications:* various articles in professional journals; *office address:* Ms Rosa Elena Simeon, Academia de Ciencias de Cuba, Industria y San José, Zona 2, Havana, Cuba.

SIMHA, Ettia; Israeli, Prime Minister's Adviser on the Status of Women; *office address:* Mrs Ettia Simha, Office of the Prime Minister, 3 Kaplan Street, Hakirya, Jerusalem 91919, Israel; *phone:* (02) 639211.

SIMMEN, Rosmarie; Swiss, Member of the Nationalrat; *born:* 10 September 1938, Zürich, Switzerland; *children:* three; *education:* pharmacy studies; *party:* Christlichdemokratische Volkspartei der Schweiz (CVP, Christian Democratic Party of Switzerland); *political career:* Mem. of the Zürich Cantonal Cncl., 1983-87; Mem. of the Ständerat for Solothurn, 1987-; *professional career:* pharmacist; *office address:* Frau Rosmarie Simmen, Ständerat/Conseil d'Etat, Secretariat-General, Parlamentsgebäude, 3003 Berne, Switzerland; *phone:* Berne 619711.

SIMON CALVO, Irma; Spanish, Deputy; *born:* 21 September 1949, Vall d'Uxó, Castellón, Spain; *education:* *party:* Partido Socialista Obrero Español (PSOE, Spanish Socialist Workers' Party), 1977; *political career:* former city councilwoman, Vall d'Uxó, Castellón; Deputy, PSOE, Castellón, 1983-89, re-elected 1989-; third secretary, Mesa del Parlamento, 1986-; *office address:* Ms Irma Simón Calvo, Congreso de los Diputados, Fernán Flor 1, Madrid 14, Spain.

SIMONIS, Heide; German, Member of the Bundesrat; *born:* 4 July 1943, Bonn, West Germany; *parents:* Dr. Horst Steinhardt and Sophia Steinhardt (née Brück); *married:* Prof. Dr. Udo, 1967; *languages:* English, French; *education:* grammar school for girls, Abitur (matriculation), 1962; Univs. of Erlangen, Nürnberg, Kiel, Economics and Sociology Degree, 1967; *party:* Sozialdemokratische Partei Deutschlands (SPD, Social Democratic Party of Germany), 1969; *political career:* alderman, Kiel, 1971-76; mem. of District Exec. Cttee., SPD, Kiel, 1972-76; mem. of Bundestag, 1976-88; Minister of Finance, Schleswig-Holstein, 1988-; mem. of Bundesrat, May 1988-; *professional career:* lecturer of German, Univ. of Lusaka, Zambia, 1967-68; German tutor, Goethe Institute, 1970-71; German tutor, Radio and Television Services, NHK, 1970-71; marketing researcher, Triumph International, Tokyo, Japan, 1970-71; careers adviser for college leavers and graduates, Federal Office of Employment, Kiel, 1972-76; *publications:* social and economic publications; *clubs:* mem. of Trade Union for Public and Transport Services; *private address:* 2352 Bordesholm, West Germany; *office address:* Frau Heide Simonis, Bundesrat, 5300 Bonn 1, West Germany.

SIMONS, Barbara; German, Member of the European Parliament; *born:* 16 June 1929, Wolfenbüttel; *party:* Socialist Group of European Parliament, S; *political career:* MEP, 1984-; mem. Development and Co-operation Cttee; *professional career:* teacher; *office address:* Frau Barbara Simons, European Parliament, Centre Européen, Plateau de Kirchberg, BP 2929, Luxembourg.

SIMPSON, Hon. Portia; Jamaican, Minister of Labour, Welfare and Sports; *office address:* The Hon.

Ms Portia Simpson, Ministry of Labour, Welfare and Sports, 1F North Street, P.O. Box 481, Kingston, Jamaica; *phone:* (92) 29500.

SINGH, Digvijay Narain; Indian, Deputy Minister of Finance; *office address:* Ministry of Finance, North Block, New Dehli 110 001, India; *phone:* (11) 3012611.

SINGH, Pratibha; Indian, Member of the Rajya Sabha; *born:* 7 July 1929, Salemgarh, District Gorakhpur, Uttar Pradesh; *parents:* C.P.N. Singh; *married:* the late Kunwar Prem Raj Singh, 1941; *children:* one s; *education:* Women's College, Patna, BA; *party:* Congress Party; *political career:* Pres., Child Welfare Council, Punjab, 1953-58; Pres., Red Cross Society Punjab, 1953-58; Mem., Child Welfare Council, Bihar, 1962-; Mem., Red Cross Society, Bihar, 1962; Mem., Bihar Legislative Assembly, 1962-69; Mem. of the Rajya Sabha, 1970-; Mem., Executive Cttee., Indian Council for Child Welfare, 1976, re-elected, 1977; Chmn., Bal Sahyog, 1984-; Mem., All India Congress Cttee; *interests:* welfare of women, children and the Harijans; *professional career:* established Saket Home for Handicapped in Chandigarh; started the scheme for Indian Holiday Home at Taradevi near Shimla; *recreations:* walking, reading, film, drama; *private address:* Village Sursand, District Sitamarhi, Bihar, India; *office address:* Shrimati Pratibha Singh, Rajya Sabha, Parliament House, New Dehli 110 011, India; *phone:* (11) 389977; 389997.

SINGH, Usha; Indian, Minister of State for Tourism; *office address:* Smt. Usha Singh, Ministry of Tourism, Transport Bhavan, Parliament St., New Dehli 110 001, India; *phone:* (11) 383816.

SINT, Marjanne; Dutch, President of the Labour Party; *born:* 24 July 1949, Amsterdam; *married:* H. G. van Noordenburg, 1985; *languages:* Dutch, English, German; *education:* Univ. of Amsterdam; IMEDE Business School; *party:* Partij van de Arbeid (PvdA, Labour Party); *political career:* Pres., PvdA, 1987-; *professional career:* mem., Staff,: Ministry of Economic Affairs, 1974-77; Ministry of Culture Health and Social Affairs, 1977-79; Economics Editor, Intermediair, 1979-80; Chief Editor, 1980-81; Publisher, UNU Business Publications, 1981-87; *publications:* Tussen wal en schip, etnische minderheden in Nederland, 1980; Economy over crisis, 1982; *recreations:* literature, poetry, music, modern art, architecture; *office address:* Mevr. Marjanne Sint, Partij van de Arbeid, Nicolaas Witsenkade 30, 1017 ZT Amsterdam, The Netherlands.

SISULU, Nontsikelelo Albertina; South African, President of the Federation of South African Women and President of the United Democratic Front; *born:* Tsomo district, Transkei, South Africa; *married:* Walter Sisulu, 1944; *public role of spouse:* General Secretary of the ANC, sentenced to life imprisonment in the Rivonia trial; *children:* five; *education:* trained as nurse, Johannesburg Non-European Hospital; *party:* Federation of South African Women; United Democratic Front (UDF); *political career:* joined ANC Women's League, active in Federation of South African Women, to which the Women's League was affiliated, 1948; involved in Defence Campaign, women's protest against passes, 1956, campaign against introduction of bantu education; during latter campaign her Orlando West home served as a classroom for community schools, which continued until unregistered schools were made illegal; detained for three months, 1963; placed under banning orders, 1964-83, including ten years of house arrest; charged with furthering aims of ANC by attending funeral, 1982, found guilty, 1984 and sentenced to four years imprisonment, sentence set aside on appeal; elected unopposed as Transvaal Pres. of UDF, while in custody awaiting trial, 1983; charged with high treason along with 15 other Mems. of South African Workers' Union, UDF, Natal Indian Congress, Transvaal Indian Congress and Release Mandela Cttee., charges were dropped against 12 of 16 including Sisulu, following collapse of state evidence on revolutionary politics, 1985; restriction order placed on her again, 1988; formed part of delegation of prominent Soweto residents in rent crisis, 1988; part of UDF delegation to meet Pres. George Bush, 1989, invited to Washington as part of broad consultations between US admin. and South African Leaders; now serves on Cttee. to re-establish ANC Women's League; *office address:* Ms Nontsikelo Albertina Sisulu, Parliament, Cape Town, South Africa; *phone:* (012) 403-2911.

SITI ZAHARAH HJ SULAIMAN, Datuk Dr.; Malaysian, Member of the House of Representatives; *born:* 24 April 1949, Lanchang, Mentakab, Pahang; *married:* Mr Samaruddin Md Rejab; *children:* four; *education:* Sultan Abu Bakar School, Kuantan, Pahang; MARA Institute of Technology; State Univ. of New York, Albany, USA, BA (Hons.); Hawaii Univ., USA, MA in Psychology and Education; Cornell Univ., USA, Ph.D. in Education Administration and Organisation Studies; *party:* Barisan Nasional (National Front Coalition Party); *political career:* Dewan Bahasa dan Pustaka, Kuala Lumpur; elected MP for Mentakab, Pahang, Barisan, 1986; Deputy Minister in Prime Minister's Department, 1986; elected UMNO Supreme Council Mem., 1987; *honours and awards:* Knight Commander of The Most Distinguished Order of the Crown of Pahang; *office address:* Datuk Dr. Siti Zaharah Hj Sulaiman, Prime Minister's Department, Tingkat 7 Bangunan Yayasan Selangor, Jalan Bukit Bintang, 55100 Kuala Lumpur, Malaysia.

SKINNER, Mary Just; American, Vermont State Senator; *born:* 7 July 1946, South Bend, Indiana, USA; *married:* Scott Skinner; *children:* two; *education:* Barnard College, AB, 1968; Columbia Univ. School of Law, JD, 1971; *party:* Democratic Party; *political career:* Vermont State Senator, Washington County District, 1979-; Delegate, Democratic National Convention, 1984 and 1988; *memberships:* Vermont and Washington County Bar Assns; *professional career:* lawyer; *office address:* Ms Mary Skinner, Box 412, Montpelier, Vermont 05602, USA.

SMET, Miet; Belgian, Secretary of State for the Environment and Social Emancipation; *born:* 5 April 1943, St. Niklaas; *parents:* Albert Smet and Irma Smet (née Ivens); *religion:* Catholic; *languages:* Dutch, French, English; *education:* grad., Catholic Training Centre for Social Sciences; *party:* Christelijke Volkspartij (CVP, Christian Social Party), 1961; *political career:* Chwn., C.V.P., Lokeren, 1971-90; Pres., C.V.P. Working Party, 'Women and Society', 1973-1983; Chwn., Commission for Women's work, Ministry of Employment and Labour, 1974-1985; Mem., Parliament, 1978-; Mem., National Policy Cttee. A.C.W., 1984-; Mem., National C.V.P. Exec. Cttee.; Official Belgian Representative, U.N.O. World Conferences on the Situation of Women, 1975-1980-1985; Secretary of State for the Environment and Social Emancipation Women, 1975, 1980, 1985; Deputy, CVP, 1978-; mem. of Cttee. of Nat. Policy ACW, 1984-; Sec. of State for Environment and Social Emancipation, Nov. 1985-; *interests:* external affairs, Europe, environment, women, labour; *professional career:* Press Attaché, Cabinet of Minister of Regional Economy, 1972; Scientific Counsellor, Research Cttee., Mens en Ruimt, 1964-71; *private address:* Durmelaan 4/5, 9100 Lokeren, Belgium; *office address:* Ms Miet Smet, Secretariat for the Environment and Social Emancipation, Place Quetelet 7, 1030 Brussels, Belgium.

SMIT-NAARENDORP, Ellen; Suriname, Minister of Health; *office address:* Ms Ellen Smit-Naarendorp, Ministry of Health, Gravenstraat 64, Paramaribo, Suriname.

SNOWE, Olympia Jean; American, Member of the House of Representatives; *born:* 21 February 1947, Augusta, Maine, USA; *parents:* the late George John Bouchles and the late Georgia Bouchles (née Goranites); *married:* John McKeenan; *religion:* Greek Orthodox; *education:* Univ. of Maine, BA, 1969; *party:* Republican Party; *political career:* Maine State Rep., 1973-77; Vice Chwn., Auburn Republican City Cttee., Maine, 1974-; Mem., Govt. Advisory Cttee. on Univ. of Maine and Govt. Positive Action Cttee., 1975; alternate delegate, Republican National Convention, 1976; Maine State Senator, 1977-78; Member of the House of Reps., 2nd District, Maine, 1979-; Mem., International Operations Foreign Affairs Cttee.; Mem., Aging Cttee. and Human Services Sub-Cttee; *private address:* 114 Nottingham Road, Auburn, Maine 04210, USA; *office* *address:* Ms Olympia Snowe, 2464 Rayburn House Office Bldg., Washington DC, 20515, USA.

SO CHAU, Hon. Yim-ping; Hong Kong, Member of the Legislative Council; *born:* 22 October 1927, Hong Kong; *children:* three; *religion:* Christian; *education:* Ying Wa Girls' School; *political career:* Mem., Legislative Cncl; *memberships:* Southern District Board; Chmn., Southern District Industrialists Assn. Ltd.; Chmn., Southern District Arts and Culture Assn. Ltd.; Mem., Cttee., Road Safety Assn. Ltd.; Pres., Western Disrict Junior Police Cell; Southern District Fight Crime Cttee.; Chmn., Community Building Cttee.; Second Vice Pres., Southern District Recreation and Sports Cncl.; Chmn., Industry Contribution Programme, 1989; Hon. Pres., The Scout Assn. of Hong Kong, Southern Island District; *professional career:* Managing Dir., New Island Printing Co. Ltd; *honours and awards:* Justice of the Peace; *office address:* The Hon. Ms Yim-ping So Chau, The Legislative Council, Government House, Hong Kong.

SOEBADIO, Prof. Dr. Haryati; Indonesian, Minister of Social Affairs; *born:* 24 June 1928, Jakarta; *religion:* Islam; *education:* elementary school, Madiun and Jakarta, 1940; junior and senior high school, Jakarta; Gemeentelijke Universiteit, Amsterdam, Holland, 1956, and Ph.D., 1971; *political career:* director general of culture, Department of Education and Culture, 1978-88; Minister of Social Affairs in the Fifth Development Cabinet, 1988-; *professional career:* lecturer in Sankrit language and literature, cultural history of ancient India, and Hindu philosophy, Faculty of Letters, Univ. of Indonesia, 1957; head, Consortium of Faculties of Arts and Philosophy, Department of Education and Culture, 1972-77; professor, Sanskrit literature and old Javanese, 1975; Dean of Faculty of Letters, Univ. of Indonesia, 1975-78; *office address:* Prof. Dr. Haryati Soebadio, Ministry of Social Affairs, Jalan Ir H Juanda 36, Jakarta Pusat, Indonesia; *phone:* (021) 341329.

SOKOLOWAKA, Wanda; Polish, Member of the Sejm; *office address:* Ms Wanda Sokolowaka, Sejm PRI, ul. Wiejska 4/6/8, 00-489 Warsaw, Poland; *phone:* (22) 28 70 01; 28 40 31.

SOLLIE, Solveig Helene; Norwegian, former Minister for Consumer Affairs; *born:* 19 April 1939, Sorum, Norway; *parents:* Sigurd Berger and Marit Elisabeth Berger (née Olsen); *married:* Finn Sollie, 1961; *children:* Nina, Sigurd Andreas, Annette, Nan Helene; *party:* Kristelig FolkeParti (KrF, Christian People's Party); *political career:* mem., Town Board of Control, Skien, from 1975, Dep. Spokesman, 1979-81; Chmn., Social Board of Control, Skien, 1981-83; mem., Borough Health and Social Cttee., Skien, 1983-; mem. of Board of Control, Borough Power Company, Skiensfjorden, 1983-; Deputy Representative, Storting, 1981-85;

Chmn., Christian People's Party's Women, 1984-; mem., Christian People's Party National Board of Control, Central Board of Control and Work Cttee., 1984-; mem. of Political Cttee. and Observer, Borough Control of Christian People's Party, Telemark, 1985-; Representative, Storting, 1985-86; mem., Finance Cttee., 1985-86; Minister of Family and Consumer Affairs, 1989-Oct.-1990; *professional career:* mem. of Hospital Board of Control, Skien, 1978-83; *office address:* Ms Solveig Sollie, Ministry of Consumer Affairs and Government Administration, Akersgt. 42, POB 8004 Dep., 0030 Oslo 1, Norway.

SOLODAR, Edna; Israeli, Member of the Knesset; *born:* 1933, Israel; *children:* one; *party:* Ma'arach (Israeli Labour party); *political career:* Mem., Knesset; *professional career:* musician; Mem. and Sec., Kibbutz Gesher; *office address:* Ms Edna Solodar, Knesset, Hakirya, Jerusalem 91000, Israel; *phone:* (02) 661211.

SOLTYK, Grazyna; Polish, Member of the Sejm; *office address:* Ms Grazyna Soltyk, Sejm PRI, ul. Wiejska 4/6/8, 00-489 Warsaw, Poland; *phone:* (22) 28 70 01; 28 40 31.

SONNTAG-WOLGAST, Dr. Cornelie; German, Member of the Bundestag; *born:* 1942; *party:* Sozialdemokratische Partei Deutschlands (SPD, Social Democratic Party); *political career:* MP for Schleswig-Holstein; *professional career:* journalist; *private address:* 2208 Glückstadt, Germany; *office address:* Dr. Cornelie Sonntag-Wolgast, Bundestag, Bundeshaus, 5300 Bonn 1, Germany.

SOUTENDIJK-VAN-APPELDOORN, Marian H.J.; Dutch, Member of the Second Chamber; *born:* 4 September 1948, Utrecht, Netherlands; *education:* Pedagogic Academy, masters in law; *party:* Christen Democratisch Appel (CDA, Christian Democratic Appeal); *political career:* Mem. general board, CDA Noord-Brabant Province; secretary CDA-women council, Noord-Brabant; Mem. of Second Chamber, 1986; *professional career:* 'scribbler' in law court; lecturer, Cath. Univ. Brotant, Tilburg; *private address:* Beekstraat 34, 5673 NA Nuenen, the Netherlands; *office address:* Mevr. Marian Soutendijk-van-Appeldoorn, Tweede Kamer der Staaten-Generaal, Binnenhof 1A, Postbus 20018, The Hague, Netherlands.

SOUTHCOTT, Heather; Australian, Senator; *born:* 1928; *public role of spouse:* Dr. of Medecine and Dr. of Science; *children:* two d; *religion:* Uniting Church of Australia; *education:* AUA Pharmacy; *party:* Liberal Movement; Australian Democrats, 1977; *political career:* involved in Liberal Movement and New LM, SA; founding Mem., Australian Democrats, 1977; Sec., Australian Democrats, SA, 1977-82; involved in administration of Australian Democrat Party, 1983-, currently Vice-Pres., Administration; Mem., Mitcham, SA, House of Assembly, 1982; First Woman to be elected Nat. Pres., Australian Democrats, 1984-85, Dep. Nat. Pres., 1985-86, Nat. Pres., 1986-87, 1987-88, 1988-89, 1989-90, 1990-91; Federal Pres., United Nations Assn. of Australia, (UNAA), 1987-90, State Pres., SA Div., Mem., UNAA Cttee. on Status of Women in SA, Mem., UNAA Peace and Disarmament Cttee., 1985-; *interests:* social justice, human rights, peace making, solidarity with disadvantaged, racial and economic justice, needs of the disabled, health care, drug dependence, resolution of violence at all levels, mass media, child and home safety, development education, overseas aid, conservation of archival material and heritage items; *memberships:* Amnesty Int.; Women's Electoral Lobby; Country Women's Assn.; South Australian Cncl. of Social Services; South Australian Cncl. on the Ageing; Australian Fed. of Univ. Women; Managment Cttee., SA Unemployed Groups in Action (SAUGA); Board of Shelter SA, Community Housing Group; Board of Consumer Advocacy Program, SA; Disability Complaints Service, SA; Childrens' Week Cttee., SA; South Australian Multicultural Forum; Refugee Week Cttee. SA; Exec. Cttee., Nat. Cncl. of Women in SA; Dep. Chairperson, Older Women's Advisory Cttee.; Older Person's Advisory Cttee.; Exec. Cttee., Greenhouse Assn., SA; Convener, City Churches Outreach Group; Human Ethics Cttee., Univ. of Adelaide; Trustee, Alumni Assn., Univ. of Adelaide; Cncl. of Governors, Seymour College; Sec., Old Collegians Assn., Presbyterian Girls College and Seymore College; Convener, Seymore College Archives Cttee; *professional career:* Pharmaceutical Chemist; *clubs:* Nat. Trust of South Australia; several environmental organisations; Save the Children Fund; Royal Zoological Soc.; Friends of Botanic Gardens; Friends of Art Gallery; Friends of State Library; Friends of State Opera, State Theatre; *office address:* Ms Heather Southcott, Senate, Parliament House, Room M13, Canberra, ACT 2600, Australia; *phone:* (062) 727111.

SPAAK, Antoinette; Belgian, Member of the Chamber of Representatives; *born:* 27 June 1928, Etterbeek; *education:* Free University of Brussels, Philosophy and Arts; *party:* Front Démocratique des Bruxellois Francophones (FDF, French Speaking Democratic Front of Brussels); *political career:* Deputy, Brussels; Pres., FDF, 1977-83; MEP, 1979-84; Local Cllr., Ixelles, 1982; Minister of State, 1983-; Pres., Cncl. of French Community, Feb. 1988-; *private address:* Avenue d'Italie 35, 1050 Bruxelles, Belgium; *office address:* Mme. Antoinette Spaak, Kamer van Volksvertegenwoordigers, Palais de la Nation, Place de la Nation 2, 1000 Brussels, Belgium.

SPIVAK, Mira; Canadian, Senator; *born:* 1934, Poland; *married:* Sidney J. Spivak, 1955; *children:* Harold,

Laurie, Diane; *education:* Primary and Secondary School, Winnipeg; Univ. of Manitoba, BA Hons., Political Science and Philosophy; Univ. Siver Medal, Faculty of Arts and Science; *party:* Progressive Conservative; *political career:* Senator for Manitoba, 1986-; Mem., Senate Cttees. for Agriculture and Forestry, Legal and Constitutional Affairs, Regulations and Other Statutory Instruments, Social Affairs, Science and Technology and Transport and Communications; *office address:* The Honourable Senator Mira Spivak, Senate, Parliament Buildings, Wellington Street, Ottawa, Ontario K1A OA4, Canada; *phone:* (613) 992 4416.

SPOERRY, Vreni; Swiss, Member of the Nationalrat; *born:* 8 March 1938, Zürich, Switzerland; *children:* three; *education:* LLB, Univ. of Zürich; *party:* Freisinnig-Demokratische Partei der Schweiz (FDP, Liberal Democratic Party of Switzerland); *political career:* Mayoress of Fischenthal; Mem., Borough Exec. for Horgen, 1978-86; Mem., Zürich Cantonal Cncl., 1979-83; Mem., Nationalrat for Horgen, Canton of Zürich, 1983-; *professional career:* housewife; lawyer; *office address:* Frau Vreni Spoerry, Nationalrat/Conseil National, Secretariat-General, Parlamentsgebäude, 3003 Berne, Switzerland; *phone:* Berne 619711.

SPORNIC, Prof. Aneta; Romanian, Deputy to the Grand National Assembly; *education:* Dr. Economics; *party:* Romanian Communist Party (RCP); *political career:* Vice Chairperson, Women's Nat. Cttee., 1966-77; candidate Mem., RCP Central Cttee., 1968-79; Chairperson, Bucharest Municipal Womens' Cttee., 1968-77; Mem., Bucharest Municipal Party Cttee., 1968-; Mem., Nat. Cncl., Socialist Unity Front, Cncl. of Socialist Democracy and Unity Front, 1974; Dep., Grand Nat. Assembly, 1975, Vice Chairperson, 1975-80; Dep. Minister of Labour, 1975-79; Minister of Education and Instruction, 1979-82; full Mem., RCP Central Cttee., 1979, Mem., Political Exec. Cttee., RCP, 1979-82; Minister, State Sec. with the State Planning Cttee., 1982-84; Chairperson, State Cttee. for Prices, 1984-86; Dep. Prime Minister, 1986-87; Chairperson, Higher Sanitary Cncl., 1986; *professional career:* Univ. Professor; Pro-Rector, Academy of Economic Studies, 1967; *honours and awards:* Order of Labour, Second Class, 1981; *office address:* Prof. Aneta Spornic, Marea Adunare Nationala, Aleea Marii Adunari Nationale, Bucharest, Romania; *phone:* 16 21 50.

SSEKITOLEKO, Victoria; Ugandan, Minister of Agriculture and Forestry; *office address:* Ms Victoria Ssekitoleko, Ministry of Agriculture and Forestry, Box 102, Entebbe, Uganda.

STAELS-DOMPAS, Nora; Belgian, Secretary of the Senate; *born:* 24 June 1925, Koersel, Belgium; *children:*

225

Three; *education:* Catholic University, Leuven, Degree in Political and Social Science, 1949; *party:* Christlijke Volkspartij (CVP, Christian Social Party); *political career:* National Co-operative Senator, 1974-81 and 1985-; Provincial Senator, Brabant, 1981-85; Member, Council of Europe; Vice-Chmn., Council of Europe; Member, Western European Union; mem. of Senate Commissions for Social Affairs, Justice, Preservation of the Environment, Revision of the Constitution and Reform of Institutions; mem., Parly. Assembly Council of Europe and the Assembly of the West-European Union; *professional career:* Study Service for Christian Female Workers' Guild, 1949; Christian Workers' Movement; General Christian Workers' Union; High Council for Families; Member of the Belgian Delegation for Women's Rights at the UN in New York & Geneva; UN Congress, Mexico; *private address:* d'Huartlaan 155, 1950 Kraainem, Belgium; *office address:* Ms Nora Staels-Dompas, Senate, Palais de la Nation, Place de a Nation 1, 1000 Brussels, Belgium.

STALLER, Llona (Elena Anna) Cicciolina; Italian, Deputy; *born:* 26 December 1951, Budapest; *married:* Salvatore Mercuri, 1972; *education:* Studied Medicine and Archaeology; *party:* Partito Radicale, 1986; Gruppo Federalista Europeo Ecologista (European Federalist Ecologist Group); *political career:* Founded Partito del Sole (Sun Party)-Ecological party; Activist, anti-American and anti-Red Brigades; Anti-nuclear; Peace and post Chernobyl protests; mem. Radical Party, 1986; Participant, Extraordinary Congress of P.R, Rome, 1987; Numerous prosecutions for indecent exposure, from 1983 until the present; Sentenced to 6 months imprisonment for obscene performances at the Diva Futura erotic agency; Campaigner for the reform of laws on obscenity; elected Deputy, Rome-Viterbo-Latina-Frosinone, 1987; mem. Cttee. on Defence; *professional career:* Photo-model; Broadcaster; Film-Star (Erotic films); Featured in Playmen; Radio Luna, 1975; T.V. broadcast Proibito (Prohibited), by Enzo Biagi; Films: Incontro d'amore, Cuore di Cane, Came Bollente; Radio broadcast Acquarius, C'era due volte; Political Satire: Vorrei fare l'amore per tre; Performance: Curve deliziose (erotic); *office address:* Ms Llona Staller, Camera dei Deputati, Montecitorio, 00186 Rome, Italy.

STALLWORTH, Alma Grace; American, Michigan State Representative; *born:* 15 November 1932, Little Rock, Arkansas, USA; *parents:* Charles Russell and Lisbon Russell (née Burse); *married:* Thomas F. Stallworth, 1953; *children:* Keith B., Thomas F; *education:* Highland Park Jr. College, AA, 1955; Wayne State Univ., 1955, 1968 and 1981-82; Merrill Palmer Inst., 1968; *party:* Democratic Party; *political career:* Michigan State Rep., District 4, 1970-74 and 1983-; currently: Chwn., Public Utilities Cttee., Asst. Majority Floor Leader, Mem., Standing Cttees. on Education,

Insurance, Senior Citizens, Retirement and Public Health; Mem., Exec. Cttee., National Conference of State Legislators; founder and Administrator, Michigan Legislative Black Caucus Foundation; Mem., National Black Caucus of State Legislators; *memberships:* NAACP; Black Women's Forum of Detroit; National Black Child Development Inst.; National Order of Women Legislators; National Black Caucus of State Legislators; Top Ladies of Distinction; Archdiocese of Detroit; *professional career:* Dir., Oak Grove and Saint John African Methodist Episcopal Day Care, 1968-69; policy Assc., High Scope Education Reasearch Foundation, 1981-82; *honours and awards:* Feminist of the Year, Detroit Chapter, National Organisation of Women, 1986; Certificate of Appreciation, State Board of Education, 1986; Woman of the Year Award, Minority Women's Network, 1986; Legislator of the Year, Michigan Assn. of Children's Alliances, 1984; Distinguished Service Award, Michigan Health Assn., 1986; United Negro College Fund; Public Service Award, American Nurses Assn; *clubs:* Hon. Mem., Alpha Kappa Alpha; *office address:* Mrs Alma Stallworth, State Capitol Room 12, Lansing, Michigan 48909, USA.

STAMM, Barbara; German, Deputy Member of the Bundesrat; *born:* 29 October 1944, Bad Mergentheim; *children:* three; *religion:* Catholic; *education:* educator training; *party:* Christlich Soziale Union (CSU, Christian Social Union), 1969; *political career:* mem. of town council, Würzburg, 1972-87; mem. of Diet Bavaria since 1976; mem. of CSU Group Cttee. since 1978; Dep. Chmn., CSU Group, 1986/87; Secretary of State, State Ministry of Labour and Social Planning, Bavaria since 1987; Deupy mem. of Bundesrat, Oct. 1987-; *professional career:* educator and full-time youth worker, Diocese Würzburg, 1970; housewife, 1970-71; remedial education teacher, Children's Home, substituting head of education, Rhönkinderdorf Riedenberg/Bad Brückenau, 1973; Warden, Seamen's Children's Home, Würzburg, 1974-78; honorary warden, Seamen's Children's Home, Würzburg, 1978-; *office address:* Frau Barbara Stamm, Bundesrat, 5300 Bonn 1, West Germany.

STAMM, Judith; Swiss, Member of the Nationalrat; *born:* 25 February 1934, Schaffhausen, Switzerland; *education:* LLB; *party:* Christlichdemokratische Volkspartei der Schweiz (CVP, Christian Democratic Party of Switzerland); *political career:* Mayoress of Schleitheim; Mem. of the Great Cncl. of Luzern, 1971-84; Mem. of the Nationalrat for Luzern, Canton of Luzern, 1983-; *professional career:* juvenile court lawyer; *office address:* Frau Judith Stamm, Nationalrat/Conseil National, Secretariat-General, Parlamentsgebäude, 3003 Berne, Switzerland; *phone:* Berne 619711.

STANISSEWSKA, Grazyna; Polish, Member of the Sejm; *office address:* Ms Grazyna Stanissewska, Sejm PRI, ul. Wiejska 4/6/8, 00-489 Warsaw, Poland; *phone:* (22) 28 70 01; 28 40 31.

STARKE, Hon. Hortensia L.; Filipino, Congresswoman; *born:* Iloilo City; *parents:* Salvador Laguda and the late Paz Lopez; *married:* Raymond P. Starke; *children:* Diane, Theresa, Ramon, Mark Dennis Hodel; *education:* St. Scholastica's College; Philippine Women's Univ., Manila; Assumption Academy, Iloilo City, Piano and Voice Culture; Julilard School of Music; *political career:* Organizer, Negros Occidental Auxilliary Foundation; Congresswoman; *memberships:* Pres., New Alliance of Sugar Producers; Sonedco Planters Association; Confederation of Sugar Producers; Confederacion Ibero Americana y Filipina de Productores de Cana de Azucar; *clubs:* Women of Negros; *office address:* The Hon. Ms Hortensia Starke, The Congress of the Philippines - House of Representatives, Batasang Pambansa Bldg., Quezon City, Manila, The Philippines.

STARLING, Sandra Meira; Brazilian, Federal Deputy; *born:* 16 January 1944, Belo Horizonte; *parents:* Benedito Starling and Cecília d'Avila Meira Starling; *married:* Thales Chagas Machado Coelho; *education:* UFMG, Belo Horizonte, law, 1972 then M.Sc. in political science, 1984; *party:* Partido dos Trabalhadores (PT, Independent Labour Party); *political career:* State Deputy, Minas Gerais, 1987-91; Mem., Cttee. for the Constitution and Justice, 1987-88; Pres., Cttee. for Science and Technology, 1989-91; Federal Deputy for Minas Gerais, 1991-95; *professional career:* professor; *publications:* A Lei? Ora a Lei... Constituinte, Constituiçao e Movimentos Populares, Ed. Segral, 1986; *office address:* Ms Sandra Starling, Chamber of Deputies, Praça dos 3 Poderes, Ed. Principal, 70160 Brasilia, DF, Brazil; *phone:* (61) 225 2885.

STEDMAN, Baroness (cr. 1974, Life Peer) Phyllis Stedman; British, Member of the House of Lords; *born:* 14 July 1916, Peterborough, UK; *parents:* Percy Adams and Emmie Adams (née Cooke); *married:* the late Henry William Stedman, OBE, (Decd. 1988), 1941; *religion:* Baptist; *education:* Peterborough County Grammar Sch., until 1932; *party:* Social Democratic Party (SDP), 1981; *political career:* county Cllr., 1946-75; mem., House of Lords, 1974-; Baroness-in Waiting (Govt. Whip), 1975-78; Parly. Under-Sec., Dept. of Environment, 1978-79; Whip, SDP, 1981, Chief Whip, 1986-88; SDP Spokesman on Local Govt., New Towns, 1981-; Environmental Protection, 1987-; Leader, Social Democrat Peers, 1988-91; *interests:* local govt., transport, new towns, countryside, conservation, European matters, defence; *memberships:* Vice-Pres., Assn. of DCs, 1980-; Vice-Pres., Nat. Assn. of Local Councils, 1983; Vice-Pres., Assn. of CCs, 1986-; Vice-Chmn., Building Socs. Assn., 1985-90; *professional career:* asst. librarian, 1932-41; group officer, Nat. Fire Service, 1941-44; Company Sec. and Dir., EW Stedman Ltd., Rose Growers and Landscape Contractors, 1944-74; mem., Independent Broadcasting Authority, 1974-75; mem., Peterborough Development Corp., 1972-72; *honours and awards:* OBE, Queen's New Year Honours, 1964; Life Peerage, 1974; *clubs:* Nat. PHAB, 1979-; Fire Services Nat. Benevolent Fund, 1975-; *recreations:* reading, countryside; *private address:* 1 Grovelands, Thorpe Road, Peterborough PE3 6AQ, UK; *office address:* Baroness Stedman, House of Lords, London SW1A 0PW.

STEFFEY, Lela Gardner; American, Arizona State Representative; *born:* 8 August 1928, Idaho Falls, Idaho, USA; *parents:* Orawell Gardner and Mary Ethel Gardner (née Owen); *married:* Warrem D. Steffey, 1973; *children:* Barry G., Bradley C., Barton P., Dean, Wayne, Susan, Luann, Scott W; *religion:* Latter-Day Saints; *education:* Univ of Idaho, Moscow, 1947-48; Univ. of California, San Diego, 1960-70; Grossmont College, California, 1960-70; Grad., American Inst. of Banking; *party:* Republican Party; *political career:* Dir., Region Six, Arizona Federation of Republican Women, 1981-83-; Arizona State Representative, district 29, 1983-; Chair, Counties and Municipalities, Banking and Insurance, Judiciary and Govt. Operations Cttees., 1983-; delegate, Republican national Convention, 1984; Mem., Revenue and Taxation Cttee., Arizona State Govt; *memberships:* Mesa Museum Advisory Board; National Order of Women Legislators; Mesa Community Cncl., Board Dir., 1985-; founder, Arizona Child Education and Safety Inc., Dir., 1985-; *professional career:* Exec.-Sec., Bank of America, San Diego, 1949-52; loan officer and asst. cashier, 1961-73; Exec.-Sec., General-Dynamics Astro, 1960-61; real estate agent, Steffey Realty, 1975-; *honours and awards:* Appreciation Award, Maricopa County Republican Cttee., 1978-81; Lincoln Bust Award, 1980; *clubs:* founder, Arizona Womens' Assn.; American Mothers Assn.; Arizona Historical Society; *office address:* Mrs Lela Steffey, 1439 East Ivyglen Street, Mesa, Arizona 85203, USA.

STEINHAUER, Waltraud; German, former Member of the Bundestag; *born:* 8 February 1925, Velbert/Rheinland, West Germany; *religion:* Protestant; *education:* elementary school; study at the Academy of Employment, 1952-53; *party:* Sozialdemokratische Partei Deutschlands (SPD, Social Democratic Party of Germany), 1951; *political career:* member of sub-district Exec. Cttee., SPD; town councillor, Siegen, 1956-74; chmn., SPD group, town council, Siegen, 1963-69; member of district assembly, Siegen, 1966-85; alderman; dep. mayor, Siegen, 1969-74; member of regional Exec. Cttee., SPD Western Westfalen, since 1969; member of party Exec. Cttee., since 1972; dep. regional chmn., SPD, since Jun. 1974; former mem. of Bundestag, party list of Nordrhein-Westfalen; *professional career:* trained industrial clerk; industrial clerk, iron foundry, 1943-48; member of Industriegewerkschaft Metall (IGM, Metal Workers' Union), since 1946; employee, Deutscher Gewerkschaftsbund (DGB, German Trades Union Confederation), district association Düsseldorf-Mettmann, Velbert, from Jul. 1948; legal secretary for social and employment law, DGB, district association Siegen-Wittgenstein, 1953-65; chmn., DGB, district association Siegen-Wittgenstein, 1965, on leave since 1977; member of self-government, County Insurance Authority Westfalen; *office address:* Frau Waltraud Steinhauer, Bundeshaus, 5300 Bonn 1, West Germany.

STEINMETZ, Kaye H.; American, Missouri State Representative; *married:* Bob Steinmetz; *children:* Mark, Steven, Richard, Stacey; *education:* grad., Columbia College, Missouri; Univ. of Missouri, Columbia, additional studies; *party:* Democratic Party; *political career:* Missouri State Rep., District 74; Mem. and Chwn., Children, Youth and Families Cttees.; Mem., Social Service and Medicaid Cttees., Ecucation Cttee., Appropriations Cttee. for Social Service and Corrections, Employment Security Cttee. and Joint House and Senate Missouri-St. Louis Airport Cttee.; Missouri House Rep.; alternate delegate, National Conference of State Legislators; Mem., Governor's Conference on Education, 1976 and Governor's Conference on Children and Youth; Mem., White House Conference on Aging; Mem., Missouri State Advisory Board on School Nurses and Parents as First Teachers; Mem., Advisory Board for Court of Appeal's Special Advocates; *memberships:* Board of Dirs., National Order of Women Legislators; Missouri State Miss Scholar Program Inc.; Missouri PTA; *honours and awards:* Women of Achievment Award, 1975; Outstanding Young Woman of the Year, 1972; Democrat Meritorious Service Award, St. Louis Globe; Ten Best Legislators List, Missouri Times; *office address:* Ms Kaye Steinmetz, 13 Longhenrich Drive, Florissant, Missouri 63031, USA.

STENIUS-KAUKONEN, Minna Marjatta; Finnish, Member of the Eduskunta; *born:* 19 July 1947, Kuopio, Finland; *parents:* Martti Jaakko Stenius and Reeta Annikki Lehtinen (née Miettinen); *married:* Erkki Kaukonen, 1981; *education:* M. Sc. (Eng.), 1971; *party:* Demokraattinen Vaihtoehto (Deva, Democratic Alternative); *political career:* mem. of Eduskunta, 1975-; *professional career:* Virke Oy, 1972; Sr. Asst. (Tutor), Univ. of Technology, 1972-73; Sr. CE, Occupational Safety and Health District of Häme, 1973; *office address:* Ms Minna Stenius-Kaukonen, Eduskunta, 00102 Helsinki, Finland.

STEPNIAK, Maria; Polish, Member of the Sejm; *office address:* Ms Maria Stepniak, Sejm PRI, ul. Wiejska 4/6/8, 00-489 Warsaw, Poland; *phone:* (22) 28 70 01; 28 40 31.

STEPOVA née Appeltová, Vlasta Anna Marie, C.Sc.; Czechoslovakian, Minister of Trade and Tourism in the Czech National Government; *born:* 7 June 1938, Letohrad, Czechoslovakia; *parents:* Leopold Wilhelm Appelt and Marie Appeltová née Turková; *married:* Milos Marcel Step, 1963; *public role of spouse:* director of the State Energy Inspectorate; *children:* Jiří, Lucie, Adam; *religion:* Catholic; *languages:* Czech, English, Russian; *education:* Prague School of Economics, B.Sc., 1956-61; Bratislava School of Economics, M.Sc./C.Sc., Sociology; *party:* Civic Forum, 1989; *political career:* Dep. for Southern Bohemia, Czech National Assembly, 1990-; Minister of Trade and Tourism, Czech National Govt., 1989-; *professional career:* senior Exec., Inst. of Trade Research, 1961-89; *publications:* Ekonomické aspekty druhého bydlení, 1985; Typologie ceskoslovenského spotrebitele, 1988; Analyza vyvoje zivotního zpusobu, 1986; Kvalitativní prognóza vyvoje spotreby, 1987; *clubs:* Civic Movement Ministers Club; *recreations:* gardening, travelling, swimming, theatre, music, reading; *private address:* Praha 2, Anny Letenské, Czechoslovakia; *office address:* Vlasta Stepová, Urad vlády CR, Lazarská 7, 113 48 Praha 1, Czechoslovakia.

STEWART, Christine; Canadian, Member of the House of Commons; *born:* 3 January 1941, Hamilton, Ontario, Canada; *parents:* Morris Alexander Leishman and Laura Anne Leishman (née Doherty); *married:* David T. Stewart Q.C., 1963; *public role of spouse:* Member of the Canadian Bar Association and Commissioner of the Ontario Police; *children:* Douglas, John, Catherine; *religion:* Roman Catholic; *languages:* English, Spanish, some French; *education:* Neuchâtel Junior College, Switzerland, 1958-59; Univ. of Toronto School of Nursing, Canada, B.Sc., 1959-63; *party:* Liberal Party, 1982; *political career:* MP for Northumberland, 1988-; opposition critic, Canadian International Development Agency, 1988-; Mem., Standing Cttee. on External Affairs and International Trade, 1988-; Mem., Sub-Cttees. on International Debt and International Human Rights, 1988-; *interests:* international development, domestic social security issues, international human rights, external affairs; *memberships:* Exec.Dir., Horizons Development Agency, a non-sectarian charity charity supporting development programmes in Central America, 1986-88; founder and co-Exec. Dir., Horizons of Friendship, 1973-86; African emergency Aid Project Selection Cttee., 1986-87; *professional career:* volunteer worker, Honduras, 1971-72; nurse, Coburg District General Hospital, 1965; public health nurse, 1963-65; *honours and awards:* Paul Harris Fellow Award, Rotary Club; Hon. Mem., FEDECOH, a Honduran development agency; *recreations:* music, reading, hiking, camping, skiing, outdoor activities; *office address:* Mrs Christine Stewart, House of Commons, Parliament Buildings, Wellington Street, Ottawa, Ontario K1A OA6, Canada; *phone:* (613) 957 3744; *fax:* 952 0874.

STILLING-PEDERSEN, Inger; Danish, Member of the Folketing; *born:* 26 July 1929, Pindstrup, Randers, Denmark; *parents:* Jens Stilling Pedersen and Johanne Marie (née Neilsen); *married:* Arne Christensen, 1988; *religion:* Protestant; *languages:* Danish, English; *education:* Aarhus Teacher Training College, final exams, 1961; *party:* Kristeligt Folkeparti (CPP, Christian People's Party), 1971; *political career:* Mem. of the Folketing, for Aarhus 1973-79 and 1984-; Vice-Chairperson, CPP Parly. Group, 1984-87, Chairperson, 1987-88, Sec., 1988-; Mem., Cttee. on Road Safety; *interests:* health, social, juridical and public transport issues; *professional career:* teacher, Nyuang School, Randers, 1961-76 then Head mistress, 1976-; *honours and awards:* Cross of the Order of Chivalry, the Queen of Denmark, 1988; *publications:* articles in various magazines and newspapers; *clubs:* Exec. Cttee., Frontier Union, 1974-, Chairperson, Local Branch, 1980-; *private address:* Kirstensminde 22, Romalt, DK-8900, Randers, Denmark; *office address:* Ms Inger Pedersen, Folketing, Christiansborg, 1240 Copenhagen K, Denmark.

STIRBOIS, Marie-France; French, Deputy to the French National Assembly; *born:* 11 November 1944, Paris 8e, France; *parents:* M. and Mme. Charles; *married:* the late Jean-Pierre Stirbois, 1969; *public role of spouse:* politician; *children:* Nathalie, Christophe; *religion:* Catholic; *languages:* English, German; *education:* teaching certificate for secondary level English; *party:* Front National (FN); *political career:* regional Cllr., 1986-; city Cllr. for Dreux, 1988-; elected Deputy for Dreux replacing Martial Taugourdeau, 1989; *interests:* family, culture, defence of the French identity; *professional career:* manages printing press; *recreations:* tennis, walking, music; *office address:* Mme. Marie-France Stirbois, L'Assemblée Nationale, 126 rue de L'Université, 75355, Paris, France; *phone:* Paris 40 63 60 00; *fax:* Paris 42 60 99 03.

STOCKER-MEIER, Monika; Swiss, Member of the Nationalrat; *born:* 1 July 1948, Turgi; *children:* two; *education:* diploma in Adult Education, Univ. Freiburg; Academy for Adult Education, Luzern; *party:* Grüne Partei der Schweiz (Green Party of Switzerland); *political career:* Mayoress of Abtwil; Mem. of the Nationalrat for Canton of Zürich, 1987-; *professional career:* social worker; *office address:* Frau Monika Stocker-Meier, Nationalrat/Conseil National, Secretariat-General, Parlamentsgebäude, 3003 Berne, Switzerland; *phone:* Berne 619711.

STOIZMAN, Maria Joanna; Polish, Member of the Sejm; *office address:* Ms Maria Joanna Stoizman, Sejm PRI, ul. Wiejska 4/6/8, 00-489 Warsaw, Poland; *phone:* (22) 28 70 01; 28 40 31.

STRAND GERHARDSEN, Tove; Norwegian, Minister of Labour and Government Administration; *born:* 29 September 1948, Solor; *married:* Rune Gerhardsen; *public role of spouse:* Project Co-ordinator; *education:* Oslo Univ., degree in Economics, 1971; *political career:* Mem., Oslo Town Cncl., 1971-75; political Sec., Ministry of Trade and Shipping and Ministry of Finance; Minister of Health and Social Affairs, 1986-89; Minister of Labour and Govt. Admin., Nov. 1990-; *professional career:* Head of Div., Ministry of Consumer Affairs and Govt. Admin., 1978; Head of Dept., National Hospital, Oslo, 1982-86; *office address:* Ms Tove Strand Gerhardsen, Ministry of Local Government and Labour, Mollergaten 43, P.O. Box 8112 Dep, 0032 Oslo 1, Norway; *phone:* (02) 34 90 90; *fax:* 349545.

STRANGE, Ebba Marie; Danish, Member of the Folketing; *born:* 15 April 1929, Flensburg, Germany; *parents:* Henrik Lassen Henriksen and Helena Petersen; *married:* Asbjorn Strange, 1950; *children:* Lena, Morten; *languages:* Danish, English, German; *education:* teacher training college, qualified kindergarten teacher, 1948-50; *party:* Socialist People's Party (SPP), 1959; *political career:* MP, Århus, 1973-; Chwn., SPP Parly. Group; Vice-Chwn., Folketing Legal Cttee; *interests:* education, legal and criminal policy, developing countries, women's policy; *memberships:* Amnesty International; Social Pædagoisk Forening; Mellem Folkeligt Samuuirke; Danmarks Natur Fredningsforening; *professional career:* kindergarten teacher, Copenhagen, 1950-57; educator in children's homes, 1957-64; teacher, high-school for kindergarten teachers, 1964-85; *publications:* Social Pædagogik I oz II, 1977; Pas På Boernene, 1984; To Katte Blivertil, 1972; Kuinder i Politik, 1984; Klager over Politet, 1986; *office address:* Ms Ebba Strange, Folketing, Christiansborg, 1240 Copenhagen K, Denmark.

STRANGE, Baroness (16th in line, cr. 1628) Jean Cherry Drummond; British, Member of the House of Lords; *born:* 17 December 1928, London, UK; *parents:* John Drummond of Megginch, Rt. Hon. Lord Strange and Violet Drummond (née Buchanan-Jardine); *married:* Capt. Humphrey Drummond of Megginch, MC, 1952; *public role of spouse:* Chairman of Scottish Society of Authors; *children:* Adam, Charlotte, Humphrey, Amelie, John, Catherine; *religion:* Church of England; *languages:* French; *education:* Oxenfoord Castle School, Midlothian; Miss K.M. Hobbs Tutorial, Guildford; Perth Secretarial Coll., secretarial certificate, 1947; St. Andrew's Univ., MA, 1951; Cambridge Univ; *party:* Conservative Party, 1986;

political career: Chmn., Glencarse Junior Unionists, 1946-52; Chmn., Caledonian Schools Sale, 1971; House of Lords, 1986-; mem., All Party Defence Studies Group; mem., International Parliamentary Union; mem., Commonwealth Parly. Assn.; mem., All Party Arts and Heritage Group; *interests:* defence, foreign affairs, children and family life, conservation, arts and heritage; *professional career:* Chmn., Megginch Farming Co., 1966-; *publications:* Love From Belinda, 1961; Lalage In Love, 1962; Creatures Great And Small, 1968; Love Is For Ever, 1988; *clubs:* Scottish Socy. of Antiquaries (Fellow); Cons. Peers Assn., Scottish Peers Assn; *private address:* Megginch Castle, Errol, Perthshire PH2 7SW, Scotland, UK; *office address:* Baroness Strange, House of Lords, London SW1A 0PW.

STRAUSS, Annette; American, Mayor of Dallas, Texas; *married:* Theodore Strauss; *children:* Nancy, Janey; *religion:* Jewish; *education:* Rice Univ., Houston, Texas; Univ. of Texas, Austin, BA, 1944; Columbia Univ., New York, MA, 1945; *political career:* former Mem.-at-Large, Dallas City Cncl.; Mayor, Dallas, 1987-; *memberships:* Dallas United Nations Assn.; Dallas History Soc.; Women's Cncl. of Dallas; Dallas Heritage Soc.; Dallas Assn. for Retarded Citizens; Jewish Federation of Dallas; *professional career:* Mem., Development Board, Univ. of Texas, Austin and Dallas Institute of Humanities and Culture; Mem., Board of Dirs., Kennedy Center for Performing Arts, Dallas Symphony Orchestra, Nat. Jewish Hospital and the Children's Medical Center; *honours and awards:* Woman of the Year, Nat. Jewish Hospital, 1965 and Humanitarian Award, 1978; Human Relations Award, American Jewish Cttee., 1971; Brotherhood Award, Nat. Confederation of Christians and Jews, 1972; Linz Award, 1975; Voluntary Community Service Award, Dallas History Soc., 1981; Fundraiser of the Year, Dallas County, 1982; *office address:* Ms Annette Strauss, 1500 Marilla, Dallas, Texas 75201, USA.

STROSSEN, Nadine; American, President of the American Civil Liberties Union (ACLU); *education:* Harvard Law School, USA, JD, 1975; Harvard-Radcliffe College, AB, 1972; *political career:* Mem., National Board of Dirs., ACLU, 1983-; National Exec. Cttee., 1985-; National Counsel, 1986-91; National Pres., ACLU, 1991-; *interests:* constitutional law, civil liberties, international human rights; *memberships:* Exec. Cttee., Human Rights Watch, 1989-91; Board of Dirs., Asia Watch, 1987-, Vice-Chwn., 1989-91, Middle East Watch, 1989-91, Coalition to Free Soviet Jewry, 1984-; Advisory Board, Soviet Jewry Legal Advocacy Centre, 1987-; Steering Cttee., New York Legal Cncl. for Soviet Jewry, 1987-; ACLU Advisory Cttee. on Reproductive Freedom Project, 1983-; National Legal Cttee., American Jewish Cttee., 1988-91; Advisory Board, New York Law School Journal of Human Rights, 1988; *professional

career: prof. of law, New York Law School, 1989-; Adjunct Prof., Columbia Univ. Grad. School of Business, Jan.-June 1990; visiting Prof. of law, New York Law school, Sept. 1988-Feb. 1989; Assc. Prof of Clinical Law, New York Univ. School of Law, Sept. 1987-Sept. 1988; Asst. Prof. of Clinical Law New York Univ., Sept.1984-Aug. 1987; Partner, Harvis & Zeichner, New York City, 1983-84; Assc. Attorney, Sullivan & Cromwell, New York City, 1978-83; Assc. Attorney, Lindquist & Vennum, Minneapolis, 1976-78; Judicial Clerk, Minnesota Supreme Court, 1975-76; editor, Harvard Law Review, 1975; Mem., Board of Dirs., National Coalition Against Censorship, 1988 and The Fund for Free Expression, 1990-; many other lectures and speeches on civil rights and other issues on the international and national domestic circuit; *honours and awards:* Ten Outstanding Young Americans, US Jaycees, 1986; The Outstanding Young People of the World Award, Jaycees Int., 1986; Outstanding Contribution to Human Rights, 1988-89; *publications:* Michigan Dept. of State Police V. Sitz: A Roadblock to Meaningful Judicial Enforcement of Individual Rights, 1991; Regulating Campus Hate Speech: A Modest Proposal?, 1990; Introduction to Symposium on Developments in Civil Rights and Employment Discrimination, 1990; Recent US and Int. Judicial Protection of Individuals Rights: A Comparative Legal Process Analysis and Proposed Synthesis, 1990; The Real ACLU, (with Mary Ellen Gale), 1990; many other articles between 1986 and 1988; *office address:* Ms Nadine Strossen, New York Law School, 57 Worth Street, New York, New York 10013, USA.

STURGULEWSKI, Jane Arliss; American, Alaska State Senator; *born:* 27 July 1927, Blaine, Washington; *parents:* Thomas Roe Wright and Henrietta Vanderlinden; *children:* Bernard Jr; *education:* Univ. of Washington, BA, 1949; *party:* Republican Party; *political career:* Chair, Greater Anchorage Planning and Zoning Commission, 1968-75; Commander, Anchorage Charter Commission, 1975; Mem., Capitol Site Select Cttee., 1975-76; Chair, Legislation Cttee., Alaska Municipal League, 1976-78; Vice-Chair Capitol Site Planning Commission, 1977-78; Alaska State Senator, 1978-; *memberships:* League of Women Voters; National Assn. of Parliamentarians; *professional career:* currently Dir., Denali Drilling Inc.; formely Dir., Alaska Pac Bancorp; *clubs:* YMCA; *office address:* Ms Jane Sturgulewski, 2957 Sheldon Jackson, Anchorage, Alaska 99508, USA.

SUBLET, Marie-Josèphe; French, Deputy; *born:* 10 February 1936, Lyons, France; *parents:* Léopold Feschet and Marie Feschet (née Fenon); *married:* Bernard Sublet, 1960; *religion:* Roman Catholic; *languages:* English; *education:* St Just High School, Lyon, university entrance examination; Technical College, Lyon, physical education diploma; *party:* Parti Socialiste (PS, Socialist Party), 1972; *political career:*

Mayor of Feyzin, Rhône, 1977-89; Deputy for Rhône, 1981-; *interests:* employment law, social issues human rights, women's rights, arbitration; *professional career:* physicist's aide, 1958; home help, 1961; director of home help service, 1971; *clubs:* League of Human Rights, 1981; *recreations:* cooking; *private address:* BP85, 69553 Feyzin Cédex, France; *office address:* Mme. Marie-Josèphe Sublet, L'Assemblée Nationale, 126 rue de L'Université, 75355 Paris, France.

SUCHOCKA, Hanna; Polish, Member of the Sejm; *office address:* Ms Hanna Suchocka, Sejm PRI, ul. Wiejska 4/6/8, 00-489 Warsaw, Poland; *phone:* (22) 28 70 01; 28 40 31.

SUGANO, Etsuko; Japanese, Member of the House of Representatives; *born:* 8 December 1942; *education:* Minato High School; *party:* Japan Communist Party (JCP); *political career:* former Vice-Chairperson, JCP Osaka Prefectural Assembly; former Dir., JCP Osaka Prefectural Women's and Children's Bureau; elected for Osaka 3, 1990-; Mem., House of Reps. Cttee. on Communications, 1990-; *office address:* Ms Etsuko Sugano, House of Representatives, 1-7-1 Nagata-cho, Chiyoda-ku, Tokyo 100, Japan; *phone:* (03) 5815111.

SULLIVAN, Jean; American, Member of the Republican Party National Executive Committee of Alabama; *born:* 9 May 1928, Selma, Alabama, USA; *parents:* Arthur Goldsby Sample and Roberta Sample (née Wood); *married:* Ira Oliver Sullivan, 1947; *children:* Arthur F., Ira Kent, James A., Connie Jean, Teresa Anne; *religion:* Methodist; *education:* Alabama College; *party:* Republican Party; *political career:* Exec. Mem., Dallas County Republican Cttee., Alabama, 1962-; delegate, Alabama State Republican Convention, 1962-68; Pres., Dallas County Republican Women, 1964-67; delegate, Republican National Women's Conference, 1964-67; Mem., Alabama State Republican Executive Cttee., 1966-; Vice-Chair, 1969-72; candidate, Alabama State Rep., 1970; Republican National Committeewomen, Alabama, 1972-; Mem., Republican National Exec. Cttee., 1974-; *memberships:* Chair, Glenn Andrews for Congress Campaign; Dallas County Rehabilitation Board; Women for Constitutional Govt; *honours and awards:* Outstanding Den Mother of Boy Scouts, 1956-60; *clubs:* Elks Emblem Club; CofC; Capitol Hill Club; Selma City Cncl. PTA; *office address:* Ms Jean Sullivan, 311 Cresthaven Ct., Selma, Alabama 36701, USA.

SULLIVAN, Kathryn Jean; Australian, Member of the House of Representatives; *born:* 8 March 1942, Brisbane, Queensland, Australia; *education:* Univ. of Queensland, BA and post grad. studies in accounting and business admin; *party:* Liberal Party, 1960; *political career:* State Sec., Young Liberals, Queensland, 1961-63 and Vice-Pres., 1963-64; Life Mem. of Young Liberals,

conferred, 1964; Exec. Mem., trade union for teachers in Independant Schools, 1964-66; founding Vice-Pres. then Pres., Univ. of Queensland Employees Assn., played a key role in the formulation of first industrial award for clerical staff, until 1974; Mem., Federated Clerks Union; Mem., Liberal Party State Executive, Queensland, 1974-77, 1979-81 and 1982-83; elected to Senate for Queensland, 1974, re-elected 1975, 1977 and 1983; youngest woman ever elected to Australian Parliament at the time of her election in 1974; Mem., joint House Cttee., 1974; Mem. and Chwn., several Senate Standing Cttees. and Estimates Cttees., 1974-84; Asst. Whip in the Senate, 1975-77; Mem. then Chwn., Coalition Parly. Policy Cttees. on Rural Affairs, Tourism, Education, Youth Affairs, Employment and Training, 1976-79, then Sec., 1985-88; Conferences, Delegations and Visits: Mem., Govt. Delegation to Japan and China, 1977; Mem., Commonwealth Delegation to Bangladesh, India and Sri Lanka, 1978; visited Phnom Penh with USA Congressional Women's Delegation, 1979; Mem., Australian Delegation to UN World Conference on Women, Copenhagen, visited Kampuchean refugee camps and Afghan refugee camps in Pakistan, 1980; Govt. Parly. Rep. on Australian Delegation to 35th Gen. Assembly of UN, 1980; Chwn., Senate House Cttee., 1981-83; Mem., Joint Standing Cttee. on the New Parliament House, 1981-89; Mem., Observer Delegation to 8th Gen. Assembly, AIPO, Jakarta, 1985 and Kuala Lumpur, 1988; Shadow Minister for Home Affairs and Admin. Services, 1983-84; elected for Moncreiff, Queensland, 1984, re-elected 1987 and 1990; first woman ever elected to both Senate and House of Reps.; Chwn., Coalition Parly. Policy Cttee. on Immigration and Ethnic Affairs, 1985-90; Exec. Mem., Amnesty International Parly. Group, 1986-; Vice-Pres., Australian Parly. Assn. for UNICEF, 1987-; Dep. Chwn., House of Reps. Standing Cttee. on Employment, Education and Training, 1987-90; Dep. leader Australian Parly. Delegation to Fiji, Western Samoa, Vanuatu, and Solomon Islands, 1989; Dep. Chwn. of Cttees., House of Reps., 1990-; Australian Parly. Opposition delegate and Dep. leader, bi-annual world conferences of the Inter-Parly. Union, 1990-93; *memberships:* Trustee, Queensland Children's Leukaemia Soc.; Patron: Beenleigh Eisteddford; Beenleigh Police Citizens' Youth Welfare Assn.; Endeavour Foundation (Gold Coast); Gold Coast Primary Schools Sports Assn.; Gold Coast Basketball Inc.; Southport Soccer Club; South-Eastern Queensland Sub-Chamber of Queensland Chamber of Agricultural Socs.; Canungra Show Sec.; Vietnam Vets. Assn. of Australia (Gold Coast Branch); Queensland Vice-Patron, Foundation 21; Associate Fellow, Australian Inst. of Management; Hon. Vice-Pres., Nat. Cncl of Women (Queensland); Hon. mem.: Australian Nat. Univ. Alumni; Beta Sigma Phi; ESA Women International; Springwood/ Rochdale Lioness Club; Young Liberal Movement (Queensland Div.); mem.: Amnesty International; Australian-American Assn.;

Australia-Britain Soc.; Australian Federation of Univ. Women; Beaudesert and District Health and Welfare Assn.; Country Women's Assn. (Queensland); Equal Opportunity Practitioners' Assn.; Family Planning Assn.; Friends of the Centre; Jim Killen Young Liberal Foundation; Nat. Foundation for Australian Women; National Trust of Queensland; Queensland Women's Electoral League; Red Shield Club; Royal Overseas League; Schizophrenia Fellow; Stockman's Hall of Fame and Outback Heritage Centre; Wongaburra Soc.; Zonta; *professional career:* mathematics and English teacher, 1964-66; Univ. of Queensland Administrative Officer, 1966-74; part-time lecturer, Queensland Institute of Technology, 1971-73; part-time Adult Education lecturer, 1971-73; *recreations:* theatre, reading, cookery, gardening, Australian Rules Football and basketball; *office address:* Ms Kathryn Sullivan, House of Representatives, Parliament House, Room M80, Canberra ACT, 2600, Australia; *phone:* (062) 726383.

SUNDBERG, Ingrid Elver; Swedish, Member of the Riksdag; *born:* 28 January 1925, New York, USA; *parents:* Carl August Jacobsson and Brit Jacobsson (née Rundquist); *married:* Ulf Carl Åke Sundberg, 1945; *children:* Katarina, Carl, Jonas, Mårten; *religion:* Protestant, Lutheran; *languages:* English, German, French; *education:* Stockholm University, Fil kand in Chemistry, Mathematics and Mechanics, 1945-50; *party:* Moderata Samlingspartiet (Moderate Party), 1950; *political career:* Chairwoman of the Parliamentary Cultural Cttee., 1982-; MP, 1982-; many other positions; *interests:* Cultural Affairs; *professional career:* teacher, 1950-60; Vice-Chwn., S. Region Nordbanken; *honours and awards:* Knighthood, the Order of the Northern Star; Honourable member of the Helsingkrona Student's Club, Lund University; *publications:* Possibility to Choose; *clubs:* Zonta; Falsterbo Golf Club; *recreations:* skiing, golf; *private address:* VÄstergaten 38, 23010 Skanör, Sweden; *office address:* Ms Ingrid Sundberg, Riksdag, Fack, S-100 12 Stockholm, Sweden.

SUSKIEWICZ, Halina Elzbieta; Polish, Member of the Sejm; *office address:* Ms Halina Elzbieta Suskiewicz, Sejm PRI, ul. Wiejska 4/6/8, 00-489 Warsaw, Poland; *phone:* (22) 28 70 01; 28 40 31.

SÜSSMUTH, Dr. Rita; German, President of the Bundestag; *born:* 17 February 1937, Wuppertal, Germany; *children:* one d; *religion:* Catholic; *education:* school leaving exam., 1956; studied romance languages and literature, Münster, Tübingen, Paris; state exam. for grammar school teaching; post graduate studies, educational sciences, sociology and psychology; Dr. of Philosophy, 1964; *party:* Christliche Demokratische Union (CDU, Christian Democratic Party); *political*

career: Mem., Scientific Advisory Cttee., Family Affairs, Federal Ministry of Youth, Family Affairs and Health, 1971-85; Mem., Commission for the Elaboration of the 3rd Report on the Situation of Families, 1977; Mem., Federal Advisory Cttee. on Youth Problems, 1982; Chairperson, Commission for the Elaboration of the 7th Report on the Situation of Young People, 1984; Vice-Pres., Family Assn. of German Catholics, 1980-; Chairperson, Commission of Marriage and the Family, Central Cttee. of German Catholics, 1982-; Chairperson, Federal Expert Cttee. on Family Policy, CDU, 1983; Federal Chairperson, Women's Assn. within the CDU, 1986-; Minister for Youth, Family Affairs, Women and Health, 1986-; Mem. of the Bundestag, 1987-, Pres., 1988-; *professional career:* Asst., Univ. of Stuttgart and Osnabrück, 1963-66; lecturer, College of Education, Ruhr, 1966; Prof., Ruhr Univ., Bochum, 1969; Full Prof. of Educational Sciences, Teacher Training College, Ruhr, 1971; Prof., Educational Sciences, Dortmund Univ., 1980-; Dir. Research Institute, Frau und Gesellschaft (Women and Society), Hanover, 1982; *office address:* Dr. Rita Süssmuth, Bundestag, Bundeshaus, 5300 Bonn 1, Germany.

SUTHERLAND, Countess of (24th in line, Scotland, cr. 1235) Elizabeth Millicent Janson Sutherland; British, Member of the House of Lords; *born:* 30 March 1921; *parents:* the late Lord Alistair Leveson Gower, MC, and Baroness Osten Driesen; *married:* Charles Noel Janson, 1946; *children:* three s., one decd., one d; *religion:* Church of England; *languages:* French, Italian; *education:* Queen's Coll., Harley Street and abroad; *party:* Conservative Party; *political career:* mem., House of Lords, 1963-; *interests:* land use, forestry, conservation of historic buildings; *memberships:* Patron. Highland Hospice, Inverness; *professional career:* Land Army, 1939-40; nurse and laboratory technician, Raigmore Hospital, Inverness, 1940-43; laboratory technician, St. Thomas's Hospital, London, 1943-45; fmr. Chmn., Trentham Gardens Ltd., Staffs.; Chmn., Dunrdoin Castle Ltd., Dir., (non-exec), and fmr. Chmn., The Northern Times; *clubs:* Patron, Scottish Red Cross, Sutherland Branch; Chief of Clan of Sutherland; *recreations:* reading, travelling, swimming; *private address:* 39 Edwardes Square, London W8, UK; House of Tongue, Lairg, Sutherland, Scotland; *office address:* The Countess of Sutherland, House of Lords, London SW1A 0PW.

SUVOVA, Dr. Hana; Czechoslovakian, Member of the Narodni Rada (Czech National Council); *born:* 2 June 1958; *party:* Komunistická Strana Ceskoslovenska (KSC, Communist party of Czechoslovakia); *office address:* Dr. Hana Suvová, Ceská národní rada, Snemovní 4, 110 00 Praha 1, Czechoslovakia; *phone:* (02) 2105.

SUZUKI, Kikuko; Japanese, Member of the House of Representatives; *born:* 2 August 1935; *education:* Chuo Univ; *party:* Japan Socialist Party (JSP); *political career:* former Mem. of Human Rights Protection Cttee.; elected for Tokyo 1, 1990; Mem., House of Reps. Cttee. on Judicial Affairs and on Construction, 1990-; *professional career:* lawyer; *office address:* Ms Kikuko Suzuki, House of Representatives, 1-7-1 Nagata-cho, Chiyoda-ku, Tokyo 100, Japan; *phone:* (03) 5815111.

SWILDENS-ROZENDAAL, Willie (Wilhelmine); Dutch, Member of the Second Chamber; *born:* 17 February 1945, the Hague, Netherlands; *parents:* Johan Willem Rozendaal and Hermina Rozendaal (née Kording); *married:* Pieter Paul Swildens, 1965; *children:* Pieter, Co; *languages:* French, German, English; *education:* Gymnasium (eg. A-levels), Gouda; 1957-64; Univ. of Amsterdam, law, 1964-68; Univ. of Amsterdam, LLM, 1980-81; *party:* Partij van de Arbeid (PvdA, Labour Party), 1972; *political career:* Secretary, PvdA, district North-Holland North, 1975-81; Mem., Provincial Board, North-Holland, 1982-87; Mem., Second Chamber, 1986-; *interests:* nature, agriculture, environment, spatial order, water policies, justice, sexual assault, homosexual emancipation and equal rights; *professional career:* Assitant to Mem. of Second Chamber, 1981-86; *clubs:* Protection of Birds, Monuments of Nature, North-Holland Nature, and others; *office address:* Mevr. Willie Swildens-Rozendaal, Tweede Kamer der Staten-Generaal, Binnenhof 1A, Postbus 20018, The Hague, Netherlands.

SY DIALLO, Mata; Senegalese, Minister-Delegate for Emigration; *office address:* Ms Mata Sy Diallo, Assemblee National, Place Tascher, Dakar, Senegal; *phone:* 23 10 99; 21 16 29.

SYNODINOU, Anna; Greek, Member of Parliament; *party:* Nea Demokratia (ND, New Democracy Party); *political career:* MP, A' Athens, 1974-85; MP, A' Athens, 1989; Alternate Minister of Social Services, 1977-80; *professional career:* actress; *office address:* Vouli, Parliament Building, Syntagma, Greece.

T

TABAKAUCORO, Adi Tamari Finau; Fijian, Minister for Women, Social Welfare and Culture; *education:* Adi Cakobau School, 1955-62; Suva Grammar School, 1963; Victoria Univ. of Wellington, New Zealand, BA, 1964-67; Auckland Secondary Teachers College, Epsom, New Zealand, 1968; *political career:* Training Officer, Dept. of Localisation and Training, 1969; Assistant Secretary, Ministry of Social Welfare and Urban Development and Housing, 1971; Assistant Secretary, Central Planning Office, 1975; Program Assistant, United Nations Development Programme, South Pacific Office, 1976; Mem., National Economic Council, 1986; Mem., Great Council of Chiefs; Minister for Women, Social Welfare and Culture, 1987-; *professional career:* Junior Fellow, Institute of Social and Administrative Studies, Univ. of the South Pacific, 1981, Fellow in Social Administration, 1982, Fellow in Development Planning, 1985; *office address:* Ms Adi Tabakaucoro, Ministry for Women's Affairs and Social Welfare, 5A and 5B Ma'afu Street, Flagstaff, Suva, Fiji; *phone:* 312681; 312908.

TADDEI, Blenda Maria; Italian, Deputy; *born:* 8 September 1946, Castelfranco di Sotto, Pisa; *education:* Teaching qualification; *party:* Partito Democratico della Sinistra (PDS, Party of the Democratic Left); *political career:* Prov. and Regional Leader, UDI; mem. Fed. Cttee., Pisa; mem. Regional Committee; Tuscany, PCI, 1976; Councillor and Assessor, 1980-; Mayor of S. Croce sull' Arno, 1985-; mem. Nat Council of League of Autonomous Authorities and Local Powers; elected Deputy, Pisa-Livorno-Lacca-Massa Carrara, 1987; Sec. Cttee. on Budget, Treasury, and Planning; *professional career:* Administrator; *office address:* Ms Blenda Taddei, Camera dei Deputati, Montecitorio, 00186 Rome, Italy.

TAINA (née Jussila), Anneli Kristiina; Finnish, Member of the Eduskunta; *born:* 21 June 1951, Imatra, Finland; *parents:* Toivo Aleksanteri Jussila and Jenny Alma (née Lamppu); *married:* Heikki Jorma Taina, 1972; *religion:* Lutheran; *languages:* Finnish, English; *education:* Univ. of Tampere, MA Political Science, Social Politics, 1970-75; *party:* Kansallinen Kokoomus (KoK, Coalition Party), 1968; *political career:* Mem. of the Eduskunta; Vice-Pres., Cttee. on Social Welfare and Health; Mem., City Cncl., Tampere; Vice-Pres., Women's Union of the Coalition Party, 1990-; *interests:* social politics; *office address:* Ms Anneli Taina, Eduskunta, 00102 Helsinki, Finland.

TAKASAKI, Yuko; Japanese, Member of the House of Councillors; *born:* 6 November 1948; *education:* Hokkaido Univ; *party:* Japan Communist Party; *political career:* elected for Hokkaido, 1990; Dir., House of Cllrs. Special Cttee. on Industry, Energy and Resources, 1990-; *memberships:* Executive Cttee., Sapporo Lawyers' Assn; *office address:* Ms Yuko Takasaki, House of Councillors, 1-7-1 Nagata-cho, Tokyo 100, Japan; *phone:* (03) 5813111.

TAKEMOTO MINK, Patsy; American, Member of the House of Representatives; *born:* 6 December 1927, Maui, Hawaii; *parents:* Mitama Takemoto and Suematsu Takemoto; *married:* John Francis Mink, 1951; *children:* Gwendolyn; *religion:* Protestant; *education:* Univ. of Hawaii, BA, 1948; Chicago Law School, DL, 1951; *party:* Democratic Party; *political career:* Charter Pres., Young Domocrats, Oahu, 1954-56; State Pres., Young Democrats,, Hawaii, 1956-58; Hawaii State Rep., 1956-58; National Vice-Pres., National Young Democrats, 1957-59; Hawaii State Senator, 1958-59 and 1962-64; Member of House of Reps. for Hawaii, 1965-77; Sec., 89th Democrat Congressional Club, 1965-77; Mem., Congressmen for Peace Through Law, 1965-67; Chwn., US-China Cttee., 1969-71; Mem., Foreign Policy-World Order Cttee.; Vice-Pres., Democratic Study Group, 1967-71 and 1975-77; Vice-Chwn., Task Force on Education, 1971; Mem., Congressional Reform Task Force, 1971; Mem., Advisory Cttee. on State-Urban Relations, Cncl. of State Govts., 1968; Mem., Commission on Rules Review, Democrat National Convention, 1969-71; American Cncl., Young Political Leaders, 1969-71; National Advisory Board, National Movement for the Student Vote, 1971; Vice-Pres., American Democratic Action, 1973-77, Pres., 1978-81; delegate, Democrat National Convention, 1960, 1972 and 1980; Mem., Credentials Cttee., 1980; delegate, Democrat National Mid-Term Conference, 1974; Asst. Sec.-of-State for Oceans and International Environmental and Scientific Affairs, 1977-78; Mem., Honolulu City Cncl., 1983-87, Chwn., 1983-85; *memberships:* American Assn. for UN; NAACP; Hawaii Assn. to Help Retarded Children; Rural and Univ. YWCA; Planned Parenthood; National Women's Law Centre; Public Citizen;

professional career: lecturer, Univ. of Hawaii, 1952-56, 1959-62 and 1979-81; attorney-at-law, 1953-65; *honours and awards:* Hon. Degrees: LLD, Lindenwood College, 1965; LHD, Wilson College, 1965; Duff's Inst.; Chaminade College, 1975; Syracuse Univ., 1976; Whitman College, 1982; Alii Award, 4-H Clubs Hawaii, 1969; Freedom Fund and Recognition Award, Honolulu NAACP, 1971; Rehabilitation Service Madallion, 1971; Distinguished Humanitarian Award, St. Louis YWCA, 1972; Human Rights Award, American Federation of Teachers, 1975; *office address:* Mrs Patsy Takemoto Mink, P.O. Box 4452, Honolulu 96812, Hawaii.

TAKEMURA, Yasuko; Japanese, Member of the House of Councillors; *born:* 5 December 1933; *education:* Seiwa College; *party:* Japan Socialist Party (JSP); *political career:* elected once as House of Reps. and now as House of Cllrs. for Hokkaido, 1990; Dir., House of Cllrs. Special Cttee. on Okinawa and Northern Problems and Mem., House of Cllrs. Cttee. on the Budget, 1990-; *clubs:* Cttee. person of YWCA; *office address:* Ms Yasuko Takemura, House of Councillors, 1-7-1 Nagata-cho, Tokyo 100, Japan; *phone:* (03) 5813111.

TAKLA, Dr. Laila; Egyptian, Member of the People's Assembly and Member of the Executive Committee of the Inter-Parliamentary Union; *office address:* Dr. Laila Takla, People's Assembly, Magles Al-Shaab Street, Cairo, Egypt; *phone:* (02) 3545000.

TALL, Aminata; Senegalese, Minister-Delegate for Literacy and the Promotion of National Languages; *office address:* c/o Ministry of National Education, rue Calmette et René Ndiaye, BP 699, Dakar, Senegal.

TAM, Hon. Maria Wai-chu; Hong Kong, Member of the Executive and Legislative Councils; *born:* 2 November 1945, Hong Kong; *education:* St. Paul's Co-Education College, Hong Kong; London Univ., LLB; *political career:* Chmn., Transport Advisory Cttee.; Mem., Council of the Chinese Univ. of Hong Kong; Mem., Education Commission; Mem., Hong Kong Assn. of Business and Professional Women; *professional career:* Barrister-at-Law; mem. of Gray's Inn; *honours and awards:* CBE, Justice of the Peace; *clubs:* Hon. Mem., Zonta Club of Hong Kong; *office address:* The Hon. Ms Maria Tam, The Legislative Council, Government House, Hong Kong.

TAM WONG, Hon. Rosanna Yick-ming; Hong Kong, Member of the Executive and Legislative Councils; *born:* 15 August 1952, Hong Kong; *parents:* Wong Chun Chung (father) and Poon Chor Ying (mother); *married:* Alfred Tam Yat-cheung, 1979; *public role of spouse:* paediatric consultant; *children:* two; *religion:* Christian; *languages:* English, Cantonese, Mandarin; *education:*

St. Stephen's Girls' College; Univ. of Hong Kong, B.Soc.Sc.; Univ. of Toronto, Canada, MSW.; London School of Economics and Political Science, Univ. of London, UK, M.Sc.; Chinese Univ. of Hong Kong and HKCSS, Diploma in Executive Management; *political career:* Chwn., Commission on Youth; Mem., Exec. Cttee., Hong Kong Council of Social Service; Chwn., Social Welfare Advisory Cttee.; Mem., Fight Crime Cttee.; Mem., Standing Cttee. on Young Offenders; Mem., Broadcasting Authority; Mem., Court of the Univ. of Hong Kong; Mem., Council of the Univ. of Hong Kong; Mem., Departmental Advisory Cttee. for Public and Social Administration, City Polytechnic of Hong Kong; Mem., Hong Kong Cttee. for UNICEF; Mem., Management Cttee. of Hong Kong Christian Service; Mem., Vocational Training Cncl.; Ex-officio Mem., Po Leung Kuk Advisory Board; *interests:* social services, youth services; *memberships:* Hong Kong Social Workers Assn; *professional career:* General Sec., The Hong Kong Federation of Youth Groups; *honours and awards:* Ten Outstanding Young Persons' Award, 1985; Justice of the Peace, 1989; OBE, 1990; *clubs:* Zonta Club of Hong Kong; *recreations:* reading, music; *private address:* D6 Senior Staff Quarters, Queen Mary Hospital, Pokfulam Road, Hong Kong; *office address:* The Hon. Mrs Rosanna Tam Wong, Suite 906, Duke of Windsor Social Service Bldg., 15 Hennessy Road, Wanchai, Hong Kong.

TARDIF, Monique B.; Canadian, Member of the House of Commons and Parliamentary Secretary to the Solicitor General of Canada; *born:* 8 January 1936, Quebec, Canada; *children:* three; *languages:* French, English; *education:* Collège des Ursulines, Quebec City, Classical Studies, BA, 1956; Univ. of Laval, Quebec City, law studies, 1965; *party:* Progressive Conservative Party (PCP); *political career:* Gen.-Sec., Interministerial Cncl. on Road Security, participated in the development of the road security code, co-ordinated the implementation of the new code by those concerned; Mem. of the Board of Governors, Office for Consumer Protection, 1980-81, Vice-Pres., 1981-84; Mem. of Parliament for Charlesbourg, House of Commons, 1984-; Observer, Exercice 'Brave Lion', Northern Norway, with Canadian Parly. delegation from the Standing Cttee. on National Defence, 1986; Delegate, annual meeting of Cttee. on Parly. Affairs in Brazil, (part of the Association international des parlementaires de langue française, International Association of French-Speaking Parliamentarians), 1986; Parly. Sec. to the Minister of Regional Industrial Expansion, active in the dismantling of FIRA, in creation of Investment Canada through Bill C-15, involved in creation of Bill C-23 for services and programs for small businesses, Bill C-66, reorganization of Canada Development Corp., active on Standing Cttee. on Regional Industrial Expansion, consideration of departmental appropriations, privitizaion of the Havilland, Industrial and Regional Development

Program (IRDP), 1985-86; Parly. Sec. to Minister of National Health and Welfare, active in Parly. proceedings on passage of the legislation on pharmaceutical products, Bill C-22, involved in the development of National Approaches to Action Against Family Violence, intensive collaboration in formulation of Senior Citizens' Independence Program, 1986-88; represented Canadian Govt., World Health Assembly, Geneva, 1987; Parly. Sec. to Minister of National Health and Welfare, Parly. Sec. to Minister of State for Seniors Citizens, 1986-88; re-elected to Parliament for Charlesbourg, House of Commons, 1988; Parly. Sec. to Minister of Supply and Services, 1989; Parly. Sec. to Solicitor General of Cananda, 1991; *memberships:* Mem., Board of Governors, Grands Ballets Canadiens, Montreal, Pres., Quebec Section; *professional career:* Mem., Board of Governors, Quebec Automobile Insurance Company, 1978-81; Dir., Consumer Protection Service, Automobile Club of Quebec, 1976-80, responsible for media relations and for relations with the Quebec Govt., review and study of bills pertaining to automobile insurance, consumer protection, energy conservation, highway code; weekly column in Soleit, Quebec City; monthly column, Protégez vous, (magazine); series of radio broadcasts at Radio Canada; interviews for TV program Consommateurs avertis (consumers alerted); *clubs:* representative of Quebec Automobile club at the Canadian Automobile Assn; *office address:* Mme. Monique Tardif, House of Commons, Parliament Buildings, Wellington Street, Ottawa, Ontario K1A OA6, Canada; *phone:* (613) 957 3744; *fax:* 952 0874.

TARJAN, Dr. Anna; Hungarian, Political Secretary of State at the Ministry for the Environment and Regional Policy; *born:* 27 August 1932, Lenti, Hungary; *parents:* József Tajnafoi and Anna Tajnafoi (née Keseru); *married:* Dr. László Tarján, 1957; *children:* Katalin, Zsuzsanna; *religion:* Roman Catholic; *languages:* Hungarian, German, Latin, English; *education:* Univ. of Forestry, Sopron, M.Sc., forestry, 1955, environmental engineering, 1977, Dr.Sc., 1982; *party:* Independent Small-Holders' Party (ISHP); *political career:* political Sec.-of-State, 1990-; Mem., National Board Political Commission, ISHP, 1990-; Mem., of Parliament, 1990-; *interests:* economic politics; *memberships:* National Assn. of Forestry; *professional career:* forest engineer, Somogy County, 1955-60; Senior Officer, Forestry Office, 1960-77; Inspector, National Authority for the Environment and Nature Conservation, Somogy County, 1977-79; Sec., Environment and Nature Conservation, Somogy County Cncl., 1979-89; Dir., Forest Economy, Forest Office, Somogy County, 1989-90; *honours and awards:* Széchenyi Medal, National Environmental Authority, 1977; Medal for the Development of the Human Environment, NEA, 1987; Pro Urbe Medal, Hungarian Assn. of Architects, 1989; *publications:* Dél-Balaton és környéke, 1984; Somogy megye védett természeti értékei, 1989; around 30 technical articles, since 1970; *clubs:* Environmental Protection Club; *recreations:* active in tourism clubs; *private address:* H-1054., Budapest, Bank u. 3., Hungary; *office address:* Dr. Anna Tarján, Országgyűlés, Kossuth L. tér 1-3, Budapest V, Hungary; *phone:* 22 5058; 22 5059.

TASCA, Catherine; French, Minister for Francophony; *born:* 13 December 1941, Lyons, France; *parents:* Angelo Tasca and Alice Tasca (née Naturel); *children:* Laura; *education:* first degree in law; Institute of Political Studies, Paris, diploma; National School of Administration, 1965-67; *political career:* civil administrator, Ministry of Culture, 1967-72; director, Grenoble Cultural Office, 1972-77; member of Commission for Quality of Radio and Television Broadcasts and member of Economic and Social Cttee. of Rhône-Alpes Region, 1974-77; Chmn. of Board of Experts for Assistance to Theatrical Companies in Ile de France Region, 1985-86; member of National Commission for Communication and Liberties, 1986-88; Minister Delegate, Ministry of Culture, Communication, Major Works and the Bicentenary, with special responsibility for Communications, 1988; Minister for Francophony; *professional career:* representative to National Office for Arts Broadcasting 1977-78; administrator of l'Ensemble Intercontemporain, orchestra, 1978-82; co-director of Nanterre-Amandiers Theatre, 1982-86; *office address:* Mme. Catherine Tasca, Ministry of Foreign Affairs, 7 rue de Talleyrand, 75007 Paris, France.

TAYLOR, Ann (Winnifred Ann); British, Member of Parliament; *born:* 2 July 1947; *parents:* the late John Walker and Doreen Walker (née Bowling); *married:* David Taylor, 1966; *children:* one s., one d; *education:* Bolton School; Bradford University; Sheffield University; *party:* Labour Party; *political career:* mem., Assn. of University Teachers; Cllr., Holmfirth Urban District Cncl., 1972-74; Member of Parliament for Bolton West, 1974-83, and Dewsbury, 1987-; PPS to Sec. of State for Education and Science, 1975-76, and to Sec. of State for Defence, 1976-79; Asst. Govt. Whip, 1977-79; Opposition Front Bench Spokesman on Education, 1979-81, on Housing, 1981-83, on the Home Office 1987-88, and on Environment, 1988-; *interests:* education; Home affairs; housing; environmental policy; *professional career:* part-time tutor, Open University; Monitoring Officer, Housing Corp., 1985-87; *honours and awards:* Hon. Fellow, Birkbeck College, University of London; *office address:* Mrs Ann Taylor, House of Commons, London SW1A OAA.

TAYLOR, Selina; Ghana, Secretary in the PNDC Secretariat for the National Commission for Women and Development; *office address:* Ms Selina Taylor,

Commission for Women and Development, The Castle, Osu, PO Box 1627, Ghana.

TAZDAIT, Djida; French, Member of the European Parliament; *born:* 8 April 1957, Algeria, North Africa; *parents:* Tazdait and Bakouri; *religion:* Muslim; *languages:* Arabic, French, English, Italian, Berber; *education:* Charvieu College (Rhône) BEPC, La Martinière Grammar School (Lyon) BACFT, Faculty of Medecine Alexis Carrell, Lab. Assistant in applied Biology, Faculty of Lyon II, sociology (psychology), Audiovisual; *party:* allied to the Green group at the European Parliament; *political career:* Member of the Commission for jurisdiction and the law of the citizen; Member of the commission for social affairs; Member of the commission for women's rights; Vice President of the EEC/Maghreb delegation (President Cheysson); First vice president of the commission of enquiry against racism in Europe; MEP, 1989-; *interests:* Rights of man, migratory tendencies, immigration, women, social issues, racism, audiovisual, television, journalism, sciences, north/south relations; *professional career:* Film director - Rhône Alpes 'Escale Image', 1982-8912/06/82 - 18/06/89; *clubs:* President of the JALB (Associating Young Arabs of Lyon and its surroundings), 1981-; Founding member of 'Escale Image'; *private address:* 5 rue de la Platière, 69000 Lyon BP 1062, France; *office address:* Mlle. Djida Tazdait, European Parliament, Centre Européen, Plateau de Kirchberg, BP 2929, Luxembourg.

TEAGUE, Marjorie; American, Executive Director of the Republican Party of New Mexico; *born:* 15 March 1935, La Grande, Oregon, USA; *parents:* William Garrett and Stella Garrett (née Rogers); *married:* Arthur William Teague, 1956; *children:* Edmond, Laura; *languages:* English, French; *education:* Northwestern School of Business, Portland, Oregon, Assc. Degree in Business Management, 1953-54; *party:* Republican Party, 1956; *political career:* Vice-Chwn. then Exec. Dir., Republican Party of Bernalillo County, New Mexico, 1981-84; Finance Dir., Republican Party of New Mexico, 1985; Exec. Dir., Republican Party of New Mexico, 1986-; *interests:* candidate recruitment, party organisation; *memberships:* Republican National Cttee.; Epsilon Sigma Alpha (ESA); *professional career:* Admin. Asst., Federal Aviation Agency, Pendleton, Oregon, 1961-69; proprietor, Marje's Wine Factory, Portland, Oregon, 1977-79; *honours and awards:* Outstanding Performance Award, FAA, 1966, 1967; Sustained Superior Award, FAA, 1968; Ousstanding Member Award, FSA, 1963; Volunteer Mother of the Year, Salem Schools, 1971; Oustanding Service Award, Republican Party of New Mexico, 1991; *clubs:* Rio Rancho Golf and Country Club; *private address:* 4910 Simon Drive NW, Albuquerque, New Mexico 8714, USA; *office address:* Mrs Marjorie Teague, Republican Party of New Mexico, P.O. Box 36900, Albuquerque 87176, USA.

TEALDI, Giovanna Maria; Italian, Deputy; *born:* 11 August 1942, Mondovi, Cuneo; *party:* Democrazia Cristiana (DC, Christian Democratic Party); *political career:* Deputy, Cuneo-Alessandria-Asti, 1987; mem. Cttee. on Public and Private Work; *professional career:* Dir., Travel Agency; *office address:* Ms Giovanna Tealdi, Camera dei Deputati, Montecitorio, 00186 Rome, Italy.

TEDESCO TATO, Giglia; Italian, Senator; *born:* 22 January 1926, Rome, Italy; *party:* Partito Democratico della Sinistra (PDS, Party of the Democratic Left); *political career:* mem. Catholic Communist Movement; mem. Central Cttee. of PCI from 1960; mem. Leadership, PCI from 1984; Employee, Ministry for the Constituent Assembly, Ministry of Treasury and Ministry of Labour; Leader, Nat. League of Co-operatives 1956; Head of Nat. Cttee. on Co-operatives; mem. International Co-operatives Alliance; Represented Italy in Central Cttee. of International Guild of Co-operatives, 1948-56; mem. Nat. Secretariat, FGCI, 1956- 59; mem. Italian Women's Union, 1945; Leadership Cttee. 1949; mem. Nat. Presidency, from 1959; Mem Nat. Executive from 1968; mem Nat. Cttee. from 1978-82; mem. International Democratic Women's Federation; mem. Congresses, Delegations, Study Groups on Women's Problems and Social Problems in all European countries and USA; elected Senator, Arezzo, 1968-76; mem. Cttee. on Justice; mem. Cttee. on authorisations to prosecute; mem. Executive of Cttee. on Supervision of Radio-TV Services; Sec. of Parly. Group; mem. Secretariat of Study Centre for initiatives for reform of the State; re-elected Senator, Montevarchi, 1976-; mem. Cttee. on Justice; Vice-Pres. of Parly. Group; re-elected Senator, 1979; Vice Pres. of Parly. Group; mem. Regulatory Body; mem. Parly. Delegation to NATO Assembly; mem. Cttee. on Constitutional Affairs; *office address:* Ms Giglia Tedesco Tato, Senato della Repubblica, Palazzo Madama, 00100 Rome, Italy.

TEED, Nancy Elizabeth; Canadian, Senator; *born:* 26 February 1949, Saint John, New Brunswick, Canada; *married:* William H. Teed; *public role of spouse:* Saint John Lawyer; *children:* Jennifer, Harrison; *party:* Progressive Conservative; *political career:* Senator; elected to New Brunswick Legislative Assembly, Mem. for Saint John South, 1978, re-elected 1982; New Brunswick Cabinet, Minister of Social Services, 1982; Minister of Health and Community Service, 1985; Minister responsible for the Alcoholism and Drug Dependency Commission; *memberships:* New Brunswick Red Cross Soc.; Saint John Heritage Trust; YMCA Women's Network; *professional career:* owned and managed several businesses in Saint John; owns interior decorating business, Interiors with Distinction; Mem., Board, Exec. Cttee., Nat. Capital Commission; Chairperson, Saint John Salvation Army Advisory Board; Corporate Sec., Exec. Cttee., Saint John Market

Square Corporation; *honours and awards:* Honoured by Canadian Assn. for the Mentally Retarded for her work and support, 1986; *office address:* The Honourable Senator Nancy Teed, Senate, Parliament Buildings, Wellington Street, Ottawa, Ontario K1A 0A4, Canada; *phone:* (613) 992 4416.

TEGELAAR-BOONACKER, Haty; Dutch, Member of the Second Chamber; *born:* 3 September 1930, Weesp, Netherlands; *party:* Christen Democratisch Appel (CDA, Christian Democratic Appeal); *political career:* Mem. of town council, Rijswijk, 1966-86; active Mem. of town council, Rijswijk, 1980-86; Pres. Head Office CH-Women; Pres. Dutch Section of European Women Union; vice Pres. CHU and CDA; Mem. of Second Chamber, 1986-; *professional career:* mathematical statistician, TNO; *private address:* Utrechtseweg 20, 6866 Ck Heelsum, the Netherlands; *office address:* Mevr. Haty Tegelaar-Boonacker, Tweede Kamer der Staaten-Generaal, Binnenhof 1A, Postbus 20018, The Hague, Netherlands.

TENNET, Elizabeth; New Zealander, Member of Parliament; *parents:* Maurice Tennet and Maurice Tennet; *married:* John Francis Galvin, 1978; *public role of spouse:* solicitor; *children:* one; *languages:* English; *education:* Victoria Univ., Wellington; *party:* Labour Party; *political career:* mem., Wellington Polytechnic Council and Wellington Business Development Board; chaired, Wellington Harbour City Conference, the Govt. Employment Promotion Conference, Labour Women's Council and the Wellington Labour Regional Council; Union secretary; mem., National Executive of the Labour Party; MP for Island Bay; *professional career:* research worker for the Arbitration Court; factory inspector in the Labour Department, union secretary; *honours and awards:* 1990 Commemorative Medal; *recreations:* tramping and piano; *private address:* PO Box 7353, Wellington South, New Zealand; *office address:* Ms Elizabeth Tennet, C/O Parliament Buildings, Wellington, New Zealand.

TERBORG, Margitta; German, Member of the Bundestag; *born:* 23 September 1941, Bunzlau/Schlesien; *children:* two; *religion:* Protestant; *education:* elementary school; University of Bremen, from 1969; state examination in social paedagogy, 1972; *party:* Sozialdemokratische Partei Deutschlands (SPD, Social Democratic Party of Germany), 1965; *political career:* member of Socialist Youth of Germany - The Falcons, 1960-65; member of Exec. Cttee., SPD Nordenham, since 1965; member of sub-district, SPD Wesermarsch, since 1968; member of town council, Nordenham, 1968-81; dep. mayor, 1972-76; chmn., SPD Nordenham, since 1975; mayor, 1976-80; member of district assembly, Wesermarsch, since 1976; recording clerk; member of regional Exec. Cttee., SPD Weser-Ems, since 1980; mem. Bundestag,

Delmenhorst-Wesermarsch-Oldenburg-Land; *professional career:* training as children's nurse, 1956-59; group leader at kindergarten, 1959-63; teacher at professional training school, 1972-78; practical school examinations for youth leaders, Niedersachsen, 1975; teacher at special school, 1978-80; member of Gewerkschaft Öffentliche Dienste, Transport und Verkehr (ÖTV, Trade Union for Public and Transport Services); *clubs:* Arbeiterwohl fahrt (AWO, Labour Welfare Organisation); Reichsbund; *private address:* 2890 Nordenham, West Germany; *office address:* Frau Margitta Terborg, Bundeshaus, 5300 Bonn 1, West Germany.

TERPSTRA, Erica G.; Dutch, Member of the Second Chamber; *born:* 26 May 1943, the Hague, Netherlands; *children:* two; *languages:* Dutch, English, German, French; *education:* Univ. of Leiden, sinology; *party:* Volkspartij voor Vrijheid en Democratie (VVD, People's Party for Freedom and Democracy); *political career:* Mem. of Second Chamber, 1977-; Mem. of County Council of Utrecht, 1987-91; *interests:* development co-operation, public health care of elderly, policy of handicapped people, welfare; *memberships:* National Committee for Refugees; National Revalidation Fund; Board, Univ. of Amsterdam; Global Forum of Parliamentary and Spiritual Leaders; Global Cttee. of Parliamentarians on Population and Development; *professional career:* journalist; *honours and awards:* Knight of the Oranje-Nassau Order; Cross of Honour of the Royal House of Oranje; Knight of the Order of the Dutch Lion; Olympic Medallist, swimming, Rome, 1960, Tokyo, 1964; *private address:* Soesterveste 20, 3432 Rk Nieuwsegein, The Netherlands; *office address:* Mevr. Erica Terpstra, Tweede Kamer der Staten-Generaal, Binnenhof 1A, Postbus 20018, The Hague, Netherlands.

TERRY, Mary Sue; American, Attorney General of Virginia; *born:* 28 August 1947, Martinsville, Virginia, USA; *parents:* Nathaniel Chatham Terry and Nannie Cooper Terry; *religion:* Baptist; *education:* Univ. of Richmond, Westhampton College, Virginia, BA, 1969; Univ. of Virginia, Charlottesville, MA, 1970 and JD, 1973; *party:* Democratic Party; *political career:* Attorney General of Virginia; *professional career:* lawyer, private practice, 1973-; Chwn., Board of Dirs., First Nat. Bank Stuart, Virginia; *office address:* Ms Mary Terry, P.O. Box 369, Stuart, Virginia 24171, USA.

TER VELD, Elske; Dutch, Secretary of State for Social Affairs and Employment; *born:* 1 August 1944, Groningen, Netherlands; *parents:* Romke Bertus ter Veld and Christina ter Veld (née Stappershoef); *languages:* Dutch, English, German, French; *education:* Higher Professional School, Academy for social and cultural work, 1963-68; *party:* Partij van de Arbeid

(PvdA, Labour Party), 1966; *political career:* Mem. of Second Chamber, 1981-89; Pres., Secretary for Women, FNV/NVV (trades unions), 1972-81; Sec. of State for Social Affairs and Employment, Nov. 1989-; *professional career:* leader, working training for youth, training centre Assen, 1968-70; Pres., Communal House for Young People, De Heerd Groningen, 1970-72; *publications:* Vrouw en Beleid, Polak & v. Gennep, SARA, 1985; *office address:* Mevr. Elske Ter Veld, Ministry of Employment and Social Security, Cinna V. Hannoverstraat 4, POB 90001- 250g LV, The Hague, The Netherlands.

TESTA, Simone; Seychelles, Minister of Education; *office address:* Ms Simone Testa, Minister for Education, Information and Youth, PO Box 648, Mount Fleuri, Seychelles.

TEUBNER, Maria Luise; German, former Member of the Bundestag; *born:* 3 November 1951, Ratingen; *religion:* none; *education:* Geschwister School grammar school, Ratingen, Abitur (advanced matriculation examination), 1970; University of Freiburg, sociology, philosophy, history, Germanic studies, 1970-75; state examination in German and history, 1975; *party:* Die Grünen (Green Party), 1984; *political career:* member of municipal council, Lahr, 1984-87; spokesman of Die Grünen group, municipal council, Lahr, 1984-87; member of Gewerkschaft Erziehung und Wissenschaft (GEW, Trade Union for Education and Science); mem. of Bundestag, party list of Baden-Württemberg, 1987-90; *professional career:* asst. teacher, Schools of Commerce, Lahr, 1976-77; secondary school teacher (civil servant) of German, history and social studies, Schools of Commerce-Integrated Professional Secondary School, Lahr; *clubs:* Society for Endangered Peoples; Bund für Umwelt und Naturschutz Deutschland (BUND, Society for the Environment and the Conservation of Nature); *office address:* Frau Maria Teubner, Bundeshaus, 5300 Bonn 1, West Germany.

THALÉN, Ingela; Swedish, Minister of Health and Social Affairs; *born:* 1 October 1943, Gothenburg, Sweden; *parents:* Erland Ericsson and Sara Ericsson (née Ström); *party:* Sveriges Socialdemokratiska Arbetarepartiet (SAP, Swedish Social Democratic Labour Party); *political career:* mem. Young Social Democrats, 1965-68; mem. Stockholm Labour District, 1968, 1978-79; mem. SAP, Party Board, 1969; mem. Stockholm County Council, 1970-72 and Gothenburg Labour district, 1975-78; political sec., Järfälla municipality, 1979-81; mem. municipal council working cttee., 1981-87; municipal cnclr., Järfälla, 1982-87; chmn., municipal council, 1983-87; Cabinet Minister and Minister for Labour, 1987-90; MP, 1988-; Cabinet Minister and Minister of Health and Social Affairs, 1990-; *professional career:* Girl Guides, 1961; Tornburg Lundberg Ltd., 1962-65; Are Ltd., 1972-74;

Renés Paint and Perfume, 1979; *private address:* Vibblabyvägen 10, 175 41 Järfälla, Sweden; *office address:* Ms Ingela Thalén, Ministry of Health and Social Affairs, Jakobsgt. 26, 103 33 Stockholm, Sweden.

THATCHER, Rt. Hon. Margaret Hilda, PC 1970; British, Member of Parliament; *born:* 13 October 1925; *parents:* the late Alfred Roberts; *married:* Denis Thatcher, 1951; *children:* one s., one d. (twins); *education:* Kesteven and Grantham High School; Somerville College, Oxford University, MA, BSc; *party:* Conservative Party; *political career:* Member of Parliament for Finchley, 1959-; Joint Parliamentary Sec., Ministry of Pensions and National Insurance, 1961-64; Front Bench Spokesman on Pensions and National Insurance, 1964; Opposition Front Bench Spokesman on Housing and Land, 1965-66, and on Treasury, 1966-67; Chief Opposition Spokesman on Power, 1967; mem. Shadow Cabinet, 1968; Shadow Minister for Transport, 1968, for Education, 1969; Sec. of State for Education and Science, 1970; Shadow Sec. of State for the Environment and Opposition Treasury Spokesman, 1974; Leader of the Conservative Party, 1975-90; Prime Minister and First Lord of the Treasury, 1979-90; *professional career:* Research Chemist, 1947-51; barrister 1954; *clubs:* Worshipful Company of Grocers (Hon. Freeman 1980); Hon. Bencher 1975, Hon. Master 1983, Gray's Inn; Royal Soc. (Fellow 1983); Carlton Club; *recreations:* music; reading; *office address:* The Rt. Hon. Margaret Thatcher, House of Commons, London SW1A OAA, United Kingdom.

THOMA, Maria; Greek, Member of Parliament; *party:* Panelliniou Socialistikou Kinema (PASOK, Panhellenic Socialist Movement), 1989; *political career:* MP, PASOK, Achaia, 1989; founding member of the Organisation of Scientists of PASOK, Patras; *professional career:* lawyer; *office address:* Vouli, Parliament Building, Syntagma, Greece.

THOMPSON, Marjorie; American, Chairwoman of the Campaign for Nuclear Disarmament, United Kingdom; *born:* St. Louis, Missouri, USA; *education:* Woodrow Wilson High School, Long Beech, California, USA, 1974; grad., Colorado College, USA, history (Hons.), 1978; London School of Economics, UK, MA, West European Politics, 1979; *political career:* joined Aldermaston, Burghfield, Greenham Link-Up and converted to CND, 1983; Parly. Officer, CND and responsible for establishing a national network of CND Parly. monitors, 1983-87; researcher foe Ann Clwyd, MP, 1987; elected Vice-Chwn., CND, 1987; Parly. Officer, Royal College of Nursing, 1988-90; elected Chwn., CND, 1990-; advisor, Royal College of Nursing Dept. of Policy and Practice (working with AIDS, Breast Care, Leukaemia, Cancer and Pollution Care nurses), Feb. 1991-; *professional career:* travelled and worked as waitress, 1980; Temp. at the World Bank, 1980; aide to Republican congressman and lobbyist on Capitol Hill, 1981-82; educational Admin., Holy Loch US base, UK, 1982; volunteer, Cardiff Peace Shop, Wales, 1983; worked for HTV during General Election, 1983; *publications:* numerous articles in The Times, The Guardian and The Independent; *recreations:* skiing, swimming, theatre, reading and writing fiction; *office address:* Ms Marjorie Thompson, Campaign for Nuclear Disarmament, 22-24 Underwood Street, London N1 7JG, United Kingdom.

TICHY-SCHREDER, Ingrid; Austrian, Member of the Nationalrat; *born:* 3 December 1941, Vienna, Austria; *education:* grammar school (science-orientated); commercial academy course for final school year students; *party:* Österreichische Volkspartei (ÖVP, Austrian People's Party); *political career:* senior official, Viennese Chamber of Industry, 1975-; mem. of the Industrial Sector Social Security Board; mem. of Nationalrat, for Vienna, 1979-; appointed to management team of project, Woman in the Business World 1982-, Federal Chamber of Industry; Vice-Pres. of Federal Chamber of Industry; *professional career:* worked in family business, 1960- and now executive partner; mem. of Specialist Commission for Young Industry, 1971- and Chmn. for Vienna, and Federal Chmn., 1974-76; *office address:* Frau Ingrid Tichy-Schreder, Nationalrat, Dr. Karl Renner Ring 3, 1017 Vienna, Austria.

TIDICK, Marianne; German, Deputy Minister-President of Schleswig-Holstein; *born:* 1 November 1942, Hamburg, Germany; *parents:* Werner Gütschow and Ingeborg Nicolaus; *married:* Dr. Frank Uwe Tidick, 1969; *languages:* English, French; *education:* primary and secondary education, Hamburg; Dame Allan's Girls School, Newcastle-Upon-Tyne, UK; Matriculation, Hamburg, 1962; Hamburg, German, English and American studies, 1962-66; studies in USA 1966-67; first state exam., 1968, second state exam, Hamburg, 1970; *party:* Sozialdemokratische Partei Deutschlands (SPD, Social Democratic Party of Germany), 1974; *political career:* Minister for Federal Affairs and Deputy Minister-Pres., Schleswig-Holstein, May 1988-; *professional career:* student adviser, Hamburg, 1970-71; spokesperson, Federal Ministry for Education and Science, 1971-76; Man. Dir., Youth Foundation e.v., 1976-87; Gen. Sec., Federal District Commission for Educational Planning and Research development, 1987-88; *clubs:* I G Medien; *office address:* Frau Marianne Tidick, Landeshaus, D-23 Kiel, West Germany.

TIMM, Dr. Helga; German, former Member of the Bundestag; *born:* 11 July 1924, Hamburg, West Germany; *education:* Hamburg Elementary and High School; Univ. Hamburg, History Latin, Educational Theory, 1946-52; Hamburg, Ph.D., 1952; *party:* Sozialdemokratische Partei Deutschlands (SPD, Social Democratic Party of Germany), 1946; *political career:* mem. of Bundestag, 1969-90; *professional career:* Scientific asst., Unesco Inst. of Youth, Gautting/Upper Bavaria, 1953-65; Lecturer and Co-Dir. of Academy of Labour, Univ. Frankfurt/Main, 1965-; *honours and awards:* Grand Cross of the Order of Merit of the Federal Republic of Germany with star, 1986; *office address:* Dr. Helga Timm, Bundeshaus, 5300 Bonn 1, West Germany.

TINSMAN, Maggie; American, Iowa State Representative; *born:* 14 July 1936, Moloine, Illinois, USA; *parents:* Francis Neir and Elizabeth Neir; *married:* Hovey Tinsman, 1959; *children:* three; *education:* Univ., of Colorado, BA; Univ. of Iowa, MSW; *party:* Republican Party; *political career:* Mem., Scott County Supervisor, 1978-88, Chwn., 1987; Chwn., Iowa Advisory Commission for Inter-Govt. Relations, 1982-84; Commissioner, Iowa Dept. of Elder Affairs, 1983-88; currently Iowa State Senator, District 20; Pres., Women Officials National Assn. of Counties, 1984-86; Sec. and Treasurer, Iowa Supervisor Assn., 1988; *memberships:* Steering Cttee., Quad Cities Vision of Future; Exec. Cttee., Quad Cities Development Group; *professional career:* Information, Referral and Assistance Service of Scott and Island Counties; *clubs:* Davenport/Bettendorf C of C; State Farm Bur; Leadership Iowa Alumni; Jr. League; American Lung Assn.; Pi Gamma Mu; Phi Beta Kappa; *office address:* Mrs Maggie Tinsman, State Capitol, Des Moines, Iowa 50319, USA.

TIRIA, Kumari Sushila; Indian, Member of the Rajya Sabha; *born:* 6 February 1956, Kaluakhamam, Orissa; *parents:* Rupnarayan Tiria; *education:* Karanjia College; Regional College, Bhubaneswar, BA, B.Ed; *party:* Congress Party; *political career:* Mem., All Orissa Tribal Assn., SUSAR, 1982-86; Gen. Sec., District Youth Congress, 1984-85; Joint Sec., Pradesh Youth Congress, Orissa, 1985-86, Gen. Sec., 1986-87; Mem. of the Rajya Sabha, 1986-; Gen. Sec., Indian Youth Congress, 1988-; Mem., Social Welfare Board, Orissa; Mem., District Rural Development Agency; Mem., District Development Board, Mayurbhanj; *professional career:* teacher, 1972-82; mem., Governing Board, Jashipur College; Sita Devi Women's Technical College, Jashipur; Panchpira Women's College, Karanjia; *clubs:* Shibaj Club; Nirachakra Club; Sec., Jatiya Mahila Sangh, Jashipur, Mayurbhanj; *recreations:* reading, writing, singing, household work, drama, music; *private address:* Kaluakhamam, P.O. Rugudi, Via Tato, P.S. Jashipur, District Mayurbhanj, Orissa, India; *office address:* Shrimati Kumari Tiria, Rajya Sabha, Parliament House, New Dehli 110 011, India; *phone:* (11) 389977; 389997.

241

TIRIKATENE-SULLIVAN, Hon. Whetu (Tini Whetu Marama); New Zealander, Member of Parliament; *born:* 9 January 1932; *parents:* Sir Eruera Tirikatene; *married:* Dr. Denis John Sullivan, 1967; *children:* one s., one d; *religion:* Ratana Christian; *languages:* English, Maori; *education:* Victoria Univ., Wellington, Diploma in Social Sciences and BA; Australian National Univ., Canberra, Dr. in political science; *party:* Labour Party; *political career:* elected MP for Southern Maori, after death of her father, 1967-; Minister of Tourism and Associated Minister of Social Welfare, 1972-75; Minister for the Environment, 1974; served on Parly. select cttees. on Maori Affairs and Electoral Law; mem., Caucus cttees. on Maori Affairs, Women, Social Services and Community Affairs; *interests:* youth affairs, family affairs, health, education, women's affairs and electoral law (i.e. effective education for children and youths and health education, working to remove prevailing inequality for all Maori New Zealanders and for the recognition of the diginity of girls and women); *professional career:* social worker, Maori and child welfare; *clubs:* patron of various New Zealand Youth Organisations; *recreations:* sport and culture, former instructor, Victoria Univ. Sports Club; *private address:* 9 Setsan Way, Ngaio, Wellington, New Zealand; *office address:* The Hon. Ms. Whetu Tirikatene-Sullivan, House of Representatives, POB 18041, Wellington, New Zealand; *phone:* (04) 719199; *fax:* (04) 4990704.

TISH, Kelly; American, North Dakota State Representative; *married:* John Kelly; *children:* three; *education:* Univ. of Maryland, BA; *party:* Democratic Party; *political career:* North Dakota State Rep., District 21, 1975-; Mem., Constitutional Celebration Cttee.; Mem., State Appropriations Cttee; *memberships:* Close Up Foundation; *office address:* Mrs Kelly Tish, 404 S. University Drive, Fargo, North Dakota 58103, USA.

TIZARD, Dame Catherine Anne; New Zealander, Governor General of New Zealand; *born:* 4 April 1931; *married:* Robert James Tizard, divorced 1983, 1951; *public role of spouse:* former Parliamentary Minister, retired 1990; *children:* one s., three d; *education:* Univ. of New Zealand, BA, 1964; *political career:* Auckland City Cllr., 1971-83, Mayor, 1983-90; Gov.-Gen. of New Zealand, Nov. 1990-; *professional career:* tutor in Zoology, Univ. of Auckland, 1965-83; *honours and awards:* Justice of the Peace, 1981; Dame Commander, 1981; OBE, 1981; *recreations:* music, drama, visual arts, scuba diving, cryptic crosswords; *private address:* 84A Beresford Street, Freemans Bay, Auckland, New Zealand; *office address:* Dame Catherine Tizard, Office of the Governor General, Private Bag, Government House, Wellington, New Zealand; *phone:* (04) 898055; (09) 686015; *fax:* (04) 603255.

TOCINO BISCAROLASAGA, Isabel; Spanish, Deputy; *born:* 9 March 1949, Santander, Spain; *parents:* Jose and Irene; *married:* José Manuel Bartolomé; *children:* seven; *religion:* Catholic; *languages:* Spanish, French, English; *education:* Dr. of Law, nuclear energy (cum laude), Complutense Univ., Madrid, 1973; *party:* Partido Popular (PP); *political career:* former Vice-Pres., Partido Popular and Speaker of Education Policies, Spanish Parliament; AP, co-ordinator of women's issues, Democratic Conservative Association; Deputy, AP, Madrid, 1986-89; re-elected for Cantabria, 1989-; speaker, PP; *interests:* foreign and economic affairs; *memberships:* Royal Academy of Lawyers; International Association of Nuclear Law; Spanish Nuclear Society; International Confraternity of Researchers; Institute of Law on Electricity, Brazil; *professional career:* professor of civil law, Complutense Univ., Madrid; *honours and awards:* degree and doctorate prize, Blasco Ramirez Foundation, 1971-73; Condesa Viuda de Maudes Foundation Prize, 1972; Cross of San Raimundo de Peñafort, 1974; Explosives Rio Tinto prize, 1983; *publications:* Aspectos legales del riesgo y daño nuclear de las centrales nucleares, 1975; Daño nuclear y medio ambiente, 1981; Centrales nucleares y medio ambiente, 1981; co-author, Bulletin du Droit Nucléaire; Revista Energia Nuclear; Reflexiones en torno al concepto de derecho civil; *private address:* Génova 13 E-28004, Madrid, Spain; *office address:* Ms Isabel Tocino Biscarolasaga, Congreso de los Diputados, Fernán Flor 1, Madrid 14, Spain.

TOGUCHI, Tamako; Japanese, Member of the House of Representatives; *born:* 16 December 1937; *education:* Tokyo Univ; *party:* Japan Socialist Party (JSP); *political career:* elected for Tokyo 4, 1990; Mem., House of Reps. Cttee. on Social and Labour Affairs, 1990-; *memberships:* President of Welfare Assn; *professional career:* Staff Researcher of Metropolitan Institute of Psychopathology; *office address:* Ms Tamako Toguchi, House of Representatives, 1-7-1 Nagata-cho, Chiyoda-ku, Tokyo 100, Japan; *phone:* (03) 5815111.

TOMINOVA, Zdena; Czechoslovakian, former Spokesperson for Charter 77, writer and dissident; *born:* 7 February 1941; *education:* Philosophy graduate, 1968; *political career:* signed declaration of Human Rights Movement Charter 77; dismissed from post, 1977; Spokesperson, Charter 77, 1979-80; *professional career:* writer; interpreter; lived in England since 1980; *publications:* literary works published in underground; *office address:* Ms Zdena Tominova .

TOMSIC, Vida; Yugoslavian, Member of the Council of Federation of the League of Communists of Yugoslavia; *born:* 1913, Ljubljana, Yugoslavia; *party:* League of Communists of Yugoslavia (LCY), 1934; *political career:* elected to Central Cttee., LCY, 10th

Congress, 1974; Mem., Cncl. of Federation, 1982-; *honours and awards:* Spomenica, 1941; *office address:* Ms Vida Tomsic, Central Committee of the League of Communists of Yugoslavia, Novi Beograd, bul. Lenjina 6, Yugoslavia.

TONGUE, Carole; British, Member of the European Parliament; *born:* 14 October 1955, Lausanne, Switzerland; *parents:* Walter Archer Tongue and Muriel Esther (née Boyes); *married:* Chris Pond, 1990; *public role of spouse:* Director of Low Pay Unit; *religion:* Quaker Attender; *languages:* French, German, Spanish; *education:* Brentwood County High School, 1967-74; Loughborough University, BA Hons., Government and French, 1974-77; *party:* Labour Party, 1980; *political career:* MEP for London East, 1989-, Socialist Group; Deputy Leader of the British Labour MEPs; member: Co-operative Party, Campaign for Nuclear Disarmament, END, SERA, Council of ISDD, RIIA; trade union memberships: MSF, GMB; Trustee of Women's Legal Defence Fund; *interests:* economic and industrial policy, car and electronic industries, environment, peace and disarmament, equal opporunities; *memberships:* Royal Institute of Int. Affairs; *professional career:* Administrator/Secretary; *publications:* articles in House Magazine, 1988-; Where Labour is Conservative, New Socialist, 1988; articles on Europe, electoral reform; *recreations:* music - piano/cello, horse riding, tennis, all the arts; *private address:* 97a Ilford Lane, Ilford, Essex; *office address:* Ms Carole Tongue, European Parliament, 97-113 Rue Belliard, 1040 Brussels, Belgium.

TÖRNQVIST, Kerttu Annikki; Finnish, Member of the Eduskunta; *born:* 18 March 1942, Pielisjärvi, Finland; *parents:* Veikko Matti Ikonen and Ksenia Ikonen (née Hirvonen); *married:* Lauri Ilmari Törnqvist, 1960; *children:* Ilpo, Solja, Päivi; *education:* Elementary School; various professional courses; *party:* Svomen Sosialidemokraatinen Puolue (SDP, Finnish Social Democratic Party); *political career:* Mem., Lieksa Town Cncl., 1976 and Vice-Chmn., 1979; mem. of Eduskunta, 1983; mem., Karelia Province Admin. Board, 1984; Chmn., North-Karelian Provincial Union Admin. Board, 1985; *professional career:* Shop asst., E-liike, 1957-63; Shop Man., 1963-74; shopkeeper, 1974-83; mem., Admin Cncl., E-co-op. Eka, 1984; *recreations:* Politics; *office address:* Ms Kerttu Törnqvist, Eduskunta, 00102 Helsinki, Finland.

TORRES MARQUES, Helena de Melo; Portuguese, Deputy; *born:* 8 May 1941, Lisbon, Portugal; *education:* Licenciate of Economics, Higher Inst. of Economic and Financial Sciences, Lisbon Univ; *party:* Partido Socialista (PS, Socialist Party); *political career:* former Secretary of State for Local Administration; former Dir. General of Regional and Local Action; former Pres., Cttee. on Social and Economic Affairs, Council of

Europe; former Mem., Directive Cttee. for European Regional and Local Administration; former Portuguese Representative, Tourism Commission, OECD; Deputy, Assembly of the Republic, 1983-; Pres., Antero de Quental Foundation; Mem., PS Political Cttee. and PS National Committee; Vice-Pres., Parly. Cttee. on Economics, Finance and Planning; *professional career:* former Assistant Lecturer, Higher Inst. of Economics, Lisbon Univ.; Economist, Central Planning Department; *publications:* Turismo-Actividade Motora do Desenvolvimento Regional; Ribatejo Zona de Opupaçao dos Tempos Livres da Populaçao de Lisboa; O Turismo como actividade Económica e Social; O Emprego no Sector do Turismo; Críaçao de um Mercado Abastecedor no Algarve; Definiçao da Politica de Credito no Sector do Turismo; Dois Novos Indicadores para a Análise das Eleiçoes Municipais: A Organizaçao e a Implantaçao Partidária a Nível Regional; Contribuiçao para o Estudo das Autarquias Locais em Portugal; As Finanças Locais em Portugal-Legislaçao e Análise Crítica; O Orçamento Geral do Estado e a Lei de Finanças Locais; Os Transportes Municipais e a lei de Finanças Locais; A Análise Crítica ao Livro Branco Sobre a Regionalisaçao; Delimitaçao dos Investimentos entre a Administraçao Central, Regional e Local; A Política Regional na CEE Alargada; Consideraçoes sobre a Regionalizaçao em Portugal; Princípios de Autonomia Antárquica; Portuguese Administrative Organization and Government Finance System; *office address:* Ms Helena Torres Marques, Assembléia da República, Palacia de S Bento, 1296 Lisboa Codex, Portugal.

TOSSI BRUTTI, Graziella; Italian, Senator; *born:* 8 December 1938, Brescia, Italy; *education:* State University, Milan, degree in Jurisprudence; *party:* Partito Democratico della Sinistra (PDS, Party of the Democratic Left); *political career:* Campaigner for Referenda campaigns on divorce, abortion and sexual violence; Head of Justice section, Fed. PCI, Perugia; mem. Leadership and Fed. Committee; Founder mem., Leadership of DUNA Association (National Women Artists' Union); mem. Leadership Cttee. of Centre for Legal and Political Studies, Umbrian Region; elected Senator, Perugia (II), 1987; mem. Regulatory Body and Sec. Cttee. on Constitutional Affairs; *professional career:* Defence Counsel, lawyer, (Supreme Court); Assistant to Chair of Criminal Law, Milan University, 1962-66; *office address:* Ms Graziella Tossi Brutti, Senato della Repubblica, Palazzo Madama, 00100 Rome, Italy.

TRAUTMANN, Catherine; French, Member of the European Parliament; *born:* 15 January 1951; *party:* Parti Socialiste (PS, Socialist Party); *political career:* MP for Bas-Rhin, 1986-88; Sec. of State, Ministry of Social Affairs; MEP, 1989-; *office address:* Mme. Catherine Trautmann, Hôtel de Ville, 9 rue Brulée, 67000 Strasbourg, France.

TRAXLER, Gabrielle; Austrian, Member of the Nationalrat; *born:* 16 September 1942, Digne Basses Alpes, France; *education:* French girls' grammar school, matriculation, 1961; courses in office skills, shorthand, typing and book-keeping; *party:* Sozialistische Partei Österreichs (SPÖ, Socialist Party of Austria); *political career:* official, Association of Socialist Secondary School Students; Women's Sec., Austrian Federation of Trade Unions; senior official, Chamber of Workers' and Employees, Vienna; district councillor, Vienna, 1978-83; mem. of Viennese Provincial Assembly, 1978-83; Mem. of Nationalrat for Vienna, 1983-; secretary to specialist commissions, Union of Hotel, Tourist Industry and Private Service Employees (domestic servants and home helps); *professional career:* shorthand typist in veneer factory; secretary, Institut Français; *office address:* Frau Gabrielle Traxler, Nationalrat, Dr. Karl Renner Ring 3, 1017 Vienna, Austria.

TRAYWICK, Flo Crisman Neher; American, Member of the Republican National Cttee. for Virginia; *born:* 9 May 1924, Lynchburg, Virginia, USA; *parents:* Clarence Raymond Weber and Flo Elizabeth Weber (née Crisman); *married:* Heber Venable Bainbridge Traywick, 1945; *children:* Heber Venable Jr., Crisman Neher, Robin Bolling, Charles M. Williams; *religion:* Methodist; *education:* Randolph-Macon Women's College, Virginia, BA, 1978; *party:* Republican Party; *political career:* Legislative Aide, Virginia Nat. Assembly, 1979-86; Mem., Republican Nat. Cttee., Virginia, 1984-; Board Mem., Virginia Federation of Republican Women, 1984-; Congressional Candidate, District 6, Virginia, 1986; *memberships:* Virginia School of Arts, Lynchburg, Virginia; Daughters of Colonists; *professional career:* Treasurer, Air Pollution Cent Products and Pres., Valley Incinerators Inc., Richmond, Virginia; *office address:* Ms Flo Traywick, P.O. Box 3092, Lynchburg, Virginia 24503, USA.

TRENZ, Erika; German, former Member of the Bundestag; *born:* 15 February 1947, München, West Germany; *children:* one; *education:* schools providing a general education; *party:* Die Grünen (Green Party), 1984; *professional career:* trained construction draughtsman; trained administrative employee, clerical service; activity in the areas of youth work, educational psychology and authorization of advance maintenance allowances, city administration, Saarbrücken, for eight years; *office address:* Frau Erika Trenz, Bundeshaus, 5300 Bonn 1, West Germany.

TREPPLER, Irene; American, Missouri State Senator; *born:* 13 October 1926, St. Louis County, Missouri, USA; *parents:* Martin and Julia Hagemann; *married:* Walter J. Treppler, 1950; *children:* John M., Steven A., Walter W., Diane V. Anderson; *religion:* United Church of Christ; *party:* Republican Party; *political career:*

Missouri State Rep., District 106, 1972-82, District 100, 1983-84; alternate delegate, Republican National Convention, 1976, delegate, 1984; Missouri State Senator, District 1, 1984, re-elected, 1988-; *memberships:* National Order of Women Legislators; National Federation of Republican Women; *honours and awards:* Republican of the Year, John Marshall Club, 1984; *clubs:* Lemay, Affton and Oakville CofC; *office address:* Ms Irene Treppler, 4681 Fuchs Road, St. Louis County, Missouri 63128, USA.

TROEDSSON, Ingegerd; Swedish, First Deputy Speaker and Vice-President of the Moderate Party; *born:* 5 June 1929, Vaxholm, Sweden; *parents:* Emil Johan Cederlöf and Gerd Cederlöf (née Wibom); *married:* Tryggve Bengt Johan Troedsson, 1949; *public role of spouse:* professor; *children:* Vigg, Susanne, Viveca, Ulf, Erik; *religion:* Protestant; *languages:* Swedish, English; *education:* Stockholm University, BA, 1951, M.Pol., political science, 1952; *party:* Moderata Samlingspartiet (Moderate Party), 1957; *political career:* Municipal Cllr., Norra Trögd and Enköping City Cncls., 1959-70 and 1971-76; Member of the Rikstag since 1974; First Deputy Speaker, 1979-; Deputy member of the Taxation Cttee., 1974-76; 1978-79, 1985-87 and 88-; mem. of the Social Affairs Cttee., 1974-76, 1978-79 and 88-; mem. of the Social Security Cttee., 1985-88; mem. of the Foreign Affairs' Panel of lay assessors, 1980; Member of the Taxation Cttee., 1979-85; 1987-88; Member of the Speakers' Conference, 1979-; mem. of Parliamentary War Delegation, 1979-; mem. of the Council of the Bank of Sweden, 1982-85; Deputy member of the Swedish Delegation to the Nordic Council, 1979-82; Cabinet Minister in the Social Department, Minister of Health, 1976-78; Member of the survey on Social affairs, 1967-76; mem. the survey on Tax Equalisation Benefits 1975-76; mem. the survey on female priests, 1979-81 and the Family Economy Committee; 1979-83; mem. the Housing Benefit Cttee., 1979-83; mem. the Cttee. on Deficit Contributions, 1980-83; mem., 1983 National Registration Cttee., 1983-88; mem. the Cttee. on differentiated VAT, 1983; mem. the Pensions Legislation Preparation group, 1985-; Deputy Chairwoman of Moderata Samlingspartiets Women's Federation, 1965-75; Member of the board of Moderata Samlingspartiet, 1966-76, 1978- and 2nd Deputy Chairwoman, 1987-; Member of the Panel of lay assessors on pensions, 1960-63; mem. the Local Education Authority, 1961-70 and the Panel of lay assessors on Sickness Insurance, 1962-65; Member of the Central Panel of lay Assessors on Social Matters, 1971-76; mem., the Electoral Cttee., 1973-76; *interests:* social welfare, taxation, economics and ideological issues; *memberships:* Board Mem., Riksskatteverket, 1979-88; Pres., Riksdagens Revisorer, 1979-82; Board Mem., The Central Bank of Sweden, 1982-85; Board Mem., Comfidencen, 1985-; Vice-Pres., Moderate Party, 1988-; Board mem., Konung Gusta V:s jubileumsfond, 1988-; Mem., Senate Cncl., Univ. of Uppsala, 1988-; *professional career:* Board mem.: Euroc, 1979-; Skandinaviska Elverk 1979-85, the Vegete-companies, 1981-86; Svenska Dagbladet Foundation, 1981-; WASA Life, 1987-; Skandinaviska Enskilda Banken 1987-; The Surveying Department, 1974-76; The Inspectorate of Taxes, 1979-88; *publications:* Hög tid för ny familjepolitik, 1962; Om tryggheten, 1964; Aktiv Vårdpolitik, 1966; Vårdkris, 1966; Att få ta ansvar, 1967; Politik för 70-talet, 1969; *private address:* Hakesta, S-190 61, Grillby, Sweden; *office address:* Mrs Ingegerd Troedsson, Riksdag, Fack, S-100 12 Stockholm, Sweden.

TRUMPINGTON, Baroness (cr. 1980, Life Peer) Jean Alys Barker; British, Minister of State for Agriculture, Fisheries and Food; *born:* 23 October 1922; *parents:* the late Arthur Edward Campbell-Harris; *married:* the late William Alan Barker, 1954; *children:* one s; *party:* Conservative Party; *political career:* Landgirl to David Lloyd George, 1939-41; Sec. to Viscount Hinchingbrooke, 1949-52; councillor, Cambridge City Council, 1963-73, and Mayor, 1971-72; councillor, Cambridge County Council, 1973-75; General Commissioner of Taxes, 1975-83; Chmn., Airline User's Cttee., 1979-80; UK delegate, UN Status of Women Commission, 1979-81; mem., Board of Visitors, HM Prison, Pentonville; mem., Mental Health Review Tribunal; House of Lords, 1980-; Baroness in Waiting (Government Whip), 1983-85; Spokesman for the Home Office Dept. of Health and Social Security and Foreign and Commonwealth Office, 1983-85; Parly. Under-Sec. for Health and Social Security, 1985-87; Parly. Sec. at Min. of Agriculture, 1987-90; Minister of State for Agriculture, 1989-; *professional career:* Naval Intelligence, 1941-45; European Central Inland Transport Organisation, London and Paris, 1946-49; JP, 1972; *honours and awards:* Honorary City Councillor, Cambridge, 1975; Hon. Fellow, Lucy Cavendish College, Cambridge; *clubs:* Folkestone Racecourse (Steward); *recreations:* antiques, cookery, bridge, golf, needlepoint; *office address:* Baroness Trumpington, Ministry of Agriculture Fisheries and Food, Whitehall Place, London SW1A 2HH.

TSOUDEROU, Virginia; Greek, Member of Parliament; *born:* 24 June 1924, Iracleo, Crete; *parents:* Emmanuel J. Tsouderos and Maria Tsouderos (Thiakaki), 1950; *children:* one s., two d; *religion:* Greek Orthodox; *languages:* Greek, English, French, Spanish; *education:* Oxford Univ., UK, MA, economics, politics, philosophy; Minnesota Univ., USA, MA, public finance; *party:* Enosi Dimokratikou Kentrou, 1974-78; Komma Demokratikou Socialismou (KODISO, Democratic Socialist Party), 21 Mar. 1979; Nea Demokratia (ND, New Democracy Party); *political career:* MP, EDIK, 1974-77; MP, independent, 1978-81; MP of State, 1985-89; MP, A' Athens, 1989-90; MP of State, 1990-; New Democracy Party Spokesperson,

1990; *memberships:* Economist Assn.; Amnesty International; Hon. Pres., Family Planning Assn.; Assn. of Greek Women; Vice-Pres., Assn., Friends of Macedonian Historical Museum; *professional career:* economist FAO, IMF columnist, 1960-67; *honours and awards:* Woman of Europe for Greece, 1988; Greek Academy for Publications of Historical Archives; *publications:* Historical Archives Emmanuel Tsouderos 1941-44; With Europe as a Compass; Discussion with a Citizen; Libraries in Greece; Medical Care; *recreations:* swimming, hiking; *private address:* Vasileos Georgiou II 14, 106 74 Athens, Greece; *office address:* Ms Virginia Tsouderou, Vouli, Parliament Building, Syntagma, Greece.

TU, Hon. Elsie; Hong Kong, Member of the Legislative Council; *born:* 2 June 1913, Newcastle Upon Tyne, United Kingdom; *married:* Andrew Tu; *education:* Durham Univ., BA; Durham Univ., Diploma of Education; *political career:* Vice-Chmn., Urban Council; *professional career:* Supervisor, Mu Kuang Schools; *honours and awards:* CBE; *office address:* The Hon. Mrs Elsie Tu, The Legislative Council, Government House, Hong Kong.

TURCO, Livia; Italian, Deputy; *born:* 13 February 1955, Cuneo; *education:* Classical Secondary Education; *party:* Partito Democratico della Sinistra (PDS, Party of the Democratic Left); *political career:* mem. Nat. Secretariat PCI; Councillor, Turin; then Regional Councillor, Piedmont; elected Deputy, Rome-Viterbo-Latina-Frosinone, 1987; and for Turin-Novara-Vercelli-Decided on the latter; mem. Cttee. on Justice; *professional career:* Teacher; *office address:* Ms Livia Turco, Camera dei Deputati, Montecitorio, 00186 Rome, Italy.

TURNER, Betty; American, Mayor of Corpus Christi, Texas; *born:* Yonkers, New York, USA; *married:* Jack Rice; *children:* two; *education:* Vasser College, BA; Texas A & I, MA; *political career:* former City Cllr., Corpus Christi; Mayor, 1987-; *professional career:* former sales manager, publishing co., Texas; currently real estate broker; *honours and awards:* Women and Men in Careers Award, 1988; *office address:* Ms Betty Turner, P.O. Box 9277, Corpus Christi, Texas 78469, USA.

TURNER OF CAMDEN, Baroness (cr. 1985, Life Peer) Muriel Winifred Turner; British, Member of the House of Lords; *born:* 1923; *party:* Labour Party; *political career:* fmr. Asst. Gen. Sec., Assn. of Scientific, Technical and Managerial Staffs; mem., Equal Opportunities Cmn., Occupational Pensions Board; mem., House of Lords, 1985-; Opp. Spokesman on social security, 1987-, employment, 1987-; *private address:* 87 Canfield Gardens, London NW6, UK; *office* *address:* Lady Turner of Camden, House of Lords, London SW1A 0PW.

TURUNEN, Eeva Annikki; Finnish, Member of the Eduskunta; *born:* 22 June 1933, Valkjärvi, Finland; *parents:* Urho Viljo Viljanen and Anna Lyyti Viljanen (née Hölttä); *married:* Mauri Heikki Kalevi Turunen, 1955; *children:* Harri, Timo; *education:* Turku, Primary School Teacher, 1955; Jyväskylä, Subject Teacher (general subjects), 1962; *party:* Kansallinen Kokoomus (Kok, National Coalition Party); *political career:* Mem., Joensuu Town Cncl., 1977; mem., Parish Cncl., Joensuu Evangelical- Lutheran Church, 1979; 1st Vice-Chmn., Joensuu Town Cncl., 1981; MP, 1988-; *professional career:* Primary School Teacher, 1955-58, Joensuu; Secondary School Teacher, 1958- 62; Part-time Teacher, Eastern-Finland Teachers' Training Coll., 1963-69; Part-time Teacher, Joensuu Free Workers' Institute, 1967-71; General Subjects Teacher, Comprehensive School, 1974; *honours and awards:* Cross for Merit, Order of the Lion of Finland; *publications:* Columnist in Karjalainen (newspaper); *office address:* Ms Eeva Turunen, Eduskunta, 00102 Helsinki, Finland.

TUZCU, Sadan; Turkish, Member of the National Assembly; *office address:* Ms Sadan Tuzcu, National Assembly, TBNN, Ankara, Turkey.

TYBERGHIEN-VANDENBUSSCHE, Maria-Ludovika; Belgian, Senator; *born:* 6 September 1939, Izegem, Belgium; *children:* Four; *party:* Christelijke Volkspartij (CVP, Christian Social Party); *political career:* Provincial Councillor, West-Vlaanderen, 1974-77; Town Councillor, Houthulst, 1977-; Deputy for Veurne-Diksmuide-Oostende, 1977-81; Senator for Veurne-Diksmuide-Oostende, 1981-; mem., Senate Commissions for National Affairs, Int. Commerce, Defence, Education and Science; Interparliamentary Consultant to the Benelux Council; mem. Flemish Council Cttees. for Culture, Environment, Preservation of Nature, Sport and Tourism; mem., Interparliamentary Cttee. of the Dutch Language Union; *private address:* Predikboomstraat 20, 8151 Houthulst, Belgium, tel 051-501479; *office address:* Ms Maria-Ludovika Tyberghien-Vandenbussche, Senate, Palais de la Nation, Place de a Nation 1, 1000 Brussels, Belgium.

TYKKYLÄINEN, Marja-Liisa; Finnish, Member of the Eduskunta; *born:* 4 October 1945, Kontiolahti, Finland; *parents:* Pekka Synkkö and Ellen Katri Maria Synkkö (née Keronen); *education:* Commercial Technician, 1974; *party:* Suomen Sosialidemokraattinen Puolue (SDP, Finnish Social Democratic Party); *political career:* Mem., Kuopio Town Cncl., 1978; mem., Presidential Electorate, 1982; mem. of Eduskunta, 1983-; *interests:* Chmn., Kuopio Music Cttee, 1979; *professional career:* Youth Leader, 1963-68; Leader and Man., Children's Camp, 1963-73; Office Sec., 1978-79; Office Man., 1979-83; *office address:* Ms Marja-Liisa Tykkyläinen, Eduskunta, 00102 Helsinki, Finland.

U

UBAIDULLAEVA, Reno Akhatovna; Soviet, Member of the Council of the Union; *party:* Communist Party of the Soviet Union; *political career:* elected from the Soviet Women's Cttee. to the Cncl. of the Union; Mem., Cncl. of the Union Commissions on Labour, Prices and Social Policy; *professional career:* Dep.-Dir., Economics Inst., Uzbek SSR Academy of Sciences, Tashkent; *office address:* Ms Rano Akhatovna Ubaidullaeva, Institute of Economics, Uzbek SSR Academy of Sciences, 700170 Tashkent, Ul. Muminova 9, Uzbek SSR, USSR.

UCHTENHAGEN-BRUNNER, Dr. Lilian; Swiss, Member of the Nationalrat; *born:* 7 September 1928, Olten, Switzerland; *parents:* August Brunner and Elisabeth (née Netzer); *married:* Dr. Ambros Uchtenhagen, 1956; *education:* Schools in Olten and Neuchâtel; Univ. of Basel; London School of Economics and Political Science, GB; *party:* Sozialdemokratische Partei der Schweiz (Social-Democratic Party); *political career:* mem. of various expert commissions on economic problems and of EFTA Consultative Cttee.; Pres., Co-op., Zurich and Cttee. of Management Co-op., Switzerland; mem. of Municipal Cncl., Zurich, 1970-74; mem. of Nationalrat, concerned with economics, public finance, science and research; *professional career:* teacher; psychiatric aide in clinic, Hartford, Conn., USA; travel in USA and Mexico; mem. of various groups dealing with youth problems, drug addiction and social work; Cncl. of management, Genossenschaft Zentralbourg Ltd; *publications:* thesis, Grenzen der Staatsverschuldung, 1955; *clubs:* Swiss Institute of Arts; various Women's Associations; *private address:* Lenggstrasse 31, Zurich, Switzerland; *office address:* Dr. Lilian Uchtenhagen-Brunner, Nationalrat/Conseil National, Secretariat-General, Parlamentsgebäude, 3003 Berne, Switzerland.

UGRIN, Dr. Emese; Hungarian, Member of the Országgyülés; *party:* Christian Democratic People's Party (KDNP); *office address:* Dr. Emese Ugrin, Országgyülés, Kossuth L. tér 1-3, Budapest V, Hungary; *phone:* 22 5058; 22 5059.

ULMER, Frances Ann; American, Alaska State Representative; *born:* Madison, Wisconsin, USA; *parents:* George Charles Ulmer and Lois Caroline Ulmer (née Radke); *married:* William T. Council, 1977; *children:* Amy, Louis Charles; *religion:* Presbyterian; *education:* Univ. of Wisconsin, Madison, USA, BA, 1969, JD, 1972; *party:* not affiliated; *political career:* Dir., Alaska Division, Policy, Development and Planning, 1977-81; Chair, Alaska Coastal policy Cncl., 1979-81; ; Mem., Exec. Board, Cncl. State Planning Agencies, 1979-81; Chair, Juneau Comprehensive Planning Cttee., 1982; Mem., Juneau Planning Commission, 1983; Mayor, Juneau, 1983-85; Mem., Advisory Board, US Mayoral Conference, 1984-; Chair, Special Cttee. on Precedural Reform, 1985-; Alaska State Representative, 1987-; *memberships:* League of Women Voters; League of Business and Professional Women; Alaska Municipal League; US Mayoral Conference; *professional career:* Staff mem., Bur of Competition, Federal Trade Commission, 1972-73; staff Mem., Alaska Legislative Affairs Agency, 1973-75; Legislative Asst. to Governor Jay Hammond, 1975-77; *honours and awards:* Alaskan Woman of the Year; *office address:* Ms Frances Ulmer, 17700 Angus Way, Juneau, Alaska 99801, USA.

ULRICH-VÖGTLIN, Ursula; Swiss, Member of the Nationalrat; *born:* 13 June 1947, Olten, Switzerland; *children:* two; *education:* diploma in Zoology, Univ. of Basel; *party:* Sozialdemokratische Volkspartei der Schweiz (SDP, Social Democratic Party of Switzerland); *political career:* borough Cllr. for Olten, 1981-; Mem. of the Solothurn Cantonal Cncl., 1985-; Mem. of the Nationalrat for Olten, Canton of Solothurn, 1987-; *professional career:* secondary school teacher, biology; *office address:* Frau Ursula Ulrich-Vögtlin, Nationalrat/Conseil National, Secretariat-General, Parlamentsgebäude, 3003 Berne, Switzerland; *phone:* Berne 619711.

UMIDI SALA, Neida Maria; Italian, Deputy; *born:* 21 December 1948, Milan; *education:* Diploma, Accountancy; *party:* Partito Democratico della Sinistra (PDS, Party of the Democratic Left); *political career:* mem. Exec. Cttee. of Labour, Milan; Gen. Council FIDAC; mem. Nat. Leadership, FIDAC; elected Deputy, Milan-Pavia, 1983; mem. Commission on Finance and Treasury; re-elected Deputy, 1987; Sec. Cttee. on Finance; *professional career:* employee, Credito Italiano (Bank); *office address:* Ms Neida Umidi Sala, Camera dei Deputati, Montecitorio, 00186 Rome, Italy.

UNGAR, Klára; Hungarian, Member of the Országgyűlés; *party:* Federation of Young Democrats (FIDESZ); *office address:* Ms Klára Ungár, Országgyűlés, Kossuth L. tér 1-3, Budapest V, Hungary; *phone:* 22 5058; 22 5059.

UNRUH, Trude; German, former Member of the Bundestag; *born:* 7 March 1925; *married:* Helmut, 1944; *children:* Helmut, Ingbert; *party:* Überpartei der Grauen (The Greys); *professional career:* Founder and Federal Chwn., Grey Panther since 1975; Bness man. and chief sec.; Founder, Grey Panther Magazine, 1983; Grey Panther National Academy for self-administration; *publications:* Aufruf zur Rebellion, 1984; Trümmerfrauen, 1987; *office address:* Frau Trude Unruh, Bundeshaus, 5300 Bonn 1, West Germany.

UNSOELD, Jolene; American, US Representative for Washington; *born:* 3 December 1931, Corvallis, Oregon, USA; *married:* the late Willi Unsoeld, 1951; *public role of spouse:* mountain climber and educator; *children:* Regon, Krag, Terres, Devi (Decd.); *religion:* Atheist; *education:* Oregon State Univ., 1949-51; *party:* Democratic Party; *political career:* Mem., Democrat Nat. Cttee., 1983-; Washington State Rep., 22nd legislative district, 1985-89; Mem., Environmental Affairs, Energy, Utilities and Higher Education Cttees.; Mem., Select Cttee. on Clean-up of Puget Sound; appointed Board Mem., Washington State Inst. for Public Policy, Jan. 1985; Mem., Northwest Citizens Forum on Defence Waste, 1986-; Congressional Caucus Mems.: Women's Issues; Rural Health Care; Democratic Study Group; Arms Control; Environment and Energy; Export Task Force; Populist; Arts; Human Rights; Democratic Caucus Task Force on Govt. Waste; US Rep., District 3, Washington, 1988, re-elected, 1990; *memberships:* Mem.,Democratic National Cttee., 1980-88; Mem., Thurston County Democratic Central Cttee., 1972-88; Better Govt. League of Thurston County, 1984-90; Instigator of Capitol Lake Restoration Cttee., 1985; Co-Chwn., Citizens Toxic Clean-up Campaign, 1987; Democratic Study Group, Western Region Rep., 1991-; *professional career:* full-time unpaid citizen lobbyist, accomplishments include: retention of protection of privacy legislation; protection of access provisions of Public Records Act and legislative and voter approval to bring certain state-appointed officials under the financial reporting requirements of the Public Disclosure Act; Dir., English Language Inst. (teaching English through the US Info. Service), Kathmandu, Nepal, 1965-67; *honours and awards:* Vietnam Veterans of America Special Recognition Award, 1990; Trout Unlimited 1990 Betty Winn Memorial Award for Legislator of the Year; Farmers Union Award, 1990; Legislator of the Year,

The Washington Assn., 1990; Friend of the Award for effective leadership in Controlling Driftnet Fishing, 1990; Gun Rights Defender of the Month, Citizens Cttee. for the Right to Keep and Bear Arms, Dec. 1990; recognised for 100% voting record, 101st Congressional Session, Children's Defense Fund and National Cncl. of Senior Citizens, 1991; *publications:* Who Gave? Who Got? How Much?; *office address:* Ms Jolene Unsoeld, 1508 Longworth House Office Building, Washington DC 20515-4703, USA.

UOSUKAINEN, Riitta Maria; Finnish, Minister of Education; *born:* 18 June 1942, Jääski, Finland; *parents:* Reino Vainikka and Aune Vainikka (née Ruohonen); *married:* Toivo Verneri Uosukainen, 1968; *public role of spouse:* Major; *children:* Antti; *religion:* Lutheran; *languages:* Finnish, Swedish, German, English; *education:* Helsinki Univ., MA, 1969; L. Phil., 1970; *party:* Kansallinen Kokoomus (KoK, National Coalition Party); *political career:* Mem., Imatra Town Cncl., 1976; 1st Vice-Chmn., 1980; mem. of Eduskunta, 1983-; Vice-Chmn., Karelia Province, 1986; *interests:* education, science, culture; *professional career:* Teacher of Finnish, Imatrankoski Sixth Form, 1969; Instructor in Native Tongue, Kyme Province, 1976-83; *honours and awards:* Silver Medal for Merit, Finnish Women's Assn. of Physical Education; *publications:* (In collaboration) Osviitta, 1979; Linkki, 1981; Äidinkielen sampo I- III, 1982-84; *clubs:* Zonta International; SKS; Liver; *private address:* Olkinuoraneatu 11, 55910 Imetra, Finland; *office address:* Ms Riitta Uosukainen, Eduskunta, 00102 Helsinki, Finland.

URBANOWICZ, Anna; Polish, Member of the Sejm; *office address:* Ms Anna Urbanowicz, Sejm PRI, ul. Wiejska 4/6/8, 00-489 Warsaw, Poland; *phone:* (22) 28 70 01; 28 40 31.

URBZASKA, Botenna; Polish, Member of the Sejm; *office address:* Ms Botenna Urbzaska, Sejm PRI, ul. Wiejska 4/6/8, 00-489 Warsaw, Poland; *phone:* (22) 28 70 01; 28 40 31.

UTSUNOMIYA, Mayumi; Japanese, Member of the House of Representatives; *born:* 3 November 1949; *education:* Ehime Univ; *party:* Japan Socialist Party (JSP); *political career:* elected for Ehime 1, 1990; Mem., House of Reps. Cttee. on Judicial Affairs and on Environment, 1990-; *professional career:* lawyer in practice; *office address:* Ms Mayumi Utsunomiya, House of Representatives, 1-7-1 Nagata-cho, Chiyoda-ku, Tokyo 100, Japan; *phone:* (03) 5815111.

V

VALADAO, Maria Bahia Peixoto; Brazilian, Federal Deputy; *born:* 19 August 1931, Anicuns, Goiás; *parents:* Moysés Pereira Peixoto and Agripina Bahia Peixoto; *married:* Ary Ribeiro Valadao; *children:* Ary Filho, Lúcia Maria, Ronaldo, Liliam, Márcio; *education:* Catholic Univ. of Goiás, Goiania, law, 1966-70; studies in the USA of the North American penitential system, 1973; *party:* Partido Democrático Social (PDS, Social Democrat Party); *political career:* Delegate to UNICEF as Pres. of the State Cttee. for Int. Children's Year, 1980; special mission to Europe in the interests of the state of Goiás, 1981; State Co-ordianator for Community Development, Ministry of the Interior, Goiania, 1981; Federal Deputy for Goiás, 1991-95; *professional career:* lawyer; *office address:* Ms Maria Valadao, Chamber of Deputies, Praça dos 3 Poderes, Ed. Principal, 70160 Brasilia, DF, Brazil; *phone:* (61) 225 2885.

VALENT, Dacia; Italian, Member of the European Parliament; *born:* 12 February 1963; *party:* Partito Democratico della Sinistra (PDS, Party of the Democratic Left); *political career:* MEP, 1989-; *office address:* Ms Dacia Valent, European Parliament, Centre Européen, Plateau de Kirchberg, BP 2929, Luxembourg; *phone:* Luxembourg 43001.

VALLENTINE, Josephine; Australian, Senator; *born:* 30 May 1946, Perth, Western Australia; *married:* Peter John Fry, 1972; *children:* two d; *religion:* Quaker; *education:* BA, Diploma in Education, Western Australia; Teacher's Certificate, Graylands Teachers' College, Western Australia; *party:* Nuclear Disarmament Party, 1984-85; The Greens (Western Australia), 1990-; *political career:* elected to the Senate for Western Australia, 1984, 1987, 1990-; Committee Service: Mem. of the Joint Standing Cttee. for Foreign Affairs, Defence and Trade, 1987-; *interests:* disarmament, social justice, ecological sustainability, participatory democracy; *professional career:* teacher; *office address:* Ms Josephine Vallentine, PO Box 137, West Perth 6005, Australia.

VALLI MUTHUSAMY; Malaysian, Senator; *political career:* currently, Pres. of MIC Wanita; concurrently, Senator, Parliament of Malaysia; *professional career:* serves on the Board of some companies; *office address:* Ms Valli Muthusamy, MIC Wanita, Menara Manickavasagam, 7th Floor Jalan Rahmat, 50350 Kuala Lumpur.

VAN DER MEER, Marie-Anne; Dutch, Member of the First Chamber; *born:* 18 May 1936, Hengelo, Netherlands; *parents:* Anne van der Meer and Jeanne, Louise van der Meer (née Kleinbussink); *party:* Partij van de Arbeid (PvdA, Labour Party), 1958; *political career:* Mem. First Chamber, 1983-; *office address:* Mevr. Marie-Anne van der Meer, Eerste Kamer der Staaten-Generaal, Binnenhof 22, Postbus 20017, The Hague, Netherlands.

VAN ES, Andrée C.; Dutch, Member of the Second Chamber; *born:* 26 January 1953, The Hague, Netherlands; *education:* Science of law, specialising in science of leading in constitutional study direction; *party:* Pacifistisch Socialistische Partij (PSP, Pacific Socialist Party); Groen Links (Green Left); *political career:* aid, PSP Second Chamber group; Mem. of Second Chamber, 1981-; Pres. PSP group in Second Chamber until September 1989; *professional career:* worked at JAC (centre for young people with problems), Amsterdam; *private address:* Jan Luykenstraat 26, 1071 CP Amsterdam, the Netherlands; *office address:* Mevr. Andrée van Es, Tweede Kamer der Staaten-Generaal, Binnenhof 1A, Postbus 20018, The Hague, Netherlands.

VAN HEEMSKERCK PILLIS-DUVEKOT, Sari; Dutch, Member of the Second Chamber; *born:* 2 May 1940, Goes, Netherlands; *education:* sec. ed.; One year studying in USA; secretary diploma from Schoevers; *party:* Volkspartij voor Vrijheid en Democratie (VVD, People's Party for Freedom and Democracy); *political career:* policy-developer, Rotterdam town-council; Mem. of town council; Pres. of VVD group in town council; treasurer, Foundation Organisation Women in the VVD; Mem. of Dutch delegation to General Meeting of UN, 1981; Mem. of Standing Cttees. for Defence (first Spokeswoman), Foreign Affairs, Art and Culture; Mem., NATO Assembly; Mem. of Second Chamber, 1982-; *professional career:* used to work in advertising and marketing; policy developer Zeeuwse Vrouwenraad; General Secretary, Federation LSB; mem., Board of Dutch Dance Theatre; mem., Board of Dutch Broadcasting Organisation; *private address:* Celebesstraat 20, 2585 TJ, The Hague, The

Netherlands; *office address:* Mevr. Sari van Heemskerck Pillis-Duvekot, Tweede Kamer der Staten-Generaal, Binnenhof 1A, Postbus 20018, The Hague, Netherlands.

Van HEMELDONCK, Marijke; Belgian, Member of the European Parliament; *born:* 23 December 1931; *party:* Socialistische Partij (SP, Socialist Party); *political career:* trade unionist; MEP 1982-; *private address:* Sterneplein 3, 1050 Brussels, Belgium; *office address:* Mevr. Marijke Van Hemeldonck, European Parliament, Centre Européen, Plateau de Kirchberg, BP 2929, Luxembourg; *phone:* Luxembourg 43001.

VANIA, Lúcia (Lúcia Vania Abrao Costa); Brazilian, Federal Deputy; *born:* 15 October 1944, Cumari, Goiás; *parents:* Abdala Abrao and Rita Gonçalves; *married:* Irapuan Costa Jr; *children:* Carlos Frederico, Ana Carla, George Henrique; *education:* UFG Goiania, communications, 1979-82; Oxford Univ., UK,post-grad studies in political science, 1985; *party:* Partido do Movimento Democrático Brasileira (PMDB, Party of the Brazlian Democratic Movement); *political career:* Federal Deputy for Goiás, 1987-91 and 1991-95; *professional career:* journalist and professor; *office address:* Ms Lúcia Vania, Chamber of Deputies, Praça dos 3 Poderes, Ed. Principal, 70160 Brasilia, DF, Brazil; *phone:* (61) 225 2885.

VAN NIEWENHAVEN, Jeltje; Dutch, Member of the Second Chamber; *born:* 2 August 1943, Weststellingwerf, Netherlands; *education:* MULO; librarian training; *party:* Partij van de Arbeid (PvdA, Labour Party); *political career:* help to Pres. of PvdA; Mem. Nat. group Red Women in PvdA; Mem. of Second Chamber, 1981-82 and 1983-; *professional career:* librarian, History of Art Institute of Univ. of Leiden; librarian, Wiardi Beckman Foundation; *private address:* De Lairessestraat 3', 1071 NR Amsterdam, the Netherlands; *office address:* Mevr. Jeltje van Niewenhaven, Tweede Kamer der Staaten-Generaal, Binnenhof 1A, Postbus 20018, The Hague, Netherlands.

VAN RIJN-VELLEKOOP, Drs. Leni; Dutch, Member of the Second Chamber; *born:* 17 November 1936, Rotterdam, Netherlands; *parents:* P.C Vellekonigs and G.Kllivenhoven; *married:* G.F.J. Van Rijn, 1960; *public role of spouse:* technical economic adviser; *children:* one; *languages:* English, German, some French; *education:* HBS-B (sec. ed.); Kweekschool for teachers, mathematics and trade knowledge, masters in economics; *party:* Partij van de Arbeid (PvdA, Labour Party); *political career:* Mem. of town council, Krimpen aan den Jissel; Mem. of Rijmond Cncl.; Mem. of Provincial States of Zuid-Holland; Mem. of Second Chamber, 1987-; *interests:* environment, economics, finances; *professional career:* teacher; committed

employee, environment policies, Openbaar Lichaam Rijmond; *private address:* Zwanenkade 116, 2925 AT krimpen aan den Ÿssel, the Netherlands; *office address:* Drs. Leni van Rijn-Vellekoop, Tweede Kamer der Staaten-Generaal, Binnenhof 1A, Postbus 20018, The Hague, Netherlands.

VANSTONE, Amanda Eloise; Australian, Senator; *born:* 7 December 1952, Adelaide, South Australia; *education:* BA, LLB, Adelaide; Graduate Diploma in Legal Practice, Marketing Studies Certificate, SAIT; *party:* Liberal Party; *political career:* Policy Chairperson, Liberal Party Women's Council, South Australia, 1979-82; Liberal Party Policy Co-ordinator, South Australia, 1982-84; Delegate, Liberal Party Federal Council, 1983; elected to Senate for South Australia, 1984-; Committee Service: Mem. of the Senate Standing Cttee. for Regulations and Ordinances, 1985-87; for Standing Orders, 1986-87; Mem. of the Senate Legislative and General Purpose Standing Cttee. for Finance and Govt. Operations, 1985-87; Mem. of the Senate Estimates Cttee. F, 1985-87 and 1987-; E, Mar.-Jun. 1987; Mem., Opposition Shadow Ministry, 1987-; Shadow Special Minister of State, 1987-; Spokesman on Status of Women, 1987-; on Australian Capital Territory, 1987-; *office address:* Ms Amanda Vanstone, Senate, Parliament House, Room M13, Canberra, ACT 2600, Australia; *phone:* (062) 727111.

VARGA LESTAR, Mária; Hungarian, Member of the Országyúlés; *office address:* Ms Mária Varga Lestar, Országyúlés, Kossuth L. tér 1-3, Budapest V, Hungary; *phone:* 22 5058; 22 5059.

VARGANE, Piros Ildikó; Hungarian, Member of the Országgyúlés; *party:* ASZ; *office address:* Ms Piros Ildiko Vargáné, Országgyúlés, Kossuth L. tér 1-3, Budapest V, Hungary; *phone:* 22 5058; 22 5059.

VARPASUO, Päivi Paula Annikki; Finnish, Member of the Eduskunta; *born:* 21 December 1945, Vihti, Finland; *parents:* Eero Olavi Varpasuo and Hilja Annikki Varpasuo (née Wallentin); *education:* B. Political Science, 1969; M. Sc., 1970; *party:* Kansallinen Kokoomus (KoK, National Coalition Party); *political career:* Mem., Vihti Municipal Cncl., 1969 and Chmn., 1977-83, 1985; mem., Parish Cncl., Vihti, 1975; mem. of Eduskunta, 1985; 1st Vice-Chmn., Central Cncl., Helsinki Regional Planning Authority, 1985; Chmn., Right-wing Temperance Movement, 1985; *interests:* Chmn., Vihti Socy., 1983; *professional career:* Sec., Town Planning, Espoo Borough, 1970-71; Information and Travel Officer, Espoo Town, 1971-73; Dep. Head of Information, (Ibid), 1974-75; Head of Information, Finnish Municipal Assn., 1975; *honours and awards:* Knight of the Order of the Lion of Finland; *publications:* Kunnallinen tiedottaminen (with

Haikonen and Kivistö), 1977; *office address:* Eduskunta, 00102 Helsinki, Finland.

VARTANIAN, Elsie; American, New Hampshire State Representative; *born:* 19 July 1930, Haverhill, Mass., USA; *married:* David, 1952; *religion:* Congregational; *education:* MacIntosh Business School; *party:* Republican Party; *political career:* Vice-Chwn. and Committeewoman, Northeast Region Republican National Cttee; *memberships:* Salem, New Hampshire and National Assn. of Realtors. New England Caucus of Women Legislators; National Order of Women Legislators; *professional career:* owner and Pres., Elsie Vartanian Real Estate Inc; *honours and awards:* Distinguished Service Award, Governor's office of Voluntarism, 1987; *office address:* Ms Elsie Vartanian, 44 Brady Avenue, Salem, New Hampshire 03079, USA.

VASQUEZ NAVA, María Elena; Mexican, Comptroller-General of Mexico; *office address:* Ms María Elena Vasquez Nava, Office of the Comptroller-General, Avenida Insurgenes Sur 1735, 10 Piso, 01020 Mexico DF.

VAYSSADE, Marie-Claude; French, Member of the European Parliament; *born:* 8 August 1936; *party:* Parti Socialiste (PS, Socialist Party); *political career:* municipal and regional govt.; MEP, 1979-; *private address:* 78 rue Maréchal Oudinot, 54000 Nancy, France; *office address:* Mme. Marie-Claude Vayssade, European Parliament, Centre Européen, Plateau de Kirchberg, BP 2929, Luxembourg; *phone:* Luxembourg 43001.

VEIEROD, Tove; Norwegian, Minister of Health and Social Affairs; *born:* 19 September 1940, Harstad; *married:* Tom Veierod; *public role of spouse:* Information Officer at Norsk Hydro; *political career:* Dep. Chair, Exec. Cttee., Norwegian Braodcasting Corp., until 1990; Mem., Troms County Exec. Board, until 1990; Minister of Health and Social Affairs, Nov. 1990-; *memberships:* former Chair, North Norway Arts Festival and Troms County College Board; Mem., North Norwegian Cultural Cncl; *professional career:* former secondary school teacher; State Sec., Ministry of Culture and Scientific Affairs, 1986-89; *office address:* Ms Tove Veierod, Ministry of Health and Social Affairs, Akersgaten 42, P.O. Box 8011 Dep, 0030 Oslo 1, Norway; *phone:* 902) 34 90 90.

VEIL, Simone Annie; French, Member of the European Parliament; *born:* 13 July 1927, Nice, Alpes-Maritimes, France; *parents:* André Jacob and Yvonne Jacob (née Steimetz); *married:* Antoine Veil, 1946; *children:* Jean, Claude-Nicolas, Pierre-François; *education:* Lycée, Nice; Faculty of Law, Paris, graduate in Law; Diploma from Institute of Political Studies, Paris; *political career:* incumbent attaché, Ministry of Justice, 1957-59;

attaché, Ministry of Justice, 1959-70; Technical Advisor to Cabinet of René Pleven, Keeper of the Seals; Sec. Gen., High Magistrates Cncl., 1970; mem. of Administrative Cncl. of ORTF, 1972; Minister of Health, 1974-77; Pres. of Cncl. of Information about Electro-Nuclear Energy, 1977; Minister of Health, responsible for Social Security, 1977-79; MEP, Jun. 1979-; Pres. European Parliament, 1979-82; Pres. of Commission on Legal Affairs, 1982-84; Pres. of Liberal Democratic and Reformist Group, 1984-89; retired as magistrate, 1985; Pres. French Cttee. for the European Year of the Environment, 1987; Pres. of Cttee. for the European Year of Cinema and Television, 1988; mem., European Parliament Cttee. on the Environment, Public Health and Consumer Protection; *honours and awards:* Doctor honoris causa, Univ. of Princetown, 1976, Weizmann Institute, 1976, Hebrew Univ. of Jerusalem, Univ. of Yale, USA, Univ. of Edinburgh, UK, Univ. of Cambridge, 1980, Univ. of Urdino, Italy, Univ. of Georgetown, 1981, Yeshiva Univ., New York, Univ. of Sussex, UK, 1982, Free Univ. of Brussels, 1984; Knight of National Order of Merit; Award for Prison Administration; Athenes Prize, Onassis Foundation, 1980; Charlemagne Prize, 1981; Louise Weiss Foundation Prize, 1981; Louise Michel Prize, 1983; Jabotinsky Prize, 1983; Prize for Daily Courage, 1984; Eleonore and Franklin Roosevelt Foundation Prize, 1984; Living Legacy Award, San Diego, 1987; Johanna Lowenheuz Prize, 1987; Thomas Dehler Prize, Munich, 1988; Univ. of Brandeis, USA, 1989; *publications:* L'Adoption, données médicales, psychologiques et sociales, 1969; *private address:* 11 Place Vauban, 75007 Paris, France; *office address:* Mme. Simone Veil, European Parliament, Centre Européen, Plateau de Kirchberg, BP 2929, Luxembourg.

VENNEGERTS, Christa; German, former Member of the Bundestag; *born:* 4 August 1951, Meppen/Ems; *party:* Die Grünen (Green Party); *political career:* member of Middle Class Advisory Board, Federal Ministry of Economics; mem. of Bundestag, party list of Baden-Württemberg, 1987-90; *professional career:* practical work experience in banking; practical work experience, technical economic association; *office address:* Frau Christa Vennegerts, Bundeshaus, 5300 Bonn 1, West Germany.

VENTER, Elizabeth Hendrina; South African, Minister of National Health and Population Development; *born:* 9 December 1938, Krugersdorp, South Africa; *parents:* Dick and Bettie Stapelberg; *married:* Dr. H.S. Venter, 1963; *children:* two s; *religion:* Dutch Reformed Church; *languages:* Afrikaans, English; *education:* Carletonville Afrikaans High School, matriculation; Univ. of Pretoria, BA Social Work, MA Social Work, Ph.D. Social Work; *party:* National Party; *political career:* Pres., SAVF, Transvaal, 1980-84; nominated Mem. of Parliament, 1984-; Hon. Pres., of SAVF;

Chair, Federale Vroueraad-Volkbelang, Cncl. of 28 Afrikaans women's cultural socs.; Mem., of standing Cttee. on National Health and Population Development and Mem. of the joint Cttee. investigating establishment of family courts; Mem., managing Cttee. NP Pretoria Regional Board; Mem. NP Transvaal Exec. Cttee. and Federal Board; Mem. of caucus study groups on Constitutional Development, Justice, Health and Welfare Services, Local Management, Housing and Works and National Health and Population Development; Mem. of Parliament for Innesdal, 1989-; Minister for National Health and Population Development, 1989; *interests:* the development of people; *professional career:* social worker, Suid-Afrikaanse Vroue Federasie (SAVF), 1960s; marriage guidance Cllr., Pretoria; *honours and awards:* Highest Award of the ATKV Vrou en Moederbeweging; The Paul Harris Fellowship Award of the Rotary Club, Carltonville; Newsmaker of the Year and various other awards; *office address:* Ms Elizabeth Venter, Private Bag X9070, Cape Town, South Africa, OR, Private Bag X399, Pretoria, South Africa.

VERANO-YAP, Hon. Lorna L.; Filipino, Congresswoman; *born:* 17 July 1951; *parents:* Felisberto M. Verano and Trinidad Lizarranga; *married:* Adelberto F. Yap; *public role of spouse:* first Senior Aide-de-Camp of President Aquino; Colonel, Philippine Air Force; *children:* two; *religion:* Roman Catholic; *languages:* Filipino, English, Spanish, French; *education:* Univ. of the Philippines, AB, Speech and Drama (Cum Laude), and credits for Law; *party:* Liberal Party; *political career:* founding leader, Alyansa Para sa Kaganapan ng Katarungan sa Pasay; founding mem., 21 August Movement; Vice Pres. for New Membership and Steering Cttee. for the House; Vice Pres., National Executive Cttee. Liberal Party; Congresswoman; *interests:* human rights advocate; consumer prtectionist; exponent of small businesses; champion of the poor; nationalist; land reform and anti-feudal measures advocate; fighter of monopolies; combinations and trust arrangements; *professional career:* Editor-in-Chief, Univ. of the Philippines Lady Vanguards Gazette; National Sales Manager, Xerox Philippines; Gov., Manila Int. Futures Exchange; *honours and awards:* Most Outstanding Congresswoman of the Philippines, 1989-90; Pines Universal Awards; Top Ten Lawmakers, 1988; *private address:* 178 Swallow Drive, Greenmeadows, Quezon City, Philippines; *office address:* The Hon. Ms. Lorna Verano-Yap, The Congress of the Philippines - House of Representatives, Batasang Pambansa Bldg., Quezon City, Manila, The Philippines.

VERHÜLSDONK, Roswitha; German, Parliamentary Secretary of State for the Family and Senior Citizens; *born:* 26 April 1927, Oberspay, Kreis St. Goar; *parents:* Rudolf Woll and Josephine Woll (née Henkel); *married:* Eduard Verhülsdonk, 1949; *children:* Ursula, Michael;

religion: Roman Catholic; *languages:* English, French; *education:* Hilda Grammar School, Koblenz, matriculation, 1947; Joh. Gutenberg Univ., Mainz, philology studies, 1947-49; *party:* Christlich Demokratische Union (CDU, Christian Democratic Union), 1964; *political career:* acting chair person, CDU/CSU group in the Bundestag; mem. of state Cttee. and district Cttee. of Rhineland-Palatinate; acting federal representative of the CDU Women's Union; mem. town council; Koblenz; mem. of Bundestag, 1972-; Parly. Sec. of State for the Family and Senior Citizens; *professional career:* lecturer, youth and adult education, Catholic Adult Education Organisation, 1966-72; *honours and awards:* Federal Merit Cross, 1st Class, 1983; Baronhood, Stein, Rhineland-Palatinate, 1986; Grand Federal Merit Cross, 1988; *clubs:* Chairperson, Women's Catholic Community, Bistum Trier; Central Committee of German Catholics; Committee, Caritas- Verband, Koblenz; *recreations:* music, sport; *private address:* Kurfürstenstr. 91, Koblenz D54, West Germany; *office address:* Frau Roswitha Verhülsdonk, Bundeshaus, 5300 Bonn 1, West Germany.

VERMA, Usha; Indian, Member of the Lok Sabha; *born:* 7 April 1933, Muria Billahra Village, Bilasanda Taluk, Pilibhit District; *parents:* the late Shri Atma Ram Verma; *married:* the late Shri Balgovind Verma; *children:* two s., two d; *education:* privately educated; *party:* Congress (I); *political career:* Pres., Uttar Pradesh Consumer Samiti; Pres., Nursing Cncl.; Exec. Pres., National Federation of Railway Porters, Vendors and Caterers; Mem., Lok Sabah; *interests:* upliftment of backward and downtrodden women, child welfare in rural areas, conservation; *recreations:* cookery, gardening, reading religious books; *private address:* Usha Nikunj, Mohalla Bhur, Gola Gokaran Nath, Lakhimpur Kheri District, Uttar Pradesh, India; *office address:* Smt. Usha Verma, Lok Sabha, Parliament House, New Dehli 110 011, India; *phone:* (11) 381825; 377102.

VERMA, Veena; Indian, Member of the Rajya Sabha; *born:* 1 September 1941, Jaipur, Rajasthan; *parents:* P.N. Raizada; *married:* the late Shrikant Verma, 1967; *children:* one s; *education:* Rajasthan Univ., MA, Sociology; *party:* Congress Party; *political career:* Mem. of the Rajya Sabha, 1986-; Vice Pres., Indian Council of World Affairs, 1986-; Hindi Salahkar Samiti, Ministries of Home Affairs, Human Resource Development, 1986-, and Ministry of Welfare, 1987-; Mem., Executive Cttee., Indian Writers Union, 1986-; Mem., General Assembly of Indian Council for Cultural Relations, 1986-; Mem., Village Development Dept., Govt. of Madhya Pradesh, 1986-; Mem., All India United Women's Forum, 1987-; Mem., Chhattisgarh Vikas Pradhikaran, 1987-; *memberships:* National Council, All India Skilled Manpower Association, 1986; *professional career:* Patron, United Children's

Movement, 1986-; Patron, Cancer Society of Bilaspur, 1986-; *clubs:* Inner Wheel Club, Delhi and North Zone, 1986-; *recreations:* modern Hindi poetry, travelling abroad, computers, gardening, classical Indian music; *private address:* Tilak Nagar, Bilaspur, Madhya Pradesh, PIN - 495001; *office address:* Shrimati Veena Verma, Rajya Sabha, Parliament House, New Dehli 110 011, India; *phone:* (11) 389977; 389997.

VERSNEL née Schmitz, Machteld Maria; Dutch, Member of the Second Chamber; *born:* 8 September 1940, Bilthoven, The Netherlands; *parents:* Willy Karel Emil Schmitz and E.C.J. Schmitz (née Blömer); *married:* Johan Freedy Versnel, 1968; *public role of spouse:* civil servant City of Utrecht; *children:* Diederik, Roderik, Nolfert; *languages:* Dutch, English, French, German, Indonesian; *education:* R.U. Utrecht, history, 1959-66; *party:* Democrats 66, (D66), 1966; *political career:* regional organiser, D66, Utrecht, 1967-68; Mem., Utrecht City Cncl., 1970-74, 1978-79, 1982-86; Mem., National Party Board, 1975-78; Chwn., Political Education Centre, 1986-89; Mem., Parly., 1989-; *interests:* environmental planning, housing, adult education, welfare, internal affairs; *professional career:* functionary, Utrecht Univ. Museum, 1961-72; civil servant, Home Office, The Hague, 1986-89; *recreations:* tennis, swimming, reading; *private address:* Parkstraat 41, 3561 PE, Utrecht, The Netherlands; *office address:* Mevr. Machteld Versnel, Tweede Kamer der Staten-Generaal, Binnenhof 1A, Postbus 20018, The Hague, The Netherlands.

VESPAGET, Josephine M.; Dutch, Member of the Second Chamber; *born:* 25 January 1946, Helmond, Netherlands; *children:* two; *education:* gymnasium-A; sociology; *party:* Partij van de Arbeid (PvdA, Labour Party); *political career:* active Mem. of town council, Zeist; Secretary-Treasurer of the Evert Vermeer Foundation of the PvdA (for development affairs); Mem. of Second Chamber, 1986-; *interests:* development co-operation, women and art, Southern Africa; *professional career:* employee NSKV; employee Open School; leading employee art education; *publications:* Various on art education, women and art, Southern Africa; *private address:* Nieuwe Boschstraat 28, 4811 CX Breda, the Netherlands; *office address:* Mevr. Josephine Vespaget, Tweede Kamer der Staten-Generaal, Binnenhof 1A, Postbus 20018, The Hague, Netherlands.

VÉZINA, Monique; Canadian, Minister of State for Employment and Immigration; *born:* July 1935, Rimouski; *children:* four; *party:* Progressive Conservative; *political career:* former Chairperson, Commission of Secondary Education; former Mem., Superior Cncl. of Education; Minister for External Relations, 1984-86; Minister of Supply and Services, 1986-87; Minister of State for Transport, 1987-88;

Minister of State for Employment and Immigration, 1988-; Minister of State for Senior Citizens, 1988-; *professional career:* Dir. and Chairperson, Federation of Popular Banks, Desjardins du Bas Saint-Laurent, then Sec. and Dir.; Chairperson, Gérardin-Vaillancourt Foundation; Mem., Board of Dirs., Rimouski Chamber of Commerce; Mem., Board of Dirs., Soc. Immobilière de Quebec; former Vice-Pres., Soc. of Automobile Insurance Companies of Quebec; *office address:* Mme. Monique Vézina, House of Commons, Parliament Buildings, Wellington Street, Ottawa, Ontario K1A OA6, Canada; *phone:* (613) 957 3744; *fax:* 952 0874.

VICK, Kathleen; American, Vice Chair of the Louisiana State Democrat Party; *born:* 1938, New Orleans, Louisiana, USA; *married:* Kendall Vick; *education:* Wellesley College, BA, 1960; Tulane Univ. Grad. School, 1962; *party:* Democratic Party; *political career:* Special Asst. to Chmn. Goals for Louisiana Cttee., 1968-70; Board Mem., Independent Women's Organisation and Sth. Louisiana Women's Democratic Organisation; Sec., Democrat Alliance of Louisiana; National Committeewoman, Louisiana Young Democrats, 1968-71; Mem., Louisiana Commisssion on Status of Women, 1971-74; formely: delegate, Democrat National Convention, 1972, 1976, 1980, 1984, 1988; Mem., Rules Cttee., 1980, 1984, Chwn., 1988; Hunt Commission, 1980; Compliance Review Commission, 1980-84; Arrangments Cttee., 1984; Charter Mem., Women's Political Caucus; Board Mem., Democrat Inst. for International Affairs; Mem., Economic Advisory Cttee, Regional Planning Commission; currently: Mem., Democrat State Chmns. Assn.; Mem., Governors Job Training Advisory Cncl.; Chwn., Compliance Assistance Commission, Democrat National Cttee; *memberships:* Inter-racial Cncl. for Business Community; Louisiana Priorities for the Future; Regional Transit Auth. for Greater New Orleans Area, Chwn., 1980-; *professional career:* currently Pres., Program Consultants Inc.; partner, Regency Imports/Experts Inc; *honours and awards:* Outstanding Woman of Achievment, 1980; Outstanding Planning Contribution to the State of Louisiana, 1979; *office address:* Mrs Kathleen Vick, 1235 Washington Avenue, New Orleans, Louisiana 70130, USA.

VICKERS, Deanna; American, Idaho State Representative; *born:* 23 December 1940, Flandreau, South Dakota, USA; *married:* Lee; *children:* Damon, Warren, Dionne; *religion:* Roman Catholic; *education:* North West Montana State Univ.; Univ. of Texas; *party:* Democratic Party; *political career:* Idaho State Rep., District 6; *memberships:* Idaho Energy Resources Policy Board, 1980-83; *professional career:* former Civic Leader and Dental Hygienist; *office address:* Ms Deanna Vickers, 807 St. Lewiston, Idaho 83501, USA.

VICKERS, Baroness (cr. 1975, Life Peer) Joan Helen, MBE; DBE; British, Member of the House of Lords; *parents:* the late Horace Cecil Vickers; *education:* St. Monica's Coll., Burgh Heath; Paris; *party:* Conservative Party; *political career:* contested Poplar, 1945; MP (Cons.), Plymouth Devonport div., 1955-74; Cons. delegate, Council of Europe and WEU, 1967-74; mem., House of Lords, 1975-; *professional career:* served with BRCS in SE Asia; Pres., Inst. of Qualified Private Secs., 1969-; Pres., Int. Friendship Assn., 1969-; Pres., Int. Bureau for Suppression of Traffic in Persons; Status of Women Cttee., London Centre for Homeless Young Persons, 1977-; Chmn., Nat. Centre for Cued Speech for the Deaf; Chmn., Greater London Red Cross Blood Transfusion Service; Pres., European-China Assn; Chmn., Anglo-Indonesian Soc; *honours and awards:* MBE; Netherlands Red Cross; DSC; Freedom of City of Plymouth, 1982; *recreations:* reading, fishing, gardening, travel; *private address:* Manor House, East Chisenbury, Pewsey, Wilts., UK; *office address:* Baroness Vickers, House of Lords, London SW1A 0PW.

VIK, Anne Petrea; Norwegian, former Minister of Agriculture; *born:* 8 January 1933, Trondenes, Norway; *parents:* Jarle Kornelius Kristiansen and Jette Marie Kristiansen; *married:* Per Vik, 1955; *education:* Sixth Form College, 1950; Telecommunication Course, 1951; School of Home Economics, 1954; *party:* Independent; *political career:* mem., Borough Board of Control, 1972-76; Chmn., Schools Board of Control, 1976-79; mem. County Council, 1980; Deputy Representative, County Cttee.; mem., County Cultural Cttee.; Minister of Agriculture, 1989-Oct.-1990; *professional career:* employee, Televerket (Telecommunications Company), 1951-55; Deputy Teacher, 1950-68; Farmer, Own Farming Concern, 1955; mem. of Board of Control Farm Women's Federation, Troms, 1965-73; mem. of Board of Control, Norwegian Farm Women's Federation, 1973-79; Chmn., Norwegian Farm Women's Federation, 1979; member of Board of Control, Norwegian Farmers Federation, 1979-83; mem., Norwegian Agricultural Science Research Council; *office address:* Ms Anne Vik, Ministry of Agriculture, Akersgt. 42, POB 8007 Dep., 0030 Oslo 1, Norway.

VIRGIL-GIRON, Rebecca; American, Secretary-of-State for New Mexico; *born:* 4 September 1954, Taos, New Mexico, USA; *parents:* Felix W. Virgil and Cecilia Virgil (née Santistevan); *married:* Rick Giron; *children:* Andrew; *education:* grad., New Mexico State Univ; *political career:* Sec.-of-State, New Mexico; *memberships:* Young Democrats; National Assn. of Secs.-of-State; League of Women Voters; Mexican American National Women's Assn.; Sickle Cell Cncl. of New Mexico; Museum of New Mexico Foundation; *honours and awards:* Outstanding Young Woman of America, 1986; *private address:* P.O. Box 135, Albuquerque, New Mexico 87503, USA; *office address:* Mrs Rebecca Virgil-Giron, 400 State Capitol, Sante Fe, New Mexico 87503, USA.

VISIEDO NIETO, Antonia Angelina; Spanish, Deputy; *born:* 18 April 1957, Santiago de la Ribera, Murcia, Spain; *education:* degree in psychology; *party:* Partido Socialista Obrero Español (PSOE, Spanish Socialist Workers' Party); *political career:* in charge of Secretariat for Women's issues, President's cabinet of Murcia autonomous government; Deputy, PSOE, Murcia, 1986-89, re-elected 1989-; mem., Cttee. on Justice and Interior; *professional career:* clinical psychologist; *office address:* Ms Antonia Visiedo Nieto, Congreso de los Diputados, Fernán Flor 1, Madrid 14, Spain.

VISNOVCOVA, Petronela; Czechoslovakian, Deputy to the Slovak National Council; *born:* 1 June 1922; *education:* Bratislava Technical College, 1945-48; *party:* Komunistická Strana Ceskoslovenska (KSC, Communist party of Czechoslovakia); *political career:* nominated as candidate Mem., CP of Slovakia for elections to Nat. Assembly for drafting Constitution, 1946; Mem. of Staff, Commissariat for Trade, 1950-56, Dep. Commissioner, 1956-57, First Dep. Commissioner for Trade, 1957-60; Mem., Cncl., West Slovak Regional Nat. Cttee. and Chairperson, Trade Commission, 1960-64; mem., Exec. Cttee., CSSR Cttee. of Women in Slovakia, 1963-69; Dep, Slovak Nat. Cncl., 1964, 1968, 1976, 1981, 1986-; Commissioner for Trade and Chairperson of Trade Commission, Slovak nat. Cncl, 1964-68; Mem., Presidium, Slovak Nat. Cncl., 1964-; Mem., Presidium, Central Cttee., CSSR Union of Women, 1967-69; Mem., Chamber of Nations and Chairperson, Foreign Policy Cttee., Mem. of Presidium and Chamber of Nations, Federal Assembly CSST, 1969-81; Chairperson, Cttee. for Nat. Cttees. of Slovak Nat. Cncl., 1969-; Dep. Chairperson, Tourism Cttee. of Slovak Socialist Republic, 1979; *office address:* Ms Petronela Visnovcova, Slavenská národná rada, Októbrové nám. 12, 800 00 Bratislava, Czechoslovakia; *phone:* (07) 311500.

VLIEGENTHART, Margo A.; Dutch, Member of the Second Chamber; *born:* 18 July 1958, Utrecht, Netherlands; *education:* gymnasium-B; psychology; *party:* Partij van de Arbeid (PvdA, Labour Party); *political career:* worked for PvdA Second Chamber Group, policy making about welfare; Pres., Young Socialist in PvdA; Mem. of Party board; Mem. of Second Chamber, 1987-; secretary of PvdA, 1989-; *private address:* Van Pabstlaan 40, 2274KG Voorburg, the Netherlands; *office address:* Mevr. Margo Vliegenthart, Tweede Kamer der Staaten-Generaal, Binnenhof 1A, Postbus 20018, The Hague, Netherlands.

VOLKHOLZ, Sybille; German, Deputy Member of the Bundesrat; *born:* 17 March 1944, Dramburg, Pommern; *parents:* Bruno Schuster and Diny Schuster (née Robben); *education:* secondary school; Univ., graduate in sociology; teacher training college; *party:* Die Grünen (The Greens); *political career:* Vice-Pres., Teachers' Trade Union in Berlin, GEW, 1979-89; Senator for Schools, Professional Training and Sport, Berlin, 1989-90; Dep. Mem., Bundesrat for Berlin, 1991-; *interests:* educational policy, democratic rights and representation; *professional career:* teacher, Berlin, 1972-89; *office address:* Ms Sybille Volkholz, Bundesrat, 5300 Bonn 1, Germany.

VON ALEMANN, Mechthild; German, Member of the European Parliament; *born:* 29 January 1937, Seebach/Thuringia; *children:* one s; *languages:* English; *party:* Freie Demokratische Partei (FDP, Free Democratic Party), 1966; *political career:* actively engaged in local politics in Düsseldorf, 1966-; mem. FDP exec., MEP, 1979-84, 1989-; Gen. Sec. Federation of European Liberals and Democrats, 1985-; *professional career:* librarian in firms of management consultants, 1968-; *office address:* Frau Mechthild von Alemann, European Parliament, Centre Européen, Plateau de Kirchberg, BP 2929, Luxembourg.

VRHOVCAK, Ivanka; Yugoslavian, Member of the Federal Chamber of the Federal Assembly; *born:* 1933, Pusenka, near Pluj, Yugoslavia; *party:* League of Communists of Yugoslavia (LCY), 1954-; *political career:* elected to Central Cttee. at 10th Congress of LCY, 1974; Mem., LCY Statutory Commission, 1982-; Mem., Federal Assembly, 1982-; *professional career:* public relations official, Ljubljana; *office address:* Ms Ivanka Vrhovcak, Savezna Skupstina, Yugoslavia.

VUCANOVICH, Barbara; American, Member of the House of Representatives; *born:* 22 June 1921, Camp Dix, New Jersey, USA; *parents:* Thomas F. Farrell and Ynez Farrell (née White); *married:* George Vucanovich, 1965; *children:* Patty Cafferata, Michael Dillon, Kenneth Dillon, Thomas Dillon, Susan Anderson; *religion:* Catholic; *education:* Manhattanville College, New York, 1938-39; *party:* Republican Party; *political career:* Mem., House of Reps., 2nd District, Nevada, 1983-; Asst. Regional Minority Whip; Mem., Administration, Appropriations Cttee.; Interior and Insular Affairs Cttee.; ranking Mem., Mining Sub-Cttee.; Mem., Exec. Cttee., Republican Study Cttee. and Republican Research Cttee., US House of Reps.; Mem., Steering Cttee., Travel and Tourism Caucus; Mem., Environment and Energy Study Conference; Mem., Pro-Life Caucus, Arts Caucus, Human Rights Caucus, Copper Caucus, Mining Caucus, Insurance Caucus; Mem., Congress Aviation Forum; *memberships:* St. Mary's Hospital Guild; *professional career:* owner, Welcome Aboard Vacation Centre, 1970-74; *clubs:* Soroptomists International; Emblem Club; Reno Republican Women's Club; *recreations:* golf, flying; *office address:* Mrs Barbara Vucanovich, 540 Riverview Circle W., Reno, Nevada 89509, USA.

WAGNER, Sue Ellen; American, Lieutenant-Governor of Nevada; *born:* 6 January 1940, Portland, Maine, USA; *parents:* Raymond A. Pooler and Kathryn Pooler (née Hooper); *married:* Dr. Peter Wagner, 1964; *children:* Kirk, Kristina; *religion:* Episcopal; *education:* Univ. of Arizona, BA, 1962; Northwestern Univ., Evanston, MA, 1964; *party:* Republican Party; *political career:* Mem., Mayor's Advisory Cttee., Reno, 1973-84; Chwn., Blue Ribbon Task Force on Housing, 1974-75; Mem., Washoe County Republican Central Cttee., 1974-84; Mem., Nevada State Republican Central Cttee., 1975-84; Nevada State Assemblywoman, 1975-83; Mem., Nevada Legislative Commission, 1976-77; delegate, Social Service Cttee., Cncl. of State Govt.; Nevada State Senator, District 3, 1980-; Mem., Ways, Means, Judiciary, Electoral, Legislative Function, Education and Transport Cttees., Nevada State Senate; *memberships:* American Assn. of Univ. Women; Reno Chapter, Business and Professional Women; *professional career:* Asst. Dean, Ohio State Univ., 1963-64; teacher, history and American Govt., Catalina High School, Tucson, Arizona, 1964-65; reporter, Tucson Daily Citizen, 1965-68; currently, special advisor to the Pres., Desert Research Inst., Sparks, Nevada; *honours and awards:* Thomas Campbell Award for Outstanding Sophomore Woman, Univ. of Arizona, 1960; Merrill P. Freeman Medal for Outstanding Senior Woman, 1962; Kappa Alpha Theta National Grad. Scholarship and Phelps-Dodge Post Grad. Fellowship, 1962; Outstanding Legislator, Nevada Young Republicans, 1976; One of 10 Outstanding Young Women in America; Outstanding Legislator Award, State Young Republicans; Woman of the Year, Reno Business and Professional Women; Outstanding Young Woman in America Award; *publications:* Diary of a Candidate; On People and Things; *office address:* Mrs Sue Ellen Wagner, 845 Tamarack Drive, Reno, Nevada 89509, USA.

WALLEY, Joan Lorraine; British, Member of Parliament; *born:* 23 January 1949; *parents:* the late Arthur Walley and Mary Emma Walley; *married:* Jan Ostrowski, 1981; *children:* two s; *education:* Biddulph Grammar School; Hull University; University College, Swansea; *party:* Labour Party; *political career:* Lambeth Councillor; Member of Parliament for Stoke-on-Trent North, 1987-; Opposition Spokesperson on Environmental Protection and Development, 1988-; *interests:* environment; health; *professional career:* Alcoholics Recovery Project, 1970-73; Planning Dept., Swansea City Cncl.; Local Govt. Officer, Wandsworth London Borough Cncl.; Vice-Pres., Inst. of Environmental Health Officers; NACRO Development Officer; *recreations:* music; swimming; walking; *office address:* Ms Joan Walley, House of Commons, London SW1A OAA.

WALLSTRÖM, Margot; Swedish, Minister with special responsibility for Ecclesiastical, Equality and Youth Affairs (Ministry of Public Administration); *office address:* Ms Margot Wallström, Riksdag, Fack, S-100 12, Stockholm, Sweden; *phone:* Stockholm 786 4000.

WALTERS, Shirley (Mary Shirley); Australian, Senator; *born:* 31 August 1925, Sydney, NSW, Australia; *parents:* the late Sir Eric Harrison KCMG KCVO and the late Mary Harrison; *married:* Dr. David John Walters, 1949; *public role of spouse:* Consultant Obstetrician and Gynaecologist, Hobart; Alderman, Hobart City Council; *children:* four; *religion:* Presbyterian; *languages:* English; *education:* qualified nurse; *party:* Liberal Party; *political career:* elected to the Senate for Tasmania 1975-; Committee Service: Mem. of the Senate Standing Cttee. for Library, 1976-; Chairperson for Library Bicentenary Publications, 1981-83; for Regulations and Ordinances, 1981-83; Mem. of the Senate Legislative and General Purpose Standing Cttee. for Community Affairs, 1987-; for Social Welfare, 1976-87 and Chairperson, 1980-83; Mem. of the Senate Select Cttee. for Industrial Relations Legislation, May-Oct. 1982; for Private Hospitals and Nursing, 1981-87 and Chairperson, 1981-83; for Volatile Substance Fumes, 1984-85; for Video Material, 1984-85; for the Human Embryo Experimentation Bill 1985, 1985-86; Mem. of the Senate Estimates Cttee. D, 1977-78 and 1987-; Chairperson of C, 1978-81; G, 1981-83; B, 1983-86 and 1986-87; F, Mar.-Jun. 1987; Mem. of the Joint Select Cttee. for the Family Law Act, 1978-80; for Video Material, 1985-; Conferences, Delegations and Visits: Mem., OECD Council of Europe Parly. Symposium on Development Co-operation, Paris, 1978; Mem., 68th Inter-Parly. Union Annual Conference, Havana, 1981; leader, Opposition Members' Delegation to Japan, 1984; Mem. of Council of HRH Duke of Edinburgh 6th Commonwealth Study Conference; Mem., Joint

Standing Cttee. on Federal Policy, 1978-79; Mem., Liberal Party State Executive,, Tasmania, 1981-82; Parly. Sec., 1987-89; Mem., Australian Bicentennial Authority Board, 1986-89; *memberships:* cttee. mem., Southern Region, National Trust of Australia; *professional career:* General Nursing Certificate, Royal Prince Alfred Hospital, Sydney, Australia, 1947; *clubs:* The Queen Mary Club, Hobart, Tasmania; *recreations:* gardening; *private address:* 80 Nelson road, Sandy Bay, Tasmania 7005; *office address:* Ms Shirley Walters, GPO Box 760 H, Hobart, Tasmania 7001.

WALZ, Ingrid; German, Member of the Bundestag; *born:* 1936; *party:* Freie Demokratische Partei (FDP, Free Democratic Party); *political career:* MP for Baden-Württemberg; *professional career:* self-employed saleswoman; *private address:* 7000 Stuttgart 1, Germany; *office address:* Ms Ingrid Walz, Bundestag, Bundeshaus, 5300 Bonn 1, Germany.

WANGCHUCK, HRH Princess Sonam Chhoden; Bhutanese, Representative of His Majesty to the Ministry of Finance; *born:* 26 July 1953, Zurich, Switzerland; *married:* Tsewang Jurmed Rixin, 1979; *children:* two; *memberships:* Pres., National Women's Assn., 1981-; *professional career:* Chwn.: Royal Insurance Corp., 1975-; Druk Air Corp., 1981-; Royal Civil Service Commission and Royal Monetary Authority, 1982-; *office address:* HRH Princess Sonam Chhoden Wangchuck, Ministry of Finance, Tashicho Dzong, Thimphu, Bhutan; *phone:* 2338.

WANG JIALIU; Chinese, Alternate Member of the Chinese Communist Party 13th Central Committee; *born:* 1929, Pinghu County, Zhejiang Province; *party:* Chinese Communist Party; *professional career:* mem., Central Cttee., Communist Youth League, 1957-66; Deputy Sec., Beijing Branch, Communist Youth League, 1960-66; Alternate mem., Chinese CP 12th and 13th Central Cttee., 1982-; mem., Standing Cttee., Beijing CP, 1982-; *office address:* Wang Jialiu, The Communist Party of China, Beijing, The People's Republic of China.

WAN SHAOFEN; Chinese, Member of the Chinese Communist Party 13th Central Committee; *born:* 1931, Nanchang City, Jiangxi Province; *education:* Zhongsheng Univ., economics, 1948-49; qualified as lawyer through self-study, 1984; *party:* Chinese Communist Party; *political career:* Mem., 6th, 7th National People's Congress for Jiangxi; Mem., Standing Cttee., Jiangxi Province CCP, 1984-88, Leading Sec., 1985-88; Mem., CCP 12th, 13th Central Cttees. 1985-; Dep. Dir., United Front Work Dept., CCP Central Cttee., 1988-; *memberships:* Dep. Sec., Nanchang Branch, Communist Youth League, 1955; Alternate Mem., Central Cttee., Communist Youth League, 1958-66; Chwn., Jiangxi Province Branch, Women's

Federation, 1983-85, Mem., Exec. Cttee., 1983-85; Vice-Pres., Federation of Trade Unions, 1988-; *office address:* Wan Shaofen, The Communist Party of China, Beijing, The People's Republic of China.

WAPPIS, Dr. Elisabeth; Austrian, Member of the Nationalrat; *born:* 2 May 1952, Wölfnitz; *education:* federal grammar school (science orientated) matriculation, 1970; University of Graz, biology; exam for teaching certificate (magisterium), 1975, Ph.D., 1981; *party:* Österreichische Volkspartei (ÖVP, Austrian People's Party); *political career:* mem. of Exec., Austrian Teachers' Union, Chairperson, Women's Movement, Klagenfurt, 1985-; provincial Vice Chairperson, ÖVP; *professional career:* AHS teacher of biology, and of physics and chemistry as subsidiary subjects, Klagenfurt First Federal Grammar School, 1976-; mem. of Austrian Teachers' Federation; *office address:* Dr. Elisabeth Wappis, Nationalrat, Dr. Karl Renner Ring 3, 1017 Vienna, Austria.

WARNOCK, Baroness (cr. 1985, Life Peer) Helen Mary Warnock, DBE; British, Member of the House of Lords; *born:* 14 April 1924; *parents:* the late Archibald Edward Wilson and Ethel Mary Wilson (née Schuster); *married:* Geoffrey James Warnock, 1949; *public role of spouse:* Vice-Chancellor, Oxford Univ., 1982-86; *children:* two s., three d; *religion:* Church of England; *education:* St. Swithun's, Winchester; Lady Margaret Hall, Oxford; *party:* Cross-Bencher; *political career:* Chmn., Cttee. of Inquiry into Special Educ., 1974-78; mem., Royal Cmn. on Environmental Pollution, 1979-84; Chmn., Cttee. of Enquiry on Human Fertility and Embryology, 1982-84; mem., House of Lords, 1985-; *interests:* educ., broadcasting, medicine, the environment; *professional career:* Fellow and Tutor in philosophy, St. Hugh's Coll., Oxford, 1952-66, Research Fellow, 1972-84, Sr. Resident Fellow, 1976-84; Headmistress, Oxford High Sch., 1966-72; Mistress, Girton Coll., Camb., 1985-; *honours and awards:* D.B.E.; Hon. Degrees: Melbourne, Glasgow, Essex, Exeter, York, Liverpool, London, Warwick, Manchester; *publications:* books on ethics and educ.; *recreations:* music, gardening; *private address:* Brick House, Axford, Marlborough, Wilts., United Kingdom; *office address:* Baroness Warnock, House of Lords, London SW1A 0PW.

WARREN, Mary Alice; American, Member of the Republican National Committee for North Carolina; *party:* Republican Party; *political career:* Mem., Republican National Cttee., North Carolina, 1983-; *office address:* Ms Mary Alice Warren, 707 Chester Road, Winston-Salem, North Carolina, 27107, USA.

WARRINGTON-BETTS, Leah; American, Chair of District Thirty-six Democrat Committee; *born:* 19 November 1932, Harbeson, Delaware, USA; *parents:* John Samuel Warrington and Anna K. Warrington (née

Walls); *married:* Nelson Franklyn Betts, 1949; *children:* Robert Neldon, Harry John; *religion:* Methodist; *education:* Delaware Technical and Community College, GED, 1973; *party:* Democratic Party; *political career:* Mem., District 36 Democrat Cttee., Delaware, 1965-, Chair, 1975-; delegate, Democrat National Convention, 1976 and 1988; Vice-Chair, Delaware State Democrat Party, 1986; town Councilwoman, Milton, Delaware, 1989-; *memberships:* Mem., Violent Crimes Compensation Board, Wilmington, 1975-, Vice-Chair, 1985-; American Cancer Society; International Assn. of Crime Victims Commission; *professional career:* Sec., Sussex County Democrats Exec. Cttee., Delaware, 1973-; *honours and awards:* Justice of the Peace; National Award, Crime Victim Commission, 1981; *clubs:* CofC; Milton CofC; Saint Jude's Bike-a-Thon; *office address:* Mrs Leah Warrington-Betts, 113 Magnolia Street, Milton, Delaware 19968, USA.

WARSHAW-FREEDMAN, Sandra; American, Mayor of Tampa, Florida; *born:* 21 September 1943, Newark, New Jersey, USA; *parents:* Joseph Warshaw and Ruthe Warshaw (née Abovitz); *married:* Michael Jay Freedman, 1965; *public role of spouse:* attorney; *children:* two s., one d; *religion:* Jewish; *education:* Univ. of Miami, Florida, BA, government, 1965; *party:* Democratic Party; *political career:* Mem., Tampa City Cncl., Florida, 1974-83, Chwn., 1983-86; Mem., Downtown Development Auth., 1977-78; Mayor, Tampa, Florida, 1986-; increased size of police force by 20% through $6.5 million crime package, 1989; helped create city's first bi-racial cttee. to promote greater understanding and communication; organised city's first march against hate crimes; created partnerships with private industry for economic development programmes to stimulate minority business and provide youth job training; *interests:* re-vitalisation of neighbourhoods with special emphasis on housing, law enforcement, growth management and community relations; controlling drug-related crime rates; *memberships:* Mem., Board of Dir., Florida League of Cities; Tampa Bay Performing Arts Centre; Athena Society; Tampa Museum; CofC Cttee. of 100; Boys and Girls Club of Tampa; Arts Cncl. of Tampa; NAACP; Board of Dirs., Florida Gulf Symphony; *honours and awards:* Human Rights Award, City of Tampa, 1980; Spessard L. Holland Memorial Award, Tampa Bay Cttee., for Good Govt., 1975-76; Women Helping Women, Soroptomist International of Tampa, 1981; Status of Women Award, Zonta Club of Tampa II, 1986; Women of Achievement Award, Business and Professional Women, 1986; *office address:* Mrs Sandra Warshaw-Freedman, City Council City Hall, 201 E. Kennedy Blvd., Tampa, Florida 33602, USA.

WATERS, Maxine; American, US Representative for California; *born:* St. Louis, Missouri, USA; *married:* Sidney Williams; *children:* Karen, Edward; *religion:*

Christian; *education:* California State Univ., Los Angeles, BA Sociology; *party:* Democratic Party; *political career:* California State Rep., 1976-90; first woman in history of California elected to chair Assembly Democratic Caucus; US Rep., District 29, California, 1990-; Mem., Cttees. for Banking, Finance and Urban Affairs and for Veterans' Affairs, 1990-; Mem., Nat. Select Cttee. on the Education of Black Youth and nat. Steering Cttee. of the Centre for the Study of Youth Policy; Mem., Women's Legislative Lobby; *memberships:* Mem., Advisory Boards: Bhopal Justice Campaign; California Peer Counselling Assn. Advisory Cttee.; Advisory Cncl., Los Angeles Women's Foundation; Women for the Rosa Parks Sexual Assault Centre; Nat. Advisory Board of the Centre for Study of Sport in Soc.; founding Mem., Nat. Commission for Economic Conversion and Disarmament; Mem., Board of Dirs., Nat. Women's Political Caucus; *professional career:* Mem., Board of Dir.; Centre for Nat. Policy; Clara Elizabeth Jackson Carter Foundation (Spelman College); Cncl. for State Govt.; Int. Children's Centre; Jobs with Peace; Nat. Minority AIDS project; Women for a Meaningful Summit; Essence Magazine; TransAfrica Foundation; *honours and awards:* honourary doctorates: Spelman College, Atlanta; North Cardina State Univ.; A&T State Univ; *office address:* Ms Maxine Walters, 1207 Longworth House Office Buildings, Washington DC 20515, USA.

WEBER, Beate; German, Member of the European Parliament; *born:* 12 December 1943, Reichenberg; *parents:* Fritz Asher and Uta Asher; *education:* Heidelberg Univ. and Heidelberg Teaching College, Institute of Interpreting; *political career:* MEP, 1979-; *professional career:* teacher, 1968-79; *publications:* Die Abgeordneten Europas, 1984; Dicke Lufte in Europa, 1987 (co-author); *private address:* Sickungstr. 1, D 6900 Heidelberg, West Germany; *office address:* Frau Beate Weber, European Parliament, Centre Européen, Plateau de Kirchberg, BP 2929, Luxembourg.

WEBER, Monika; Swiss, Member of the Ständerat; *born:* 18 March 1943, Zürich, Switzerland; *education:* BA Phil., studied philosophy and political science in Zürich and Geneva; *party:* Independent and Evangelical Faction; *political career:* Mem. of the Zürich Cantonal Cncl., 1971-83; Mem. of the Nationalrat, 1982-87; Mem. of the Ständerat for Zürich, 1987-; *professional career:* Gen.-Sec., Swiss Business Assn.; former Pres., Forum for Consumers (Women's Assn.); *office address:* Frau Monika Weber, Ständerat/Conseil d'Etat, Secretariat-General, Parlamentsgebäude, 3003 Berne, Switzerland; *phone:* Berne 619711.

WEGNER, Dr. Konstanze; German, Member of the Bundestag; *born:* 1938; *party:* Sozialdemokratische Partei Deutschlands (SPD, Social Democratic Party);

political career: MP for Baden-Württemberg; *professional career:* historian; housewife; *private address:* 6800 Mannheim 1, Germany; *office address:* Dr. Konstanze Wegner, Bundestag, Bundeshaus, 5300 Bonn 1, Germany.

WEGRZYN, Malgorzata; Polish, Member of the Sejm; *office address:* Ms Malgorzata Wegrzyn, Sejm PRI, ul. Wiejska 4/6/8, 00-489 Warsaw, Poland; *phone:* (22) 28 70 01; 28 40 31.

WEILER, Barbara; German, Member of the Bundestag; *born:* 17 September 1946, Düsseldorf, West Germany; *children:* one d; *education:* elementary school; school of commerce, Mittlere Reife (intermediate high school certificate), 1963; language studies, United Kingdom, 1½ years; *party:* Sozialdemokratische Partei Deutschlands (SPD, Social Democratic Party of Germany), 1970; *political career:* member of Easter March Movement, since 1962; citizens' representative, Willich/Kreis Viersen, 1971; member of local Exec. Cttee., SPD, 1972-81; member of sub-district Exec. Cttee., SPD, 1974-79; member of Exec. Cttee., Jungsozialisten (Young Socialists), 1974-79; town councillor, Willich/Kreis Viersen, 1975-85; member of Exec. Cttee., Working Group for Education, 1977-85; party secretary, SPD, district of Fulda, 1985-87; mem. of Bundestag, party list of Hessen, since 1987; *professional career:* commercial clerk, secretary, managing clerk, specialist adviser, in industrial firms, 1965-85; member of Industriegewerkschaft Metall (IGM, Metal Workers' Union), 1971-84; member of Gewerkschaft Handel, Banken und Versicherungen (HBV, Trade Union for Commerce, Banks and Insurance); lay assessor for youth, 1977-80; *clubs:* Arbeiterwohlfahrt (AWO, Labour Welfare Organisation); Parents' Association Hessen; Association of Single Mothers and Fathers; *office address:* Frau Barbara Weiler, Bundeshaus, 5300 Bonn 1, West Germany.

WEISS STEINBERG, Cathey; American, Senator; *born:* 2 October 1942, Wilkes-Barre, Pennsylvania, USA; *parents:* Stanley M. Weiss Sr. and Miriam Weiss (née Cohen); *children:* Jill, Lauren; *religion:* Jewish; *education:* Carnegie Mellon Univ., BA, 1964; Univ. of Pittsburgh, M.Ed., 1965; *party:* Democratic Party; *political career:* Georgia State Rep., District 46, 1977-; Mem., Georgia State Democratic Cttee., 1978-; Vice-Chwn., Pension Cttee., National Conference of State Legislators; *memberships:* Childrens Aid Society, Philadelphia, 1967-68 and 1970-71; Mem., Citizens Advisory Board, Georgia Mental Health Inst., 1977-80; Mem., Advisory Board, Atlanta Cncl. Campfire, Atlanta Legal Aid Society, 1980-; Co-Chwn., Foetal Alcohol Syndrome Task Force; Mem., Advisory Board Neighbourhood Justice Centre; National Cncl. of Jewish Women; League of Women Voters; Hadassah;

professional career: social worker, Sheltering Arms Children Service, New York, 1965-67; Mental Health Centre, Fitchberg, Mass., 1968-69; *honours and awards:* One of Atlanta's Twenty Outstanding Women, 1978; Legislators Award, Georgia Conference of Social Welfare, 1980; Freedom Award, Georgia Federation of Democratic Women, 1982; NEBPW Woman of the Year, 1984; *office address:* Mrs Cathey Weiss Steinberg, 1732 Dunwoody Place, Atlanta, Georgia 30324, USA.

WENTZ, Janet Marie; American, North Dakota State Representative; *born:* 21 July 1937, McClusky, North Dakota, USA; *parents:* Charles Neff and Martha Schindler; *married:* Thomas Arthur Wentz, 1957; *children:* Elizabeth, Karin, Thomas; *religion:* Methodist; *education:* Westmar College, 1955-57; Univ. of Minnesota, 1960-62; Minot State College, 1967-70; *party:* Republican Party; *political career:* North Dakota State Rep., District 41, 1974; Chwn., Judiciary Cttee. and Mem., Political Sub-divisions and Joint Constitutional Revenue Cttees., North Dakota House of Reps; *memberships:* Organisation of Women Legislators; Court Service Admin. Cttee.; North Dakota United Methodist Rep., North Dakota Conference of Churches, 1973-; League of Women Voters; *professional career:* registered securities Rep; *office address:* Mrs Janet Wentz, 505 8th Avenue SE, Minot, North Dakota 58701, USA.

WEYEL, Gudrun; German, Member of the Bundestag; *born:* 1927; *party:* Sozialdemokratische Partei Deutschlands (SPD, Social Democratic Party of Germany); *political career:* MP for Rheinland-Pfalz; *professional career:* study adviser; *private address:* 6252 Diez, Germany; *office address:* Ms Gudrun Weyel, Bundestag, Bundeshaus, 5300 Bonn 1, Germany.

WHITE, Baroness (cr. 1970, Life Peer) Eirene Lloyd White; British, Member of the House of Lords; *born:* 1909; *parents:* the late Dr. Thomas Jones, CH; *married:* the late John Cameron White, 1948; *education:* St. Paul's Girls' Sch.; Somerville Coll., Oxford; *party:* Labour Party; *political career:* mem., Nat. Exec. Cttee. of Lab. Party, 1947-53, 1958-72; MP (Lab.), East Flint, 1950-70; Chmn., Fabian Soc., 1959; Parly. Under-Sec., Colonial Office, 1964-66; Minister of State for Foreign Affairs, 1966-67, for Wales 1967-70; Chmn. of Lab. Party, 1968-69; mem. House of Lords, 1970-; Chmn., Land Authority for Wales, 1976-80; Dep. Chmn. Metrication Board, 1972-76; mem., Royal Cmn. on Environment Pollution, 1974-81; British Waterways Board, 1974- 80; Univ. Grants Cttee., 1977-79; Principal Dep. Chmn. of Cttees., and Chmn., ECs Select Cttee., House of Lords, 1979-82; a deputy speaker, 1979-89; *interests:* environmental affairs, higher educ; *professional career:* a journalist, 1945-50, previously in Min. of Labour; Council, Univ. of Wales; Chmn., Univ. of Wales; Inst. of Science and

Technology, 1983-88; Vice Pres. U.W. College of Cardiff, 1989-; *clubs:* Royal Cmmw. Soc; *private address:* 64 Vandon Court, Petty France, London SW1H 9HF, UK; *office address:* Baroness White, House of Lords, London SW1A 0PW.

WHITMIRE, Kathryn Jean; American, Mayor of Houston, Texas; *born:* 15 August 1946, Houston, Texas, USA; *parents:* Karl Niederhofer and Ida Reeves; *married:* the late Jim Whitmire, 1967; *religion:* Methodist; *education:* Univ. of Houston, Texas, BBA, 1968, MS, 1970; *party:* Democratic Party; *political career:* Controller, Houston, Texas, 1977-81 then Mayor, 1982-; *memberships:* Pres., Texas Municipal League, 1989-90; Juvenile Diabetes Foundation; Pres., US Confederation of Mayors, 1989-90; Trustee, Univ. of Houston Foundation; Co-Chwn., Nat. League of Cities Int. Economic Development Taskforce; Mem., Exec. Cttee., Greater Houston Partnership; *professional career:* former Audit Mgr., Coopers and Lybrand, Houston; former Faculty Mem., Dept. of Business Management, Downtown College,Univ. of Houston; *honours and awards:* Distinguished Alumna Award, College of Business Admin., Univ. of Houston, 1979; Distinguished Alumnas Award, Alumni Organisation, Univ. of Houston, 1982; Public Service Award, 1982; Woman of Year, Texan Women's Political Caucus, 1982; Int. Business Award, Houston World Trade Assn., 1985; Michael A. DiNunzio Award, US Confederation of Mayors, 1985; Human Relations Award, American Jewish Cttee., 1986; Humanitarian Award, Int. New Thought Alliance, 1986; Distinguished Professional Woman, Cttee. on the Status of Women, 1986; *office address:* Ms Kathryn Whitmire, P.O. Box 1562, Houston, Texas 77251, USA.

WIBBLE, Anne Marie; Swedish, Member of the Riksdag; *born:* 13 October 1943; *parents:* Bertil Gotthard Ohlin and Evy Ohlin (née Kruse); *married:* Jan Arne Wibble, 1966; *children:* Petra Charlotte Deepa, Monica Kanaka; *religion:* Protestant; *languages:* English, French, German; *education:* St Anne's School, Charlottesville, USA, 1959-60; Higher School Certificate, HAL, Kungsholmen, Stockholm, 1957-62; Graduate, Stockholm School of Economics, 1962-66; Stanford Univ., USA, M.A. Econ., 1966-67; Stockholm School of Econ., Licentiate in Economics, 1967-73; *party:* Folkpartiet Liberalerna (Liberal Party), 1962; *political career:* mem. of Riksdag for the Stockholm Admin. Province, 1985; Deputy Chairman of the Parliamentary Finance Cttee., 1986-; Member of the Liberal Party Board, 1987-, the Party Executive, 1986-, and the board of Liberal Party MPs, 1986-; Member of the National Debt Board, 1988-; Expert in the Government Co-ordination Chancellery, 1980-82; Clerk in the Liberal Party's Parliamentary Chancellery, 1982-83; Head of Liberal party Parly. Chancellery, 1983-86; *interests:* economics, taxation, foreign trade; *professional career:* teacher in national economics,

Stockholm School of Economics, 1966-77; Investigator Regional Planning Office of Stockholm County Council, 1977-80; *publications:* Nymerrantilism Oca Ekonipol, 1970; Svense Finanspol i Teori Prartir, 1971 Selektiv Generell Ekonomisk Pol, 1973, all above by Institute of Research into Economics, Debatt Artiklar, Ekonomisk Debatt, Dagspress, 1980; *clubs:* Liberal Party Women's Assoc.; Society for National Economics; Liberal Economics Club; *office address:* Ms Anne Wibble, Riksdag, Fack, S-100 12 Stockholm, Sweden.

WIDDECOMBE, Ann Noreen; British, Parliamentary Under-Secretary of State for Social Security; *born:* 4 October 1947; *parents:* James Murray Widdecombe, CB, OBE and Rita Widdecombe; *religion:* Church of England; *education:* Royal Naval School, Singapore; La Sainte Union Convent, Bath; Birmingham University; Lady Margaret Hall, Oxford University; *party:* Conservative Party; *political career:* founder mem. and Vice-Chmn., Women and Families for Defence; Vice-Chmn., Nat. Assn. of Conservative Graduates, 1974-76; Cllr., Runnymede District Cncl., 1976-78; mem., Gas Consumers Cncl., 1984-86; Member of Parliament for Maidstone, 1987-; Parl. Under-Sec. of State for Social Security, 1991-; *interests:* defence; education; abortion; health; *professional career:* Marketing Dept., Unilever plc., 1973-75; Senior Administrator, London University, 1975-87; *recreations:* reading; researching Charles II's escape; riding; theatre; *private address:* 9 Tamar House, Kennington Lane, London SE11 4XA, UK; *office address:* Miss Ann Widdecombe, House of Commons, London SW1A OAA.

WIECZOREK-ZEUL, Heidemarie; German, Member of the Bundestag; *born:* 21 November 1942, Frankfurt, Main, West Germany; *education:* High school leaving examination, 1962; Johann-Wolfgang-Goethe Univ. Frankfurt, Teacher training degree; *party:* Sozialdemokratische Partei Deutschlands (SPD, Social Democratic Party of Germany), 1965; *political career:* cttee. mem., SPD, 1984; mem. of SPD presidency since 1986; mem. of Bundestag (Hesse list); town councillor, Rüsselsheim, 1968-72; mem. of Kreistag GroßGerau, 1972-74; mem. of SPD District cttee., South Hesse, 1972-85; Federal chmn., Young Socialists, 1974-77; mem. of European Parliament, 1979-87; mem. of Party cttee. since 1984; dep. chmn., 1985; chmn., 1988; *professional career:* Teacher, Friedrich-Ebert School, Rüsselsheim, 1965-74; teacher, Georg-Büchner School, Rüsselsheim, 1977-78; mem. of EU and GEW; chmn., European Coordination Office, International Youth Assns., 1977-79; *office address:* Frau Heidemarie Wieczorek-Zeul, Bundeshaus, 5300 Bonn 1, West Germany.

WILCZYNSKA, Zofia; Polish, Member of the Sejm; *office address:* Ms Zofia Wilczynska, Sejm PRI, ul.

261

Wiejska 4/6/8, 00-489 Warsaw, Poland; *phone:* (22) 28 70 01; 28 40 31.

WILDE, Hon. Fran (Francis Helen); New Zealander, Member of Parliament; *born:* 1948, Wellington, New Zealand; *children:* three; *education:* St Mary's College; Wellington Polytechnic, BA, political science; Victoria Univ. of Wellington, diploma of journalism; *party:* Labour Party; *political career:* parliamentary researcher, Legislative department; joined Labour Party, 1972; held numerous posts including electorate chairperson and executive mem. of Labour Party's regional council; former editor, Labour Party newspaper; elected to Parliament for Wellington Central, 1981; mem.: Select Cttee. on Commerce and Energy; Select Cttee. on Official Information; Parly. Opposition Spokesperson on State Services; re-elected to Parliament, 1984-87; Govt. Whip, 1984-87; chairperson, Govt. Administration Select Cttee., 1984-87; mem., Standing Orders Select Cttee.; successfully sponsored two private mems. bills; Homosexual Law Reform Bill and Adult Adoption Information Bill; re-elected to Parliament, 1987-; Associate Minister of Foreign Affairs, 1987-90; Associate Minister of Conservation, 1987; Minister for Disarmament, 1988-90; Associate Minister of External Relations and Trade, 1988-90; Minister of Tourism, 1989-90; convener of the Wellington Regional MPs Lobby; *interests:* activie in the peace movement and in support of feminism; *professional career:* newspaper and radio journalist; operated her own publicity and public relations business; mem., Council of Victoria Univ. of Wellington; *recreations:* reading, theatre, music, travel; *office address:* The Hon. Ms Frances Wilde, House of Representatives, POB 18041, Wellington, New Zealand; *phone:* (04) 719199; *fax:* (04) 4990704.

WILL-FELD, Waltrud; German, former Member of the Bundestag; *born:* 11 June 1921; *married:* Dr. Wilhelm; *children:* two s; *religion:* Protestant; *education:* High school, Traben-Trarbach, leaving examination, 1939; Univ. Marburg, Maths and physics discontinued studies; *party:* Christlich Demokratische Union (CDU, Christian Democratic Union), 1968; *political career:* mem. of Kreistag Bernkastel-Wittlich, 1969-; mem. of Bundestag, 1972-90; *professional career:* tax authority and adviser, 1950- and 1960-; *office address:* Frau Waltrud Will-Feld, Bundeshaus, 5300 Bonn 1, West Germany.

WILLIAMS, Karen; American, Tennessee State Representative; *born:* 5 September 1950, Memphis, Tennessee, USA; *parents:* Robell Williams and Rubye Williams; *religion:* Episcopalian; *education:* Univ. of Arkansas, BA, 1972; Memphis State Univ., JD, 1976; *party:* Republican Party; *political career:* Tennessee State Rep., 1983-; *memberships:* Assn. of Women Attorneys; Republican Career Women Club;

professional career: lawyer; *honours and awards:* Outstanding Female of the Year, Young Republicans, 1983; *office address:* Ms Karen Williams, 147 Jefferson No. 600, Memphis, Tennessee 38103, USA.

WILMS, Dr. Dorothee; German, Member of the Bundestag; *born:* 11 October 1929; *parents:* Lorenz Wilms and Lieselotte Wilms (née Schiedges); *religion:* Roman Catholic; *languages:* English, French; *education:* leaving exams, 1950; political economy and sociology studies, diploma political economist, 1950-54; Univ. of Cologne, Dr. rer. pol, 1956; *party:* Christliche Demokratische Union (CDU, Christian Democratic Union), 1961; *political career:* acting federal secretary, CDU, 1974-76; mem. Bundestag, 1976-; parliamentary secretary, CDU/CSU group in the Bundestag, 1980-82; Federal Minister of Education and Knowledge, 1982-87; Federal Minister for Intra-German Relations, 1987-91; *interests:* foreign affairs, economics; *professional career:* science lecturer, acting head of the Education, Employment and Social Policy Department and mem. of Secretariat of the German Industrial Institute, Cologne, 1955-73; *honours and awards:* Grand Federal Merit Cross of the Meritorious Order of the German Federal Republic, 1985; Grand Federal Star Merit Cross of the Meritorious Order of the German Federal Republic, 1989; *publications:* various articles and essays on educational, social and women's political issues and German politics; *office address:* Dr. Dorothee Wilms, MdB Bundehaus, 5300 Bonn 1, Germany.

WILMS-KEGEL, Heike; German, former Member of the Bundestag; *born:* 19 October 1952, Bremen, West Germany; *religion:* Protestant (Free Church); *education:* Tannenbusch grammar school, Bonn, Abitur (advanced matriculation examination), 1971; University of Bonn, medicine, qualified physician, 1979; *party:* Die Grünen (Green Party), since 1983; *political career:* mem. of Bundestag, party list of Rheinland-Pfalz, 1987-90; *professional career:* asst. surgeon, 1979-80; asst. doctor of radiology, radiotherapy and oncology, 1980-82; ward doctor, Special Clinic of Psychosomatic Medicine, Bad Tönisstein, 1982-87; member of International Physicians for the Prevention of Nuclear War (IPPNW); *office address:* Frau Heike Wilms-Kegel, Bundeshaus, 5300 Bonn 1, West Germany.

WILSON, Elizabeth; American, Member of the Republican National Committee; *born:* 7 November 1941, Bessemer, Alabama, USA; *parents:* James Clay Smith and Mary Elizabeth Smith (née Veitch); *married:* William Roberts Wilson Jr., 1970; *children:* William Roberts III; *religion:* Episcopal; *education:* Univ. of Alabama, BS, 1963, MA, 1969; *party:* Republican Party; *political career:* Mem., Jackson County Exec. Cttee., 1973-; alternate delegate, Republican National

Convention, 1976 and 1984; delegate, Miss. State Republican Convention, 1972, 1976, 1980 and 1984; founder and 1st Pres., Jackson County Republican Women, 1973-75; 3rd Vice-Pres., Miss. State Federation of Republican Women, 1978-80, 1st Vice-Pres., 1982-84, Pres., 1984-88; Mem., Republican National Cttee., 1988-; *memberships:* Pascagoula Civic Guild; Pascagoula-Moss Point Jr. Auxillary; *clubs:* Singing River Yacht Club; *private address:* 808 Swordfish Drive, Pascagoula, MS 39567, USA; *office address:* Mrs Elizabeth Ann Wilson, 31 Polo Drive, Jackson, MS 39211, USA.

WINTER, Daria Portray; American, Chair of the Washington DC Democrat Committee; *born:* 7 September 1949, Washington DC, USA; *married:* Reginald C. Winter, 1973; *children:* Michael Alan; *religion:* Episcopal; *education:* Univ. of Virginia. MA, 1973; *party:* Democratic Party; *political career:* Alternate Democrat National Committeewoman, 1979-; delegate, Democrat National Convention, 1984-; Mem., Electoral College, 1984; Chair, Washington DC Democrat Cttee., 1984-; *memberships:* National Education Assn.; National Black Womens' Caucus; Assn., State Democratic Chmn.; Women's Political Caucus; Democratic National Cttee. Black Caucus; Democratic National Cttee. Women's Caucus; Democratic National Eastern Regional Caucus; Democratic National Cttee; *professional career:* English instructor, Univ. of DC; *honours and awards:* National Endowment for Humanities Fellowship, Univ., of Virginia, 1977; Fellowship, George Washington Univ., Ph.D. program, 1988-89; *office address:* Mrs Daria Portray Winter, 1107 K Street NE, Washington DC, 20002, USA.

WINTERTON, Ann (Jane Ann); British, Member of Parliament; *born:* 6 March 1941; *parents:* Joseph Robert Hodgson and Ellen Jane; *married:* Nicholas Winterton MP, 1960; *children:* two s., one d; *education:* Erdington Grammar School for Girls; *party:* Conservative Party; *political career:* mem., West Midlands Conservative Women's Advisory Cttee., 1969-71; Member of Parliament for Congleton, 1983-; mem., Agricultural Select Cttee.; Sec., All Party Pro-Life Group; *interests:* agriculture; chemical industry; pharmaceutical industry; textile industry; 'think-British' campaign; transport; Southern Africa; *clubs:* South Staffordshire Hunt (Joint Master, 1959-64); *recreations:* cinema; music; riding; skiing; tennis; theatre; *private address:* Whitehall Farm, Newbold Astbury, Congleton, Cheshire; *office address:* Mrs Ann Winterton, House of Commons, London SW1A OAA.

WISDOM, Jane; American, Member of the Nevada State Assembly; *born:* 1 May 1932, Hagerstown, Maryland, USA; *children:* Charles Patrick; *religion:* Protestant; *education:* Maryland Univ.; National

Security School of Languages; *party:* Democratic Party; *political career:* Mem., Nevada State Assembly; Mem., Nevada and Clark County Democrat Central Cttees; *memberships:* Mem., Univ. Medical Centre Foundation Board; Salvation Army; Business and Professional Women; *clubs:* Clark County Women's Democrat Club; Nevada Opera and Theatre Assn.; Nike House; *office address:* Ms Jane Wisdom, 210 S. Mallard Street, Las Vegas, Nevada 89107, USA.

WISE, Audrey; British, Member of Parliament; *born:* 4 January 1935; *parents:* George Crawford Brown and Elsie Crawford Brown; *married:* John Wise; *children:* one s., one d; *party:* Labour Party; *political career:* Member of Parliament for Coventry South West, 1974-79, and for Preston, 1987-; elected first woman Pres., Union of Shop Distributive and Allied Workers (USDAW), 1991-; Mem., Labour Action for Peace, Campaign for Nuclear Disarmament, Nicaragua Solidarity; Mem., Commons Select Cttee. on Health; Mem., Labour Party National Exec. Cttee., 1982-87; *interests:* environment; health; poverty; nuclear disarmament; women; trade unionism; *memberships:* the Soil Assn; *professional career:* former shorthand typist; *publications:* Women and the Struggle for Workers' Control; Eye Witness in Revolutionary Portugal; *recreations:* organic gardening; *office address:* Mrs Audrey Wise, House of Commons, London SW1A OAA.

WISNIEWSKI, Prof. Dr. Roswitha; German, Member of the Bundestag; *born:* 23 September 1926, Stolp, Pomerania; *parents:* Bruno Wisniewski and Edith Wisniewski (née Berndt); *education:* Lessing School, Stolp; Univ. Berlin (Humboldt and Free), Marburg, Bohn German Studies, Classics, Philology, Theology; habilitation qualification, 1960; *party:* Socialdemokratische Partei Deutschlands (SPD, Social Democratic Party of Germany); *political career:* mem. of Bundestag since 1976; *professional career:* lecturer, Univ. Berlin/Free since 1960; professor (non-budgetry, unscheduled), 1965; ordinary professor Cairo, Heidelberg, 1967; President, German-Egyptian Society since 1982; Professor of German Philology; *publications:* Mittelhochdeutsche Grammatik, 1956, 9th edition, 1984 (with Helmut de Boor); Die Darstellung des Niflungenuntergangs in der Thidrekssaga, 1961; Kudrun, 2nd edition, 1969; Deutsche Grammatik, 1978; Kreuzzugsdichtung, 1984; Dietrichdichtung, 1986; Handbuch für Frauenfragen (with Bischof Hermann Kunst), 1988; *office address:* Prof. Dr. Roswitha Wisniewski, Bundeshaus, 5300 Bonn 1, West Germany.

WOLLNY, Lieselotte; German, former Member of the Bundestag; *born:* 26 February 1926, Hamburg, West Germany; *children:* five; *religion:* Protestant (Lutheran); *education:* elementary school, 1932-36;

secondary school, 1936-43; day student at private school, to prepare for Abitur (advanced matriculation examination), Oct. 1944-45; *party:* Independent; *political career:* labour service, 1942; auxiliary war service, air force (Luftwaffe), 1943-44; member of Citizens' Initiative for the Protection of the Environment, Lüchow-Dannenberg, since 1978; member of Exec. Cttee., Citizens' Initiative for the Protection of the Environment, since 1979; member of municipal council, Hoehbeck, for an independent group, 1982-86; alderman; mem. of Bundestag, Die Grünen party list of Niedersachsen, 1987-90; *professional career:* housewife; *office address:* Frau Lieselotte Wollny, Bundeshaus, 5300 Bonn 1, West Germany.

WONG, Dr. Aline K.; Singaporean, Senior Minister of State at the Ministry of Health; *born:* 13 May 1941, Hong Kong; *married:* Prof. John Wong; *children:* two s; *education:* Univ. of Hong Kong, BA (Hons.) economic and Pol.Sci., 1962; Univ. of California, Berkeley, USA, MA sociology, 1964, PhD., 1970; *party:* People's Action Party, (PAP); *political career:* MP, Changkat, 1984-; Chwn., Govt. Parly. Cttee. on Health and Environment, 1987; Chwn., Women's Wing, Peole's Action Party, 1989-; Senior Minister of State at the Ministry of Health, 1990-; *professional career:* lecturer, Dept. of Sociology, Univ. of Singapore, 1971, senior lecturer, 1976; Head of Research, Systems and Research Dept., Housing and Development Board, 1983-84; Assc. prof., Dept of Sociology, Univ. of Singapore, 1985; *recreations:* reading, music; *office address:* Dr. Aline Wong, Ministry of Health, College of Medicine Building, 16 College Road, Singapore 0316; *phone:* 2237777.

WONG, Hon. Elizabeth; Hong Kong, Member of the Legislative Council; *born:* 1937; *education:* Hong Kong, BA (Hons.); Dip. Ed; *political career:* Administrative Officer, 1969, 1975, 1978, 1982, 1987; Administrative Asst., Social Welfare Dept., 1970; Asst. Financial Sec., 1973-75, 1977; Commissioner for Recreation and Culture, 1982; Deputy Sec., Home Affairs, 1983-84; Deputy Commissioner, Assessment Office, 1984; Deputy Sec., Lands and Works, 1984-86; Deputy Sec., Academy for Performing Arts, Municipal Services Branch, 1985-86; Deputy Sec., Recreation and Culture, Municipal Services Branch, 1986; Director of Social Welfare, 1987; *office address:* The Hon. Mrs Elizabeth Wong, The Legislative Council, Government House, Hong Kong.

WOOD-FELTON, Dorothy; American, Georgia State Representative; *born:* 1 March 1929, Tulsa, Oklahoma, USA; *parents:* George Fetter Wood and Ima Wood (née Chrominster); *married:* Jethro Jerome Felton Jr., 1953; *children:* Jethro Jerome III, Frank Bryan; *religion:* Methodist; *education:* Univ. of Arkansas, Fayetteville,

BA, 1950; *party:* Republican Party; *political career:* Mem., Personnel Board, Fulton County Govt., Georgia, 1973-75; Georgia State Rep., Ditsrict 22, 1975-; Mem., Education, Legislation and Congressional Reappointment and State Planning and Community Cttees.; Georgia House Rep; *memberships:* Mem., Board of Dirs.: Protestant, Radio and TV Centre; Leadership Atlanta Girls Club; Wesley Community Centre; Trustee, Campbell-Stone North; Citizens Advisory Cttee. to Fulton County School; League of Women Voters; Board of Georgia Society to Prevent Blindness; *professional career:* reporter and society editor, Tulsa Tribune, Oklahoma, 1950-53; freelance public relation, 1953-74; Mem., Advisory Board, Juvenile Court; *honours and awards:* Outstanding Community Service National Award, Delta Gamma; Lifetime Mem. for Outstanding Work in Education, North Fulton PTA; Distinguished Service in Health Education, Medical Assn., Georgia, 1980; Atlanta Journalists' Constitutional Award; Mover and Shaker in Nartto Fulton County, 1984; *clubs:* United Methodist Women; *office address:* Mrs Dorothy Wood-Felton, 465 Tanacrest Drive NW, Sandy Springs, Georgia 30328, USA.

WOZNIAK, Teresa; Polish, Member of the Sejm; *office address:* Ms Teresa Wozniak, Sejm PRI, ul. Wiejska 4/6/8, 00-489 Warsaw, Poland; *phone:* (22) 28 70 01; 28 40 31.

WÜRFEL, Uta; German, Member of the Bundestag; *born:* 19 August 1944, Bad Wiessee/Tegernsee; *children:* two; *education:* high school; Diploma for Doctor's Assistants, München; Diploma for Secretaries, Ingolstadt; Diploma for foreign language assistance, Washington D.C., USA; *party:* Freie Demokratische Partei (FDP, Free Democratic Party), 1976; *political career:* research asst. for employment, health, family and social affairs, FDP group, regional parliament, Saarland; chmn., county special Cttee. for women and family policy, 1982; district chmn., FDP Saarplatz-Kreis, since 1982; dep. chmn., Federal Commission for Equality and Family Policy, FDP, since 1984; recording clerk; mem. of Bundestag, party list of Saarland, since 1987; *professional career:* position at Institute of Aircraft Medicine; position at Test Flight Centre 61; position at German Observer Group, Aberdeen Proving Ground, Maryland/USA; housewife and mother, for 14 years; *clubs:* German Children's League (member of governing board); German Family Association Saar (chmn., until 1986); *office address:* Frau Uta Würfel, Bundeshaus, 5300 Bonn 1, West Germany.

WU WENYING; Chinese, Minister of Textile Industry; *born:* 1932, Changzhou City, Jiangsu Province; *party:* Chinese Communist Party; *political career:* Dep. Sec., Changzhou Municipality CCP, Jiangsu Province, 1982-83; Alternative Mem., CCP 12th Central Cttee., 1982-

85; Minister of Textile Industry, 1983-; Mem., CCP 12th, 13th Central Cttees., 1985-; *memberships:* Vice-Pres., Women's Federation; *office address:* Wu Wenying, Ministry of Textile Industry, 12 Dongchangan Jie, Beijing, People's Republic of China; *phone:* 5129542.

WU YI; Chinese, Alternate Member of the Chinese Communist Party 13th Central Committee; *born:* 1938, Wuhan City, Hubei Province; *education:* Beijing Petroleum Institute, 1962; *party:* Chinese Communist Party, 1962; *political career:* Alternate mem., Chinese CCP 13th Central Cttee., 1987-; Vice-Mayor, Beijing Municipality, 1988-; *professional career:* Dep. Manager then Party Sec., Beijing Yanshan Petrochemical Corp., 1983; *office address:* Wu Yi, The Communist Party of China, Beijing, The People's Republic of China.

X

XIE XIDE; Chinese, Member of the Chinese Communist Party 13th Central Committee; *born:* 1920; *education:* Smith College, Massachusetts, USA, MA, 1947-49; Massachusetts Institute of Technology, USA, Ph.D., 1949-51; *party:* Chinese Communist Party; *political career:* Mem., CCP 12th, 13th Central Cttees., 1982-; *professional career:* teacher, Theoretical Mechanics, Elementary Physics, Solid Physics, and Semi-conductor Theory in Physics Dept., Fudan Univ., 1952-77; Vice-Pres., Fudan Univ., Shanghai, 1978-83; Mem., Presidium, Academy of Sciences, 1981-; Mem., Scientific Council, Academy of Sciences, 1981-; Pres., Fudan Univ., in Shanghai, 1983-88 Director, American Studies Centre, Fudan Univ., 1985-; *office address:* Xie Xide, The Communist Party of China, Beijing, The People's Republic of China.

XING ZHIKANG; Chinese, Alternate Member of the Chinese Communist Party 13th Central Committee; *born:* 1930; *education:* college, Shanghai, 1946-48; *party:* Chinese Communist Party, 1946; *political career:* Alternate mem., Chinese CCP 12th and 13th Central Cttee., 1982-; Chmn., Shanghai Branch, Women's Federation, 1986-; mem., Executive Cttee., Women's Federation, 1988-; *office address:* Xing Zhikang, The Communist Party of China, Beijing, The People's Republic of China.

Y

YAMANAKA, Ikuko; Japanese, Member of the House of Councillors; *born:* 19 April 1932; *education:* Waseda Univ; *party:* Japan Communist Party; *political career:* former Cttee. person of Central Cttee. of Zendentsu; third time elected for National; Mem., House of Cllrs. Cttee. on Communications and Mem., JCP Presidium, 1990-; *office address:* Ms Ikuko Yamanaka, House of Councillors, 1-7-1 Nagata-cho, Tokyo 100, Japan; *phone:* (03) 5813111.

YIANNAKOU, Marietta; Greek, Minister of Health, Welfare and Social Security; *office address:* Ms Marietta Yiannakou, Ministry of Health, Welfare and Social Security, Odos Zalokosta 10, Athens, Greece.

YIN CHANGMIN; Chinese, Alternate Member of the Chinese Communist Party 13th Central Committee; *born:* 1923, Qingjiang County, Jiangxi Province; *education:* graduate, Biology Dept., Zhongshan Univ., 1945; *party:* Chinese Communist Party; *political career:* Alternate mem., Chinese CCP 12th Central Cttee., 1982-86; mem., Standing Cttee., Hunan Province CCP, 1983-85; mem., Chinese CCP 12th Central Cttee., 1986-87; Alternate mem., Chinese CCP 13th Central Cttee., 1987-; *professional career:* Assc. Professor, Hunan Teachers College, 1953-66; professor and Dir., Hunan Teachers College, 1979-83; Vice-Chwn., Hunan Branch, Association for Science and Technology, 1982, Chwn., 1987; *office address:* Yin Changmin, The Communist Party of China, Beijing, The People's Republic of China.

YOSHIDA, Kazuko; Japanese, Member of the House of Representatives; *born:* 6 May 1949; *education:* Women's College of Fine Arts; *party:* Japan Socialist Party (JSP); *political career:* former Dir. of a Consumers' Co-operative Society; elected for Tokyo 6, 1990; Mem., House of Reps. Cttee. on Commerce and Industry, 1990-; *professional career:* School teacher; *office address:* Ms Kazuko Yoshida, House of Representatives, 1-7-1 Nagata-cho, Chiyoda-ku, Tokyo 100, Japan; *phone:* (03) 5815111.

YOSHIKAWA, Haruko; Japanese, Member of the House of Councillors; *born:* 26 November 1940; *education:* Chuo Univ; *party:* Japan Communist Party; *political career:* former Vice-Chmn., JCP Diet Policy Cttee.; Dir., House of Cllrs. Cttee. on the Cabinet and Cttee. Persons; Mem., JCP Central Cttee., 1990-; *professional career:* School teacher; *office address:* Ms Haruko Yoshikawa, House of Councillors, 1-7-1 Nagata-cho, Tokyo 100, Japan; *phone:* (03) 5813111.

YOUNG, Baroness (cr. 1971, Life Peer) Janet Mary Young; British, Member of the House of Lords; *born:* 23 October 1926; *parents:* John Norman Leonard Baker and Phyllis Marguerite Baker (née Hancock); *married:* Geoffrey Tyndale Young, 1950; *children:* Alexandra, Rosalind, Juliet; *religion:* Church of England; *education:* Dragon Sch., Oxford; Headington Sch.; schools in the USA; St. Anne's College, Oxford, politics, schools philosophy, economics; *party:* Conservative Party; *political career:* cllr., Oxford City Council, 1957, Alderman and Leader of the Cons. group on the Council, 1967; mem., House of Lords, 1971-; Baroness in waiting (govt. whip in the House of Lords), 1972-73; parly. under-sec. of state, Dept. of the Environment, 1973-74; Minister of State, Dept. of Educ. and Science, 1979-81; a vice-chmn. of Cons. Party Organisation, 1975-83, dep. chmn., 1977-79; Chllr. of the Duchy of Lancaster, and Leader of the House of Lords, 1981-82; Minister in charge of Civil Service Dept., 1981, and of Mgt. and Personnel Office, Nov. 1981-83; govt. spokesman for Wales, 1982; Lord Privy Seal and Leader of the House, 1982-83; Minister of State, Foreign and Cmmw. Office, 1983-87; *professional career:* Dir., UK Provident Instituion, 1975; mem. British Railways Western Region Advisory Board, 1977; co-Chmn., Women's Nat. Cmn., 1979-83; Dir., Nat. Westminster Bank, 1987-; non-exec. Dir., Marks and Spencer, 1987-; Vice-Pres., The West India Cttee.; trustee, Lucy Cavendish Coll., Camb.; Chmn., Independent Schools Joint Council, 1989-; DL, Oxfordshire, 1989-; *honours and awards:* Hon. Fellow, Institution of Civil Engrs.; Hon. Fellow, St. Anne's Coll., Oxford; hon. DCL, Mt. Holyoke Coll., USA; *clubs:* Univ. Women's Club; *recreations:* music; *office address:* Baroness Young, House of Lords, London SW1A 0PW.

Z

ZAKHAROV, Olive (Alice Olive); Australian, Senator; *born:* 19 March 1929, Kew, Victoria, Australia; *parents:* Robert Hay and Alice Hay, 1954; *children:* Jeanne, Martin, Robin; *religion:* Atheist; *languages:* English, French; *education:* BA, Melbourne; Accredited Course in Teacher Training, Melbourne STC; Graduate Diploma Ed. Couns. (RMIT); *party:* Australian Labor Party; *political career:* Delegate, Labor Party State Conference, Victoria, 1972-85; Executive Mem., Diamond Valley Federal Electoral Assembly, 1972-75; Executive Mem., Labor Party Montmorency Branch, 1973-83; Mem., Victoria Health and Welfare Policy Cttee., 1977-83; elected to Senate for Victoria, 1983-, re-elected 1984 and 1987; Committee Service: Mem. of the Senate Standing Cttee. for Publications, 1983-85; for the House, 1985-87, and 1988-; for Regulations and Ordinances, May 1984, Feb.-Sep. 1985, and 1990-; Mem. of the Senate Legislative and General Purpose Standing Cttee. for National Resources, 1983-87 and Chairperson, 1985-87; Chairperson for Community Affairs, 1987-; for Environment, Recreation and the Arts, 1987-90; Mem., Joint Statutory Cttee. for Australian Security Intelligence Organisation, 1990-; Mem. of the Senate Select Cttee. for Private Hospitals and Nursing Homes, 1983-87; for Video Material, 1984-85; for the Embryo Experimentation Bill, 1985, 1985-86; Mem. of the Senate Estimates Cttee. D, 1983-85, 1987-88 and 1990-, then Chair, Nov. 1990-; Chairperson of E, 1985-86; Chairperson of F, 1986-87; Mem. of the Joint Select Cttee. for Video Material, 1985-, for Employment, Education and Training, 1990-; Parly. Representative on the Council of the Australian National Univ., 1984-86; Conferences, Delegations and Visits: Mem., Australian Govt. Delegation to UN World Conference for the End of the Decade for Women, Nairobi, 1985; Mem., Parly. Delegation to the European Institutions, the North Atlantic Assembly and Finland, 1987; Temporary Chair of Cttees., 1987-; Mem., Parly. Liaison Group on AIDS; Special Parly. Adviser to the Minister Assisting the Prime Minister on Violence Against Women; Govt. Rep., Cncl. for Equal Opportunity in Employment; *memberships:* Victorian Secondary Teachers' Association; Australian Psychological Society; National Parks Association; Wilderness Society; Australian Conservation Foundation; Amnesty International; Social Biology Resources Centre; Humanist Society; Australian Film Institute; World Women Parliamentarians for Peace; Campaign for International Co-operation Disarmament; Psychologists for the Prevention of War; Rationalist Society, Victorian AIDS Trust; National Trust; Australian National Gallery; *professional career:* school counsellor; teacher; registered psychologist; market research interviewer; pathology assistant; clerk; shop assistant; mail officer; waitress; fruit picker; psychiatric nurse; *private address:* 23a Swallow Street, Port Melbourne, Victoria 3207, Australia; *office address:* Ms Olive Zakharov, PO Box 95, Melbourne, Victoria 3207, Australia.

ZALEHA BT ISMAIL, Datin Paduka Hajjah; Malaysian, Deputy Minister of Transport; *born:* 18 May 1936, Batu Laut, Kuala Langat, Selangor; *children:* three; *education:* Sekolah Melayu Sungai Pelek, Sepang, 1942-45; Sekolah Melayu Bagan Lalang, Sepang Kecil, 1945-46; Sekolah Menengah Perempuan Methodist, Kuala Lumpur, 1947-55; Sekolah Menengah St. John's, Kuala Lumpur, 1956-57; Univ. Malaya, Singapore, 1957-60; Univ. Malaya, Kuala Lumpur, BA (Hons.) 1960-61; *party:* Barisan Nasional (National Front Coalition Party); *political career:* Political Secretary to Welfare Minister, 1974-78; Selangor State Assemblywoman for Permatang, Barisan, 1978; Mem., Selangor State Cabinet (Exco) 1978-82; MP for Tanjung Karang, 1982; re-elected MP for Salayang, Selangor, 1986; Parly. Secretary, Ministry of Land and Regional Development, 1986-87; Deputy Minister of Transport, 1987-; elected UMNO Supreme Council Mem., 1978, re-elected, 1981; Vice-Pres., UMNO Wanita; *professional career:* part-time DJ, Radio Malaysia, (RM) 1951-61, then assistant programmer, 1961-62, then assistant organiser, Malay Services, 1962-65 and finally organiser, English Service Programme, 1965-68; lecturer and part-time tutor, Univ. Malaya, 1965-71; Encyclopedia Officer, Dewan Bahasa dan Pustaka (DBP), 1968-71, deputy head, Educational Books Section, 1971-74; *honours and awards:* Companion of The Order of The Crown of Selangor, 1979; Officer of The Most Esteemed Order of The Defender of The Realm, 1979; Commander of The Order of The Crown of Selangor, 1980; *office address:* Datin Paduka Hajjah Zaleha BT Ismail, Ministry of Transport, 5th-7th Floors, Wisma Perdana, Jalan Dungun, 50616 Kuala Lumpur, Malaysia.

ZENELAJ, Shpresa; Albanian, Member of the Albanian Workers' Party Central Committee; *party:* Albanian Workers' Party (AWP); *political career:* candidate Mem., AWP Central Cttee., 1971-, full Mem., 1982-; *professional career:* Pro-Rector, Enver Hoxha Tirana Univ., 1970; *office address:* Ms Shpresa Zenelaj, Albanian Workers' Party, Tirana, Albania.

ZHANG GUOYING; Chinese, Member of the Chinese Communist Party 13th Central Committee; *born:* 1935, Dongquan County, Guangdong Province; *party:* Communist Party of China, 1954; *political career:* Dep. Party Sec. for Baoting County, 1965-66, for Rehua County, 1976-82, for Huijang Prefecture, 1982-83; 1st Sec., Women's Federation, 1983 then Vice Chairperson; Mem., CCP 12th, 13th Central Cttee., 1985-; *office address:* Zhang Guoying, The Communist Party of China, Beijing, The People's Republic of China.

ZHAO DI; Chinese, Alternate Member of the Chinese Communist Party 13th Central Committee; *born:* 1939; *party:* Chinese Communist Party; *political career:* Vice-Mayor, Kaifeng City, 1982; mem., Standing Cttee., Henan Province CCP, 1983-; Deputy Dir., Organization Dept., Henan Province CCP, 1983-84; Deputy Sec., Henan Province CCP, 1984-; Alternate mem., Chinese CCP 12th and 13th Central Cttee., 1985-; *office address:* Zhao Di, The Communist Party of China, Beijing, The People's Republic of China.

ZIA, Begum Khaleda; Bengali, Prime Minister, Minister for Establishment, Information and Mineral Resources and Leader of the Bangladesh Nationalist Party; *married:* the late Pres. Ziaur Rahman, murdered 1981; *public role of spouse:* President of the Republic of Bangladesh, 1977-81; *party:* Bangladesh Nationalist Party; *political career:* led Bangladesh Nationalist Party in first democratic election in 20 years, Feb. 1991; set to form coalition govt. with Jamaat-i-Islami Party, Mar. 1990; Prime Minister of Bangladesh and Minister for Establishment, Information and Mineral Resources, 1991-; *office address:* Begum Khaleda Zia, Prime Minister's Secretariat, Gono Bhaban, Sher-e-Banglangagar, Dhaka, Bangladesh; *phone:* 328292; 418989.

ZIOLKOWSKA, Wieslswa; Polish, Member of the Sejm; *office address:* Ms Wieslswa Ziólkowska, Sejm PRI, ul. Wiejska 4/6/8, 00-489 Warsaw, Poland; *phone:* (22) 28 70 01; 28 40 31.

ZÖLCH-PALMER, Elisabeth; Swiss, Member of the Nationalrat; *born:* 24 April 1951; *parents:* Samuel Balmer and Gertrud; *married:* Franz Zölch, 1981; *religion:* protestant; *languages:* French, English, German; *education:* secondary school, school leaving certificate, 1961-71; University of Bern, barrister, 1971-77; *party:* Parti Suisse de l'Union Démocratique - Schweizerische Volkspartei (SVP, Swiss People's Party); *political career:* District Cllr., 1977-81; mem. of Nationalrat, 1987-; *interests:* government and state affairs, educational issues; *professional career:* lawyer; *clubs:* mem., several organisations; mem., Swiss Community Association; *private address:* Herrengasse 4, Bern, 3011, Switzerland; *office address:* Frau Elisabeth Zölch-Palmer, Nationalrat/Conseil National, Secretariat-General, Parlamentsgebäude, 3003 Berne, Switzerland.

ZSLEWSKA, Teresa; Polish, Member of the Sejm; *office address:* Ms Teresa Zslewska, Sejm PRI, ul. Wiejska 4/6/8, 00-489 Warsaw, Poland; *phone:* (22) 28 70 01; 28 40 31.

ZUFFA, Grazia; Italian, Senator; *born:* 8 August 1945, Piasco, Cuneo, Italy; *children:* Irene; *education:* Degree in Letters, 1970; *party:* Partido Democratico della Sinistra, (PDS); Partito Comunista Italiano (PCI, Italian Communist Party), 1970; *political career:* Mem. Women's and Feminist movements; Leader of PCI, Florence from 1977, then in Tuscany as head of Women's Committee; mem. Central Cttee. PCI from 1986; and Councillor, Florence; elected Senator, Florence (II) 1987; mem. Cttee. on Hygiene and Health; Minister for Youth Politics, PDS Shadow Cabinet, 1989-; *professional career:* Writer from its inception, for 'Rosa' (feminist magazine); and 'Donne e politica', 'Reti', 'Memoria' and other women's reviews; *office address:* Ms Grazia Zuffa, Senato della Repubblica, Palazzo Madama, 00100 Rome, Italy.

ZUGIC-RIJAVEC, Silvija; Yugoslavian, Member of the Vojvodina League of Communists' Provincial Committee; *party:* League of Communists of Yugoslavia (LCY); *political career:* Mem., Central Cttee., LCY, 1982; Mem., Presidium, LC of Vojvodina, 1986; Mem, Vojvodina LC Provincial Cttee., 1986; *office address:* Ms Silvija Zugic-Rijavec, Vojvodina Provincial Committee, League of Communists of Yugoslavia, Novi Beograd, bul. Lenjina 6, Yugoslavia.

PART II
STATISTICAL
SURVEY

STATISTICAL SURVEY OF WOMEN IN WORLD POLITICS

Certain trends and anomalies are evident from a study of the statistics presented in the tables below. Only 12% of national representatives worldwide are female. Out of the 156 territories covered in this survey, there are only seven whose head of state is female and four whose Prime Minister is female. See the note to *Table 1* for a complete list of these countries.

Table 2 shows that the percentage of women in the legislatures of the Developed Regions, Asia and the Pacific, and Latin America and the Caribbean is much the same at 12-13%. However, by comparing the figures for women in the legislature and women in the Cabinet it is possible to deduce that a woman is only half as likely to reach Cabinet level in Asia and the Pacific or Latin America and the Caribbean than in the Developed Regions.

Table 3 reveals that even within the Developed Regions there are nine countries, including the UK and Japan, that do not have any female Cabinet Members. It is only in the Scandinavian countries that women are approaching parity with men in the occupation of Cabinet level posts, with Norway topping the league at 47%.

It is also noteworthy that Africa has 11 Ministers for Women's Affairs (or the equivalent), as compared to three or four in each of the other regions, but around four times less women in legislatures than the other three regions.

In *Table 4* the figures for the Developed Regions show that the total percentage of women in the legislatures has fallen by nearly 6%, from 1987 to 1991. A closer examination of the statistics reveals that this is mainly due to a fall in the number of women representatives in Eastern Europe, coinciding with democratic elections having been held in these countries during this period.

Criteria

The following tables provide statistics relating to the numbers of women holding positions (elected or otherwise) as Head of State, Prime Minister or equivalent, member of the cabinet or member of the national legislature in the global political arena. Where possible, figures relating to the percentage of women in national legislature in previous years have been included. For ease of reference the data are presented in groups relating to geographic or economic region, with separate tables for each position.

All figures have been verified as of July 1991. Those that appear in parenthesis have been verified by regional representatives of the respective government, but have not been supported by documentary evidence. A pictorial representation of the data included in these tables is given in the maps that appear at front and back of this book.

For many countries no data were available and in some cases the national legislature had been recently dissolved, accordingly the tables are not exhaustive.

Inclusion in these tables does not imply any democratic credentials. Simply those countries for which data were available are included.

Table 1
Female Share of National Leadership Posts, July 1991

Head of State			Prime Minister (or equivalent)		
Total	Women	%	Total	Women	%
169(153)	23(7)*a*	13.6(4.1)	169	4*b*	2.4

Note: Figures in brackets exclude the 16 territories (besides the UK) whose Head of State is HM Queen Elizabeth II.

a   The following countries have female heads of state:
Denmark; Iceland; Ireland; Netherlands; Nicaragua; Philippines; UK

b   The following countries have female Prime Ministers:
Bangladesh; Dominica; France; Norway

Source: national government and embassy press offices.

Table 2
Female Share of Cabinet and National Legislative Posts, by Region, July 1991

	Cabinet			Legislature		
	Total	Women	%	Total	Women	%
Developed regions	656	68	10.4	15,339	1,974	12.9
Asia and the Pacific	904	28	3.1	10,460	1,196	11.4
Latin America and the Caribbean	506	32	6.3	4,167	378	9.7
Africa	869	48	5.5	5,513	128*a*	2.3*a*
World	2,935	176	6	35,479	3,935	11.1
of which: OECD countries *b*	479	63	13.2	10,115	1,287	12.8

a   Figures are approximate only as data are unavailable for this region

b   See Table 3 for countries included in this heading.

Source: distibution of seats between men and women in National Parliaments - statistical data from 1945 to 30 June 1991, Inter-Parliamentary Union, Geneva; national government and embassy press officers

Table 3
Female Share of Cabinet Level Posts, July 1991
Developed Regions

Country	Total in Cabinet	Total Women	%
Albania	15	2	13.3
Australia *d*	17	1	5.9
Austria *d*	17	3	17.6
Belgium	17	0	0
Bulgaria	19	1	5.2
Canada *d*	39	7*a*	18.0
Czechoslovakia	16	1	6.3
Denmark	19	4	21.1
Finland *d*	17	7	41.2
France *d*	33	4*b*	12.1
Germany *d*	22	4*a*	18.2
Greece *d*	29	1	3.4
Hungary	17	1	5.9
Iceland *d*	11	1	9.1
Ireland *d*	14	1	7.1
Italy *d*	33	2	6.1
Japan *d*	13	0*c*	0
Luxembourg *d*	12	1	8.3
Malta	10	0	0
Netherlands *d*	14	3*b*	21.4
New Zealand *d*	20	2*a*	10.0
Norway *d*	19	9	47.4
Poland	20	0	0
Portugal *d*	17	0	0
Romania	25	0	0
Spain *d*	18	2	11.1
Sweden *d*	22	8	36.4
Switzerland *d*	8	0	0
USSR	64	1	1.6
United Kingdom *d*	22	0	0
United States *d*	18	2	11.1
Yugoslavia	19	0	0
Total	656	68	10.4

a   Figure includes a Minister for Women's Affairs

b   In addition, there are three female government members who are not in the Cabinet

c   In addition, there is one female government member who is not in the Cabinet

d   OECD members as indicated, plus Turkey

Asia and the Pacific

Country	Total in Cabinet	Total Women	%
Afghanistan	39	2	5.1
Bahrain	18	0	0
Bangladesh	12	1	8.3
Bhutan	7	2	28.6
Brunei Darussalam	11	0	0
Cambodia	27	1	3.7
China	49	3	6.1
Cyprus	11	0	0
Fiji	20	2a	10.0
Hong Kong	15	3	20.0
India	16	1	6.2
Indonesia	32	1a	3.1
Iran	22	1a	4.6
Iraq	24	0	0
Israel	21	0	0
Jordan	25	0	0
N. Korea	51	2	3.9
S. Korea	28	0	0
Kuwait	18	0	0
Laos	21	1	4.8
Lebanon	31	0	0
Malaysia	26	1	3.9
Maldives	16	0	0
Mongolia	15	1	6.7
Myanmar	9	0	0
Nepal	14	1	7.1
Pakistan	21	0	0
Papua New Guinea	29	0	0
Philippines	25	1	4.0
Saudi Arabia	23	0	0
Singapore	14	0	0
Solomon Islands	15	0	0
Sri Lanka	24	1a	4.2
Syria	36	1	2.8
Thailand	21	1	4.8
Tonga	11	0	0
Turkey	28	1	3.6
Vanuatu	9	0	0
Vietnam	36	0	0
Yemen	34	0	0
Total	904	28	3.1

a   Figure includes a Minister for Women's Affairs

Latin America and the Caribbean

Country	Total in Cabinet	Total Women	%
Argentina	9	0	0
Bahamas	15	0	0
Barbados	13	1*b*	7.7
Belize	15	0	0
Bolivia	18	0	0
Brazil	12	1	8.3
Chile	17	1	5.9
Colombia	13	1	7.7
Costa Rica	19	2*c*	10.5
Cuba	44	2	4.5
Dominica	11	1	9.1
Dominican Republic	18	1	5.6
Ecuador	14	0	0
El Salvador	13	1	7.7
Grenada	10	1*a*	10.0
Guatemala	14	1	7.1
Guyana	17	4	23.5
Haiti	12	0	0
Honduras	14	1	7.1
Jamaica	18	1	5.6
Mexico	25	2	8.0
Nicaragua	13	0	0
Panama	10	0	0
Paraguay	12	1	8.3
Peru	14	0	0
Puerto Rico	17	3	17.6
St Kitts & Nevis	10	1*a*	10.0
St Lucia	11	0	0
St Vincent/Grenadines	10	1*a*	10.0
Suriname	11	1	9.1
Trinidad & Tobago	17	3*b*	17.6
Uruguay	13	0	0
US Virgin Islands	8	0	0
Venezuela	19	1	5.3
Total	506	32	6.3

a   Figure includes a Minister for Women's Affairs

b   In addition, there is one female government member who is not in the Cabinet

c   In addition, there are two female government members who are not in the Cabinet

Africa

Country	Total in Cabinet	Total Women	%
Algeria	24	2	8.3
Botswana	9	1	11.1
Burkina Faso	21	3*b*	14.3
Burundi	23	2*a*	8.7
Cameroon	29	1*a*	3.4
Central African Rep	18	1	5.6
Congo	18	1	5.6
Cote d'Ivoire	20	3*a*	15.0
Egypt	27	1	3.7
Equatorial Guinea	21	0*c*	0
Gabon	26	1	3.8
Gambia	12	1	8.3
Ghana	22	2*bc*	9.1
Guinea	23	0	0
Guinea-Bissau	39	3*a*	7.7
Kenya	32	0	0
Lesotho	15	1*a*	6.7
Libya	6	1	16.7
Madagascar	22	0	0
Malawi	9	0	0
Mali	21	2*a*	9.5
Mauritania	21	0	0
Mauritius	19	1*a*	5.3
Morocco	31	0	0
Mozambique	22	0	0
Namibia	21	2	9.5
Niger	19	1*ad*	5.3
Rwanda	20	0	0
Sao Tome & Principe	9	1	11.1
Senegal	25	1*a*	4.0
Seychelles	10	3	30.0
Sierra Leone	23	0*f*	0
Somalia	6	0	0
South Africa	20	1	5.0
Sudan	21	0	0
Swaziland	12	1	8.3
Togo	19	1*a*	5.3
Tunisia	23	0	0
Uganda	20	4*ec*	20.0
Tanzania	19	2*a*	10.5
Zaire	31	0	0
Zambia	19	1	5.3
Zimbabwe	22	3	13.6
Total	869	48	5.5

a	Figure includes a Minister for Women's Affairs
b	In addition, there are two female government members who are not in the Cabinet
c	The Minister for Women's Development is not a member of the Cabinet
d	In addition, there is one female government member who is not in the Cabinet
e	In addition, there are five female government members who are not in the Cabinet
f	In addition, there are two female government members who are not in the Cabinet

Sources: national government and embassy offices.

Table 4
Female Share of Cabinet Level Posts, July 1991
Developed Regions

Country	Year of Women's Enfranch- isement	Total in Legis- lature	Women in Legis- lature	% 1991	% 1987	% 1975
Albania	1945	250	72	28.9	28.8	33.2
Australia	1901	224	23	10.2	6.1	0
Austria	1918	264	44	16.7	11.5	7.7
Belgium	1948	396	37	9.3	7.5	6.6
Bulgaria	1944	400	34	8.5	21	18.8
Canada	1918	402	55	13.7	9.6	3.4
Czechoslovakia	1920	300	28	9.3	29.5	26
Denmark	1915	179	54	30.2	29.1	5.6
Finland	1906	200	62	31	31.5	23
France	1944	898	69	7.7	6.4	1.6
Germany	1919	662	167	25.2	15.4	5.8
Former German Democratic Republic	-	500	-	-	32.2	31.8
Greece	1952	300	14	4.7	4.3	2
Hungary	1945	387	27	7	21	28.7
Iceland	1915	63	14	22.2	20.6	5
Ireland	1918	226	18	8	8.4	2.8
Italy	1945	954	102	10.7	12.9	3.8
Japan	1945	764	40	5.2	1.4	1.4
Luxembourg	1919	60	8	13.3	14.1	5.1
Malta	1947	69	2	2.8	2.9	3.6
Netherlands	1919	225	55	24	14.4	4.6
New Zealand	1893	97	16	16.5	14.4	4.6
Norway	1913	165	59	36	34.4	15.5
Poland	1918	560	68	12.1	20.2	15.9
Portugal	1931-76	250	23	9.2	8	7.6
Romania	1929-46	506	15	3	34.4	15.2
Spain	1931	558	69	12.4	6.4	-
Sweden	1921	349	132	38	28.5	21.4
Switzerland	1971	246	33	13	14	7.5
USSR	1917	2791	446	16	34.5	32.1
United Kingdom	1918-28	1844	125	6.4	6.3	4.3
United States	1920	539	31	5.8	5.3	3.7
Yugoslavia	1946	308	48	15.6	18.8	15
Total		153,339	1,974	12.9	18.7	11.8

Asia and the Pacific

Country	Year of Women's Enfranch- isement	Total in Legis- lature	Women in Legis- lature	% 1991	% 1987	% 1975
Afghanistan	-	427	-	-	-	-
Bangladesh	1947	300	30	10	9.1	4.8
Bhutan	1953	150	-	-	1.3	-
Cambodia	-	-	-	-	-	-
China	1949	2978	(743)	(25)	21.2	22.6
Hong Kong	-	57	13	22.8	-	-
India	1950	543	48	8.8	8.3	4.3
Indonesia	1945	500	62	12.4	-	7.2
Iran	1963	270	4	1.5	1.5	-
Iraq	1980	250	27	10.8	13.2	-
Israel	1948	120	7	5.8	8.3	6.7
Jordan	1973	120	(1)	(0.8)	0	0
North Korea	1946	687	(138)	(20.1)	21.1	20.9
South Korea	1948	299	6	2	2.5	5.5
Lebanon	-	99	(1)	(1)	0	0
Malaysia	1957	246	13	5.1	5.1	3.2
Maldives	1932	48	(2)	(4.2)	-	-
Mongolia	1923	370	(6)	(1.6)	24.9	22.9
Nepal	1951	140	(6)	(4.3)	5.8	-
Pakistan	1947	237	(25)	(10.5)	8.9	4.1
Papua New Guinea	-	106	0	0	0	-
Philippines	1939	224	22	9.8	-	-
Singapore	1948	84	4	4.8	3.8	0
Solomon Islands	1945	38	1	2.6	0	-
Sri Lanka	1931	225	6	4.2	4.8	-
Syria	1949	250	(21)	(8.4)	9.2	2.7
Thailand	1932	357	10	2.8	3.5	1.1
Tonga	-	30	0	0	0	-
Turkey	1934	450	6	1.3	3.0	-
Tuvalu	-	12	(1)	(8.3)	-	-
Vanuatu	1980	46	-	-	0	-
Vietnam	1946	496	88	17.7	17.7	-
Yemen	1970	301	-	-	0	-
Total		10,460	1,291	12.3	6.7a	7.6a

a   Average figure

Latin America and the Caribbean

Country	Year of Women's Enfranch- isement	Total in Legis- lature	Women in Legis- lature	% 1991	% 1987	% 1975
Argentina	1952	300	20	6.7	5.0	9.0
Bahamas	-	65	5	7.7	4.0	
Barbados	-	49	7	14.3	4.0	8.0
Belize	-	36	1	2.8	4.0	
Bolivia	1952	157	-	-	4.0	-
Brazil	1934	524	30	5.7	5.3	0.3
Chile	-	167	(10)	(6.0)	-	-
Costa Rica	1949	57	7	12.3	10.5	5.3
Cuba	1934	510	171	33.5	33.9	-
Dominica	1951	30	5	16.7	12.9	-
Dominican Rep	-	150	-	-	5.0	-
Ecuador	1928	71	(5)	(7.0)	1.4	-
El Salvador	-	60	12	20	3.3	-
Grenada	-	28	-	-	12.5	-
Guatemala	1945	100	-	-	7.0	-
Guyana	1966	65	(10)	(15.4)	11.9	-
Honduras	1957	128	11	8.6	5.2	-
Jamaica	-	81	7	8.6	11.7	3.8
Mexico	1953	464	82	17.7	10.8	5.0
Nicaragua	1955	92	(15)	16.3	13.5	-
Panama	1941	58	(4)	(7.0)	6.0	-
Paraguay	1962	108	-	-	1.7	-
Peru	-	240	(14)	(5.8)	5.6	-
Puerto Rico	-	78	7	9.0	-	-
Suriname	1948	51	-	-	12.9	5.1
Trinidad & Tobago	-	66	9	13.6	16.7	2.8
Uruguay	1932	130	-	-	0	0
Virgin Islands	-	16	4	-	25.0	-
Venezuela	1947	245	(44)	(18)	3.9	2.7
Total		4,167	480	11.5	8.2	4.2

Africa

Country	Year of Women's Enfranch-isement	Total in Legis-lature	Women in Legis-lature	% 1991	% 1987	% 1975
Algeria	1962	295	7	2.3	2	-
Angola	1975	319	-	-	15	-
Benin	1956	206	-	-	4	-
Botswana	1966	40	2	5	5	0
Cameroon	1946	180	-	-	14	6
Cape Verde	1975	83	-	-	15	2
Comoros	1956	42	-	-	0	-
Congo	1963	133	(19)	(15)	10	-
Cote d'Ivoire	1956	175	-	-	6	9
Djibouti	1946	65	-	-	0	-
Egypt	1956	458	10	2.2	4	2
Equatorial Guinea	1963	60	-	-	3	6
Gabon	1960	120	-	-	13	4
Gambia	-	51	-	-	-	0
Guinea-Bissau	1977	150	-	-	15	-
Kenya	1956-63	202	2	1.0	2	4
Madagascar	1959	137	-	-	2	-
Malawi	-	109	11	10.1	-	7
Mali	1956	82	2	2.4	4	-
Mauritius	1956	70	5	7.1	6	-
Morocco	1963	306	0	0	0	0
Namibia	-	72	(5)	(7)	-	-
Niger	-	93	(5)	(5.4)	-	-
Rwanda	1961	70	-	-	13	-
Sao Tome & Principe	-	51	-	-	12	-
Senegal	1945	120	-	-	12	4
Seychelles	-	25	-	-	24	-
Sierra Leone	-	127	6	4.7	-	1
Somalia	1956	177	-	-	-	4
South Africa	1979	177	5	2.8	4	-
Swaziland	-	70	5	7.1	2	-
Togo	1956	77	3	3.9	5	-
Tunisia	1956	141	6	4.2	6	3
Uganda	-	278	45	16.2	-	-
Tanzania	1959	244	15	6	-	8
Zaire	1960	222	12	5.4	4	11
Zambia	-	136	7	5.1	3	5
Zimbabwe	1957	150	18	12.0	9	-
Total		5,513	128	2.3	7.1a	4.2a

a   Average figure

Sources: The World's Women 1970-1990 Trends and Statistics, United Nations, New York, 1991; Distribution of seats between men and women in National Parliaments - Statistical Data from 1945 to 30 June 1991, Inter-Parliamentary Union, Geneva, 1991; national government and embassy press offices.

PART III
BIOGRAPHICAL
INDEX

BIOGRAPHICAL INDEX

People's Republic of Bangladesh
Ganaprojatantri Bangladesh

Barbados

Kingdom of Belgium
Koninkrijk België

Republic of Benin
République du Benin

Kingdom of Bhutan
Druk-Yul

Central African Republic
République Centrafricaine

Republic of Chad
République du Tchad

People's Republic of China
Zhōnghuá Rénmin Gonghéguo

Republic of Colombia
República de Colombia

People's Republic of the Congo
République Populaire du Congo

Republic of Costa Rica
República de Costa Rica

Republic of Côte d'Ivoire
République de la Côte d'Ivoire

Commonwealth of Dominica

Dominican Republic
República Dominicana

Arab Republic of Egypt
Jumhuriyat Misr Al-Arabiyah

Republic of El Salvador
República de El Salvador

Republic of Equatorial Guinea
República de Guinea Equatorial

Fiji

Republic of Finland
Suomen Tasavalta

Republic of France
République Française

Republic of Gabon
République Gabonaise

Republic of the Gambia

Federal Republic of Germany
Bundesrepublik Deutschland

Republic of Hungary

Republic of Iceland
Lýdveldid Ísland

Republic of India
Bharat

Republic of Indonesia
Republik Indonesia

Jamaica

Japan
Nippon

Republic of Poland

Republic of Portugal
República Portuguesa

Republic of Romania
Republica România

St Kitts and Nevis

St Vincent and the Grenadines

San Marino

Sao Tomé and Principe

Republic of Senegal
République du Sénégal

Republic of Seychelles

Republic of Singapore
Republik Singapore

Solomon Islands

Republic of South Africa
Republiek van Suid-Africa

Spain
Estado Español

Democratic Socialist Republic of Sri Lanka
Sri Lanka Prajatantrika Samajawadi Janarajaya

Republic of Suriname
Republiek Suriname

Kingdom of Swaziland
Hulumende

Kingdom of Sweden
Konungariket Sverige

Confederation of Switzerland
Sweizerische Eidgenossenschaft

Syrian Arab Republic
Al-Jamhuriyah Al-Arabiyah Al-Suriyah

Taiwan
Republic of China

United Republic of Tanzania
Jumhuri ya Muungano wa Tanzania

Kingdom of Thailand
Prathes Thai

Republic of Togo
République Togolaise

Republic of Trinidad and Tobago

Republic of Turkey
Türkiye Cumhuriyeti

Tuvalu

Republic of Uganda

United Kingdom of Great Britain and Northern Ireland

United States of America

309

Union of Soviet Socialist Republics
Soyuz Sovyetskikh Sotsialisticheskikh Respublik

Republic of Venezuela
República de Venezuela

Socialist Republic of Vietnam
Cong-Hoa Xa-Hoi Chu-Nghia Viêt-Nam

Socialist Federal Republic of Yugoslavia
Socijalistička Republika Jugoslavija

Greenland

Iceland

United Kingdom

Ireland

Alaska

Canada

Azores   Portugal   Spa

Maderia

United States

Canary Islands   Morocco

● Bermuda

Hawaiian Islands

Mexico   Bahamas

Western Sahara

ATLANTIC

Cuba

Dominican Republic

Mauritania   Senegal

Belize   Jamaica

Cape Verde Islands

PACIFIC

Honduras   Haiti

OCEAN

Mali

Guatemala
El Salvador   Nicaragua

Gambia
Guinea Bissau   Guinea

Barbados

OCEAN

Trinidad & Tobago

Costa Rica   Guyana

Sierra Leone   Ivory Coast

Panama   Venezuela   Surinam

Liberia

Colombia   French Guiana

Ecuador

Equi

Peru

Ascension

Society Islands

Brazil

St Hel

Tahiti

Bolivia

Chile   Paraguay

Argentina

Tristan da Cunha

Uruguay

Falkland Islands

Sth. Georgia

BOWKER-SAUR

Who's Who

OF

WOMEN IN WORLD

POLITICS